The London Women's Handbook

D1422323

Produced and Published by
the GLC Women's Committee

© 1986 GLC Women's Committee
Produced and Published by the GLC
   Women's Committee

Typeset by P·W·L

Printed for GLC Supplies Department
   (CRS) by Howard Hunt Litho Ltd
   2/86

Designed by Dianne Ceresa
Illustrations by Judy Stevens

Thanks to all women, inside and
   outside the GLC Women's
   Committee Support Unit, who
   helped make this Handbook
   possible. Thanks also to the GLC
   Supplies Department for their
   assistance and co-operation.

ISBN 7168 16369

Contents

Message from the Chairperson of the Women's Committee

Dear Sisters,

I am delighted to be able to introduce this Handbook for women in London produced by the GLC Women's Committee. It's the first Handbook of its kind and will be a vital resource for women.

The Handbook outlines the ways women are under-resourced, disadvantaged, discriminated against, and marginalised — in spite of being 52% of the population! But it also shows women's strength — our resourcefulness and ability to fight for and create the services and facilities we need. The Handbook will be an important asset for women who want to claim what's theirs — with information on what women are entitled to, what's available, and how and where to find it. Use it!

The Handbook also reflects the wide range of the work and activities of the GLC Women's Committee and will remain as a reminder of everything the Committee has achieved.

The GLC Women's Committee was the first to be set up in Britain, and in its four years achieved a great deal. It brought women's needs regarding local authority services to the centre stage. It brought rapid and significant change in GLC policies in important areas such as transport and planning. It made available the largest single source of funds for women and gave grants to much-needed and high quality innovative projects run by and for women. It produced a wide range of information on issues relating to women. It sought out women's views widely to find out what they wanted. It explored the ways different groups of women are additionally disadvantaged and discriminated against — especially Black and ethnic minority women, women with

disabilities, lesbians and older and young women — and sought to challenge this discrimination and re-direct resources, in GLC policy work and grant-aid.

The GLC Women's Committee sought to change things for women in London — and we succeeded in many ways. The abolition of the Council has stopped all this just as it was taking root, but all the achievements and experiences have not been lost. There are many resources available to women in London — use this Handbook to make the most of them!

Valerie Wise

What Is In This Handbook?

This Handbook aims to give information about services and facilities in London which women might use. It covers services and facilities which borough councils, government departments, community projects, local groups, charities and women's projects provide.

The Handbook is the first of its kind. It looks at many of the issues facing women living and working in this enormous and varied city and then draws together all the places women can go to get more information and advice, to take action or to take part in organisations which are working in London.

Why a Handbook for Women?

The Handbook has been produced because women do have particular problems, needs and demands - the pattern of women's lives is quite different from men's. Women carry the main responsibility for bringing up children, for looking after families, for work at home, for looking after people who are ill, disabled or frail. It is estimated that half a million women are caring for people who need care - that does not include children! At the same time the majority of women have to earn an income, and many are responsible, alone, for earning an income for themselves and their family. 40% of London's households are headed by women. 80% of single parents are women. Most women only have access to the lowest paid, unskilled and low status jobs and, overall, women still receive on average only two thirds of the income received by men.

Discrimination operates from the earliest age - girls receive a different education, get less training, have fewer opportunities. So women have fewer skills, lower earning capacity and are forced into the low paid sector. Domestic responsibilities shape and reinforce women's unequal position. Access to housing and other major facilities is very limited for women - discrimination and poverty mean most women get access to these things through men and through marriage. So many public institutions and services have been designed on the assumption of women's dependency and inequality - the tax, social security, immigration and pensions systems all reinforce that inequality and discriminate against women. Women face violence, sexual harassment and rape in the home, on the streets and in the work place. In addition, many women are profoundly disadvantaged by the impact of racism, or because they are not able-bodied or not heterosexual.

The Services Women Use

The public and social services, which should and could make such a difference to women's lives by providing support, and therefore greater opportunities, have never been good enough and have been dramatically affected by government cutbacks in recent years. The status of women has been undermined too - the shift towards equality in the 70s has been replaced by a 'back to the home' philosophy from government. The media and the advertising industry have always undermined women's dignity and status - by projecting women as stupid, as sex objects.

There has been hardly any recognition of the fact that over half the population faces this range of disadvantage and that services and facilities can be shaped around that reality. The people who design them, who think up policies and who run them are largely men. They have always operated on the basis of designing or planning or running things for a mythical 'Londoner' or 'patient' or 'client' who is neither male nor female (but is actually male when you look at the end results of their work).

Take health, for example. There are experiences unique to women like pregnancy and childbirth. There are illnesses and diseases which only women get. Many women suffer from stress, anxiety, depression - related to their relative poverty, their enormous responsibilities, their limited options, and to racism. Women make up the bulk of the elderly population. At the same time, the medical profession and the health service is run by men; there are scarcely any women-only health facilities and the few there are have been cut; preventive health care has low status and priority (which contributes to GPs' 'treatment' of so many women with valium); real community care does not exist; many women experience medical care as highly unsatisfactory with their symptoms ignored or denied, treatment unsympathetic and lack of information throughout. This major rift between women's health needs and health care is made even more ludicrous and unjust when the facts of women's predominant caring role and their dominance in all the lowest status health service jobs (nursing auxilliaries, domestics) is looked at too.

As women, therefore, we not only consume services, but in many cases are the majority of workers within them. Yet this is not reflected within the social policy that shapes these services, and neither do we receive a proportional share of the services in relation to our numbers. It is for this reason that we believe it is right that women should be aware of what services exist and what demands they may make on those services.

How do London's Services Measure Up?

A review of the services and resources in London reveals alarmingly few government services which are designed for women or which offer women anything in particular. Indeed, they are some of the most rigid, unexciting, distanced and discriminatory. The Sex Discrimination Act not only exempted the government itself from the effect of the Act in many areas, such as social security, it also did not put a duty on government to take any positive steps to look at its own arrangements and to re-organise so that women's needs and interests are promoted.

Women are prime users of local borough council services - like housing, social services, and childcare - and have a lot of direct contact with council offices. A lot of councils have not recognised the needs of women and, also, do not respond positively and sympathetically to people in their own area. They have, sadly, a reputation for frustrating bureaucracy. Some of the boroughs contacted in this exercise did not want to give us, in the GLC, any information! We know that users will find the same problem - and more so. Some are beginning to change - the introduction of decentralised offices which means access to all services is through one office is one recent and notable change. Some councils have good information services.

The Arrival of Women's Committees

Within local government, however, we have seen the very exciting development of Women's Committees. The GLC and eleven other London boroughs have set up Women's Committees - to identify women's needs and interests, and then to work to re-shape the council's own services to meet those. They also consult women, and provide information and resources directly to women in the community. They have not been going for very long, and often don't have enough resources themselves. But they do represent the first positive recognition that a lot can be done to change the way services are provided in this city, so that they meet real needs and extend opportunities to all Londoners. The Women's Committees start from the assumption that policy makers should ask women what they need. That involves asking the many different constituencies of women, in particular those who face the most severe disadvantage such as Black and ethnic minority women, older women, lesbians and women with disabilities. And the answers have been clear, informed and loud. The Committees have looked at housing policy, transport, social services policies and identified where they are ignoring women or reinforcing women's problems. For example, the first ever policy review and survey of women and public transport showed that far more women than men use public transport but for different purposes. It also showed that the fare system means women pay more for their use of public transport. No-one had looked into the question before!

The Committees have all recognised that women themselves are providing their own services, such as childcare or advice services in local communities. They have rarely received recognition or funding and so have run on voluntary effort and fundraising. They are designed by and run by local women, which means they are really meeting needs. They are often innovative and more flexible than Council or government services. Providing funding to maintain, develop and equip those groups has been seen as a vital part of extending opportunities for women.

All the Committees have found a warm response from women, a great demand for change and a lot of scope for real change. The same approach can and should be applied by all local authorities, as well as to other government public institutions such as the National Health Service (NHS), Department of Health and Social Security (DHSS), national voluntary organisations. Now more Women's Committees are springing up, and there is increasing pressure to see their work become a responsibility of all authorities.

Women and the Voluntary Sector

The third way in which a lot of the services available in London are provided is by the voluntary sector. There are different strands in the voluntary sector - the traditional charitable or church organisations, self-help groups, campaigning groups, local projects. Again, the traditional self-financing voluntary sector has been more concerned with doing things for people, and although these projects play a large role in some services, they have not seen the need to consider women's position or the position of Black people, when carrying out their work. London has also seen the blossoming of another sort of project - those run by local people, by women, by Black people, for themselves. Many of these groups began as campaigning groups, but from the experience of successful campaigning they have grown into groups providing community based services. Many nursery and childcare projects, for instance, started with a small group of mothers meeting together to demand facilities, who then went on to organise and run childcare projects. Local government funding has been instrumental in the growth of this voluntary sector. However the distribution of funding is not evenly spread through London or the country as a whole. Many local authorities continue to fund groups which are providing what they may consider to be 'cheap' services - for example, community based voluntary sector projects for old people, because it is cheaper than running services themselves. Others will not fund anything but the most 'respectable' mainstream organisations.

The last four years have seen major changes in the pattern of funding for voluntary groups because of the GLC's commitment to supporting them. The Council has considered the voluntary sector to be a vital element in the network of facilities which are needed by Londoners. It has been committed to resourcing the voluntary sector properly. Over 2,500 groups have been funded - in every area and of every kind. It has also taken its own commitment to extending equal opportunities for Black people, women, lesbians and gay men, people with disabilities and helped and encouraged the voluntary sector to shape itself to the needs of all members of the community. All funded groups are monitored from an equal opportunities perspective.

The GLC Women's Committee has had a major impact - over 500 women's projects have been funded with a total budget of £11 million in 1985/6. 12% of all full-time childcare places in London are funded; women's centres offering a wide range of advice, childcare, educational, training and leisure facilities have been funded for many areas; projects providing architectural, design and computing services are funded. Some of the most interesting voluntary sector projects for women can therefore be found in London.

Many of the projects funded through the Ethnic Minorities, Grants, Arts and Recreation, Transport, and Housing Committees will be much more approachable by women, too, because of the work done to promote awareness among them.

The Future of the Handbook

The Handbook lists all the organisations and bodies we have been able to draw together at this stage. It is by no means comprehensive - we know there are more projects, more organisations and agencies. Gathering the information was difficult precisely because it does not exist in one place. Even collecting information on GLC funded groups was not straightforward. The Handbook ought to be continually developed and updated - and it would have been if the Council and therefore the Women's Committee were not abolished. At the time of going to print we are hoping to find a 'home' for the Handbook and an organisation/authority which will update it regularly.

At the same time, a much more difficult job could also be done - starting to analyse the projects, boroughs, agencies and giving an indication of the quality of their services for women. Do they run things for women - are women employed in them, are women on the management committee, are women's issues a concern, do they direct any information or advertising at women, are the needs of Black women catered for, is the building accessible, are there childcare facilities...?

At the time of writing, the GLC Women's Committee is scheduled for abolition. The government has made no arrangements for its work to continue. We are not giving up though - we are looking for ways through the London Boroughs, that the vital London-wide work for women can be carried on.

How to use the Handbook

The first sections of the Handbook are about some of the issues and problems women face and where to go for more information, advice, practical help, others who share the problem, support, services. The *introduction* to each section gives some background to the issue, describes the current debates and ideas about the issue, looks at what women have done and are doing and details the action the GLC has taken on it. Then follow the *listings* of organisations, groups and authorities with their addresses, telephone numbers, opening hours and where possible a summary of their activities and how accessible they are for women with disabilities. Useful publications are also listed at the end of each section. These sections, listed alphabetically, cover Black and ethnic minority Women, carers, childcare and children, disability, education and further education, employment and unemployment, family relationships and the law, funding for voluntary organisations/groups, health, housing, immigration and nationality, lesbians, media and arts, older women, peace, planning, policing, prison, prostitution, sport, training, transport, violence against women, young women.

The second major part of the Handbook is printed on pink paper and is called Borough Information. The Borough Information section lists MPs, councils, women's centres and advice centres on a borough by borough basis. Many of these listing also appear in the topic sections but they are brought together in Borough information to make it easy for women to identify important local facilities.

Again, the listings aim to give name, address, telephone number, hours, outline of facilities, access information.

The third short section is called Women's Resources and Campaigning. It looks at how women organise campaigns, groups, services, projects and lists some of the key women's resource centres in London where you can get further information and advice.

Finally, the index at the back should help you to find the right page(s) for a particular topic. It is in alphabetical order.

Whenever possible you will be referred to other useful or relevant sections in the Handbook. This cross-reference is always written in brackets as (see **Employment and Unemployment**) or (see **Housing**). If you are being referred to a particular bit of Housing, it will say (see **Housing**, racial harassment), or (see **Media and Arts,** women's publications).

Collecting the information for the Handbook has been an enormous job. We do not have complete or full information on every listing. In particular, we have not been able to find out how accessible all the projects and authorities are to women with disabilities. Where we have found out we have used a Code to describe the access. The code uses the letters A, P or N. Access A means the building is accessible to wheelchair users. Access P means there is access to part of the building or that access is possible with help. Access N means the building does not provide any. In some cases, home visits can be arranged. If you are planning to visit and are concerned about access it is always worth phoning first. Also where we have no code you can phone the group or authority to establish the position. By doing so more people will be encouraged to consider the issue of accessibility.

It has not been possible to investigate all listings to establish how aware they are of women's issues; whether they run things just for women; whether women get a good service. Similarly, it has not been possible to establish whether the needs of Black and ethnic minority women, lesbians, older or younger women, or women with disabilities are fully met. What we have done is show by an asterisk (*) which projects have been funded by the GLC Women's Committee. That means that the Committee supported the aims of the project and considered it was meeting women's needs. It also means the Committee's conditions that the project be available and accessible to all women will have been operating, and that the project has had to consider that.

The details are as accurate as we have been able to get them - some are bound to be wrong already and others will soon be out of date. If so try a similar organisation or one listed as an important information-giving project on the issues you are concerned with.

Codes used in the Handbook

*Projects funded by GLC Women's Committee

A Accessible to wheelchair users (not necessarily with accessible toilet)

P Part of premises accessible to wheelchair users

N Not accessible to wheelchair users

Black and Ethnic Minority Women

This section brings together listings and presents information which, it is hoped, will be useful to Black and other ethnic minority women. Many of the organisations listed here appear elsewhere in the Handbook, but the purpose of this section is twofold for it aims not only to reflect the issues of particular concern to Black and ethnic minority women, but also to highlight the contribution which Black and ethnic minority women are making in some of the areas outlined.

The limitations in attempting to encapsulate concerns of such a wide range of women from so many different backgrounds in the section are obvious, but Black and ethnic minority women share the common experience of discrimination on grounds of race, ethnicity, religion and national origin, and on the whole have been denied the rights and recognition which is their due. Many ethnic groups, particularly Black groups, are under- or un-represented in policy and decision-making arenas at both a local and regional level and in the public and private sector alike. This has undoubtedly had an adverse effect on their access to resources of all kinds and in the delivery of services to their communities. What is remarkable is the energy and determination which has been demonstrated by women from these backgrounds in fighting their oppression and setting up alternative structures to service their own and the wider community, while at the same time insisting on their right to full participation in this society.

London has the greatest concentration of Britain's Black people who constitute over 15% of the population. It is not known what the precise percentage is as the official statistics which enumerate non-British born Black heads of household exclude the native-born population. What is certain is that along with other ethnic groups they make up a sizeable population of the capital's citizens. Many of these groups have had a long association with Britain and although a small percentage are migrant workers and recent newcomers, the majority have been settled here for a considerable period of time ranging from centuries to several generations, and have made a significant contribution to the economic, social and cultural life of the city. Of the two main Black communities - African/Afro-Caribbean and Asian, 54.25% of the first group (African/Afro-Caribbean) and 39.49% of all Asians in Britain live in

London. Within London itself African/Afro-Caribbean communities are concentrated in the Inner London boroughs of Wandsworth, Lambeth, Southwark, Lewisham and Hackney with a sizeable community in Brent, while 78% of Asian background people are concentrated in the band of boroughs in northwest London from Barnet through Brent and Ealing to Hounslow. In addition, there are also Asian communities in east London boroughs such as Newham and Tower Hamlets.

Black and ethnic minority women have established a wide range of self-help and voluntary organisations in order to supplement and in some cases fill the gaps in the provision of public and welfare services which they need. They are also increasingly becoming involved in the economic activity areas by setting up organisations specifically concerned with training and employment creation. From the earliest times they have been concerned with childcare and the provision of sound anti-racist education of their children. This can be seen in the Saturday/ Supplementary schools movement and the establishment of groups concerned with the issues of fostering and adopting as well as parental support. The link between women's caring responsibilities and women's position as workers has been of crucial importance to Black and ethnic minority women who have always had higher economic activity rather than other women in the society. They are concentrated in four main areas of the economy; clerical, sales and service industries and the professional and technical sectors which includes the nursing services. 80% of Black and migrant women are in semi-skilled and unskilled manual occupations and clothing, food, drink and electrical assembly - working long hours for low pay. Education, therefore, in the widest sense has been a constant theme for women from these backgrounds, linked not only to personal self advancement, but as a means of improving the lot of whole communities though attaining better remunerated and safer jobs.

The legal and civil status of the different Black and ethnic minority communities varies in accordance with the origin of the community and the period of settlement. A combination of factors, including a declining demand for labour, growing discontent and racial violence in inner city areas, and the lack of access to power both nationally and internationally of particularly the Black population led to the introduction of immigration controls. Immigration legislation discriminates specifically against Black people and while earlier acts were designed to keep Black people out of Britain, more recent legislation such as the Nationality Act serves to redefine civil and welfare rights of Black settlers in Britain. (See Immigration and Nationality).

The commonly shared colonial experience of many Black and ethnic minority workers in Britain have been a basis for common struggle against institutional and state racism. Black and ethnic minority women's experience of racism in education, housing, welfare services, with the police and of immigration rules are very similar. And it is the similarity of these experiences as well as the shared experiences of British colonialism in their countries of origin that have led to many Black and ethnic minority women coming together to organise. Hence the definition of Black has become politicised and now denotes for many people a commonly shared experience of colonialism, racism, discrimination and exploitation. Black and ethnic minority women's experience is often different from that of white women in all areas of their lives as they are affected not only by the sexism prevalent in society but also by racism.

Irish Women

There are over a quarter of a million Irish-born women, in addition to second generation Irish women living in London. Their reasons for coming here are varied, but related in the main to economic, social and political conditions at home. Like Black and other ethnic minority groups there is a connection between the historical relationship between Britain and Ireland and the pattern of immigration. At one stage in this century over 43% of Irish people became emigrants. Many came to England. Their work has traditionally been in the service industries - cleaning, catering and caring for the sick and elderly - work that has been undervalued and underpaid.

It is assumed that because the majority of Irish people are white that they do not experience racism, but many of the stereotypes through which the Irish are depicted can be equated with racist stereotypes, and they issue from the phenomenon of cultural imperialism and economic exploitation which amounts to anti-Irish racism. The Irish have taken many of the same routes as Black and other ethnic minorities in dealing with discrimination and Irish women too are at the forefront of providing the support structures for their communities. Self-help and voluntary activity are a common feature of all these communities and the listings under this section include many of the organisations which have been thus established.

Jewish Women

The Jewish community in London is, in fact, a network of many varied communities, made up of people from widely diverse backgrounds. Some have families established here for many generations; others, many with most of their family killed by the Nazis, are more recently established. There are Jews in all social classes, and of all political perspectives. Despite the assumption behind anti-semitism, there is no stereotypical Jew. Nor are all Jews, or even most Jews, white. Approximately two-thirds of the world's Jews have African, Asian or middle Eastern origins: Black Jews suffer white racism (including from white Jews) as well as anti-semitism.

Jewish women are sometimes depicted as being more oppressed than other women by virtue of their religion/culture. This again can be an anti-semitic assumption about Jewish family life, which is varied and in any case not necessarily more patriarchal than that of many other religions, including Christianity. Jewish women also vary in their views on Israel: some take a strongly Zionist point of view (which is in itself complex), others are anti-Zionist, and others seek to define and take action around the many difficult contradictions that arise - including the anti-semitism that can be unleashed towards Jewish women over this issue.

Whatever the difference of background and political and religious belief, all Jewish women share the experience of anti-semitism, which in London and other metropolitan areas is on the increase, along with other manifestations of racism. This is causing many Jewish women to seek and support each other. In some cases, women are rejecting former efforts to be 'assimilated' by, for instance, changing their surnames and first names (disguised by parents and grandparents protecting their families) back to Jewish forms, and becoming active in campaigning for Jewish peoples' issues, building networks against anti-semitism, in all its forms.

This section is ordered as follows: ***Black and Ethnic Minority Women's Groups, Ethnic Minority Organisations.***

Black and Ethnic Minority Women's Groups

African Refugee Women's Group, c/o African Refugee Housing Action Ltd, 25 Leighton Road, NW5, or 42 Albany Street, NW1. Support/advice group.

Arab Women's Group, c/o Outwrite, Oxford House, Derbyshire St, E2.

Armagh Co-ordinating Committee, Tindlemanor, 52-54 Featherstone Street, EC1.

Asian Women's Aid,* (703 4319/4291). Refuge for Asian women, with childcare and developmental workers.

Asian Action Group,* 30 Willoughby Road, Hornsey, N8 (341 3802). Asian Women's Action Group provides cultural activities, racism and sexism awareness courses, and publishes a magazine. Open 10am - 6pm, and when refurbished will be open 10am - 9pm.

Asian Women's Network,* Tindlemanor, 52-54 Featherstone St, EC1Y 8TR (251 9276). Library and information service for Asian women.

Asian Women's Forum,* c/o Asian Centre, 8 Caxton Road, N22 (889 6938).

Asian Women's Resource Centre,* (Brent), 134 Minet Ave, NW10 (961 5701). Girls' work, classes, advice/info/ referral (for people with disabilities as well as general). Open 10-5pm Mon-Fri.

Bangladesh Women's Association,* 91 Highbury Hill, N5.

Battersea Black Women's Group,* 248 Lavender Hill, SW11 (228 8532). Open only Sundays 4pm onwards. Creche provided. Discussion meetings on general issues. Aims to involve Black women in public affairs in Wandsworth. No wheelchair access.

Black Women's Radio Group, c/o Local Radio Workshop, 12 Praed Mews, W2.

Black Women for Wages for Housework, PO Box 287, King's Cross Women's Centre, NW6 (837 7509).

Brent Black Women's Group, 11-12 Donovan Court, Eston Crescent, NW10 (961 3337/965 2477/965 0047). Creche and access. Classes, workshops, lunch club and occasional health speakers. Open 10am - 5pm Mon - Fri.

Brixton Black Women's Centre,* Mary Seacole House, 41a Stockwell Green, SW9 (274 9220). No creche, no access. General advice & information, community work. Open 10am - 6pm, (Thursdays till 10pm).

Camden & Islington Black Sisters, c/o Law Centre, 146 Kentish Town Rd, NW5 (485 6672).

Centre for Black Women,* 136 Kingsland High Road, PO Box 29, E8. Creche, no access. Advice & information, playgroup. Young single mothers group, library with Black literature, history and culture, elderly black women's club, racism awareness, health and sickle cell sessions. Open 9am - 5pm Mon - Fri.

Claudia Jones Organisation,* 103 Stoke Newington Church St, N16 (241 1646). Access and creche. Advice and info on education, health etc. Recreational activities. Open 9.30am - 5.30pm Mon - Fri.

Croydon Asian Women's Group, c/o Secretary, 9 Howden Road, SE25 (653 1565). No premises, organises activities on issues of health, education, welfare, Asian culture, local community affairs, and has a youth project. Creche.

Cypriot Women's League, 96 Palmerstone Road, N22.

East London Black Women's Organisation,* 747 Barking Road, Plaistow, E13 (552 1169). No access. Creche occasionally. Workshops and classes. Open 9.30am - 5.30pm Mon - Fri.

Saturday school 2 - 5pm.

Eleanor Street Women's Group, 8 Eleanor Street, Bow, E3. (Self-help by residents of official travellers' site).

Eritrean Women's Association, PO Box 7007, WC1 (794 6931).

FAEERU Women's Group, 116 Ladbroke Grove, W10 (221 2007).

Grainne Mhaol Collective,* 26 Boscombe Road, W12. Closed group documenting the history, culture, struggles and activities of Irish Women in London.

Greenwich Asian Women's Centre,* c/o Macbean Centre, Macbean Street SE18 (854 1188).

Greenwich Asian Women's Group, c/o Asian Resource Centre, LEB Buildings, Macbean St, SE18.

Hackney Muslim Women's Council,* 101 Clapton Common, E5 (809 0993). Creche, no access. Playgroup, classes and talks. Open 9-7pm Mon - Fri, 10-12 Sat, 11 - 1 Sun.

Hackney Pakistan Women's Centre,* 42 Stamford Hill, N16 (806 3289). Open 9.45am - 6pm Counselling service and wide range of cultural/recreational activities. Variety of classes and translation service.

Haringey Black Women's Group,* c/o Old Somerset School, Lordship Lane, N17 (802 0912).

Hounslow Asian Women's Community Centre,* 126 Hanworth Road, Hanworth, Mddx. (572 2484). No creche, partial access. Language and sports classes. Open 9.30am - 5.30pm.

Iranian Women's Support Group, c/o Spare Rib, 27 Clerkenwell Close, EC1.

Irish Women in Islington Group,* Cabin X, 25 Horsell Road, N5 (609 8916/7325).

Jewish Women's Centre Group, c/o Sisterwrite, 190 Upper Street, London N1. Group formed with the aim of setting up a Jewish women's centre in London.

Jewish Women's Oral History Project, Southbank House, Black Prince Road, London SE1.

Latin American Women's Group - CARILA,* 29 Islington Park Street, N1 (359 2270).

Lewisham Asian Association Women's Section, 170 New Cross Road, SE14.

London Irish Women's Centre,* 59 Stoke Newington Church St, N16 (249 7318). Irish language and cultural classes, social club, children's classes etc. Admin address - Cabin Y, 25 Horsell Road, N5. 609 8916 Open 9.30am - 6.30pm Mon - Fri.

London Jewish Feminist Group, c/o AWP, Hungerford House, Victoria Embankment, WC2 (836 6081).

Milap Ladies' Group, Milap Day centre, Town Hall Annexe, Southall, Mddx. (843 1893).

Millan Asian Centre, 59 Trinity Rd, SW17 (767 8628). Access but no creche. Legal advice, classes, playgroup, mother & toddler group, after school care.

Muslim Women's Welfare Association, 200 Capworth St, E10 (539 7478).

Peckham Black Women's Group,* c/o St Giles Parish Hall, Benhill Rd, SE5 (701 2651). Creche and access. Workshops, counselling, discussions. Open 10am - 5pm Mon - Fri.

Philippine Women's Support Committee, BM Box 758 WC1 3XX (603 1873).

Polish Women's Group, c/o 165 Lyndhurst Road, N22 (881 3285). Discussion Group.

Pragati Asian Women's Association,* 9 - 13 Nicoll Road, NW10 (965 8643).

Shepherds Bush Black Women's Group, c/o 119 or 139 Becklow Road, W12.

Soloettes, c/o League of Jewish Women, Woburn House, Upper Woburn Place, London WC1. Social club for Jewish women who are single, divorced, separated or widowed. They hold meetings, arrange outings and weekends away etc. There is one group in Redbridge and another in North London.

Somali Women's Group, c/o Oxford House, Derbyshire St, E2.

Southall Black Women's Centre,* 86 Northcote Avenue, Southall, Mddx. (843 0578).

Southwark Muslim Women's Association,* Old Bellenden School, Bellenden, SE15 (732 8053). Creche, no access. Workshops, language classes. Open 10am - 9pm approx. Mon, Wed, Fri open late.

SWAPO Women's Council, 96 Gillespie Road, N5 (359 9116/7).

Tamil Women's League,* c/o 3 Canonbury St, N1 (226 2367).

Turkish Women's Project, c/o Thornhill Neighbourhood Project, Orkney House, 199 Caledonian Road, N10.

Union of Turkish Women in Britain,* 129 Newington Green Rd, N1. (226 7544).

United Black Women's Action Group, c/o Wood Green Community Centre, Stanley Road, N15 (802 0911).

West Indian Women's Association,* 71 Pound Lane, NW10. (451 4827).

Yehudit - Jewish Women's Theatre Group, Contact c/o 388 4625.

Ethnic Minority Organisations

Projects and Resources based at 5a Westminster Bridge Road:

Asian Sheltered Residential Association Co. Ltd.

Black Media Workers Association

Black Teens Magazine

Black Trades Union Solidarity Movement

Confederation of Indian Organisation

Federation of Afro-Asian Sports

Multi-lingual Print Shop

National Association of Asian Youth

Open Access Project Co. Ltd.

Racism Awareness Programme Unit

Searchlight

Standing Conference of Ethnic Minority Senior Citizens

West Indian Standing Conference

There is also a conference hall which can hold 175 people, as well as meeting rooms available for hire. Hours 9.00am to 10.30pm seven days a week. Access A. Tel 928 8108

Aboriginal Land Rights Support Group, 192 Burdett Road, E3 4AA.

The Africa Centre, 38 King St, WC2E 8JT (836 1973). General African community centre with regular theatre and music events, meetings and discussions. Also restaurant, bookshop and meeting space for hire. Hours - 9.30am to 5.30 pm weekdays (phone for programme of events). Access: A to ground floor rooms only.

African Refuge Housing Action Ltd, 42 Albany Street, NW1. Campaigning group and Housing Association - women's group attached.

Black People's Information Centre, 301 Portobello Road, W10. (969 9825)

Board of Deputies of British Jews, Woburn House, Upper Woburn Place, London WC1. (387 4044). Can give information about Jewish organisations, clubs, synagogues etc.

Bolivian Working Group, 29 Islington Park Street, N1.

Brent Irish Cultural Centre, 76-82 Salisbury Road, NW6 6NY.

Chile Democratico,* 95-97 Old Street, EC1V 9JJ (278 3329)

Chinese Information & Advice Centre,* 152-156 Shaftesbury Ave, WC2 (836 8291). Mainly advice and support. Has autonomous women's section. Open Mon to Wed and Fri 11am - 5pm. Closed Thurs. Access N.

Chinese Welfare Project,* Sailors Palace, 680 Commercial Road, E14 7HA. (515-5598)

Commonwealth Centre, Kensington High St, W8 6NQ, (603 4535). Cultural central centre with particular interest in Black Commonwealth communities. Facilities include cinema, theatres, workshops and seminar spaces, bookshops, exhibitions, restaurants, cafes. Phone for programme. Access A.

Comunidad - Latino Americana Magazine (CLAM), 2 Warwick Crescent, Beauchamp Lodge, W2.

Eritrean Relief Association, 391 City Road, EC1.

Haringey Travellers' Support Group, c/o Mr I Ashton, Area 4, Social Services, 115 King's Road, Woodgreen, N22.

Indo-Chinese Project, Greencoat House, 10 Francis Street, SW1p IDH. (834 5911)

Iranian Centre,* 465a Green Lanes, N4 (341 5005/348 9115). Community centre providing language classes, musical events, socials, classes on Iranian culture, literature and exhibitions. Open 10am - 5pm Tues to Fri (closed 1 - 2pm. Access N.

Irish Centre, 52 Camden Square, NW1 (485 OO51). General cultural and social activities, also with advice and information available. Hours - 9.30am to 5.30pm weekdays (closed 1-2pm lunch), 9.30am - 12.30pm Sat. Phone for details. Access A.

Jewish Employment Action Group. (205 7168 or 954 1201). Offers advice and assistance to people suffering antisemitism at their workplace.

Jewish Socialist Group, Box JSG, BM 3725, London WC1N 3XX, (587 1506). This group has a women's caucus.

Jewish Welfare Board, 221 Golders Green Rd, London NW11 9DW. (458 3282). Contact for your nearest day centre.

Kurdish Cultural Centre, 13-15 Stockwell Road, SW9.

Lambeth Irish in Britain Representation Group, 245a Coldharbour Lane, SW9 8RR

Latin American Advisory Committee (LAAC), Beauchamp Lodge, 2 Warwick Crescent, W2.

Latin American Community Project, 10 Bernays Grove, SW9 8DF. (737 3617)

Latin American House Association, 97 Caledonian Road, N1 9JY.

Liberation Cuba Resource Centre, 313/5 Caledonian Road, N1. (607 0465)

London Interpreting Project, 245a Coldharbour Lane, SW9 8RR.

London Roadside Travellers Group, Box 18, Kingsland High Street, E8 2NS

Millan Asian Community Centre,* 59 Trinity Rd, SW17 75D. (767 8718/9/0, 767 8628/9/0)

National Gypsy Education Council, c/o Mr N Lee, 7 Taylor Court, Clays Lane, E15

Pakistan Welfare Association, 21 South Park Rd, SW19. (542 6176)

Polish Social and Cultural Association, 238-246 King St, W6 ORF (741 1940) Largest Polish library outside Poland, cafe, restaurant, theatre, social events. Open 9am - 11pm weekdays (12 midnight Fridays/Saturdays) 10 - 11am Sundays. Access A.

Portuguese Community Centre, 7 Thorpe Close, W10. (969 3890)

Rastafarian Advisory Centre, 17a Netherwood Road, W14.

Sephardi Women's Guild, 2 Ashworth Road, London W9. (289 2573).

Somali London Community & Cultural Association (SLCCA), 17 Victoria Park Square, Bethnal Green, E2.

Turkish Education Group,* 129 Newington Green Road, N1. (359 4315) Classes, youth clubs, children's groups, creche, interpreting, translating, library.

Turkey Solidarity Campaign, BM Box 5965, WC1N 3XX.

Ujamaa Centre, 14 Brixton Road, SW9. (582 5590)

Union of Jewish Students, 1 Endsleigh Street, London WC1 0DS, (387 4646 or 380 0111). The UJS has a women's officer and a women's group.

Vietnamese Association Services, 3 Ravensdale Gdns, SE19. (771 5199)

Westway Site Support Group, c/o Ms T Suddaby, 26d Powis Square, W11. (Residents and Workers on official travellers' site)

Carers

It is difficult to estimate the number of carers because of the hidden nature of caring in the home - indeed many carers do not even recognise themselves as such. The Equal Opportunities Commission suggests that in London alone there are some 500,000 unpaid carers looking after people at home with physical and mental disabilities, elderly people needing care and children with disabilities under 16 years.

Caring is seen by society as traditionally 'women's work', and within the family it is almost always women who are responsible for maintaining the household routine and looking after relatives and friends with chronic illnesses and disabilities.

Most women are carers for much of their lives in one form or another. Married women care for small children, then ageing parents, often with mental and physical handicaps, and finally as ageing women themselves, for elderly husbands and perhaps other people with disabilities. Single women carers very often do not have the *choice* to lead a 'normal' life. Their lives revolve around looking after others and consequently result in almost total isolation. This often continuous but changing spectrum of caring responsibilities means that at any time large numbers of women are actively involved in providing care for other people. They are forced to fit caring tasks around their other work and at the expense of leisure pursuits. There is more pressure placed upon them either to give up their jobs altogether, especially among single women, or to take low-paid, often part-time employment near to home, which makes them vulnerable in the competitive labour markets and in the long run reduces their entitlement to pensions etc.

Black and ethnic minority women looking after a friend or relative are often more inadequately housed, with lower incomes, and are more likely to be employed in low-paid and physically exhausting work, thus limiting their capacity to care for family dependants. Many professionals assume that ethnic minority carers will be able to call upon the extended family but in many cases they have moved away from the family network or are separated by racist immigration laws denying or endlessly delaying entry to family members. Social workers often do not ensure that ethnic minority carers get the services they need. Nor is provision always taken up by Black and ethnic minority women especially where English is not the first language and more interpreters should be available.

It is not only racist and sexist assumptions which lead to the difficulties women face as carers. The rising demand for, and costs of, public caring services, along with political unwillingness to expand resources, has led to the development of community care as a solution. This idea is further supported by increasing criticism of the care provided by institutions. However, research into community care shows that the reality of 'community' is that women within the family are taking responsibility for caring. As a result of pressures on local authorities, causing them to reduce spending and thus limit resources, social services tend to act only in response to crisis and breakdown within families over-stressed by the burden of caring.

Women as carers should have a real choice over whether they prefer to care for their friend or relative in the home or seek paid employment outside. This choice is denied partly because the responsibilities of caring restrict employment opportunities and disrupt career patterns and partly because the resources to allow the positive choice to be a carer are not available. Funding must be made available for adequate finances and back-up services designed to maximise the independence of people with chronic illnesses or disabilities, and alternatives to 'community care' as a cheap solution provided. See Residential Care in the Community below. (Also see Disability and Childcare and Children)

In response to this the GLC Women's Committee organised a Conference on 22 September 1985. Over 270 carers attended. One woman was quoted as saying she had not left the house in 6 years.

Listed below are some of the demands from carers who attended the Conference.

● A better support system should be available to all caring at home, non-means tested, and including respite care in or outside the home.

● Institutionalised racism in the existing services serves to make Black women even more invisible as carers and to limit their access to services which are theirs by right. Recognition of women as carers must take into account the needs of Black women, reflect their interest and involve Black people in all stages of the decision-making.

● Carers want status, recognition, an identity, with pay for the work they do. They also need information, training, access to advice and these should be made available soon.

- Services should be provided whatever the handicap and whatever the age of the child. Carers should not have to fight between themselves for resources.

- Carers should be treated on a par with professionals, since they are the key person, along with the children.

- As of right, all carers should have payment for the work they do.

- There must be much more awareness of what is available for the terminally ill and their carers. Professionals must be made more aware so that they can pass information on at the appropriate moment.

- Both Voluntary and Statutory organisations concerned with carers must make their services applicable to Black and ethnic minority people, and the 'colourblind' approach is not acceptable. There must be proper recognition of racism in the caring services and steps must be taken to change this.

- The social situation should be structured so that young carers feel confident to identify themselves in a way that their position is not jeopardised ie, being taken into care themselves.

- Money should be made available to help young people under 16 in the practical work of caring. From 16 upwards caring should be considered as waged labour for those that choose it.

- More money should be available for the practical costs of access. The DHSS appeal structure has no democratic system to appeal against money paid out. The response to appeals etc., is too long - help is needed more quickly. Evaluation of money needs should be more realistic.

- The local authorities should provide more education and experience of disability for their service provider base, with direct consultation with carers and people with disabilities. There is a lack of individual contact, and a lack of practical experience and awareness of disabilities.

There are a number of groups and organisations which can give support and/or provide resources for carers and the person they care for. Also, ring your local Social Services Department, as most have officers dealing with carers and information about carers' benefits and carers' groups.

This section is ordered as follows: *Caring for Elderly People/ Parents, Incontinence, Mental Handicap/Mental Illness, Caring for Children with Disabilities, Caring for Adults with Disabilities, Caring for Terminally Ill People, Care Attendant Schemes, Aids and Equipment, Housing, Mobility/Transport, Publications.*

Caring for Elderly People/ Parents

Age Concern Greater London, 54 Knatchbull Road, SE5 9QY (737 3456). Age Concern is a Community Resource for pensioners and their families. Most local Age Concerns run clubs and day centres, or pop-in centres. Each of these can be a focus of social activity. Families contact Age Concern groups for local information about facilities and services: most areas in Greater London have one borough-wide Age Concern. Some boroughs do not. They have two or more local groups. Contact Age Concern Greater London for the addresses of smaller local groups, or look in the telephone book under Age Concern.

National Council for Carers and Elderly Dependants Ltd, 29 Chilworth Mews, W2 3RG (262 1451).

Pensioners' Link Central Office, 17 Balfe Street, N1 9EB (278 5501/2/3/4).

Council and Care for the Elderly, 131 Middlesex Street, E1 7JF (621 1624).

Help the Aged, 32 Dover Street, W1A 2AP (499 0972).

Southall Old People's Welfare Association, 43 Minterne Avenue, Norwood Green, Southall, Middlesex (574 5654).

(The) Calabash Centre, George Lane, SE13.

Incontinence

Incontinence laundry services are provided by the following Local Authorities: Newham, Tower Hamlets, Kensington and Chelsea, Greenwich, Lambeth, Islington, Southwark, Waltham Forest, Wandsworth and Hackney.

You would normally qualify if you are elderly, live alone or with an elderly carer and you are incontinent. Contact Social Services for information about this service.

Mental Handicap/Mental Illness

(See **Disability**)

Portugal Prints, Parish House, Portugal Street, WC2. A Print and Arts Workshop for people recovering from mental illness, aiming to help workers lead a more independant life away from hospital.

Caring for Children with Disabilities

(Also see **Childcare; Disability**)

Association of Parents with Vaccine Damaged Children, 2 Church Street, Shipston-on-Stour, Warwickshire, CV36 4AP.

The Children's Society, 108 Alderman Hill, N13 (886 4769).

Children's Legal Centre, 20 Compton Terrace, N1 2UN (359 6251/2).

Children's Aid Team, 662 High Road, N17 (808 4965). See Childcare Section of this book.

Caring for Adults with Disabilities

(Also see **Disability**)

Many carers experience feelings of isolation and loneliness, and the opportunity to talk with carers and gain their support can very often lessen these. There is a network of local support groups which have been started by carers themselves. New groups are starting all the time.

Association of Carers, Lilac House, Medway Homes, Balfour Road, Rochester, Kent, 6QU (0634 8131981). The Association of Carers is the national organisation which provides advice and information on all aspects of caring. It has a vast database of information ranging from local support groups to rights and benefits for individuals, and will tell you of your local group as well.

Contact A Family, 16 Strutton Ground, SW1 (262 2695).

(SPOD) Sexual and Personal Relationships of the Disabled, 286 Camden Road, N7 0BJ (607 8851).

Sisters Against Disablement, c/o WRRIC, 52-54 Featherstone Street, EC1 (251 6332).

Caring for Terminally Ill People

During the 1960's and 70's the concept of community care changed from a policy of care *in* the community to one of care *by* the community. Care *in* the community could be defined as the professional provision of services in local residential and daycare centres, and in the recipients' homes. However, instead of the state providing facilities and support in small residential units or through domiciliary services which could enable people to remain in the community outside large institutions, care and support has been increasingly regarded as a 'natural' function of the family.

St Christopher's Hospice, Lawrie Park Road, SE6 6DZ (778 9252), and St Joseph's Hospice, Mare Street, E8 (985 0861). Working to improve the quality of life for people with advanced malignant and neurological diseases. If a patient is admitted the whole family remains the focus of care and is often involved as part of the caring team.

Care Attendant Schemes

(Also see **Disability**)

Continuous caring can create stress and strain on carers and there are schemes operating which can provide attendants and 'sitters' to take over the caring role within the home for periods ranging from a few hours to a few weeks.

The Association of Crossroads Care Attendant Schemes, 94a Coton Road, Rugby, Warwickshire, CV24 4LN (0788 61536). Your local Social Services should have a list of what schemes are available in your own area (see phone book, listed under your borough).

Local Women's Royal Voluntary Service (WRVS), see your phone book.

Community Service Volunteers, 237 Pentonville Road, N1 (278 6602).

British Red Cross, 9 Grosvenor Crescent, SW1X 7EJ (235 5454). Many local branches, see phone book.

Home Helps - Contact your local Social Services Dept.

Cheshire Foundation Family Support Services, 26-29 Maunsel Street, SW1P 2QN (828 1822).

Grace (Nursing Home Advisory Service), Leigh Corner, Leigh Hill Road, Cobham, Surrey.

Winged Fellowship Trust, 2nd Floor, 64-66 Oxford Street, W1N 9FF (636 5575/5886).

NCVO Community Care Project, 26 Bedford Square, WC1 (636 4066).

LVSC Neighbourhood Care Project, 68 Chalton Street, NW1 (388 024).

Aids and Equipment
(Also see **Disability**)

Invalids at Home Trust, Sarah Lomas, 19 Grasmere Avenue, Preston Road, Wembley, Middlesex. Grants for equipment and help. (Also see Disability)

Housing

Habinteg Housing Association, 6 Duke's Mews, W1M 5RB. This was set up in 1971 and is a specialist housing association which provides purpose-built accommodation within the community for people with physical disabilities and their families. There are at present 4 schemes in London: Islington, Haringey, Southwark and Hammersmith (also, see Housing).

Mobility/Transport
(See **Disability**)

London Dial-A-Ride (Federation of London Dial-A-Rides), St Margarets, 25 Leighton Road, NW5 2QD (482 2325). The Dial-A-Ride schemes are for those who are unable to use the bus or tube who need door-to-door transport. The fares for the service are equivalent to bus fares. The service has paid, trained drivers and the vehicles are wheelchair accessible, designed to meet the needs of those using the service. In most cases travel is limited to between 5-9 miles and it is usually necessary to book several days before travel. Your Local Social Services will have a list of a scheme available in your area, or telephone 482 2325.

Useful Reading

Children with Disabilities and their Families, A review of research S. Baldwin and C. Glendinning, A. Walker (Ed), Philip Duckworth £7.95.

Disability in Britain, Martin Robinson, 1981.

Caring for the Elderly and Handicapped: Community Care Policies and Women's Lives, Equal Opportunities Commission, EOC 1982 (free).

The Experience of Caring for Elderly and Handicapped Dependants: Survey Report, EOC, EOC, March 1980 (free).

Behind Closed Doors, EOC, a report on the public response to an advertising campaign about discrimination against married women in certain social security benefits, EOC, December 1981 (free).

Looking after Granny: The Reality of Community Care, A. Flew, New Society 9 October 1980.

The Extra Costs of Disabled Living, M. Hyman, (National Fund for Research into Crippling Diseases, 1977. £2.00).

The Supporters of Confined Elderly Persons in the Community, National Institute for Social Work Training, 1983.

Family Care for the Handicapped Elderly: Who Pays? M Nissel and L Bonnerjea, (Policy Studies Institute, 1982. £3.00).

A Labour of Love: Women, Work and Caring: J. Finch and D. Groves (Eds), (Routledge 1983. £5.95).

Caring: Experiences of Looking After Disabled Relatives, A. Briggs and J. Oliver, (RKP 1984. £5.95).

Old Age Abuse, M. Eastman, (Age Concern, 1984. £5.00).

Take Care of Your Elderly Relatives, McKenzie, Loval, Gray and Muir (Allen & Unwin £5.95).

Help at Hand, Association of Carers.

All the above are available from the Association of Carers, Lilac House, Medway Homes, Balfour Road, Rochester, ME4 6QU, Kent (0634 813981).

Disability Rights Handbook: A guide to rights, benefits and services for all people with disabilities and their families, (The Disability Alliance ERA £2).

Chance or Choice, Community Care and Women as Carers, GLC publication.

Women as Carers - GLC Women's Committee Directory of services available in the 32 London boroughs.

Who Cares for the Carers? EOC.

Ask the Family, NCVO.

Help Starts Here, National Children's Bureau.

Childcare and Children

This section recognises that women in this society have the primary responsibility for childcare and that women on a low income are particularly disadvantaged. However, the recognition of women's primary responsibilities for childcare does not incorporate an acceptance of women's traditional role or the major impact this has on women's wider role in society. There are a number of major issues currently to be considered with regard to childcare - these are some of the issues:

- State policies towards children and childcare tend to assume that the nuclear family is the norm (mother, father, and on average, two children) yet in Greater London only 13% of families currently fit this pattern. The needs of single parents, who are predominantly women, thus go unrecognised, as also does the continuing key role of the extended family network in some communities.

- Women's childcare responsibilities can be perceived as a major factor in their failure to move on to positions of authority, security or influence in our society. The acute shortage of childcare provision prevents women from taking up employment, educational or leisure opportunities that would otherwise be available to them.

- There are few childcare agencies or projects which have developed an effective anti-racist policy from a race equality perspective. There is a tendency, for example, for such aspects as differing dietary needs to be neglected in childcare provision. However this is more frequently acknowledged as part of a multi cultural approach to childcare than the need for white childcare workers to examine their project's overall policies and their own ingrained attitudes and practices towards Black children using their facility.

- The need for positive images of Black children in play materials, reading matter and posters etc is comparatively unrecognised

- Many childcare projects express a desire to cater for the needs of children with disabilities so that those children can enjoy an integrated approach to play and childcare. However, the necessity for additional resources - for funding of special needs workers, provision of further training and special equipment etc, need considerable care and attention paid to them before children with disabilities are taken into 'mainstream' provision. Another key issue is how to tackle the adverse attitudes that 'able-bodied' children and indeed, parents, often have towards children with disabilities.

• Children who are experiencing, or who have experienced, sexual abuse from adults have special needs which must be dealt with sensitively and appropriately. The extent to which sexual abuse is prevalent in our society has only comparatively recently been documented, analysed, and the damaging psychological impact examined. This is in contrast to the recognition of other forms of physical and psychological violence towards children.

• There are a range of issues with regard to children 'in care' - as to when and whether children should be taken into care, and whether racist attitudes towards Black families result in a larger proportion of Black children being taken into care. There are a number of issues about the nature of fostering and adoption as alternatives to a protracted stay for a child in a children's home. There are also current debates with regard to fostering and adoption about how to meet the needs of Black children who are to be fostered or adopted. The debates deal with the published research which exposes the 'identity crisis' of Black children placed with white families. One major question here is why Black single parents who have wished to provide a foster home or to adopt have not been considered by local authorities or voluntary agencies to be suitable 'adoptive families'.

• Lesbian mothers have been struggling to raise public awareness of the discrimination against them, and the resultant bias in judgments made on custody cases. Invariably, judgment has been made in favour of the child's father on the grounds that a lesbian is an unfit mother. This issue highlights the nature of heterosexism and the influence of heterosexist attitudes on the State's policies towards childcare. Lesbians also point out that the image of the so-called 'normal' family in play materials, children's books and games is prevalent. Consequently there is a formation of negative attitudes to lesbians and gays and alternative household arrangements from an early age. The wider issue of the restricting impact of heterosexism on the lives of all adults and children in our society in terms of our sexuality and the freedom to choose life styles other than the so called 'normal' family, is totally under recognised.

There are a range of other major issues that are being examined and publicised by many of the projects listed in this section, such as the provision of appropriate training for childcare, the need for workplace nurseries, the need for adequate child benefits, and support for parents under stress. The issues highlighted all relate closely to the equal opportunity policies adopted, and practised by the Greater London Council.

The abolition of the GLC, in conjunction with rate-capping legislation and the assumptions underlying present government policies towards women and the family, will together have a major impact on children and childcare in London.

The GLC Women's Committee in 1985 funded 220 childcare projects which have no guarantee of alternative funding from 1 April 1986. Government proposals for future funding of the voluntary sector, taken in conjunction with the impact of the Rates Act in several local authorities in London, indicate that no more than a handful of childcare projects will be funded in 1986/87 by alternative sources.

In 1984/5 the Women's Committee has provided £6m in grant aid to provide 2,500 childcare places in London. Thus, the Committee provides at least 12½% of all childcare provision in London. Total provision in London amounts to only 40% of the actual need, so there will be a massive impact on the lives of women and children in London when this funding ceases at 31 March 1986.

The GLC Women's Committee has made efforts to prioritise applications from Black and ethnic minority projects or projects which have positive anti-racist and other equal opportunity policies. The cessation of the funding will have implications for the nature of the remaining provisions in London.

Those projects which are well established, perhaps London wide or national organisations, will have a greater chance of receiving alternative funding than the 200 plus, local projects, a large proportion of which are catering for a significant number of Black and ethnic minority children. The resultant 'knock-on' effects of the loss of women's employment in the voluntary sector and of the loss of childcare places for children whose parents' employment may depend upon that provision, cannot be under-estimated.

The listings in this section provide information about a wide range of projects and organisations concerned with children and childcare. The underlying theme to this section is the recognition that childcare provision in London is grossly inadequate, that existing provision tends to have been established on a piecemeal, unplanned and under-funded basis and that provision is often inappropriate or insensitive to the needs of Black and ethnic minority parents and children who constitute a significant proportion of the population in London.

This section is ordered as follows: *Adoption and Fostering, Black and Ethnic Minority Groups, Child Abuse, Childcare Campaigns, (0-5 and 5-11 age groups), Child Minders, Children In Care, Children with Disabilities, Children's Rights and Welfare, Education Support Groups, Entertainment, Lesbian Mothers, Parents Under Stress, Single Parents, Under Fives Provision - Co-ordinating Groups.*

Adoption and Fostering

British Agencies for Adoption and Fostering, 11 Southwark Street, SE1 1RQ. (407 8800). This agency will provide information on adoption procedure, availability of adoptive children and agencies in each borough.

The New Black Families Unit, 121-123 Camberwell Road; SE5 (703 1089). The only independent Black organisation set up to find foster and adoptive parents from the Black community. The unit is interested in hearing from Black families and single women with a positive Black identity, commitment and the skills needed to look after and care for a child.

Independent Adoption Service, 160 Peckham Rye, SE22. (703 1088). This organisation finds permanent families for children of all ages, particularly older children and ethnic minority children. It has a very active programme for encouraging Black families to adopt.

Black and Ethnic Minority Groups

The following is a list of organisations and groups either concerned with developing anti-racist policies in nurseries and schools and implementing those policies, or are directly involved with childcare provision for Black and ethnic minority children.

Camden

Black Parents Group, c/o John Oke, 70 Leverton Street, NW5.

Bengali Boys and Girls group, Kings Cross Neighbourhood Centre, 51 Argyle Street, WC1 (833 4740). Access: N.

Bengali Workers Action Group, 1 Robert Street, NW1. (388 7313). Organises womens groups with creches, youth projects, language and religion classes. Access: N.

Camden Women's Bus, * 213 Eversholt Street, NW1. (380 0304).

Community Centre, 173 Arlington Road, NW1 Tel: 267 3019. Organises under-fives group and after school club.

Chinese Welfare Project, * 152-156 Shaftesbury Avenue, WC2. (836 8291).

Fitzrovia Nursery Group (for Asian and Chinese children), 24 Warren Street, W1. (387 1516).

Hopscotch, Asian Mother and Toddlers Group, * Basement, St Richards House, Eversholt Street, NW1 (387 8747).

Camden Committee for Community Relations, 58 Hampstead Road, NW1. (387 1125), Organises five nurseries and four are playgroups with special emphasis on the needs of Black and ethnic minority children. Access: P.

Greenwich

Charlton Training Centre, Charlton, SE18. (317 9636 ext 44).

Hackney

Claudia Jones Organisation,* 55 Stoke Newington Church St, N16 (808 9330).

Mixifren Association, 38 Cranwich Road, N16 (800 5969).

Hammersmith and Fulham

Speak Pre-School Language Group,* 47 Ashchurch Grove, W12 9BU. (743 7677).

Haringey

Nktewa Community Nursery for Black Children,* 10 Hornsey Park Road, Hornsey, N8. (888 0102).

Tottenham Single Parents Group, Approach Road, Tottenham Green, N15. (801 6492/804 6188).

Asian Women's Forum,* Wood Green Shopping City, Wood Green, N22. (882 2446).

Willan Road Nursery,* 3 Willan Road, Broadwater Farm, N17. (808 1196).

Islington

Black and in Care, 20 Compton Terrace, N1. (359 6251).

Union of Turkish Women in Britain,* 129 Newington Green, N1. (226 7544).

Turkish Education Group,* 129 Newington Green Road, N1.

Lambeth

Asian Community Action Group, 322 Brixton Road, SW9. (733 7494).

Consortium of Ethnic Minorities in Lambeth, 403-405 Brixton Road, SW9. (733 1236/7)

Gresham Supplementary Education Scheme, 1 Gresham Road, SW9.(733 0690).

Ifeoma, 3-5 Gresham Road, SW9.(733 7617).

Knight's Hill Day Nursery,* 55 Casewick Road, West Norwood, SE27. (761 2267).

Latin American Children's Project,* 14 Brixton Road, SW9. (582 5590).

Myatts Field Mobile Creche,* c/o Myatts Field Health Centre, Patrios Road, SW9. (735 9171 x207).

One Love Playgroup, 4 Harcourt House, Albian Avenue, SW8. (622 6076).

Southwark

Southwark Council for Community Relations organises a supplementary school and mother and toddlers group. Ring for details. (703 1906).

Building Blocks, Castlemead Estate, The Rampway, Camberwell Road, SE5. (701 4418).

Wandsworth

Asian Parents' Group, 12 Ascot Road, SW17 (767 0617). Access: N.

Battersea Black Women's Group, c/o York Gardens Community Centre, Lavender Road, SW11. (223 7961).

Wandsworth Council for Community Relations organises the Millan Community Project, which organises supplementary schools for ethnic minority children. Ring. (767 3631).

The Federation of Black Self-Help Group, 361 Clapham Road, SW9 may be able to give information on community-based Black childcare initiatives in your area.

London-wide

Commission for Racial Equality, Elliot House, 10/12 Allington Street, SW1. (828 7022). The CRE's Education Department is producing a book on anti-racist strategies in childcare aimed at parents and trainee workers.

Child Abuse

(And see **Violence Against Women** for sexual abuse of children)

National Society for the Prevention of Cruelty to Children (NSPCC), 67 Saffron Hill, EC1. (242 1626). Acts to prevent the physical and mental abuse of children. Gives advice, counselling and practical help, and puts you in touch with their regional offices.

Parents Anonymous, 6-9 Manor Gardens, Islington, N7. (263 8918). Offers a strictly confidential telephone service to any parent who may have problems with her babies, toddlers or older children. Staffed by other parents with a team of professional workers.

Childcare Campaigns

The organisations listed below are campaigning for recognition of the needs of children under five and their parents and for an extension of existing provision. Some of these organisations can provide information about provision in their local area.

National Childcare Campaign, * Wesley House, 70 Great Queen Street, WC1 5AY (405 5617). Brings together all local childcare campaigns in the country, to co-ordinate and campaign for under fives childcare provision. Access: P.

Greenwich Childcare Campaign, * 84 Wellington Gardens, SE7. (858 8272).

Haringey Childcare Campaign, Community Playservice, The Lodge, Church Lane, N17. (808 7604)

Islington Under Fives Action Group, 145 Thorpsdale Road, N4 (272 9916).

Lewisham Childcare Campaign, 179 Deptford High Street, SE8 (691 3550).

Parents Forum, Mansfield House, 310 Barking Road, E13 (476 2324).

Southwark Childcare Campaign, 2-6 Peckham Road, SE5. Tel: (701 7535).

Thomas Coram Foundation for Children, 40 Brunswick Square, WC1. (278 2424). A research organisation with many projects adoption agency, adolescents' project, day centre for under 5's. Access: A.

Voluntary Organisations' Liaison Committee for the Under Fives (VO/CUF), 130 City Road, EC1 (250 0806). Provides a forum for the development of ideas on provision for the under 5s, and for the dissemination of information.

Wandsworth Childcare Campaign, 84 Beathwaite Road, SW11

Workplace Nurseries Campaign, Room 205, Southbank House, Black Prince Road, SE1 7SJ. (582 7199).

The following organisation campaigns and co-ordinates on provision for the 5-11's age group:

The National Out of School Alliance, Oxford House, Derbyshire Street, Bethnal Green Road, E2. (739 4787). This is the major organisation supporting and encouraging community based out of school schemes and local authority provision in schools, youth clubs, etc through advice, information, training and research. They will give advice on how to set up a playscheme, or how to find an existing one in your area.

Childminders

National Childminding Association, 204-206 High Street, Bromley BR1 1PP. (464 6164). Campaigns, co-ordinates and provides information on childminding, especially good childminding practice and information on how to find a childminder. Access: N.

Greater London Childminding Association, 87 Chudbergh Road, Brockley, SE4 1JX, (690 0201). Co-ordinates local groups and develops good standards of childminding through the provision of education and training for childminders. It also acts as a resource and information centre for people wishing to obtain details about childminding in London.

Wandsworth Childminders Association, Room 66, 11 Theatre Street, Battersea, SW11. (228 7182). Provides support to childminders and organises events to publicise childminding within the borough.

Children In Care

A Voice for the Child in Care, 60 Carysfort Road Hornsey N8 348 2588. This organisation aims to arrange for children in care to have access to an independent person, and to improve the professional practice in work with children growing up in care.

Family Rights Group, 6-9 Manor Gardens, Holloway Road, N7 (272 7308/4231). A group of social workers, lawyers and others who want to improve the law and practice relating to children in care. Access: N.

Rights of Women 52-54 Featherstone Street, EC1, (251 6911). Takes up these and variations on issues relating to children in care.

National Association of Young People in Care (NAYPIC), Sales House, 28A Manor Row, Bradford BD1. An independent organisation set up to help local care groups keep in touch start new groups and take up issues raised by local groups. Run by and for young people.

Children With Disabilities

There are a wide range of organisations and projects dealing with different aspects of children's disabilities: (See Disability, Health).

ACTIVE (with Toy Libraries Assoc.), Seabrook House, Darkes Lane, Potters Bar, Herts. EN6. (Potters Bar 44571). Aims to help children with disabilities and adults to lead more active and independent lives by using, encouraging and supporting a do-it-yourself approach to play, leisure and communication aids. Also encourages formation of local ACTIVE groups.

Association for all Speech Impaired Children, 347 Central Markets, Smithfield EC1 (236 3632/6487). Runs an information and support service for parents and campaigns for better facilities for children with speech and language disorders. Access: N.

Assocation for Spina Bifida and Hydrocephalus, 22 Upper Woburn Place, WC1 (388 1382). Access: A.

Association for the Welfare of Children in Hospital, Argyle House, 29-31 Euston Road, NW1. (833 2041). Supports sick children and their families.

Contact A Family, 16 Strutton Ground, SW1 (222 3969/2695). Introduces and links families with children with disabilities. Access: N.

Disability Alliance, 25 Denmark Street, WC2 (240 0806). Gives advice on disability rights and produces an annual handbook. Advice line 2-4 pm, Mon-Fri.

Down's Children's Association, 4 Oxford Street, W1 (580 0511/2). Helps parents and professionals with the care, treatment and training of Down's Syndrome children. Nationwide self-help groups and London resource centre.

Dyslexia Foundation, 133 Gresham Road, Staines, Middlesex TW18. (Staines 59498). Educational assessments and specialist tuition for dyslexics of all ages and specialist training for teachers.

EXODUS, 12 Park Crescent, W1 (636 5020). Campaigning group for alternative sites of care for all children diagnosed as mentally handicapped and resident in long-stay wards.

GLAD (Greater London Association for Disabled People), 1 Thorpe Close, NW10 (960 5799). Gives advice and information to people with disabilities and their families.

Haemophilia Society, P.O. Box 9, 16 Trinity Street, SE1 (407 1010). Provides advice, support and assistance to people with haemophilia and their families. Access: A.

Handicapped Children in Hackney, Huddleston Centre, 30 Powell Road, E5. (985 8869).

Handicapped Adventure Playground Association, Fulham Palace, Bishops Ave., SW6 (736 4443). Access:A.

Harrow Parents' Association for Hearing Impaired Children, 54 Hazeldene Drive, Pinner, Middlesex HA5 (868 3287). Aims to increase public awareness of the needs of hearing impaired children. Arranges outings and meetings and gives support.

Hyperactive Children's Support Group, 59 Meadowside, Angmering, Sussex. Aims to help and support hyperactive children and their families.

Institute of Child Psychology, 6 Pembridge Villas, Wll. (229 4759).

Jewish Association for the Physically Handicapped, 14 Soho Street, Wl (437 8716). Runs clubs for all ages and a holiday home.

MENCAP (Royal Society for Mentally Handicapped Children & Adults), 123 Golden Lane, ECl (253 9433). Welfare rights, counselling, education, residential accommodation, holidays, information and specialised books and publications. Encourages and supports the formation of regional groups. Access: A.

National Association for Deaf-Blind and Rubella Handicapped, (SENSE), 311 Grays Inn Road, WCl (278 1005). Helps and supports deaf-blind young people and their families.

National Autistic Society, 276 Willesden Lane, NW2 (451 3844/5). Provides information advisory services for parents and professionals. Runs seven schools, adult community hostel and day care centre. Access: A.

National Deaf Children's Society, 45 Hereford Road, W2 (229 9272/4). Advice on welfare, education and services for deaf children and their families and information on all aspects of childhood deafness. Access: N.

National Demonstration Centre, Pinderfields General Hospital, Aberford Road, Wakefield, Yorks. WFl (Wakefield 375217 ext 2510/2263). Information and advice on all aspects of living

with a disability, specialising in paediatrics.

National Eczema Society, Tavistock House North, Tavistock Square, WCl (388 4097). Access: N.

National Toy Libraries Association, Seabrook House, Darkes Lane, Potters Bar, Herts. EN6. (Potters Bar 44571). National body for over 1200 toy libraries for children, especially those with special needs.

Physically Handicapped and Able Bodied (PHAB), Tavistock House North, Tavistock Square, NWl (388 1963). Promotion of the integration of people with disabilities into the community. Access: A.

Royal Association for Disability and Rehabilitation, (RADAR), 25 Mortimer Street, Wl (637 5400). Co-ordinating body for over 400 member organisations working in the areas of access, education, employment, housing and welfare for people with disabilities. Access: A.

Royal National Institute for the Blind (RNIB), 224 Great Portland Street, Wl (388 1266). Education services, training, employment, homes, hostels, special aids and schools for blind people. Access: A.

Royal National Institute for the Deaf (RNID), l05 Gower Street, WCl (387 8033). Provides personal services. Protects the interests of all deaf people. Access: N.

Shaftesbury Society, 112 Regency Street, SWl (837 7444). Special schools and hostels for young people and provides holiday centres for people with a physical or mental handicap and elderly people with a disability.

Spastics Society, 12 Park Crescent, Wl (636 5020).

Voluntary Council for Handicapped Children, National Children's Bureau, 8, Wakeley Street, ECl (278 9441). To advance and assist in promotion of scientific research into the needs of children with a disability, and to disseminate the results to the public.

Children's Rights and Welfare

Children's Legal Centre, 20 Compton Terrace, N1 (359 6251). Aims to clarify, develop and improve the laws and policies affecting children and young people.

Child Poverty Action Group, 1 Macklin Street, WC3 (242 3225/9149). Provides welfare rights advice and publishes annual guides to social security benefits.

Justice for Children, 35 Wellington Street, WC2 (836 5917). Provides advice and information service for parents, children and social workers and campaigns on the juvenile justice system. Access: N.

National Association for Maternal and Child Welfare, 1 South Audley Street, W1 (491 2772). Promotes education in matters concerning the welfare of mothers and young children, including a range of leaflets on child care.

Maternity Alliance,* 59-61 Camden High Street NW1. (388 6337), is an organisation that campaigns for improvement in rights and services for parents and babies, and has leaflets explaining how to claim for all benefits you may be entitled to. Access: N.

National Association for Maternal and Child Welfare, 1 South Audley Street, W1 (491 2772). Promotes education in matters concerning the welfare of mothers and young children, including a range of leaflets on child care. Access: N.

Education Support Groups

(And see **Education**)

Advisory Centre for Education, 18 Victoria Park Square, E2 (980 4596). ACE produces information material on subjects of importance to parents, ranging from education welfare benefits to racism and sexism in schools.

British Association for Early Childhood Education, Studio 3/2, 140 Tabernacle Street, EC2.(250 1768). Encourages the provision of nursery schools and day care and promotes the interests of young children generally. Ring for information on local groups. Access: P.

Campaign Against Sexism and Sexual Oppression in Education, 17 Leamington Road, NW6.

National Association for Multi-Racial Education, PO Box 9, Walsall, WMidlands, WS1 3SF. An independent assessment and advisory service on all aspects of education.

National Campaign for Nursery Education, c/o 33 High Street, SW1 (828 2844).

Entertainment

What's on for Youngsters is a comprehensive guide to children's entertainment and facilities in GLC parks, open spaces and historic houses. Pick up a free copy from your local reference library or park, or ring 633 1707 and ask for a copy to be sent to you. Your local library will also have information on leisure activities and facilities in your borough.

Kidsline (222 8070) is a phone-in information service that gives information on local playschemes and other facilities, what's on in children's theatre, museums etc. Also offers ideas on cheap or free outings in London. Open everyday after school from 4-6pm and from 9am till 4pm every weekday during school holidays.

Artsline (388 2227/8) is another phone-in information and advice service on arts and entertainment in Greater London for people with disabilities and special needs. Useful for access information and availability of creches at specific venues. Open Mon to Fri 10am-4pm, Sat 10am-2pm.

City Limits and *Time Out*, weekly 'what's on' magazine from newsagents, both have weekly listings columns of children's events. newsagents.

Lesbian Mothers

Rights of Women*, 52/54 Featherstone Street, EC1. (251 6577), is a collective campaign around a range of women's issues and has set up lesbian custody project to monitor the way that lesbian mothers are dealt with by the legal system, social services, and schools. The project is also involved in informing women legal workers on the issues involved in lesbian custody cases. ROW also has a lesbian custody worker who can give advice, information and support. The lesbian custody group is made up of lesbian mothers and lesbian legal workers, and welcomes new members. ROW has produced *Lesbian Mothers on Trial*, from

ROW (above) £1.50 A report compiled from experiences of lesbian mothers in child custody cases.

Parents Under Stress

(And see Child Abuse, above)

Association for Post Natal Illness, c/o 7 Gowan Ave. SW6. (831 8996).

Baby Life Support Systems (BLISS), 44 Museum Street, WC1. Supplies equipment for premature babies.

CRYSIS (882 4720/886 5848), (for mothers with crying babies), 63 Putney Road, Enfield EN3. Access: N.

Network, c/o Belmont House, 187 St. Albans Road, Watford, Herts. Links mothers suffering from post natal depression with contacts.

Newpin, (New Parent Infant Network), Sutherland House, Sutherland Square, Walworth, SE17 (703 5271). Resource centre, information service and support programme for young families by local mothers in Southwark area.

Parents Anonymous, 6-9 Manor Gardens, N7, (263 5672/263 8918). Designed to offer help to parents who are likely to abuse their child/ren due to their own suffering. Runs Parents Lifeline, 24-hour crisis phone service on above numbers.

Stillbirth and Neonatal Death Society, (SANDS), Argyle House, 29-31 Euston Road, NW1 (833 2851). Provides support for parents who have suffered a stillbirth or lost a new born baby, and increases awareness of professionals and general public to needs of bereaved parents.

Single Parents

Gingerbread, 35 Wellington Street, WC2 (240 0953). Supports lone parents and their children by providing advice on financial, social and legal problems, and by the social and practical activities of over 300 local self help groups and a holiday schemes. Access: N.

The National Council for One Parent Families, 255 Kentish Town Road, NW5 (267 1361). Campaigns, co-ordinates and provides information on issues of women to single parents and their children. Advice Mon, Tues, Thurs, Fri 9.15 - 5.15. Access: N.

Under Fives Provision - Co-ordinating Groups

(Some of these projects also provide information on provisions for 5-11 year olds) See also Childcare Campaigns, above.

Barnet Play Association, 5 Oakleigh Gardens, N20 (446 6510).

Brent Under Fives Centre, Willesden Sports Centre Stadium, Donnington Road, NW10 (459 6469).

Ealing Under Fives Liaison Group, 7-21 Kings Street, Acton, W6 (993 3890).

Hackney Under Fives*, c/o Centerprise, 136 Kingsland High Street, E8 (254 9145).

Haringey Under Sevens Coordinating Committee, Tottenham Town Hall, Approach Road, N15 (808 1000 ext 248).

Inner London Pre-School Playgroups Association, 314-316 Vauxhall Bridge Road, SW1 (828 1401). Access: N.

Islington Under Fives Action Group, c/o David Michael, 145, Thorpedale Road, N4 (272 9916).

Islington Play Association, c/o West Library, Bridgeman Road, Islington, N1 (607 9637/8).

Inter-Change, 15 Wilkin Street, NW5 (267 9421). Runs a drop-in Centre for under-fives, organises children's festivals and develops community education projects.

Wandsworth Latchkey Development Group,

Wandsworth Pre-school Playgroups Association, Battersea Town Hall, Theatre Street, SW11. Tel: 228 7024. Access: P.

Harriet Tubman Books, 27/29 Grove Lane, Birmingham, B21 9ES.

Letter Box Library, Children's Books Co-operative, 1st Floor, 5 Bradbury Street, N16 8JA.

National Childminding Association, 204/206 High Street, Bromley, Kent, BR1 1PP.

New Beacon Books, 76 Strand Green Road, N4.

VOLCUF, Thomas Coram Foundation, 40 Brunswick Square, WC1N 1AZ.

Useful sources for publications

Afro Caribbean Educational Research Project, Wyvil School, Wyvil Road, SW8 2TJ.

Anti Sexist Resources Guide, Centre for Learning Resources, 275 Kennington Lane, SW11 5QZ.

Arawidi Ltd, 10 Dyson Road, Leytonstone, E11 1LZ.

The Book Place, 13 Peckham High Street, SW15.

Children's Rights Workshop, 73 Balfour Street, SW17.

Disability

There are about 200,000 women with some kind of disability living in London, all of whom encounter a multitude of obstacles in the course of day-to-day life. Many of these obstacles are physical - the result of policy, planning and design in which their needs have been ignored. Many will arise from the ignorant and oppressive attitudes prevalent in our society which rejects all those who do not conform to the acceptable stereotypes - heterosexual, white and able-bodied. Women with disabilities have to fight against the combined oppressions of sexism, handicappism and a greatly aggravated economic powerlessness; this is particularly true for Black women with disabilities who also experience racism.

The impact of a disability on an individual and her immediate family can be very serious. Earning power is much less than for able-bodied women, and this situation is often aggravated by the need for another member of the family to take on the responsibility of caring for a family member with a disability. The social security benefit system is seriously inadequate, as are resources to provide adequate housing, aids and equipment. Access to public facilities and transport is severely restricted and a person with disabilities is likely to be treated differently in public.

People with disabilities are often regarded with sympathy and as in need of welfare help or charity handouts. The charitable sector, which has for long dominated work around disability, is usually organised and run by able-bodied people. In the absence of adequate state provision, people with disabilities often have to rely on charities for basic assistance. This poses additional problems for Black and ethnic minority women with disabilities, for whom the charitable sector has made virtually no provision. There are few translators and little information in different languages, and no recognition of their own culture, traditions and religions. The charitable sector's ethos, directly or indirectly, informs most current thinking on disability. Even people who generally hold 'radical' views are likely to regard disability as an 'unfortunate condition' which requires special help and special provision.

By contrast, disability organisations run by and for people with disabilities, including feminist groups such as SAD and GEMMA, regard disability as a fundamental political issue. They argue that access and other provision for people with disabilities should not be special provision - but should, rather be available as part of 'normal' or 'ordinary' provision. People with disabilities are not an 'unfortunate' sector of society, but part of an oppressed group which is systematically denied access to much of the available provision, and which is discriminated against in every part of life. These organisations point out that every time able-bodied people plan events or take part without protest in activities which are not accessible to people with disabilities, they are actively perpetuating this discrimination. They also emphasise that the factors which are shared by people with disabilities such as harassment, discrimination and other negative treatment are much more significant than the differences which result from the varying disabilities themselves.

This approach to disability has been reflected in the work of the GLC's Disability Resources Team, which was established, significantly, with a high proportion of workers who themselves have disabilities. A main priority has been to ensure that people with disabilities have a major say in or control over provision which affects their lives, including access to all 'ordinary' provision. Within the Women's Committee Support Unit of the GLC, the Equalities Team had a brief to ensure that issues of concern to women with disabilities were taken into account in all the work of the Women's Committee. So, for instance, projects funded by the Women's Committee were asked to consider physical access and other participation aids they provide, contact with disability organisations, services they offer to women with disabilities, employment policies, books, posters and other resources, as well as action they can take to challenge handicappist attitudes amongst workers or users. Childcare projects are asked about the integration of children with disabilities, and asked to work to challenge negative attitudes on disability from able-bodied children. Information has been prepared to help groups consider what actions they can take.

In recognition of the discrimination faced by women with disabilities in London the GLC Women's Committee had a reserved place for a co-opted member with a special brief on disability issues as well as an advisory member on disability. In addition, the work of the Committee - on transport, planning, recreation and so on - took account of the needs of women with disabilities.

Abolition of the GLC will certainly mean that much of this work will be dropped, and there will be no central organisation in a position to give a lead to local authorities to continue work of this kind.

This section covers the main areas of concern to women with disabilities, and those caring for an adult or child with a disability. Mental illness and mental handicap have been included within this section as women in these situations share many of the experiences of women with a physical disability. As space in the Handbook is limited and organisations concerned with disability are numerous, only main sources have been listed. A more comprehensive list of disability organisations is printed annually in the excellent *Disability Rights Handbook,* produced by the Disability Alliance. (£2.20, available from them post free: 25 Denmark Street, WC2 (240 0806).

This section is ordered as follows: **General Disability Associations, Mental Health, Learning Disability, Access, Aids and Equipment, Black and Ethnic Minority Women with Disabilities, Children, Education, Employment, Help at Home, Housing, Legal, Personal Relationships, Sport, Transport and Mobility, Welfare Benefits, Organisations Concerned With Specific Disabilities: Blind and partially-sighted, Cancer, Deaf and hearing impairment, Disabling illness, Injury, Surgery, Useful Reading.**

General Disability Associations

In almost every London borough there is a disability association and these are affiliated to GLAD, the Greater London Association for Disabled People. These local associations are the best source for providing information or advising where to get it from. Some have guides to other organisations in their locality. For information about your local association contact GLAD's central office:

GLAD, 336 Brixton Road, SW9 (274 0107). GLAD's central office operates an information service and has a range of leaflets on topics such as benefits for people with disabilities, holidays, clubs and aids. In addition, GLAD publishes a quarterly journal, the only regular, widely available publication for Londoners with disabilities.

Jewish Blind and Physically Handicapped Society, 118 Seymour Place, W1H 5DJ (262 2003). Has sheltered accommodation in North and South London.

Liberation Network of People with Disabilities, c/o Townsend House, Green Lanes, Marshfield, Chippenham, Wilts.

Network for the Handicapped Ltd, 16 Princeton Street, WC1 (831 8031/7740). Free advice centre for handicapped people and their families.

RADAR, (Royal Association for Disability and Rehabilitation), 25 Mortimer Street, W1 (637 5400). A co-ordinating body dealing with most aspects of concern to people with disabilities. Produces some useful publications.

SAD, (Sisters Against Disablement), c/o Women's Reproductive Rights Information Centre, 52-54 Featherstone Street, EC1 (251 6332). A group of women with disabilities who meet to discuss the issues of feminism and disability. Produces Newsletter and meets third Sunday in every month.

Union of Physically Impaired Against Segregation, c/o Flat 2, St Giles Court, Dane Road, W13 (579 9679).

Mental Health

(And see **Health**)

The psychiatric profession still operates circular arguments as to what constitutes mental 'health'. Normality is viewed as the ability to fit reasonably comfortably into the behaviour and attitudes expected by society, according to gender, sexuality, race and class. This can have disastrous implications for women whose 'mental health' will be defined in terms of a 'feminine psyche' which many women consider to have been defined by a historically misogynist and racist male academic and therapeutic establishment. These stereotypes of 'normality' are particularly devastating to women who are Black or who belong to an ethnic minority, or are lesbians.

The idea of a 'cure' all too often means some form of pressure on the patient to accept and conform to oppressive stereotypes and/or to adjust to, rather than struggle against, whatever conditions have caused her to break down. Attitudes within the system towards Black women, lesbians, mothers, incest survivors, victims of domestic violence are considered by many women's groups to be generally negative. Blame is placed on the victim who needs to be 'cured'. Women are very vulnerable to being detained ('sectioned') against their will, under the Mental Health Act.

GPs, therapists and hospitals usually resort to the control of symptoms by the use of drugs, ECT and in extreme cases, psycho-surgery. There are now much stricter controls on the long-term prescription of minor tranquillisers which are seriously addictive but the system is still built around the widespread use of both minor and major tranquillisers, in spite of their appalling side-effects.

There are a number of organisations concerned with researching mental health, supporting, advising or offering therapy, and promoting critical attitudes towards an oppressive mental health system.

The following groups can give general advice and assistance:

Afro-Caribbean Mental Health Association, 48 East Lake Road, SE5 9QL (737 3604). Befriending and support services for Afro-Caribbean psychiatric patients and others of Afro-Caribbean origin with mental health problems, their families and friends. They want to expand into a community care centre providing community care, counselling, psychotherapy, group therapy etc. Can also give advice on rights including legal, housing, etc.

Greenwich Black Women's Health Project, St Mary's Church, Green Law Street, SE18 (854 3766). Can give support and advice to women with mental health problems.

(For other Black women's Mental Health groups - see **Health**.)

Irish Women's Mental Health Group, c/o Islington Women and Mental Health, Caxton House, 129 St. Johns Way, N19 (281 2345).

Islington Women and Mental Health (281 2345). Feminist project arising out of discussions with local women of their needs. Counselling phone-line for any woman needing support, information and advice ranging from depression, psychiatric care and its alternatives, drugs/alcohol dependency, anxiety, stress, isolation etc. Leaflet available.

London Women and Mental Health, c/o AWP, Hungerford House, Victoria Embankment, WC2. Feminist discussion, research and information group, open meetings last Wednesday of the month at AWP, 7 pm.

MIND, 22 Harley Street, W1 (637 0741). Concerned with all aspects of mental health from a radical point of view. Has a free list of local Mental Health Associations. Advice Unit (9.30-5 pm Mon-Fri) can advise on any aspect of mental health including legal advice. Publishes a variety of useful leaflets and a bi-monthly journal *Open Mind* (£5 pa for individuals, £4 to MIND members, £7 to organisations).

Women in MIND is a working group researching women's mental health needs. They have produced a pamphlet on women and mental health and are working on a book which will promote the need for women-only resources. Contact at MIND, above.

Women's Health Information Centre,* 52 Featherstone Street, EC1 (251 6580). Can give information on mental health rights, general advice and referral.

Women's Action for Mental Health, c/o 7 Mackay House, White City Estate, W12. For information on drug dependency (including alcohol), therapy, depression etc, see **Health**, Mental Health.

Learning Disability

Women with learning disabilities may be denied the right to make choices about their lives on the grounds that they 'can't know' what they need. As children, most will have been educated in special schools, completely segregated from other children, and consequently will have encountered additional difficulties in making friends at home. Adults with learning disabilities are likely to live in segregated provision, or at home with little contact with others outside the family. Day Centres or sheltered workshops are also segregated, and provision is generally extremely badly resourced, and limited in its scope. Many mentally handicapped adults still live in the big mental handicap hospitals around London, where an initial disability has been greatly compounded by years of institutionalisation. Women with learning disabilities may be denied the right to have control of their own money or possessions, to form relationships, or to bear children - or to care for children they do have.

Advocacy Alliance, 115 Golden Lane (off Old Street), EC1 (253 2056). Trains volunteers to represent mentally handicapped people's interests in hospitals.

BIMH, British Institute of Mental Handicap, Wolverhampton Road, Kidderminster, Worcestershire (0562 850251). Run conferences and workshops on the use of micro-electronics.

Campaign for Mentally Handicapped People, 12A Maddox Street, W1 (491 0727). Campaigning organisation which supports and encourages integration of and participation by people with learning disabilities.

Children's Legal Centre, 20 Compton Terrace, N1 (359 6251). Offers legal advice and assistance to young people with learning disabilities, particularly in relation to institutions, social services, etc.

Jewish Society for the Mentally Handicapped, Stanmore Cottage, Old Church Lane, Stanmore, Middlesex (954 7528).

MENCAP, 123 Golden Lane, EC1 (253 9433). Royal Society for Mentally Handicapped Children and Adults.

Access

The right of people with disabilities to access to public places and resources is very rarely recognised, or, often limited and inappropriate. For example, many venues which are wheelchair-user accessible may have wheelchair-inaccessible toilets or changing rooms, or seating arrangements which mean that a woman with disabilities may not sit with her friends.

'Access' tends to be thought of in terms of wheelchair-user access only, and many groups and venues which are unable to provide full wheelchair access feel that they cannot do anything. Access means considering all kinds of physical disability, including making the spoken or written word accessible to women whose sight or hearing is impaired. Sisters Against Disablement has produced a detailed access code which includes many of the features which determine whether a venue or event will be accessible. Where there is limited space, a more restricted code - such as the one used in this handbook - may be more appropriate. Failure to use a code discriminates against women with disabilities. The use of a code will also highlight areas which could be improved immediately within the resources available.

Some boroughs have accessible public toilets which use the National Key Scheme (NKS). Further information and keys (price £2) are available from RADAR. *The Nicholson London Guide: Access in London* gives access details, and *City Limits* weekly magazine provides limited access guides to places of entertainment. Both are available from London newsagents. Some local boroughs also have access guides. Information about travel is given later in this section.

Artsline (388 2227) is a phone-in information and advice service on arts and entertainment in Greater London for people with disabilities and special needs. Useful for access information and availability of creches at specific venues. Open Mon-Fri 10 am-4 pm, Sat 10 am-2 pm.

Sportsline (222 8000) is a phone-in information and advice service on sports activities which includes detailed information for people with disabilities. Open seven days a week 10 am-6 pm.

For information about travel and mobility see later in this section under **'Transport and Mobility'.**

Aids and Equipment

Aids Advice Centre, 215 Gray's Inn Road, WC1 (833 0084) (24 hour ansaphone). Display of aids and professional assessment and advice on aids given.

Alternative Talking Newspaper Collective, PO Box 35, 136 Kingsland High Street, E8 2NS. A collective run by blind and partially sighted people with sighted allies producing left wing/feminist tapes.

Breakthrough Trust, The Hall, Peyton Place, Greenwich, SE10 8RS (853 5661). Offers an information service run by deaf people on all aspects of hearing impairment and advice on environmental aids. Displays in certain boroughs. Contact above number for details.

Disabled Living Foundation, 380-384 Harrow Road, W9 2HU (289 6111). An aid centre with an exhibition of a wide variety of aids and equipment. They give detailed advice and information. This is the largest centre in London. Visits by appointment only.

Electronic Aids Loan Service, Willowbrook, Swanbourne Road, Mursley, Bucks MK17 0JA (029672 533). Information and advice, free short-term loans of electronic aids. Phone or write for details enclosing 9″ x 4″ sae.

REMAP, Thames House North, Millbank, SW1P 4QC (834 4444 ext. 4112). A panel of volunteer engineers and remedial therapists, who design and supply individual aids, adaptations and modifications. The service is free.

Royal National Institute for the Blind, 224 Great Portland Street, W1N 6AA (388 1266). RNIB sells over 500 special aids which are on show, together with other equipment and gadgets. It also offers an education advisory service and a Talking Book Service.

Black and Ethnic Minority Women with Disabilities

Racism in the NHS, in local authority and voluntary organisations, and from individuals means that Black and ethnic minority women with disabilities face particularly severe discrimination.

Black women with disabilities may be singled out for particularly serious racist abuse as well as direct physical attacks. Within institutions concerned with disability, working class and Black women are less likely to be referred to specialist doctors and to receive decent quality aids and equipment they require. Food and activities in day centres generally do not take account of cultural or religious requirements of Black and ethnic minority women. Less emphasis is placed on research into diseases (eg sickle cell anaemia and thalassaemia) which particularly affect Black and ethnic minority people. Few organisations make interpreters available for women whose first language is not English, and printed information is rarely translated into other languages.

Where helpers and carers are used, little effort is made to ensure they speak the mother tongue of the person they are assisting. Many Black people with disabilities rely for their main support on local Black voluntary groups, who may have few resources but may be more willing to offer assistance or are forced to rely on friends or relatives.

Afro-Caribbean Mental Health Association, 48 East Lake Road, SE5 (737 3604). Befriending and support service for Afro-Caribbean people.

Afro-Caribbean Self Help Voluntary Organisation, 48 East Lake Road, SE5.

Asha Asian Women's Resource Centre, c/o 27 Santley Street, SW4 (737 5901/ 274 8854).

Black Health Workers and Patients Association, Annexe B, Tottenham Town Hall, High Road, N15 (808 1000).

Brent Asian Women's Resources Centre, 134 Minet Avenue, Harlesden, NW10 (453 0243).

Brent Black Mental Health Project, 13 Nicoll Road, Harlesden.

Brent Sickle Cell Centre, Willesden Hospital, Harlesden Road, NW10. (459 1291 x 235) Access: A.

Jewish Society for the Mentally Handicapped, 140 Wembley Road, Wembley.

Lambeth Sickle Cell Information Centre, Swan Mews, 2 Stockwell Road, SW9 (737-3588).

Southall Black Women's Centre, 86 Northcote Avenue, Southall, Middlesex (843 0578).

Children
(See also **Childcare and Children** and

also Legal Rights below.)

ACTIVE (with Toy Libraries Association), Seabrook House, Darkes Lane, Potters Bar, Herts, EN6 (Potters Bar 44571). Aims to help children with disabilities and adults to lead more active and independent lives by using, encouraging and supporting a do-it-yourself approach to play, leisure and communications aids. Also encourages formation of local ACTIVE groups.

Association for all Speech Impaired Children, 347 Central Markets, Smithfield, EC1 (236 3632/6487). Runs an information and support service for parents and campaigns for better facilities for speech and language-handicapped children.

Association for the Welfare of Children in Hospital, 29-31 Euston Road, NW1 (833 2041). Supports sick children and their families and works to ensure that health services are planned for them. Have produced leaflet for Indian parents in five languages

Breakthrough Trust, The Hall, Peyton Place, SE10 (853 5661). Works for the integration of deaf and hearing children and adults, mainly through education authorities and social services departments. Also runs an advice centre for parents and children, with library and demonstrations of environmental aids. Access: A.

Child Growth Foundation, 2 Mayfield Avenue, W4 (995 0257). Supports parents of children with growth disorders and funds research. Phone or write for information/appointment.

Child Poverty Action Group (see Welfare Benefits below)

Children's Aid Team, 643 High Road, N17 (808 4965). Support and advice for families of mentally handicapped people.

Contact A Family, 16 Strutton Ground, SW1 (222 3969/2695). Introduces and links families with a handicapped child and offers mutual support and advice.

Down's Children's Association, 4 Oxford Street, W1 (580 0511/2). Helps parents and professionals with the care, treatment and training of children with Down's Syndrome. Nationwide self-help groups and London resource centre.

Dyslexia Foundation, 133 Gresham Road, Staines, Middlesex, TW18 (815 9498). Educational assessments and specialist tuition for people of all ages who are dyslexic, and specialist training for teachers.

EXODUS, 12 Park Crescent, W1 (636 5020). Campaigning group for alternative sites of care for all mentally handicapped children in long-stay wards.

Family Tree Pre-School Unit (Autism), Holybush House, Hadley Green, Barnet, Herts (449 0431). Provides education and management of children up to 12 years with specific learning disabilities resulting from infantile psychosis.

Handicapped Adventure Playground Association, Fulham Palace, Bishop's Avenue, SW6 (736 4443).

Handicapped Children in Hackney, Huddleston Centre, 30 Powell Road, E5 (985 8869). Pre-school playgroup, holiday playschemes, girls group and other provision.

Harrow Parents' Association for Hearing Impaired Children, 54 Hazeldene Drive, Pinner, Middlesex, HA5 (868 3287). Educates the public in their approach to deaf children. Arranges outings and meetings and gives support. Access: A.

Hyperactive Children's Support Group, 59 Meadowside, Angmering, Sussex. Aims to help and support hyperactive children and their families.

Institute of Child Psychology, 6 Pembridge Villas, W11 (229 4759).

Jewish Child's Day, 183-189 Finchley Road, NW3 (328 1557). Aims to help children in need.

KIDS (National Society for Deprived and Handicapped Children), 16 Strutton Ground, SW1 (222 1517).

MENCAP (Royal Society for Mentally Handicapped Children and Adults), 123 Golden Lane, EC1 (253 9433). Welfare rights, counselling, education, residential accom-modation, holidays, information and specialised books and publications. Encourages and supports the formation of regional groups.

National Association for Deaf, Blind and Rubella Handicapped, (SENSE), 311 Grays Inn Road, WC1 (278 1005). Helps and supports deaf-blind young people and their families.

National Autistic Society, 276 Willesden Lane, NW2 (451 3844/5). Provides information advisory services for parents and professionals. Runs six schools, adult community hostel and day care centre.

National Deaf Children's Society, 45 Hereford Road, W2 (229 9272/4). Advice on welfare, education and services for deaf children and their families and information on all aspects of childhood deafness. Access: N.

National Demonstration Centre, Pinderfields General Hospital, Aberford Road, Wakefield, Yorks, WF1 (Wakefield 375217 ext. 2510/2263). Information and advice an all aspects of living with a disability, specialising in paediatrics.

National Federation of Gateway Clubs, 117-123 Golden Lane, EC1 (253 9433). Youth clubs for young people with learning disabilities.

National Toy Libraries Association, Seabrook House, Darkes Lane, Potters Bar, Herts, EN6 (Potters Bar 44571). National body for over 1,200 toy libraries for children, especially those with special needs.

Physically Handicapped and Able-Bodied (PHAB), Tavistock House North, Tavistock Square, WC1 (388 1963). Promotion of the integration of physically handicapped people into the community. Access: A.

Shaftesbury Society, Regency Street, SW1 (837 7444). Special schools and hostels for physically and mentally handicapped young people and holiday centres for the elderly people and people with disabilities.

Voluntary Council for Handicapped Children, National Children's Bureau, 8 Wakeley Street, EC1 (278 9441). To advance and assist in promotion of scientific research into the needs of handicapped children, and to disseminate the results to the public. Access: A.

Voluntary Organisations Liaison Council for Under Fives, c/o Thomas Coram Foundation, 40 Brunswick Square, WC1 (278 8365). Federation of voluntary organisations working together to improve services for under fives and their families through interdisciplinary collaborative projects. Access: A.

Education

At present most children with moderate or severe disabilities are educated in segregated 'special' schools. Under the 1981 Education Act, children with disabilities have the right to be educated in ordinary schools and to any special resources they may need to be provided within that school. This is limited, however, to a level of provision which the authority decides is consistent with the efficient education of that student and others in the school. A report by ILEA's Fish Committee, published in July 1985, came out strongly in favour of integrated provision for all children with disabilities. (And see **Childcare and Children** and **Education**)

Advisory Centre for Education, 18 Victoria Park Square, E2 (980 4596). Access: A.

Children's Legal Centre, 20 Compton Terrace N1 (359 6251).

ILEA produces its own guide to the Education Act (1981) and listings of groups active in education. See also Report of the Fish Committee, July 1985, into special education.

MENCAP (see above), can advise on the education of mentally handicapped children.

Parents Campaign for Integrated Education, 27 Woodnook Road, SW16 (789 4944/677 9828). Self-help group of parents and professionals in ILEA campaigning for the interests of children with special needs and their integration to mainstream education. Can put parents in contact with local groups.

RADAR (see above). Also gives advice and information and publishes a free guide to the Education Act (1981).

Employment

Under the Disabled Person (Employment) Act 1944 and 1958, employers of 20 or more people are required to employ 3% disabled staff. In reality, this quota is rarely fulfilled. There is a penalty fine of £500, but prosecutions are rare. Furthermore, there is still no legislation outlawing discrimination against people with disabilities. Women with disabilities face double discrimination in seeking training and employment and this situation is worsening in the current climate as the least powerful groups are hit disproportionately. Women with disabilities are often pressurised by DROs (Disablement Resettlement Officers) to seek work at low wages and with poor career structure, or special training leading to sheltered employment without prospects. In addition, DROs, ATCs (Adult Training Centres) etc and sheltered work schemes often prioritise white men, seeing them as 'most in need' of a job. And employers are generally unwilling to invest in equipment which would allow women with disabilities to realise their potential. At the same time it is important to recognise that there are women with disabilities who do not want or cannot undertake paid employment. (See also **Employment and Unemployment**).

Disablement Resettlement Officers are based at job centres to help disabled people find work and advise on training for employment. The DRO can arrange special assistance, eg, adaptations to employers' premises. Contact your local DRO at a job centre near you (telephone your local disability association to find out where your nearest DRO is based).

Haringey Disablement Association, c/o Tottenham Town Hall, Town Hall Approach, N17 (801 5757). Seeks to link unemployed people with disabilities and job opportunities within Haringey. Access: A.

Lady Margaret Hall Settlement Project; 460 Wandsworth Road, SW8 (622 9455). Developing employment opportunities for women with disabilities in Lambeth and Wandsworth. Access: A.

Opportunities for the Disabled, 1 Bank Buildings, Princes Street, EC2R 8EU (726 4963). Employment service (no fees) specialising in jobs for people with disabilities. Write or phone for application form. Access: A.

Outset, Drake House, 18 Creekside, SE8 (692 7141). Works to establish sheltered workshops using new technology to deploy skills of people with disabilities in providing administrative and financial services to local businesses and voluntary organisations.

Sheltered Industrial Groups. Provides work for a small group of people with learning disabilities in sheltered setting. In Hounslow there is a SIG which employs ten gardeners with learning disabilities and two supervisors. For information about local SIG's contact DRO as above.

Help at Home

Crossroads Care Attendant Schemes, National Office, 29 Coton Road, Rugby, Warwickshire CV21, (0788 73653) for details of schemes in many parts of London. Provide care assistants who will come in to help look after a disabled person at home or give support to the whole family. Some of the London boroughs have their own Crossroads Scheme and the local associations should be able to give contacts. For Local Schemes, Contact your local disability association or social services for alternative Care Schemes or contact your local Social Services for home help, adaptations, aids, and meals on wheels. (Also see **Carers**)

Housing

As a result of the way housing is planned and built, people with disabilities are often segregated from the rest of the population. Housing design for people with disabilities usually follows the assumption that all people with disabilities are single and want to live alone. There is a lack of warden-supported accommodation and very little flexibility in housing provision for people with disabilities. (Also see **Housing**)

Anchor Housing Association, 13-15 Magdalen Street, Oxford. Provides warden-supported housing for people over retirement age. Priority given to those in poor housing conditions.

Cheshire Homes, L. Cheshire House, 26-29 Mausel Street, SW1P 2QN. Provides permanent homes for disabled people and admission given on need. Some accommodation for married couples with disabilities.

Habinteg Housing Association Ltd, 6 Duke's Mews, W1M 5RB. Provides purpose built flats and bungalows. Each scheme has warden service.

John Grooms Association, 10 Gloucester Drive, Finsbury Park, N4 2LP. Offers a variety of housing from institutional setting to self-contained flats.

National Federation of Housing Associations, 30-32 Southampton Street, WC2E 7HE. Publishes guide to Housing Associations.

SHAC (The London Housing Aid Centre), 189a Old Brompton Road, SW5 0AR. Will give housing advice to single people and families and also gives advice on tenancy.

Legal

Advocacy Alliance, 115 Golden Lane, EC1Y 0TJ (253 2056). Trains volunteers to represent mentally handicapped people's interests. Access: N.

ARCH (Advice and Rights Centre for the Handicapped), 49 Old Street, EC1. Local advisory service in Islington offering assistance on legal problems and advice on benefits for people with disabilities.

Children's Legal Centre, 20 Compton Terrace, N1 (359 6251). Aims to clarify, develop and improve the laws and policies affecting children and young people.
Access: A.

Court of Protection, 25 Store Street, WC1E 7BP. Concerned with the management of estates of people suffering a mental impairment and unable to manage their own affairs.

Free Representation Unit, First Floor, 3 Middle Temple Lane, EC4Y 9AA. Will represent claimants before various statutory tribunals, supplementary benefit appeals and give other forms of legal assistance. Referrals through CABs, law centres etc only.

Justice for Children, 35 Wellington Street, WC2 (836 5917). Provides advice and information service for parents, children and social workers and campaigns on the juvenile justice system.

Legal Action Group, 28a Highgate Road, NW5. A group of lawyers concerned to improve legal services to the community.

Rights of Women,* 52-54 Featherstone Street, EC1 (251 6577). The group acts as a pressure group to support legislation of benefit to women, and also provides advice on legal rights to women.

(And see **Borough Information** for advice/legal centres.)

Personal Relationships

Brothers and Sisters Club, BMB+S, WC1N 3XX. For deaf and partially hearing lesbians and gay men.

GEMMA, BM Box 5700, WC1V 6XX. A club for disabled/able-bodied lesbians to lessen the isolation caused by disability and offer access to feminist/lesbian literature.

SPOD (Committee on Sexual and Personal Relationships of the Disabled), 286 Camden Road, N7 0BJ (607 8851). Can advise and counsel people with disabilities by correspondence and where required offer counselling. Advisory leaflets available. Access: A.

There are also a number of pen-friend organisations:

Circle, 30A Wellington Parade, Blackfen Road, Sidcup, KENT. Magazine (edited by Mr T Simmons) encouraging world-wide friendships. Pen-friend list supplied to members.

Friends by Post, 6 Bollin Court, Macclesfield Road, Wimslow, Cheshire, SK9 2AP. Offer conversation by correspondence to try to combat loneliness.

Friendship Register, 29 Goldstone Way, HOVE, E. Sussex, BN3 7PA. Voluntary organisation for making friends in Sussex. Have formed Pen-friend Register for disabled and handicapped people.

International Correspondence Service, PO Box 10, Matlock, Derby. Free pen-friendship service for disabled people.

'**Yours**' Pen-Friends, PO Box 126, Watford, Herts. Pen-friend service for older people.

Sport

There are several sports facilities for women with disabilities. Contact the recreation departments of your local borough (see **Borough Information**), Social Service departments, or ring:

Sportsline (222 8000) which advises on sports/activities for women and facilities for women with disabilities.

British Sports Association for the Disabled, BSAD London Regional Officer, The Cottage, Tottenham Sports Centre, 703 High Road, N17 (801 3136). Organises and gives information on sports activities for people with disabilities. Access: A.

GLAD Directory of Clubs You can order this listing of over 700 clubs for people with disabilities in Greater London from GLAD, 1 Thorpe Close, W10 5XL.

The Islington Women's Sports Club, George Orwell School Annexe, Duncombe Road, N19 (800 0471).

Transport and Mobility

Access to public transport is also limited for people with disabilities. Much could be done, even with limited resources, to make public transport more accessible but in the present climate such moves are unlikely. In the absence of an appropriate public transport system, various initiatives have been taken to provide transport for people with disabilities, although this can have the effect of further segregating people with disabilities and shifting the onus from the provision of suitable public transport.

Phone your local disability association, Social Services or other local transport group for information on schemes for people with disabilities.

Mobility allowance is the social security benefit (£20 a week at the moment, there is usually an annual increase) to help with the cost of transport for severely disabled people.

To claim you must be unable or virtually unable to walk. Claim Form N1 211 is available in Post Offices and DHSS offices.

Free bus and tube passes (subject to restrictions on travel times) are available from your Social Security office if you are a registered blind or disabled person.

Community Transport groups often have at least one fully accessible vehicle fitted with a tail lift. See **Transport**.

Dial-a-Ride is a door-to-door bus service with adapted vehicles for people with disabilities unable to use public transport. Fares are public transport rates. Book well in advance. Some Dial-a-Rides have a 'local only service' which means local trips possibly could be booked with only a day's notice and some have reciprocal arrangements with other boroughs. Check for full details with Central Dial-a-Ride below, for your local service.

Federation of London Dial-a-Ride, 25 St Margaret's, Leighton Road, NW5 (482 2325).

Orange Badge Scheme: Parking is very difficult in London. Most boroughs have an Orange Badge Scheme provided free by Social Services. This allows you to park for up to 2 hours on a yellow line or for an indefinite time, without cost, at a parking meter. Contact the Social Services Department of the Town Hall in your area for information on parking. In a few boroughs, eg Camden and Westminster, the Orange Badge Scheme is invalid in certain areas.

Welfare Benefits

As a result of lack of access to suitable employment, many women with disabilities are dependent on social security benefits. Again, they will face discrimination both as women and as people with disabilities. The system works on the assumption that married women are supported by their husbands. As women often work in low-paid or part-time jobs and may break their career pattern in order to raise children, their entitlement to contributory benefits is adversely affected. The rules are complex and mystifying, and claiming as well as living from benefits is often frustrating and humiliating.

Child Poverty Action Group, 1 Macklin Street, WC2 (242 3225/9149). Provides welfare rights advice and publishes annual guides to social security benefits.

Disability Alliance, 25 Denmark Street, WC2 8NJ (240 0806). Gives advice on social security benefits. Publishes *Disability Rights Handbook* (£2.20) available post free.

Disablement Income Group (DIG), Attlee House, Toynbee Hall, 28 Commercial Road, E1 6LR (247 2128 and 6877). Provides an advisory service for disabled people on benefits and services. Also a campaigning group working to establish an adequate income even for people with disabilities.

DHSS Leaflet Unit, Stanmore, Middlesex. Free benefit leaflets can be obtained from the DHSS Leaflet Unit.

Organisations Concerned with Specific Disabilities

Blind and partially-sighted

Partially Sighted Society, 4 Delamare Close, Breaston, Derbyshire, DE7 3UE (03317 3036). Helps partially sighted people.

Royal National Institute for the Blind (RNIB), 224 Great Portland Street, W1N 6AA (388 1266). Concerned with all aspects of blind people's living: rehabilitation, training, homes, education, employment, aids, Moon, Braille, reference library and Talking Books Library. Counselling service offered in employment, rehabilitation and education.

Cancer

Bacup, 212/123 Charterhouse St, EC1 (608 1785/6) Specialist counsellors will give inquirers (patients or families) up-to-date information on treatment and general advice/support.

Cancer After Care and Rehabilitation Society (CARE), Lodge Cottage, Church Lane, Timsbury, Bath, Avon, BA13 1LF (0761 70731). A society conducted by people who have had cancer, and who now seek to advise, encourage and help others especially when diagnosis, treatment or recovery may be impeded by fear.

Cancer Information Association, 2nd Floor, Marygold House, Carfax, Oxford, OX1 EF (0865 46654). Provides an advisory service on guidance and the recognition of early symptoms.

Women's National Cancer Control Campaign, 1 South Audley Street, W1Y 5DQ (499 7532). Concerned with measures for the prevention and early detection of cancers of the cervix and of the breast. Leaflets are available on request (send sae).

Cancer Help Centre, 7 Downfield Road, Clifton, Bristol 8. Advice about an alternative, holistic, approach to cancer, based on diet and other therapies including visualisation, homoeopathy, acupuncture.

Disabling Illness

Action for Research into Multiple Sclerosis (ARMS), 11 Dartmouth Street, SW1H 9BL (222 3224). Has 24-hour counselling service (222 3123). Promotes research and self-help for MS with centres offering advice on diet, physiotherapy and hyperbaric oxygen therapy.

Arthritis and Rheumatism Council, 41 Eagle Street, WC1R 4AR (405 8572). Access: A. Can give general information on rheumatic disease. Eight hundred local branches.

Arthritis Care, 6 Grosvenor Crescent, SW1X 7ER (235 0902). Will give advice on welfare and legal matters, aids, homework, research into social and welfare problems. More than 200 branches.

Association for Spina Bifida and Hydrocephalus, Tavistock House North, Tavistock Square, WC1 (388 1382). Access: A.

British Epilepsy Association, Crowthorne House, New Wokingham Road, Wokingham, Berkshire, RG11 3AY (0344 773122). Help and advice groups in London.

Chest, Heart and Stroke Association, Tavistock House North, Tavistock Square, WC1H 9JE (387 3012). Offers advice and help to those suffering from asthma, bronchitis, lung cancer, angina, coronary thrombosis and stroke. Publishes educational literature cassettes, and a magazine entitled Hope. Access: A.

Haemophilia Society, PO Box 9, 16 Trinity Street, SE1 (407 1010). Provides advice, support and assistance to people with haemophilia and their families.

Multiple Sclerosis Society of Great Britain and Northern Ireland, 286 Munster Road, SW6 (381 4022). Many local branches - see phone book. Encourages research and offers a comprehensive welfare and advice service.

Muscular Dystrophy Group of Great Britain, Nattrass House, 35 Macaucay Road, SW4 0QP (720 8055). Primarily a research association but gives advice and help. Has local branches.

National Eczema Society, Tavistock House North, Tavistock Square, WC1H 9SR (388 4097). Access: A.

Parkinson's Disease Society of the UK Ltd, 81 Queen's Road, SW19 8NR (946 2500). Sponsors medical research and offers information and advice for sufferers and their families on problems arising in the home.

Poliomyelitis, Bell Close, West End Road, Ruislip, Middlesex, HA4 6LP (Ruislip 75515). Help and advice.

Sickle Cell Society, c/o Brent Committee, 16 High St, Harlesden, NW10 4LY (And see Health for local groups and clinics).

Spastic Society, 12 Park Crescent, W1N 4EC (636 5020). Information, advice, runs schools centres, hostels.

Deafness and hearing impairment

British Association of the Hard of Hearing, 6 Great James Street, WC1N 3DA. Offers information and advice.

British Deaf Association, 38 Victoria Place, Carlisle, CA 1HU (0288 48844). Branches throughout the country to help all deaf people including those without speech. Organises manual communication skills project and educational courses. Publishes sign language books.

Royal Association in Aid of the Deaf and Dumb, 27 Old Oak Road, Acton, W3 (743 6187). Promotion of the social, general and spiritual welfare of deaf people.

Royal National Institute for the Deaf (RNID), 105 Gower Street, WC1 (387 8033). Provides personal services.

City Literacy Institute, Stukeley Street, WC2. Centre for the deaf. Courses, including signing. (See **Education**, Further Education).

Injury

Headway National Head Injuries Association, 17 Sherwood Rise, Nottingham, NG5 1AG (0602 622382).

Spinal Injury Association, 5 Crowndale Road, NW1 1TU (388 6840). Offers information on all aspects of injury.

Sight Impairment

Partially Sighted Society, 4 Delamare Close, Breaston, Derbyshire, DE7 3UE (03317 3036). Helps partially-sighted people. Access: A.

Royal National Institute for the Blind (RNIB), 224 Great Portland Street, W1N 6AA (388 1266). Concerned with all aspects of blind people's living: rehabilitation, training, homes, education, employment, aids, Moon, Braille, reference library and Talking Books Library. Counselling service offered in employment, rehabilitation and education. Access: A.

Surgery

Colostomy Welfare Group, 38-39 Eccleston Square, SW1V 1PB (828 5175). Provides a free welfare service for people who have had, or are about to have, a colostomy operation. Strives to allay anxiety and help with adjustment.

Mastectomy Association of Great Britain, 26 Harrison Street, WC1H 8JG (837 0908). Offers non-medical help to patients following a mastectomy operation. Volunteer helpers nationwide. Free booklets (SAE required).

Useful Reading

Advice for Disabled People, produced by GLAD (Greater London Association for the Disabled). An easy-to-read book (in large print) on the main facilities, amenities and information useful to people with disabilities. Available from GLAD, 1 Thorpe Close, W10 5XL.

Care in the Air, pamphlet for passengers with disabilities wanting to travel by plane. Air Transport Users' Committee, 129 Kingsway, WC2B 6NN.

The Cancer Journals, Audre Lorde. (Sheba Feminist Publishers £2.95). Concerns Mastectomy.

Compass - The Direction Finder for Disabled People, R. Rock, a cheap comprehensive book on facilities and information throughout the country. Each organisation or amenity listed is given a short summary which is a useful guide. Written by a disabled woman for disabled people. Also available from RADAR, 25 Mortimer Street, W1 (637 5400).

Directory for the Disabled - A handbook of information and opportunities for disabled and handicapped people, Darnborough and Kinrade. Published by RADAR, very comprehensive book but expensive. RADAR produce a wide range of publications. Phone or write for full details: RADAR, 25 Mortimer Street, W1 (637 5400).

Disability Rights Handbook, updated each year by Disability Alliance, 25 Denmark Street, NW1 4JL, £2.20. A very comprehensive guide to welfare rights with extensive list of disability organisations.

Down There: An Illustrated Guide to Self-Examination, (Only Women Press 75p.)

Equipment for the Disabled, Mary Marlborough Lodge, Nuffield Orthopaedic Centre, Oxford. Lists of aids which are very practical everyday articles but more sophisticated equipment is also included.

Guide for the Disabled Traveller, published by the Automobile Association, available free to their members from AA Centres (see phone book). Lists over 300 British hotels suitable for travellers with disabilities, plus motoring information, European touring information and suggested continental tours with lists of suitable accommodation.

Holidays for the Disabled, a comprehensive holiday guide produced by RADAR, £1.50 from WH Smith. Or contact RADAR, address as above.

Images of Ourselves - disabled women talking, editor Jo Campling, Routledge Kegan and Paul. A collection of short biographies by disabled women of all ages and disabilities. £4.95.

London - A Guide for Disabled Visitors, London Tourist Board, 26 Grosvenor Gardens, SW1 0DU. Lists all the major attractions in central and outer London also lists hotels and restaurants. A useful guidebook.

London for the Disabled, F. Lockhart, Ward Lock Ltd. Useful little pocket book on facilities and amenities in London for people with disabilities.

London Women and Mental Health Newsletter, c/o AWP, Hungerford House, Victoria Embankment, WC2. Send SAE for details.

More Equal Than Some is a study of the employment needs of women with disabilities in Lambeth written mainly in their own words. Available free to individuals from Lady Margaret Hall

Settlement, 460 Wandsworth Road, SW8 (622 9455). (£2.25 to funded group).

Motoring and Mobility for Disabled People, Darnborough and Kinrade, RADAR. £3.00.

Our Bodies Ourselves, editors Angela Phillips and Jill Rakusen, (Penguin £7.95). A health book by and for women.

Outdoor Pursuits for Disabled People, N. Croucher, published by Disabled Living Foundation. Comprehensive book written by disabled person for disabled people. £8.95.

Parents Handbook No. 4 on 'Aids for the handicapped' is a useful indicator of what is available. From the Spastics Society, 12 Park Crescent, W1N 4EQ.

The Source Book for the Disabled, G. Hale, (Heinemann £9.95). A useful comprehensive book on what's available for people with disabilities with helpful illustrations, particularly sections on independent living.

Education and Further Education

This section is divided into two main parts. The first deals with primary and secondary schooling. The second covers further education, with a brief look at higher provision (degree courses at polytechnics and universities etc).

Primary and Secondary Education

Universal state education is meant to provide all children with a free education involving the systematic learning of basic skills, a challenging programme for acquiring knowledge and more advanced skills, continuity, assessment of individual needs and the recording of progress. In reality the education available to many children falls short of these objectives because of reductions in education spending and because of sexist and racist attitudes and practices. Girls end up with fewer and different qualifications than boys. Despite comprehensive schooling, it is boys from white middle class families who still benefit most and who are most likely to move on to university and who consequently will have better job prospects. ILEA statistics for 1981 show that although more girls than boys achieved five or more CSEs or higher grade 'O' levels, fewer girls applied for and got the three or more 'A' levels needed to apply to university. Girls also tend to enter for arts subjects while boys are more likely to obtain qualifications in maths and sciences. These differences crucially affect women's choices of work and their levels of pay.

Reasons for these differences are social pressures on girls, the expectations and attitudes of teachers, parents and often of the girls themselves, and the way girls are treated at school. In particular, attitudes and behaviour to and expectations for Black and ethnic minority girls, girls with disabilities and for girls who are lesbians or daughters of lesbians limit their participation and achievement at school.

Studies (for example see Spender in **Useful Reading** below), have shown that boys, through their behaviour, are more demanding both of teacher time and laboratory and computer use and girls often lose out drastically. The curriculum may theoretically now be open for girls to take science and technical subjects but no allowance is made of the problems associated with such a choice in terms of early childhood stereotyping with girls encouraged into a caring role and boys encouraged to explore and be adventurous. This stereotyping continues into school life and is heightened by the position of the staff: few women or Black teachers in positions of authority, women concentrated in arts subjects and the part-time posts, women as cleaners, meal providers, secretaries etc. In addition, no account is taken of the pressure girls are under to conform in the eyes of their peers, ie that girls should be feminine, not brainy swots, and there is a corresponding drop-off in girls' achievements in their teens.

Teachers' expectations and attitudes about girls also contribute to the problem. Assumptions that a woman's primary role will be 'wife and mother' influence the advice teachers give girls, the education routes they suggest girls should take and the extent to which girls are pushed to take exams. For example some teachers make assumptions based on race, class, sexuality and gender about who should be withdrawn from mainstream schooling. When children do not want to go to school, the assumption is often made that there is something wrong with the child rather than something wrong with the school itself or the system the child is in.

Black parents in particular are critical of the way many schools are organised and structured and of the curriculum and the way it is taught, as well as of the discriminatory attitudes and behaviour that their children often experience at school.

According to the 1981 Education Act, parents and pupils have the right to make specific demands for a young person's schooling and should be consulted before any major decisions are made. In practice parents are rarely consulted and parents, particularly Black parents, who are critical of their children's schools are told to transfer their children if they don't like the way the school operates. As a result, Black parents have set up a network of pressure and support groups to challenge racism in schools and to argue for the type of schooling they want for their children. In some cases, Black parents have set up alternative Saturday schools or daily supplementary schools (see Local Organisations, Parents' Groups and Supplementary and Saturday Schools below).

Some initiatives are being taken to combat sexism, heterosexism and racism in schools: teachers and librarians have to some extent become aware of the need for text books, fiction and other materials which challenge race and gender stereotypes; girls-only sessions at lunchtime and after school are being run. The Inner London Education Authority (ILEA), the body responsible for education in the Inner London boroughs, has begun to respond to this need for change. Resource centres have been established to produce and promote the use of anti-sexist and anti-racist materials in schools. The curriculum has been opened up to girls and teachers are receiving in-service training better geared to multi-racial, non-sexist education.

In the outer boroughs, with the exception of Brent and Haringey, there is as yet little evidence of any real commitment by the education authorities to a positive policy for equal opportunities in education. Furthermore, throughout the country the massive central government cuts in education spending have meant reductions in staff and resources, damaging both existing educational provision and those initiatives designed to make it fairer. The listings below provide useful places to contact if you are worried about your own schooling or that of your child. For general enquiries about free school meals, school transfer and other general information, contact your local education authority. For independent advice about the rights of pupils and parents, contact the Advisory Centre for Education, your local law centre, the Citizens Advice Bureau or the CRC (see **Borough Information**). There are a number of Black Parents' Groups which offer support and advice, and the Lesbians in Education group is open to parents as well as teachers and staff. For children with learning disabilities see **Disability**. There are also other agencies specialising in children's rights, for example the Children's Legal Centre will advise on expulsion and suspension. For addresses see below and Childcare and Children.

This section is ordered as follows: *Advice and Support Groups for Parents and Carers; Local Organisations, Parents' Groups and Supplementary and Saturday Schools; Equal Opportunities in Education - Campaign Groups and Resource Centres; Local Education Authorities: ILEA, Outer London Boroughs; Bookshops, Materials, Resource Centres; Useful Reading.*

Advice and Support Groups for Parents and Carers

Advisory Centre for Education (ACE), 18 Victoria Park Square, E2 9PB (980 4596). A registered charity, independent of central or local government. The only national, full-time education watchdog pressing for a fairer education system. ACE also have a specialist worker, critically assessing 'special needs'. Produce regular Bulletin (six per year, £7.50) and have published many useful handbooks and information sheets, including *Special Education Handbook* (£3.00) and *Education Law Guides* and *Governor Handbooks*. Send sae for list of publications and fact sheets.

Campaign for Advancement of State Education (CASE), The Secretary, 4 Hill Road, Carshalton, Surrey. National organisation which campaigns for a first class state education service throughout life, with equal educational opportunity for all, regardless of where they live, their home circumstances, their ability, sex, race or religion. Send sae for information about local groups.

Children's Legal Centre, 20 Compton Terrace, N1 2UN (395 9392). Independent national body concerned with laws and policies which affect children and young people. Free advice and information service by telephone and letter. Will advise on suspensions, expulsions, etc. Produce a leaflet on young women's contraception rights (post-Gillick).

Education Otherwise, 25 Common Lane, Hemingford Abbots, Cambridgeshire (0480 63130). Provides information and advice about educating your child at home. Send 9" x 4" sae for details.

National Association of Governors and Managers (NAGM), c/o 81 Rustlings Road, Sheffield S11 7AB. Non-party association which presses for greater involvement of governors in the education system and for their development and training. For information on local groups in outer London contact above address. Inner London branch, c/o 22 Croftdown Road, NW5 1EH (485 3739).

National Association for Multi-Racial Education (NAME), PO Box 9, Walsall, West Midlands WS1 3SF. Aims to play an active role in making the changes required in the education system to further the development of a just and equal non-racist society. The national organisation encourages and co-ordinates the work of local groups all over the country and there are several active groups in the outer London boroughs. Also publishes six-monthly journal and termly newsletter. For information send sae to above address.

National Confederation of Parent/ Teacher Associations, Greater London Federation, c/o Mr Philip Stephens, 22 Camplin Road, Kenton, Harrow, Middlesex. Aims to encourage co-operation between home and school. Useful leaflets and publications available. Send sae for further information.

National Council for One-Parent Families, 255 Kentish Town Road, NW5 2LX (267 1361). Campaigns on behalf of one-parent families, provides information and an advice service, publishes a teaching pack for schools and resource lists. Phone for appointment to visit library and information office.

Parents' Campaign for Integrated Education in London, 25 Woodnook Road, SW16. Organisation to support all parents of children with special needs in London.

Parents' Enquiry, 16 Honley Road, SE6 2HZ. Help and counselling agency for gay teenagers and their parents to try to sort out family and school problems and put families in touch with each other. Pen pal service.

Right to Comprehensive Education (RICE), c/o 36 Broxash Road, SW11 6AB. (228 9732).

Special Education Division, Department of Education and Science, York Road, SE1 7PH (928 9222 x3335)

Local Organisations, Parents' Groups and Supplementary and Saturday Schools

Citizens Advice Bureau (CABs) and Law Centres are important sources of advice and information. Their usefulness on issues related to education varies from borough to borough. Hackney CAB and Stockwell and Clapham Law Centre both offer a specialist service in education matters. For the address of your local organisation see **Borough Information.**

Community Relations Councils (CRCs) are also very useful sources, particularly for Black parents and parents from ethnic minorities. They should be able to advise on supplementary (Saturday) schools and parent support groups. The councils in the inner boroughs have an education liaison officer based in them. For addresses see **Borough Information.** Some have produced helpful publications.

Camden
Afro-Caribbean Parents' Group, c/o Social Services, 156 West Lane, NW6

Camden Black Parents' and Teachers' Group, c/o 146 Kentish Town Road, NW5

Greenwich
Chinese Association Family Project, 36 Earlswood Road, SE10 (858 2410) Supplementary School and Language School.

Hackney
Hackney Black People's Association, Stoke Newington Road, N16

H.E.A.D.S, Rectory Road, N16 (254 2852)

Haringey
Haringey Multicultural Resource Centre for Under Fives, 66 Turnpike Lane, N8 (889 7641)

John Loughborough School, Holcombe Road, N17 (808 7837)

Islington
Escuela 'Nino Luchin', Sixth Form Centre, Chillingsworth Road, N5 (354 2951).

CARILA, 29 Islington Park Street, N1.

Lambeth
West Indian Parents' Action Group, c/o 7 Canterbury Crescent, SW9.

Mafalda, c/o Brixton Black Women's Centre, 41A Stockwell Green, SW9 (622 6285).

Lewisham
Lewisham Parents' Education Action Group, 56 Pascoe Road, SE13 5JB

Escuela 'Amanacer', Albany Centre, Douglas Way, SE8 (965 0257) Saturday School, 11-3.30 pm.

Newham
Newham Parents' Centre, 745-747 Barking Road, E13 9ER.

East London Black Women's Group, 66B Sebert Road, E7 (552 1169). Supplementary School, Sat 2-5 pm, ages 4-18 years.

Tower Hamlets
Muslim Parents' Association, c/o 13E Hoe Street, E17 4SD

Waltham Forest
Afro-Caribbean Education Project, 593 High Road, E10 (556 0602)

Wandsworth
Asian Parents' Group, c/o Millan Centre, 59 Trinity Road, SW17

Wandsworth Association of School Parents (WASP), c/o 36 Broxash Road, SW11 6AB

West Indian Parents' Group, c/o Telegraph Hill Neighbourhood Centre, Telegraph Hill, SE14

West London

West London Tamil School, Stanhope Middle School, Mansell Road, Greenford, Middx (927 1170/940 5939)

Equal Opportunities in Education - Campaign Groups and Resource Centres

Afro-Caribbean Education Resource Project (ACER), Wyvil School, Wyvil Road, SW8 2TJ (627 2662). Promotes and produces multi-cultural materials for use in schools, including videos. Competitions for young Black writers.

All London Teachers Against Racism and Fascism (ALTARF), Unit 216, Panther House, 38 Mount Pleasant, WC1X 0AP (278 7856). Works with teachers, children and parents challenging racism. Aims to combine anti-racist and anti-sexist education. Phone for appointment.

Anti-Racist Education Resource Centre, Mawbey School, Coopers Road, SE1 (237 3824). Four teachers seconded by ILEA working as an anti-racist strategies team collecting and disseminating information and resources; working closely with other teachers to write and produce materials; offering support and training in anti-racist strategies to ILEA staff. Access: N (but will visit).

Anti-Sexist Working Party, contact J Granados, Grasebrook Primary School, Lordship Road, N16 (802 4051). Group of primary school teachers aiming to challenge sexism in the curriculum of primary schools. Have produced exhibition; participate in in-service work.

Brent Curriculum Development Support Unit, Donnington Road, NW10 (459 3205). Helps produce non-sexist and non-racist teaching materials and works with teachers on classroom projects. Lends books and videos. Mon-Fri 9 - 5.30.

Campaigning Against Sexism and Sexual Oppression in Education (CASSOE), 7 Pickwick Court, SE9 4SA (857 3793). A small voluntary group - mainly a newsletter collective. An information service which aims to support the many individuals and groups directly involved in the various campaigns against sexism and sexual oppression in education. The newsletter publicises groups, their activities, relevant contact addresses and any resources. Contributions and new people to join welcome. Subscription £2.50 per year.

Campaign to Impede Sex Stereotyping in the Young (CISSY), 177 Gleneldon Road, SW16 2BX (677 2411). A small, self-funded and voluntary organisation. Aims to promote children's books which go some way towards challenging traditional sex role bias by means of publicising, bibliographies and recommendations

Caribbean Teachers' Association, 8 Camberwell Green, SE5 (708 1293). Aims to promote the educational interests of the Black community. Members are people of Caribbean or African origin who work in the field of education. The association runs a daily supplementary school and provides an educational counselling service. Contact the co-ordinator for further information.

Centre for Urban Educational Studies (CUES), Robert Montefiore Secondary School, Vallance Road, E1 5AD (377 0040). A specialist teachers' centre concerned with multi-cultural and urban education. Main concerns include challenging class-bias, racism and sexism in schools. Reference library with collection of anti-sexist books for children and teachers. Phone for appointment. Library: Mon-Fri 11 am to 5 pm.

East London Whole School Project, Robert Montefiore Secondary School, Vallance Road, E1 5AD (377 9934).

Team of teachers visiting primary, infant and secondary schools to help promote anti-racist and anti-sexist initiatives.

Gay Teachers' Group, BM/Gay Teacher, WC1N 3XX. A supportive, campaigning and educational group working for gay rights in education. Membership is open to all people interested/working in education. Aims to reach gay teachers (often under a great deal of pressure and afraid to meet others) who can use the organisation for mutual support. Not all members are out gay teachers. The area of curriculum development is an ongoing consideration. Holds an annual conference, publishes books and a termly newsletter.

Greenwich Afro-Caribbean Education Resource Unit, 105 Plumstead High Street, SE18 (854 2662). Concerned with issues of racism and sexism in education. Provides advice and support to parents and children.

Group Against Sexist Practice (GASP), Newham Inservice Education Centre, Credon School, Credon Street, E13. A group of teachers who have produced a mobile exhibition and publish occasional papers. Paper Four, entitled *Confronting gender bias: a resource book*, contains information on using books, advertisements and activities to raise awareness and challenge sexual stereotypes. Free with 30p sae.

Lesbians in Education, c/o AWP, Hungerford House, Victoria Embankment, WC2. A support and campaign group for all lesbians in education - pupils, students, teachers, youth workers, technicians or other workers in schools, colleges, etc. Meets once a month at A Woman's Place, Hungerford House, Victoria Embarkment, WC2 (836 6081).

National Union of Students Women's Campaign, 461 Holloway Road, N7 6LJ (272 8900). Campaign to co-ordinate the activities of women students, giving information to and developing NUS's and student unions' awareness about anti-sexism and the involvement of women in all student activities. Developing Women in Education pack.

Newham Equal Opportunities Network (NEON), c/o Sara Bonnell School, Deanery Road, E15 (534 6791). A group of women teachers from primary and secondary schools concerned about the under-achievement of girls in Newham schools. Decided their first task was to raise the level of commitment on the issue in the borough. A conference was held and a pack of materials produced. Pack available, free, from Research Department, Newham Education Office.

Resource Centre for Asian Studies, Robert Montefiore School Building, Vallance Road, E1 5AD (377 9937). Offers services to schools, colleges, AEIs and community groups. Collects publications; develops teaching aids and materials to promote multicultural approaches within the school curriculum with particular reference to Asia. Reference library and loan service.

Society of Teachers Opposed to Physical Punishment (STOPP), 18 Victoria Park Square, E2 9PB. Group of teachers opposed to the use of physical punishment in schools.

Women's Education Group (WedG),* Drama and Tape Centre, Princeton Street, WC1 (242 6807). WedG is a feminist collective committed to anti-racism and anti-sexism. Have set up a Women's Education Resource Centre and produce *GEN*, anti-sexist education magazine, available in bookshops or by subscription. Involved in self-defence for girls (video and teaching pack). Also runs Black Women's Creativity Project. Ring for details.

Women in NUT, 83 Banbury House, Banbury Road, E9 7EB. Holds meetings, shares resources and practices, holds conferences, produces newsletter, campaigns. Write for details.

Local Education Authorities (LEAS)

The Inner London Education Authority (ILEA)

ILEA services the 12 inner boroughs and the City of London and is divided into ten divisions, each with its own divisional education officer. The Education Welfare Service is at the same address except where indicated.

Division 1
Hammersmith & Fulham, Kensington & Chelsea: 50 Brook Green, W6 7BJ (603 3388).

Division 2
Camden, City of Westminster: 3-4 Picton Place, W1M 5DD (486 0190).
Education Welfare Service, 10/11 Bulstrode Place, W1 (486 0190).

Division 3
Islington: Northstar House, 556-564 Holloway Road, N7 6JW (262 7727).

Division 4
Hackney: 41 Stamford Hill, N16 5SR (802 1331).

Division 5
City of London, Tower Hamlets: Harford Street, Mile End Road E1 4PY (790 1288)

Division 6
Greenwich: Riverside House East, Beresford Street, SE18 6DF (855 3161)

Division 7
Lewisham: Capital House, 47 Rushey Street, SE6 4AT (698 4633)

Division 8
Southwark: 2 Camden Square, SE15 5LE (703 0855)

Division 9
Lambeth: 50 Acre Lane, SW2 5SS (274 6288) Education Welfare Service: 45b Streatham Hill, SW2 4TS (671 0051).

Division 10
Wandsworth: 78 Garratt Lane, SW18 4TB (874 7262).

If you are in any doubt about whom to contact, or if you want general information, ring or write to: ILEA Information Centre, Room 80, County Hall, SE1 7PB (633 1066).

ILEA Education Liaison Service There are 12 Education Liaison Officers (one in each inner London borough) who work with ethnic minority communities. Their work involves liaising with and advising the educational establishments and the minority communities to help promote better understanding and co-operation between them. Black and ethnic minority parents/childcarers can contact these liaison officers for advice on educational issues and also to get in touch with parent support groups. Ask for the Education Liaison Officer. They are located in your local Community Relations Council (CRC) premises. (see **Borough Information**).

ILEA Equal Opportunities Unit, Room 526, County Hall, SE1 7PB (633 8191). Aims to develop and promote equal opportunities policies within ILEA, both as an employer and as an education service. At present the unit has a race equality and sex equality team in relation to education, but the equal opportunities officers in the employment branches also deal with disablement and sexual orientation. Wheelchair access. Mon-Fri 9 am to 5 pm.

ILEA Equal Opportunities Inspectorate, Room 578, County Hall, SE1 7PB (633 1474). Promotes and supports the implementation of equal opportunities for girls and boys throughout ILEA and provides inservice courses for teachers and lecturers in anti-sexist education. Responsible for Girls' Work: Leah Thorn, Yvonne Field. Room 463 (633 1237).

Multi-Ethnic Inspectorate, Room 528a, County Hall, SE1 7PB (633 8551). Responsible for multi-ethnic education throughout ILEA and provides inservice courses for teachers and lecturers in anti-racist education. There is a multi-ethnic co-ordinator in every division. For your division see above.

Outer London Boroughs Education Authorities

Barking and Dagenham
Chief Education Officer, Town Hall, Barking, Essex IG11 7LU (594 3880).

Barnet
Chief Education Officer, Town Hall, Friern Barnet, N11 3DL (368 1255).

Bexley
Director of Education, Town Hall, Crayford DA1 4EN (303 7777).

Brent
Director of Education, PO Box 1, Chesterfield House, 9 Park Lane, Wembley HA9 7RW (903 1400). Brent Advisory Teachers for Equal Opportunities, Chesterfield House, as above.

Bromley
Director of Education, Sunnymead, Bromley Lane, Chislehurst BR7 6LH (467 5561).

Croydon
Director of Education, Taberner House, Park Lane, Croydon CR9 1DH (686 4433).

Ealing
Chief Education Officer, Hadley House, 79/81 Uxbridge Road, W5 5SU (579 2424).

Enfield
Chief Education Officer, Civic Centre, Silver Street, Enfield EN1 3ES (366 6565).

Haringey
Chief Education Officer, 48-62 Station Road, N22 4TY (881 3000). Advisory teacher for Equal Opportunities: Helen Cairns, ext 3209.

Harrow
Director of Education, PO Box 22, Civic Centre, Harrow HA1 2UW (863 5611).

Havering
Director of Educational Services, Mercury House, Mercury Gardens, Romford RM1 3DR (Romford (70 66999).

Hillingdon
Director of Education, Civic Centre, High Street, Uxbridge UB8 1UW (Uxbridge (0895) 50111).

Hounslow
Director of Education, Civic Centre, Lampton Road, Hounslow TW3 4DN (570 7728).

Kingston
Director of Education, Guildhall, Kingston-upon-Thames, KT1 1EU (546 2121).

Merton
Director of Education, Station House, London Road, Morden SM4 5DR (542 8101). Advisory teacher on Equal Opportunities: Kate Myers.

Newham
Director of Education, 29 Broadway, Stratford E15 4BH (534 4545). Advisory teacher for Equal Opportunities: Joan McKenna.

Redbridge
Director of Educational Services, Lynton House, 255 High Road, Ilford, Essex IG1 1NN (478 3020).

Richmond
Director of Education, Regal House, London Road, Twickenham TW1 3QB (891 1433).

Sutton
Director of Education, The Grove, Carshalton, SM5 3AL (661 5000).

Waltham Forest
Chief Education Officer, Municipal Offices, E10 5QJ (539 3650).

Bookshops, Materials, Resource Centres

The following is a selection of organisations and bookshops which specialise in anti-sexist, anti-racist materials and books and offer resources to both parents and teachers. (A list of London bookshops and facilities available to women can also be found in **Media and Arts**).

Black Ink, 258 Coldharbour Lane, SW9 (733 0746). Collects, publishes, distributes and promotes Black people's writing. Readings and discussions in and out of schools. Bookstalls available. Mon-Fri 11am - 5pm.

Black Women's Centre, 41 Stockwell Green, SW9 (274 9220). Tues-Fri 10-6. Provides a place where Black women can come together for support, help and encouragement. There is an information and advice service available on matters such as housing, education, social security and welfare benefits. The centre has a reference library, an art and craftwork room and a creche and is open to Black women of all ages and with all interests. Runs a summer project for children 5-16.

Bookplace/Peckham Publishing Project, 13 Peckham High Street, SE15 (701 1757/0720). Community bookshop. Publishing project and Adult Education Centre Bookshop is wheelchair accessible. Creche facilities. Offers teachers books, advice on anti-sexist and anti-racist books. Publishes writing by students and other local people. Mon, Tues, Wed, Fri, Sat 10am to 6pm.

Bookspread, 58 Tooting Bec Road, SW17 (767 6377). Judy Hall's Bookspread runs book-related events, such as storytelling, workshops, author and illustrator visits. Takes books out in the form of displays and exhibitions with activities. Offers help and advice to those with reading difficulties. Newsletter every two months distributed to all ILEA schools. Mon, Tues, Wed, Fri 10am to 5pm; Thurs, 10am to 9pm; Sat 10am to 3pm.

Centerprise, 136 Kingsland High Street, E8 (254 9632). Multi-purpose community centre with bookshop giving high priority to children's books, working class writing and history. Always willing to discuss issues with teachers on appointment basis. Can arrange for writers to visit schools and can supply books for stalls/school bookshops. Tues, Wed, Fri, Sat 10.30am - 5.30pm; Thurs, 10.30am - 2 pm.

Cockpit Gallery, Princeton Street, WC1 (405 5334). Exhibitions for hire by any educational establishment - hire fees negotiable (free to schools within ILEA). Several anti-sexist and anti-racist exhibitions, many co-produced with school students, about their lives and ideas.

Dalston Children's Centre, 112 Greenwood Road, E8 (254 9661). A community centre based around the needs of children and those who look after them - mainly women. Works in an anti-racist, anti-sexist, anti-herterosexist, anti-authoritarian way. Runs under-five groups, after school clubs, junior and senior girls nights. Has a small library, videos and adult education classes. Mon-Fri 10 am - 6 pm.

Fawcett Library, City of London Polytechnic, Old Castle Street, E1 7NT (283 1030). Britain's main historical research library on women, containing much current material. Subjects include: women's studies, employment, education, suffrage, political and legal rights, sexuality, violence against women etc. Research facilities for teachers, older students. Bibliofem is the largest source of academic material on women in UK and is available on microfiche. (Term-time) Mon 1 pm to 8.30pm; Tues-Fri 10am to 5pm; (vacations) Mon-Fri 10am to 5pm.

Feminist Library and Information Centre, Hungerford House, Victoria Embankment, WC2N 6PA (930 0715). Lending library. Borrowers pay subscription according to income - free use to all on premises. Aims to make material accessible and available to as many women as possible.

ILEA: Learning Resources Branch, Marketing and Publicity Section, Centre for Learning Resources, 275 Kennington Lane, SE11 5QZ (633 5971). Produces a range of learning materials for children and teachers - packs, books, teacher's notes, jigsaws, audio-cassettes, video cassettes. Most LRB materials are also available to users outside the ILEA, either directly or through national publishers and distributors as indicated in the catalogues. Contact the above address for information, catalogues, order forms. Equal Opportunities Librarian: Sue Adler.

Lambeth Toys, 130 - 146 Ferndale Road, SW4 (733 3729). Developing multi-racial materials for use in schools.

Letterbox Library, 1st Floor, 5 Bradbury Street, N16 8JN (254 1640). Children's bookclub specialising in non-sexist books. Members pay one-off fee of £2.50 and receive quarterly catalogue and newsletter. Mon-Fri 9.30 am - 3.15 pm (please ring first).

Resources and Information for Girls, 25 Bayham Street, NW1 (387 7450). Aims to develop resources for girls and young women and to initiate and support girls groups. Works with statutory services particularly in Camden. Liaises with teachers on curriculum issues. Mon-Fri 10 am to 6 pm; girls' groups Tues, Wed, Thurs pm.

Mrs Robinson's Bookshop, Shop 3, Benson House, Hatfields, SE1 (633 9507). A place where parents, teachers and librarians can find a great variety of multi-ethnic, non-sexist and foreign language books not normally available under one roof. Specialises in children's books. Mon-Fri 11 am to 6 pm, Sat 10.30 am to 5 pm.

Soma Books, 28 Kennington Lane, SE1. Carries books from Asian subcontinent in a range of languages. Also Afro Caribbean titles, and books in dual-text. Outlet also at Commonwealth Institute, Kensington High Street, W8 (603 4535).

Southwark Equal Opportunities (Nursery) Group, Lyndhurst Grove, SE15 (701 9577). Exhibition showing sex stereotyping in cards, comics, toys, books (including reading schemes). Very useful to initiate discussion with teachers and parents. Available for loan.

Tressell Publications, 139 Carden Avenue, Brighton, Sussex BN1 8NH (0273 561464). A publishing co-operative owned and controlled by classroom teachers.

Women's Education Resource Centre,* ILEA Drama and Tape Centre, Princeton Street, WC1 (242 6807). The centre contains books, posters, videos, journals etc. and examples of teachers' work. Open to all women interested in and involved in education. Maintains a contact network and the centre can be used by women for meetings.

Women's Film, TV and Video Network,* 79 Wardour Street, W1V 3PH (434 2076). Provides an information and support network. Information sheets on a range of topics available for use in schools. Would like to do sessions in schools, youth clubs, etc for girls. Phone for opening times.

(Also see **Young Women** and **Media and Arts**).

Useful Reading

Journals and newsletters: The following journals/newsletters can provide a useful source of information on current issues and developments in education. Contact the organisations for up-to-date details of subscription rates, availability.

ACE Bulletin, (Formerly WHERE). Advisory Centre for Education, 18 Victoria Park Square, E2 (980 4596). Six per year, £7.50. For everyone concerned with education. Includes major articles, ACE news, advice and information, series on parents and the law, and digest (listing of publications).

Cassoe Newsletter, 7 Pickwick Court, SE9 4SA (857 3793). Six per year, £2.50 (£1 unwaged). Essential reading. Information, contacts, resources and current news and good practice in education.

Dragon's Teeth, NCRCB (National Committee on Racism in Children's Books) Notting Hill Methodist Church, 7 Denbigh Road, W11 2SJ. Four per year, £3 (£5 institutions). Produced by NCRCB. Valuable for its articles and reviews, which frequently have an anti-sexist, as well as anti-racist, perspective.

English Magazine, English Centre, Sutherland Street, SW1 (821 8011). Three per year, £4. Self-financing magazine, produced for teachers of English, with much in it of interest to parents, librarians and other teachers. Frequently has features/articles specifically on gender issues.

GEN, Women's Education Resource Centre, ILEA Tape and Drama Centre, Princeton Street, WC1 (242 6807). Three per year, £1.50 per issue. An anti-sexist education magazine providing forum for debate about feminist/anti-sexist education and space for girls and women to share their experiences of the educational process.

Issues in Race and Education, 11 Carleton Gardens, Brecknock Road, N19 5AQ. Quarterly, £2.50 (£4 for institutions). Journal on race, incorporating a strong anti-sexist perspective.

Multi-racial Education, Journal of the National Association for Multi-racial Education (NAME), PO Box 9, Walsall, West Midlands WS1 3SF. Six monthly journal with articles, reviews, Branch news. Send sae for subscription/membership details.

Working with Girls Newsletter, National Association of Youth Clubs, Keswick House, 30 Peacock Lane, Leicester LE1 5NY. Bi-monthly newsletter published - mainly concerns youth work, but relevant to teachers, and all those developing girl-centered work and anti-sexist youth projects.

Reports, Handbooks and Books

(Also see radical and feminist bookshops for the large range of books on education from an anti-racist, anti-sexist perspective.)

ACE Publications, 18 Victoria Park Square, E2 9PB (980 4596). Publication list available with sae. Includes handbooks which cover education (eg *Special Education Handbook*) and range of information sheets (eg *Sex Discrimination in Education; Parents and Reading*).

Anti-Sexist Resources Guide ILEA Centre for Learning Resources, 275 Kennington Lane, SE11 5QZ (633 5971). Information especially useful to those working with the secondary age range, both in schools and youth work but also of interest to colleges, primary and special schools, parents and the wider community. Listings of organisations working to improve understanding of the issues in anti-sexist education, women's organisations, bookshops and bookclubs, publishers, distributors, ILEA and selected material resources.

'Black Girls in a London Comprehensive' by Mary Fuller in *Schooling for Women's Work* (see below)

'Do you provide equal educational opportunities?' A guide to good practice in the provision of equal opportunities in education (revised edition) EOC, 1982, free. Available from EOC, Overseas House, Quay Street, Manchester M3 3HN. (061 833 9244).

Equal Opportunities for Girls and Boys, a report by the ILEA inspectorate 1983, £1.00 (ILEA) £1.50 (non-ILEA). Available from ILEA Information Centre, County Hall, SE1 7PB (633 1066).

'An equal start - Guidelines for those working with the under-fives'. EOC, free. Available from EOC see above.

Gender and Schooling, A study of sexual divisions in the classroom, Michele Stanworth (Hutchinson £1.95).

Gender and the secondary school curriculum. EOC 1982, free, address as above.

Improving Primary Schools, report of the committee on primary education under the chair of Norman Thomas, 1985 and *Improving Secondary Schools*, report of the committee on secondary education under the chair of Dr David Hargreaves, 1984, £7.50 each (including p & p) from ILEA Learning Resources Centre, 275 Kennington Lane, SE11 5QZ.

How Children Fail, John Holt (Pelican £2.95)

How the West Indian Child is Made Educationally Subnormal in the British School System Bernard Coard, New Beacon Books 1971.

Invisible Women: The schooling scandal, Dale Spender (Writers and Readers £3.95).

Learning to Lose: Sexism and Education, Dale Spender & Elizabeth Sarah

Further Education

Although there are very many courses of different types available in London, women are till concentrated in 'traditional' types of courses - secretarial, nursery nursing, hairdressing, etc - whereas men tend to opt for either technical subjects or courses that lead on to higher qualifications or better jobs. The Inner London Education Authority (ILEA) has a policy to increase access to education for people who in the past have been left out - women, working class and Black and ethnic minority students - and some colleges have created special posts to look at ways of eliminating sexist and racist practices. However, in times of cuts, these are often the sort of posts that disappear first, and it is only with pressure from women's groups and unions that ILEA's equal opportunity policy will actually be put into practice.

There is a great imbalance in teaching posts, where men still tend to hold the higher positions and dominate the areas of maths and science. Cutbacks in spending on staff training schemes means that women are even less likely to gain promotions, therefore providing even fewer models for young women to aspire to.

Most colleges in London now see the 16-19 year age group as the priority, and therefore most money goes in their direction. This disadvantages older women who are returning to work after raising children or who were not able to train when they were younger. However, some colleges have set up special courses aimed at women returning to work or who wish to try a new area of work. There is also an increasing emphasis on Youth Training Scheme (YTS) courses in colleges, and there is a considerable debate about the effectiveness of these schemes and particularly about the treatment women students receive on them.

Childcare provision is still non-existent in most educational establishments and this is a major factor preventing women from taking further education courses, particularly those which demand full-time attendance. Many colleges have creche campaigns but only a very few have been successful in actually setting up creches.

Other than English as a Second Language (ESL) courses, there is very little provision aimed specifically at Black and ethnic minority students. A few colleges positively encourage Black people to apply for courses. Where colleges do particularly welcome and offer courses for Black and ethnic minority students, this is noted in the listings below.

Many colleges are still not physically able to cope with students with disabilities and indeed often see the presence of disabled students as a nuisance. New posts are being created especially to help students who have special needs, but very often there is a need to improve the physical condition of the college and the attitudes of staff and other students.

However, don't let any of that put you off! Remember, a college or any other body cannot legally exclude you from any course on the basis that you are a woman. If you find any resistance from a college where you are wanting to do, for example, a construction course, take it up immediately with one of the organisations listed under 'Discrimination' in Training. Also see Training for details of women-only courses and other training schemes.

This section contains information about the provision of education for post-16 year olds and concentrates on courses below degree level, although some sources of information on degree level education are given under Higher Education below.

This section is ordered as follows: *16-19 Year Olds; Post 19s; Choosing a Course; Entry Requirements; Fees; Grants; Disability Access and Facilities; Where to Study; Open University; Women's Studies; Colleges of Further Education, Adult Education Institutes, WEA and Educational Advice Centres in Inner London Boroughs; Colleges etc in Outer London Boroughs; Higher Education; Useful Reading.*

16-19 Year Olds

Many school leavers, either disillusioned with their experience in school or simply wanting a change of environment, may decide to go to a college of further education to take a traditional 'O' or 'A' level course, or to do subjects that schools may not be equipped to teach. If you want advice about colleges etc, go to your local Careers Office (addresses in phone book or library) who have a duty to advise you about further education.

If you are at work, you may wish to take a day release course at a college, and your employer should allow and indeed encourage you to do this.

Post 19s

Unfortunately, there is no legal right to education once you're over 19. However, councils do have a duty to provide opportunities for adults to study, and there are no age limits.

Choosing a Course

The first step is to decide what type of course is right for you. Education Advice Centres have been set up specifically to advise adults on education and training opportunities, and these are listed later by borough. If there isn't one near you, your local library should have details of courses and women's centres and unemployed centres (see **Employment** and **Unemployment**) also have information. A publication called *Floodlight* lists all ILEA classes in colleges and adult education institutes and is on sale June to Sept. If you are interested in training for a skill, see **Training**.

If you don't know what you really want to do or what you are looking for, many colleges and institutes have set up special courses for women who want a chance to use their minds again but aren't quite sure what direction they want to go in. These are usually called Fresh Start or New Horizons, or similar titles, and are available in most parts of London.

Entry Requirements

Most courses at Colleges of Further Education (CFEs) and Higher Education establishments ask for a certain number of CSEs, 'O' or 'A' levels before you can start. However, as mentioned above, it is the policy of the ILEA to encourage women back into education and therefore in many cases the college will recognise the years a woman has spent in childcare or at work and will accept her without 'O' or 'A' levels. Some colleges offer ACCESS courses, which are designed for people who would like to go to polytechnic or university but who do not have any 'A' levels.

Fees

Once you reach 18, you have to start paying for courses. Each local authority has a different charge, but generally speaking full-time courses are quite expensive, especially if you are considered to be an 'overseas student'. You will have to read very closely the prospectus of the college that you are interested in.

Nowadays, many colleges have developed courses lasting 21 hours or less, because then you can study without losing unemployment or supplementary benefit. In ILEA colleges, there is a charge of £1 per year for any number of classes up to 21 hours, if you are:

● resident in the ILEA area and

● receiving unemployment or supplementary benefit, or

● over 60, or

● enrolling on a literacy (including mother tongue), basic education or English as a second language course, or

● enrolling in family workshops or other provision for groups together in a family situation.

If you live outside the ILEA area, your local Council may offer similar concessionary fees. Ask for details at your local library, Citizens' Advice Bureau, Unemployed Centre or Women's Centre (see **Borough Information**).

Grants

The general rule is that the only courses for which you are guaranteed a reasonable grant, are those at Higher Education level, ie those which usually need two 'A' levels or equivalent to get in.

If you get a place on such a course, and you have not had a mandatory award in the past, you are usually legally entitled to a grant. There are other eligibility conditions which you should check with your local Education Authority - most produce a local guide to grants and awards.

Your local Authority *may* also consider making a discretionary award where a mandatory award is not payable. However, each application is considered on its own merits and the awards office of your local Education Authority is the only place that can give you a very accurate idea of what you will be entitled to.

The telephone numbers from which you can get the local guide and further information are as follows:

ILEA (633 1066), **Barking and Dagenham** (594 3880), **Barnet** (368 1255), **Bexley** (303 7777), **Brent** (903 1400), **Bromley** (464 3333), **Croydon** (686 4433), **Ealing** (579 2424), **Enfield** (366 6565), **Haringey** (881 3000), **Harrow** (836 5611), **Havering** (0708 66999), **Hillingdon** (0895 50529), **Hounslow** (570 7728), **Kingston Upon Thames** (546 2121 ext 2616), **Merton** (542 8101), **Newham** (534 4545), **Redbridge** (891 1433), **Richmond** (891 1433), **Sutton** (661 5000), **Waltham Forest** (539 3650)

Disability Access and Facilities

As many colleges are divided into several sites, with some courses on split sites, it isn't possible to give complete access information in this section. A special guide to facilities and courses for people with disabilities (latest edition 1982) for all post-school educational institutions in London and the south is available from:

Regional Advisory Council, Tavistock House South, Tavistock Square, WC1H 9LR (388 0027).

Deaf and partially hearing students - advice on facilities and courses available from: **Centre for Deaf and Partially Hearing Students**, City Literacy Institute, Stukeley Street, Drury Lane, WC2 5LJ.

Where to Study

The three main types of establishments offering courses are:

Adult Education Institutes (AEIs), which have traditionally offered courses in a wide range of leisure/recreational subjects and have been innovative in the area of courses for women. Most AEIs do not run courses which lead to qualifications (there are a few exceptions), and attendance is part-time, day or evening.

Further Education Colleges (CFEs), which were originally set up to provide education and training for particular jobs, but which now offer a wide range of courses which can lead to recognized qualifications, on a full- or part-time basis or on a day- or block-release from employers. Most CFEs do not offer 'advanced' further education, ie degrees or diplomas.

Colleges of Higher Education/Polytechnics/Universities, which offer 'advanced' further education. This means that the normal requirement to do a course there is two 'A' levels, but, as at CFEs, it may be possible for mature students to be admitted without formal qualifications.

Hillcroft - A College for Women Hillcroft is unique in that it is the one residential college in Britain for women only. It is therefore highly conscious of its responsibility for preparing women students more adequately for the future. A recent step in this direction has been the College's introduction into its Arts and Social Studies based curriculum of a Computer Studies course, as well as a course covering aspects of Science and Technology.

A short course programme has recently been set up which complements the full-time courses. The purpose of the programme is to strengthen links with the local community. At the same time it meets an increasingly evident need for a structured introduction to the techniques of learning. Course topics include Study Skills, Women in Literature, Images of Women in Film, Values in Society, Vegetarian Cookery, Gallery and Theatre Going.

For further information, please contact Margaret Horne, Hillcroft College, South Bank, Surbiton, Surrey, KT6 6DF.

But remember, education does not only take place in these institutions. **The Workers Education Association** (WEA), 9 Upper Berkeley Street, W1H 8BY(402 5608) London District, 32 Tavistock Square, WC1 (387 8966) is actively involved in women's education and runs a wide range of classes in community based premises. Their addresses are listed by borough below.

There are also many community organisations, women's centres and unemployed workers' centres that run courses or education programmes, including some particularly for Black and ethnic minority women, eg the Black Women's Centre in Haringey and the Bengali Women's Education and Training Project in Bermondsey. For details, contact your local library, women's centre (see **Borough Information**) or unemployed centre (see **Employment** and **Unemployment**).

The Open University

The London Region of the Open University is based at Parsifal College, 527 Finchley Road, NW3 7BG (794 0575) Access: A. Besides the courses leading to degrees and other qualifications, the OU runs a range of short Community Education Courses for parents, for consumers and on health which include Children 5-10, Parents and Teenagers, Consumer Decisions, Energy in the Home and Health Chores and Planning Retirement.

You can also buy packs of self-standing OU material such as a programme of scientific and technical updating courses; in service education for teachers (including Reading Development which leads to the OU's only diploma, the Diploma in the Reading Development) and packs on children, language, literature and racism in the community.

Other areas of study include Health and Social Welfare which includes The Handicapped Person in the Community and is intended as training for professional and volunteer workers. There are also packs on Abuse in Families, Management Education and Personal and Cultural Education. These courses all last the same time and run the same academic year as undergraduate courses. Packs can be obtained at any time.

Women's Studies

Many AEI and WEA branches run classes in women's studies, and women's centres often run courses.

The Polytechnic of Central London, 309 Regent Street, W1 (580 2020) runs a Diploma in Women's Studies course.

Feminist Library, First Floor, Hungerford House, Victoria Embankment, WC2 (930 0715). They have a library; lists of research projects and women's studies courses; large journal collection. Also produce a useful directory of women's studies courses. Access: N, but will service women downstairs in A Woman's Place. Opening times: Wed-Sat 11am-5.30pm; Thurs open till 7pm.

The Fawcett Library, housed in the City of London Polytechnic, is the major resource for the history of feminism and women in general. It operates on a subscription basis. For more information, contact Catherine Ireland, Fawcett Librarian, Calcutta House, Old Castle Street, E1 7NT (283 1030 x570). Access: A.

The University of Kent at Canterbury, c/o Graduate Office, Canterbury, Kent, CT2 7N7 (0227 66822), runs a post-graduate course in women's studies. Access: P.

New women's studies courses are advertised in publications like *Spare Rib* and *City Limits*. *Floodlight* is the ILEA guide to adult education courses and it has a women's section - on sale June-September in chain stores like W H Smiths (50p).

Colleges of Further Education, Adult Education Institutes, WEA and Educational Advice Centres in Inner London Boroughs

Some examples of colleges offering *vocational* training for women only or of interest to women are listed in **Training**.

Camden

Camden Adult Education Institute, 87 Holmes Road, NW5 3AX (267 1414). An extensive programme of day and evening classes, many of which have creche facilities available. Of special note: Camden's facilities for classes in the field of art - from designing and making clothes; printing in a variety of mediums; fine art classes and practical workshops. Classes are available in basic skills; reading, writing, speaking English. Numeracy is taught in practical contexts. Many classes are run for women only. Courses are also available in art, music, liberal studies, history, psychology, movement, dance and keep fit (eg aerobics and yoga). General information is available on 267 1414. Access: P.

The Central Institute of Adult Education, Longford Street, NW1 (388 7106/7). The following four main centres are open to adults during the day and the evening. Headquarters, Longford Street, NW1, Creche. Access: A. Bolt Court Centre, 6 Bolt Court, EC4 (off Fleet Street). Chequer Centre, Chequer Street, EC1 (off Bunhill Row),

Creche. Access: A, ground floor. Christopher Hatton Centre, Laystall Street, EC1 (off Rosebery Avenue), Creche. Access: A, ground floor. The Institute does not provide on-site parking facilities, except in very special circumstances for people with disabilities. A variety of courses are available - the emphasis being on self-help, people and community activities.

The City Literacy Institute, (City Lit Centre for Adult Studies), Stukeley Street, Drury Lane, WC2B 5LJ (242 9872). The City Lit provides a variety of courses, during the day and evening. Departments offer courses in humanities, science, speech and drama, music, languages and art. The Department of Humanities offers a women's studies course to which all women are welcome. The centre also runs a variety of return to study courses - both full-time, part-time and on a self-programme basis. An advisory service is available to support individual student learning. A Centre for the Deaf is available. This provides a service for people who are born deaf, those who have acquired a hearing loss, for stammerers and dysphasic people and for hearing unimpaired people who are in contact with the hearing impaired. Signing courses taught. City Lit Centre for the Deaf will advise on colleges teaching courses for deaf and partially-hearing students. Access: A.

Working Men's College, Crowndale Road, NW1 1TR (387 2037). Mainly academic courses, some part-time evening courses.

Kingsway Princeton College, Sidmouth Street, Grays Inn Road, WC1 (and branches) (278 0541). YTS, Pre-TOPS, TOPS; Return to Work/Study; Skylight: for students who need tuition in basic skills; Wider Opportunities for Women - 'Access' courses: FE, law, science, foundation in social and community work. Pre-Access: working in the community. Access: N.

Mary Ward Centre, 42 Queen Square, WC1N 3AQ (831 7711). The centre offers a variety of courses including computer literacy, computer programming and word processing. About half of each course consists of instruction; the remainder of the time is used for practice by individual students under supervision. Some facilities for women with disabilities and partial creche facilities (Tues). Access: P.

Camden Adult Learning Advice, 58 Phoenix Road, NW1 (388 4666)

See also neighbouring boroughs of Islington and City/Westminster.

City/Westminster

Marylebone-Paddington Institute, Amberley Adult Centre, Amberley Road, W9 (286 1900/7792). Offers a great range of courses across the curriculum in both day and evening classes. Educational home visiting is available to students with special needs. ESL classes for minority groups, and women only groups are available. 'Access' to higher education schemes are run and also Return to Study, a non-examination based, one-year course, preparing students for a variety of examination courses. Access: A.

Paddington College, Elgin Avenue, W9 2NR/Beethoven Street, W10 (969 2391). Many courses of specific in-

Thameside Adult Education Institute, Admin HQ, (855 9044) Burrage Grove, SE18 7LJ (854 6908). Offers: basic skills classes; return to study, women's lives and writing; women and health; ESL classes (information available on 790 5991) - as well as a wide range of classes for adults in the community. Access: P.

Woolwich College, Villas Road, SE18 (855 3933). Basic skills, New beginning courses, MSC funded vocational training courses, return to work or study, Access courses: BEd, science, maths or engineering. No women only courses but tries to provide for the needs of the community especially women and ethnic minorities. Access: N.

Education Advice Centre, Greenwich Education Training Advice, 12/14 Wellington Street, SE18 (854 2993). Access: A.

See also neighbouring borough of Lewisham.

Hackney

Hackney Institute, Chelmer Road, E9 6BZ (533 2427). Strongly supports the needs of local people in its day and evening provision. Some women-only courses in car maintenance, woodwork and self-defence. Fresh Start for Women part-time courses. Subjects: history, English, science, typing, family work, health, with students eventually choosing what to study. Essentially a preparation for further education. The Institute also offers basic numeracy and literacy classes, women's workshops, working in the community, ESL, etc. Access: P.

Hackney College, Stoke Newington Centre, Ayrsome Road, N16 (and branches) (809 2480). Full-time and part-time courses. General basic education, ESL, painting/decorating, brickwork/carpentry, joinery, electrical and mechanical engineering, technology, computing, microprocessing. Pre-training for firefighters (GLC funded). Second chance courses for those who wish to return to work or study (GLC funded). Access courses:

youth and community education, science. All departments welcome applications from women. The college, with the support of the Equal Opportunities Committee, is working towards improving and extending the facilities and opportunities that can be made available to women. Partial creche provision is available. A support unit for women is being developed especially for women participating in technical courses. Access: P.

Cordwainers Technical College, Mare Street, Hackney E8 3RE (985 0273) A range of unusual courses in leather trades, saddlery etc. Access: P. See **Training** for further details of courses.

Hackney Education Advice Service, 263 Mare Street, E8 (986 8446).

Hackney WEA, K Worpole, 43 Lordship Park, N16 (800 7901).

See also neighbouring boroughs of Islington and Tower Hamlets.

Hammersmith and Fulham

Fulham and South Kensington Institute, Beaufort House, Lillie Road, SW6 1UF (385 6166). This institute is very involved in women's studies and offers a variety of courses, for example: assertion training; women and health; images of women; self defence for women. The institute also runs a Return to Study course (a one year part-time course giving the opportunity to take English and Maths 'O' level). Individual counselling is an important part of the course. Access: A.

Hammersmith and West London College, Gliddon Road, Barons Court, W14 9BL (741 1688). Full-time and part-time courses. Basic skills, English as a foreign language (EFL), business studies, technical courses in brickwork, plastering/joinery, painting/decorating, shopfitting, plumbing, return to study. Access: A.

Education Advice Centre, Sue Thurston, Education and Training Advice for Adults, 241 Kings Street, Hammersmith, W6 (741 8441). Access: A.

See also neighbouring boroughs of

terest to women/adults in the community. Variety of Access courses, basic skills provision, ESL classes, multi-skills workshop classes, wider opportunities for women. Access A.

Central London WEA, for information write to: Fred Osborne, 32 Tavistock Square, EC1.

See also neighbouring boroughs of Camden and Kensington and Chelsea.

Greenwich

South Greenwich Institute, Haimo Road, Eltham, SE9 6DZ (850 3632/3503). Classes of particular interest are available to those seeking tuition in basic skills. Specific courses are available to the disabled and the unemployed. Access: A.
Kensington and Chelsea.

Islington

Islington Adult Education Institute, Shepperton Road, N1 3DH (226 6001). Return to Study courses, Fresh Start part-time courses in anatomy and physiology for women, Black studies for women, psychology for women, science for women. If you like the idea of returning to study, there are many ways the Institute can help. You will probably find an introductory course to your subject in the programme and in the 'fresh start' courses. You can even get coaching about how to study effectively. For information about women in adult education contact Ruth Lesirge (226 9190). Access: P.

City and East London College, Pitfield Street, N1 (253 6883) (and branches). Pre-TOPS, TOPs (including for adult returners); basic skills, ESL, adult foundations courses, Access: business studies, teaching, social work, librarianship, university preparation course.

North London College, 444 Camden Road, N7 OSP (609 9981). Pre-TOPS; NACRO scheme; short courses in adult studies, return to studies, further skills for adults - working in the community, designing and making craft goods, DIY, engineering, sports

leadership. Part-time studies. Access: N.

Islington WEA, Mike Parsons, 35 Frankham House, Frankham St. SE8 (692 9245(eve); 928 2099(day)).

See neighbouring boroughs of Camden and Hackney.

Education and Advice Centre, Education Advice Service for Islington Adults, ILEA Learning Materials Service, 12 Barnsbury Road, N1. (226 9143).

Kensington and Chelsea

Chelsea Westminster Adult Education Institute, Branches at: Marlborough School, Draycott Avenue, SW3 3AP (589 2044); Park Walk School, Park Walk SW10 OAY (352 2895); Pimlico School, Lupus Street, SW1V 3AT (828 3578 6-9 pm); Buckingham Gate Branch, Castle Lane, SW1 (828 9614). A 'drop in' centre for English as a second language is available. Day time classes at the Lupus Street Branch have a qualified child tutor available to supervise children of all ages. Basic skills classes in English and maths are available. Of great importance to women, The Chelsea Westminster Adult Education Institute offers advice and counselling to help prepare individual course of study. A variety of courses is available to enable women develop their own potential - for example, New Horizons, Second Chance, Return to Study, Fresh Start and Open College courses offer a variety of ways back to study or training to acquire new skills.

Hammersmith and North Kensington Adult Education Institute, Addison and Wornington Branches (960 4171 or 960 2693). A variety of courses are offered to local people and the Institute reflects particularly the needs of women. Fresh Start and Return to Study packages, literacy, ESL, basic mathematics. Courses can be set up to meet the particular needs of students, eg welfare rights, women's studies, steel band, running community organisations, Arabic for social workers,

Black history and literature, Alternative medicine. Creche facilities at Wornington during day - early enrolment essential to avoid disappointment. Also facilities for people with disabilities at Wornington. No creche or facilities for people with disabilities at Addison.

See also neighbouring boroughs of Hammersmith and Fulham and City and Westminster.

Education Advice Centre, Deborah Lowen and Mana McClew, Hammersmith & North Kensington AEI, Wornington Road, W10 5QQ.

Lambeth

Lambeth Institute, Strand Centre, Elm Park, SW2 2EH (671 1300/0026). Lambeth Institute promotes through its educational facilities the self-development of adults in a multi-racial community. **Lambeth Educational Opportunities**, an information advice service, provides educational guidance to any member of the public. (671 2961).

Brixton College of FE, 56 Brixton Hill, SW2 (737 1166). YTS and TOPS courses. Full-time and part-time courses. Basic skills classes. English as a second language (ESL). Access courses for teaching, social work, electrical and electronic engineering, social science. Few women-only classes. Some branches accessible for wheelchair users.

South London College, Knights Hill, SE27 (670 4488). Basic skills classes, ESL, science, food, science, flexi-study maths/English and other 'O' level subjects, MSC funded courses. Particular emphasis on the recruitment of women and ethnic minorities for Access in business studies. Access: A.

Southwark and Lambeth WEA, M.L. Tichelar, 5 Thornton Avenue, SW2 (274 7722 ext 2050 (day); 671 0547 (eve)).

Lambeth Education Opportunities, Strand Centre, Elm Park, SW2 2EH (671 2961). Mon-Thurs 10-2, Wed 4-7.

See also neighbouring boroughs of Southwark and Wandsworth.

Lewisham

Ravensbourne Adult Education Institute, Lewisham School, Ewhurst Road, Brockley, SE4 1AG (690 0720). Provides facilities for the adult community and offers creche facilities at three branches during the day. The Institute also provides special classes for people with disabilities and offers women-only ESL classes. Access: P.

South Lewisham Institute, Malory School, Lancelot Road, Downham, Bromley BR1 5EB (698 4113). Creche provided at most daytime centres. Wide range of classes including Second Chance maths and English and courses of Women Today (including Assertion Training, Women Writers etc,). Access: P.

South East London College, Lewisham Way, SE14 1UT (692 0353). Offers a wide range of full-time and part-time courses. Business studies, Computer studies, foundation in electronics, skills sampling course, ESL classes. Access courses: to BEd (at Goldsmiths College) - full-time one year course of particular interest to women and ethnic minorities; to design technology (at Avery Hill). Has Switch on to Science course for women, see **Training** for details. Access: P.

Goldsmiths College, University of London, School of Adult and Community Studies, Lee Centre, 1 Aislibie Road, SE2 (692 7171). Courses in community and youth work, making Experience Count, New Horizons. Women only classes in ESL. The Lee centre (852 4700) has creche facilities.

Lewisham Education Advice Project, c/o Deptford Library, Lewisham Way, SE14 6PF (692 4265).

See also neighbouring boroughs of Greenwich and Southwark.

Southwark

Southwark Institute, Queens Road Centre, St. Mary's Road, SE15 2EA (639 1178). A variety of classes for women available including: ESL (women only) and ESL via the Industrial Language Unit. Special classes for mentally and physically handicapped people also are available and the Institute also has special facilities to enable blind people to read via the new Opticon Machine. Access: P.

Southwark College, (various sites) (928 9561). Offers a variety of provision. Pre-TOPs in business studies, TOPs secretarial, basic skills classes for adults and those with special needs, full-time and part-time ESL classes, Access courses in: humanities and social science, science/maths and computing, modern languages. Flexi study for 'O' and 'A' level courses.

Morley College, 61 Westminster Bridge Road, SE1 7HT (928 8501). Offers a comprehensive programme of adult education. Full-time and part-time day courses for women returning to study and ESL. The College makes every attempt to offer this work to students in as flexible and approachable a way as possible. Thus courses are held in the morning, at lunch-time, in the afternoon, the rush-hour and the evening. Access: A.

Southwark and Lambeth WEA, Mike Tichelar, 5 Thornton Ave, SW2 (274 7722 ext 2050 (day); 671 0547 (eve)).

Education Advice Centre, INSET, Information and Advice Network on Southwark Education and Training, 175 Rye Lane, SE15 (635 9111/2).

See also neighbouring boroughs of Lewisham and Lambeth.

Tower Hamlets

Tower Hamlets Institute, 4 Smithy Street (off Jubilee Street), E1 3BW (790 3358). Language Department (790 5991). A wide range of day and evening full-time and part-time classes. Extensive provision in Basic Education and ESL classes (including Bengali and Urdu) for women in the community. Fresh Start courses offering language support and opportunity to prepare for maths and English 'O' level. Many classes available to women with disabilities. Some creche facilities. Access: P.

Tower Hamlets WEA, Ms D Jones, The Tower Hamlets Arts Project, 178 Whitechapel Road, London E1 (247 0216). Access: P.

Education Advice Centre, Kevin Burton, The Education Shop, 75 Roman Road, E2 (981 3164). Access: P.

See also neighbouring borough of Hackney.

Wandsworth

Putney and Wandsworth Adult Education Institute, Manresa House, Holybourne Avenue, SW15 4JF (789 8255). Aims to provide a comprehensive and flexible range of courses for adult community. Courses include Second Chance, Fresh Start study group. Some creche facilities available. Art courses at Putney School of Art (788 9145). Access: P.

Streatham and Tooting Institute, Adare Centre, Mountearl Gardens, Leighan Court Road, SW16 2PW (Main office 677 3522). Provides day and evening classes. Of particular interest: Return to Study, a part-time course available to adults and especially those with ESL needs; family workshops (parents' with children); classes in old people's homes and day centres Hopes to extend this service to housebound elderly people and to the mentally handicapped. Access: A.

Clapham Battersea Institute, 6 Edgley Road, SW4 6EL (622 2965). Day time and evening provision, with partial creche support facilities, are available over a wide range of subject areas. Courses of particular interest to women include women and the law, women's car maintenance, women and literature, women's magazines, women and self defence and women and stress. For details of these courses phone Alison Tomlin (228 6723). Women with disabilities should phone Liz Jones (673 6244) or Joan McGee (675 5109) so that special arrangements could be made for them to attend classes. Other courses include New

Horizons: a 10 hours a week course for people who speak English as a second language or those who left school without qualifications and want to try new subjects like following the news; history and you; drama; writing. Popular Planning: a joint GLC/Clapham-Battersea project looking at how local people can have more say over the economic decisions which affect their lives. Women's Sports Night (Thurs): seven different activities. There is creche provision at five branches and family workshops, where parents learn alongside their pre-school children, at 12 locations.

Westminster College, Battersea Park Road, SW11 (720 2121). Pre-TOPs, TOPs MSC funded vocational training courses. First Step Forward - flexi study, basic skills courses. See also **Training** for details of vocational fashion course. Access: P.

Vauxhall College of Building and FE, Belmore Street, Wandsworth Road, SW8 (928 4611). A range of MSC funded vocational training courses. Full-time and part-time technical and construction course. Offers two women only courses: Construction and Land Use Foundation Course and Women's Painting and Decorating Course - see **Training** for details. Access: P.

South West London College, Tooting Broadway, SW17 0TQ (672 2441). Basic skills, ESL, MSC funded vocational training courses, return to work to study. Access to accountancy. Access: A.

South Thames College, Wandsworth High Street, SW13 2PP (870 2241). Basic skills classes, ESL, MSC funded vocational training courses, return to work or study course. Access courses with special reference to social sciences and community studies. Particular emphasis is placed in many courses on the needs of ethnic minorities and women. Access: N.

Education Advice Centre for Adults, Ros Gillham, Wandsworth Education Shop, 86 Battersea Rise, SW11 (350 1790)

Wandsworth WEA, Rose Taw, 18 Gaskarch Road, SW12 (673 1905).

See also neighbouring boroughs of Lambeth and City/Westminster.

Colleges of Further Education, Adult Education Institutes in Outer London Boroughs

Barking and Dagenham

Barking College of Technology, Dagenham Road, Romford RM OXU (70 66841). A variety of equal opportunities courses run in conjunction with NE London Polytechnic. Access courses. Return to Study. Access: P.

Barking College of Adult Education, Fanshaw Crescent, Dagenham (595 3237). Full-time and part-time evening courses available to both women and men: leisure/keepfit; secretarial; music; arts; courses in construction, engineering, woodwork, electrical maintenance and technical management. ESL and basic skills classes (literacy/numeracy). Of special interest to women: Barking Women's Action Group, 5 Brook Avenue, Dagenham (593 5056). Access: P.

Barnet

Barnet College, Wood Street, Barnet, Herts (440 6321) and Hendon College. The Williams Building, The Burroughs, Hendon, NW4 4DE (202 3811). Both of these colleges offer a variety of courses which are available to both men and women. Traditional 'O' and 'A' level courses are run on both full-time and part-time basis. Hendon College has an adult studies department: for advice and information contact Mrs Jones (202 3811). Access: P.

WEA, K Carter, 7 Fernstanton Avenue, N12 (445 3193)

Bexley

Erith College, Tower Road, Belvedere, Kent DA17 6JA (03224 42331). Offers full-time and part-time courses in traditional subject areas as well as day release secretarial courses, TOPs training programme in shorthand/audio typing, accounts and bookeeping. Access: N.

Bexley Adult Education Centre, Bexley Health (303 2541), Crayford (0322 521463)
Sidcup (300 3054). These centres are working to support adult students, especially women. Some creche facilities are available to support women students during the day. A pilot Access course is being run at the moment and further provision is planned. ESL courses are available. Leisure and academic subjects are offered and confidence building, and personal development is seen as a priority for many students. Principal Adult Education Officer: (303 7777 ext 590).

Brent

Willesden College of Technology, Denzil Road, NW10 2XD (451 3411) offers a wide range of courses full-time and part-time, evening. Of particular interest to women - a variety of short courses are available including Skills tasters, Return to Work and women wishing to get further advice and information may contact Miss Pipash. Access: N.

WEA, Ms S Boserup, 93 Braemar Avenue, NW10 (452 8584).

Bromley

Bromley College of Technology, Rookery Lane, Bromley, BR2 8HE (462 6331). Traditional and academic courses are available, but of special interest: MSC funded 18 week courses in secretarial, audio typing; typing and shorthand. Both courses include an introduction to computer literacy and office technology. Return to Work - a course which is designed for women with some previous experience in the field of office work. The curriculum includes shorthand, audio typing, word processing and the use of micro-computers. Access: A.

Orpington College of Further Education, Department of General Education, The Walnuts, High Street, Orpington. Traditional and academic courses are available as well as MSC funded TOPs: 18 week secretarial course, 17 week audio typing. Access: A.

Croydon

Croydon College, Fairfield College Road, Croydon CR9 1DX (688 9271). Short courses for women who wish to return to office work; 'Women into Management', a part-time course under the 21 hour rule - applications are welcome from women without formal qualifications. Work preparation courses, with special provision for ESL students. Also a variety of two hour courses designed for women are available during both day and evening. They include: assertiveness training and self defence. No creche facilities. Margaret Davey, the adult students' adviser is available for information (686 4433 ext 2292). Access: P.

WEA Miss E M Godwin, 44 Langdale Road, Thornton Health, CR4 7PP (689 5300).

Haringey

Haringey College, Park Road, Bounds Green N11 2QF (888 7123). Haringey's education policy places special attention on the needs of adult students, women students and those from ethnic minorities. Haringey College offers a wide variety of courses, many of which fall under the 21 hour rule - (claimants are charged a concessionary £1.00 fee). The Faculty of Performing Arts and Education offers a 21 hour Access course, which leads to a DHE at Middlesex Polytechnic. ESL courses are available including Language for Study, Language for Living, ESL Foundation in Business Studies. Working in the Community: course is available to women who need to gain the basic skills and confidence to seek employment in the field of community work. It may also be suitable for women who wish to proceed to professional qualification courses. Women from ethnic minorities are especially welcome. The College also offers a variety of Starting Work courses; an MSC Preparatory course; a variety of ESL courses including an introductory course to Business studies, and, separately, one linked to craft skills; and one called English for Academic purposes - language for studying; a one year Pre-Certificate course in the teaching of community languages for those who do not have formal teaching qualifications. Also computing and information technology courses. Return to Study business/office skills. There is also a 'Drop In' skills centre open to the community. Anyone can attend this 'learn by appointment' scheme, which is available between 10 and 4 am. Further information from Barbara or Heather on 888 7123. Fresh Start in Science and Technology for women over 19. See Training for details. Access: P.

Haringey Adult Education Institute, White Hart Lane, N22 (888 0952), Muswell Hill, N10 (883 9241). Leisure and recreation classes are available over a wide range of areas, including self defence, Asian studies, ESL classes for Asian women, basic skills classes and adult literacy/numeracy classes. Further information available on 888 0952. Access: A in some buildings.

Haringey Women's Training and Education Centre, Lordship Lane, N17 (801 6233) open 9.30am-5pm. Courses from assertiveness to carpentry, plumbing, electronics and computing as well as short training courses. See also Training. Access: A.

WEA Mr G Alston, 4 Connaught Gardens, Muswell Hill, N10 (883 9275).

Harrow

Harrow College of Further Education, Hatch End Centre, Uxbridge Road, Hatch End, Middlesex HA5 4EA (428 0121). Topics covered: maths, communication skills, seminars on general topics. The college also offers: Second Chance courses (part-time evening), TOPs courses, ESL classes, short course in computer studies (a basic introduction to computers in a 10 week course), basic skills, adult literacy and numeracy, flexi-study system for students who need to work mostly from home, mainly in the area of maths. Access: P.

WEA Ms L Ferrer, 73 Preston Road, Wembley, Middlesex (908 0678)

Havering

Havering College of Adult Education, Dury Falls Campus, Wingletye Lane, Hornchurch, RM11 3TB (04024 40832). A variety of leisure, recreation and vocational courses are available, as well as academic studies. Courses include 'O' and 'A' levels, DIY, secretarial/typing and shorthand, basic education, adult literacy, EFL classes. Access: P.

Hendon College of Further Education, Department of Adult and Community Studies, The Burroughs, Hendon, NW4 (202 3811). Hendon College offers courses for adults to Return to Study. Access: A.

WEA, Mrs J Paul, Oak House, Parson Street, Hendon, NW4 1QJ (203 0724)

Hounslow

Hounslow College (568 0244) A variety of non vocational, part-time courses are offered to the community. Women students are welcomed to join any of the following: DIY, electrical engineering, plumbing, printmaking, glassblowing. ESL courses are available. Access: P.

Southall College Beaconfield Road, Southall, UB1 1DP (574 3448) An extensive range of courses. Access: P.

Spring Grove Education Centre, Spring Grove, Isleworth TW7 4HG (568 3697) offers a range of part-time day and evening classes including recreational and leisure subjects, ESL, basic skills and adult literacy.

WEA, Mrs J Bates, 8 Burton Gardens, Hounslow, Middx TW5 ODF (570 3148)

Kingston on Thames

Kingston College, Kingston Hall Road, Kingston, KT1 2AQ (546 2151). Traditional studies are offered as well as Return to Study. This course is particularly geared to women returners. No academic qualifications are needed. It offers daytime study in GCE subjects, English language, literature, maths, computer studies, biology, history. Classes are timetabled to suit the needs of mothers, between 10am and 12 noon and 1-3pm. Access: P.

WEA, Miss M Renshaw, 8 Wyburn Court, 22 Ewell Road, Surbiton, Surrey, KT6 6HX (390 2998)

Merton

Merton College, London Road, Morden (640 3001) offers a variety of courses and welcomes women applicants especially in non-traditional areas. The Engineering Departments offers part-time and full-time courses in motor-cycle mechanics, musical instrument technology, repairing musical instruments, computer studies. Access course: part-time day and evening, linked to higher degrees at Kingston Poly especially in the field of arts and social sciences. Return to Study: a course designed for adults especially women, who need not have academic qualifications. Tutorial support is available to give individual guidance. Short courses: Wider Opportunities, TOPs (eg three weeks full-time) in business studies areas. TOPs evening course on 'Starting Your Own Business'. Access: P.

Merton Institute of Adult Education, Whatley Avenue, SW20 9SN (543

9292). Pre-TOPs 18 week full-time MSC funded in secretarial studies, computer studies, engineering, These courses aim to help students improve their job prospects. Special needs students are offered two term full-time courses in basic skills and craft areas. Part-time courses - day and evening with some daytime creche provision- in self defence, 'Drop In' back to work courses. Basic skills, literacy and numeracy workshops. Improving English and maths (0-5 creche provision), 'O' level English Language, maths (creche facilities), especially for women who wish to proceed to teaching qualifications. Fresh Start available to all adults wishing to return to study. The course concentrates on developing basic skills and confidence and covers current affairs. Back to Work: especially for women who wish to return to work or who want to change careers. Personal effectiveness development and basic skills in work contexts are the main curriculum emphasis. Access: P.

WEA, Miss Olive Craig, 33 Imperial Gardens, Cedars Avenue, Mitcham, Surrey (623 3556 (day); 640 9336 (eve)).

Newham

East Ham College, High Street South, East Ham, E6 4ER (472 1480) and West Ham College, Welfare Road, Stratford, E15 (555 1422). The Borough of Newham is keen to promote opportunities for adults, especially women and those from ethnic minorities. East Ham College offers a number of courses of special interest to women: 21 hour course - The Asian Women's Project; ESL Access to Computing; Access to Dip ME and NE London Polytechnic in social science and language areas. Both East Ham and West Ham Colleges offer TOPs courses, ESL classes for the community, basic skills and adult literacy/numeracy provision. Both colleges offer part-time and full-time day and evening courses in a wide variety of subjects and skills areas and welcome enquiries from women. Access: P to some sites.

Newham Parents' Centre, Docklands Training Program Ex-engineers Building, Royal Victoria Dock, SE16. (511 1012). Provides a variety of training courses for women; childcare; women's studies, computer and keyboard skills. Nursery available. Access: P.

WEA, R Phillips, 3 Osborne Road, Forest Gate, E7 OPJ (534 7410 (eve); 472 2000 (day)).

Redbridge

Redbridge Technical College (599 5231) Barley Lane, Romford RM6 4XT. Courses available for adults wishing to return to study or work, particularly some part-time courses for women returners, eg Wider Opportunities for Women. No creche. Access: P.

Redbridge Institute of Adult Education, Valentines High School, Cranbrook Road, Gants Hill, Ilford, Essex (554 4400). Part-time day and evening classes in a range of subjects. Access: P.

WEA Miss M Shrubb, 168 Auckland Road, Ilford, Essex (518 0119).

Richmond

Richmond Adult and Community College, Clifden Centre, Clifden Road, Twickenham, TW1 4LT (891 5907). Fresh start: a programme of special interest to women who would like to proceed to degree courses in the area of social sciences. No academic qualifications required, applicants will be interviewed. TOPs courses available in the business studies areas, eg typing/word processing; typing/ shorthand; information technology. EFL; grades 1-6. ESL; a variety of classes - all mixed groups. Basic education: a 'Drop In' centre is run where adults may improve basic skills particularly literacy and numeracy. Back to Business: full-time 10-13 week course for people with professional qualifications who wish to acquire skills in computing. The college provides an

Educational Guidance Service, contact Chris Mills (891 5907 ext 403). Access: A.

WEA, Mrs S Dequin, 16 Kinnarid Avenue, Chiswick, W4 (994 0692).

Uxbridge

Uxbridge Technical College, Park Road, Uxbridge, Middlesex (0895 30411). New opportunities for women. Phone for a guide to mature women who wish to return to work or further study. Access: A.

WEA Mrs D Costelloe, 8 Bishops Close, Hillingdon, Middx. (0895 38187).

Higher Education

All the above information (with the exception of the MA in Women's Studies at Kent University) concerns courses below degree level. However, if you want to proceed to degree or post-graduate level the following publications are helpful:

Opportunities in Higher Education for Mature Students, CNAA, 344-345 Gray's Inn Road, WC1X 8PB. Free.

Directory of First Degree and Diploma of High Education Courses and Directory of Post-graduate and Post-Experience Courses, CNAA, 344-354 Grays Inn Road, WC1X 8PB, free.

Grants to Students: A Brief Guide, applies to those ordinarily resident in England and Wales only. Room 2/11, Department of Education and Science, Elizabeth House, 39 York Road, SE1 7PH and from Local Education Authorities, free.

Mature Students: a brief guide to university entrance, Committee of Vice-Chancellors and Principles, 29 Tavistock Square, WC1H 9EZ, free.

Sponsorship offered to students by employers and professional bodies for first degrees, BEC and TEC higher awards and comparable courses, available from careers services, public libraries or in cases of difficulty from Manpower Services Commission, Careers and

Occupational Information Centre, Sales Department (CW), Moorfoot, Sheffield S1 4PQA price (Jan 1983) £1.50 including postage.

Birkbeck College, London University, Malet Street, WC1 7HX (637 9563) specialises in part-time degrees and has many mature students.

Useful Reading

Libraries, youth centres, Job Centres etc often display useful information about local courses and are excellent places to look. Courses of particular relevance to women are often advertised (especially near the beginning of terms) in *Spare Rib* (monthly) women's liberation magazine, on sale in newsagents.

Floodlight, ILEA, Information Centre, County Hall, SE1 (633 1066), 50p, and in newsagents like Smiths, July-September. Lists all FE courses, has special women's section.

Life Doesn't End at UB40, produced by London Weekend Television, Free, (222 8070).

Second Chances: The Annual Guide to Adult Education and Training Opportunities, National Extension College, 18 Brookland Avenue, Cambridge B2 2HN (0223 316644).

Returners, National Advisory Centre for Careers for Women, Drayton House, 30 Gordon Street, WC1H OAX.

Employment and Unemployment

More than two-thirds of women between 16 and 60 in London are in paid work or looking for work. Paid employment is therefore an issue of direct concern to the vast majority of women in London and to most is the single most important means of gaining the financial independence which is necessary for many other aspects of women's liberation.

Most women in London work in low paid, traditionally female occupations. Despite the Equal Pay Act the average wage for women in full-time jobs in Greater London in 1984 was only two-thirds of men's and the Low Pay Unit has estimated that at least a half a million women in London are low paid. The main reason for women's continuing low pay is that women are concentrated in 'women's work' where there are no men with whom they can directly compare themselves for equal pay purposes. Nearly half of all working women in Greater London are concentrated in just one occupation - clerical work. The majority of the rest work in other 'service' occupations such as cleaning, catering, hairdressing, selling, nursing, teaching and social work. Less than a quarter are employed in manufacturing industry and they are concentrated in the least well-paid industries - clothing, food processing and electrical assembly.

Nor has the Sex Discrimination Act helped women to enter non-traditional areas of work. Women are still under-represented in skilled manual occupations, in scientific and technical jobs, in the so-called 'higher' professions and in supervision and management and in higher grades of administration. Another reason for women's low pay is that many women's skills are both unrecognised and under-valued simply because it is women who possess them. Furthermore, many women work in industries where men are also low paid, such as personal services, clothing and distribution.

Women's opportunities at work are affected by their position in the family. Women's primary responsibility for housework, childcare and increasingly, the care of the elderly, limits the hours many women can work and the jobs they can take and therefore structures their career patterns. The lack of adequate childcare, school holiday provision and help with elderly dependants means that many women have little or no choice in whether they work, where they work and when they work. Their access to employment is also limited by their greater reliance on often inadequate public transport and the absence of good employment opportunities locally. Many women, nearly a third in London, are part-time workers who tend to have lower pay and status, fewer fringe benefits and more limited career opportunities. Particularly vulnerable are homeworkers who are often forced to work in the home at extremely low rates without even the minimal protection of employment legislation.

Another crucial factor is the way women are perceived and treated in the labour market. Women workers are still largely seen as marginal, temporary and their earnings as 'pin-money'. Women encounter both subtle and direct discrimination in the labour market as well as industry and career structures and hours of work based on traditional male career patterns. Despite the Sex Discrimination Act, employers continue to discriminate against women for certain jobs and women are much less likely than men to receive training, even in predominantly female industries. (See **Training**). Added to lack of opportunities at work is the problem of sexual harassment.

London's workforce is segregated by race as well as gender, with Black and ethnic minority women forced into the lowest paid jobs of all - cleaning and catering work in schools, hospitals, offices, shops and hotels and unskilled work in declining areas of manufacturing such as clothing. Black and ethnic minority women are much more likely to work in poor and even dangerous conditions, in sweatshops or as homeworkers. Their concentration in London in the public services makes them particularly vulnerable to the effects of cuts and privatisation and their jobs are often the first to go. Language difficulties and the constant worry of immigration checks and controls are further barriers to Black and ethnic minority women finding and keeping jobs. Opportunities for training and promotion for Black and ethnic minority women are even more limited than those for white women, and their unemployment is increasing at a faster rate, particularly among young women.

Women with disabilities are also particularly disadvantaged in the labour market. It is assumed even more for women with disabilities than for able-bodied women that they are likely to be economically dependent, that they do not need training for skilled and responsible jobs, that they will not seek paid work, or if they do, that it will not be in skilled or responsible jobs. Many more women with disabilities than able-bodied women are unemployed and those women with disabilities who are in paid work tend to be trapped in extremely low paid jobs. Many of the problems that women with disabilities face are those which other women face, but that these are aggravated by an even greater degree of economic powerlessness, the lack of suitable transport and by the additional problem of inadequate access to buildings and unsuitable equipment used at work.

Lesbians experience discrimination in the labour market both as women and as homosexuals. It is likely that most lesbians find their choice of jobs and promotion opportunities limited primarily because they are women, and they suffer the additional fear of losing their jobs if they 'come out'.

Many women in London are being hit by increasing unemployment and by worsening pay and conditions of employment. Official unemployment figures for women in London have doubled over the last five years. More than 110,000 women are registered as unemployed and it is estimated that at least half as many again are unemployed and available for work, but not registered as unemployed. Young women and Black and ethnic minority women have been particularly affected. Over a third of registered unemployed women are under 25. Black women's rate of unemployment is significantly higher than white women's and it is calculated that Black women's rate of unemployment rises 3% for every 1% rise in the overall unemployment rate for women. The main reason for this is active discrimination against Black and ethnic minority women in the labour market. A local survey in Haringey found that 76% of Black women left school with some qualifications (as compared with 45% of white women), but nevertheless experienced longer periods of unemployment and often were forced to take jobs that did not reflect their experience or qualifications.

Women with disabilities are also particularly likely to be both unregistered and unemployed. A recent report showed that although many women with disabilities wanted to work, they didn't register because they felt it was impossible to get a job.

Many women in London work in jobs and sectors which are particularly vulnerable to changes in technology. The introduction of micro-electronics threatens women's jobs in offices, banks and shops and in factories and warehouses. While new technology has removed the need for strength from some traditionally male jobs and created a new set of skills, women are not gaining access to the new and better paid jobs created by new technology or to the training needed to move into new areas of work and new skills. Instead, they are confined to the more menial and repetitive jobs, but with new health hazards and increased levels of stress.

Cuts in public services are also affecting many women in London - both as employees and as users. The reduction in teaching and nursing jobs, the introduction of contract cleaning and other cuts to cleaning staffs, cuts to school meal services and so on all affect women's opportunities to work, and increase the amount of caring work they have to do, unpaid in the home. With increasing privatisation of public sector jobs, already low paid and vulnerable women have either lost their jobs altogether or been forced to work with worsened pay and conditions of employment.

Women in London are also affected by the recession and the way that industry is reorganising. Women are over-represented in sectors such as clothing which are in severe decline. When industry contracts, semi-skilled and unskilled jobs, where most women are concentrated, are often the first to go. For example, more than 22,000 jobs (30% of all women's jobs in engineering in London and a much greater proportion than of men's) disappeared in just three years.

The GLC has worked to improve women's employment opportunities in a variety of ways. As a large employer of women, it made a positive commitment and put considerable resources into improving the opportunities of its women staff. Two workplace nurseries were set up, training schemes were introduced to give women a second chance to gain qualifications, job sharing and improved opportunities for part-timers were brought in and all personnel procedures were revised. The Council also used its purchasing power to influence the employment practices of employers in the private sector by requiring all potential suppliers or contractors to the Council to comply with the Sex Discrimination and Race Relations Acts.

The GLC also played a strong role in preserving and creating jobs in London through the work of the Greater London Enterprise Board which gives financial and other support to London enterprises and funds co-operatives. GLEB has created or saved more than 3,000 jobs, nearly half (45%) of which are women's jobs. 200 of the 450 jobs in co-operatives created with the help of GLEB and the London Co-operative Enterprise Board are women's jobs. The GLC has also helped to provide the training women need to get jobs in areas of work traditionally done by men. The Greater London Training Board funded more than 250 women-only training places with childcare facilities and/or allowances to enable women to go on them. It also prioritised women and Black and ethnic minority people on all its courses. (See **Training**) Finally, the Women's Committee funded more than 200 childcare projects which enabled women to take up training places or to work (see Childcare and Children).

This section is ordered as follows: *Black and Ethnic Minority Women; Childcare; Creating Your Own Employment; Employment Rights; Homeworkers; Lesbians; Low Pay; Part-time Work and Job Sharing; Resources for Women Workers; Sexual Harassment; Training; Unemployment; Women with Disabilities.*

Black and Ethnic Minority Women

Many Black and ethnic minority women work out of economic necessity, to supplement a low family income or because they are the sole earner in the family. Black and ethnic minority women work longer hours than white women but at lower hourly rates. They are even more concentrated in the lower paid sectors of the economy than white women. Racism, fears of immigration checks and both racist and sexist harassment all contribute to stress and insecurity and make women vulnerable to exploitation and active discrimination by employers. Some organisations dealing specifically with employment issues are:

Open Access, 5 - 5a Westminster Bridge Road, SE1 (928 9941). A job placement agency serving the needs of Black women and men, helping them to identify their training and employment needs and break into fields of employment from which they have been traditionally excluded.

Black Trade Union Solidarity Movement, 5-5a Westminster Bridge Road, SE1 (928 8108). Network and resources for all Black workers in London and elsewhere.

Black Workers Resource Centre, This is a new group being set up. Further information will be available from Open Access and other organisations listed below.

Migrant Workers' Organisations

Migrant Resource Centre, 2 Denbigh Place, SW1 (630 5842). London-wide resource for all migrant workers.

Women's Group of the Philippines Support Group, St. Francis of Assissi Community Centre, Pottery Lane, W11 (603 1813/221 0356).

Latin American Advisory Committee, Beauchamp Lodge, 2 Warwick Crescent, Harrow Road, W2 (289 7277).

Carila, Latin American Women's Group, 29 Islington Park Street, N1 (359 2270).

Chile Solidarity Campaign Women's Section, 129 Seven Sisters Road, N7 (272 4298).

Federation of Italian Immigrant Workers and Families, 80a Dean Street, W1 (437 4138).

INCA/CGIL (Italian Workers' Organisation), 124 Canonbury Road, N1 (359 3701)

Portugese Workers Association, Centro "25 April", 7 Thorpe Close, W10.

Federation of Spanish Immigrants Associations, 116 Ladbrook Grove, W10 (351 2697).

Iranian Community Centre, 465a Green Lanes, Haringey (341 5005)

Chinese Information and Advisory Centre, c/o Weefit Tay, 152/6 Shaftsbury Avenue, WC2 (836 8291).

Confederation of Indian Organisations, 5-5a Westminster Bridge Road, SE1 (836 8108).

Tower Hamlets International Solidarity, Oxford House, Derbyshire Street, E2 (739 9093). Support for Bangladeshi women in Tower Hamlets.

Union of Turkish Women in Britain, 129 Newington Green Road, N1 (226 7544).

Maendeleo Project (379 6889)

Africa Centre, King Street, WC2 (836 1973). Support for African women workers throughout London.

Arab Women's Group, c/o Outwrite, Oxford House, Derbyshire Street, E2 (739 4575)

Tamil Women's League, 23a Sumatra Road N5 (435 9584).

National Union of Eritrean Women in Europe, PO Box 7007, WC1 (837 2936/7).

Childcare

A major problem for women wanting to return to work or already at work is the absence of good quality childcare with hours that suit working parents, particularly for children under two. State provision is extremely limited, most voluntary and private schemes offer only part-time or limited hours, and only a handful of London employers have workplace nurseries (and the decision by Inland Revenue to tax employees on the employer's contribution to the cost of a workplace nursery place has made the use of those workplaces nurseries which do exist much more difficult for women to afford). There is very little after school and holiday provision for school-age children. Most women are forced to rely on relatives or childminders, or make do with a variety of ad hoc arrangements.

The GLC has funded several workplace nurseries, more than 200 community-based childcare schemes (see Childcare and Children) and various groups campaigning to improve childcare provision in London. The GLC also set up two 50-place nurseries for its own staff and provided financial assistance for employees using other childcare provision.

Listed below are a few groups campaigning for better childcare provision. For further and more detailed information on local and other childcare campaigns, see **Childcare and Children**.

The Workplace Nurseries Campaign, Room 205, South Bank House, Black Prince Road, SE1 (587 1546).

National Childcare Campaign, Wesley House, 70 Great Queen Street, WC2B 5AX (405 5617). Campaigns for under fives provision.

National Out of School Alliance, Oxford House, Derbyshire Street, Bethnal Green Road, E2 (739 4787). Campaigns for and co-ordinates provision for the 5 to 11 age group.

A useful publication is *Who Cares*: A GLC guide to funding and evaluating daycare facilities for under-fives in London, GLC 1985. Several unions (for example the NUJ and NALGO) and the EOC publish booklets on how to negotiate for and set up a workplace nursery.

Creating Your Own Employment

Many women, fed up with being unemployed or with the low pay, sexism, and racism of most existing jobs, have begun to create their own employment opportunities, either by setting up as collectives or cooperatives or as individual self-employed workers. Working in a co-operative in particular can give you more flexibility in relation to childcare arrangements and a greater opportunity to learn and use a range of skills. But starting a business or a co-operative is hard work, and often involves long hours of work tor low pay, particularly while you are trying to get the business or co-operative established. It is worth while looking carefully at the advantages and disadvantages of both types of organisation before making a firm decision. There are several places you can turn to for advice if you want to set up a co-operative:

London Co-operative Enterprise Board, 11-13 Charterhouse Buildings, EC1H 7AN (608 1141) helps finance co-operatives.

Greater London Enterprise Board, 63-67 Newington Causeway, SE1 (403 0300). Finance for co-operatives.

Community Accountancy Services, The Works, 105a Torriano Avenue NW5 2RX (482 2866). Accountancy services to co-ops.

Co-operative Advisory Group Ltd., 272-276 Pentonville Road, N1 9JY (833 3915). Co-operative and business consultants.

London ICOM (Industrial Common Ownership Movement), Unit 7, Bradbury Street, N16 (249 2837). Advice, publications, and model articles for co-operatives.

ICOM Women's Link Up, 393-395 City Road, EC1 (837 7020). Training for women wanting to set up and run co-operatives.

For information about what your borough can offer, contact the Industrial Liaison Officer at your local Town Hall except in Camden, Haringey, and Lewisham, which have their own co-operative development staff:

Camden Enterprise Ltd, 57 Pratt Street, W1 (482 2128)

Haringey Borough Council, 4th Floor, 98/100 High Road, N22 (881 3000 ext 3003).

Lewisham Borough Council, Town Hall Chambers, Rushey Green, SE6 4RY (690 4343 ext 630).

However, you may be able to get more immediate help from your local Co-operative Development Agency (CDA):

Brent CDA, 192 High Road, Willesden, NW10 (451 3777)

Central London CDA, 80 Waynefleet Square, W10 6UJ (968 7744)

Croydon CDA, 99 London Road, Croydon, Surrey, CR9 2QN (686 1966)

Ealing CDA, Charles House, Bridge Road, Middlesex UN2 4BD (574 4724).

Feltham Community Association Co-op Resources Centre, Feltham Community Centre, Hanworth Road, Feltham, Middlesex (751 4618)

Greenwich Employment Resources Unit, 311 Plumstead High Street, SE18 IJX (310 6695/6)

Hackney CDA, 16 Dalston Lane, E8 3AZ (254 3743/4829)

Hammersmith and Fulham Community Enterprise Development Agency, 16 Askew Crescent, W12 (740 7271)

Hammersmith and Fulham CDA, Bishop Creighton House, 378 Lillie Road, SW6 7PH (381 4446/748 3020 ext 5300)

Haringey Economic Development Unit, 98-100 High Road, Wood Green, N22 (881 3000 ext 3343)

Harlesden People's Community Council Co-operative Development Worker, Bus Garage Project, Brentfield, Harrow Road, NW10 (965 2223)

Islington CDA, 177 Upper Street, N1 1RG (226 2783)

Kingston and Richmond CDA, Clarence Chambers, Fairfield West, Kingston, Surrey KT2 60H (549 9159/5099)

Lambeth CDA, Co-op Centre, Mowll Street, SW9 6BG (582 0003)

Newham CDA, 55 West Ham Lane, E15 (519 2377)

Shalom Centre, 395 High Street North, E12 6TL (472 3571). Workshop space and equipment for co-operatives in Newham.

Southwark CDA, 135 Rye Lane, SE15 (639 0134)

Tower Hamlets CDA, 84 Whitehorse Road, E1 (791 0450)

Waltham Forest CDA, 160 High Street, E17 7JS (520 0460).

Advice on setting up your own small business is available from:

London Enterprise Agency, 69 Cannon Street, EC4N 5AB (236 2676). Advice, training and links with investors, possible partners, managers, and new business opportunities.

Small Firms Service, Ebury Bridge House, 2-18 Ebury Bridge Road, SW1 (730 8451). Government service providing information and advice to small firms.

Project Fullemploy Resource Bank, Unit 120, Clerkenwell Workshops, 31 Clerkenwell Close, EC1 (251 6037). Information, free publications and advice to help people set up and run their own businesses.

Spitalfields Small Business Association, 170 Brick Lane, E1 6RU (247 1892)

Wandsworth Enterprise Development Agency, Unity House, 56-60 Wandsworth High Street, SW18 4LN (870 2165)

If you are drawing unemployment benefit you may be eligible for the Government's Enterprise Allowance Scheme. Ask at your local Job Centre for details.

Employment Rights

Employees have certain rights laid down for them in law. These include contracts of employment, dismissal and redundancy, health and safety, maternity provision, equal pay and sex and race discrimination. Some workers are also covered by protective legislation which limits the hours they can work or where they can work, or by Wages Councils which set minimum wages for workers in their industry. Your best protection, however, is to join a union. Most unions negotiate for better terms and conditions than the statutory provision and your union will advise and represent you if you have a problem.

If you have a problem, contact your union and/or any relevant women's group (see Resources for Women Workers below). If your problem is a legal one you may also need to contact your nearest law centre (see Borough Information).

Useful publications on employment rights and union agreements are:

Rights at Work, Jeremy McMullen, Pluto Press, 2nd edition.

Women's Rights in the Workplace, Tess Gill and Larry Whitty, Pelican Books, 1983, is very useful but out of print, try libraries.

Industrial Relations Review and Reports, 67 Maygrove Road, NW6 (328 4751) and Incomes Data Services (IDS), 140 Portland Street, W1 (580 0521/9). Both publish regular information on various aspects of employment and employment rights. Both publish details of significant cases and some analysis of agreements. Expensive to subscribe but available from libraries.

Labour Research Dept, 78 Blackfriars Road, SE1 (928 3649) Information, research and publication about rights, collective bargaining and individual companies, free to affiliated organisations.

Department of Employment Gazette (monthly) also publishes regular articles on employment law, and pay and practices.

The Equal Pay and Sex Discrimination Acts

The Equal Pay and Sex Discrimination Acts came into force at the end of 1975. They offer women limited avenues for improving pay and opportunities at work.

Women in London still earn only two-thirds of men's average hourly rates, despite the Equal Pay Act 1970 (as amended). One reason why the Act has had such a limited effect is that it provided for equal pay for 'like work' and for work 'rated as equivalent' under a job evaluation scheme, but many women are in jobs where there are no men with whom to compare themselves and where there is no job evaluation. After a successful European Commission case against the UK in March 1982, the Government introduced the Equal Pay (Amendment) Regulations 1983 which allow a woman doing a different job from that of a man to claim that her work is equal in value to his, whether there is a job evaluation scheme or not. This amendment has led to more than 100 equal value cases, some of which have been won at industrial tribunal.

Detailed information on the Equal Pay Act and how to use it are available in: *No More Peanuts: an evaluation of women's work*, Jo Morris 1983, £2.50 NCCL. 21 Tabard Street, SE1 4LA (403 3888).

The Equal Opportunities Commission, Overseas House, Quay Street, Manchester, M3 3HN (061 833 9244), the **Department of Employment** (see phone book for local offices) and the **TUC**, Congress House, Great Russell St. WC1 636 4030) also supply information on this legislation as well as other useful publications on topics such as job evaluation.

If you think that your work is underpaid or undervalued in relation to that of a man where you work, you should first of all contact your union and/or your local law centre or women's or other resource centre for advice and help to prepare your case.

The **NCCL**, 21 Tabard St, SE1 (403 3888) and **ROW**, 52-54 Featherstone Street, WC2 (328 0465), in particular will help and advise on cases. The NCCL in some cases can provide legal representation and the EOC gives legal support for some cases. Taking a case to industrial tribunal is difficult and stressful and you will need support.

The Sex Discrimination Act 1975 makes unlawful discrimination on the grounds of sex (and of being married). The Act covers two types of discrimination:

• direct discrimination, where a person treats you less favourably than she/he treats or would treat a man.

• indirect discrimination where a condition or requirement is applied equally but which is such that the proportion of women who can comply with it is considerably smaller than the proportion of men and which cannot be justified by the employer. Such a condition or requirement must also be to your detriment because you cannot comply with it.

It is also unlawful to victimise someone for bringing proceedings under the Act. The Act covers advertisements, recruitment, transfer and promotion, training, benefits and dismissal. There are some exceptions: companies with five or less employees (this is due to be changed), genuine occupational qualifications for particular jobs, and special treatment for women in connection with childbirth and pregnancy or retirement and death benefits.

The Act overall has had a limited impact. While it has made discrimination less overt it has not prevented direct discrimination nor has it changed the way in which established structures, practices and attitudes interact to limit women's opportunities even when there is no intention to discriminate. One reason is that the Act as it stands does not allow positive discrimination (except in some circumstances with respect to training, see Training), thus making it difficult to take measures to overcome the effects of past discrimination and to break down barriers.

Detailed information on the Act is available from the NCCL, EOC and the Department of Employment (see above). If you feel you have a case, again contact your union first and/or your law centre, women's project, NCCL etc as for equal pay cases. Again taking a case is difficult and remedies offered in law are limited. For example, in most cases, an individual who wins a case on recruitment gets compensation rather than the job.

In general, the law cannot be relied upon as an instrument for fighting sexism at work. Comprehensive equal opportunities clauses in collective agreements must be fought for, as well as effective programmes to ensure that policies are turned into practice.

Women in many industries and unions have formed networks or groups to collectively organise, campaign for and to monitor changes to practices within their industry and to advise and support one another. These groups are listed in Resources for Women Workers below.

Some employers, under pressure from women and the unions, have set up positive action programmes. These are voluntary agreements to take positive steps to encourage and help women to move up in the organisation.

Positive Action for Women: The Next Step, Sadie Robarts, with Anna Coote and Elizabeth Ball, NCCL, provides information on how to go about negotiating a positive action programme. **The Equal Pay and Opportunity Campaign**, 45 College Cross, N1 and many of the networks mentioned above can supply information on initiatives in specific industries.

Maternity Rights

Women's maternity rights under law are very limited and many women are not entitled to those that exist because either they have not got sufficient length of service or do not earn enough to qualify. However, all women are entitled to the following two rights regardless of employment status, length of service, amount earned, or size of employer:

- The right to time off work without loss of pay for ante-natal care
- The basic state maternity grant.

Other rights dependent on length of service and size of firm or amount of social security contributions are:

- The right to claim unfair dismissal and take a case to industrial tribunal if you are dismissed purely or mainly on grounds of pregnancy. If you are unable to do your job (because for example of hazardous chemicals) your employer must offer you suitable alternative work if it is available. To qualify for this protection, you must have worked for the same employer for 12 months (or 2 years if your employer employs fewer than 20 people or if you started work after June 1985).

- The right to reinstatement into your job or a similar job for up to 29 weeks after the birth of your baby. This means that you can take maternity leave for up to 11 weeks before and 29 weeks after the birth without losing your right to your own or a similar job. Women working for a firm employing 5 or less people do not qualify for reinstatement at all. Otherwise, women must have worked continuously for the same employer for at least 2 years to qualify or for 5 years if they work between 8 and 16 hours per week. It is estimated that more than a third of all full-time women workers and the majority of part-time workers do not qualify for this right.

- The right to six weeks maternity pay at 90% of basic pay. Again, a two year qualification period is required.

- The right to a weekly maternity allowance which women can claim for 11 weeks before the birth and 7 weeks after. To qualify, women must have paid full national insurance contributions on sufficiently high earnings over a specified period in the previous tax year. According to the Department of Employment more than 2] million part-time employees (nearly all of them women) earned less than the minimum required in 1984 and thus were not entitled to maternity benefit.

The law in this area is changing and not always clear. Also, trade unions in some areas have succeeded in negotiating maternity, paternity and parental leave agreements which are considerably better. For advice and information on maternity rights, contact your trade union, ROW (see above), a law centre or a trade union support unit, or women's employment project (see below). The NCCL Rights of Women Unit, 21 Tabard Street, SE1 4LA (403 3888) publishes a useful booklet *Maternity Rights for Working Women* and the Maternity Alliance, 59-62 Camden High Street, NW1 (388 6337) provides leaflets explaining how to claim all the benefits you may be entitled to.

Health and Safety at Work

Many of the jobs done by London's women are extremely hazardous. Even office jobs, such as word processing, can be harmful. Some legal protection is available, but this generally depends on strong trade union organisation to ensure that it is implemented. If you are worried abut conditions in your workplace contact your union first of all. If you haven't got a union contact Women and Work Hazards (see below) for advice.

The Health and Safety at Work Act 1974 requires employers to ensure the health, safety and welfare of their employees 'as far as is reasonably practicable'. It is administered by the Health and Safety at Work Executive who employ inspectors. The Factories Act 1961 and the Offices Shop and Railway Premises Act 1963 also impose minimum standards of cleanliness and decoration of premises, overcrowding, ventilation, lighting, sanitation etc and are enforced by health and safety inspectors and local authority environmental health officers. Look under Health and Safety Executive in the telephone directory for a list of its different sections.

Common law also imposes a duty on an employer to take reasonable care for the safety of employees by providing a safe place of work, a safe system of work, adequate plant and equipment and competent staff. If you are injured at work or become ill as a result of your employer's negligence, with the help of a solicitor you can sue your employer for damages.

For information on health hazards contact:

The London Hazards Centre, 103 Borough road, SE1 (261 9550). Information and resources on health and safety at work for all London workers.

Women and Work Hazards Group, c/o BSSRS, 9 Poland Street, W1. Information and resources on women's health and safety at work for women throughout London and elsewhere.

Protective legislation

The hours and conditions of women doing manual jobs in factories (places where people are employed doing manual labour) are restricted by the Factories Act 1961 and the Hours of Employment (Conventions) Act 1936. The rules are complicated but one of their main effects is to prevent women working at night unless there is an exemption order in force which can be granted for the purposes of 'maintaining or increasing the efficiency of industry or transport' but not simply because women want to work during hours forbidden by law. But women employed solely in cleaning (including night cleaners) are excluded from the protection of these laws which are also not affected by the Sex Discrimination Act.

Women are also subject to restrictions on working with lead and radioactivity.

Homeworkers

If you do work for someone in your home or the home of someone else, you are a homeworker. Many homeworkers work at home because of childcare problems or illness or disability. Many homeworkers earn very low wages for long hours. Some areas of homeworking are covered by Wages Councils where minimum rates are set by law (see Low Pay below). Very few homeworkers are in trade unions and thus are particularly vulnerable to exploitation. The following projects give support and advice to homeworkers:

Greenwich Homeworkers Project, Lower Ground Floor, Claymill House, Raglan Road, SEl8 7HY (854 9841). Information and resources for homeworkers in the Greenwich area.

IVAC Community Employment Unit, 322 Upper Street, Islington, Nl (226 4690). Information and resources for Islington homeworkers.

Lambeth Women and Work Project, Lady Margaret Hall, 460 Wandsworth Road, SW8 (622 9208). Information and resources for homeworkers in Lambeth

Migrant Services Unit, 68 Chalton Street, NWl (388 0241). Information and resources for migrant homeworkers in the Camden area.

Southwark Community Voluntary Group, 135 Rye Lane SE15 (732 7232) works with Southwark homeworkers.

Low Pay Unit, 9 Upper Berkeley Street, WlH 8BY (262 7278). Information and advice for homeworkers throughout London and elsewhere.

In addition, several local authorities such as Haringey, Hackney, Camden and Southwark have their own homeworking officers, who can be contacted care of the Town Hall or Civic Centre, in the relevant borough.

The following unions organise and represent homeworkers:

NUHKE (National Union of Hosiery and Knitwear Workers), South England Area Office, 3 Parade Court, Bourne End, Bucks (06285 25298). Trade union for hosiery and knitwear workers.

NUTGW (National Union of Tailor and Garment Workers), London Area Office, 16 Charles Square, Nl 6HP (739 5504). Trade union for garment workers.

GMBATU (General and Municipal Boilermakers and Allied Trades), Southern Region, J P Cooper House, 205 Hook Road, Chessington, Surrey (397 8881). General trade union for manufacturing and some service workers.

TGWU (Transport and General Workers Union), South East Area Office, 173 Clapham Road, SW8 (274 3251). General trade union for manufacturing and some service workers.

NUJ (National Union of Journalists), Freelance Branch, 314 Grays Inn Road, WCl 8DP (278 1812). Trade union branch which represents home-based proof-readers, copy-editors, indexers, etc., as well as journalists and photographers.

ASTMS (Association of Scientific, Technical and Managerial Staff), 79 Camden Road, NWl (267 4422). Trade union which will take home-based white-collar staff, including computer staff into membership and negotiate for them.

See also list of migrant workers organisations under Black and Ethnic Minority Women above, some of which can give advice and support to homeworkers and other low paid workers.

Lesbians

There are no laws specifically aimed at protecting lesbians from discrimination of any sort. In theory if you are sacked because you are a lesbian you can claim unfair dismissal under the general principles of the Employment Protection Act. But tribunals have upheld the sacking of lesbians and gay men for other reasons, eg a clerk was dismissed for wearing a 'lesbians ignite' badge because it was seen as offensive to customers and colleagues (Boychuk v. H. J. Simmonds 1977 EAT) and an odd-jobber working at school, who was not required to have contact with children, was dismissed even though there was no evidence of his involvement with children or that homosexuality made this more likely (Saunders v. Scottish National Camps Association 1980 EAT).

For resources which give support and advice to lesbians, See **Lesbians**. One project which concentrates exclusively on lesbian employment issues is:

Greater London Lesbian Employment Rights, Room 205, South Bank House, Black Prince Road, SE1 (587 1636) Campaigning, information and resources on employment rights for lesbians throughout London.

Low Pay

It is estimated that nearly half a million women in London are low paid. Black and ethnic minority women on average earn less per hour than white women and are more likely to work in low paid jobs and industries. Part-time workers are less likely to be in trade unions and are generally on the lowest pay levels. Other groups of workers who are frequently exceptionally poorly paid are women with disabilities and older women. Another factor is the systematic undervaluing of women's work (see equal pay in Employment Rights above). In some industries where union organisation has been weak and conditions are correspondingly poor (eg, hotel and catering, the clothing industry, shops, laundries and hairdressers), Wages Councils make orders for minimum rates (and holidays). If you think you are being underpaid, and your work may be covered by a Wages Council, you can complain to the Wages Inspectorate, London and South Eastern Region, Hanway House, Red Lion Square, WC1 (405 8454). However, the existence of Wages Councils is currently under threat by recent Government proposals for their abolition. By far the most effective way of increasing your wage levels is through collective negotiation by your trade union (see Resources for Women Workers below for details of the appropriate union for your type of work).

The Low Pay Unit, 9 Upper Berkeley Street, W1H 8BY (262 7278). Campaigns on the issue of low pay and can provide help and advice as well as a range of useful publications on low pay - both in general and within specific industries.

Women's Rights in the Workplace, Tess Gill and Larry Whitty, Pelican, 1983, has several chapters on understanding your pay and how to negotiate a better deal.

Part-time Work and Job Sharing

Women's inferior bargaining position in the workplace is partly a product of the restricted hours which many women can work due to domestic commitments and, in some cases, actual legal restrictions on working hours. A third of London's employed women work part-time and so lose out on benefits available to full-time workers.

Many part-time workers have lower pay, worse terms and conditions, and fewer fringe benefits than full time workers. Most employment protection rights, eg the right to claim unfair dismissal, redundancy payments and maternity leave, apply only to those workers who have been required to work, or who have actually worked, 16 or more hours a week (for 1 or 2 years continuously, depending on the right claimed) or 8 or more hours a week for 5 years continuously.

Many part-timers are also excluded from the statutory sick pay scheme (SSP) which is supposed to provide a flat rate benefit payable by employers and reimbursed to them by the state, for most workers who are off sick for up to 8 weeks. Those who earn on average less than the 'lower earnings limit' below which you do not pay social security contributions (from April 1984 to April 1985 it was £34), in the 8 weeks before going sick are not entitled to SSP.

A European Court decision (Jenkins V. Kingsgate l981) established that it is unlawful to set lower rates for part-time women workers unless they can be justified on non-discriminatory business grounds. However, to claim equal pay the part-timer must be able to find a man employed on broadly similar work or 'work of equal value'.

One way to improve your situation if you are a part-timer is to join your union and campaign for pro-rata pay and terms and conditions for all part-time workers.

Job sharing is one of the means that women have developed to work shorter hours while retaining (on a pro-rata basis) the benefits of full-time working, including more interesting types of work. For information on job-sharing contact:

New Ways to Work, 309 Upper Street, Nl (226 4026). Information, advice and publications for women wishing to jobshare throughout London and elsewhere. London-wide jobshare register.

Hackney Jobshare Project, 380 Old Street, ECl (739 0741). Resources and information for Hackney women wishing to jobshare including jobshare register.

Lewisham and Southwark Jobshare Group, c/o ll Stavely Close, Asylum Road, Peckham SEl5 (732 2898). Campaigning, information and advice group open to existing or would-be jobsharers in Lewisham and Southwark.

Lewisham Jobshare Register, Personnel Department, Lewisham Town Hall, Catford, SE6 (690 4343 ask for Jo Morris). Jobshare register for women in Lewisham wishing to apply for Council jobs.

NATFHE Employment Register, 21 Huntspill St., SWl7 (879 3881). For part-time teaching vacancies.

A useful guide to rights for part-time workers:

Part-time Workers need Full-time Rights, Ann Sedley, NCCL.

Resources for Women Workers

There are comparatively few resources in London specialising in the industries where most women work. This section lists: women's employment projects; resource centres and networks and trade unions catering specifically for particular industries or groups of workers; trade union resource centres, and sources of information about employers.

If your problem is a legal one, relating to your employment rights, you should contact your trade union (see below), or your nearest law centre or citizens' advice bureau (see **Borough Information**).

Women's Employment Projects

These projects provide a wide range of resources for women workers:

Haringey Women's Employment Project, 1B Ringslade Road, N22 (889 6599).

Lambeth Women and Work Project, Lady Margaret Hall, 460 Wandsworth Road, SW8 (622 9208).

Lewisham Women's Employment Project, 179 Deptford High Street, SE8 (691 3550).

There are also a wide range of women's training projects in London. See **Training** for details.

Resource Centres and Networks

The following resource centres and networks provide advice and support for workers in specific industries and often work with the unions in them. The women's groups or networks have developed to give advice and support to women in specific industries who are trying to break out of women's work, change policies and practices, and improve their pay and opportunities in their industry. Most hold regular meetings and produce bulletins or newsletters.

Office Work, Banking and Finance

City Centre, 32-35 Featherstone Street, EC1 (608 1338). Provides information, advice and resources for office workers, especially those in the City of London.

Women in Banking, Kathryn M. Riley, Manager, Personnel, Royal Bank of Canada, 99 Bishopsgate, EC2 (920 9212). Network for women in banking.

Hotel, Catering and Shop Work

SWAAP, (Service Workers Action and Advisory Project), Carlisle House, 8 Southampton Row, WC1 (405 8984). Advice and resources for shop, hotel and catering, contract cleaning and hostel workers throughout London.

Central London Law Centre, 13 Ingestre Place W1 (437 5764). Advice and resources for shop, hotel and catering workers in central London.

North Kensington Law Centre, 74 Goldbourne Road, W10 (946 7473). Advice for hotel and catering workers in Kensington.

Hackney Trade Union Support Unit, 489 Kingsland Road, E8 (245 6685). Resources and organisational support for Hackney shop workers.

Health Workers

London Health Emergency, 335 Gray's Inn Road, WC1X 8PX (833 3020). Resources and advice for health workers throughout London and elsewhere.

There are also local Health Emergency projects, or similar organisations in some areas which are specifically concerned with threats to jobs due to cuts in expenditure and/or privatisation and which support workers who are trying to defend their jobs and improve pay and conditions and the services provided.

Barking and Dagenham Health Emergency, 14 Porters Avenue, Dagenham, Essex. (592 5038).

Brent Health Emergency, 2 Tavistock Road NW10 (453 1280).

Camberwell Health Emergency, c/o 42 Braganza Street, SE17 (582 0996).

Hackney Health Emergency Liberty Hall, 489 Kingsland Road, E8 (254 6689).

Hammersmith and Fulham Health Emergency, 42 Fulham Palace Road, W6 (748 0682)

Haringey Health Emergency, Tottenham Community Project, 628 High Road, N17 (801 5460).

Harrow Health Emergency c/o Resource Centre, 4-16 Peterborough Road, Harrow (864 7446).

Hillingdon Health Emergency, 9a Yiewsley High Street, West Drayton, Middlesex (0895 444658).

Islington and Hornsey Health Emergency, Caxton House, 129 St. John's Way, N19 (272 1772).

Lewisham and North Southwark Health Emergency, c/o 42 Braganza Street, SE17 (582 0996).

Merton Public Services Project, 240 Merton Road, SW19 1EQ (543 8155).

Tower Hamlets Health Campaign, St Margarets House, 21 Old Ford Road, E2 (980 0445).

SCAT (Services to Community Action and Tenants), 31 Clerkenwell Close, EC1 (253 3627). Research, information and advice on fighting privatisation in the NHS throughout London and elsewhere.

Media and Communications

Women in Libraries, Sherry Jesperson, 8 Hill Road, NW8. Works to improve position of women working in libraries.

Women in Media, BM WIM, WC1N 3XX (380 0517). Networking group open to all women working in the media.

Women in Publishing, 1 Ortygia House, 6 Lower Road, Harrow, Middlesex HA2 0DA (864 1957). Network, training sessions, directory and monthly newsletter open to all women in the book trade

WFVTN (Women's Film, Video and Television Network), 23 Frith Street, W1V 5TS (434 2076). Information, directory, campaigning and mutual support network for women working or wanting to work in film, television or video in London or elsewhere.

Women in Entertainment, 7 Thorpe Close, W10 (969 2292). Campaigning and information network, directory, conference and events for women in the performing and other arts in London and elsewhere.

Black Media Workers Association, c/o Black Trade Union Solidarity, 5a Westminster Bridge Road, St. George's Circus, SE1 (928 8108). Network and directory open to Black media workers in London and elsewhere.

Fleet Street Nursery, 4th floor, Wesley House, 70 Great Queen Street, WC2 5AX (405 5617) or Mike Pike (278 2332 x3234). Creche campaign for media workers in central London. 25 place nursery will be opening in Holborn in early 1986.

Manufacturing

Valuable research on a number of manufacturing industries has been carried out in the various trade union support units listed at the end of this section. Additional resources on manufacturing industries where large numbers of women work include:

Women Working Worldwide, c/o War on Want, 467 Caledonian Road, N7 9BE (609 0211). Research and international networking for women in the clothing, textile and electronics industries.

Hackney Trade Union Support Unit, 34 Dalston Lane, E8 3AZ (249 8086). Provides specialist support and resources for workers in the clothing industry in Hackney.

CAITS (Centre for Alternative Industrial and Technological Systems), Polytechnic of North London, Holloway Road, N7 8DB (607 7079). A general resource for workers in manufacturing industry, particularly those working in multiplant companies, throughout London and elsewhere.

London Women and Manual Trades, 52-54 Featherstone Street, EC1 (251 9192/3). Networking, support and campaigning group of women in manual trades throughout London. Resource centre, library and publications.

Women in Printing Trades, Group open to women in the printing trades throughout London and elsewhere. For video and details of group ring Cinema of Women (251 4978).

Women and Construction Advisory Group, Room 201, South Bank House, Black Prince Road, SE1 (587 0028/ 1802). Advice centre working with employers and women in the building trade, gives advice on training and is developing a register of women looking for work in the industry so that they can be informed of relevant vacancies.

Computing, Engineering and Technology

Women and Computing, Wesley House, 70 Great Queen Street, WC2 (430 0655). Networking and support group and resource centre for women in the computing industry throughout London.

Women Into Science and Technology (WIST), Union Office, Imperial College, Prince Consort Road, SW7 (leave messages on 589 5111). Campaigning and support group for women in scientific or technical training or employment.

Women in Telecom (WIT), c/o Denise McGuire, STE Office, Room 117, Holborn Centre, 120 Holborn, EC1N 2TE (936 2137/3207). Network of women in Telecom.

Women's Engineering Society, 25 Foubert's Place, W1V 2AL (437 5212 ext 39). Promotes the study and practice of engineering among women.

Management and professional

Women in Management, Elizabeth Harman, 74 Cottenham Park Road, Wimbledon, SW20 0TB.

City Women's Network, Hilary Sears, 58 Coleman Street, EC2R 5BE. Network of professional working women in the City. The aim of the organisation is to encourage women to seek executive, professional and managerial positions.

General:

IVAC Employment Unit, 322 Upper Street, N1 (226 4690).

Trade Unions

As women enter the labour force in greater numbers they have increasingly joined trade unions and pressured for change. Over the last ten years, unions have begun to take up women's needs and demands. Issues such as abortion (once seen as a 'social' rather than work-related issue), job-sharing, maternity leave, sexual harassment, and positive action (in a few cases) all have come on to the Trades Union Congress (TUC) and union's agendas as women have organised and lobbied. Nonetheless, unions are still largely male-dominated and relatively few women (NUPE is a notable exception) hold positions on national executives or as full-time officials. Furthermore, despite some gains and despite attempts by women to get negotiators to tackle other issues of importance to them, such as hours of work, collective bargaining strategies are still largely based on the notion of the 'family wage' and on assumptions that what matters above all is the wage. Some unions now have women's officers or women's groups operating within them who are campaigning to win their union's support for women's

demands. Contact them through the unions listed below. The TUC has a Women's Advisory Committee, contact Anne Gibson, Congress House, 23-28 Great Russell Street, WC1B 3LS (636 4030 ext 158) and the South East Region of the TUC (SERTUC) has an Equal Opportunites Committee, Caxton House, 13-16 Borough Road, SW1 0LA (636 4030 ext 214). Both are campaigning within the TUC and unions for better opportunities for women and provide useful information for women.

The best way to protect yourself at work is to join the appropriate union. If you don't know which one is appropriate, or if you need advice on how to organise in your workplace, contact your local trade union resource centre (see below) or the TUC.

White collar workers
(office workers, banking and finance workers, civil and other public service workers)

AUEW/TASS (Amalgamated Union of Engineering Workers, Technical, Administrative and Supervisory Section), Onslow Hall, Little Green, Richmond, Surrey (948 2271). Trade union for office workers in the engineering industry.

APEX, (Association of Professional, Executive, Clerical and Computer Staff), 22 Worple Road, SW19 4DF (947 3131). A general trade union for white-collar staff.

ASTMS, (Association of Scientific, Technical and Managerial Staffs), 79 Camden Road, NW1 9ES (247 4422). A general trade union for white-collar staff.

BIFU (Banking, Insurance and Finance Union), 17 Hillside, Wimbledon, SW19 4NL (946 9151). Trade union for banking, insurance and finance workers.

CPSA (Civil and Public Services Association), 215 Balham High Road, SW17 7BN (672 1299). Trade union for office workers in the Civil Service except those in high-grade or technical jobs.

GMBATU/MATSA (General, Municipal, Boilermakers and Allied Trades Union, Managerial and Technical Staff Association), Thorne House, 152 Brent Street, Hendon, NW4 2DP (202 8272). The white-collar section of GMBATU is a general union for office workers.

IRSF (Inland Revenue Staff Federation), Douglas Houghton House, 231 Vauxhall Bridge Road, SW1V 1EH (834 8254). The appropriate trade union for Inland Revenue staff on professional and technical grades.

NALGO (National and Local Government Officers' Association), 1 Mabledon Place, WC1H 9AJ (388 2366). Trade union for office workers in local authorities, hospitals and nationalised industries.

SCPS (Society of Civil and Public Servants), 124/130 Southwark Street, SE1 0TU (928 9671). Trade union for higher grade Civil Servants.

SOGAT '82 (Society of Graphical and Allied Trades), Sogat House, 274-288 London Road, Hadleigh, Benfleet, Essex SS7 2DE (0702 553131). Trade union for clerical staff in the printing and publishing industries.

TGWU/ACTSS (Transport and General Workers Union, Association of Clerical, Technical and Supervisory Staff), 218 Green Lanes, N4 2HB (800 4281). The white-collar section of the TGWU is a general trade union for office workers.

TSSA (Transport Salaried Staffs Association), Walkden House, 10 Melton Street, NW1 2EJ. Trade union for white-collar staff working for British Rail.

Shopworkers, Catering and Hotel Work

USDAW (Union of Shop, Distributive and Allied Workers), Dislike House, Malet Street, WC1E 7JA (580 8641). Trade union for shop workers.

Hotel and Catering Workers' Union, 4-6 Dukes Road, WC1 (388 7326). Part of the GMBATU, this is a specialist union for hotel and catering workers.

TGWU Catering Section, Drummond House, 203-209 North Gower Street, NW1 (387 7242). The catering section of the TGWU trade section.

Health Service Workers

COHSE (Confederation of Health Service Employees), Glen House, High Street, Banstead, Surrey SM7 2LH (07373 53322). Trade union representing nursing, administrative and ancillary staff in hospitals.

NUPE (National Union of Public Employees), Civic House, 20 Grand Depot Road, SE18 6SF (854 2244). Primarily a trade union for public sector manual workers, NUPE also represents some nursing and administrative staff in the Health Service.

HVA (Health Visitors Association), 36 Eccleston Square, SW1V 1PF (834 9523/ 821 0310). Trade union for health visitors (the only TUC-affiliated union which is almost entirely female in membership).

The white-collar unions NALGO and ASTMS (see above) also have a substantial presence in the NHS, as does the GMBATU (see below) among manual workers.

Education

AUT (Association of University Teachers), United House, 1 Pembridge Road, W11 3HJ (221 4370). Trade union for university teachers.

NATFHE (National Association of Teachers in Further and Higher Education), Hamilton House, Mabledon Place, WC1H 9BH (387 6806). Trade union for teachers in polytechnics and adult education colleges.

NUT (National Union of Teachers), Hamilton House, Mabledon Place, WC1H 9BH (387 2442/387 9191). Trade union for teachers in infant, primary and secondary schools.

Non-teaching white-collar staff in education tend to be represented by ASTMS or NALGO (see above) and manual staff by NUPE (see above).

Media and Communications

ACTT (Association of Cinematograph, Television and Allied Technicians), 2 Soho Square, W1V 6DD (437 8506). Trade union for film and television workers.

Equity (British Actors Equity Association), 8 Harley Street, W1N 2AB (636 6367/637 9311). Trade union for actors.

ETA (Entertainment Trades Alliance), 155 Kennington Park Road, SE1 4JU (735 9068). Formed as a result of the amalgamation of the ABS and NATTKE, this is now the trade union for most BBC staff and for ancillary, craft and some technician grades in ITV, as well as non-acting staff in theatres and cinema and Bingo workers.

MU (Musicians Union), 60-62 Clapham Road, SW9 0JJ (582 5566). Trade union for musicians.

NUJ (National Union of Journalists), Acorn House, 314-320 Gray's Inn Road, WC1X 8DP (278 7916). Trade union for journalists, photographers and editorial staff in newspapers, books, magazines, radio and television.

UCW (Union of Communication Workers), UCW House, Crescent Lane, SW4 9RN (622 9977). Trade union for post office workers.

NCU (National Communications Union), Greystoke House, 150 Brunswick Road, W5 1AW (998 2981). Trade union for British Telecom staff.

Manufacturing

AUEW (Engineering Section), 110 Peckham Road, SE15 5EL (703 4231). Trade union representing a wide range of members in metal-based manufacturing industries.

EEPTU (Electrical, Electronic, Telecommunications and Plumbing Union), Hayes Court, West Common Road, Bromley BR2 7AU (462 7755). Trade union which represents skilled electricians as well as semi- and unskilled electronics workers, including substantial numbers of women workers in the electronics industry.

GMBATU (General, Municipal, Boilermakers and Allied Trades Union), Thorne House, Ruxley Ridge, Claygate, Esher, Surrey KT10 0TL (78 62081). General union representing unskilled and semi-skilled workers in a wide range of manufacturing industries.

NGA (National Graphical Association), Graphic House, 63-67 Bromham Road, Bedford, Bedfordshire MK40 2AG (0234 51521). Trade union for skilled print workers.

NUHKW (National Union of Hosiery and Knitwear Workers), South England Area Office, 3 Parade Court, Bourne End, Bucks (06285 25298). Trade union for workers in hosiery and knitwear.

NUTGW (National Union of Tailor and Garment Workers), London Area Office, 16 Charles Square, N1 6HP (739 5504). Trade union for workers in the garment industry.

SOGAT '82 (Society of Graphical and Allied Trades), SOGAT House, 274-288 London Road, Hadleigh, Benfleet, Essex SS7 2DE (0702 553131). Trade union representing most shop floor women workers in the paper, printing and publishing industries.

The Tobacco Workers Union, 9 Station Parade, High Street, Wanstead, E11 1QF (989 1107). Trade union for tobacco workers.

TGWU (Transport and General Workers Union), Transport House, Smith Square, Westminster, SW1P 3JB (828 7788). General union representing a wide range of workers throughout the manufacturing industry.

Construction

AUEW (Construction Section), Construction House, 190 Cedars Road, Clapham, SW4 0PP (622 4451). Trade union representing workers on large construction sites such as power stations, civil engineering projects and chemical factories.

UCATT (Union of Construction, Allied Trades and Technicians), UCATT House, 177 Abbeville Road, Clapham, SW4 9RL (622 2442). Trade union for all workers in the construction industry.

Other Public Sector

ASLEF (Associated Society of Locomotive Engineers and Firemen), 9 Arkwright Road, Hampstead, NW3 6AB (431 0275/435 6300). Trade union for skilled railway workers.

NUR (National Union of Railwaymen), Unity House, Euston Road, NW1 2BL (387 4771). Trade union representing all grades of railway workers.

FBU (Fire Brigades Union), 59 Fulham High Street, SW6 3JN (736 2157). Trade union for fire fighters.

NUPE (National Union of Public Employees), Civic House, 20 Grand Depot Road, SE18 6SF. (854 2244). Primarily a trade union for public sector manual workers.

Trade Union Resource Centres

These centres provide resources and information for existing trade unionists and those wishing to join unions in their areas. In some cases they also serve the needs of local women's groups and community groups.

Barking and Dagenham Link, 14 Porters Avenue, Dagenham, Essex RM8 2AQ (595 4252/3).

Battersea and Wandsworth Trade Union Support Unit, Junction Resource Centre, 248/250 Lavender Hill, SW11 (228 1163/4).

Brent Local Economy Resource Unit, 389 High Road, NW10 (459 6221/2).

Camden Trades Council Support Unit, c/o Camden Unemployed Action Centre, 102 St Pancras Way, NW1 (485 6352/624 9718).

Cities of London and Westminster Trades Council Resource Centre, 40 Tachbrook Street, SW1 (828 0393).

Croydon Trade Union Support Unit, 49c South End, Croydon, Surrey CR0 1BF (686 0219).

Hackney Trade Union Support Unit, Liberty Hall, 489 Kingsland Road, E8 (245 6685)

Haringey Trade Union Support Unit, 628 High Road, N17. (801 9464).

Harrow Trades Council Resource Centre, 4-6 Peterborough Road, Harrow on the Hill, Middlesex HA1 2BQ (864 7422).

Hillingdon Trades Union Council Resource Centre, 9a High Street, Yiewsley, West Drayton, Middlesex UB7 7QG (West Drayton (0895) 444659).

Hounslow Trade Union Support Resource Centre, 18 Staines Road, Hounslow, Middlesex TW3 3JS (572 3764).

Kensington and Chelsea Trade Union Support Unit, 49-53 Kensington High Street, W8 (937 2511/3248).

Merton Research and Resource Centre, 240 Merton Road, SW19 1EQ (542 6223).

Southwark Trades Council Support Unit, 42 Braganza Street, SE17 3RJ (582 0996).

Sutton and District Trades Council Resources Centre, 6 Grove Road, Sutton, Surrey SM1 1BG (661 7210).

Tower Hamlets Information, Research and Resources Centre, Oxford House, Derbyshire Street, E2 (739 3630).

Waltham Forest Trade Union Resource Centre, 547-551 Leytonstone High Road, E11.

Sources of Information about Employers

London Transnationals Information Centre, Octavia House, Ayres Street, SW1 (403 7550). Free resources, information and education on transnational companies operating in London.

CIS (Counter Information Service), 9 Poland Street, W1 (439 3764/6541). Publications and research on companies and industries affecting workers throughout London.

CAITS (Centre for Alternative Industrial and Technological Systems), Polytechnic of North London, Holloway Road, N7 8DB (607 7079). Free resources for workers in manufacturing industry, particularly those working in multi-plant companies.

London Industrial Strategy, GLC, 1985, This document analyses the key industrial sectors in London, including domestic work and childcare, office work, cleaning and homeworking. The **London Financial Strategy** examines financial institutions in the city.

International Defence and Aid to Southern Africa, 64 Essex Road, N1 (359 9181). Free information on companies which operate in South Africa.

EIRIS (Ethical Investment Research and Information Service), 9 Poland Street W1 (439 2771). Free investment monitoring service.

For information about your employer, consult Entel cards, *Who Owns Whom*, *Macarthy cards*, *Kompass Directory*, *Directory of Directors*, Company Annual Reports, Trade Journals and directories, press cuttings in the reference section of your local public library or in:-

City Business Library, 55 Basinghall Street, EC2.

London Business School Library, Sussex Place, Regents Park, NW1 (262 5050).

You can obtain company records on microfiche from:

Companies House, 55 City Road, EC1 (253 9393). But you must pick them up in person and will require access to a microfiche reader to decipher them.

To make contact with women's employment projects in other countries, and help develop international links with women employed by your employer or industry, contact:

WISER (Women's Information, Self-Education and Research) Links, Archway Development Education Project, 173 Archway Road, N5 (341 4403). Resource centre, library and network for women throughout London and elsewhere.

Sexual Harassment

Sexual harassment is unwanted, 'unreciprocated and unwelcome comments, looks, actions, suggestions or physical contact that is found objectionable and offensive and that might threaten an employee's job security or create an intimidating working environment' (GLC Equal Opportunities Code of Practice definition). It can include offensive sexist images, embarrassing remarks, leering and physical assaults. Sexual harassment per se is not unlawful, but a recent tribunal upheld the dismissal on grounds of gross misconduct of a manager who had been sexually harassing a clerk in his office.

Some unions and companies have agreed that sexual harassment is a disciplinary offence. If you think that you or a colleague are being sexually harassed, first contact your union. For more information and advice on this issue see:

Sexual Harassment at Work, Ann Sedley and Melissa Benn, National Council for Civil Liberties, 21 Tabard Street, SE1 4LA, 1982.

Sexual Harassment at Work: A TUC Guide for Trade Unionists, TUC, Great Russell Street, WC1B 3LS, 1983.

Sexual Harassment is a Trade Union Issue, NALGO, 1 Mabledon Place, WC1H 9AJ, 1983.

Women and Harassment at Work, Nathalie Hadjifotiou, Pluto Press, 1983.

Training

For information on training courses see **Training** and **Further Education**. Networks to provide advice and support for women wanting to train for traditionally male jobs are listed under Resource Centres and Networks above.

Unemployment

This section covers signing on for unemployment benefit and women's signing on campaigns. It also lists unemployment centres, groups and projects and useful campaigns and publications. See also **Training** for ideas on where to train for new skills and Creating Your Own Employment (above) for ideas on how to start a co-operative.

Signing on for unemployment benefit

In October 1982 the government introduced new benefits regulations which made it harder for women with children or other dependants to sign on. Women who are not registered are not entitled to benefit and do not show up in the statistics. They may also be excluded from certain government-funded training schemes (such as the Community Programme) designed for the unemployed.

You are probably entitled to unemployment benefit if you are not working and want a paid job or if you have done one of the following between April 1984 and April 1985 (to get benefits in 1986):

a) Had a job where you paid full national insurance contributions; b) Signed on; c) Attended a full-time training course such as TOPS; d) Received one of the following: maternity allowance, sickness benefit, unemployment benefit, invalidity pension, invalid care allowance, injury benefit, unemployability supplement. For further information contact your nearest Women's Signing On Campaign or local Citizens' Advice Bureau or Welfare Rights Centre (see **Borough Information**).

Even if you are not eligible for benefit, there are still good reasons to sign on:

● If you sign on, you can apply for a pass to grant you free or reduced entry to all local Authority sports and leisure facilities.

● If you sign on, your UB40 will get you in cheaper to some cinemas, clubs, concerts, exhibitions, theatres etc.

● If you sign on, your UB40 can get you cheap education and training courses. The ILEA for example will only charge you £1 for any number of adult education courses.

● If you live with a man who gets Supplementary Benefit, now or in the future, once you have signed on for at least six months you will be able to ask the DHSS to pay Supplementary Benefit to you. You will also be able to claim Supplementary Benefit for your household if the man you live with gets a wage or student grant which is lower than the Supplementary Benefit level, or your husband is out of the country and not supporting you.

- Much women's unemployment is hidden because they don't register. Signing on means you are counted.

The GLC printed and distributed a leaflet in several languages encouraging women to sign on for unemployment benefit and funded several locally-based women's signing on campaigns (WSOCs) who provide information on and help with signing on. WSOCs are also often involved with wageless women locally in campaigning against discrimination against women in the benefits system as a whole. They are also often involved in setting up other projects such as job-sharing, childcare, training courses and social projects. Most WSOCs were funded by the GLC and employ one worker or two job-sharers.

Women's Signing On Campaigns

Brent: c/o Brent Unemployed Workers' Centre, 387-389 High Road, Willesden, NW10 (459 2799).

Camden: c/o Camden Unemployed Action Centre, (see below for address).

Catford: c/o Catford Unemployment Centre,

Greenwich: c/o Greenwich Action Group on Unemployment,

Hackney: c/o Hackney Centre for the Unemployed. Kit on how to set up a WSOC available from centre. Workers available to run workshops on how to set up a campaign.

Hounslow: c/o Hounslow Centre for the Unemployed, 18 Staines Road, Hounslow, Middlesex, (572 6347).

North Kensington: c/o North Kensington Unemployed Centre, Telford Road, W10 (969 6515)

Southwark: c/o Southwark Women's Centre, 2-6 Peckham High Street, SE15, (701 2564/703 1062). Signing on pack available: What signing on can mean to you: how to sign on; married women's reduced national insurance contribution; single parents and signing on.

Unemployed Centres/ Groups/Projects

There are unemployed centres or projects operating in nearly every London borough. They are sponsored by local trades councils, local authorities and the GLC. They all provide information and advice about signing on, benefits and other unemployment related issues and are usually involved in local campaigning to improve or change conditions for the unemployed eg: campaigning against cuts in social security, against DHSS 'snoopers', for improved facilities at unemployment and social security offices and for concessions for the unemployed. These centres tend to be white male dominated and have not concerned themselves in the past with issues of prime importance to Black, married, single parent or disabled women for example.

This dominance of white men is being successfully challenged in many centres particularly by the provision of women's days. Contact your local women's centre (see **Borough Information**) for the information or advice you want, should you not be able to get it from your unemployment centre. However, it is important that we make demands of our unemployed centres for creches, women's days and resources for women's campaigns, courses and events so that wageless women are recognised as being a central part of the unemployed.

Barnet Unemployed Group, 9 Tillingham Way, N12 7EN, (452 2273).

Bexley Unemployed Group, Trinity Place, Broadway, Bexleyheath, Kent.

Brent Unemployed Workers Centre, 387-389 High Road, Willesden, NW10 (459 2799). Opening hours: Weekdays 9 - 5pm, WSOC (See above). Access: P

Camden Unemployed Action Centre, 102 St. Pancras Way, N1 (485 6352).

Catford Unemployment Centre, 20 Holbeach Road, Lewisham, SE6, (690 0338). New centre opens March. Plans: Women's day. Creche. WSOC. Courses: Small business and workers co-ops. Access: P.

Croydon Unemployed Centre, 49c Southend, Croydon, Surrey CRO 1BF, (686 0796). Opening hours: Mon, Wed, Fri 10 - 4.30pm. Printing facilities, training given to women's groups, WSOC. Access: N.

Greenwich Action Group on Unemployment, Building A, The MacBean Centre, MacBean St, Woolwich, SE13, (854 4984). Opening hours: Weekdays 9.30 - 4. Irregular womens events, Campaign against social security cuts, Monthly newsletter. Access: P.

Hackney Centre for the Unemployed, 485 Kingsland Road, Hackney, E8, (249 8994). Opening hours: Weekdays 10.30 - 4.30. Wageless women's group Tuesday am. Creche. WSOC. Access: P.

Hammersmith and Fulham Unemployed Centre, 190 Shepherds Bush Road, W6 7NL, (603 1831). Opening hours: Weekdays 9 - 5. Women's woodwork classes, Irregular creches, daily cheap lunch-time canteen, monthly centre magazine. Access: N.

Haringey Trade Council Centre for the Unemployed, c/o Tottenham Community Centre, 628 High Road, N17, (801 5629). Opening hours: Weekdays 10.00 - 4.00. Irregular women's events.

Women's self-defence classes. SERTUC benefits charter and fuel campaign. Claimants union. Access: N.

Hearsay Young Women's Unemployment Project, 17 Brownhill Road, Lewisham, SE6, (697 2152).

Hounslow Trade Union Support Unit and Centre for the Unemployed, 18 Staines Road, Hounslow, Middlesex (672 6347). Opening hours: Weekdays 9.30 - 5.30. WSOC. Local childcare campaign; SERTUC benefits charter campaign (Heather Tipton), bimonthly newsletter. Access: N

Ilford and District Jobless Centre, 203 Ilford Lane, Co-op Hall, Ilford, Essex, (940 2298).

Islington Action Group on Unemployment, 355 Holloway Road, N7, (607 8271). Opening hours: Weekdays 1 - 5. Mon cheap lunches 12 - 2. Access: P.

Kingston Unemployed Workers Centre, 10a Fairfield Road, Kingston-Upon-Thames, Surrey, (549 9158). Opening hours: Weekdays 10 - 4.

Lewisham Unemployed Action Group, The Albany, Douglas Way, Lewisham, SE8, (692 0231). Opening hours: Mon, Tues, Thur, Fri 10 - 4, Wed 10 - 6, Women only. Creche. Women's craft, assertion training and massage classes. Access: A.

Newham Centre for the Unemployed, 1 Eve Road, Stratford, E15, (519 4135). Opening hours: Weekdays 10 - 5. Wageless Women's group Wed 10.30 - 5.00. Access: A.

North Kensington Unemployed Centre, Telford Road, W10, (969 6516). Opening hours: Wed women only. Creche 10 - 5. Womens keep-fit. Self-defence classes. Tue 10 - 5. WSCO. Access: P.

Richmond and Twickenham TUC Unemployed Centre, Richmond United Reformed Church, Quadrant Road, Richmond, Surrey, (940 2298).

Southwark Unemployed People's Centre, 83 Peckham High Street, Southwark, SE15, (703 9011/2). Opening hours: Temporarily closed, women contact Southwark Women's Centre.

Tower Hamlets Centre for the Unemployed, 20 Watney Market, E1, (981 6515). Opening hours: Weekdays 10 - 4; Thurs pm casework; Tues 1pm onwards, women's group; women's rights and local health campaign; Bi-monthly centre magazine. Access: P.

Waltham Forest Centre for the Unemployed, Markhouse Road, Walthamstow, E17 8BD (520 3838). Opening hours: Weekdays 9 - 5. Irregular women's events. Access: A.

Haringey Women's Employment Project, 1b Ringslade Road, N22 (889 6599). Research comparing Black and white women's position in the labour market in Haringey in relation to unemployment, training, qualifications, earnings and promotion.

Lewisham Women's Employment Centre, 179 Deptford High Street, Deptford, SE8, (691 3550). Opening hours: Mon, Tues, Wed 10 - 4, Fri 10 - 1, Tues evenings 6 - 9.30. Book and hand tools lending libraries, duplicating facilities, meeting rooms free to wageless women.

Campaigns

Action for Benefits, c/o SCPS, 124-130 Southwark Street, SE1 OTU, (928 9671). Launched at the end of 1984 by the DHSS trade unions and various campaigning groups with the intention of defending the social security system against further governmental cuts and to extend the benefits system to provide a better service. Bi-monthly free newspaper Action for Benefits.

Campaign Against Racist Checks In Dole Offices, contact: Hackney Centre for the Unemployed (249 8994) or your local unemployed centre. Due to the enormous success of this campaign attempts to introduce racist monitoring practices into Unemployment Benefit Offices have been 'permanently suspended' by the Government. The campaign is therefore likewise suspended.

National Campaign Against Social Security Cuts, (0632 812242).

SERTUC, Committee for unemployed members' women's working party. Contact: Heather Tipton, Secretary, Hounslow Unemployed Centre, (572 3764); Sally Billens, Hackney Centre for the Unemployed, (249 8994). SERTUC holds an annual women's conference for unwaged women.

TUC Unemployed Charter Campaign, also contact Heather Tipton (572 3764).

Federation of Claimants' Unions, The Rights Shop, 296 Bethnal Green Road, E2, (739 4173). Resources and support for local claimants unions; charter for claimants; conferences; publications. Contact your local Claimants' Union via the Federation, Unemployed Centre or Citizens' Advice Bureau and see below for Federated Claimants' Unions.

Claimants unions work with Tenants Associations, Pensioners groups and other local groups on campaigns relevant to the local area, for example, Islington Claimants Union (c/o Starting Point, 11 Barnsbury

Road, N1 (837 8078)) campaigns for concessions on public transport, in shops and cafes, to improve conditions in unemployment and DHSS offices; for the Right to Fuel campaign, and to bring into use 2,000 empty council properties in Islington.

East London Claimants' Union, Dame Colet House, Ben Jonson Road, Stepney Green, E1 (790 9070), (Wed 7pm).

Bethnal Green Claimants' Union, 296 Bethnal Green Road, Bethnal Green, E2 (739 4173), (Tues 2pm).

Haringey and Islington Claimants' Union, Crouch Hill Recreation Centre, Hillrise Road, N14 (272 7569), (Wed 2pm).

Barnsbury Claimants' Union, 11 Barnsbury Road, N1 (837 8078), (Fri 10am).

Kingston Claimants' Union, c/o 16 Gainsborough Road, New Malden, Surrey.

Ponders End Claimants' Union, Common Room, Curlew House, Almer Road, Ponders End, (Thurs am).

Hendon Claimants' Union, St Peters, 25 Cricklewood Lane, NW2, (Thurs 6pm).

Southwark Claimants' Union, c/o S.U.P.A., 83 Peckham High Street, SE15, (Wed pm).

Newham Claimants' Union, 53 West Ham Lane, E15, (Every other Mon 7.30pm).

Ilford Claimants' Union, c/o Ilford Jobless Centre, 203 Ilford Lane, Ilford, (514 5116), (Wed 2pm).

Tottenham Claimants' Union, c/o Unemployment Centre, 628 High Road, N17, (Tues 1pm and Thurs 1pm).

Hackney Claimants' Union, Old Fire Station, 61 Leswin Road, N16, (Fri 2 - 4).

Women with Disabilities

Women with disabilities face double discrimination both in finding work and in the workplace. Under the Disabled Persons (Employment) Acts 1944 and 1958, employers with more than 20 regular workers must employ a quota of registered disabled workers (usually 3%) and if they are employing less than their quota, they cannot fill a vacancy with a non-disabled person unless exempt. The penalty is a fine of £500 but prosecutions are rare.

It is, of course, not enough simply to put pressure on employers to meet their minimum quota. There needs to be a change of attitude, which leads them to redesign jobs and equipment, training courses and the working environment to meet the needs of people with disabilities so that they can be fully intergrated into the workforce and gain access to jobs which make full use of their abilities and skills.

Organisations which provide advice and support and campaign on the issue of disabilities are listed under **Disability**. Projects which give advice on employment issues and disability are:

Disablement Resettlement Service MSC, Pennines Centre, 20/22 Hawley Street, Sheffield S1 3GA (0742 753275).

Pathway, 273 Garrett Lane, SW18, (871 1572). Employment of mentally handicapped people.

New Ways to Work, 309 Upper Street, N1 (226 4026).

Opportunities in The City, 1 Bank Building, Princes Street, EC1 (726 4963).

Association for Disabled Professionals, The Stables, 73 Pound Road, Banstead, Surrey SM7 2AU (07373 52366).

Jobability, Haringey Disablement Association, Room 16, Tottenham Town Hall, Approach Road, Haringey, N15 (808 4964).

Southwark Enterprise for Employment of Disabled People, 4-5 Milledge Corner, Rotherhithe New Road, SE16 3AD (231 9156/7).

Outset, 92-94 Tooley Street, SE1 (278 6921).

Lambeth Accord, 336 Brixton Road, SW9 7AA (274 2299).

Useful Reading

Able to claim: A study of take-up of disability benefits, Ruth Cohen, Action Research Project, Islington Peoples Rights, 2 St Pauls Road, N1. £1 plus post and packaging.

Action for Benefits, 124 - 130 Southwark Street, SE1 0TU. Bi-monthly free newspaper.

On The Dole, £1 to claimants, £2 to non-claimants; *Strikers' Handbook* 50p and 75p. Federation of Claimants Unions, 296 Bethnal Green Rd, E2.

Redundancy—booklet from Hackney Centre for the Unemployed.

Housing Benefit in Waltham Forest, a CAB publication, from 167 Hoe Street, E17. Underlines how disastrous the scheme has been for many claimants.

Immigrants and the Welfare State: A guide to your rights. Chapeltown CAB.

Lost Giros: How to replace them, Merseyside Welfare Rights Centre, Ground Floor TUC Centre, 24 Hardman Street, Liverpool L1 9AX. £1.

Rights Guide to Non-Means Tested Social Security Benefits and Rights Guide to Means Tested Social Security Benefits. Child Poverty Action Group, £3.50.

Single and Pregnant: A guide to benefit. One Parent Families, 255 Kentish Town Road, NW5 2LX. Free to claimants.

State Benefits 1985: A guide to trade unionists. Labour Research Dept, 78 Blackfriars Road, SE1 8HF. 85p.

Welfare Rights Bulletin, CPAG. Welfare Rights Advisory Service, Citizens Rights Office, 1 Macklin Street, WC2 5NH. Bi-monthly magazine. £1.

Women's Signing On Campaign Pack, Southwark WSOC, c/o Southwark Womens Centre, 2-6 Peckham High Street, SE15. Free.

How to Set up a WSOC, Hackney Centre for the Unemployed, 485 Kingsland Road, Hackney, E8.

Family Relationships and the Law

Despite the strength of the 'happy ever after' idea, most women have difficult experiences or choices at some times in their personal lives - over/in marriage or living with a man; having a sexual relationship with a man or woman; having children, with a partner or alone; over the breakdown of a relationship, separation or divorce; over further relationships or remarriage; over the death of a partner.

Very few women find these issues problem-free, not least because the role women have in 'the family' is one of the main sources of the discrimination they have in every aspect of life. Women's role caring for and bringing up children, caring for dependants and doing the bulk of domestic work restricts their access to paid work and other opportunities.

Talking over difficulties with a friend, a partner, or a counsellor (perhaps from the Marriage Guidance Council) or in a women's group can be a real help. Many women feel they have found ways of keeping up or strengthening a relationship by doing those things. They can identify changes needed and ways of working towards them. Even where a woman wants to leave a relationship there are often many reasons why it is not an easy option.

This section refers women to other sections in the Handbook which list advice and counselling organisations.

Many aspects of family relationships are bound up with the law and legal issues and present women with further difficulties because 'family law' is conservative in its nature, reflecting and reinforcing traditional views of women's role in the family. The law which deals with such vital issues as rights within marriage and custody of children, is not based on any notion of promoting equality of opportunity or recognition of discrimination against women. The legacy of Victorian views of women's role in the family is still obvious in today's laws. In those days a woman lost her right to control her own property on marriage and her husband had sole custody of the children of the marriage. Today judges assume women should receive a one third share (not a half) of any property on the breakdown of a marriage. (See *The Cohabitation Handbook* listed below). The process of law making, and the judiciary are dominated by white, upper and middle class men. The implications of this for women, and particularly for Black and ethnic minority women, lesbians and working class women, are that their needs and concerns are not considered or protected by the framework of family law.

Women have always campaigned for improvements in family law and have demonstrated the ways in which it currently reinforces women's inequality. Issues of the outdated and unnecessary status of 'illegitimacy', the racism of nationality laws built on women's position in marriage, custody of children for lesbian mothers, the failure of the maintenance system as support for women or children, the need for quick and effective remedies for women experiencing violence - all have been actively taken up. Women have developed their own support systems - legal advice, women's aid refuges, support groups for women going through custody cases and so on.

There are better models for a system of family law in other countries and some women have begun to call for a complete review of the basis of the legal framework here. One idea is that the law should be based on the concept of 'the household' and that there would be rules governing rights - to benefits, property, custody - between people sharing a household. It would mean that other kinds of relationships, such as those between relatives sharing a home or cohabitees or lesbian couples, would fall properly within the legal framework.

Meanwhile, there are still important legal aspects to be aware of whether you are single, married or cohabiting, for instance in the areas of rape, consent to abortion or sterilisation, entitlement to benefits, tax allowances, entitlement to state pensions via a man's National Insurance contributions, rights of occupation and to a share in property, immigration rules. You can be advised on these by the agencies listed in Borough Information.

The Women's Committee has looked into several aspects of family law and its impact on women's lives such as new regulations on rights to social security benefits for married women. The Committee has also funded women's advice services, campaigning groups and research. The GLC has funded advice agencies across London and London-wide coordinating bodies which are concerned to see that women's needs for advice are met.

This section is ordered as follows: *Legal advice, Advice/counselling, Useful Reading.*

Legal advice

Try a legal advice centre, law centre, CAB or women's advice service first. They will put you in touch with solicitors if you then need a solicitor. See **Borough Information.**

Rights of Women*, 52-54 Featherstone Street, EC2 (251 6577). Free legal advice service for women on Tues and Thurs eve 7-9pm. Write or phone. They also have a list of sympathetic solicitors. Advice for lesbians leaving marriages, especially re custody.

Divorce County courts: can give you the free official booklet on *Undefended Divorce.*

The Divorce Registry, Somerset House, WC2.

Barnet County Court, Kingmaker House, Station Road, New Barnet, (449 0881).

Bromley County Court, Court House, College Road, Bromley, (464 9727).

Croydon County Court, Law Courts, Barclay Road, Croydon, (681 2533).

Edmonton County Court, 59 Fore Street, (807 1666).

Ilford County Court, Buckingham Road, Ilford. (478 1132).

Kingston-upon-Thames County Court, St. James Road, Kingston-upon-Thames (546 8843).

Advice/counselling

(See **Borough Information** —Women's Centres, **Childcare and Children, Health, Lesbians, Older Women, Violence Against Women, Young Women).**

Marriage Guidance Council, London Office (including all Inner London Centres) 76a New Cavendish Street, London, W1. (580 1087).

Barnet, Haringey & Herts, 5 Woodhouse Road, N12. (445 9549).

Bromley & District, 83 Tweedy Road, Bromley. (460 6832).

Central Middlesex,(for Brent, Ealing, Harrow & Hillingdon), 1 High Street, Wealdstone (427 8694).

Enfield Office, Southgate Town Hall, Green Lanes, N13. (886 0615).

Kingston-upon-Thames, 29 St. James Road, (549 3318).

Merton, 30 Worple Road, SW19. (946 1788).

Jewish Marriage Council, 529b Finchley Road, NW3. (794 5222/8035), Counselling - Marital and Personal, 2 Somerset Road, NW4. (203 6311).

Useful Reading

The Cohabitation Handbook, A Rights of Women guide to the law, Bottomley et al, (PLUTO 2nd ed. 1984) available in bookshops.

Women's Rights - a Practical Guide, Coote and Gill.

On Getting Divorced, Consumers Association, (3rd ed. 1982)

Family Law and Social Policy, John Eekelaar (2nd ed. 1984)

The Law and Sexuality, Steve Cohen and others (Grass Roots Books and Manchester Law Centre) available in bookshops.

Making the Break, Carew-Jones and Watson (Penguin)

Leaving Violent Men, Val Binney and others, (Womens Aid Federation).

Women in Law, Brophy and Smart (RKP).

Lesbians on Trial, Rights of Women (see above).

Funding for Voluntary Groups

This section identifies sources of funding for women's projects in London and highlights some of the key issues facing projects run by and for women, to meet their needs.

The emphasis on key issues rather than sources of funding is indicative of the current climate. Scant recognition is given to women's needs within the voluntary and public sectors by central government and by charities and trusts. Some local authorities, particularly the GLC, have recently been concerned about women's funding and the allocation of financial resources.

Women in London, although forming the majority of the population, are treated as a minority. Like most minority groups and communities in this society women suffer discrimination in every sphere of life.

There is little recognition of the contribution made in the national interest by women in both the paid and, in particular, unpaid work that they do. 'Voluntary' work has traditionally been seen as a proper and natural sphere of activity for women, an extension of their caring role in the home, an outlet for their organising skills and energies and as 'something' to keep them occupied while men got on with the real business of running the world. This view of 'voluntary' work for women is out of tune with the realities of today. Voluntary work has expanded and shifted in emphasis until it is more commonly associated with self-help, with communities organising to do for themselves what was once done for them as a favour. It is about communities organising to lay claim to the physical and financial resources once given to them as a 'dole'.

Within London currently, thousands of groups - some based in local areas, some serving a section of the community - meet, make plans for activities and services they need, and find ways of providing those. Community centres, advice centres, youth clubs, childcare groups, cultural groups exist in every part of the city. Women's organisations and groups vary enormously in how they run and what they do. They are very active and the numbers increase all the time as women face so many problems in everyday life which no-one else is necessarily trying to solve and have both the skills and commitment with which to organise.

The voluntary sector, which this section focuses on, perpetuates the discrimination that women experience by accepting their labour, talents and skills but excluding them from policy and decision-making. Women, when given recognition, tend to be treated as an homogeneous group which further exacerbates the levels of discrimination experienced by particular groups and communities of women such as Black women or older women. These women have to fight multiple battles to have their needs recognised and met.

Institutional sources of funding (statutory and non-statutory) need to re-evaluate their funding policies and resource allocation to take account of women's needs on a general and specific basis. And women's groups do need income. They require funds to provide the infrastructure for their organisations - the buildings, equipment, furniture and fittings, office supplies etc, without which they are seriously limited. They need funds to pay their employees, who are only 'voluntary' to the extent that they work in the non-state social services sector of the economy. They need funds to train their employees to operate the complex technology of today's world, simply to keep abreast in the field of service delivery. The range of women's organisations covered in this Handbook, which is by no means exhaustive, will give you an idea of the volume of resources required. Women are setting up and running nurseries and pre-school facilities for the under-Fives, which must meet standards of health and safety laid down by law. It requires an investment of over £100,000 just to set up these facilities, and information centres which, given the small mainly local scale of their operations, require even more the information storage and retrieval systems to make them workable. Advice and referral services generate costly overheads in terms of telephone, mailing and advertising.

Further development is required on equal opportunities policy development and implementation programmes in the voluntary, public and private sectors that would assist in improving the profile of women's organisations and projects and their funding.

Funders need to provide the financial resources to enable women to run efficient and effective projects in terms of:

- Freehold purchase and leasing of adequate property
- Capital for bringing buildings up to the standard required to meet project needs and relevant legal considerations
- Training - in house and out house (employee relations, financial management, fund raising, organisation development,

marketing, management development, equal opportunities, public relations and research)

- Equipment and running costs - particularly reflecting special needs eg disabled women, specialist books etc

The GLC like other funding sources has been funding voluntary organisations for a considerable time and it has, mainly through its adoption and implementation of an equal opportunities policy, given recognition to the specific needs of women. The consequence has been that some 14% of its grant aid for 1984/5 went to women's projects and over 20% of the grants processed during that period were women's projects.

The Women's Committee has been the most significant funding committee - over 500 projects have been funded during the last three years with a total of about £30m. The range of projects and policy considerations included:

- Strategic Projects - projects which played a strategic role in the voluntary sector. These included projects which provide resources to new or existing women's organisations, helping them to start up and providing ongoing professional and technical advice which would not otherwise be available or which would only be available at commercial or professional rates

- Equalities Projects - Specific groups of women are particularly discriminated against even within the general overall disadvantaged position of women within society, and the Committee has had a commitment to funding resources for such groups of women.

- Projects which are of the specific types listed below were considered if they fell into the priority areas outlined above

- Childcare - Black and ethnic minority childcare projects, innovative training projects for childcare workers including childminders, projects which maintained existing childcare provision in London, projects for children under two years old, projects having an outreach role, and projects which catered for the needs of children with disabilities

- Health - Projects working towards preventive health care for women in the following areas: Black and ethnic minority womens health projects, projects concerned with women as carers, projects which aimed to maintain and extend specialist women's health facilities, community-based women's health projects servicing local areas. Also projects dealing with the needs and concerns of women working in the health services

- Women's Centres/Resource and Information Centres -
  i) projects which made accessible technical skills and resources to women and women's groups such as: computing and information technology; libraries; printing; surveying; building; law; architecture; mechanical skills; translation services.
  ii) projects which were concerned to inform women of rights, entitlements and opportunities; projects which offered women support or counselling.
- Campaigns and Conferences - organised by women around issues which affect their lives and which contribute to the knowledge and awareness of women's issues generally.

There is an urgent need to maintain and to continue to develop resources managed by women for women in London. This need and the urgency for it to be met is amplified by the abolition of the GLC.

This Handbook is part of our endeavour to help women's organisations to survive when that source of funding dries up. In acknowledging the funding crisis which will ensue for the voluntary sector, it is not the intention to leave you demoralised and depressed but to encourage you to make demands on other sources of funding, to continue to campaign for women's rights and for the right of your communities to define their needs and have them met, for the right of the voluntary sector to be acknowledged as an important and valid area of economic activity.

This section provides some useful information on possible sources of funding for women organising in the community. It is difficult to obtain as comprehensive a listing as the volume and wide-ranging nature of the organisations currently set up and run by women in the voluntary sector merits. Although women have traditionally had to fill the gaps in community services not provided by the state, there are very few funding agencies which specifically earmark funds for women's organisations.

The main possible sources of statutory funding for women in 1986/7 are 'transitional funding', which is provided by local authorities, using additional short term funding from the government, and funding from the Richmond Scheme (details available from the London Voluntary Service Council - see listings).

Women's organisations must refuse to go backwards: women's groups must continue to make demands on public funding and begin to make more demands on trusts and industry for funding which is our right.

Wherever you apply for money, you will often need to make an application for funding as part of a (non-profit-making) group. This can mean some degree of formal organisation such as a constitution, a treasurer and a secretary. Advice on how to organise yourselves if you are a new group wanting funding (eg model constitutions), should be available from your law centre, women's centre (or women's committee support unit in your borough - see **Borough Information**).

Whilst there is potential for women's groups to raise money outside government sources, those groups set up to provide social services or information will suffer greatly from cuts and the abolition because it will nearly always be impossible to charge for those services.

The money that groups get falls into two categories: *capital*, which is money for non-recurring expenses, such as purchase of equipment or premises, major improvements to buildings; and *revenue*, which is your recurring expenses, such as wages, rent, repairs, bills, etc.

Raising money takes time and determination. You cannot afford to get depressed by rejections but must be optimistic that you will get the funding you need - somehow!

This section is ordered as follows: *Statutory funding, Trusts, Funds from industry, Starting your own community business or co-operative, Other ways to get money for your group, General and Professional advice, Useful Reading.*

Statutory Funding

The following two publications are useful guides to obtaining statutory funding:

Raising Money from Government, ed Michael Norton, Directory of Social Change, 1981, £2.95. A guide to getting money from national and local government and quangos, including the Urban Programme and the Manpower Services Commission's various employment programmes.

Sources of Statutory Money: A Guide for Voluntary Organisations available from the National Council for Voluntary Organisations, 26 Bedford Square, WC1 (636 4066).

Government bodies which give funding are:

Department of Energy: Capital grants for insulation/energy advice projects which serve the needs of elderly, disabled or people on welfare benefits. Contact: Gill Owen, Neighbourhood Energy Action, Information Centre, 2-4 Bigg Market, Newcastle Upon Tyne, NE1 1UW (0632 614789).

Department of the Environment - The Urban Programme: The Urban Programme is the collective name given by Government to separate schemes for assisting local authorities and community organisations in urban areas.

Traditional Urban Programme: 'Trad-UP' is open to all local authorities *without* Partnership or Programme Authority status (see below). Participating authorities usually advertise for bids from community organisations following the issue of a government circular. This circular appears once a year normally in midsummer, and sets out criteria and priorities for funding.

Circular 25 stated that projects put forward should meet one or more of the following criteria: economic regeneration; environmental improvement; attracting private sector assistance; developing skills of voluntary organisations; assisting the unemployed; meeting the needs of ethnic minorities; complementing statutory services; reducing crime or alleviating its effects; encouraging self help in the community; meeting the needs of the under-fives; developing parental involvement in their children's education and welfare; and providing sports and leisure facilities for children including holiday projects. In addition to this all projects must fulfil three general criteria - namely that they operate in or for the benefit of an area of special social need; that they aim to alleviate either directly or indirectly the deprivation identified in the area; and that they must be politically neutral.

Partnership and Programme Authorities: Seven London Boroughs have an enhanced status under the Urban Programme and receive annual allocations of between £4.5m-£13.5m for expenditure on statutory and community organisation projects. The criteria for acceptable projects are similar to those outlined above for Trad UP. The government gives main importance to economic regeneration projects, then to those making an environmental improvement and lastly to those with a social orientation.

Apply to your local authority, for grants under the Urban Programme - Chief Executives' Department at your Town Hall.

Lambeth Partnership, Inner City Unit, Lambeth Town Hall, Brixton, SW2 (274 7722 x2269/2050).

Hackney Partnership, Inner City Unit, Hackney Town Hall, Mare Street, E8 (986 3123 x490/542).

Islington Partnership, Inner City Unit, Police Development Office, Town Hall, Upper Street, N1 2UD (226 1234 x3141).

The four Programme Authorities are:

Brent 903 1400 x8257 **Hammersmith and Fulham** 748 3020 x2275 **Tower Hamlets** 980 4831 x106 **Wandsworth** 871 6181

For general advice and enquiries on the Urban Programme contact:

Department of the Environment, Inner Cities Directorate, 2 Marsham Street, SW1 3EB.

National Council of Voluntary Organisations, Inner Cities Unit and Information Department, 26 Bedford Square, WC1B 3HU (636 4066).

Your local Council for Voluntary Service (ring your Town Hall for details - see **Borough Information**).

Department of the Environment, Housing Department Grants via local authorities or The Housing Corporation to housing associations and housing co-operatives for projects to bring property to a 'minimal habitable standard'. Although not registered as a housing co-operative, many women's groups have successfully got funding by making arrangements with a local housing association, for example for women's refuges or work with homeless girls. For information about these grants contact:

Housing Corporation, Maple House, 149 Tottenham Court Road, W1P OBN (387 9466).

National Federation of Housing Associations, 30-32 Southampton Street, WC2E 7HE.

You can also contact your local housing department or local housing association. (See **Housing**).

The budgets of the Housing Corporation and local authorities have been drastically cut but there may be statutory 'topping-up grants' involving the elderly, disabled, or drug addicts, and single-parent families.

Urban Programme (see above) and Health Authorities can make contributions to voluntary hostels.

Home Office The Home Office can provide running costs of hostels for discharged prisoners and homeless offenders. Information from:

The Department of Health and Social Security, Alexander Fleming House, Elephant and Castle, SE1 6BY (407 5522).

Home Office (Voluntary Services Unit), 50 Queen Anne's Gate, SW1H 9AT (213 7079). Funds mainly directed to projects involving 'alienated youth' or ex-offenders.

European Funding: European Social Fund of the EEC

This is actually an employment and training fund giving revenue grants only: particularly for the over 25s, women wanting to return to work, disabled women, migrant women, retraining in new technology or new management techniques. For further details and a copy of ESF Guidelines contact: Department of Employment, Overseas Division (OB2), Caxton House, Tothill Street, SW1H 9NA (213 4293).

Funding from Local Authorities

The London boroughs give grants and loans for capital and revenue expenses to voluntary and community organisations, community businesses and co-ops which operate within their boundaries. Most have certain general conditions and criteria for funding and they vary in the amounts they will give and for what length of time they will provide funding.

To find out what your borough will fund, see the following contact list. Town Hall addresses are in **Borough Information**. (You will also find details there on boroughs with women's and/or ethnic minority committees; if relevant to your project, also contact them for advice on funding).

Barking: Director of Social Services,

Civic Centre, Dagenham, Essex.

Barnet: Mr Marsden, Principal Manager Officer, Voluntary Organisations.

Bexley: Steve Pittam (303 7777 x2393).

Brent: Policy Co-ordinator (903 1400 x8270); Jo Noble, Community Development Officer (903 1400 x8257).

Bromley: The Chief Executive's Office, Town Hall, Bromley.

Camden: Mr B Barford (278 4444 x2003).

Croydon: Mr B Pavitt, Co-ordinator, Croydon Voluntary Services (654 8100).

Ealing: Mr H Lobstein, Voluntary Services Adviser (579 2424 x2409).

Greenwich: The Community Development Team (884 8888 x2098/2099).

Hackney: Winston Brewster, Community Development Officer (986 3123 x485/544 or 533 0216).

Hammersmith and Fulham: Travis Merrill, Community Development Officer (748 3020 x349).

Haringey: Ms Del Burra, Haringey Community Development Unit (881 3000 x3522).

Harrow: Mr F Blakemore, Community Work Co-ordinator (863 5544).

Havering: Mr D Turner, Community and Volunteer Officer (706 6999).

Hillingdon: Voluntary Services Liaison Officer - ring Town Hall.

Hounslow: Mr L McSwain, Voluntary Services Officer (570 7728 x3355).

Islington: Kristina Glenn, Social Services (607 2747).

Kensington and Chelsea: Graham Taylor, Clerk to the Voluntary Organisations Liaison Committee (937 5464 x614).

Kingston: Mr T Butcher, Social Services (546 2121 x3441).

Lambeth: The Community and Grants Unit Leader, Lambeth Town Hall.

Lewisham: Mr Reg Castree (698 6121 x342).

Merton: Merton Voluntary Bureau (543 0099; 540 0345).

Redbridge: c/o Town Hall.

Richmond: Children's Division: Mr T Earland (940 9575); Elderly: Mr H J Trussler (891 1422); Specialist: Mr T Dean (894 5544).

Southwark: Mr M Canter, Community Development Team (703 6311 x2084/2260).

Waltham Forest: Mrs Hazel Perrott, Organiser Waltham Forest Volunteer Centre (521 6266).

Westminster: Miss Helen Moss, Clerk to the Grants Sub-Committee (828 8070 x2735).

If your group operates over the whole of London, or is not eligible for funding by your local authority for some reason, contact: The Principal Adviser on grants, London Boroughs Association, Taverner House, Park Lane, Croydon (686 4433 x2488).

Greater London Enterprise Board, 63-67 Newington Causeway, SE1 6BD (403 0300). This was set up as the main job-creating arm of the GLC. Funding for co-ops. In 1984 it set up the London Co-operative Enterprise Board to deal with applications for loans up to £25,000 which has set aside over half its funds for women, ethnic minorities, gays and people with disabilities. (For more information on co-ops, see **Employment**.)

Inner London Education Authority, EO/CC Branch, County Hall, SE1 (633 6291). Gives grants for educational activities.

Overseas Development Ministry, El and House, Stag Place, SW1. Gives small grants for exchange visits and conferences for the benefit of developing countries, particularly for girls and young women.

Funding from Quangos and other government bodies

Equal Opportunities Commission, Overseas House, Quay Street, Manchester, M3 3HN (061-833 9244). Gives grants for research or educational activities and also for conferences. Project must help eliminate sex discrimination or promote equality of the sexes. Grants can be as small as £200 but rarely more than one full-time salary and normally only for one year. They do not give capital grants, nor do they fund purely local projects. Women should discuss their project with staff at the EOC before submitting applica-'ions.

Greater London Arts Association, 25-31 Tavistock Place, WC1H 9SF (388 2211). Capital grants made for workshops, equipment, publicity; revenue grants after one year of project funding for salaries.

London Docklands Development Corporation, West India House, West India Dock, E14 (515 3000). Gives grants to some voluntary groups and organisations in Docklands. Docklands Boroughs (see above) also fund some groups.

National Council for Civil Liberties (NCCL),* 21 Tabard Street, SE1 4LA (403 3888). Campaigns for equal treatment and rights. Cobden Trust is their research and education trust.

Commission for Racial Equality, Elliott House, 10/12 Allington Street, SW1E 5EH (828 7022). Funds organisations which are concerned with the promotion of equal opportunity and good relations between racial groups.

Arts Council of Great Britain, 105 Piccadilly, WC1V 0AV (629 9495). Revenue grants to established companies; grants for specific projects; individual bursaries and awards; capital grants for 'housing the arts'.

Nature Conservancy Council, Calthorpe House, Calthorpe Street, Banbury, OX16 8EX (0295 56701). Nature conservation; aim of projects must be to protect flora, fauna, geological or physiographical features of interest for study or research.

Greater London and South East Council for Sport and Recreation (Sports Council), 160 Great Portland Street, W1N 5TB (580 9092). Funds youth organisations and other bodies which include sport and physical activities in their general programme.

Crafts Council, Crafts Advisory Committee, 12 Waterloo Place, SW1Y 4AV (930 4811). Funds artists/craftsperson at the outset of their careers.

Manpower Services Commission - many different funding programmes for youth and community. Look in the *Guide for Voluntary Organisations* available from National Council for Voluntary Organisations, 26 Bedford Square, WC1.

Countryside Commission, 25 Savile Row, W1X 2BT (734 6010). Groups concerned with facilities for the enjoyment of the countryside, conservation and provision of public access.

Trusts

There are two kinds of charities: those that give money away, and those that carry out charitable acts. Trusts (those charities which give money away) often fill in the gaps between statutory programmes, doing unpopular work which government may not want to do. They give away money to charities which undertake work they would like to support.

Trusts and foundations give about £300 million each year to charity. The money which they give away mainly consists of the interest on their capital assets. They have tax-exempt status and get tax relief on charitable donations, so it is in their financial interest to make donations.

Trusts are diverse and independent bodies, administered by small groups of people accountable only to themselves. They can be part of a large organisation (eg Sainsbury's) or may be simply a small family trust. Trustees are nearly all white, male and middle/upper class.

Charities and trusts do not generally make revenue grants but rather capital grants, of widely varying amounts. Laws limit charity-giving to 'nonpolitical' activities. This obviously benefits the status quo and women's groups may have to tailor their applications accordingly.

Charities often want to innovate, therefore they may like to provide starter money until someone else takes over or a project becomes self-supporting. Charities can also sometimes be persuaded to fund projects which are preventive in nature rather than patching up, for example educational or development work.

There are thousands of charities and trusts listed in the *Directory of Grant-Making Trusts* (see below). Women are beginning to approach these trusts for money: bear in mind that the amounts you will receive will vary considerably and generally will not cover wages. It is always worth re-applying to trusts and always thank them when you do get a donation.

Some of the publications listed below give details of the obligations of groups which receive money from trusts. If you are or become a charity yourselves you will have certain legal obligations. And some trusts can only give money to other charities, so if you are not a charity you would have to apply to an intermediary body for the money. For advice on how to become a charity, ask you local law centre (see **Borough Information**).

Central Register of Charities, Charity Commission, St Albans House, 57-60 Haymarket, SW1Y 4QX (214 6000). Keeps a list of smaller trusts which are not listed in *The Directory of Grant-Making Trusts* (see below).

Charities Information Bureau, 161 Corporation Street, Birmingham B4 6PT, (021 236 1264). Has information on grant-making trusts listed according to categories of recipients.

Directory of Grant-Making Trusts, 1983, £39 (in your local library reference section). Lists thousands of grant-making trusts, classified by category, giving values of assets and grants, types of projects supported, names of trustees, etc.

The Funding Register for Ethnic Minority Self-Help Groups, compiled by Carole F. Willis, Home Office Research Unit, HMSO, 1979. Details of where groups can get funding, from statutory sources or trusts.

Raising Money from Trusts, ed Michael Norton, Directory of Social Change, 1981, £2.95. Describes what trusts are, how to find the right trust, how to make a good application.

National Council for Voluntary Organisations' Reference Library (26 Bedford Square, WC1) contains directories for funding from international bodies or for international projects, cross-cultural studies or study tours: *Guide to European Foundations, Foundation Directory (USA), Directory of World Foundations*, and others.

The organisations listed below are known to have funded women's or ethnic minority groups and it may be worth trying them first, as choosing trusts to approach can be quite arbitrary:

Allen Lane Foundation, 6 Bloomsbury Square, WC1A 2LT.

British Council of Churches, Community and Race Relations Unit, Division of Community Affairs, 10 Eaton Square, SW1W 9BT.

BBC Broadcasting Support Services, 252 Western Avenue, W3 6XJ.

Barrow Cadbury Fund Limited, Barrow Geraldine S. Cadbury Charitable Trust, J & L.A. Cadbury Charitable Trust, The Secretary, 2 College Walk, Selly Oak, Birmingham B29 6LE.

Capital Help-Line, Capital Radio, Euston Centre, Euston Road, NW1 (388 1288).

The Chase Charity, Calton Younge, General Secretary, 77 Gloucester Road, SW7.

Christian Aid, 240 Ferndale Road, SW9 (733 5500).

City Parochial Foundation, BH Woods MBE, 10 Fleet Street, EC4Y 1AU.

Leonard Cohen Trust, 13 Rosslyn Hill, NW3.

Commonwealth Countries League, 5 Belsize Park Gardens, NW3.

Ford Trust, Central Office, Eagle Way, Brentwood, Essex.

Norman Franklin's Charitable Trust No. 2, Messrs Lawford and Co, 2 Field Court, Gray's Inn, WC1R 5EJ.

Calouste Gulbenkian Foundation, UK and Commonwealth Branch, 98 Portland Place, W1N 4ET.

The Hilden Charitable Fund, A Rampton, Gort Lodge, Sudbrook Lane, Richmond, Surrey.

P H Holt Charitable Trust, The Secretary, c/o Ocean Transport and Trading Ltd, India Buildings, Liverpool L2 ORB.

Kleinwort Benson (Trustees) Ltd, 20 Fenchurch Street, EC3.

Lambeth Endowed Charities, 127 Kennington Road, SE11.

The Leigh Trust, Clive M. Marks, FCA, Marks Green and Co, 44a New Cavendish Street, W1M.

John Lewis Partnership, Charity Manager, John Lewis, Oxford Street, W1.

Marks & Spencer, Charity Manager, Michael House, Baker Street, W1.

Methodist London Mission Department, 1 Central Buildings, Matthew Parker Street, SW1.

North Kensington Amenity Trust, 1 Thorpe Close, W10.

Northmoor Trust, The Secretary, 36 Carlton Hill, NW8

Oxfam, 274 Banbury Road, Oxford (0865 56777).

The Queen's Silver Jubilee Trust, Harold Haywood, OBE, 8 Buckingham Street, WC2.

Radley Foundation, 89a Blackheath Hill, SE10 8TJ.

Joseph Rowntree Charitable Trust, LE Waddilore, Beverley House, Shipton Road, York YO3 6RB.

Royal Silver Jubilee Trusts, The Director, 8 Buckingham Street, WC2.

Sainsbury Charitable Trust, HL de Quelterville, 13 New Row, St Martin's Lane, WC2N 4LF.

SHELTER National Campaign for the Homeless, 157 Waterloo Road, SE1.

Shell UK Ltd, Head Office, PO Box 148, Shell Mex House, Strand, WC2.

The Tudor Trust, 15 Young Street, Kensington, W8.

The Thames Help Trust, Thames TV Ltd, 306-316 Euston Road, NW1.

Violet Melchett Trust, 14 Allcroft Road, NW5.

Wates Trust, Sir John Henniker-Major KCMG, 1260 Lord Road, Norbury, SW16 4EG

Funds From Industry

Another source of funding for women's groups is industry, which can donate money, goods or services. Companies generally prefer to give away relatively small amounts to more groups. You could be lucky and get a company to make a deed of covenant to your group. This means they will give a fixed amount over a period of four or more years.

Large companies operating in a particular area may feel themselves responsible for serving the community in some way and may give to social service groups, environmental or recreational activities.

You could also try to get money from local businesses - usually by just going in, or there may be local Business Association which could help. Publications to consult:

A Guide to Company Giving, 1984 Directory of Social Change, ed Michael Norton, £8.95.

Industrial Sponsorship and Joint Promotions, Directory of Social Change, £2.95. How charities, arts organisations and events organisations can get money from industry for joint commercial schemes.

Raising Money from Industry, ed Michael Norton, Directory of Social Change, 1981 £2.95. A comprehensive guide covering the scope and nature of company giving, how to approach them, lists companies giving £50,000 or more, raising money from The City.

Starting Your Own Community Business or Cooperative

For details about setting up and financing a small business or co-operative see Employment. Also apply for information on funding to: London Co-operative Enterprise Board, GLEB, 63-67 Newington Causeway, SE1 6BD (403 0300).

Other Ways To Get Money For Your Group

There are many other ways to raise small amounts of money for your group. Radio and TV stations often give free air time for you to publicise your activities and to ask for donations, especially if there is a particular item you want to buy. Jumble sales, fairs, fetes and raffles, and benefits are also ways to earn money and publicity. You can also approach rich and/or famous people who you think might wish to support your activities with a donation or a regular contribution.

Banks are useful if you are running some kind of business: they give loans and overdraft facilities. However, they generally want some kind of security or personal guarantees for the money they lend and they will, of course, want to be confident that your venture will be successful. Some banks have a Community Sponsorship Programme which could be a source of funding.

General and Professional Advice

National Council for Voluntary Organisations (NCVO) 27 Bedford Square, WC1 (636 4066) is the key national body which co-ordinates voluntary sector organisations and campaigns and promotes public awareness on issues affecting the interests of the voluntary sector in the UK. It provides advice and information and publishes *Raising Money for Women: A Survivors Guide for women's organisations*, Marion Bowman and Michael North, Bedford Square Press, spring 1986. Price and

further details from NCVO

London Voluntary Service Council (LVSC) 68 Chalton Street, NW1 (388 0241) is a London-wide co-ordinating and comparing body which aims to promote the interests of voluntary sector organisations and projects in London. LVSC organises regular meetings, conferences and workshops on current issues having implications for community projects. The Community Development worker works with women's group and will give information and advice. There are local councils for Voluntary Services (CVSs) carrying out the same function is every borough. For addresses and phone numbers, see Funding from Local Authorities (above) or contact LVSC.

Groups funded by the GLC may be able to give your organisation some general advice: women's centres are listed under **Borough Information.** Law centres (also under **Borough Information**) will advise on constitutional matters regarding the Sex Discrimination Act, if you want your project to make women-only (or girls' only) provision. Further general and professional advice may be obtained from:

Community Accountancy Project, 34 Dalston Lane, E8 3AZ (249 7109). For groups in Hackney.

Community Accountancy Services, The Works, 105a Torriano Avenue, NW5, (482 2866). Accountancy services to co-operatives.

Community Accountants, Lambeth Inner City Consultative Group, 10 Gernay's Grove, SW9 8DF (737 3617). Advice for groups in Lambeth.

Directory of Social Change, 9 Mansfield Place, NW3 1HS. A registered charity providing information, advice, training, research services and several publications on funding. They do however sometimes charge for their services.

Kentish Town Women's Workshop, 169 Malden Road, NW5 (267 0688). Gives advice sessions on fund-raising for women's groups, including trusts.

Will help with grant applications.

Microsyster, Wesley House, 70 Great Queen Street, WC2 (430 0655). A feminist computer collective offering service to women's groups.

Groups campaigning to maintain funding for women's projects are:

Women's Campaign, Local Government Campaign Unit, 5/7 Tavistock Place, WC1, (387 9893). Campaigns around rate-capping legislation.

Community Development Worker, London Voluntary Service Council, 68 Charlton Street, NW1. (388 0241). Working with women's groups to maintain funding.

Fund-Raising: a handbook for minority groups, Directory of Social Change (see above), £1.50. A guide to raising money for ethnic minority group projects produced in conjunction with the Commission of Racial Equality.

The Future of Voluntary Organisations: Report of the Wolfenden Committee, Croom Helm, London 1978. Looks at the role of voluntary organisations, their financial prospects, how measures to counter unemployment benefit voluntary organisations, recommendations for the future.

Useful Reading

Accounting and Financial Management for Charities, £2.25 explains in simple terms how basic accountancy systems work; sections on budgeting and costing a project for fund-raising. (388 0241).

Charitable Status: a practical handbook, Andrew Phillips with Keith Smith, Inter-Action, London 1982, £2.50. A brief guide to charity law and how it affects charities.

Charity Law and Voluntary Organisations, Report of the Goodman Committee, Bedford Square Press, London. Present legal position of charitable giving and recommendations for changes to reflect greater needs of certain groups in society, eg women, Black people and ethnic minorities.

Charity Statistics 1983/84, Charities Aid Foundation, 48 Pembury Road, Tonbridge, Kent TN9 2JD. Gives details of charity giving in 1983/84.

The Charity Trading Handbook, £4.95. How to earn money through trading, eg Christmas cards, thrift shops, promotional items etc.

Fund-Raising: a comprehensive handbook, Directory of Social Change (see above), £3.25. A practical and comprehensive guide to different aspects of fund-raising for charities.

Health

This section recognises the major concerns of women as users of the health services, as carers of other adults, people with disabilities and children.

This section also recognises that decision-making in the health services is dominated by white men who occupy the more highly paid professional and managerial posts and who take a leading role on such bodies as District Health Authorities. Women, especially Black and ethnic minority women, whilst being the majority of staff employed, tend to be employed at lower levels, in poorly paid unskilled work such as cleaning or catering and are badly unrepresented on decision-making bodies.

There is scarcely any recognition in the health service of women's specific health needs and concerns, and of their lay role in preventive care and policy, in planning and decision-making within the health service.

There are a number of major health issues. These are some of them.

• Generally, the benefits of preventive health care and a holistic notion of health are not widely accepted in the health services. These concepts involve an acceptance of the influence of environmental factors such as housing and other social factors on an individual's health and thus directly link such concerns as the continuing shorter life expectancy of working class people including Black and ethnic minority people, to the conditions that they experience at home and at work. Such conditions including chemical hazards, adversely affect the health of working class people and this fact is not taken into account in terms of preventive health care.

• There are major issues with regard to reproductive rights - contraception and the control of women's fertility, abortion and a woman's right to choose when to have a child, artificial insemination by donor and in vitro fertilization and a woman's ability to conceive, how to conceive and the promotion of her giving birth to a healthy child. There is a disturbing lack of comprehensive information on contraception in all languages, and abortion is not consistently available. Black and ethnic minority women have testified to racist practices operated by medical staff. When seeking advice on their pregnancy they face considerable pressure to have an abortion.

• There are issues in relation to ante natal care and childbirth - the advice and support available before childbirth, and the question of a woman's autonomy when faced with an array of technological equipment and drugs, during birth itself. This increase in the use of technology causes childbirth to become a very alienating experience for a large number of women. This experience begins at the ante natal stage where clinics are increasingly overloaded and women do not feel they are treated as individuals. The centralisation of maternity facilities shows the overall rapid move to centralisation of key health facilities for women. This leads to a further depersonalisation of medical treatment. Women and children then face the practical difficulty of having to travel several miles for hospital treatment.

• There is a scarcity of women-only provision, and it is not only women who want contraception who want treatment by a woman doctor. Lesbians too often prefer women-only medical services, and the death of these has a specific adverse implication for lesbians needing health care.

• Mental health and mental handicap have been under funded and under recognised in our health services, with inadequate attention paid to the long-term needs of sufferers or forms of treatment, support and care which would maximise the autonomy and potential of individuals. The role of women as carers is crucial and is an increasingly exploited role, as large psychiatric hospitals are closed and their patients discharged to local communities without supportive funding or assistance to their relatives, neighbours or helpers who will mainly be women. The high level of dependence on drugs and lack of community involvement in psychiatric hospitals causes patients to become institutionalised and to find it very difficult to make the adjustment to life in a local community.

• Black and ethnic minority groups point out the frequency of racist notions and inappropriate diagnosis and treatment of psychiatric conditions in Black and ethnic minority people.

• Women are several times more likely than men to receive treatment for a psychiatric condition, so these issues have a major impact for women.

• Massive cuts in financial provision to District Health Authorities, particularly in London, are having a significant impact on women in their predominant role as carers. The media has given emphasis to the need for expensive mechanical technology such as scanners, but this has not focused on the impact of the closure of long-stay psychiatric and geriatric wards with the consequent acute need for care and support in local communities. Community care is a popular concept with wide ranging support, yet without adequate finance or back up from local health services, community care will result in an intolerable physical and psychological burden being placed on large numbers of women and an unsatisfactory level or quality of care of those long-stay patients no longer resident in hospital.

- This has a particular impact for older women whose health concerns tend to be under recognised and under funded. The cost of providing health care for an ageing population escalates massively yet there is a wealth of resources to deal with the combined effects of a range of disabilities and conditions that affect older women, who tend to live longer than men.

- Pressure from the current Government to privatise services like cleaning and catering within the health services has a particular effect on women's employment because women do most of this work. The move to privatise results in extensive job losses for women, the employment of women on even lower rates of pay without adequate conditions of employment or attention paid to aspects such as health and safety, and generally a lowering of standards to the extent that concern is being expressed by environmental health officers in some authorities.

- Black and ethnic minority women users of the health services suffer institutional racism with a damaging effect on their experience of seeking health advice and treatment. Disorders such as Sickle Cell Anaemia and Thalassemia have been under recognised and under researched with the resulting marginalisation of these conditions, lack of understanding of the diagnosis and treatment and inattention to the vital need to counsel sufferers and families and to monitor the incidence of such disorders.

This section covers a very wide range of organizations and agencies concerned with aspects of health and health care. If you would like suggestions as to which publications are relevant on specific women's health issues please contact the Women's Health Information Centre (address and phone number in listings). The listings are divided into two sub-sections and are ordered as follows:

Section 1 (General and London-wide Groups/Services) - General Health Information Groups, Black and Ethnic Minority Women's Health Groups, Community Health Projects/Self-Help Groups, Community Health Councils, Well Woman Clinics, Alternative medicine. Section 2 (Topics in Alphabetical Order) - Bereavement, Cancer, Drugs, Alcohol and Smoking, Eating and Weight, Health Workers, Heart and Blood Disorders, Mental Health, Occupational Health, Reproductive Health, Teeth.

1. General and London-wide Groups/Services

General Health Information Groups

Healthline, is a confidential telephone information service (introduced by the College of Health in London) giving tape recorded advice and information. Ring 980 4848 any evening between 6pm. and 10pm. A list of the tapes available can be obtained for £1 from The College of Health, PO Box 499, E2 9PV.

London Community Health Resource,* 68 Chalton Street, NW1 (388 0241). General information for community health groups, community workers, health professionals and anyone interested in community involvement in health. LCHR produces a bi-monthly newsletter and organizes regular meetings and discussions on a range of community health issues, and produces *London Health Action Network*, a directory of local health projects and campaigns, community health councils and London-wide health groups or organizations. Access:N

The Patients' Association, Room 33, 18 Charing Cross Road, WC2 (240 0671) gives information on patients' rights and can advise individuals who have problems in dealing with the health services. Access P: they occupy 2 small rooms but there's a lift to their floor, no toilet for people with disabilities.

Women's Health Information Centre,* 52-54 Featherstone Street, EC1 (251 6580). A London-wide source of information on women's health issues and women's health groups. WHIC collects and classifies journal articles, newspaper reports, pamphlets and books on women's health issues; maintains a register of women's health groups, self-help groups, well women campaigns and voluntary organizations concerned with health; and produces a quarterly newsletter. (However, they don't have the resources to give clinical advice or counselling, nor keep lists of clinics, feminists doctors or alternative practitioners). Access A : One step at front but ramp available, toilet for women with disabilities, 1st floor.

Women's Reproductive Rights Information Centre, * also at 52-54 Featherstone Street, EC1Y 8RT (251 6332) referred to throughout this section as WRRIC, campaigns and informs on issues concerned with reproduction and fertility control: pregnancy testing, contraception, abortion, sterilisation, morning after contraception, sexuality, infertility, reproductive health (including health at work) and technology. They are also working on a London-wide survey on abortion, contraception and sterilisation facilities. The centre gives information and support to women who do not know where to find the help they need or who have been refused access to facilities, who have experienced problems eg with a contraceptive method, or who have experienced abuses within the health system. WRRIC also produced a bi-monthly newsletter and organizes meetings on reproductive rights issues. Runs support groups for post-abortion, infertility, and Artificial Insemination by Donor (AID). Access as above.

Black and Ethnic Minority Women's Health Groups

Black Health Worker's and Patients Group, 259a High Road, Tottenham, N15 (809 0774) Main areas of work: supporting Black workers in their struggles, pushing for better treatment of Black patients and monitoring racism and racist policies on health. Access: N but will visit at home if required

Black Women's Health Group, Black Women's Centre, 41a Stockwell Green, SW9 (274 9220), Meets fortnightly on Thurs evenings 7.30 - 9.30. Access: N

Foundation for Women's Health Research and Development (FOWARD), * Africa Centre, 38 King St, WC2E 8JT (379 6889). Women's development agency promoting good health and education amongst women and children (particularly in Africa). Has links with women's groups in Africa. In UK special Mandeleo project (African mother and child health campaign) provides education and counselling service (particularly concerned with female circumcision). Access: P

Greek Cypriot Women's Health Group, * Cypriot Centre, Earlham Grove, N22 (881 2329), available Mon-Thurs 10am - 5pm. Lift for access being built.

Greenwich Black Women's Health Project, * 39 Wellington Street, Woolwich, SE18 (854 3766). Recently moved into new premises the group is developing a drop-in centre for advice and counselling on the following: women's self-help health groups, mental health, outreach work on women's health to isolated women in the area. Access: P

Haringey Greek Cypriot Women's Health Group, * Social Services Centre, 14a Willoughby Road, N8 (341 1100 x59). Aims to provide specialised health information, to act as referral agency, to establish a support system amongst women and to increase their knowledge of and confidence in the NHS. Also contact Cypriot Centre, Earlham Grove, London N22 (881 7826).

London Black Women's Health Action Project, * Wickham House, 10 Cleveland Way, E1 4TR (790 2424). Areas of work cover Black and ethnic minority women's health in general in this country and internationally. Particularly involved in fighting to stop female circumcision in London and internationally. Access: A

Maternity Services Liaison Scheme * Brady Centre, Hanbury Street, E1 (377 8725). Team includes Bengali and Somali workers - community-based linkworkers befriending and escorting women during pregnancy and after the birth. Accompany women to hospitals, clinics etc.

Multi-Ethnic Women's Health Project, c/o City & Hackney CHC, 210 Kingsland Road, E2 8EB (739 6308). For greater understanding of health needs of ethnic minority women, innovating several new projects. Works in conjunction with the Mothers' Hospital in Hackney. Access A

Organisation for Sickle Cell Anaemia Research (OSCAR), 22 Pellat Grove, Wood Green, N22 (889 4844/3300). A national organization, carries out and sponsors research into sickle cell anaemia. Access: N

Sangam Association for Asian Women, 235/237 West Hendon Broadway, NW9, (202 4629). Counselling and advice in women's health. Access: N

Sickle Cell Society, Willesden Hospital, Harlesden Road, Wood Green N22 (451 3293). The Society helps to support sickle cell sufferers by fund raising events, and by bringing together those affected and their families. Membership open to any person who supports objectives of the Society Regular Newsletter. Donations welcome. Access A

NHS Sickle Cell Counselling Centres: Phone first for appointment as most of these centres are only open for short periods during the week. As below:

Brent Sickle Cell Centre, Willesden General Hospital, Willesden, NW10 3RY (459 1292 Ext 235). Access: A

City and Hackney Sickle Cell Centre, St Leonards Hospital, Nuttal St, N1 5LZ, (739 8484 Ext 369). Access: A

Haringey Community Health Clinic, Prince of Wales Hospital, Tynemouth Rd, N1J (808 1081). Access: A

Islington Sickle Cell Centre, St. David's Wing, Royal Northern Hospital, Holloway Rd., N7 (272 7777). Access A

Lambeth Sickle Cell Centre, Swan Mews, Stockwell Road, SW9 9EN (737 3588).

Southall Black Women's Centre, (Afro-Caribbean and Asian Women), 86 Northcote Avenue, Middlesex, UB1 2AZ (843 0578). Advice on health care and holds occasional workshops on health related matters. Access: N

Thalassaemia Society, 107 Nightingale Lane, N8 7QY, (348 0437). Access: N

Community Health Projects/ Self-Help Groups

Albany Health Project, The Albany, Douglas Way, Deptford, SE8, (692 0231). Neighbourhood based health project which includes women's health groups, offers free pregnancy testings. Also, advice and information to young people. Access A

Balham Family Centre, 91 Bedford Hill, SW12, (673 4350). Tues and Thurs 10.30-12.30. Offers free pregnancy testing and information about contraception, abortion and pregnancy. Free pregnancy testing Tues 6-7pm at the Health Centre opposite Balham Family Centre. Access: N

Bethnal Green Women's Health Group, 296 Bethnal Green Road, E2 OAG (739 4173). Claiming group Weds am, drop-in health group Weds pm. Access: A

Brent Women's Health Collective, c/o Brent Women's Centre, High Road, Willesden, NW10. Access: N.

Caxton House Community Education Project, Caxton Hse, 129 St John's Way, N19 (263 3151/2). As part of their general education programme they co-ordinate weekly women's health groups. Access: P

East London Health Project, 9 Bruce Road, E3 3HN (981 6104). Produce prints on a range of health issues, including women's health.

Fulham Girls' Project, 683 Fulham Road, SW6, (736 7696). Young women's health - including sexuality, menstruation, contraception, pregnancy, childbirth as well as drug abuse and mental health.

Haringey Women and Health Centre,* Annexe C, Tottenham Town Hall, N15 (801 3152). Provides advice on NHS and alternative health provisions, distributes info on health and self help groups in borough and provides support to individuals having difficulty with health services. Black women's health group Tues afternoon, Asian women's group Thurs. Access: P

Health in Homerton, 282 Banister House, Homerton High St, E9 (533 1525)
Long established local community health project, focus on women and pensioners' health. Access: N

Lambeth Girls' Project, c/o Vauxhall Primary School, Vauxhall Street, SEll 5LG (735 8803/4). Concentrates on young women's health. Access: P

Lambeth Women and Children's Health Bus,* East House, South Western Hospital, Landor Rd, SW9 (737 7151). The health bus visits eight different sites a week.

North Paddington Community Darkroom, 510 Centre, 510 Harrow Road, W9 (969 7437). Produced photographic exhibitions on 'Women & Health' covering all aspects of womens' health work, housing, costs, alternative medicine, NHS etc. Access: A

Stockwell Health Project, c/o Lady Margaret Hall Settlement, 460 Wandsworth Road, SW8 (622 9455). Access: P

Tower Hamlets Information Research and Resource Centre, Oxford House, Derbyshire St, E1 (739 3630). Produce leaflets on women's health clinics, maternity provision in TH general resource centre.

Waterloo Health Project, St John's Church, Waterloo Road, SE1 (633 0852). Neighbourhood community health project which includes self-supporting women's health group.

Women and Health, 155 Arlington Road, NW1 (267 3637).

Community Health Councils

The CHC is an independent body which aims to represent the interests of the public in the National Health Service. It is your link with the NHS - you should contact your CHC if you have useful ideas or criticisms about the NHS in your area; or if you have a problem or complaint that you need help with; or if you want some information about the local health services.

See below for local CHCs.

Barnet CHC, 104 Watling Avenue, Burnt Oak, Edgware, Middx, (959 2038). Access: P

Bexley CHC, 11a Upton Road, Bexleyheath, Kent DA6 8LQ, (301 0920). Works closely with Bexley Council for Racial Equality on matters of health and social security. Access: P

Bloomsbury CHC, 114 Hampstead Road, NW1 2LT, (387 6789/0). Access: P

Brent CHC, Rear Block, 16 High Street, Harlesden, London NW10, (961 2028). Access: P

Bromley CHC, 40B Masons Hill, Bromley, Kent BR2 9JG, (464 0249). Access: P

Camberwell CHC, 75 Denmark Hill, SE5 8RS, (703 9498). Access: P

City & Hackney CHC, 210 Kingsland Road, E2 8EB, (739 6308). Access: P

Croydon CHC, 28 Lennard Road, Croydon CRO 2UL (680 1503). Access: N

Ealing CHC, 119 Uxbridge Road, W7 (579 2211). Access: P

Enfield CHC, Highlands Hospital, Worlds End Lane, Winchmore Hill, N21 1PN (360 5566). Access: P

Greenwich CHC, 23 Anglesea Road, SE18 (317 9994). Produces leaflets translated in main Asian languages.

Riverside CHC (Hammersmith & Fulham) 42 Fulham Palace Road, W6 (748 0639) or 50 Tufton Street, SW1 (222 6957).

Hampstead CHC, 124 Heath Street, NW3 (794 9953). Access P

Haringey CHC, 332 High Road, N15 4BN (808 1694). Access: A

Harrow CHC, 3rd floor, 102 College Road, Harrow, HA1 1EF (863 6432). Access: P

Hounslow & Spellthorne CHC, 55 Church Road, Ashford TW15 2TA (695 9548). Access: P

Hillingdon CHC, 65 Bellmont Road, Uxbridge, Middx (0895 57858). Access: A

Islington CHC, Manor Gardens Centre, 6-9 Manor Gardens, N7 6LA (263 7207). Access: A

Kingston & Esher CHC, 41c Victoria Road, Surbiton, KT6 4JN (399 8415). Access: P

Lewisham & North Southwark CHC, 13 Catford Broadway, SE6 (690 8777). Access: A

Merton & Sutton CHC, 29 West Street, Sutton, Surrey, SM1 SJ1 (642 6405).Access: N

Newham CHC, Rooms 33 and 34, Lord Lister Health Centre, 121 Woodgrange Rd, Forest Gate, E7 (555 5331 ex 38/44). Access: P

Paddington CHC, 82 Westbourne Grove, W2 4UN (221 4018). Access: P

Redbridge CHC, Fourth Floor, Ilford Chambers, 11 Chapel Road, Ilford. Access A

Richmond, Twickenham & Roehampton CHC, 222 Upper Richmond Road West, SW14 8AH, (878 0265). Access: N

Tower Hamlets CHC, 23 New Road, E1 (247 7858). Access: N

Waltham Forest District CHC, 608 High Road, Leytonstone, E11 3DA (539 7180). Access: N

Wandsworth CHC, 1 Balham Station Road, SW12 9SG (673 8820/8829). Access: P

West Lambeth CHC, 2-4 Cleaver Street, SE11 (582 3288/3238). Access: P

Inquiries about changes of addresses of individual CHC should be made to the office of the steering committee from the National Association of CHCs, at 362 Euston Road, NW1 (388 4943/4 or 388 4814).

Well Woman Clinics

The following is a list of Well Woman Clinics. Some of these are attached to Family Planning Clinics and include those that offer family planning services, and in many cases, checks on health, screening for breast and cervical cancer etc. Well Woman clinics are held on certain days only so phone for information and appointment. Local Community Health Councils (above) can advise on new clinics, changes of address etc. Not all are staffed by women doctors: check first.

London Postal Area E:

Greenwood Clinic, Peel Grove, E2 (980 5866). Tues - Bengali Teaching, Weds pm. Bengali interpreter at baby clinic. Access: N

Shoreditch Health Centre, 210 Kingsland Road, E2 (739 8351). 2nd Tues in the month only - 9.30am to 11.30am. Access N

Wellington Way Centre, 1A Wellington Way, Bow Road, E3 4YE (980 3510). Access: A

Lower Clapton Centre, 36 Lower Clapton Road, E5 OPB (986 7111) 1st and 3rd Fri in the month only - 1.30 to 4.30pm. Access: P

Richmond Road Clinic, 136 Richmond Road, E8 (254 6374) Fri 1.30 - 3.30pm. Access: P

Elsdale Street Centre, 28 Elsdale Street, E9 (533 0031) 3rd Tues in the month only - 1.30 - 3.30pm. Access: N

Granleigh Health Clinic, Trinity Close, E11 (539 8565). Access: N

Church Road Clinic, Church Road, E12 (478 3521) Wed aft - once a month. Access: A

Bath Street Health Centre, 60 Bath Street, EC1 9JH (251 3535). Fri 9.30am. Access: N

Finsbury Health Centre, Pine Street, EC1 (837 00031). Family planning only. Access: A

City of London F.P. Clinic, Public Services Building, Milton Court, Moore Lane, EC2 (985 4442). Access: N

London Postal Area N

River Place Health Centre, Essex Road, N1 (226 4491), Thurs 9.30am. Access: A

John Scott Health Centre, Green Lanes, N4 (800 0111). 2nd & 4th Fri in the month only - 9.30 - 11.30am. Access: A

Highbury Grange Health Centre, 115 Highbury Grange, N5 (359 4121). Tues 9.30am. Access: N

Goodinge Health Centre, Goodinge Close, North Road, N7 (607 6799). Thurs 5.30pm fortnightly. Access: N

Manor Gardens Centre, 6-9 Manor Gardens, N7 (272 4231). Thurs 9.30am. Access: A

Crouch End Health Centre, 45 Middle Lane, N8 (341 2045). Tues aft. Access: A

Weston Park Clinic, 23a Weston Park N, N8 (348 8467). Tues aft.

Medical Centre, 150 Fortis Green, N10 (444 9753). 2nd & 4th Mon morning each month. Family planning clinic. Access: A

Barton House Centre, 233 Albion Road, N16 (249 5511). 1st Tues in the month - 9.30am to 11.30am. Access: P

Fountayne Road Health Centre, 1a Fountayne Road, N16 (806 3311), 4th Tues in the month - 1.30 - 3.30pm. Access: A

Medical Centre, 131 Park Lane, N17 (808 5833). Fri am. Access: P

Health Centre, 8 Stuart Crescent, N22. 2nd & 4th Wed eve - 5.30pm.

Gospel Oak Health Clinic, Lismore Circus, NW5 (267 3211). Mon morning, Tues aft and eve and Wed aft. Access: P

Solent FHC, 9 Solent Road, NW6 (794 7533). Tues eve, Wed eve, Fri aft (except last in month). Access: N

Belsize Priory Health Clinic, 208 Belsize Road, NW6 (328 1700). Tues eve and Thurs aft and eve. Access: N

London Postal Area S

Bermondsey Health Centre, 108 Grange Road, SE1 (237 2285). Alternate Mon's 5.15 - 6.30pm. Access: N

Camberwell Health Authority: Requests for appointments to Well Woman Clinics should be made either in writing or by phone to: The Community Health Services Office, 'B' Block GAF Site, King's College Hospital, Denmark Hill, SE5, (274 6222 Ext 2410).

Boundfield Road Health Centre, SE6, (698 3585). 2nd Tues aft 1.30pm to 3.30pm and 3rd Thurs eve 5.30 - 7.30pm. Access: N

South Lewisham Health Centre, 50 Conisbrough Crescent, SE6 2SS, (698 8921). 1st Wed of each month - 9.30 - 12 noon. Access: N

Waldron Health Centre, Stanley Street, SE8 (691 4621). Alternate Tues 6pm to 7pm. Access: A

Lee Health Centre, 2 Handen Road, SE12 (318 4431). Thurs 6.30pm to 8.30pm. Family Planning (852 1772) Tues, Wed, Thur. Access: A

Amott Road Clinic, 60a Amott Road, SE15. Alternate Thurs am.

South East London General Practitioners' Centre, St May's Road, SE15. Wed afternoons.

Jenner Health Centre, 201 Stanstead Road, SE23 (690 2231). Friday morning 9.45am to 12noon. Access: N

Sydenham Green Health Centre, 20 Holmshaw Close, SE26 (778 1333). Alternate Fri 1.30pm to 3.30pm. Access A

West Norwood Health Clinic, 39 Lancaster Ave, SE27. Wed am. Access: P

West Lambeth Health Authority, 66 McCall Close, (off Jeffreys Rd) SW4 (720 6551 Ext 50); Manor Health Centre (622 2293); Streatham Health Centre (764 5268/9); Moffat Clinic (735 4169); Streatham Hill (674 7178); Ferndale Road (733 8581); Barley Mow (928 5921).

Loughbrough Clinic, Barrington Road, London SW9. Every Thurs a.m. & alternate Tues eve.

World's End Health Centre, 519-529 Kings Road, SW10 (351 5555). Mon p.m. 1.30pm to 3.30pm. Access: A

Wandsworth Health Authority (SW11/12/18), information obtained by phoning (672 0317) - 9.30am to 4.30pm Mon to Fri.

St Christopher's Clinic, Wheeler Court, Plough Road, SW11. Wed 2pm to 3.30pm & 5.30pm to 7pm. (223 7222). Access: P

Stromont Health Clinic, 5-11 Stromont Road, SW11 (228 4104). Tues 1.30pm to 3pm & 6pm to 7.30pm & Thurs 5.30pm to 7pm. Access: N

Bridge Lane Health Centre, 20 Bridge Lane, SW11 (223 4211). Tues 9.30am to 11am & Tues 5.30pm to 7pm. Access: A

Doddington Health Centre, 311 Battersea Park Road, SW11 (622 6463). Tues 1.30pm to 3.30pm & Wednesday 5.30pm to 7pm. Access: A

Balham Health Centre, 120 Bedford Hill, SW12 (673 1201). Wed 6pm - 7.30pm & Thurs 9.30am - 11am. Access: A

St James' Hospital, Sarsfeld Rd, Balham SW17 (672 1222). Mon 6pm - 7.30pm & Fri 2pm - 3.30pm. Access: A

Brocklebank Health Centre, 249 Garrett Lane, SW18 (870 1341). Mondays 6.15pm to 7.30pm. Access: A

Fairfield Health Clinic, Fairfield Street, SW18 (870 6173). Thurs 5.30pm to 7pm & Thurs & Fri 9.30am to 11am. Access P

London Postal Area W

Cloister Road Clinic, Cloister Road, Acton, W3 (992 6460). Access: N

Chiswick Health Centre, Fishers Lane, Chiswick, W4 (995 8051). Access A

Raymede Clinic, Telford Road, W10 (960 0233). Access: P

St Stephen's Clinic, St Stephen's Road, Greezywater, Enfield (804 1074). Appointments to be made at 100 Church Street, Enfield, Tues 2.00pm to 4.30pm by appointment only.

Elm Park Clinic, Abbs Cross Lane, Elm Park, Hornchurch, (04024 43681). Access: P

Grange Park Clinic, Lansbury Drive, Hayes, (573 1022). Wed 9.30am (most weeks). Access: P

West Mead Clinic, West Mead, South Ruislip, (845 5888). Wed 9.30am. Access: P

Ruislip Manor Clinic, Dawlish Drive, Ruislip Manor HA4 9SF (71 35003). Access: P

Ickenham Clinic, Long Lane, Ickenham, (71-37286). Wed 9.30am. Access: P

Uxbridge Health Centre, George Street, Uxbridge, (0895-31925). Thurs 9.30am (most weeks). Access: A

Laurel Lodge Clinic, Harlington Road, Uxbridge, (0895-31221). Fri 9.30am. Access: N

Northwood Health Centre, Neal Close, Northwood, (65-27744). Fri 1.30pm (2nd & 4th Fri). Access: A

Harefield Health Centre, Rickmansworth Rd, Harefield (420 2944). Fri 1.30pm (2nd & 4th Fri). Access: P

Kingston and Esher

Molesey Clinic, (The Forum) Walton Road, (Molesey 979 6464). Acess: N

Hook Clinic, 1 Gosbury Hill, Chessington (397 5737). Access: N

The Dittons Clinic, Watts Road, Thames Ditton (398 0914). Access: P

Hawks Road Clinic, Hawks Road, Kingston (546 1115). Access: N

Acre Road Clinic, 204 Acre Road, Kingston (546 5812). Access: P

Roselands Clinic, 163 Kingston Road, New Malden (942 0800). Access: N

Manor Drive Clinic, 3 Manor Drive, Worcester Park (390 1111). Access: P

Hampton Wick Clinic, 20 Seymour Road, Hampton Wick, (977 6552). Access: N

Kings Road Clinic, Kings Road, Richmond, (940 9879). Access: P

Windham Road Clinic, Windham Road, Richmond, (948 1763 or 940 0522). Access: N

Victoria Drive Clinic, 67 Victoria Drive, SW19, (788 1525). Access: P

Sheen Lane Health Centre, Sheen Lane, SW14, (878 7561). Access: A

Eileen Lecky Clinic, 2 Clarendon Drive, Putney, SW15, (788 2236). Access: P

Teddington Clinic, Queens Road, Teddington, (977 8131). Access: A

St John's Health Centre, Oak Lane. Access: P

Whitton Clinic, Hospital Bridge Road, Whitton, (894 4293). Access: N

Feltham Clinic, Cardinal Road, Feltham, Middlesex (890 2469). Access: A

Hanworth Clinic, Grove Crescent, Hanworth, Middlesex.

Heston Health Centre, Cranford Lane, Heston, Middlesex, (570 6451). Access: P

Hounslow and Spelthorne Health Centre, 92 Bath Road, Hounslow, Middlesex, TW3 TDL (570 7715). Access: P

Isleworth Clinic, Busch Corner, Isleworth, Middlesex, (560 4308). Access: P

Shepperton Health Centre, Balcham Road, Shepperton, Middlesex.

Spelthorne Clinic, Feltham Hill Road, Middlesex.

Spring Road Health Centre, Spring Road, Lower Feltham, Middlesex (890 6598). Access: P

Staines Health Centre, Knowle Green, Staines, Middlesex TWl8 lXD (0784 5941). Access: P

Stanwell Health Centre, Hadrian Way, Stanwell, Middlesex.

Sunbury Health Centre, Green Street, Sunbury, Middlesex (0932 787861). Access: A

Central

Elizabeth Garrett Anderson Hospital, 144 Euston Rd, NW1 (387 2501/ 4646 x 225) Clinics: 9-11.30 a.m. Mon-Fri. 1.30-3.00 pm Mon-Thurs. Appointments must be made well in advance.

Alternative Medicine

Women's Natural Health Centre, c/o Kentish Town Women's Workshop, 169 Malden Road, Kentish Town, NW5 (267 5301). Women's health generally - homeopathy, psychotherapy, osteopathy, acupuncture and a herbalist counselling and self-help courses on alternative medicine. Phone between 9-10 am for appointment. Access: P

New Approaches In Cancer, c/o Seekers Trust, Addington Park, Maidstone ME 19 5BL (0732 848336).

The British Acupuncture Association & Register, 34 Aldermay St, SW1V 4EU. Will tell you your nearest acupuncturist.

The British College of Naturopathy & Osteopathy, 6 Netherhall Gardens, NW3 5RR, (435 7830). List local practitioners. Access: N

British Homeopathic Association, 27a Devonshire St, W1N 1RJ. List local practitioners. (Westminster) LW National. Access: N

The British School of Osteopathy, 1-4 Suffolk St, SW1 4HG, (930 9254/8). Access: P

Institute for Complementary Medicine, 21 Portland Place, W1N 3AF, (636 9543). Access: A

Royal Homeopathic Hospital, Great Ormond Street, WC1N 3HR, (837 3091). For a list of GP's who practise homeopathy in your area. Access: A

South London Feminist Therapy Centre, 43 Killyon Road, London SW8, (622 0148) (see above under Mental health). Access: N

2. Specific Health Topics

Bereavement

Cruse, Cruse House, 126 Sheen Road, Richmond, Surrey TW9 1UR, (940 9047). Counselling, practical information and advice for the recently widowed and their families. Network of London groups. Access: P

Compassionate Friends, 6 Denmark St, Bristol, BS1 5DQ (0272 292778). Self help group of bereaved parents offering help and understanding to those who have recently lost a child. Telephone answering service in almost every county in UK.

Gay Bereavement Project, Unitarian Rooms, Hoop Lane, NW11 8BS, (837 7324).

London Bereavement Project Group, 68 Chalton Street, NW1, (388 0241). Counselling on bereavement. Jewish Counselling. Access: P

National Association of Widows, c/o Stafford District Voluntary Service Centre, Chell Road, Stafford ST16 2QA, (0785 45465). Pressure group and self help organization with over 100 branches throughout country to support and advice all widows and to help them get back on their feet. Also concerned to fight for the financial anomalies which widows have to face.

Self Help Group on Child Bereavement, 23 Woolwich Road, Bexley, Kent.

The Still Birth Association, 8 Cambridge Rd, Sidcup, Kent, (309 0542).

Stillbirth & Neonatal Death Society, (SANDS), Argyll House, 29-21 Euston Rd. NW1 25D, (8332851/2). Coordinate a national network of befriending parents. Access: N

Women's Therapy Centre, * 6 Manor Gardens, N7, (263 6200 between 2 - 4 pm). Access: P

Healthline (980 4848) tape 88.

Also, many Age Concern (Pensioners') and Pensioners Link groups run bereavement counselling services.

Cancer

Association for New Approaches to Cancer, c/o Seekers Trust, Addington Park, Kent, MEl 95BL (0732 848336). Access: P

Cancer Link, 12 Cressy Road, NW3 2LY (267 8048). Provides information for cancer patients, their families and members of the helping professions together with back-up for support groups. Access: P

Health Education Council, New Oxford Street, WC1A 1AH, (631 0930). Publishes booklets and posters on a wide range of health topics including sickle cell, breast cancer. Publications in Asian languages.

Healthline, 980 4848, ask for tape relevant to particular cancer.

Mastectomy Association, 26 Harrison Street, Kings Cross, WC1(837 0908). Maintains a register of 1500 volunteers who have themselves had a mastectomy. A new patient can be put in touch with a local volunteer for help, advice and encouragement. Publishes leaflets and offers advice on a wide range of topics. Access N

Marie Curie Foundation, 28 Belgrave Square, SWl 8QG (235 3325). Access: A

Medic-Alert Foundation, 9 Hanover Street, W1R 9HF (449 2261). Provides identification discs for persons suffering from hidden medical problems. A patient who has had radiotherapy or developed lymphoedema should not have injections, vaccinations, or blood tests in the arm on the side of the mastectomy, or blood tests in the arm in the side of the mastectomy. Access: N

National Society for Cancer Relief, Michael Sobell House, 30 Dorset Square, NW1 6QL (402 8125). Provides individual financial assistance to those in need. Application is made via Social Services or the Community Nursing Service. In conjuction with the NHS, it is building up a number of continuing care units to provide short-stay specialist care for in-patients and those living at home. Access: N

SW Thames Regional Cancer Organization, Education and Information Officer, Block E, Royal Marsden Hospital, Downs Road, Sutton, Surrey, (643 8901 Ext 284). Access: A

Women's National Cancer Control Campaign, 1 South Audley Street, W1Y 5DQ, (499 7532). Produces films, posters, and leaflets aimed at improving women's knowledge of cancer and the importance of monthly self-examination of breasts. Also provides speakers for women's groups. Runs a fleet of mobile screening units equipped to provide clinical examination of the breasts. Screening programmes for Asian and Black women's groups. Currently producing leaflets in several Asian languages. Access: N

Drugs

Blenheim Project, 7 Thorpe Close, W10 5XL (960 5599/930 4688). Publications for women, women oriented support, counselling. Arranges home visit for the disabled. Access: N

City Roads, 356 City Road, EC1, (278 8671). Private Residence for drug users. Access: N

Drugs, Alcohol and Women Nationally * (DAWN), Boundary House, 91-93 Charterhouse St, ECL (250 3284). Campaigns on behalf of women with drug/alcohol problems. Access: N

Institute for the Study of Drug Dependence, 1-4 Hatton Place, Hatton Gardens, ECl (430 1991). (Library only). Access: N

Narcotics Anonymous, PO Box 246, SW10 (351 6794). Can put you in touch with a local group.

Open Door, c/o Hornsey Young People's Consultation Service, 12 Middle Lane, Crouch End, N8 HPO (348 6235). Counselling for 13-25 year-olds. Access: P

Release, c/o 347a Upper Street, N1 (485 4440). 24 hour emergency telephone (603 8654), limited counselling on drug use and referral. Access: N

Standing Conference on Drug Abuse, 3 Blackburn Road, NW6, (328 6556/430 2341). National co-ordinating body for voluntary projects concerned with drug abuse.

TRANX, 17 Peel Road, Wealdstone, Middlesex, (427 2065). Self-help groups for tranquiller users (and ring Health Line 980 4848, ask for tape number 7.

Alcohol

Accept Clinic,* 200 Seagrave Road, SW6 1RQ, (381 3155) (Hammersmith). Offers free one-to-one counselling and/or group therapy for people who have drink problems on day treatment basis. Runs women only groups, but as part of whole programme (min 2 weeks). Ring for further details.

Accept Ethnic Network, 170a Heston Road, Middlesex, TW5 0QU (577 6059).

Al-Anon Family Groups UK, 61 Great Dover Street, SE1, (403 0888). Self help groups, relatives and friends of problem drinkers. Ring or write for referral to local group. 10am to 4pm Monday to Friday.

Alcoholics Anonymous, London Regional Telephone Service, SW1, (834 8202), 140A Tachbrook Street, London SW1 2NE. Self help groups for people with drinking problems. Ring for referral to local group or write to PO Box 514, 11 Redcliffe Gardens, London SW10. 10am - 10pm every day of the year. Answerphone outside office hours.

Alcohol Counselling Service,* 34 Electric Lane, Brixton, SW9, (737 3570/3579) Free counselling, women counsellors. Black women and alcohol group.

Alcoholics Recovery Project,* 68 Newington Causeway, SE1 6OF (Head Office) (403 3369). They have shop fronts at: 6-8 Kings Cross Road, London WC1 (837 2686). Women only Tues 2-4pm; and 318 New Cross Road, London SE1, (691 2886). Women only Tues 2-4pm. Providing counselling and where appropriate, housing for people with drink problems. They run a residential programme and have a series of hostels.

Consortium, 146-150 Camberwell Road, SE5 0EE (701 2209). Access: P.

Greater London Alcohol Advisory Service, 91/93 Charterhouse Street, EC1 (253 6221).

Women's Alcohol Centre,* (Part of Alcoholics Recovery Project, see above), 254 St Paul's Road, N1 2LJ, (226 4581). Counselling and referral where appropriate, will provide referral to their residential hostels for women only.

Westminster Advisory Centre on Alcholism, 38 Ebury St, SW1W OLU, (730 1574) (Westminster).

Healthline (980 4848 Tapes nos 1,2,3.)

Smoking

ASH - Action on Smoking and Health, 5-11 Mortimer St, W1N 7RH (637 9843), (Pressure group, information & publications). For local Stop Smoking groups, contact your nearest Health Education Unit by looking in the phone book under the name of your District Health Authority or call the Health Education Council.

Healthline, (980 4848 tapes nos 133,134,135).

Eating and Weight

Anorexics Anonymous, 45A Castelnau, SW13 (748 4587). Advice for anorexics. Counselling fees on a scale. 11am - 8pm Mon to Fri. Also treats Bulimia and other eating disorders. Access: N

Anorexia and Bulimia Nervosa Association, 12 Geneva Court, Manor Road, N16.

Anorexia and Bulimia Women's Groups: (892 5945) after 9pm.

Overeaters Anonymous, PO Box 539, W11, (868 4109).

Women's Therapy Centre,* 6 Manor Gardens, N7 (263 6200). Individual and group services with some self-help groups meeting. Access: P

Healthline (980 4848, tape 119 or 121 in pregnancy).

Diet

The Vegetarian Society, 53 Marloes Rd, W8 6LA (937 7739).

Institute for Optimum Nutrition (ION), 15-17 Southend Rd, NW3 (794 4971) Access: N

Health Plus Limited, 118 Station Rd, Chinnor, Oxford OX9 4E2 (0844 5298). Access: N

Healthline (980 4848) tape 119, 121 in pregnancy; 110 diet and heart disease; 119 fibre; 120 children.

Health Workers

Black Health Workers and Patients' Group, 259a High Rd, Tottenham N15 (809 0774). Access: N

Lesbian Nurses' Group, c/o AWP, Hungerford House, Victoria Embankment, London WC2.

Radical Health Visitors' Group, c/o BSSRS, 9 Poland St, W1.

Women and Medical Practice,* 666 High Road, N17, (885 2277), A radical collective which provides advice, information, counselling on all issues of women's health. Also gives information about sympathetic doctors and alternative practitioners in Haringey. Access N, but events and and workshops held in accessible buildings.

Heart and blood disorders

Chest, Heart and Stroke Association, Tavistock House North, Tavistock Square, WC1 H9JE (387 3012). Involved in health education, research, rehabilitation, conferences, counselling and welfare services for the prevention of chest, heart and stroke illnesses. Produce books and leaflets ring for details. Access: N

Mental Health
(and see **Disability**, Mental Health)

British Association of Psychotherapy, 121 Hendon Lane, N3 3PR (346 1747). Access: N

Clinic of Psychotherapy, 26 Belsize Square, NW3 (903 6455). Treatment ranging from supportive work to full psychoanalysis. Ring for appointment. Fees to be arranged with therapist. 24 hour answering service. Access: N

Highgate Counselling Centre, Tetherdown Hall, Tetherdown, N10 (883 5427). Psychotherapeutically based counselling on emotional, family, and marital problems for people over 17. Ring for appointment, Contributory fees. 10am - 8pm Mon and Tues, 9.45am - 2.45pm Wed 10am - 6pm Thurs 10am - 1pm Fri. Answerphone outside office hours. Access: N

Institute of Psychosynthesis, 1-2 Cambridge Gate, NW1 4JN (486 2588/9). Individual counselling and help with emotional problems. Ring for appointment. Fees negotiable. 9am - 4pm Mon to Fri. Answerphone outside office hours. Access: N

National Association of Mental Health, MIND (England), 22 Harley Street, W1N 2ED, (637 0741) (Westminster) W National. Access: P

Pellin South London Feminist Therapy Centre, 43 Killyon Road, SW8 2XF (622 0148). Access: N

Psychiatric Rehabilitation Association, The Groupwork Centre, 21A Kingsland High Street, E8, (254 9753). Rehabilitation and aftercare of the mentally ill. Ring or write for appointment. Free to residents of Enfield, Hackney, Haringey and Tower Hamlets. 9.30am - 6pm Mon - Fri. Answerphone outside office hours. Access: N

Westminster Association for Mental Health, 526 Harrow Rd, W9 3QF (969 2434) Access: A

The Richmond Fellowship, 8 Addison Road, W14 8DL (603 6373). A network of therapeutic communities for people who are under emotional strain or have had a mental breakdown. It runs 37 halfway houses and lengths of stay range from 3 months to 5 years. Help towards costs is normally available from your social services department. For further details contact the Fellowship. Access: N

Women and Mental Health, c/o A Woman's Place, Hungerford House, Victoria Embankment, WC2. Campaigning group.

Women's Therapy Centre,* 6 Manor Gardens, N7 (263 6200/6209). Counselling in emotional problems, compulsive eating, anorexia nervosa and assertiveness training. Ring for appointment. Contributory fees. 2pm - 4.30pm Mon to Fri. Answerphone outside office hours. Black women's group meet quarterly, workshops for disabled women. Access: A

Phobias
Action on Phobias, 17 Burlington Place, Eastbourne, East Sussex BN21 4AR, (0323 504755). Telephone for your local group. Access: N

Depression
Albany Trust, 24 Chester Square, SW1 (730 5871). Offers a counselling service to those who are depressed with particular emphasis on working on issues about personal relationships and sexuality. Charge per session though can be waived or reduced in some circumstances. Access: N

Arbours Association, 6 Church Lane, N8 (340 7646). Provides four kinds of help to people with severe depression: a phone service where you can speak about your feelings with someone who is tolerent, sympathetic and can offer advice; a crisis centre where you may be able to stay for a short while; three long stay communities in London, and a psychotherapy clinic. Ring for fees for psychotherapy. Access : P

Healthline (980 4848) tape 90; tape 124 Post-Natal Depression.

Schizophrenia
National Schizophrenia Fellowship, 78-79 Victoria Rd, Surbition, Surrey, KT6 4NS (390 3651/2/3). Telephone for your local group. Access: N

Healthline (980 4848) Tape 91.

Groups/Projects: Mental Health
Black Mental Health Project, (453 0243) (Afro Caribbean Asian).

London Women and Mental Health Newsletter, also to set up phone lines and crisis centre, c/o A Woman's Place, Hungerford House, Victoria Embankment, WC2.

Peckham Black Women's Mental Health Group, c/o Peckham Black Women's Group, c/o St Giles Parish Hall, Benhill Road, SE5 (701 2651). Access: A

Vassall Neighbourhood Centre, 143-145 Brixton Rd, SW9 (735 1878). Mainly concerned with Mental health. Working towards providing counselling service to be developed with local groups.

Occupational Health
London Hazards Centre, Centre for Trade Union Studies, Polytechnic of the South Bank, Borough Rd, SE1 OAA.

Women and Work Hazards Group, c/o BSSRS, 9 Poland St, W1.

Reproductive Health
British Pregnancy Advisory Service (BPAS), 2nd Floor, 58 Petty France, SW1 2EU, (222 0985). Non-profit making charitable organization who provide a counselling service as well as having their own abortion facilities. They also do pregnancy testing. BPAS operate throughout Britain, also offer sterilisation (Male and female) and artificial insemination by donor (AID). Will advise lesbians on AID. Ring London office for details. Access: N

Brook Advisory Centres: London Brook, 223 Tottenham Court Road, W1 (Main Office), (323 1522). They have other centres throughout London. Ring for details or look in phone book.

Offer advice/help and information to all young people (under 26 years) on personal relationships, contraception and pregnancy, including pregnancy testing, abortion referral (where possible and desirable to NHS). Most of the services are free, financed by the NHS. Access: N

Pregnancy Advisory Service (PAS), 11-13 Charlotte St, W1 (637 8962). Non-profit making charitable organization who provide a counselling service as well as having their own abortion facilities. Also do pregnancy testings. Soon to offer AID. Counselling in various languages, eg Spanish, French, German. Access: N

Marie Stopes House, 108 Whitfield St, W1 (388 4843/0662). Offer wide range of services including abortion/contraception/sterilisation/pregnancy testing/cervical smears etc. Access: N

Campaigning Groups and Information Services

Abortion Law Reform Association (ALRA),* 88 Islington High St, N1 (359 5200). Access: N

Co-ordinating Committee in Defence of the 1967 Abortion Act (Co-ORD), 27-35 Mortimer St, W1 (580 9360). Campaign to defend '67 Abortion Act. Access: N

National Abortion Campaign, 70 Great Queen St, WC2B 5AX (405 4801). Campaign to defend and further abortion rights. Access: N

Women's Reproductive Rights Campaign,* 52-54 Featherstone St, EC1 (251 6332). WRRC campaigns around all issues of women's reproductive rights and women's rights to decide if and when to have children - namely abortion, contraception, sterilisation, infertility, reproductive health at work, reproductive technology, AID, discrimination within the NHS. Currently working on the latest round of right-wing attacks on women's control over our own bodies. Access: A

Healthline, (980 4848 tape 128).

Artifical Insemination by Donor (AID)

BPAS (see above), offer AID service, ring for details.

WRRIC (see above), offer help, advice and support. Run AID support groups: ring for details.

PAS (see above), hope to offer AID soon, ring for details.

All the above will advise lesbians wishing to have AID.

Contraception

Brook Advisory Centres, (see above), specially for young people under 26. (And see **Young Women**, family planning clinics).

BPAS (see above).

Family Planning Information Service (FPIS), 27-35 Mortimer St, W1 (636 7866). List of clinics throughout Britian, free leaflets, phone-in inquiry service. Contact your local GP, CHC for details of your women's clinic (all listed previously in this section) or you can at your local hospital. Access: N

Margaret Pyke Centre, 15 Bateman Bldgs, Soho Sq, W1 (734 9351). Information and counselling on contraception, abortion, sterilisation etc, as well as providing these services. Access: N

Marie Stopes House, (see above)

PAS (above) including morning after contraception.

WRRIC: Information and advice about all aspects of contraception methods, side effects, contraception/abortion/sterilisation etc.

WHIC: Information on all methods/side effects etc.

Send sae to either of the above organizations (addresses above in this section) for detailed reading on all types of contraception, sterilisation etc.

Healthline, (980 4848, tape no: 65).

Co-ordinating Group on Depo-Provera, WRRIC, 52-54 Featherstone St, EC1. Monitor and campaign about abuses in the use of DP - the injectible contraceptive. Access: A

Endometriosis

Endometriosis Society, 65 Holmdene Ave, Herne Hill, London SE24 9LD, (737 4764) (evenings). Voluntary organization that was formed to help endometriosis sufferers. Produced leaflets and handouts to help explain endometriosis and its orthodox and alternative treatments. Self-help meetings arranged. Access: N

Sexually Transmitted Diseases

Most London hospitals have clinics, usually called Special or Genito-Urinary (GU) Clinics. You don't need to go to your doctor first. Telephone your local hospital and ask to be put through to the Special Clinic, to make an appointment. See Healthlines below for advice on specific infections.

Terrence Higgins Trust BM AIDS WC1N 3XX (278 8745) for help, advice on AIDS (auto-immune deficiency syndrome). Send sae for leaflet. Helpline (833 2971)

The Herpes Association, 39-41 North Road, N7 9DP. Self-help organization. Sae for details, publications etc.

Healthline (980 4848) tapes: 140 (general); 136 (AIDS); 137 (gonorrhea); 138 (herpes); 141 (NSU: non-specific urethritis); 139 (syphilis).

Sterilisation

You need to be referred by your GP for NHS sterilisation. Or you can contact **Family Planning Information Service**, 27-35 Mortimer St, W1 (636 7866); **PAS**, **BPAS**, **Marie Stopes** (see earlier, under Abortion).

Hysterectomy

Hysterectomy Support Group - London, 11 Henryson Rd, SE4 1HL, **Hysterectomy Support Group Newsletter** available £1 for a year's subscription.

Infertility

Child, c/o 367 Wandsworth Road, SW8 29J (486 4289). Access: N

WRRIC (251 6332), For details of treatment, where to go etc, what to expect, what kind of treatment is available. Also run an Infertility Support Group which meets once every six weeks, ring for details.

Menopause

Menopause clinics are at the following hospitals:-

Dulwich Hospital, East Dulwich Grove, SE22 3PT.

The Hospital for Women, (Soho Hopital - part of Middlesex Hospital Group), Soho Square W1V 6JB (580 7928).

Kings College Hospital, Dept of Obstetrics & Gynaecology, Denmark Hill, SE5 9RS (274 6222).

Royal Free Hospital, Pond Street, NW3 2Q9 (794 0500).

St Thomas' Hospital, Dept of Gynaecology, Lambeth Palace Road, London SE1 7EH (928 9292).

Samaritan Hospital for Women, Marylebone Road, NW1 5YE (402 4211).

St George's Hospital, Blackshaw Road, Tooting, SW17 (672 1255).

Family Centre, Wood Street, Barnet, Herts.

Beckenham Hospital, 379 Croydon Road, Beckenham, Kent (650 0125).

For most of the above you may need a referral from your doctor. Menopause advice and support is also available from many Well Woman Clinics (see earlier in this section).

Menstrual Problems

National Association for Pre-Menstrual Syndrome, 6 Beech Lane, Guildford, Surrey, (Guildford 32573).

Pregnancy and Childbirth

La Leche League, BM 3424, London WC1V N3XX, (404 5011) Breastfeeding information and help.

Maternity Alliance,* 59-61 Camden High Street, NW1 7JL (388 6337). Campaign for improved services for new parents and babies. Black and ethnic minority groups meet quarterly. Access: N

National Childbirth Trust,* 9 Queensborough Terrace, W2 (221 3833). Mostly telephone counselling.

Pregnancy Advisory Service, 11-13 Charlotte St, W1P 1HD (637 8962). Pregnancy test £3 (Urine); Blood test £6 (Special early test). Speakers in Italian, Limited Asian, Spanish languages. Access: N

Pregnancy Advisory Service, 2nd floor, 58 Petty France, Victoria, SW1H 9EU (222 0985). Pregnancy test £2 (Urine); Blood test £5 (Special early test). Access: N

Marie Stopes House, 108 Whitfield St, W1, (388 0662). Pregnancy test £4; Blood test £8 (special early test). Access: N

The following Women's Centres in London offer **pregnancy testing**. Some also offer information about contraception, abortion and pregnancy:

Albany Health Project, The Albany Centre, 8 Douglas Way, Deptford, SE8 (692 0231 Ext 222). Offer free pregnancy testing. Also, advice and information to young people. Mon-Fri 10-4pm. Access: P

Balham Family Centre, 91 Bedford Hill, SW12 (673 4350). Offer free pregnancy testing and information about contraception, abortion and pregnancy. Tues & Thurs 10.30-12.30. And free Pregnancy testing Tues 6-7pm at the Health Centre opposite Balham Family Centre. Access: N

Brent Women's Centre,* 232 Willesden High St, NW10 (459 7660). Offer free pregnancy testing Saturday mornings 10-12 noon. Most classes for Black and Irish women. Access: A

Deptford & Lewisham Women's Centre,* 74 Deptford High St, SE8 (692 1851). Offer free pregnancy testing Mon-Fri 1-3.30pm.

Haringey Women's Centre,* 40 Turnpike Lane, Tottenham, N8 (889 3912). Offer free pregnancy testing and information and advice. Tues 6-8pm; Sat 10-12 noon. Access: P

Kentish Town Women's Workshop,* 169 Malden Rd, NW5 (267 0688). Offers pregnancy testing any weekday so long as they are given prior telephone notice. Also offers advice if the result is positive. They ask for a small donation (50p) to cover costs. Access: P. Disabled Toilets presently being built.

Newham Women's Centre, Community Links, 81 High Street South, E6 (472 6652). Offer free pregnancy testing Thurs 6.30-7.30pm. Tues (mornings) Asian womens group, mostly women who are divorced or separated. Interpreter for Hindi, Punjabi. Also Thrus - legal advice service. Access: A

Waltham Forest Women's Centre,* 5 Pretoria Avenue, E17 (520 5318). Offer free pregnancy testing. Ring the Centre first to find out times of testing. Access: N

Reproductive Technology, For further information on this subject, details of the new technology, the Warnock Report, and more, contact: WRRIC, & WHIC (see opening of listings)

Teeth

You can qualify for free dental treatment, dentures or glasses or a combination of all these on the following grounds: **Age**: Dental treatment is free for everyone under 18 and to those under 19 who are at school, college or university full-time. Dentures are free for children under 16 and those under 19 at school, college or university. Just tell the dentist you want free treatment. **Motherhood**: Expectation mothers and mothers with a child under one can get free dental treatment and dentures by signing a declaration at the the dentist. **Receiving Supplementary Benefit or Family Income Supplement**: The whole family (excluding non-dependants) qualifies for free dental treatment, dentures and glasses. All you have to do is to sign a declaration when you go to the dentist's or optician. Emergency treatment can be obtained from :

Eastman Dental Hospital, 256 Grays Inn Rd, WC1 (837 3646). Access: A

Royal Dental Hospital, 32 Leicester Sq, WC2 (930 8831).Access: A

London Hospital, Dental Dept, 57 Turner St, E1 (247 8370). Access: A

St George's Hospital, Tooting Grove, SW17. Access: A

Housing

A safe home of your own is important to everyone. Yet the issue is particularly important to women because of the obstacles and restrictions that are put in our way by the people who control housing.

First, public sector (that is council) housing is designed and provided primarily for nuclear families. This means it is usually offered to women only if they are wives or mothers. Where housing associations have stepped in more recently to provide housing for women and men without children, it has largely been for 'single' people. There has always been limited access to public sector housing for women who want to live together.

Secondly, the Conservative government has cut the amount of money borough councils can spend on housing. A shortage of new houses, together with the sale of council stock, has led to a crisis in housing in London from which women, and especially Black women, suffer most. It is more and more difficult to get housed by the local authority unless you have statutory rights under the terms of the Housing (Homeless Persons) Act 1977.

At the same time, decent private housing is also beyond the reach of most women. Whether you look at house buying, or at expensive and hard-to-find private rented accommodation, access depends on your income. In London, house prices are higher than in the rest of the country. Traditionally building societies have provided most of the loans for house purchase. It has become illegal for them to offer mortgages to women on terms which are less favourable than those offered to men. But there are many reasons why women are less likely to obtain loans.

It is almost impossible to buy your own house unless you have a well-paid job. Women are less likely to be in paid employment than men; or if they are, it is likely to be part-time and low paid. On average, women's wages are some 30% lower than men's, and Black women find themselves at the very bottom of the scale. Women take most responsibility for childcare, so the necessity of making adequate childcare arrangements cuts both their income and their employment opportunities.

Homelessness is the most acute form of housing need: the popular image of homelessness is of the vagrant male, alcoholic, sleeping rough under the arches in Charing Cross. Homelessness among women is hidden because they are not seen, in hostels or on the streets. There are fewer places for women in hostels than for men, so they are simply not counted. Women are more likely to make their own temporary arrangements with friends or family, to put up with unsatisfactory living arrangements because there is nowhere else to go.

More and more women - especially Black women - many of them single parents with young children, are forced to spend long periods in unsafe and unsuitable accommodation such as bed and breakfast establishments, reception centres and short life housing.

Black women face special problems in finding decent housing. It is harder for them to obtain rented accommodation because of racial discrimination from landlords. Members of the Black and ethnic communities, particularly Asians, tend to be forced into buying cheap, run down, inner-city properties which they cannot afford to renovate. Not only is the quality of housing bad, but they suffer more from problems of overcrowding, inadequate amenities and the attendant health risks than the overall population. In addition, racial harassment makes secure housing a real problem for many Black families.

It is essential that housing provision for women should be independent of our relationships. We are not able to make truly free choices about our lifestyles unless there is adequate secure housing for women, with no strings attached.

This section outlines some of the main problems faced by women, and some 'first things to do' in these situations. It also provides listings of housing departments, hostels, advice agencies and housing associations and is ordered as follows:*Access to Housing, Council Tenants - Further Information, Race and Housing, Housing for Women with Disabilities, Rent and Benefits, Repairs, Security of Tenure, Tenants Associations, Owner Occupiers. Council Housing Waiting List Registration/ Homelessness, Hostels, Advice Agencies, Black and ethnic minorities Housing Advice, Housing Associations, Housing Co-ops, Tenants Associations.*

Access to Housing

Rented: There are two ways of becoming a council house tenant: by registration on the waiting list, or if you are homeless.

Waiting List: You are entitled to register on the waiting list of the council in the area where you live. Some councils will also allow you to register on the waiting list if you work in their area. Check this by ringing the Waiting List Section of the council (see listings). The council will assess your application on the basis of the accommodation that you occupy, giving 'points' for things such as overcrowding or lack of facilities. You should inform them if you change your address. You may ask to see a copy of the Council's Points Scheme: this will say how points on the waiting list are awarded so you can check your own application.

If you are without children, ask the council if they have any schemes for single people, or single sharers - such as nominations to the Greater London Mobility Scheme (GLMS), 'Difficult to let' property, 'Key Workers' or other special schemes.

Homelessness: If you are homeless, or threatened with homelessness, the council will have a duty to assist you in some way, under the terms of the Housing (Homeless Persons) Act 1977. Apply to the Homeless Persons Unit at the council (see listings). It may be called the 'Homeless Families Unit' or the 'Housing Emergency Office'. You do not have to be registered on the waiting list. If you become homeless outside of office hours ring the emergency number if there is one listed. If there is no emergency number listed, ring the police.

If you have dependent children, or are over retirement age, you will be in 'priority need'. You may also be in 'priority need' if you are a young woman at risk of sexual or financial exploitation, a woman with disabilities, a battered woman at risk of further violence, or mentally ill. If you are not in 'priority need', the council must give you advice and assistance. If you are in 'priority need', the council must provide temporary accommodation for you until they have come to a final decision.

The council will also consider whether anything you have done in the past has led to your present situation - whether you have 'made yourself homeless'. If the council considers that you have made yourself homeless, it has a duty to provide only temporary accommodation. If it is decided that you have not made yourself homeless (that you are not 'intentionally homeless') then the council has a duty to ensure that permanent accommodation becomes available to you. You have a right to have any decision the council makes put in writing: this is called a 'Section 8 Notice'. If you dispute any part of the council's decision, get independent advice. (See listings).

Violence: If you live with a man and he is violent towards you, you should be accepted as 'homeless' by the council under the terms of the Homeless Persons Act. It does not matter if you have a tenancy or a home elsewhere. If you are in 'priority need' you should be given temporary accommodation. You may need assistance from an advice agency in making your application to the council, as it can be complicated (see listings), also see **Violence Against Women**.

Refugees: If you are a refugee in Britain you should also be recognised as 'homeless', whether or not you have a home or tenancy elsewhere. You may find it helpful to consult an advice agency, particularly if there is one catering for your own ethnic community.

Council House Transfers: You may wish to move because your house is too big or too small, because you are working in a different area, because of racial harassment, or because your relationship has broken down. Each council has its own policy on housing allocation and transfer, and may have a long waiting list. To apply in your own borough, and to find out their priorities, contact your Housing Department - see Waiting Lists - the same number will normally apply, or they will inform you of the correct number. Or contact your Town Hall information desk (see **Borough Information**). Racial harassment: see later in this section.

Housing Associations: Housing associations are non-profit making organisations which build or convert property to rent, at 'fair rents'. 'Fair rents' are fixed by an independent rent officer, and are usually around or a little higher than council rents. Most of the money that they use to carry out their work comes from central or local government, so at least 50% of their vacancies will be let to people 'nominated' by the local council. This means, if you have not already done so, that you should tell the local council Waiting List Department if you are interested in this type of accommodation. (See listings for details.)

Housing associations have been severely affected by government cuts, and consequently don't have many vacancies. This means that often they do not keep their own waiting lists. The best thing to do is to approach your local advice agency to discuss your problem (see listings). If local housing associations do have open waiting lists, they are likely to know.

If you are contacting a housing association directly it is best to do so in writing.

Housing associations try to help people with no other options; so if you can afford to buy, or if you are entitled to housing under the terms of the Homeless Persons Act, they will probably not be able to assist you.

Some housing associations cater especially for women, for ethnic minorities or gay people, or have special projects for disabled people. See listings later for a selection of Housing Associations, or contact:

The National Federation of Housing Associations, 175 Grays Inn Road, WC1 (278 6571).

Private Rented Accommodation: Privately rented accommodation can be the only option available to women who need somewhere to live urgently, and who are not in 'priority need' under the Homeless Persons Act. Yet it is very hard to find, often badly maintained, and usually expensive. Landlords often discriminate against people with children, people dependent on benefits or people from ethnic minorities or with disabilities.

You can find privately rented accommodation by looking in London and local newspapers; on noticeboards in local shop windows; by registering with accommodation agencies. Accommodation agencies should not charge you a fee unless you accept a place that they have found for you. If you are asked to pay just for registering, or for a list of addresses, you should contact your local advice agency. (See listings).

You may be asked to sign an agreement before you move in. This may affect your rights to stay there, to get repairs done or to register a 'fair rent'. The best thing to do is to take a copy of the agreement before you sign it to your local advice agency and ask them to explain what it means. It may be that you need accommodation urgently, and that even if it does affect your rights, you have to sign it straight away. If this is the case, read it carefully, ask for a copy, and take it to the advice agency later. At least you will know what your position is if any dispute with your landlord arises later.

For accommodation agencies, see the Yellow Pages of the telephone directory.

Hostels: Hostel accommodation varies a lot - it is provided by charities, housing associations, and commercial organisations. Many hostels provide accommodation for a particular age or ethnic group, or for people with a particular need: for example, ex-alcoholics. It is important for you to read the requirements of the hostel before ringing about vacancies. The hostels listed later in this section do take people who ring them directly. Some hostels only take people who have been 'referred' by another agency, such as an advice agency. For general information on hostels nationally contact: **National Association of Voluntary Hostels**, 33 Long Acre, WC2 (836 0193).

Guide to Women's Hostels in London, available from **SHAC** (The London Housing Aid Centre), 189a Old Brompton Road, SW5 0AR, (£2.50).

The Housing Advice Switchboard (434 2522) has carried out a survey to discover which hostels have practised racism.

Short Life Housing and Housing Co-operatives: Sometimes councils and housing associations have property that they can't afford to demolish or improve just yet. They sometimes agree to let it on a temporary basis to individuals or a group of individuals on a 'short life' basis. This can be for a few months, or for a few years. It is usually in a poor state of repair, and has to be shared communally between a number of people, and so is not very suitable for people with children. Short-life accommodation is usually cheap. If you are an individual interested in this type of accommodation, you should consider joining a Short Life Housing Group, or Co-op. You can obtain information about short life housing groups in your area from your local council, or advice agency.

If you are a group of women, wanting to share together, you may want to consider setting up your own housing co-op.

Housing co-ops are organisations of people who join together to buy or rent property together. There are various types of co-ops: management co-ops, where the property continues to belong to the council or housing association, but is managed by the group; ownership co-ops, where the property is actually owned by the co-op.

There are two types of ownership co-ops: co-ownership societies, where an individual buys a share in the house or houses, and 'sells' their share on the open market when they move on. They will get the benefit of the increased value of the property when they sell. There are very few of these type of co-ops. Also: non-equity sharing co-ops, where the individual puts in only a nominal share - usually £1 - and the house or houses remain the property of the Co-op itself. The Co-op can buy and convert property for itself, or through a development agent, such as a housing association. A number of non-equity sharing co-ops have both short life, and permanent accommodation.

Both non-equity sharing co-ops, and management co-ops are run by the tenants themselves. They usually have regular members meetings, and elect their own management committees. If you want to learn more about setting up your own co-op, contact:

Housing Emergency Office, 157 Waterloo Road, SE1 8UU (633 9377).

For information about existing housing co-ops contact:

National Federation of Housing Associations, 175 Grays Inn Road, WC1 (278 6571) (Steve Roff).

The National Federation of Housing Co-ops, 61 Corbin House, Bow Bridge Estate, E3 3BQ.

There are a number of co-ops for women or Black and ethnic minorities. See listings for selection.

Squatting: Squatting itself is not a crime. However, you can be arrested for breaking into a property or causing damage. Unless the owner gives you permission to live there, you will eventually be evicted. If the owner does want to evict you s/he will have to obtain a Court possession warrant unless s/he is a 'displaced residential occupier'. This means that s/he was living in the property at the time and was only temporarily absent. There is also a 'protected intending occupier'. This means that if the property has just been bought or let to someone who was intending to move in, that person is a 'protected intending occupier'. In these circumstances, the person displaced can call the police to remove you, and you are committing a criminal offence if you refuse to leave.

If the owner does issue a Court summons, the Court will always grant a possession warrant to the owner unless you can show that s/he gave you permission to be there. For further advice on your position contact your local advice agency or contact:

Advisory Service for Squatters, 2 St Paul's Road, N1 (359 8814) 2-6 pm.

Owner Occupation: Buying a home is a complicated process. You need to work out quite carefully what you can afford. You will need savings to pay a deposit, solicitor's fees, surveyor's fees, and to move and to furnish your home. The first step is to talk to a number of building societies to find out how much they will lend to you in your circumstances: usually between two and three times your basic salary or wages; what sort of property they will lend money to buy: you should ask particularly about older property and leasehold property; whether they will lend to people who want to buy together, how many joint borrowers will they lend to; whether they are lending to people who save with their building society only (this changes frequently, depending upon the money market).

This can help you decide where to put your savings. Once you know what you can afford, you can ask local estate agents for lists of properties in your price range.

If you are refused a loan by a building society, there are alternative sources of funds:

Councils: Councils can give money themselves for mortgages. Most councils do not have the money at the moment; however, they often have special arrangements with local building societies and can refer people to them. For more information, contact your local council's Housing Aid Centre or Mortgage Department.

Mortgage brokers: Estate agents and mortgage brokers often offer to arrange mortgages. These will usually be more expensive than through building societies, so do not think about this option unless you have been refused a loan by a building society. The mortgage will be more expensive because it will usually be an 'endowment mortgage' (see below). If you are in this situation, work out very carefully what the cost of your outgoings will be before you take on such a commitment.

Finance companies: Avoid finance companies at all costs. Interest rates are very high; advertising is often misleading; penalty clauses are severe. You could get yourself into a nasty mess!

There are two main types of mortgage:

Capital repayments mortgage: You pay a regular monthly amount, which is made up of interest and capital. In the early years, you pay mostly interest, because you are paying the interest on the outstanding capital. When the capital begins to be paid off, the amount of interest is reduced and you pay more capital. These loans are usually paid over 25 or 30 years.

Endowment mortgages: Here you pay interest only. In addition, you pay a premium, usually to a life assurance company. At the end of 25 or 30 years, you cash in your policy, and it should pay off the outstanding mortgage loan. Sometimes these policies pay out a lump sum as well. This type of mortgage is usually more expensive in terms of monthly payments than an ordinary capital repayment mortgage. It is also not always as flexible as a capital repayment mortgage.

When you have found a place that you like, you make an offer, 'subject to contract'. This means that you have not contracted to buy it if you find anything wrong with it. If your offer is accepted, you will need: i) A solicitor. You can obtain a list from a Citizens Advice Bureau (see **Borough Information**). Ring several, and compare costs. ii) A survey. Don't stint on the cost of the survey: it could be more expensive to find something substantially wrong with your house later. Any estate agent (or solicitor) will recommend a surveyor.

Your solicitor will arrange the contractual side of buying your home. For more detailed notes on house purchase, see:

Buying A Home, from SHAC (The London Housing Aid Centre), 189a Old Brompton Road, SW5 OAR, (£1.00).

Council Tenants-Further Information

When You Receive Your Offer: Sole or Joint Tenancy? If you are offered a council or housing association tenancy, you will have to decide who you want to be the tenant. You may not have a choice: the council may have a policy of giving tenancies to one person only, or to both partners in a relationship, or jointly to all sharers if they applied in a 'single sharer' scheme. You should think, however, about the advantages and disadvantages of holding the tenancy as sole tenant or joint tenant.

Married women: If you are married, both partners to the marriage have the right to live in the matrimonial home until the marriage is ended by divorce, separation, or nullity. The only way in which you can exclude your husband is by obtaining an injunction (that is, an order of the Court) against him if he is disruptive or violent. If the tenancy is in your sole name, or in joint names, you will be responsible for all the rent. If your husband is the only person in paid employment in the household, you will still be liable (that is responsible) for all the rent.

If the tenancy is in his sole name, he alone is responsible for all of the rent. If your marriage breaks down, you can apply to have the tenancy transferred into your sole name as part of the divorce or separation proceedings. You will be obliged to pay rent from that date. If the tenancy is in his sole name, and he dies, you can inherit the tenancy as long as you were living with him at the time of his death.

Unmarried women: If you are taking a tenancy with a man you are not married to, you should consider whether you are better off with a sole or a joint tenancy. If the tenancy is in his sole name, he is liable for all the rent. You will be his 'licensee' (that is, you merely have his permission to be there). He may ask you to leave if he gives you 'reasonable' notice to leave. If he dies, you can legally inherit his tenancy only if you have been living with him for one year at the time of his death.

If the tenancy is in your **joint names**, you are both equally liable for all the rent. This means that if he doesn't pay his share, you can be evicted for 'his' rent arrears. If your relationship breaks down, neither of you can ask the other to leave. If he is violent you can obtain an injunction (that is, an order of the Court) to exclude him, but this will usually be only a temporary solution.

If you have the tenancy in your **sole name**, you are liable for all of the rent. He will be your 'licensee' (that is, he will merely have your permission to be there), and you can ask him to leave as long as you give him 'reasonable' notice. If you die, he can legally inherit the tenancy as long as he has lived with you for at least one year at the time of your death.

Lesbians: Most councils do not recognise lesbians living together as 'couples' for the purposes of renting accommodation.

You may get a tenancy as 'single sharers' if the council has a special scheme of this sort. However, if you do get the opportunity of taking a council or housing association flat together, consider the following points: if the tenancy is in the name of one woman only, the tenant is legally liable for all of the rent. The other woman will be a 'licensee' (that is, she will merely have the tenant's permission to live there). The tenant may ask her to leave as long as she gives 'reasonable' notice. If the tenant dies, the other woman cannot legally inherit the tenancy.

If one woman has a council tenancy, and her lover moves in, they cannot demand as a right that the tenancy be put into both their names. You can ask the council to do this, but they are not obliged to do so. If you have a joint tenancy, then you are both equally liable for all of the rent. Neither can ask the other to leave. If one woman dies, the other can continue to live in the property as sole tenant.

Relationship Breakdown: This section applies to both council and housing association tenants. It is a rough outline of the various courses of action open to you. Before you decide, discuss the best course of action with your local advice agency, or with a solicitor. If your relationship has broken down, don't give up your tenancy or surrender it before you have had independent advice.

Married women: If you are a married woman, and your relationship has broken down, you have several options. If there is violence, you can go to a Woman's Aid Refuge. This is a house run by women for women who have suffered violence. Ring Women's Aid Federation England (WAFE) for the nearest refuge with space (251 6537). And see Violence against Women section in this book.

Refuges have an open-door policy, but space is tight and you are likely to be sharing a bedroom and other facilities. Priority may be given to women with children.

Women's Aid gives help and support with: claiming benefits from the DHSS; going to a solicitor if you need a Court injunction to prevent your husband harassing you or you need legal advice on divorce, cruelty etc.; and applying to the local housing department for accommodation. Once you are staying in the refuge you should be accepted as homeless and in 'priority need' and offered accommodation. You could see a solicitor with a view to obtaining an injunction (that is, an order of the Court) to restrain or exclude your husband from the home; and/or you could apply to the council under the term of the Homeless Persons Act (see Access to Housing above);

If there is no violence and he is not willing to leave, there may be no immediate solution to your housing problem. You will have to see a solicitor to commence proceedings for separation or divorce. You can apply to have the tenancy transferred into your name as part of the proceedings; your council may have a policy of rehousing both partners when a relationship breaks down. Ask your local independent advice agency.

Unmarried Women: If the tenancy is in your name only, you can ask your partner to leave if you give 'reasonable' notice. If you live with a man who refuses, or is violent, you can see a solicitor about obtaining an injunction (that is, an order of the Court) to exclude him from the house, or apply to the council under the terms of the Homeless Person Act. They will probably ask you to obtain an injunction. Go to a Women's Aid Refuge. Ring Women's Aid Federation England (WAFE) for advice (251 6537).

If the tenancy is in both your names, the situation is quite complicated. You will need independent advice. (For Law Centres etc., see Borough Information). If your partner is violent, you can obtain an injunction (that is, an order of the Court) to restrain or exclude him from the house. This will usually be only a temporary solution (see Violence against Women). Apply to the council under the terms of the Homeless Person Act (see Access to Housing). If the council tell you to obtain an injunction, get independent advice, go to a Women's Aid Refuge. Ring Womens Aid Federation England (WAFE) for advice (251 6537).

If you have successfully excluded your co-habitee, or divorced your husband, and the tenancy is now in your sole name but he continues to harass you, ask the council for a 'management transfer'. This is an urgent move on social grounds. Some councils are more helpful than others in this. If you need assistance, contact your local advice agency. Don't just give up your home.

Race and Housing

Discrimination Postwar Black and ethnic minority migrants to London in the 1950s and 1960s faced widespread racial discrimination in the housing field. Signs in shop windows saying 'Room To Let - No Coloureds' were all too common. As a result of this discrimination and low pay the majority of the Black and ethnic minority households were forced into the bottom end of the housing market - the run-down inner city areas which more prosperous white people were leaving behind.

The current housing position of London's Black and ethnic minority households differs significantly in several respects from white households as the table below shows.

The most dramatic differences are in the housing conditions London's Black and ethnic minority groups face. In terms of overcrowding and use of amenities they are far worse off than white Londoners. This is a result of low income and continuing racial discrimination. The results are that whether it be in the public or private

	West Indians	Asians	White
Tenure			
Owner Occupied	34%	61%	45%
Local Authority/ Housing Association	53%	17%	35%
Private Rented	13%	22%	20%
Overcrowding			
Below Bedroom Standard	18%	27%	6%
Amenities			
Lack Use of One Amenity	14%	30%	12%

(Source: *National Dwelling and Housing Survey* 1979)

sector, London's Black and ethnic minority families are still poorly housed.

Considerable research into the housing situation of London's Black and ethnic minority households has been carried out, notably by the Runnymede Trust and the Policy Studies Institute. Two main conclusions emerged with respect to the public sector - that initially it took far longer for Black and ethnic minority people to be housed compared with white households, and once they were housed it tended to be worse accommodation than that of white households.

One of the main reasons for the wait before being housed was that many London boroughs had residence qualifications. Thus however bad your housing need, you could not be housed until you had lived in the borough for three or more years. This particularly hit Black people who made up the majority of recent arrivals in the 1950s and 1960s. Most boroughs have now reduced their residence qualification and Black people have now been in London for many years. Now that they are being rehoused, it tends to be in poorer quality council housing. For example, research by the Runnymede Trust in 1975 and the London Borough of Wandsworth in 1979 found that twice as many ethnic minority households were given flats in high rise blocks than white households. To counter this the councils were urged to review their allocation policies by the House of Commons Home Affairs Committee (*Racial Disadvantage Report*, 1981) but very few have done so.

Racism is still widespread in the private sector of housing. The Commission for Racial Equality estimates that many private accommodation agencies still discriminate. An investigation into one South London estate agent revealed that Black applicants were being given details of only a few properties because of pressure from local white residents' groups.

Black Women and Housing: Black women suffer from at least two forms of discrimination. They are not only victims of racism but also of sexism. This double disadvantage is rarely recognised and thus action rarely taken. Black women are often concentrated in the worst paid and most dangerous jobs. The mental and physical stress induced by anti-social working hours and bad working conditions is compounded by poor housing. The women of the Bangladeshi community in East London, where there is a high incidence of racial attacks, are especially vulnerable. Their men are often working night shifts, leaving women and children at a time when some of the most vicious attacks occur.

Nearly 50% of all tenants are women. A disproportionate number of these are of Black or of other ethnic minority origin. A significant group are single mothers. Many of them are virtual prisoners because of the lack of creche facilities and centres where they can meet or have their children properly looked after. As a result it is very difficult for them to get a job or even to get out of the flat and have any kind of social life or to develop their potential in other ways. An additional factor is that a large number of Black single mothers come into the council housing system via the homeless channel. In general this is the channel which is allocated the poorest quality accommodation. Thus not only are they trapped; they are frequently trapped in damp, inadequate premises, often on high floors of tower blocks.

Linguistic, cultural and religious factors can further isolate Black or other ethnic minority women. Some groups of women, especially most from the Indian sub-continent, are not permitted to have contact with men unless they are part of their immediate family. This can lead to problems when the majority of the officials the woman has to deal with are men. Thus many such women are unable to receive fully their entitlements, for example housing benefit, rebates and repairs. The lack of English as a Second Language classes for women compounds these problems. The closing down of important communal resources like estate-based laundries further restricts the opportunity for Black women to socialise with other women, both Black and white. The stereotyped view held by white people is that Black and other ethnic minority households all live in extended families. Thus there is no real need to provide for Black elderly people because they will automatically be cared for by their relatives. In fact, this is not always the case. Economic and social pressures coupled with changing values mean that an increasing number of elderly Black women require accommodation. Few agencies however provide accommodation which is in any way suitable for elderly Black women, especially those who may have had little previous contact with the white community.

A further unmet housing need for Black women is the lack of suitable provision for battered Black women. A limited number of refuges have been set up in London but all but two have been developed by white-based groups largely for white women. As a result, when Black women have been referred to these hostels they have often been subjected to racism on top of all the other problems they are having to cope with. There is also little recognition of the extreme isolation a Black woman can face after the break-up of her marriage.

An increasing number of young Black women are seeking to live away from home in order to work or study. There is virtually no provision for such women to live in an environment where they are able to preserve and develop their cultural and religious heritage. This is necessary if young Black women are to realise their potential.

The Law: It is illegal for local authorities, accommodation agencies, landlords, estate agents or anyone else to discriminate against you because of your race or colour.

Section 71 of the Race Relations Act 1976 states: '...it shall be the duty of every local authority to make appropriate arrangements with a view to securing that their various functions are carried out with due regard to the need a) to eliminate unlawful racial discrimination, and b) to promote equality of opportunity, and good relations, between persons of different racial groups.'

The Commission for Racial Equality (CRE) has recommended to local authorities reviews of policies and procedures to ensure that they are not directly or indirectly discriminatory; ethnic record-keeping and monitoring systems; training programmes; and the appointment of specialist workers or individuals responsible for particular work on race and housing. The CRE can issue a non-discrimination notice to enforce such measures.

If you find you have been the victim of racial discrimination you can: a) contact your borough race relations advisors, if they have been appointed, or a local advice agency (see **Borough Information**); b) go to the CRE. The Commission has the power to support a Court case to claim compensation.

CRE, Elliot House, Allington Street, SW1 (828 7022).

Racial Harassment: Racial harassment, especially on housing estates, has been increasing over the last five years and takes many forms, including physical as well as verbal abuse. In severe cases individuals have been beaten up, seriously injured and even killed. Women and children are most at risk, particularly when men are out at work, possibly working overnight shifts. On some estates women and children have become virtual prisoners in their own homes, afraid to go out for fear of attack by gangs of white youths. There is also a rising number of racist attacks on Jewish people in their homes, and an increase in anti-semitic graffiti and threats.

In the past, local authorities have been slow to recognise or deal with the problem. Black and Asian families have been concentrated in the poorest quality housing, often because of the council's own 'points' system. Such properties may have broken windows and leaking roofs, bad drainage and damp, inducing colds, chest complaints and generally poor health. Because councils have been slow to carry out repairs, the tenants themselves have been blamed for the poor conditions and deterioration. When Black and Asian tenants have been offered better housing, they have often been afraid to take it because of intimidation by white tenants. Some council housing officials have either refused to believe reports of racial harassment or done nothing about them.

Women from ethnic minorities living in private housing are equally at risk from racial attacks. Families are often forced to remain in poor housing close to their own communities as the only form of security.

Evidence to the GLC Panel of Inquiry on Racial Harassment in London showed that the ethnic communities have little faith in the police. In many cases police were unsympathetic, hostile, or refused to take reports of racist assaults seriously. Action, if any, was slow, and even where attackers were identified the police were reluctant to prosecute.

New policies have now been agreed by the GLC and some borough councils to stop racial harassment on housing estates. There should be simple, standard procedures for reporting racial incidents, with monitoring to check what action has been taken. Training should be given for council staff on how to handle complaints (the GLC has also set up a Race and Housing Action Team in Tower Hamlets to investigate and advise on cases within 48 hours) and repairs, and the removal of racist graffiti should be carried out within 24 hours. Some councils are issuing leaflets in Asian languages, giving tenants information on what to do about racial harassment. An interpreter should always be available. Housing welfare officers from ethnic communities have also been appointed. Housing departments should liaise with community groups set up to counter racial harassment, and provide support for victims. Other initiatives include patrols of caretakers, or telephone rotas of officers, councillors, neighbours etc, prepared to 'sit' with harassed tenants.

If you suffer racial harassment you can report the incidents to a sympathetic person or organisation. This may be a caretaker, estate officer or housing welfare officer. You may prefer to go to a community group, advice agency (listed later) or even your MP. Make sure the local authority is informed. If you are a tenant the council can arrange for you to be transferred. It can also evict the offenders. Under the Housing Act 1980, the council has the power to evict tenants who break their agreements. Some boroughs include specific clauses in their tenancy agreements, or have written to tenants warning them against racial harassment. Councils can also take legal action against offenders, such as a private prosecution to recover the cost of damage, or support for the victim in claiming damages.

You can also report the incidents to the police. You can ask to speak to a Community Liaison Officer. The police should provide protection for victims if necessary. Most cases involving damage or assault are criminal, not civil matters, and offenders should be identified and prosecuted by the police.

You can also contact your local Community Relations Council (see **Borough Information**) or the **Commission for Racial Equality,** Elliot House, Allington Street, SW1 (828 7022).

A number of local organisations now exist to fight racial harassment. They include:

Community Alliance for Police Accountability (Tower Hamlets), Oxford House, Derbyshire Street, E2 (729 2652).

Greenwich Action Committee Against Racial Attacks, 1st Floor, 78 Sandy Hill Road, SE18 7AZ (855 4343).

Racial Harassment Bill Group, Chair Rizwan Razaq, c/o SHAC, 189a Old Brompton Road, SW5 0AR (373 7276).

Tower Hamlets Association for Racial Equality, Oxford House, Derbyshire Street, E2 (729 1946).

If you have suffered physical injury you may claim compensation through the Criminal Injury Compensation Board. The claim will be estimated on medical evidence and other factors such as lost earnings, and is easier if your attacker has been arrested and convicted. Get legal advice first from a law centre or solicitor. (See **Borough Information**).

Security: Security at home is a vital issue for women, especially if you are older or from a racially harassed ethnic minority. Often the design and planning of housing fails to take this into account. For instance, housing estates are built with front doors that are weak or concealed from view, allowing intruders easy access. Poor lighting is another problem. Simple improvements can be made: for instance, entryphones to the main doors of blocks of flats.

If you are a council tenant, contact your local authority or tenants' association, which may be able to lobby the council on your behalf for the necessary funding. However, money is very scarce for all council's housing improvement programmes because of government cutbacks in finance.

Allocations and Ethnic Monitoring: Many discussions about race and housing are based on opinion and myth rather than fact. One way in which a housing agency can find out what is happening with regard to the services it provides is to collect and monitor ethnic origin records. This view is shared by the government, the National Federation of Housing Associations, the Association of Metropolitan Authorities and the Association of London Authorities. It is also supported by the major, national, ethnic minority organisations.

Some people have argued that to collect ethnic origin data is a discriminatory act. This is not the case. Every applicant for a housing agency's services should be asked his or her ethnic origin, not just one particular group. Another argument against keeping ethnic origin records is that the information might fall into the wrong hands. Whilst it is vital that such data is kept confidential, almost all racial discrimination in Britain is based on skin colour. Thus, it is not necessary to have ethnic origin data to discriminate. Several reports, most recently the Commission for Racial Equality's investigations into Hackney's Housing Department, have all shown that Black and other ethnic minority groups receive worse treatment than similar white households. And this happened in an authority which at the time did not keep ethnic origin data.

Any piece of information is only as useful as the use to which it is put. This is true for ethnic origin data. A housing agency should therefore not only agree to collect ethnic origin data, but also monitor the information. The monitoring should concentrate on how many people are being housed, how long it takes before they have been housed and the quality of accommodation allocated. To ensure that this can happen it is important that ethnic data is collected for all aspects of a housing agency's work.

To collect ethnic origin data requires a clear commitment to act on the results of the monitoring. If, for example, it was found that Black and other ethnic minority households are being allocated poorer quality accommodation, then the reasons for this need to be examined. It may be that the explanation for this was that most Black families were housed because they were homeless and that the agency's policy was that all homeless families receive only one offer of poor quality property. If this was the case then the agency should consider changing this policy because it may well constitute racial discrimination as defined by the Race Relations Act 1976.

Approximately a third of the London boroughs currently collect ethnic origin housing data, as do an increasing number of housing associations. Most have found that their clients are willing to disclose their ethnic origin provided they are clear why the data is being collected and the uses to which it will be put. They also found that when they monitored the ethnic origin data different patterns did emerge for Black and white households. This confirms the view that what was found by the CRE in Hackney was typical rather than exceptional. Hackney has now decided to collect and monitor ethnic origin data to help ensure that the policies it has now adopted to eliminate discrimination are in fact working.

One London borough which has been keeping and monitoring ethnic origin records for some years now is Lambeth. Lambeth asks everybody who applies for any of its housing services to classify themselves in one of the following categories: Black (Afro-Caribbean); Black (Asian); White; Other (Please notify).

The question, which is preceded with an explanation of why the borough wants the information, is included on every application form. All staff have been trained about the need to collect the data and the uses to which it will be put for their own benefit and so they can answer any question the public might have.

Well over 90% answer the ethnic origin question. On the basis of this, regular monitoring reports are prepared to find out how many ethnic minority people need housing, how many have been housed, in what areas, and in what type of property compared to white households. In this way the borough can check whether its housing programme is being fair to all and not just one part of the local population.

Housing for Women with Disabilities

Houses are seldom planned to meet the needs of disabled women, so they face special problems in finding suitable accommodation, and there is little information on disabled women's housing needs.

In some boroughs the situation is improving slowly. In Camden, for instance, 5% of new council housing is designed for wheelchair or mobility access. Elsewhere, ground floor and first floor flats are being renovated to accommodate disabled people, including a second bedroom for single people, etc.

If you are buying a house, look for a surveyor who knows about disability and can tell you whether the building is suitable.

You can apply for a grant for improvements or alterations from your local authority. Improvement grants are made at the council's discretion, and although disabled people are given priority, there is limited money available. Intermediate grants, for extra standard amenities such as an accessible WC, are mandatory. The maximum rate of grant is 75% of the cost of the work, or 90% if you are in financial hardship. If you cannot get a grant for adaptations, contact your local Social Services Department which may be able to help with a grant or loan.

A number of councils and advice agencies are beginning to provide specialist advice for elderly home owners: eg, **Brent Elderly Home Owners Aid Service**, 3rd Floor, Imperial Life House, 390-400 Wembley High Road, Middlesex (903 4307). Ring your Town Hall Information Desk - (see **Borough Information**).

Organisations like the **Southwark Mental Handicap Consortium** (703 0838) provide housing for mentally handicapped people. Contact your local advice agency for information. (See **Disability**).

Rent and Benefits

Council Tenants: Difficulty meeting the rent: if you are unemployed or working less than 30 hours per week, you should first make a claim for supplementary benefit. Fill in Form B7 at your local unemployment office. If you are entitled to supplementary benefit you should receive 100% of your rent and rates. This means, in effect, you will have no rent to pay. You may have to pay a contribution to your rent if you pay for heating, hot water, cooking or lighting in with your rent and/or if you have people living in your household who are not dependent on you.

Private and Housing Association Tenants: Difficulty meeting the rent: if you are unemployed or working less than 30 hours per week, you should first make a claim for supplementary benefit. Fill in Form B1 from your unemployment office. If you are entitled to supplementary benefit, you should receive 100% of your rent and rates. You will receive a monthly cheque, unless you request weekly payments in writing. You may have to pay a contribution towards the rent and rates if you pay for heating, cooking, hot water or lighting in with your rents and/or if you have people living in your household who are not dependent on you.

Privately Rented Accommodation: Rent registration: if you are a 'protected tenant', you can get a 'fair rent' registered by an independent rent officer. (See Private Tenants: Security of Tenure below.) Only certain tenancies can be registered by the rent officer. If you apply to the rent officer, and you are not a protected tenant, you are likely to find yourself evicted. If you have checked your status, and you have decided that your rent can be

registered, you can get advice from most local agencies about how to apply to the rent officer. Some agencies also assist in representation at rent officer hearings. Once your rent is registered, it means that the landlord cannot legally charge more than the fair rent. The rent can only be raised every two years by application to the rent officer. Advice from agencies (see listings) and

SHAC (The London Housing Aid Centre), 189a Old Brompton Road, SW5 0AR (373 7276) Mon, Tues, Fri 1-4.30 pm, Thurs 9 am-4.30 pm.

Housing Benefit: If you are working full-time you may still be entitled to housing benefit, whether you are a tenant or an owner-occupier.

Standard housing benefit is paid to people who are not entitled to supplementary benefit. It is paid by the local authority, not the DHSS. You can have a high income and still qualify for housing benefit, according to your dependants, your earnings, and your housing expenses. If you own your own house, you will get help only with rates and not with mortgage repayments.

There are three forms of payment: rent rebates for council tenants; rent allowances for private and housing association tenants, housing co-ops, hostels, mobile homes etc; and rate rebates for owner-occupiers and tenants who pay rates.

Normally the person 'liable' for the rent/rates makes the claim, but benefit can also be paid to a 'partner' living in the house. Benefit can still be paid if the main claimant is temporarily absent (eg in hospital or prison).

People in short stay accommodation such as hostels are entitled to benefit once they have been living there for 14 days. Claim at once and press the local authority to progress the claim immediately. You can get benefit on two homes if you have moved because of violence or fear of violence. If the home is jointly occupied, benefit can be claimed by both partners and will be shared out by the local authority. It can be backdated for up to 12 months.

You can get an application form for housing benefit from your local Housing or Treasurer's Department. Your rate of benefit will be assessed by the local authority, and you should be informed in writing within 14 days of the claim being completed. If you are not happy with the decision you should ask for a review. You must write to the local authority within six weeks of the decision.

If you are in doubt about whether you qualify for supplementary benefit, apply *first* to the DHSS. If you are not entitled to SB they should advise you on claiming housing benefit and also assess you for housing benefit supplement.

Housing benefit supplement is a form of supplementary benefit but is paid by the local authority, not the DHSS. You can get housing benefit supplement if you would qualify for SB except for the fact that your income is too high. If that income falls below the SB level once your rent and rates are paid, you can make up the difference with housing benefit supplement.

Certified housing benefit is paid to people on supplementary benefit. You should not have to claim for it. The DHSS will contact your local authority and it will be responsible for making payments.

Contact your local authority or advice agency for help in claiming housing benefit, or refer to:

Guide to Housing Benefit, from SHAC, 189a Old Brompton Road, SW5 0AR, (£4.50).

National Welfare Benefits Handbook, from the Child Poverty Action Group, 1 Macklin Street, WC2B 5NH, (£3.50).

Repairs

Council Tenants: Repairs are often a problem for council tenants. The council as landlord is obliged to do certain repairs to maintain the structure and exterior of the dwelling, eg, the rooms, walls, floors and windows; the drains, gutters and pipes; the plumb-ing and sanitary installations, such as WC, bath and sinks; and the services and installations for the supply of water, gas and electricity. The landlord is only responsible for a defect that s/he knows about, or ought to have known about, so keep a record of any telephone call or visit you make to report a defect; put your complaints in writing, and keep a copy; keep items that are damaged and receipts for them if you have them. If the council still has not done the repairs after several telephone calls and letters, you should consider taking it to Court. You will need advice. Contact your local advice agency. If the defects are to a group of dwellings in your block, or to the whole estate, you may be more effective acting together, in a tenants association. If you do not have a tenants association on your estate, get advice about how to start one. (See listings below.)

Private and Housing Association Tenants: Getting a private landlord to do repairs is usually a difficult matter. Although private tenants do have two main courses of action open to them to get repairs done, before you take any action always seek advice. (See Private Tenants: Security of Tenure below.)

If you take action against a landlord when you are not a 'protected tenant', you could find yourself evicted. Don't take any action unless you are sure that you are a 'protected tenant'. The landlord does have an obligation to maintain the structure and exterior of the dwelling, eg, the roof, walls, floors and windows; the drains, gutters and pipes; the plumbing and sanitary in-stallations, such as WC, bath and sinks; and the services and installa-tions for the supply of water, gas and electricity.

The landlord is only responsible for a defect that s/he knows about, or ought to have known about so keep a record of any visit or telephone call when you reported the defect; put your complaints in writing and keep a copy; keep items that are damaged by the disrepair and receipts for them if you have them.

If your repairs are not done, you have two courses of action. Either take your landlord to Court - contact your local advice agency for advice about this - or contact your local environmental health officer. Once you have notified him/her of the disrepair, s/he has a duty to inspect. Ring your local council for the telephone number (see Borough Information). Important: if your landlord has not done the repairs, and you are getting fed up, don't just stop paying the rent, get advice.

Security of Tenure

Succession on Death and Assignment: (council and housing association tenants). You cannot normally pass your tenancy on to someone else without the permission of the council or housing association. There are four exceptions:

• If you die, your spouse (that is, someone to whom you are married) can inherit the tenancy as long as he was living with you at the time of your death. Other members of your family can also inherit the tenancy as long as they have lived with you at least one year at the time of your death. This includes a co-habitee (not woman lover), son, daughter, father, mother, grandson, grand-daughter.

• You can assign (that is pass on legally) your tenancy to someone who would have been entitled to inherit the tenancy if you had died. If you want to do this, get independent advice from a local advice agency.

• If you are married, your tenancy can be assigned (that is, passed on) to your husband, or from him to you, as part of divorce, separation or nullity proceedings.

• You can assign to another secure tenant as part of an exchange. You must first ask your Council for permission. The Council must reply within 42 days. They can refuse permission only on certain listed grounds. If the coun-

cil does not respond with 42 days, you can apply to the County Court for a declaration of your statutory rights. If you want to do this, get independent advice. Do not move without it.

If you assign your tenancy in any other circumstances, you cease to be a secure tenant, and may lose your home. The person who has taken over will be an illegal tenant, and may in due course be evicted. If you have any doubt about your status, get advice.

Subletting (council and housing association tenants): As long as you do not overcrowd the property, you may take in a lodger without asking the council or housing association for permission. A lodger is normally someone who lives with you as part of the family and shares meals with you. If you wish to sublet a room to someone who will live more independently from you, you have to ask the council or housing association for permission. The council may not refuse permission unreasonably. If you are living on supplementary benefit, or receiving housing benefit, subletting may affect your entitlement. If you want to find out more about this, get independent advice.

Security of Tenure (private tenants): If you find a privately rented flat, bedsit, or room, the first question must be - what are your rights to remain there without interference from the landlord? This is a very complicated area of law. It is also very important, because it will affect: i) your right to remain in occupation, and your right not to be evicted; ii) your right to get the rent fixed (to 'register a fair rent'); iii) your chance of getting any repairs done; iv) the rights of your family to inherit the tenancy if you die.

Recent research by Housing Advice Switchboard shows that the majority of new lettings by accommodation agencies are not secure arrangements. So, the first thing you should do is contact your local Advice Agency; take copies of any written agreement you have; take your rent book, or any receipts you have; make a note of anything that was said when you took the place on. The advice agency should then be able to tell you what your status is, and what this means.

Only tenants known as 'protected tenants' have full security of tenure, and can safely get repairs done, or get a 'fair rent' registered. Always check your status before you take action on any of these matters.

Harassment (private tenants): Most 'residential occupiers' have a right to be evicted only by proceedings in the County Court. There are very few exceptions to this rule. So act quickly - get advice. If the landlord asks you to leave; threatens or intimidates you; puts you or your belongings in the street; damages or loses or keeps your belongings, you should contact the Tenancy Relations Officer (sometimes called the Harassment Officer). S/he is employed by the local council. S/he can negotiate or conciliate in disputes between landlords and tenants, and, if necessary prosecute landlords who illegally evict or harass tenants. Alternatively, contact a solicitor. Check whether s/he does Legal Aid, and what your maximum contribution would be (that is, how much you will have to pay). Also check, if you have been evicted, whether s/he can do emergency injunctions (they are orders of the court) in cases of illegal eviction; or contact your local advice agency. If they can't take legal action on your behalf, they should be able to tell you of a Law Centre or Legal Aid solicitor who will. (See Borough Information.)

Tenants Associations

Tenants Associations are organisations made up of tenants on one estate, or in one area. All tenants in that area are entitled to attend meetings, vote, or stand for election as officers of the tenants association. Tenants associations can take up issues with the council or housing association such as repairs or estate improvements. If you don't have a tenants association in your area you can get advice on setting one up from the organisations listed later in this section. A conference for Black tenants was held by the London Tenants Organisation in April 1984. The recommendations from it included the setting up of a support, information and resource unit for Black tenants, as well as action on racial harassment, and Black co-ops. A second conference is being planned.

Owner Occupiers

Money: If after you take on a mortgage, you suffer a drop in your income, you will have to increase your income or cut your mortgage costs to avoid losing your home.

Increase your income: If you become unemployed, or are working less than 30 hours per week, claim supplementary benefit. Go to your local unemployment office and ask for Form B1. You will need to supply details about your income, savings, bank statements, and mortgage payments, etc. Once your claim is decided, you can ask for a detailed breakdown of how it has been worked out on Form A124. If you are not satisfied, get independent advice. If you are working more than 30 hours per week, consider applying for the following money benefits. **Family Income Supplement** (FIS): This is a weekly allowance for families on a low wage. Get Form FISI from your Post Office. **Housing Benefit**: This can help towards the rates and ground rent if you are a leaseholder or live in a mobile home. Apply to the council, (see Housing Benefit above). **Child Benefit**: This allowance is for each dependent child. Ask for a form from the Post Office. **One Parent Benefit**: This is for women bringing up children on their own. Get Form CH11 from the DHSS. **Rate Relief**: If you are a rated occupier, the local authority has the power to reduce or refund your rates on grounds of poverty - for instance if you have failed to claim a rate rebate and got into arrears. If you are disabled, you can get rates relief on special facilities. Contact your local authority for details. **Education Benefits**: some local councils give the following benefits. Ask at your local education office about: school clothing vouchers; study grants for children staying on at school; school fares; free school meals. **Medical Benefits**: free prescriptions, Form P11; dental charges, Form D11; free glasses, Form G11; milk and vitamins, Form MV11. Obtain these from the Post Office or DHSS.

Income Tax: Your income tax position will have changed if you are getting divorced or separated. The income tax office will not know until you tell them. If you are left on your own, you may be able to claim additional allowances.

Cut your mortgage costs: It may be possible for you to cut your mortgage costs if you have suffered a reduction in income. If you anticipate any difficulties *get advice immediately*. These are the possible courses of action: if you have an endowment mortgage, you can cut your costs by switching to an ordinary repayment mortgage (See Access to Owner Occupation); you may be able to pay interest only for a period, while you arrange your affairs or get another job; you may be able to extend the term of the mortgage, which will reduce your monthly repayments.

It is important to remember that everything suggested above is just an outline. If you are having difficulty paying your mortgage, go to a local advice agency to discuss your problem as soon as possible.

Relationship Breakdown

Married Women: If you are married, and your relationship is breaking down remember both of you have the right to live in the home until the marriage is ended. If he has behaved violently or caused distress to you and your children, you can apply for an injunction (that is, an order of the Court) to restrain him, or exclude him from the home. If the house is in his name only, you should 'register a charge' to prevent him from selling the house without your knowledge. See a solicitor about this. Do not agree to sell the house until you have had independent advice and considered all the options. Do not be put off by the thought of legal costs. You may be entitled to Legal Aid to help you with the cost of legal action. Act. Get advice.

Unmarried women: If the house is in your joint names, remember you both have rights to live there. If your partner is violent, you may be able to obtain an injunction (that is, an order of the Court) to restrain him or exclude him from the home. Do not agree to a sale of the home until you have had independent advice and considered all the options; get advice quickly.

If the house is owned solely by your partner can you establish a financial interest in the home? Have you made direct or indirect financial contributions to the deposit, or mortgage? Have you done building work on the house? You may be able to establish a claim. Was the house bought 'for the family?' You may be able to establish a claim. Did you give up something substantial in order to move in, eg a secure home? You may be able to establish a claim. If none of these apply, you may have no right to remain once you are asked to leave. Get advice quickly.

The above points are merely a summary of the most urgent things to remember. You should also get independent advice. Useful reading:

Rights Guide for Home Owners, available from: CPAG, 1 Macklin Street, WC2 5NH, and from SHAC 189a Old Brompton Road, SW5 OAR (£1.50).

Repairs: One of the biggest problems facing owner occupiers is the cost of maintenance and repair of the home. To finance the cost of the repair if you are on a limited income, consider applying for a grant from your local authority. Apply to the Home Improvement Grants Section. Some

Once you have the money, choosing a builder is a big problem. If there is one you know, or one who is recommended to you, you may be all right. If you want a woman builder in your home, contact the Women and Manual Trades group, who keep a register of women builders, electricians and plumbers. If you have any complaints about the quality of the work that your builders have done, contact your local advice agency or:

Women and Manual Trades, 52-54 Featherstone Street, EC1 (251 9192).

Council Housing Waiting List Registration/Homelessness

Barking Waiting List Registration, Housing Department, Heathway, Dagenham, Essex (592 4500). Application to the Homeless Families Unit Green Lane, Dagenham, Essex (592 4500).

Barnet Waiting List Registration, Housing Department, 65 Watford Way, Hendon, NW4 (202 8282). Application to the Homeless Families Unit, Housing Department, 65 Watford Way, Hendon, NW4 (202 8282, including emergencies out of hours).

Bexley Waiting List Registration, Housing Department, Civic Centre, Broadway, Bexleyheath, Kent (303 7777). Application to the Homeless Families Unit, Housing Department, Civic Centre, Broadway, Bexleyheath, Kent (303 7777; emergencies out of hours telephone police).

Brent Waiting List Registration, Brent Housing Aid Centre, Robert Owen House, 192 High Road, NW10 (451 0911). Application to the Homeless Families Unit, Brent House Annexe, 356-368 High Road, HA9 6BY (903 1400 ext 640; emergencies out of hours, telephone Social Services Duty Officer 903 1400).

Bromley Waiting List Registration, Housing Department, Sherman House, Sherman Road, BR1 3TG (464 3333). Application to the Homeless

grants, for essential amenities, are mandatory. Most grants, however, are discretionary, and many local authorities are cutting this area of activity. Contact your local advice agency for further information. Also consider applying for a loan from your lender or bank. If you are on supplementary benefit, the DHSS will meet the interest on loans for essential repairs. If you are not on supplementary benefit, you will have to meet the repayments yourself. Sometimes builders will offer to arrange loans through finance companies. Avoid this at all costs. The rates are usually very high, the penalties are usually heavy. If you are on supplementary benefit, or would be entitled to it if you claimed, you can apply for a 'single payment' to meet the cost of essential repairs. The money must not be available from any other source. The cost must not exceed £325 (until November 1985).

Families Unit, Sherman House, Sherman Road, BR1 3TG (464 3333; emergencies out of hours, 464 4848).

Camden Waiting List Registration, Housing Department, Bidborough House, 38 Bidborough Street, WC1 (278 4444). Application to the Homeless Persons Unit, 207-215 Instrument House, King's Cross Road, WC1 (837 4266; emergencies out of hours, 278 4444).

City Waiting List Registration Housing Department, North Office Block, Guildhall, EC2 (606 3030). Application to the Homeless Families Unit Housing Department, Guildhall, EC2 (606 3030).

Croydon Waiting List Registration, Housing Advice Centre, Taberner House, Park Lane, Croydon, CR9 3JS (686 4433). Application to the Homeless Families Unit, Taberner House, Park Lane, Croydon, CR9 3JS (686 4433; emergencies out of hours, 654 8100).

Ealing Waiting List Registration, Housing Advisory Section, Town Hall Annexe, New Broadway, W5 (579 2424). Application to the Homeless Families Unit, Town Hall Annexe, New Broadway, W5 (579 2424).

Enfield Waiting List Registration, Housing Department, Civic Centre, Silver Street, Enfield EN1 3XA (366 6565). Application to the Homeless Families Unit, Housing Department, Civic Centre, Silver Street, Enfield EN1 3XA (366 6565).

Greenwich Waiting List Registration, Housing Department, Peggy Middleton House, 50 Woolwich New Road, SE18 (854 8888). Application to the Homeless Families Unit, 121 Charlton Road, SE3 (858 7178; emergencies out of hours, 854 0366).

Hackney Waiting List Registration, Housing Advisory Centre, 287 Mare Street, E8 1EB (986 3191). Application to the Homeless Persons Unit, Housing Emergencies Section, Mare Street, E8 (986 3191).

Hammersmith and Fulham Waiting List Registration, Housing Aid Centre, 77 Glenthorne Road, W6 (748 3020). Application to the Homeless Persons Units: 77 Glenthorne Road, W6 (748 3020; emergencies out of hours fire and flood - ring 748 3020. All other emergencies ring police).

Haringey Waiting List Registration, Housing Action Centre, 13-27 Station Road, N22 (881 3000). Application to the Homeless Persons Unit, Housing Action Centre, 13-27 Station Road, N22 (881 3000; emergencies out of hours, 558 4716).

Harrow Waiting List Registration, Housing Department, Civic Centre, Station Road, Harrow, HA1 2VW (863 5611). Homeless Persons Unit, PO Box 65, Civic Centre, Station Road, Wealdstone, Middlesex (863 5611 x 2096; emergencies out of hours, 863 5611).

Havering Waiting List Registration, Housing Aid Centre, 2nd floor, Mercury House, Mercury Gardens, Romford RM1 3DT (70 66999). Homeless Persons Unit, Housing Aid Centre, 2nd floor, Mercury House, Mercury Gardens, Romford RM1 3DT (70 66999; emergencies out of hours contact police).

Hillingdon Waiting List Registration, Housing Department, Civic Centre, Uxbridge, Middx (0895 50111). Homeless Persons Unit, Emergency Housing Unit, 64 High Street, Uxbridge (0895 50111 x 3739 emergencies out of hours, 0895 50111).

Hounslow Waiting List Registration, Housing Department, Civic Centre, Lampton Road, Hounslow, Middx (570 7728). Homeless Persons Unit, Civic Centre, Lampton Road, Hounslow, Middx (570 7728; emergencies out of hours, Social Services Duty Officer 570 7728).

Islington Waiting List Registration, Housing Advisory Service, 292 Essex Road, N1 (226 3300). Homeless Persons Unit, 292 Essex Road, N1 (226 3300; emergencies out of hours, 226 1234 for Duty Officer).

Kensington and Chelsea Waiting List Registration, Housing Department, Town Hall, Hornton Street, W8 (937 5464). Homeless Persons Unit, 2nd floor, Town Hall, Hornton Street, W8 (937 5464; emergencies out of hours, 828 8070).

Kingston Upon Thames Waiting List Registration, Housing Department, Guildhall Extension, St James Road, Kingston Upon Thames (546 2121). Homeless Persons Unit, Housing Welfare Office, Guildhall Extension, St James Road, Kingston Upon Thames (546 2121).

Lambeth Waiting List Registration, Housing Advice Centre, 2-7 Town Hall Parade, Brixton Hill, SW2 (274 7722). Homeless Persons Unit Housing Advice Centre, 2-7 Town Hall Parade, Brixton Hill, SW2 (274 7722, including emergencies out of hours).

Lewisham Waiting List Registration, Housing Department, Leegate House, Lee Green, SE12 (852 4391). Homeless Persons Unit, Families Admission Centre, 340 Lewisham High Street, SE13 (690 8211, including emergencies out of hours).

Merton Waiting List Registration, Housing Department, Worsfold House, Chapel Orchard, Church Road, Mitcham (640 1931). Homeless Persons Unit, Worsfold House, Chapel Orchard, Church Road, Mitcham (640 1931; emergencies out of hours contact police).

Newham Waiting List Registration, Housing Department, 91 The Grove, Stratford, E15 (534 4545). Homeless Persons Unit, 91 The Grove, Stratford, E15 (534 4545; emergencies out of hours, 590 6060).

Redbridge Waiting List Registration, Housing Aid Centre, 9-13 York Road, Ilford, IG1 2AD (553 4133). Homeless Persons Unit Reception, Housing Department, Valentines Mansion, Emerson Road, Ilford (518 6999; emergencies out of hours, 550 2065).

Richmond Upon Thames Waiting List Registration, Housing Department, Regal House, London Road, Twickenham, TW1 3QB (891 1433). Homeless Persons Unit, 1st floor, Regal House, London Road, Twickenham, TW1 3QB (891 1433; emergencies out of hours, phone police).

Southwark Waiting List Registration At your local office: Camberwell, 92 Poulner Way, SE15 (701 6391) Dulwich; 47a East Dulwich Road, SE22 (693 3399); Peckham, 25 Ruby Street, SE15 (639 9881); Bermondsey, 1-3 Spa Road, SE16 (237 6677); Walworth, 241-471 Wendover, Thurlow Street, SE17 (701 7174); sub-office 177-179 Walworth Road, SE17 (701 0976); Rotherhithe, 153-159 Abbeyfield Road, SE16 (237 6644). Homeless Persons Unit at your local office, as above.

Sutton Waiting List Registration, Housing Department, Civic Offices, St Nicholas Way, Sutton SM1 1EA (661 5000). Homeless Persons Unit, Housing Aid Centre, St Nicholas Way, Sutton (661 5000; emergencies out of hours, contact police).

Tower Hamlets Waiting List Registration, Housing Department, Cheviot House, 227-233 Commercial Road, E1 2BU (790 1818). Homeless Persons Unit, Cheviot House, 227-233 Commercial Road, E1 2BU (790 1818).

Waltham Forest Waiting List Registration, Housing Department, 1 Wood Street, Walthamstow, E17 3JU (527 5544). Homeless Persons Unit, 1 Wood Street, Walthamstow, E17 3JU (527 5544).

Wandsworth Waiting List Registration, Housing Aid Centre, Rear of Town Hall, Wandsworth High Street, SW18 2PU (871 6817). Homeless Persons Unit Wandsworth Housing Aid Centre, Rear of Town Hall, Wandsworth High Street, SW18 2PU (871 6848 Emergencies out of hours, 871 6000).

Westminster Waiting List Registration, At District Offices: Victoria (SW1), Covent Garden (WC2) & Pimlico, District Office 1, 137 Lupus Street, SW1Y 3HE (834 7706); Marylebone (W1, NW1), St John's Wood (NW8), District Office 2, Westminster Council

House, Marylebone Road, NW1 5PT (828 8070); Paddington (W2) part of Bayswater (W9), East of Sutherland Ave (odd nos), District Office 3, North West Housing Office, 261 Harrow Road, W2 5EH (289 2221); Queens Park (W10, parts of W9) and West of Sutherland Ave (even nos), District Office 4, 3 Dowland Street, W10 4DU (696 9444), Homeless Persons Unit; Crawford Place Dwelling, 11 Crawford Place, W1 (724 2401; emergencies out of hours, 828 8070).

Hostels

Please note that inclusion in this list does not mean recommendation. Different hostels offer accommodation to different groups of women - as the hostels are listed alphabetically, please read through. General information available from:

National Association of Voluntary Hostels, 33 Long Acre, WC2 (836 0193) *Guide To Women's Hostels in London,* SHAC (London Housing Aid Centre), 189a Old Brompton Road, SW5 0AR, (£2.50).

Academy House, 42 Ladbroke Grove, London, W11 (727 7379). For students aged 18-25, mixed. Apply by letter. References required.

Ada Lewis Trust, Head Office, Knights Court, 6-8 St John's Square, EC1M 4DE (251 6091). Women only, any age. 3 hostels. Apply through Head Office.

Ada Lewis Trust, 1 Dalmeny Avenue, N7. Women only, any age. Apply to Head Office.

Ada Lewis Trust, 2 Palliser Road, W14. Any age, women only. Apply to Head Office.

Ada Lewis House, Empire Way, Wembley, Middlesex. Any age, women only. Apply to Head Office.

Alone in London Service, West Lodge, 190 Euston Road, NW1 (387 3010). 16-19, mixed. Advice, drop-in or telephone.

Alcoholics Recovery Project runs two houses for women with drinking problems. Any age. Apply through:

Women's Alcohol Centre, St Paul's Road, N1 (226 4581)

Alcoholics Recovery Project, 6 Kings Cross Road, WC1 (837 2686) 9.30 am-1 pm.

Alcoholics Recovery Project, St Anselm's Vestry, Sancroft Street, SE11 (735 6217) 10 am-12 noon.

Alcoholics Recovery Project, 318 New Cross Road, SE14 (691 2886) 9.30 am-12 noon.

Ambrosden Hostel, 1 Ambrosden Avenue, SW1 (834 1451). 18-35, mixed. Application form.

Ann Elizabeth Hostel, 30 Collingham Place, SW5 (370 4821). 18-35, women only. Telephone, turn up or write. Personal interview.

Annesley House Methodist Hostel, 2 Princes Way, SW19. Younger women 17-21, women only. Write enclosing SAE. Waiting list.

Arbours Association, 41 Weston Park, N8 (340 8125). Any age, mixed. For people in emotional crisis. Very small, intensive support.

Astor Youth & Student Services Ltd, Head Office (for reservations and information), 76 Cale Street, SW3 (352 8424/7045). For travellers and students. Younger women, 17-30, mixed. Referrals through Central Office.

Avon Hotel, 50 Norfolk Square, W2 (723 4921). For students, travellers and those needing cheap accommodation. Mixed, any age. Ring for vacancies.

Baptist Union, Newington Court, 1 Collins Road, N5 (359 2495). Students and workers. Younger women, 17-26. Write for application form. References required.

Bartrams Student Hostel, Rowland Hill Street, NW3 (794 4504). Students and workers. Younger women, 18-25, women only. Write with SAE.

Look Ahead (Beacon Hostels) Housing Association Ltd runs four hostels:

Beacon House, Castle Lane, SW1 (828 9137). People in work, seeking employment or students. 18-65, mixed. Interview.

Beacon House, 30-31 Leinster Square, W2 (229 2220). In work, seeking work, or students. 18-65, mixed. Interview.

Beacon House, 7 Dock Street, E1 (481 1326/4200). In work, seeking work, or students. 18-65, mixed. Interview.

Beacon House, Princess Beatrice House, Finborough Road, SW10 (370 0755). Students, workers, job seekers, 18-65. Ring or write.

Bristol Youth Hostel, 38 Norfolk Square, W2 (723 0114). Workers, students and travellers. Any age, mixed. Telephone.

Burlington House, Head Office, 6 St Johns Square, EC1 (251 6091).

Burlington House, Dwight Court, Burlington Place, SW6. 18-36, mixed. Through Head Office, 3 flats for disabled. Vacancies rare.

Mr and Mrs John Beech Home, 215-217 Chingford Mount Road, E4. Any age, women only. Through Head Office.

Camden Accommodation Scheme, 33 Grafton Road, NW5 (267 2953). Mail to: PO Box 373 NW1. Young homeless people 16-22, mixed. Referrals from Social Services, Probation Service, agencies and some self-referrals.

Camden Accommodation Scheme, 175 Arlington Road, NW1 (267 2953). Mail to: PO Box 373 NW1. Young homeless people 16-22, women only. Referrals from Social Services, Probation Service, agencies and some self referrals.

Camden Resettlement Unit, 2-5 Birkenhead Street, WC1 (278 6466/7). 17-60, women only. Referral by telephone on day of need essential.

Carr Gomm Society, 38 Gomm Road, SE16. For lonely people, any age, mixed. Waiting list.

CASA, 147 Brecknock Road, N19 (485 1945). For alcoholics, 25-55, mixed. Ring or write.

Cecil House, 34-35 Boswell Street, WC1 (940 9828/9). 22-70, women only. Telephone.

Cecil House, 266 Waterloo Road, SE1 (928 5752). 18+, women only. Telephone.

Centrepoint (night shelter), 65a Shaftsbury Ave, W1 (734 1075). Younger women, 16-21. Queue outside at 8pm.

Chester House Hostel, 1 Chester House, Pages Lane, N10 (883 8204). For workers and students (Methodists preferred), 18-25, mixed. Write with Church references.

Christ Today Community Trust, 31 Gillender St, E14 (515 3023). Any age, women only. Referrals mainly from agencies but some self-referrals.

Christian Alliance, Dashwood House, 6 Pembridge Square, W2 (229 7848). Workers and students. Younger women, 16-30, women only. References required.

Christian Alliance, 54 Queensgate, SW1 (589 1988). Workers and students. 17-28, women only. References required.

Christian Alliance Centre, Secker Street, SE1 (633 0128). Workers and students. 18-30, mixed. Application form, references required.

Church Army, 1 Cosway Street, NW1 (262 3818). 18-55, women only. Direct or via agency.

Church Army, 28 Greencoat Place, SW1 (834 0584). Age any, women only. Direct or via agency.

Church Army, Elgood House, 84 Bell Street, NW1 (402 4971). Workers and students. 18-55, women only. References required.

Community of All Saints, All Saints House, 82 Margaret Street, W1N 8LH (636 1490). Workers and students. Younger women, 17-21, women only. References required, vacancies rare.

Cyrenians (West London Cyrenians), Cyrenian Short Stay House, 9 Basing Street, W11 (221 1943). 16-65, single homeless, mixed. Referrals from anywhere, workers' decision.

Cyrenian Short Stay House, 57 Cambridge Gardens, W10 (696 4630). 16-65, single homeless, mixed. Referrals from anywhere, workers' decision.

Cyrenians (West London Cyrenians), Long Stay Houses, Cyrenians, 96 Barons Court Road, W14 (381 2278). All homeless people. 18-65, mixed. Prospective residents interviewed by house members.

Cyrenians, 40 Charleville Road, W14 (381 1662). All homeless people. 18+, mixed. Prospective residents interviewed by house members.

Deaconess Guest House, 90 Holland Road, W14 (603 3773). Younger women, 16-25, women only. Telephone or write.

Don Ludwig House, 372 Gray's Inn Road, WC1 (837 5318). For travellers. 15-30, mixed.

Driscoll House, 172-180 New Kent Road, SE1 (703 4175). Any age, mixed. Personal interview with manager.

Ealing Community Relations Hostel, 376 Uxbridge Road, W5 (992 4036). For Black, Asian homeless people. 16-21, mixed. Referrals 24 hours from anywhere. Generally two day referral period.

Elizabeth Baxter Hostel, 52 Lambeth Road, SE1 (928 4239). For workers. 17-56, women only. Personal interview with warden.

Elizabeth House, 94 Redcliffe Gardens, SW10 (370 1279). For ex-drug dependents and workers. 24-34, mixed. Selection through interview.

First Base, 29 Cadogan Terrace, E9 (986 7007). For homeless young people in Hackney, 16-25. Referrals from agencies and self-referrals.

Gayfere Hostel, 8 Gayfere Street, SW1 (222 6894). For students. 17-25, mixed. Bring identity card.

German Catholic Centre, Lioba House, 40 Exeter Road, NW2 (452 8566). For students and workers. 17-30, women only. Interview.

Girls' Friendly Society, 126 Queens Gate, SW7 (589 9628). For workers. Any age for short stay. 17-25 for long stay. Bookings can be made in advance.

Girls' Friendly Society, 32-34 Evelyn Gardens, SW7 (370 2121). For students. Young women, 16-21, women only. In writing. Advanced booking.

Grafton House Hostel, 278 The Vale, W3 (749 4831). Any age, mixed. Telephone for vacancies. This is a private hotel.

Grangewood Lodge Hotel, 104 Clova Road, E7 (534 0637). Any age, mixed. Telephone for vacancies. This is a private hotel.

Hostel for homeless women. 59 Greek Street, W1 (253 0201).

The Heath Hostel, 2 Holford Road, NW3 (435 9217). For workers and students. 18-30, women only. References required.

Hibbert House, 102 Albert Street, NW1 (485 4784). Students, workers and travellers. 18-25, mixed. Telephone for vacancies.

Highbury Hotel, 48 Highbury Grove, N5 (226 4002). 21, mixed. Telephone.

Holy Cross Convent, 3 Fitzjohns Avenue, NW3 (435 5249). Students only (Catholics preferred). 18-25, women only. Write. Reference required.

Home of Peace, 108 Salisbury Road, NW6 (624 4107). Women only, 35 . Ring for vacancies.

Homeless Action, 52-54 Featherstone St, EC1 (278 6688/9). Has several hostels in different parts of London. Any age, women only. Ring or write in advance for interview.

House of St Barnabas, 1 Greek Street, W1 (437 1894/5508). 17-70, women only. Referrals from agencies and self referrals.

Howard and Hillibrand Hotel, 64-65 Princes Square, W2 (727 6062). Any age, mixed. Ring for vacancies.

Howard House, 49 Princes Square, W2 (727 6062). 16+, mixed. Telephone for vacancies.

International Lutheran Students' Centre, Thanet Street, WC1 (388 4044). Students. 16-60, mixed. Written evidence of study. References required.

International Students' Housing Society, International House, Brookhill Road, SE18 (854 1418/9). Students and Trainees. 17+, mixed. References required.

International Students' House, 229 Great Portland Street, W1. Students and trainees. 18-35, mixed. Ring or write.Also includes Mary Trevelyan Hall, York Terrace East, NW1 (486 6881).

International Student Trust, 10 York Terrace, NW1 (486 6881). Students only. 18+, mixed. Application form.

Irish Centre Hostels Ltd, St. Louise, 33 Medway Street, SW1 (222 2071). Working women and students. 18-25, women only. Irish women. References required.

J D Students' House, 285 Pentonville Road, N1 (278 5385). Students and travellers. 17-28, mixed. Student card or travel documents necessary.

Jerome House, 25 Harrington Gardens, SW7 (373 2789). Students (mostly overseas). Any age, mixed. Ring or write. References may be required.

Kaleidoscope Youth and Community Project, 40-46 Cromwell Road, Kingston Upon Thames, Surrey (549 2681). Young people, 18-22, mixed. Interview at staff meeting.

Kipper, 78 Whitehorse Road, E1 (790 0637). Young homeless people. 17-25, mixed. Mostly referrals through agencies.

Lee Abbey International Student Club, 26 Courtfield Gardens, SW5 (373 7286). Students, travellers and workers. 18+, mixed. Ring or write.

London Friendship Centre, 3 Creswick Road, W3 (992 0221). Students, travellers and workers. Any age, mixed.

London Hostels Association runs 15 hostels, 13 which are open to the public. Head Office, 54 Eccleston Square, SW1 (828 3263). Workers and students. 16-55, mixed. Apply to the Head Office. References required.

Marathon House, 14 Barkston Gardens, SW5 (373 5782). Workers and students. 18-40, women only. Interview with manager.

Marian Lodge, 5 The Downs, SW20 (946 3564). 20-30. Interview. References required.

Messenger House Trust, 8 Malcolm Road, SW19 (947 0969). 18-25, mixed. Referrals via attendance at large group meetings.

Methodist International House, 4 Inverness Terrace, W2 (229 5101). Students (many from overseas). 18+, mixed. Any denomination. References required.

Methodist International House, 1-5 Lambeth Road, SE1 (735 4568). Mixed. 18+.

Methodist Youth Hostel, 1 Chester House, Pages Lane, N10. (883 8204). Workers, students and overseas visitors. 18-25, mixed. Referrals from Methodist ministers. Application form.

Montoba Hostel, 159 Fordwych Road, NW2 (452 1890). Students and trainees mainly. Any age, mixed. Telephone or write.

More House, W. London Catholic Chaplaincy, 53 Cromwell Road, SW7 (584 2040). Students in term time, visitors July/August. 18+, mixed. Early application for University year essential.

Moullin Memorial Hostel, 24-26 Mount Park Road, W5 (997 4343). Students and workers (Methodists preferred). 18-25, women only. Personal interview. Church referral preferred.

Mount Carmel, 12 Aldingham Road, SW16 (769 7674). Recovering alcoholics. 16-60, women only. Most referrals by agencies.

New Ways Trust, Link House, 66 Cheam Road, Sutton, Surrey. People on probation, or on bail. 17-25, mixed. Applicants must make a trial visit. Few women referred.

Nightwatch Hostel, 89 Wellesley Road, Croydon, Surrey (688 5031). Single homeless. 16-65, mixed. Croydon residents. Prefer agency referrals.

Nile Lodge, The Capitano Sisters, Queenswalk, W5 (997 3933). Students and workers. 18-25, women only. Any denomination. Interview. Reference required.

Norfolk House, 54 Norfolk Square, W2 (723 1359). Travellers and students. Any age, mixed. Telephone.

Olave House, World Association of Girl Guides and Girl Scouts, 45 Longridge Road, SW5 (370 2574). For past and present members of the World Association of Girl Guides, students, workers and travellers. Any age, women only.

Opus Dei, International Catholic Lay Association, Ashwell House, 29 Pembridge Square, W2 (229 3584). 18-22, women only. Any denomination. Interview and reference required.

Parchmore Church Youth and Community Centre, 55 Parchmore Road, Thornton Heath, Croydon (653 7353). Young homeless. 16-21, mixed.

Patricia House, 18 Bramham Gardens, SW5 (370 3739). Workers and students. 18-40, women only. Interview with manager.

Phoenix House, 1 Eliot Bank, SE23 (699 5748). Ex-drug users. Any age, mixed. Only people motivated to give up drugs.

Poor Servants of the Mother of God, St Gabriel's, 9 Pembridge Square, W2 (229 1424). Workers and students. Women only. Any denomination. References required.

Poor Servants of the Mother of God, St. Philomena's, 70/71 Euston Square, NW1 (387 9084). 18-25, women only. References required. Waiting list.

Portland Hostel, 36 Portland Rise, N4 (800 0787). Students. 17-30, mixed. Students' card required.

Prince Arthur House, 170 Wendling Estate, Haverstock Road, NW5 (485 9947). Young homeless. 18-30, mixed. Phone or write first, interview and then residents make final decision.

Providence Row, 50 Crispin Street, E1 (247 2159). Any age, mixed. Need a letter from referral agency.

Religious Order of Mary Immaculate, 15 Southwell Gardens, SW7 (373 3869). Workers and students. 17-26, women only. Write or ring. Interview.

Religious Order of Mary Immaculate, 44 Augustus Road, SW19 (788 9477). Workers and students (mostly from abroad). 17-22, women only. Any denomination. References required.

Riverpoint, 229 King Street, W6 (741 2888). 15-65, mixed. Need a letter from a referral agency. 7 nights only.

St Christopher, 36 Warwick Road, SW5. 17-21, mixed. Through Head Office, 53 Warwick Road, SW5 (370 1083).

St Giles Centre, Sojourner House, 5 De Crespigny Park, SE5 (703 8085). Young homeless women only, 16-21. Some self-referrals.

St. Lukes House, 25a Wincott Street, SE11 (735 8665). Alcoholics. 25-55. Must dry out first. Few women. Apply direct.

St. Monica House, Augustinian Sisters, 83 Clapham Road, SW9. Students and workers. Any age, mixed. Any denomination. References required.

St. Mungos, 83 Endell Street, WC2 (240 5431). 20+, mixed.

St. Ursula's Hostel, 16 Brooke Street, EC1 (405 7148). For workers (Church of England). 18-60, women only. Written application. Reference from priest required.

Salvation Army, Concord House, 49-51 Leinster Square, W2 (229 7388). Students. 18-30, women only (mostly from overseas). Written application form. Interview.

Salvation Army, Red Shield Hotel, 66 Buckingham Road, SW1 (222 1164). Workers (primarily in the forces). Any age, mixed. Telephone or write.

Salvation Army, Hopetown House, 60 Old Montague Street, E1 (247 1004). Any age, women only. Ring or write.

Saney Guruji Hostel, 18a Holland Villas, W14 (603 3704). Students and travellers. 18-26, mixed. Telephone.

Mrs Sawady, 18 Manstone Road, NW2 (452 1835). Students only. 18-26, women only. Telephone for interview.

Shortstay Young Homeless Project, 4 Bina Gardens, SW5 (373 0635). Young homeless. 16-25, mixed. Mainly take referrals from agencies.

Simon Community Nightshelter, House of Hospitality, 50 St Pancras Way, NW1 (388 6006).

Single Homeless Project, 63 Preston Road, E11 (530 6319). 25+, mixed. Referrals from all sources.

Single Homeless Project, 4 Tunley Road, NW10 (961 0190). 25+, mixed. Referrals from all sources.

Single Homeless Project, 57 Craven Park, Harlesden, NW10 (961 3286). 25+, mixed. Alcoholics/mentally ill. Referrals from all sources.

Single Homeless Project, 28 Lithos Road, NW3 (435 5012). 25+, mixed. Referrals from all sources.

Single Homeless Project, 43-44 The Park, W5 (840 5710). 25+, mixed. Referrals from all sources.

Sisters of Charity, St. Vincent de Paul, Loreto Club, 14 Blandford Street, (935 3229). Students and workers. 16-26, women only. Written application, two references required. Send SAE.

Sisters of Mercy, three hostels at 1,5,7 Gun Street, E1 (377 9551). Students and workers. 18-50, women only. Write or ring for application form. Interview. References required.

Sisters of St. Dorothy, International Students Centre, 99 Frognal, NW3 (794 6893). Students. 16-25, women only. Any denomination. References required.

Sisters of the Cross and Passion, St. John's House, 44 Duncan Terrace, N1 (226 9854). For business girls. 18-25. References required. Interview.

Sisters of the Resurrection, Resurrection House, 44 Ennismore Gardens, SW7 (584 1616). Students. 16-25, women only. Any denomination. References required.

Stopover, 48 Dacres Road, Forest Hill, SE23 (699 1574). Young people, 15-21, mixed. Ring or through an agency.

Susan Lawrence Hostel, 170 Kings Cross Road, WC1 (837 5919). Students and workers. 18+, women only. Interview with warden. Run by London Borough of Islington.

Sutherland House Hostel Group, 35 Bolton Gardens, SW5 (373 5877). Workers and students. 18-40, women only. Interview with manager.

Theatre Girls' Club, 59 Greek Street, W1 (402 1555). 18-60. Apply direct.

Toynbee Hall, 28 Commercial Street, E1 (247 3633). For people who live in a residential community. Any age: mostly 20-30, mixed. Apply direct. Residents undertake to do a certain amount of voluntary work each week.

Trafalgar House Trust Hostel, 4 Dean Road, NW2. Students and workers. Any age, mixed. Telephone.

Ujima Hostels, several hostels in London. Interview at Ujima Advice centres: 413-419 Harrow Road, NW10 (960 8179). For Afro-Caribbean. 18-26, mixed.

Unity, 90-92 Lancaster Road, W11 (229 2255/6). Young Afro Caribbeans. 15-20, mixed. Some self-referrals.

Vaughan House Hostel, 49 Holland Road, W14 (603 6436). Workers, students and travellers. Any age, mixed. Ring or write.

Verona Sisters, 2 Chiswick Lane, W4 (994 4951). Students and workers. 18-25, women only. Any denomination. References required. Interview. Rare vacancies.

Victoria League Students Hostel, 55 Leinster Road, W2 (229 3961). Full time students of the Commonwealth. 18-30, mixed. Ring or write.

Warwick House Hotel, 32 Warwick Road, SW5 (373 4293). Any age, mixed. Telephone. A private hotel.

West Hampstead Students' Youth Hostel, 5,8,10 Agamemnon Road, NW6 (794 9943). Anyone. 15-50, mixed. Telephone. Frequent vacancies.

William Hart House, 358 City Road, EC1. Crisis intervention for multi-drug abusers. 16-35. Self referrals.

59 Windsor Road, (Commercial Guest House), W5 (579 4299). Workers. Any age, mixed. Write or phone.

YWCA: hostels in Acton, Bayswater, Chelsea, Ealing, Earls Court, Euston, Finchley, Hampstead, Holborn, Kensington, Kings Cross, Putney, Regents Park, St. Marylebone, Victoria, Bromley, Croydon, Dagenham, Harrow. Contact Central Office for details of vacancies: YWCA, 57 Great Russell Street, WC1B 3BD (430 1524).

Advice Agencies

(Also see **Borough Information** where further advice agencies are listed.)

London-Wide Agencies:

SHAC, The London Housing Aid Centre, 189a Old Brompton Road, SW5 0AR (373 7276). Mon, Tues, Wed 1-4.30, Thurs 9.30-4.30. Telephone advice. Access: N.

Housing Advice Switchboard, 47 Charing Cross Road, WC2 (434 2522). 24 hour telephone advice for childless people. Access: N.

Alone in London Service, West Lodge, 190 Euston Road, NW1 (387 3010). Advice for young people.

National Council for One Parent Families, 255 Kentish Town Road, NW5 2LX (267 1361). Mon-Fri 9.15-5.15 by appointment. Access: N.

Shelter, 157 Waterloo Road, SE1 (633 9377).

Women's Aid Federation England, 52/54 Featherstone Street, EC1 (251 6537). Access: A.

Barnet

Barnet Housing Aid Centre (independent), 317 Regents Park Road, N3 (349 2456). Opening hours: Mon-Fri 10-1, Tues 10-1, 5-7. Phone for an appointment. Access: N.

East Finchley Neighbourhood Centre, Legal Advice Session, 42 Church Lane, N2 (444 6265). Wed 6.30-8. Access: A.

Housing Advisory Service (Council), Civic Centre, Bexleyheath, Kent (303 7777 ext 2062). Mon-Fri 9-5.

Brent

Housing Aid Centre (Council), Robert Owen House, 192 High Road, NW10 (451 0911) Mon, Tues, Wed & Thurs 9-1, Fri 9-3.45. Access: A.

Harlesden Advice Centre, 25 High Street, NW10 (965 2590). Mon 10.30-12.30, Tues 2-4, Thurs 2-4. Telephone advice outside those hours.

West London Community Law Centre, 59 Kingsgate Road, NW6 (328 4501/4523). Mon, Tues, Thurs, Fri 11-2, Wed, Thursday 4-7. Phone Mon-Fri 10-5. Except Wed am. Access: A.

Bromley

Age Concern, 86 Tweedy Road, Bromley (460 1676) Mon, Thurs 9-5; Fri 9-4.40 (Home visits done). Access: N.

Voluntary Service Council, 94 Tweedy Road, Bromley (464 2287) (Accommodation Adviser). Mon-Thurs 9.30-4.30, Fri 9.30-2.

Camden

Housing Aid Centre (Council), 83 Euston Road, NW1 (388 0331). Mon and Fri 9.30-4.30; Tues & Thurs 1-4.30. Access: A.

West Hampstead Housing Aid Centre (Council), 179-181 West End Lane, NW6 (625 0251). (Emergency No 624 4779, harassment, illegal eviction etc). Mon, Tues, and Fri 10-12, Mon, Thur, Fri 2-4; Tues 5-7. Access: P.

Inquire Neighbourhood Advice, 85 Charlton Street, NW1 (388 0226/0094). Mon, Tues, Wed & Fri 10-4. Access: P. (small door; upstairs WC).

Community Law Centre, 146 Kentish Town Road, NW1 (485 6672/5). Mon, Wed 10-5, Fri 10-4. All week for phone calls except Thurs am. Eve sessions by appointment. Access: P.

Mary Ward Centre, 42 Queens Square, WC1 (831 7009/7000). By appointment, Mon-Fri 9.30-5.30. Access: A.

Central London Community Law Centre, 13 Ingestre Place, W1 (437 5764). Mon-Fri 10-3.30 to make an appointment, Wed 12-2 and 5-7 general queries. Access: N.

Neighbourhood Advice Centre, Bedford House, 35 Emerald Street, WC1 (405 2379).

City of London

Housing Aid Centre (Council), Guildhall, EC2 (606 3030 ext 2646). Mon-Fri 9-5. Access: A.

Croydon

Housing Aid Centre, Taberner House, Park Lane, Croydon CR9 3JS (687 4433). Mon-Fri 9-5.

Croydon Housing Aid Service (CHAS) (independent) 10a Station Road, Croydon (688 7900). Mon-Fri 9.30-4. Interviews by appointment. Access: N.

Norwood/Norbury CHAS, (Independent) 22 Norbury Rise, SW16. Correspondence only.

Ealing

Ealing Housing Aid Service (EHAS) (independent), 92-94 Warwick Road, W5.

CHAS Southall (independent), Havelock Centre, Havelock Road, Southall (571 2241). Tues 4-7.

Southall Community Rights Law Centre, 54 High Street, Southall (571 4920). Mon-Fri 10-1 and 2-6, Sat 10-1. Women only advice: Tues 10-1 and 6-9.30. Creche available. Access: A.

Ealing Community Law Centre, Acton Green Methodist Church, Steele Road, W4 (993 7801). Mon-Fri 9.30-5.30; Tues 9.30-1; Thurs 2-5.30. Additional session at the Viking Centre.

Northolt Village Community Centre, Ealing Road, Northolt (845 0643). Open every morning.

Enfield

Housing Advice Service (Council), Civic Centre, Silver Street, Enfield EN1 3XA (366 6565). Mon-Fri 9-5. Access: P (three steps but can help).

Greenwich

Housing Aid Centre, Churchill House, Greens End, SE18. (854 8888). Mon-Fri 9-5. Access: N.

Greenwich Housing Rights (independent), 30-34 Hare Street, Woolwich, SE18 (853 4093). Ring for advice sessions in different locations.

Plumstead Law Centre, 105 Plumstead High Street, SE18 (855 9817). Some women only sessions: Ring for hours. Access: A.

Hackney

Wally Foster Advice Centre, Homerton Road, E9 (985 3987). Mon-Fri 9-5. Access: A.

Hackney Housing Aid Centre (Council), 287 Mare Street, E8 1EB (986 3191 x 240). Mon, Tue & Fri 9.30-4, Wed 9.30-7. Access: A.

Advice Centre, 150 Stamford Hill, N16 (985 3804). Mon-Fri 9-4.30. Access: N.

People's Advice Centre (Council), Stoke Newington Church Street, N16.

Advice Centre (Council), Templemead House, 5 Homerton Road, E9 (985 3987).

Hackney Citizens Rights Advice Bureau, Centreprise, 136 Kingsland High Street, E8.

Stoke Newington Advice Group Service, United Reform Church, 102 Manor Road, N16 (802 7949).

Hackney Law Centre, 236 Mare Street, E8 (986 8446). Mon, Wed, Thurs 10-2; Tues 5-7.

Hammersmith

Hammersmith Housing Aid Centre (Council), 77 Glenthorne Road, W6 (748 3020). Mon, Tues, Wed, Fri 9-4, Thurs 9-1. Appointment necessary except in emergency. Access: N.

Shepherds Bush Advice Centre (independent), 338 Uxbridge Road, W12 (743 6953). Mon-Fri 9.30-12.30; Tues & Fri 2-4.30; Mon & Wed 6-8. Alternative at 9.30-12. Access: A.

Threshold (Housing Advice for Single People), 126 Uxbridge Road, W12 (749 2925). Mon and Fri 10-4.30; Tues 12-6.45; Thurs 10-1; Wed 10-1; Fri 10-4.30. Access: N.

Black Information Unit, 50 St Stephens Avenue, W6 (743 7893). Telephone first.

Hammersmith and Fulham Community Law Centre, 106-108 King Street, W6 (741 4021). Appointments only. Access: N.

Fulham Legal Advice Centre, 410 Fulham Road, SW6 (731 2401). Mon, Tues, Thurs 6.30-8.30. Access: P.

Haringey

Housing Action Centre, 13-27 Station Road, N22 (881 3000). Mon-Fri 9-4.30. Tues 9-7.30. By appointment except emergencies. Access:A (WC).

Tottenham Neighbourhood Law Centre, 15 West Green Road, N15 (802 0911/2). Mon 10-6, Wed 4-7 and 7-8.30; Fri 10-2 by appt. Access: P.

Legal Advice Centre, 628 High Road, N17 (808 4754). Mon 7-9. Access: N.

Harrow

Harrow Free Law Centre, Holy Trinity Church, High Street. Wealdstone. Tues 7-8.15. Access: A. Also session at Welldon Community Centre, Welldon Crescent, Harrow. Thurs 7-8.15.

Havering

Housing Aid Centre (Council), 2nd Floor, Mercury House, Mercury Gardens, Romford RM1 3DT (70 66999). Mon-Fri 9-5. Access: A.

Hillingdon

Hillingdon Legal Resource Project, 12 Harold Avenue, Hayes, Middlesex (561 9400). Mon-Fri 10-6; Mon and Fri 6-8. Access: A.

Hounslow

Hounslow Law Centre, 51 Lampton Road, Hounslow, Middlesex (570 9505). Mon, Tues, Thurs, Fri 10-6; Wed 2-6 by appointment. Access: A.

Housing Aid Centre (Council), 94 High Street, Hounslow (570 7728 ext 3352/3). Mon-Fri 9.30-4.30, Wed 9.30-7. Access: N.

Islington

Housing Advisory Service (Council), 292 Essex Road, N1 (226 3300). Mon-Fri 9-5.

Angel Voluntary Housing Advice Service, 39 Duncan Terrace, Islington (226 3277). Mon 7-9. Access: N.

Islington People's Rights, 2 St Pauls Road, Islington, N1 (359 2010/359 7627). Mon, Tue, Thurs 10-12.30 and 2-5. All week for phone enquiries. Access: A.

Islington Community Law Centre, 161 Hornsey Road, N7 (607 2461). Hours: Access: A.

South Islington Law Centre, 131-2 Upper Street, N1 (354 0133). Tel for appointment. Access: A(WC).

Kensington and Chelsea

North Kensington Housing Aid Centre (independent), Westway. Information Centre, 140 Ladbroke Grove, W10 (969 2433). Mon 9.30-2, Wed 2.30-7; Fri 12-4.30; Sat 9.30-12. Access: A(WC).

Earls Court Advice Centre, 282 Earls Court Road, SW5 (373 7837). Mon 10-12; Tues and Thur 2.30-4; Wed 10-12. Ring for appointment at other times. Access: N.

North Kensington Law Centre, 74 Golborne Road, W10 (969 7473). Phone between 10-6. Access: A(WC).

Nucleus, 298 Old Brompton Road, SW5 (373 4005). Mon, Tue, Thurs, Fri 2-5; Wed 2-6.30; 7-9 by appointment only. Access: A.

Worlds End Neighbourhood Advice Centre, 2 Worlds End Place, Edith Yard, Kings Road, SW10 OHE (351 5749). Mon 10 and 2-4.30; Wed 2-4.30; Thurs 3-7, Fri 2-4.30. Access: A.

Lambeth

Lambeth Housing Advice Centre, (Council), 2-7 Town Hall Parade, Brixton Hill, SW2 (274 7722). Mon-Fri 10-4. Access: A.

Brixton Advice Centre, 167 Railton Road, SE24 (733 4674). Mon-Fri 10-4.

BIAS (Blackfriars Settlement), 44 Nelson Square, SE1 (928 9521). Tues 10-12; Weds 2-4. Access: N.

Lambeth Community Law Centre, 506-508 Brixton Road, SW9 (733 4245). Mon, Tues, Fri 10-12.30; Weds 6-8. Access:N.

North Lambeth Law Centre, 371 Kennington Lane, SE11 (582 4425/4373). Access: A

Waterloo Action Centre, 14 Baylis Road, SE1 (261 1404). Mon-Fri 10-2. Access: A(WC).

Centre 70, 138 Christchurch Road, SW2 (674 6671). Mon, Thurs 10-1; Tues, Fri 1-4. Reception open: Mon, Tues, Thurs, Fri 9.30-5.30. Access: A.

Clapham Advice Centre, St Anne's Hall, Venn Street, SW4 (720 8731). Mon, Wed, Fri 12-4. Access: A.

Stockwell and Clapham Law Centre, 337 Walworth Road, SW8 (720 6231). Mon-Fri 9.30-5.30 (appointment only); Wed 6-7.30 (open advice session). Access: N.

Lewisham

Housing Advisory Centre (Council), Leegate House, Lee Green, SE12 (852 4391). Mon-Fri 9.30-4.30. Access: A.

Deptford Housing Aid Centre (independent), 171 Deptford High Street, SE8 (691 1602/1300). Mon 10-2; Tues 2-5; Fri 10-1. Access: A.

North Lewisham Law Centre, 28 Deptford High Street, SE8 (692 5355). Ring for nearest session. Access: N.

Women's Advice and Counselling Service, The Albany, Douglas Way, Deptford, SE8 (692 6268). Mon 7-10.

Housing Advice Centre (Council), Vestry Hall, London Road, Mitcham (640 1931). Mon-Fri 9-5. Access: A.

Newham

Housing Aid Centre (Council), 91 The Grove, Stratford, E15 (534 4545). Mon-Fri 9-5. Access: A(WC).

Newham Rights Centre, 285 Romford Road, E7 (555 3331). Mon, Tues, Wed, Fri 9.30-11.30 and 2.30-4.30. Access: A(WC).

Canning Town Information Centre, 57 Barking Road, E16. (474 0931). Telephone for opening times. Access: A.

Redbridge

Housing Aid Centre (Council), 9-13 York Road, Ilford 1G1 2AD (553 4133). Mon-Fri 9.30-4.30. Access: A(WC).

Richmond

Housing Advisory Centre (Council), Regal House, London Road, Twickenham, TW1 3QB (891 1433). Mon-Fri 9-5. Access: A.

Southwark

Blackfriars Information and Advice (BIAS), 44 Nelson Square, SE1 (928 9521). Tues & Fri 10-12, Wed 2-4 at 56 Southwark Bridge Road, SE1. Access: A.

Southwark Law Project, 29-35 Lordship Lane, SE22 (299 1024). Tues 4.30-6.30, Fri 10.30-12.30; Thurs 5-7 at 108 Grange St, SE1. Access: A at Lordship Lane; P at Grange St.

Lordship Lane Information Centre (Council), 29 Lordship Lane, SE22 (299 1515). Mon-Fri 10-4. Access: A.

Bellenden Advice Centre, Copleston Centre, Copleston Road, SE15 (639 8447). Mon & Wed 6.30-8.30; Tues 10-12, Sat 11-1. Access: A.

Walworth Project, 186a Crampton Street, SE17 (701 1038). Mon, Tues, Thurs, 9.30-12.30, Tues 6.30-8.30 legal advice. Access: A.

Advice Centre in the Blue, 190 Southwark Park Road, SE16 (231 2471). Mon, Wed, Fri 10.30-12 and 2-3.30, Thurs 6-7.30. Access: A to shop, N to WC.

Cambridge House Legal Centre, 137 Camberwell Road, SE5, (703 3051/701 9499). Mon, Tues, Wed, Fri 10.30-12.30 and 2.30-4. Tues, Thurs, 7-8.30 by appointment. Ring first for appointment. Access: N.

Sutton

Housing Aid Centre (Council), St Nicholas Way, Sutton (661 5000). Mon-Fri 10-4. Access: A.

Tower Hamlets

Spitalfields Housing Rights and Planning Service, 192 Hanbury Street, E1 (247 2978). Ring for hours. Access: N.

Tower Hamlets Law Centre, 341 Commercial Road, E1 2PS (791 0741). Mon-Fri 10-2. Ring for hours of advice sessions. Access: A.

Housing Advice Centre, (Council), Cheviot House, 227-233 Commercial Road, E1 (790 1818). Mon-Fri 9-4.30. Access: A.

Waltham Forest

Housing Advice Centre (Council), 807 High Road, E10 (558 0033). Mon-Fri 10-6, Sat 9-1. Access: A.

Wandsworth

Housing Aid Centre (Council), Rear of Town Hall, Wandsworth High Street, London SW18 (871 6840).

Threshold Centre (for people without children), 101a Tooting High Street, SW17 (767 2121/672 2162). Mon, Wed, Fri 10-12.30, 1.30-4, Thurs 4-7. Access: A(WC).

Wandsworth Legal Resource Project, 248 Lavender Hill, SW11 (228 9462). Advice sessions throughout the borough. Ring for details.

Westminster

Citizens' Advice Bureau, Royal Court of Justice, Strand, London WC2 (405 7641 ext 3880). Mon-Fri 10-12.30 and 1.30-4.30. Access: N.

Mary Ward Centre, 42 Queen Square, WC1 (831 7009). Mon-Fri 9.30-5.30 by appointment. Access: A.

Central London Community Law Centre, 13 Ingestre Place, W1 (437 5764). Mon-Fri 10-3.30 for appointment, Wed 12-2 & 5-7 general queries. Access: N.

Pimlico Neighbourhood Aid Centre, 1-3 Charlwood Street, SW1 (821 1608). Mon-Fri 2.30-5.30, Tues 7.30-9.30 legal advice. Access: A. Also disabled self-help group starting up here.

510 Centre, 510 Harrow Road, W9 (969 7437). Mon-Fri 10.30-5. Access: A.

Paddington Advice and Law Centre, 441 Harrow Road, W10 (960 4481). Tues 10-12, Wed 4-5, Thurs 3- 4, Fri 1-2.

Black and Ethnic Minorities Housing Advice

African Refugee Housing Action Group (women), 2nd Floor, St Margarets, 23-25 Leighton Road, NW5 (482 3829). Access: N.

African Women's Association, 135 Clarence Road, E5 8EE (985 0147). Access: N.

ASHA, Lambeth Asian Women's Resource Centre, c/o 378 Coldharbour Lane, SW9 (274 8854/737 5901). Two refuges for single women and women with children. Access: N.

ASHA, Southwark, PO Box 484, SE5 0HS (703 4319). Refuge for Asian women. Access: N.

Asian Women's Resource Centre, 134 Minet Avenue, NW10 (961 5701/6549).

ASRA, 5 Westminster Bridge Road, SE1 (928 9379). Access: N.

Black Roof Women's Group, 19a Groveway, Stockwell, SW9 0AH (582 4436). Access: N.

Housing Co-op La Caye, c/o THARE, Oxford House, Derbyshire Street, E2 (729 1946). Access: N.

Haringey Young Single Homeless, Tottenham Green Education Centre, Town Hall Approach, N15 (808 9330).

Homeless Action, 52-54 Featherstone Street, EC1 (251 6783). Women only. Access: A.

Latin American Women's Rights Service, Beauchamp Lodge, 2 Warwick Crescent, Harrow Road, W2 (289 7277).

Mixifren Association, 33 Braydon Road, Stamford Hill and 38 Cranwich Road, Stamford Hill, N16 (800 5969). Advice for young black people. Three hostels for women are being opened.

Ackee Housing Project, 55 Stoke Newington Church Street, N16.

Threshold Centre, 101A Tooting High Street, SW17 (672 2162). Access: A.

UJIMA Housing Association, 413-419 Harrow Road, W9 (960 5141). Access: N.

Housing Associations
Projects for Women

Over-40 Association for Women Workers, Mary George House, 120-122 Cromwell Road, SW7 4HA (370 2507). Women only. Also runs an employment agency.

Soho Housing Association, 9 Archer Street, W1V 7HL (437 9141). Women's hostel at 59 Greek Street, W1. Access: N.

South East London Consortium Housing Association (SELCHA), 146 Camberwell Road, SE5 (701 9231/7468/ 7632). Priority to young women.

Stonham Housing Association, Octavia House, 54 Ayres Street, SE1 1EU (403 1144). Women and men, especially ex-offenders. Also girls 'at risk', women's refuges. Access: N.

Women's Pioneer Housing Association, 227 Wood Lane, W12 8HL (749 7112). Women only. Access: N.

Women's Royal Voluntary Services Housing Association, 17 Old Park Lane, W1Y 4AJ (499 6040). Mainly elderly women.

Gay People
Stonewall Housing Association, 6 Willow Bridge Road, N1 (226 3776).

Projects for Disabled People
John Grooms Association for the Disabled, 10 Gloucester Drive, N4 (802 7272).

Circle 33 Housing Trust, 26 Pancras Road, NW1 (278 3261).

London and Quadrant Housing Trust, Osborn House, Osborn Terrace, SE3 (852 9181).

Hyde Housing Association, Pembroke House, 26 Pembroke Road, Bromley, Kent, BR1 2IU (464 3322).

Habinteg Housing Association, 4 Dukes Mews, W1 (935 6931).

Raglan Housing Association, 1 St Giles Court, Dane Road, W13 (579 5213).

Shaftesbury Society Housing Association, 112 Regency Street, SW1 (834 7581).

Mentally Ill People

Windsor Walk Housing Association, c/o Dr J.L.T. Birley, Maudsley Hospital, Denmark Hill, SE5 (703 6333).

Projects for Black and Ethnic Minority Groups

ASRA, 5 Westminster Bridge Road, SE1 (928 9379).

Presentation Housing Association, 123 Kings Avenue, SW4 (671 4966).

UJIMA Housing Association, 413-419 Harrow Road, W9 (960 5141).

Others

Haringey Umbrella Housing Association, 513-521 High Road, Tottenham, N17 6SB.

West Hampstead Housing Association, 70 Kingsgate Road, NW6 (328 7542).

Action Housing Association, 407 Uxbridge Road, W3 9SU.

Battersea Churches HA Ltd, Christ Church Vestry, Candahar Road, SW11 2PU.

Bondway HA, PO Box 374, Bondway, Vauxhall, SW8.

Brent People's HA Ltd, Park House, Manor Park Road, NW10.

Contour Housing Association, 175 Lavender Hill, SW11.

Community Housing Association, 295 Kentish Town Road, NW5.

Croydon Churches HA Ltd, 77 Wellesley Road, Croydon, Surrey, CRO 2AJ.

Ealing Family HA Ltd, St. James House, 105-113 The Broadway, West Ealing, W13 9BE.

East London HA, 197 Balaam Street, E13.

Family Housing Association, 189a Old Brompton Road, SW5 0AR.

Look Ahead (Beacon Hostels), Housing Association, 189a Old Brompton Road, SW5 0AR.

Metropolitan Housing Trust, Cambridge House, 109 Mayes Road, Wood Green, N22 6UR.

New Era HA Ltd, 123 Golden Lane, EC1.

New Islington and Hackney HA, 123 Kingsland High Street, E8 2PB.

UKHT, Poland House, 167 Oxford Street, W1R 1TA.

Notting Hill Housing Trust, 46 All Saints Road, W11.

Paddington Churches HA Ltd, Electricity House, 296 Willesden Lane, NW2 5HR.

Peter Bedford Housing, 76a Liverpool Road, N1.

Richmond Churches HA Ltd, 363 Upper Richmond Road West, SW14 7NX.

St Mungo Community HT, 33 Long Acre, WC2E 9LA.

Salvation Army HA Ltd, 110 Middlesex Street, E1 7HZ.

Shepherd's Bush HA Ltd, 28-29 Eastman Road, W3 7YG.

Solon Housing Association, 381 Clapham Road, SW9 (274 9990).

Solon (Wandsworth), 49a Lavender Hill, SW11 (223 7376).

South London Family HA, 1st Floor, Rochester House, 2-10 Belvedere Road, SE19.

Springboard Housing Association, 1 Merchant Street, Bow Road, E3 4LY.

Thames Housing Association, 22 Ritherdon Road, SW17.

Threshold Single Persons Housing Association Ltd, 227a Garratt Lane, SW18 0SU (871 1244).

WPHT, 5-6 Turnpike Parade, Green Lanes, N15 3EA.

Cheshire Foundation Housing Association, 380-384 Harrow Road, W9 2HU.

North West London Housing Association Ltd, 32 The Avenue, NW6 7NP.

Housing Co-ops
Women only

Seagull, 36 Cambridge Gardens, W10 (960 4402).

London Fields Housing Co-op, 71 Shrubland Road, E8 (249 8748).

Blue Moon Housing Co-op (short-life housing), Lewisham, 132b Evelyn Street, SE8; Southwark, 25 Brook Drive, SE11; Lambeth, 26 Nursery Road, SW9.

Trafalgar Avenue Housing Co-op (short-life and permanent), 50 Trafalgar Avenue, SE15.

Black and Ethnic Minority People

Housing Co-op La Caye, c/o THARE, Oxford House, Derbyshire Street, E2 (729 1946).

Spitalfields Housing Co-op, 170 Brick Lane, E1 (247 1040). Black members only.

Amilcar Cabral Housing Co-op, 101a Tooting High Street, SW17 (767 2121).

Ekarro Housing Co-op, Flat 10, Mondragon House, 49 Guilford Road, SE4.

Shrine, 9-13 Nicoll Road, NW10.

Umoja Housing Co-op, c/o NCH, 53 West Ham Lane, E15.

Avalon Housing Co-op (Irish people), 33 Lorn Road, SW9.

Black Roof Housing Co-op, 19a Groveway, Stockwell, SW9 0AH (582 4436).

Tower Hamlets Federation of Tenants Associations, Oxford House, Derbyshire Street, E2 (739 6778).

Westminster Council Tenants' Action Group (WCTAG), Lillington Gardens Community Centre, Under Morgan House, Vauxhall Bridge Road, SW1 (834 0777).

Tenants Associations

London Tenants' Organisation, 17 Victoria Park Square, Bethnal Green, E2 9PE (981 1221). Will inform you of tenants associations in your area.

Brent Federation of Tenants' and Residents' Associations, 375 High Road, Willesden, NW10 (459 1346).

Camden Federation of Tenants' and Residents' Associations, 30 Camden Road, NW1 (267 5328).

Federation of Hackney Tenants' Associations (FOHTA), 380 Old Street, EC1 (739 3631).

Federation of Islington Tenants' Associations (FITA), 19 Highbury Place, N5 (359 8224).

Council Tenants' Tenants' Associations

Lambeth Federation of Tenants, 49 Eastlake Road, SE5 (733 1918).

Federation of Lewisham Tenants' and Residents' Associations, Wendy Block, Ladywell Lodge, 82 Ladywell Road, SE13 (690 8231).

Southwark Group of Tenants' Associations, 21 Rye Lane, Peckham, SE15 (639 6718).

Immigration and Nationality

Presently, there are approximately one million Black people of Asian and Afro-Caribbean descent out of a population of seven million living in London. Since the 1970s, workers from the Philippines, Turkey, Morocco, Greece, refugees from Latin America, Vietnam and elsewhere have also come to London. The operation of British immigration and nationality laws has been and is a crucial focus in the lives of all Black and ethnic minority people. The laws are both racist and sexist in their impact and cause distress and disruption to many Black and ethnic minority families and individuals. Many are faced with blatant discrimination before they enter Britain. Others face severe problems in bringing family members to join them. Yet others face deportation.

Immigration law and practice involve a complex set of issues to which it is impossible to do justice in a short introduction such as this. The aim of this section is to give a brief outline of how immigration legislation has developed in this country, and how women are discriminated against under the law, particularly Black and migrant women. At the end of this section, references for further reading, plus places to get more information are provided.

Black immigration to Britain in the 1950s and 60s was a direct result of Britain's colonial history in the Indian subcontinent, the Caribbean and parts of Africa. The post-war period in Britain was characterised by severe labour shortages. Britain turned to its former colonies as a source of cheap labour, and workers from the Caribbean and the Indian sub-continent were actively recruited to undertake low-paid jobs which white workers did not want to do. At this time these workers had the right of entry and settlement in Britain, since they were inhabitants of the Commonweatlh.

From the very start, however, the government of the time displayed a negative view of Black immigration. At the same time as Black workers were encouraged to meet Britain's labour needs, the government was creating a concern about the 'problems' and 'social costs' of Black settlement.

While popular racism grew - for example, anit-Black riots in Notting Hill in 1958 - the government, instead of introducing measures to combat racism, introduced the 1962 Commonwealth Immigrants Act with a view to curtailing Black immigration. This act was followed by the 1968 Act, further reducing the rights of Black people to enter Britain. Up to that point, those who came could settle here permanently.

The 1971 Act eroded the right for Black people to settle in Britain permanently. This Act replaced virtually all existing immigration laws and formed the basis of control today. People were divided up into patrials (predominantly white) and non-patrials (predominantly Black), patriality being defined in terms of being of British descent. Patrials are free from immigration control deportations and restrictions on taking employment.

A further effect of the 1971 Act was that the wives and children of Commonwealth citizens who had settled in the UK on or after the 1st January 1973 no longer had automatic right to settle.

This measure was by no means the first to discriminate against women. In fact, a key feature of immigration law is that it has never given women independent status. Rather, women are treated as appendages of men, which affects their capacity to enter the country and their right to bring in dependants. Women settled in the UK can be deported if their husband is deported. The sexism inherent in the laws affects Black/migrant and white women differently, because the former are also subjected to the racism within this legislation. For instance, the concept of patriality (1971 Act) enables women patrials to confer immigration rights on their children born abroad for the first time. However, as most Black women are not patrials, this benefits mostly white women.

The immigration laws are interpreted in practice using the immigration rules. These are often unpublished and civil servants and immigration officers at ports of entry have 'discretion'. The form and working of these rules has caused concern and protest as they are seen as reinforcing the racism and sexism inherent in the legislation.

As described above, by the late 60s and early 70s immigration had come under stringent control. The attention of the anti-immigration lobby turned to a group of people who still retained an automatic right of entry - the dependants of people already living in Britain.

In 1969, women's right to have their husbands or fiances join them in Britain was taken away. The Asian communities were hardest hit by these rules and campaigned to change the law but without much effect. By 1974 cases of white women separated from their husbands mounted and public opinion shifted dramatically against these regulations. Rules were changed, to allow husbands/fiances to enter on the same basis as wives. In order for a husband/finance to live in Britain, the couple had to have met and the husband couldn't enter for the purpose of marriage if the immigration officer had reason to believe that the marriage was one entered into primarily to obtain admission to UK. These rules have predominantly affected Asian communities but have been applied to other Black and migrant men and women.

Combined with increasing restrictions for entry into Britain, there have been increasing controls on Black and ethnic minority people living in the country. There have been police raids in places of work aimed at 'catching' so called 'illegal' immigrants. Various statutory bodies, the Department of Health and Social Security (DHSS), the National Health Service (NHS), schools and higher education authorities have been instructed by the Home Office to request passports from Black and ethnic minority people before claiming supplementary benefits, or gaining admission into hospitals, and schools. Local groups, trade unions and others have opposed these practices but despite this, they continue and seem to be increasing.

Lobbying and campaigning at local and national level has aimed to raise awareness of the issues, to make information (often complex, long and changing) available to the immigrant and migrant communities, to prevent deportation of Black and ethnic minority people, and to reunite families, through the support of local people and sympathetic MPs.

The GLC Women's Committee *Programme of Action for Women in London* (Report W550) described the views and concerns of women in London about immigration issues which had arisen at the Committee's consultation meetings. The Committee sponsored a conference in 1982 on Women, Immigration and Nationality.

A consultation conference with Black and ethnic minority women in June 1983 discussed the issues and recommendations coming out of the conference contributed to the Council's policies in relation to the issues.

The Committee considered a report (W 1185) on the outcome of a test case to the European Court of Human Rights by women affected by the Immigration Rules of 1980. The Committee welcomed the court's findings of sex discrimination in the operation of the rules but condemned the government's response to the court decision which involved making entry for dependants more difficult for both men and women.

The GLC Ethnic Minorities Unit produced several policy reports on immigration and nationality laws and argued for the repeal of immigration/national legislation and an end to immigration controls both outside the UK and within. A report on registration and naturalisation fees recommended that these fees were outrageously high and should be abolished and the results of several consultation conferences have been distributed to other local authorities, statutory bodies and voluntary groups.

With the abolition of the GLC, no single central authority will exist in London to oppose the immigration/naturalisation legislation and support organisation and campaigns which are campaigning to prevent deportations and change the law.

This section is ordered as follows: *Information and advice, Useful Reading.*

Information and advice on immigration and nationality issues

The following organisations will provide information and advice on immigration/nationality issues:

African Refugee Housing Action Group, (ARHAG), St Margarets, 23/25 Leighton Road, NW5.

Asian Centre, 17 Dalston Lane, E8 (254 4898).

Asian Women's Resource Centre, 134 Minet Avenue, NW10 (961 6549/961 5701).

Basle Court Centre for Refugees, 28 Fairmont Road, Brixton Hill, SW2 1AD.

Black Information Unit, The Hut, 50 St Stevenson's Road, W12 (743 7893).

Brent Law Centre, 190 Willesden High Road, NW10 (451 1122).

Brent Young Peoples Law Centre, 272 Willesden High Road, NW10 (451 2428).

Brixton Black Women's Centre, 41A Stockwell Green, SW9 9HZ (274 9220).

Carila, Latin American Women's Group, 29 Islington Park Street, N1 (359 2270).

Central London Community Law Centre Ltd, 13 Ingestre Place, W1 (437 5764/437 5854).

Colmena, Latin American Women's Rights Service, 2 Warwick Crescent, W2 (289 1601).

Community Centre for Refugees from Vietnam, Laos and Cambodia, 37 Peak House, Woodberry Down, N4 2NU.

Commission for Filipino Migrant Workers, CFMW, St Francis Centre, Pottery Lane, W11.

Ealing Housing Aid Service, 92-94 Warwick Road, Ealing, W5. Nirmala Sharma (840 1886).

Greenwich Asian Women's Group, Macbean Centre, Macbean Street, Woolwich, SE18 (854 1188).

Hammersmith and Fulham Law Centre, 106-108 King Street, W6 (741 4021).

Hillingdon Legal Resource Centre, 12 Harold Avenue, Hayes Middlesex (561 9400).

Hounslow Law Centre, 52 Lampton Road, Hounslow, Middlesex (570 9505).

Immigration Widows Campaigns, c/o 131/2 Upper Street, N1 (354 0133).

Iranian Community Centre, 465A Green Lanes, N4 (341 5005).

Joint Council for the Welfare of Immigrants (JCWI), 115 Old Street, EC1 (251 8706).

Migrants Resource Centre, 2 Denbigh Place, SW1

Migrant Services Unit (Part of London Voluntary Service Council, LVSC), 68 Chalton Street, NW1 (388 0241) Mary Dimech, Mandana Hendessi.

Newham Rights, 285 Romford Road, Newham, E7 (555 3331).

North Islington Law Centre, 161 Hornsey Road, N7 6DU (607 2461) Non Ardill.

North Lambeth Law Project, 381 Kennington Lane, SE11 5QY (582 4425/4373).

North Lewisham Law Centre, 28 Deptford High Street, SE8 (692 5355).

Paddington Migrants/Immigrants Employment Unit, 439 Harrow Road, W10 (960 5746).

Paddington Advice/Law Centre, 441 Harrow Road, W10 (960 4481).

Philippine Resource Centre, 1/2 Grangeway, NW6.

Plumstead Community Law Centre, 105 Plumstead High Street, SE18 (855 9817).

Refugee Action Group, 17 Deptford High Street, SE8.

Rights of Women, 374 Grays Inn Road, WC1 (278 6349). Campaigning and legal advice.

Runnymede Trust, 178 North Gower Street, NW1 4NB (387 8943). Information Centre with publications for minority groups, on housing, immigration etc. Library available. Access: N.

Southall Black Women's Centre, 86 Northcote Avenue, Southall, Middlesex (843 0578).

Southall Community Law Centre, 14 Featherstone Road, Southall, Middlesex (574 2434).

Southall Rights, 54 High Street, Southall, Middlesex (571 4920/843 0094).

Stockwell and Clapham Law Centre, 337 Wandsworth Road, SW8 (720 6233).

South Islington Law Centre, 131/2 Upper Street, N1 1QP (354 0133).

Tamil Refugee Action Group, (TRAG), 52 Acre Lane, SW2.

Tottenham Law Centre, 15 West Green Road, N15 (802 0911).

Vietnamese Refugee Community, 10 Collinson House, Lindley Estate, Commercial Way, SE15.

West Hampstead Law Centre, 220 Belsize Road, NW6 (326 4523).

Women Immigration and Nationality Group, c/o JCWI, 115 Old Street, EC1 (251 8706).

Useful Reading

Immigration Law and Practice, Lawrence Grant and Ian Martin 1982, (Published by The Cobden Trust) £10.25

World's Apart, Women under Immigration and Nationality Law, Women Immigration and Nationality Group Ed Bhahba (Pluto £4.95).

The Thin End of the White Wedges, Manchester Law Centre Immigration Handbook No.5 (Steven Cohen). Can be obtained from Manchester Law Centre, 595 Stockport Road, Longsight, Manchester.

Immigration Bulletin, Runnymede Trust.

Lesbians

The number and variety of lesbian groups in London - from Deptford Dykes to the Catholic Lesbian Sisterhood, from the Black Lesbian Support Group to GEMMA - attracts lesbians from all over the country. Compared with many parts of Britain, there are more support groups, campaigning organisations, help lines offering advice and information, and venues with women-only events and entertainment. The vast majority of these services rely upon time and energy voluntarily given — a testament to the strength of lesbians in London.

The need for lesbians to organise together is also a comment upon a society which, when it doesn't actively ridicule or threaten lesbians, attempts to marginalise their needs or ignore their existence altogether. Isolation, invisibility and enforced secrecy remain a major element in the oppression of lesbians and play a large part in persuading the heterosexual world that only 'ten per cent' of women are lesbians. In fact, if all lesbians could come out, and be open about their lives, heterosexuals would have to rethink their calculations.

Lesbians have been active in the women's movement, challenging sexism and campaigning on issues affecting *all* women - such as abortion, rape, sexual harassment and equal pay. This support, however, has not always been returned. Some heterosexual women feel that lesbians threaten the 'respectable' face of feminism and are 'extremists' who give the women's movement a bad press. Many lesbians have been angry at what they have seen as the co-option of the gay rights movement by the women's movement and have, as a result, decided to work in mixed gay groups in recognition of a common, if not identical, oppression shared by gay men. Heterosexism has also been pushed higher up the political agenda by lesbians in the women's movement since, in many ways, they have understood heterosexism to be a more accurate term than sexism to describe the ways in which men and women relate and the means by which women are kept in subservient roles to men.

Racism exists throughout society and therefore lesbian groups are no exception. The few resources that exist for lesbians, such as counselling services, directly or indirectly discriminate against Black and ethnic minority lesbians. Support networks, such as the Black Lesbian Support Group, have been set up in recognition of the different needs of Black lesbians and in the process have shattered the myth that lesbianism is only for white women.

Zami, a name first used by Audre Lorde to describe Black women-loving women, has been adopted by many Black lesbians because the term lesbian has been too closely identified with white middle-class women. The first Black lesbian conference was held in London in October 1985 called Zami, at which over 300 Black Zamis attended. The next conference is likely to be in either Leeds or Sheffield, and is part of the growing Black lesbian movement.

Young lesbian groups are also active in London, providing a space to discuss common problems and to make contact with other young lesbians, who are generally told that they are too young and immature to make any choices or decisions about their sexuality. Patronising or hostile behaviour from adults, whether parents, teachers or counsellors, often leads young lesbians to be expelled from school or made homeless. In *Something to Tell You*, a book recently published by the London Gay Teenage Group, it was shown that 11% of young lesbians are made homeless after 'coming out' to their parents. They face heavy pressure to conform to the heterosexual model or be 'cured'. In spite of all this, however, many young women 'come out' and stay out as lesbians.

It has been very difficult for many older women to live openly as lesbians; many remain in marriages and are unable to make any real choices. There are few places for older lesbians to meet and many feel that the majority of lesbian groups do not cater for their needs or recognise their different experiences, especially in relation to family life.

People with disabilities are generally assumed not to have any sexual feelings at all, or such feelings are seen as shameful and to be kept in the background. Groups such as GEMMA work to decrease the isolation felt by lesbians with disabilities and increase the sensitivity of able-bodied lesbians to recognising their needs. All too often, events are organised in inaccessible venues; information and publicity - if it is sent at all - is not taped or Brailled. Nevertheless, many lesbians with disabilities are actively challenging able-bodiedism.

Some lesbian and mixed gay groups focus their attention upon specific issues. The following points give an indication of the range of topics involved.

- Lesbians and gay men are offered no protection under the law and industrial tribunals have concurred with employers in seeing homosexuality as a just cause for dismissal. Furthermore, as a result of widespread homophobia (that is, fear of homosexuals), certain jobs are seen as particularly 'unsuitable' for lesbians and gay men - such as childcare, youth work or jobs which involve contact with the public. Some trade unions are beginning to include lesbians and gay men in job protection and equal opportunities policies but coming out is still risky, especially for lesbian mothers.

• Lesbian mothers also suffer from the punitive effects of a legal and social service system which sees lesbians as 'unfit' mothers. It is extremely rare for a judge to find in favour of lesbian mothers in child custody cases, which are occasions for blatant displays of bigotry. In response, lesbian mothers' groups have grown rapidly in London and any lesbian mothers needing support should contact **Lesbian Line** or the **Rights of Women** custody worker (see listings).

• In housing allocation, lesbian couples are rarely given the status of heterosexual couples, married or not. Many local authorities refuse to grant lesbians tenancy rights in the event of the death of a partner. Harassment of lesbians on housing estates is rarely taken seriously by local authorities. Caught between discriminatory council housing policies and expensive, low standard housing in the private sector some lesbians have formed their own housing co-ops or have joined with gay men in forming mixed gay co-ops.

• Heterosexism runs through all public services, including the health service. Any lesbian who cites her partner as 'next-of-kin' runs the risk of facing open hostility and intimidation, both verbal and physical.

• Some groups are not only working against oppressive media stereotypes of lesbians - who are seen as young, white, able-bodied, single women who want to be 'like men' - but are claiming their right to the share of the media through women's photography, film, video and radio facilities. The press reaction to the GLC's funding of lesbian groups is only one example of why such campaigns are necessary.

Since its inception, the Women's Committee has recognised lesbians as being 'doubly disadvantaged'. By popular demand, a lesbian was co-opted on to the Women's Committee and a Lesbian Working Group was set up. The Women's Committee's *Programme of Action* summarised the results of a London-wide survey, indicating the areas of most concern to lesbians. A small number of lesbian groups were funded, such as Lesbian Line, but it has also been the policy of the Women's Committee to ask all funded groups how they meet the needs of lesbians in London.

In spite of severe press hostility, the GLC stood firm in its commitment to lesbians and gay men in London by funding the Lesbian and Gay Centre and the Lesbian and Gay Charter - the first of their kind in Britain.

This section is order as follows: *Advice and Counselling, Black and Ethnic Minority Lesbians, Bookshops, Cafes, Centres, Contacts, Drama, Entertainment, Health, Housing, Legal, Lesbians with Disabilities, Lesbian Mothers, Older Lesbians, General Organisations and Groups, Work (including labour movement), Young Lesbians, Publications and Useful Reading.*

Advice and Counselling

For details of events, groups etc, or for advice, befriending and support, contact:

Gay Bereavement, Unitarian Rooms, Hoop Lane, NW11 8BS. Please enclose SAE. In emergency phone Gay Switchboard (837 7324).

Gay Switchboard, 24 hour telephone service (837 7324). Advice and information for lesbians and gay men.

Lesbian Line*, BM Box 1514 (251 6911) Mon and Fri 2-10pm; Tues, Wed, Thurs 7-10pm. There are lesbian lines all over the country so if you do not live in London, ring this number and they will tell you your nearest line.

London Friend, 274 Upper Street, N1. Telephone service (354 1846) with name only line 7.30-10pm. Youth GP Fri evening. Thurs evening women only.

Parents' Enquiry, 16 Honley Road, Catford, SE6 2HZ (698 1815). Counselling for gay teenagers and their parents.

The Walk-In Centre, 42 Turnpike Lane, N8 (888 3188). Advice and counselling, majority of staff are women.

Black and Ethnic Minority Lesbians

Black lesbians are welcome at most Black (and other) women's centres who will advise on local groups and activities. (See **Borough Information** and **Black and Ethnic Minority Women**).

Lesbian and Gay Black Group, held at Gays the Word Bookshop (see below) at 8.00pm Fri. BM Gay Black Gp, BM Box 4390, WC1N 3XX.

Black Lesbian Support Network, Brixton Black Women's Centre, 41a Stockwell Green, SW9 9H7 (274 9220/7696). Social events, advice, support. No wheelchair access.

Camden and Islington Black Lesbians, 15 Manor Gardens, N7.

Chinese Lesbian Group, 7 Marriott Road, N4.

Irish Lesbian Group, c/o LIWC, 59 Stoke Newington Church Street, N16.

Jewish Lesbian Feminist Group, c/o Box 39, Sisterwrite, 190 Upper Street, N1.

Peckham Black Lesbian Group, c/o Southwark Women's Centre, 6-8 Peckham High Street, SE15

Young Black Lesbian Group, 25 Bayham Street, Camden Town, NW1 (387 7450). Meets Tues 6-9pm.

ZAMI Conference of Black Lesbians, Brixton Black Women's Centre, 41a Stockwell Green, SW9 9H7 (274 9220/7696).

Bookshops

(See **Media and Arts**, Women's Book-sellers for fuller list of feminist book-shops, all of which stock a good range of lesbian books.)

Gays The Word, 66 Marchmont Street, WC1 (278 7654). Mon-Sat 11am-7pm, Sun 2-6pm. Gay community bookshop - newsletter produced. Also has a lesbian discussion group and a small cafè.

Cafes

The Greenhouse, Drill Hall, 16 Chenies Street, WC1 (637 8270). Women only, Mon only 6-10pm. Wholefood and vegetarian.

See also **London Lesbian and Gay Centre**, below.

Centres

Black Lesbian and Gay Centre, c/o Annex B, Tottenham Town Hall, Approach Road, N15 (855 3543)

Camden Lesbian Centre Project, 2 Malden Road, NW5 (267 1402).

London Lesbian and Gay Centre, 67/69 Cowcross Street, EC1 (608 1471). Comfortable gay and lesbian community centre. Lesbian-only space and disco. Creche, caf, bar and bookshop and a wide range of events and activities.

Contacts

If you cannot come out as a lesbian for one reason or another (work, children, family, shyness) but want to meet others, you could advertise using a Box Number (then you won't get unpleasant phone calls) in *Spare Rib* magazine (Spare Rib classifieds: for details and rates ring 253 9792, then send in your ad in writing) or the weekly listings magazine *City Limits*. Buy these magazines in any newsagent.

Drama

Gay Sweatshop, c/o Kate Owen, Drill Hall, 16 Chenies Street, WC1. Mixed regular productions. Work in schools etc.

Lesbian Drama Workshops, Cromer Street Women's Centre, 90 Cromer Street, WC1 (737 2495). Meet Thurs 8pm. Drama workshops.

Lesbian Only Theatre Group, meet Hackney Women's Centre (see Borough Information). Sun 1pm.

No Boundaries, c/o 247 Mayall Road, SE24.

Siren Theatre Co, 191 Brooke Road, E5.

Entertainment

There's at least one women-only venue/event every evening in the week. Venues frequently change. Up-to-date information is available from: Lesbian Line, Gay Switchboard or London Friend (see opening to this section). *City Limits* magazine, weekly, available newsagents. Look under Music section (Nightclubbing) and Out in the City. Also see the Action section for women-only benefits. *Spare Rib* magazine (monthly) (see **Media and Arts**, Women's Publications) also advertise women-only events. Women's Centres (see **Borough Information**) also can advise, and will advertise local women-only events on their notice-boards etc. Disco venues for lesbians, or women-only, are long-established, or going strong at the time of publication (but check with Lesbian Line etc above, or the venue, for specific lesbian or women-only evenings):

Ace of Clubs, 52 Piccadilly, W1. Sats 9.30-3.30pm. Aimed at gay women but allows entrance to gay men friends.

The Bell, 259 Pentonville Road, Kings Cross, N1 (837 5617). Women's City Disco, 8pm-12.30am Sats. Although the disco is wheelchair accessible, it tends to be noisy, dark and mainly for younger women.

Beryls at Valentinos, 344 High Street, Tottenham, N15. Saturday Nights: Lively. Large building on split-levels can be smokey and loud. 9pm-2am.

Brandy's, The Crypt, St Paul's Church, Deptford High Street, SE8, 8pm-12.00 Mon.

Bugatti's, 71 Shacklewell Lane, E8. Fri 8pm-very late. Women only.

Drill Hall, 16 Chenie's Street, WC1. Mon eves, bar, OK for meeting friends for a quiet drink.

The Entertainer - Claude's, 72 Balls Pond Road, N1. Wed night, a place Black lesbians feel happy to go. PA's from Sister Culture.

The Fallen Angel, 65 Graham Street, N1. Tues evening, women only: pleasant atmosphere can be crowded. Sun open for afternoon tea to gay men as well.

Femme Disco, The Cock, 2 Diana Place, Triton Square, NW1. 8pm-late, women only.

Garlands, 483 Hackney Road, E2. Fri 8pm-12.00pm. Women only who don't like disco music. Sat, Sun.

Lips Bar, 2 St John's Square, EC1. 8.30-12.00. Women only Mon.

London Lesbian and Gay Centre, 67-69 Cowcross Street, EC1. (608 1471) Women only discos and entertainment on Thurs and Sat nights. Day membership plus entrance to downstairs. Ring for more details.

Rackets, Pied Bull, 1 Liverpool Road, N1 (837 3218). Access: A (no access to toilet). Weds quiet, candle-lit tables, often live music, good place to meet friends and talk. Thurs and Fri nights disco, can be a little crowded.

Sappho '85 (formerly WICCA women), Upstairs Bar, Chepstow Pub, Chepstow Place, W10. Access: N.

South London Women's Centre, 55 Acre Lane, Brixton, SW2. Black lesbian discos often held on Fri nights. See press for details.

There are many more! Check as indicated - some close, new ones open. There are also many venues in outer London areas eg Wimbledon and Croydon. Contact Lesbian Line (etc) as above, and/or your local Women's Centre (see **Borough Information**).

Health

Alcoholics Anonymous Gay Group (mixed), Response Bookshop, 300 Old Brompton Road, SW5 (834 8202). Meets Wed and Sat - telephone for details.

British Pregnancy Advisory Service, 2nd Floor, 58 Petty France, SW1 (222 0985). Information and advice available on artificial insemination (AID), and see **Health**.

Dawn (Drugs, Alcohol and Women Nationally*), c/o London Council on Alcoholism, 146 Queen Victoria Street, EC4 (250 3284).

Gay Medical Information Society, BM GMIS, WC1N 3XX.

Lesbian and Alcohol Group, Women's Alcohol Centre, 254 St Paul's Road, Islington, N1 (226 4581). Mon-Fri 10am-1pm. 11.30-1 pm Wed

Lesbian Herpes Sufferers' Groups, The Herpes Association, 39-41 North Road, N7 9DP.

Western Hospital Accept Clinic, Seagrave Road, SW6 1RZ (381 3155). Lesbian group meets Fri

Women's Therapy Centre*, 6 Manor Gardens, N7 6LA (263 6200). Weekdays 1-3.30pm, phone for advice and information.

Housing

(Also see **Housing** for accommodation and housing rights).

After Six, (836 6534) 24 hour switchboard not just for lesbians and gays, but positive.

August Trust, 42 Tredegar Road, Dartford, Kent (736 6602). Home for elderly lesbians and gay men.

Blue Moon Housing Co-op, women only. Lewisham: 132b Evelyn Street, SE8; Southwark: 25 Brook Drive, SE11; Lambeth: 26 Nursery Road, SW9

Gay Housing Group, c/o London Friend, 274 Upper Street, Islington (837 7324 - Gay Switchboard).

Islington Gay Co-op Housing, 79 Crayford Road, N7.

Islington Girls' Project*, 8 Manor Gardens, N7 (263 6270). Short life housing for young lesbians.

Seagull, 36 Cambridge Gardens, W10 (960 4402). Women only.

SHAC (London Housing Aid Centre), 189A Old Brompton Road, SW5 0AK (373 7276). Publish a guide to women's hostels in London. (Details on women-only hostels - see Housing.)

Stonewall Housing Association, lesbian and gay, 69 Cowcross Street, EC1 (608 1923).

Flatshare etc: see *City Limits* (weekly listings magazine) classified ads, **(see Media and Arts)**, *Spare Rib* (monthly) magazine, and noticeboards in Women's Centres (see **Borough Information**).

Legal

Gay London Police Monitoring Group, 38 Mount Pleasant, WC1 (278 6215).

GLAD, BM GLAD, WC1N 3XX (821 7672 nightly 7-10pm). Gay legal advice service.

Lesbian and Policing Project (LESPOP),* 38 Mount Pleasant, WC1 (833 4996). Monitors policies dealings with lesbians, can also offer support to women having problems with the law.

Lesbian Custody Worker, Rights of Women (ROW), 52-54 Featherstone Street, EC1 (251 6577).

There are several groups which are active in lesbian custody matters and give social and legal support to women involved in lesbian custody cases. Contact ROW as in above listing.

Lesbians with Disabilities

Brothers and Sisters Group, BMB and S, WC1N 3XX. Social and support group for deaf and hard of hearing.

GEMMA, BM Box 5700, WC1N 3XX. Meet regularly, lesbians with or without disability, social activities, bef-riending and supportive groups. Newsletter available. Enquiries welcome in Braille or cassette.

Lesbian Disabled Group, WICCA Women, Upstairs Bar, Chepstow Pub, Chepstow Place, W2. Meet as part of WICCA every Tues at 7.30pm. Discussions and socials.

Sisters Against Disablement, c/o Women's Reproductive Rights Information Centre, 52-54 Featherstone Street, EC1 (251 6332). This is a group of feminist and lesbian-feminist women who campaign for better lives for women with disabilities.

Lesbian Mothers

For details of lesbian mother groups contact Lesbian Line. For legal advice and support contact the lesbian custody worker at **ROW** (Rights of Women), 52-54 Featherstone Street, EC1 (251 6577). ROW also has a Black women's sub-group.

Older Lesbians

London Supper Club, BCM Box 2792, WC1N 3XX. This is a social club specifically for gay women over 30.

Older Lesbian Network, c/o Lesbians at Friend, 274 Upper Street, N1 359 7371. Meets second Sat of month, social events and discussions. Befriending. Access: A.

Pink Wrinkle/Rosa Rimple. This is a social group for mature lesbians and gay men. They meet on the first Sat of each month at: Unitarian Library, Palace Gardens, W8, between 7.30pm and 9.30pm.

General Organisations and Groups

We have only included groups whose addresses etc are by Box No or at a centre of some kind. Again, if you are looking for a special group (eg writers' group) ring Lesbian Line.

Bi-sexual Group, BM/BI, WC1 3XX. Meets Heaven Disco, The Arches, Villiers Street, WC2, each Tues. Newsletter available. Please send sae A4 size.

Campaign for Homosexual Equality (CHE), c/o 274 Upper Street, N1 2UA (359 3973).

Catholic Lesbian Sisterhood, BM Reconciliation, WC1N 3XX. Meet quarterly in London.

Catholics who are Gay, QUEST, BM Box 2585, WC1N 3XX (373 7819), Fri-Sun 7-11pm.

Croydon Lesbian Support Group, Croydon Women's Centre, 13 Woodside Green, SE25, meets at 8pm.

Deptford Dykes (Deptford Lesbian Group), Deptford Women's Centre, Deptford High Street, 74 Deptford High Street, SE8 (692 1851). Meets Mon 8pm at above address. Wheelchair access difficult, but help is available.

Gay Christian Movement, BM Box 6914, WC1N 3XX (283 5165). Offers counselling service.

Gays The Word Lesbian Discussion Group, 66 Marchmont Street, WC1, meets at Gays The Word Bookshop (278 7654 for details) and occasionally goes on to Racketts or The Bell after meeting - see under Bookshops, and Entertainment above.

Greenwich Lesbian and Gay Rights Group, The Bell Pub, Haddo Street, SE10 (853 5206).

Hackney Women's Centre*, 27 Hackney Grove, E8. Lesbian Weekly Social.

Harrow Gay Unity, BM HGU, WC1N 3XX. Meets Mon 8.30pm Harrow Leisure Centre.

Kenric, BM Kenric, WC1N 3XX. This is a 'non-political' social group which arranges various activities for its members mainly in London. The group also runs a national newsletter. It is a group with a wide age range and welcomes new members.

Lesbian Country Correspondence Group, BM Lesbian Correspondence Group, WC1N 3XX. For lesbians in isolated areas.

Lesbian Feminist Artists' Group, meets 52-54 Featherstone Street, EC1. Every second Fri at 7.30pm.

Lesbian Feminist Society, c/o Merton Resources Centre, 240 Merton Road, SW19. Newsletter available.

Lesbian History Group, Wesley House, 70 Great Queen Street, WC2 (430 1076). Meets alternate Fri, 7.30pm.

Lesbians in Libraries, meet Wed 6.30pm. Ring Wesley House, as above.

Lesbian Social Group, North Paddington Women's Centre, 115 Portnall Road, W9 (969 8897). There is a regular monthly lesbian only social.

Married Lesbians, meet in the upstairs bar of the Chepstow Pub, Chepstow Place, 1 Notting Hill, first Tues of every month, 7.30pm. Access: N.

NUS Lesbian and Gay Committee, 461 Holloway Road, N7.

Open University Gay Society (OUGS), 54 Cavendish Road, N4 1RS.

Student Union Lesbian Group, c/o South Bank Polytechnic, Rotary Street, SE1.

Wages Due Lesbians, c/o The Women's Centre, 71 Tonbridge Street, WC1 (837 7509).

Working Class Lesbian Group, meets A Woman's Place, Hungerford House, Victoria Embankment, WC2, Thurs 7.30pm. Newsletter available. Access: P

Work (including labour movement)

APEX Lesbian and Gay Group, c/o LCGR, 39 Chippenham Road, W9

Camden Nalgo Lesbian and Gay Group, Camden Law Centre (485 6672).

Civil and Public Service Gay Group, 51 Charlmont Road, Tooting, SW17 9AH.

Communist Party Gay Rights Committee, 16 St John Street, EC1M 4AY (251 4406).

Gay Rights at Work, 7 Pickwick Court, SE9 (857 3793).

Gay Teachers' Group (Lesbian and Gay), BM Gay Teacher, WC1N 3XX.

Gay Welfare Workers' Group (Lesbian and Gay), c/o 100c Knightshill, West Norwood, SE27.

Haringey Nalgo Lesbian and Gay Group, 2A Brabent Road, N22.

Labour Campaign for Lesbian and Gay Rights, c/o 39 Chippenham Road, W9 (286 9692).

Labour Movement Lesbians, c/o Labour Campaign for Lesbian and Gay Rights.

Lesbian Employment Rights, Room 205, Southbank House, Black Prince Road, SE1 7SJ. Women's phone-line (587 1636). There are two lesbian workers and a separate lesbian project. Women can call in to them each Tuesday afternoon. Contact them for advice on heterosexism/anti-lesbianism in the workplace.

Lesbians In Education, c/o A Woman's Place, Hungerford House, Victoria Embankment, WC2.

Lesbians and Gays in TASS, c/o LCGR, 39 Chippenham Road, W9.

Lesbian Nurses' Group, c/o A Woman's Place, Hungerford House, Victoria Embankment, WC2. Meeting arranged, a network being set up.

Lesbians in Social Work Group, 52-54 Featherstone Street, EC1.

Nalgo Lesbian and Gay Group, Nalgo Office, c/o Town Hall Extension, 7th Floor, NW1.

NUR Lesbian and Gay Group, c/o LCGR, 39 Chippenham Road, W9.

Teachers in Further and Higher Education Gay Group, c/o 5 Caledonian Road, N1.

TGWU Lesbian and Gay Group, c/o LAGER, Room 205 South Bank House, Black Prince Road, SE1.

Unwaged Fight-Back Lesbian and Gay Group, 335 Holloway Road, N7. Meets Wed 11am-1pm.

Young Lesbians

Brent Youth Advisory Service, Chalkhill Neighbourhood Project, 369 Green Rigg Walk, Chalkhill Estate, Wembley Park (904 0911). Advice to young people, gay men and lesbians encouraged to use the service.

Camden and Islington Young Lesbian Group, c/o 8 Manor Gardens, N7 (263 6270). Meets Mon 8pm, 16-21 years.

Gay South West London Youth Group, ask for youth worker at Wands-worth Unemployment Youth Project, mixed (228 7136).

Gay Teenage Group, c/o 6-9 Manor Gardens, N7 (272 5741 phone for venue). Meets Sun 3-7pm and Wed 7-10pm, mixed lesbians and gay men.

Haringey Girls and Young Women's Project, c/o Education Office, Station Road, N22 (889 3912). Can undertake counselling, workshops and projects not just for lesbians, but pro-lesbian. Mainly under 21 years.

Help Starts Here, 168 Battersea Park Road, SW11 (720 0753/0852) Mon 2-6pm, Wed 10am-1pm, Thurs 2-6pm. Advice for under 21s, lesbians, gay men.

Lesbian and Gay Young People's Group, Ecumenical Centre, 7 Denbigh Road, W11. Meets Tues 7.30-10pm, women only 16-21 years.

Lesbian and Gay Youth Movement, BM GYM, WC1N 3XX. For lesbians and gay men under 26 years old.

Parents' Enquiry (698 1815), any reasonable time. A counselling agency for gay teenagers and their parents.

Piccadilly Centre, Subway 4, Piccadilly tube, W1 (930 0066/0274). Offers advice to young people.

South London Young Gay People, c/o Hearsay, 17 Brownhill Road, Catford, SE6 (697 2152). Meets Tues 7-10pm, 16-21 years. Access: N

West London Young Lesbians, Dept Senior Youth Officer, Kensington and Chelsea Area Youth Office, King House, 11 Westbourne Grove, W2 (727 1552).

Young Black Lesbian Group, Brixton Black Women's Centre, 41a Stockwell Green, SW9 (274 9220).

(And see also **Young Women**).

Useful Reading

For range of feminist publications, and books on/by lesbians, of which there are many, visit one of the women's bookshops or Gays The Word Bookshop - (see Bookshops in this section).

Artemis, BM PERFECT (TR), WC1N 3XX. Non-political lesbian magazine.

Compulsory Heterosexuality and Lesbian Existence, Adrienne Rich (Onlywomen Press 90p).

Contact Magazine, c/o Lavender Menace, 11a Forth Street, Edinburgh, EH1 3LE. British lesbian monthly magazine - national distribution.

Gaia's Guide, 32 Ivor Place, NW1 6DA. Guide listing bars, clubs, hotels etc worldwide. Available also in women's bookshops (see **Media and Arts**, Women's Booksellers).

Guide to Gay Custody, Action for Lesbian Parents, c/o Peaceworks, 58 Wakefield Road, Huddersfield, West Yorks. Covers problems of obtaining custody, solicitors and legal procedures.

Home Girls, a Black feminist authology, also has an excellent section on Black lesbians, ed Barbara Smith (Kitchen Table Press £9.95).

Lesbian Exchange Grapevine, c/o PO Box 162, Sheffield, S1 1UD. Newsletter of National lesbian network.

Lesbian Mothers on Trial - A Report on Lesbian Mothers and Child Custody, Rights of Women, 52-54 Featherstone Street, EC1 (251 6911/2) £1.50.

Lesbian Self-Insemination Booklet, available from Sisterwrite Bookshop, 191 Upper Street, N1.

London Disabled Lesbian/Gay Guide, GEMMA, BM Box 5700, WC1N 3XX. Also available in Braille.

London Lesbian Newsletter, available from Gays The Word Bookshop, (see Bookshops above) and Sisterwrite Bookshop, 191 Upper Street, N1.

Nice Jewish Girls, Jewish Lesbian Anthology (Persephone Press £5.40)

Onlywomen Press, 38 Mount Pleasant, WC1X 0AP. Mail order service available - publishes books by lesbians. Send sae.

Sheba Feminist Publishers, 10a Bradbury St, London N16. (254 1590) mail order service available — publishes many books by lesbians. Send sae for catalogue.

The Reach, lesbian feminist fiction, editors Mohen and Shulman (Onlywomen £2.95).

Rocking the Cradle: Lesbian mothers - a challenge in family living, Hanscombe and Forster (Sheba Feminist Publishers £3.50).

Sappho Was A Right-On Woman, Abbott and Love (Day Books £1.95)

Something To Tell You, Trenchard and Hugh Warren (London Gay Teenage Group £2.00).

Media and Arts

The adverts on street corners, the news on television, the portraits in art galleries, the plays in the West End, the programme of musicians and composers in concerts, all illustrate the inequality women face. Women's talents, skills and work are not displayed, portrayed or represented. The images of women used in the arts and by the media reinforce men's view of women as inferior and as sexual partners.

The reality of women's lives and experiences, unlike the media stereotypes surrounding us, is not represented in mainstream culture. We are rarely seen, for instance, as workers, or as independent of any relationships to men. The imagery which supposedly describes us is very restricted, amounting usually to variations on the same patriarchal themes: of mothers, wives, and heterosexual lovers in a number of subordinate relationships to men. We are rarely seen as creative outside of our biological capabilities. The artist is still regarded as male with women and Black people his exotic subject matter. There is a direct link between the pictures which are given to us and the capabilities that we are seen to have. As we are constantly pictured as supporting or servicing men or as their sexual objects for gratuitous display, so we continue to be denied any form of control. If we want ourselves to be represented in a better way it is vital that we gain access to the jobs and services which are the means of representation in our culture.

The pattern of women's employment across all the artistic and media professions is similar. Women do feature in the music business, the film, photographic and broadcasting industries but as the subject, as entertainment value, or behind the scenes in some supporting role as typists, caterers (the wonderful women in the Beeb's canteen, the majority of whom are Black) or as researchers and curators; work which is often unskilled or under-valued and which amounts to the 'caring professions' of culture. From the top decision-making white collar grades to the unionised production and technical levels, women are excluded from white and male only areas of work, on the basis that they are either untrained or unused to positions of power and control. The system perpetuates itself by the lack of training opportunities and the lack of precedents. The token successful woman, moreover, is rarely Black and never disabled or known to be gay.

To fill these enormous gaps, women in the media over the last decade have organised autonomously to provide their own resources from skills training workshops to performing, publishing and distributing outlets. A culture by and for women has been built up which draws upon and acknowledges the importance of women's experience. It seeks to challenge racist, sexist and handicappist reportage in the media, as well as the present discriminatory employment practices. Its success in London can be seen in the circulation of new writings, plays and films by women, the flourishing of publishing houses, alternative presses and Black and Asian art forms. However, if these developments which are revitalising mainstream culture are not to be re-appropriated by it or regarded as merely an alternative sub-culture then demands must continue to be made within the major areas of production and consumption by the women who are both 50% of its audience and a major element in its workforce.

In the *Programme of Action* the Women's Committee resolved to challenge the dominant images of women purveyed by public institutions and the mass media, in recognition that here is an important point of intervention for asserting all women's rights and which cuts across all aspects of the Committee's work. The Committee has worked in a number of ways to achieve this: through direct grant aiding of women's projects in conjunction with the Arts and Recreation Committee; through its own publicity, information and campaigning initiatives, two examples being the monthly bulletin and the Spot the Sexist Ads Campaign; and through policy development work with other committees, such as the Cinema Policy Working Group which was set up in 1983. The Committee has played a vital role concerning the GLC's powers with regard to cinema licensing and film certification and was instrumental in changing the GLC's rules of management to outlaw the showing of any material in places of public entertainment which incite hatred against any section of the public on grounds of colour, ethnic or national origins, sexual orientation or gender, or which promote sexual humiliation, degradation, or violence towards women. In its recent stand against offensive and violent imagery - from art exhibitions in GLC-controlled galleries to the billboard advertisements of London Transport, to the explicit selling ground of Soho cinemas, it has challenged the idea that art, whether it is in a prestigious art gallery on the South Bank, or a private club in Soho, is a purely aesthetic activity which has nothing to do with the law. With enormous support from London women the Committee has campaigned against the display of images which persistently misrepresent women and their interests. Through its own publications and in a more direct way through the resourcing of women's organisations which widely publish and distribute women's media and arts material, such as the film distributors **Cinema of Women**, **Sheba** the feminist publishing house, *Outwrite* the anti-racist anti-sexist women's newspaper and **Format** the all-women photo co-op and picture agency, the Committee has supported culture where women can actively become involved and also own it. There is no more effective strategy for supporting women artists than at the points of major public circulation.

Genuine equal opportunities initiatives and anti-sexist, anti-racist codes of practice in the media industries have yet to be achieved. The Women's Committee, in conjunction with other departments of the GLC, has pursued such policies with employers and trade unions as well as directly supporting women's cultural events. The listings which follow provide information on both the alternative networks and the mainstream training and employment bodies which women entering the industry or as consumers may find useful.

The section is ordered as follows: *Film, Video, Television and Radio - Opportunities for Women in Film and Programme-making, London-wide and National Groups, Community Activities and Classes, Formal Courses, Women's Groups Distributing Women's Film and Tapes, Other Distributors, Equipment Hire and Screening Facilities, Production Groups Making Film and Videos, Complaints about Sexist Advertising Commercials and TV Programmes; Music, Photography, Theatre, Visual Arts; Publications, Publishing and books.*

Film, Video, Television and Radio

Opportunities for Women in Film and Programme-making

The television, film, video and radio industry is one of the most male-dominated and white areas of employment in Britain. There is an alarming lack of programmes and films made by women, something which needs to change if women are to see a better representation of themselves and the world on screen and tape. Access to jobs and to training is a key element in that.

The following groups and organisations either have an interest in the involvement of women and of Black people in the film, television, video and radio industries - in some cases they have policies to this effect - and/or they are concerned about the representation of women on the air, on screen and on tape.

Many groups working at a local community level also have these interests and they are featured in the section 'Community Activities and Classes'.

London-wide and National groups

Association of Black Film and Video Workshops, c/o Black Audio Film Collective, 89 Ridley Road, Dalston, E8 (254 9527/9536). An umbrella organisation which represents Black film and video workshops in London and nationally.

Association of Cinematograph, Television and Allied Technicians (ACTT), 2 Soho Square, W1 (437 8506). Access: N. The main union for film, video and television workers. The ACTT has codes of practice on racism and sexism related to: the representation of women and Black people in programmes; attitudes in the workplace; employment practices. It has a Committee on Equality whose policy is to encourage and ensure that women and Black people enter the industry and are not kept in low grade jobs. The Committee on Equality hold an annual women's conference dealing with equal opportunities, racism, gay and lesbian and union issues. A newsletter, *Equality News*, is produced about every 2 months for ACTT members. The ACTT journal, called *Film and Television Technician*, is free for union members. The *Employment Bulletin* produced by the ACTT has a weekly jobs register for members looking for work.

Black Audio Film Collective, 89 Ridley Road, E8 (254 9527/9536). Exists to prioritise and encourage a Black film culture.

Black Women's Radio Group, c/o Local Radio Workshop, 12 Praed Mews, W2 (402 7651). They aim to challenge the white media's representation of Black people as a 'problem' and make recordings for and about the Black communities and especially Black women's activities and have made tapes covering Black conferences and Black music etc. Hope to set up a tape library.

CEDDO Film Video Workshop, 1st Floor, Seven Sisters School, Seaford Road, N15 (802 9034). A group of Black film/video makers concerned with the needs of Black people in general in relation to the industry.

Independent Film and Video Makers Association (IFVA), 79 Wardour Street, W1 (439 0460). Lobbies MPs, funding institutions and others for a better deal for film and video workers, particularly in the non-commercial, independent field. Acts as information and advice network to members. Individuals or groups may join. Reduced membership fee for students and unemployed. Will send an information package on request.

Local Radio Workshop, 12 Praed Mews, W2 (402 7651). Access: N. A non-profit making company which works with campaigning and special interest groups to make programmes for broadcast on London's local radio stations. Campaigns for access to airtime and accountability of local radio stations and their regulatory authorities. They have produced a number of reports on these issues and published a monthly publication newsreel which monitors media coverage of industrial and community issues. (See Community Activities and Classes below).

London Video Arts, 23 Frith Street, W1 (734 7410). Access: N. Non-profit-making (funded by GLC, Channel 4, GLA and BFI). Works only in video, not film. Works on a membership basis - has up to 150 members at any one time - anyone can become a member as long as they are non profit-making. Membership is £25 per year to individuals, £50 per year to groups. They produce a monthly newsletter, which can be received by associate members.

National Union of Journalists (NUJ), Head Office, Acorn House, Grays Inn Road, WC1 (278 7916). Has an Equality Council and Race Relations Working Party which strive for the rights of women and Black NUJ members within their profession. This covers news and research work in television and radio in addition to editorial work in press and publishing. Procedure for dealing with complaints against members who have breached its code of conduct. (See Complaints about sexist advertising commercials and TV programmes).

Sankofa Film and Video, Unit 5, Cockpit Yard Workshops, Northington Street, WC1 (831 0024). Black film and video group.

Society for Education in Film and Television (SEFT), Women's Media Education Network, 29 Old Compton Street, W1V 5PL (734 5455/3211).

Television Users Group (TUG), 29 Old Compton Street, W1V 5PL (734 5455/3211). TUG is campaigning for democratic access to, and control of, the film and broadcasting media; progressive and innovative television and related media; equal opportunities in all aspects of television. TUG functions as an alliance between programme-makers and viewers and a forum for debate and exchange of information. In London TUG holds monthly open meetings. TUG organises conferences and lobbies of parliament. Publishes a quarterly newsletter, called *TUG Newsletter*. Helps teachers and educators with resources and information. Annual membership £2 waged; £1 unwaged. £5 institutions.

Women's Airwaves, c/o Local Radio Workshop, 12 Praed Mews, W2 (402 7651). A voluntary part-time collective which produces radio productions and offers training by women for women which is currently limited to very occasional workshops on basic recording and production techniques. The group has an anti-racist policy, and is particularly interested in encouraging girls to explore radio. They currently produce a documentary/educational programme which is available for hire to groups and individuals.

Women's Film, Television and Video Network (WFTVN)*, 79 Wardour Street, W1 (434 2076). Access: N. Functions as an information and advice network for women who either work in the industry, or those who would like to, or those who are just interested in the field. Also endeavours to promote better opportunities for women to work in the industry, runs occasional one-off 'familiarisation sessions' which focus on particular aspects of working in the media. Produces a *Directory* of women working in, or trained in, film, video and TV (£3.50 for individuals/£8 for groups plus 50 p&p). Is compiling an *Information Folder* on women in broadcasting. Any woman may join. There are monthly meetings, six-weekly mailouts for members and an annual general meeting.

Women in Entertainment, 7 Thorpe Close, W10 (969 2292). The organisation behind the Women Live Festival, WIE are more concerned with the visual and performing arts than film, TV and video. Has two main functions: is a campaigning body, committed to improving the representation of women of all races and cultures on the media and arts. Also functions as a resources, support and information network for women working or waiting to work in the media and arts. Now has an advice worker who can advise on women's activities on these fields and on training opportunities. Has a very broad membership of women involved in a wide range of media and produces a directory of members.

Women in Sync*, Unit 5/6 Wharfdale Project, 47-51 Wharfdale Road, N1 9SE (278 2215). A women's video group whose main aim is to share skills with other women, particularly those without much experience in making tapes. They provide practical information and help for women. (See also Community Activities and Classes, and Equipment Hire and Screening Facilities).

Women's Media Action Group*, c/o A Women's Place Hungerford House, Victoria Embankment, WC2 (836 6081). Involved in monitoring and campaigning against sexism in the media. *Women's Media Action* is the bi-monthly magazine of the Women's Media Action Group (WMAG) - 1 year's subscription - £3.00. WMAG meet every Tuesday evening, 6.00 pm at A Woman's Place, Hungerford House, Victoria Embankment, WC2.

Details about local part-time and evening classes are available in *Floodlight,* a yearly publication, published in August/September by the Inner London Education Authority for inner London boroughs. Similar information is also available from outer London borough education authorities (see Education and Further Education) about local classes in their areas. Familiarisation classes and activities are available at a variety of venues in London. Some are strictly community-based while others are not limited to use by people from a particular area.

Albany Video, The Albany, Douglas Way, Deptford, SE8 (Office - 692 0231 ext 46. Distribution 692 6322). Access: P. Offer advice service and workshops in conjunction with local women's organisations in the Lewisham area.

Aphra Video, 245a Coldharbour Lane, SW9 (733 7207). Women's community video group. They work with community groups, mainly women's groups, mostly producing videos with and for women on community and women's issues and sometimes produce videos covering conferences and events. They hire out some of their tapes.

Community Activities and Classes

Association of Black Film and Video Workshops, c/o Black Audio Film Collective, 89 Ridley Road, Dalston, E8 (01-254-9527/9536). Access: P. Runs film familiarisation courses, some for Black women only.

Black Audio Film Collective, 89 Ridley Road, Dalston, E8 (01-254-9527/9536). Access: Areas of interest include anti-racist/sexist film material. Organises screenings, seminars, film familiarisation courses, some for Black women only.

Connections, Hammersmith and Fulham Community Media Project, Project Enterprise, 16 Askew Crescent, W12 9DP (740 7271 ext 8). This community project, records local events and holds some training courses - some for women only and girls only - throughout the year. Mobile facilities for outreach work with people with disabilities. Access: N.

Fantasy Factory Video, 42 Theobald Road, WC1 (405 6862). Video editing and post production company. Offers tuition in video editing at subsidised rates - 60% discount to the unemployed. Also has a print reference library giving information on training courses and facilities.

Four Corners, 113 Roman Road, E2 (981 4243). Access: P. Runs occasional semi-vocational intensive courses in specific film-making skills. Has often helped campaigning groups produce videos. Will allow use of facilities, resources and advice for would-be film/video markers. Has a positive discrimination policy in favour of women and Black people. Open Access to both individuals and groups. (See in listings Equipment Hire and Screening Facilities.)

Lambeth Video, 245a Coldharbour Lane, SW9 (274 7700). Access: N. Local access for individuals and groups from Lambeth. A resource centre which uses videos. Courses involve familiarisation with video equipment. Some women only and Black only courses.

Local Radio Workshop, 12 Praed Mews, W2 (402 7651). Access: N. Runs a 6-week 'Introduction to Radio' course and 'General Programming' course, operating in Autumn and Spring terms. ILEA funded. Covers the history and politics of radio. Emphasis on using tape recorders and machines. Courses open access.

London Film Makers Co-op, 42 Gloucester Avenue, NW1 (722 1728). Non profit-making (funded mainly by the BFI, some help from GLC), 50% women members. Functions as a production workshop, a distribution library, and a cinema (90 seats). Its workshop is open access, and runs occasional courses; including for women/black people/and unemployed/and general skill sharing workshops. (See in listings Equipment Hire and Screening Facilities.)

London Video Arts, 23 Frith Street, W1 (734 7410). Access: N. Non-profit-making (funded by GLC, Channel 4, GLA and BFI). Works only in video, not film. Works on a membership basis. Runs periodic short courses which are priority to members but which are open access.

Moonshine Community Arts Workshop Ltd., 1090 Harrow Road, Kensal Green, NW10 (960 0055). Access: P. Progressive policy in relation to women and Black people - emphasis on autonomous as well as mixed sex and race projects. Holds video workshops weekly, alternating in content rotationally from practical training on U-matic production and editing equipment to TV studies. Other workshops held at irregular intervals. Photography and printing workshops are held on a regular basis.

Retake Film and Video Collective Ltd., 25 Bayham Street, NW1 (388 9031). Asian film and video collective committed to working with community groups on projects. Community training sessions/workshops in film and video (328 3934)

Sankofa Film and Video, Unit 5, Cockpit Yard Workshops, Northington Street, WC1 (831 0024). Is committed to anti-racist, anti-sexist work. Workshops in film and video some for Black women only. Other special events organised, screenings etc. Access: P.

Walworth and Aylesbury Community Arts Trust (WACAT), 1A Wendover Thurlowe Street, Southwark, SE17. Community projects in radio, printing, photography, drama and music spread in different buildings on the estate. Local access only. Radio Section (701-9010). Access: A. Runs regular girls' groups (Tues evenings 6.30-9.00) teaching basic practical and theoretical radio skills. Is setting up a daytime women's group to offer similar skills. Runs (mixed) weekend courses functioning as an introduction to community radio, teaching skills and theory. Creche available and negligible fee (£1.00) WACAT also hold girls' project.

Women's Media Resources Project (WEFT), (WEFT at the Rio), c/o Rio Cinema, Dalston, 107 Kingsland High Street, E8 (254 6536). Shows regular programmes of independent and mainstream films and videos for women-only audiences. Space for discussions afterwards. Creche facilities possible by arrangements. Open membership to any women in London and open collective meetings.

West London Media Workshop, 118 Talbot Road, W11 (221 1859). Access: N. Runs video and photography resource courses for women and mixed groups. Video production course use camera and VHS and U-matic cameras. In conjunction with 'Connections' they run classes at Wornington Road

Adult Education Institute W10 which has creche facilities and full access.

Women's Airwaves, c/o Local Radio Workshop, 12 Praed Mews, W2 (402 7651). See National and London-wide groups.

Women in Sync*, Room 1/2, 38 Mount Pleasant, WC1 (278 2215). Runs training weekend workshops and week courses (sliding scale for unemployed etc.) weekend courses £12 waged, £6 unwaged). (See also under London-wide Groups).

Formal Courses

Two publications produced by the BFI Education Department give information about courses in the UK. *Film and Television Training* £1.00 + 40p p&p. *Studying Film and Television* £1.50 + 40p p&p.

In film and video all forms of training can be expensive. Some commercial enterprises in the field charge very high prices and so it is advisable to assess very carefully what you are getting for your money. The following organisations are mainly either commercial or are local authority or state funded. None of the courses are free. Fees vary. Ask for a prospectus and information on grant aid.

Short courses

Crosswind Films Ltd, 13 D'Arblay Street, W1 (439 1973) video and film courses. Commercial send for brochure.

National Broadcasting School, 14 Green Street, W1 (434 2411). Access: P. 3-month programming and journalism courses. Proficiency certificate. Grants may be available. Send for prospectus.

National Film and Television School, Beaconsfield Studios, Station Road, Beaconsfield, Bucks (Beaconsfield 71234). Access: A. Primarily offer in-service training and retraining in film and TV. Short courses for women and Black people funded by the GLC.

North East London Polytechnic, Greengate House, Greengate Street, E13 (590 7722). Offers two four day courses on video and editing techniques.

Polytechnic of Central London, PCL, Short Courses, 35 Marylebone Road, NW1, (486 5811). Access: P. Wide variety of courses in radio and TV. Prices vary.

South Thames College, Wandsworth High Street, SW18, (870 2241). Access: N. Short courses on TV production. About £10.00 per week for one week course if you live in the ILEA area.

St Martin's School of Art, 109 Charing Cross Road, WC2 (437-0611). Access: A. Summer School, two weeks in video production, £19.00 only. Evening classes, one evening per week for one year, in film and video production:

Full-time Courses

Croydon College, Faculty of Art and Design, Fairfield, Croydon, CR9 1DX (686 9471). One year post-graduate, 'Intermedia' course covering film and animation.

Goldsmiths' College, University of London Goldsmiths' College, New Cross, London SE4, (692 7171). Access: P. BA in Communications. Includes theoretical and practical curricula, mixing media studies with sociology as well as actually working within a chosen medium (eg film-making, radio etc). Also one-year full-time post graduate Diploma course, specialising in one of the following: video; film; animation; radio.

Harrow College of Higher Education, Northwick Park, Harrow, HA1 3TP (864 5422). Access: A. BA Hons degree in Applied Photography, Film and Television. Part-time, two year BA in Photographic Media Studies, for professional photographers who want to add to their qualifications. A purely theoretical course.

JOBFIT, Joint Board for Film Industry Training, 4th Floor, 5 Dean Street, W1 (734 5141). two year training on technical and production grades of film-making. Includes short courses on specific aspects, attachment to a variety of film, productions and individual specialisation in the 2nd year. A new scheme, GLC funded at present. Students are paid a wage of £100 pw by the scheme. JOBFIT is committed to a representative quota of women and Black students - 50% women, 25% Black/Ethnic Minority.

London College of Printing, Elephant and Castle, SE1 (735 9100). Foundation course in Media Studies: one year, practical and theoretical. BA in Photography, film and television: three years; practical and theoretical; early specialisation. Media Production and Design: four year sandwich course; placements in the media industry; practical and theoretical; covers all mediums. Diploma in Photojournalism: Applicants with experience only; one year; full-time. Radio Journalism: post-graduate diploma; one year; full-time; practical and theoretical.

Middlesex Polytechnic, 114 Chase Side, N14 (886 6599). BA Hons in Fine Art includes film and video. BA Hons in Graphic Design incorporates photography, film and TV. Post-graduate Diploma, one year, part-time in Film and TV Studies - theory and practice. Four year part-time BA Hons in Social Science - specialisation in Media Society possible. Theory only.

National Film and Television School, Beaconsfield Studios, Station Road, Beaconsfield, Bucks. (Beaconsfield 71234). Access: A. Offers three year vocational courses at post-graduate level, but degrees are not compulsory entrance requirement - talent and commitment main prerequisite. Courses cover all aspects of film and programme-making; students specialise in one field from the beginning.

Polytechnic of Central London, 35 Marylebone Road, NW1, (486 5811). Access: A. BA degree in Media Studies - radio, television and journalism. BA Film, Video and Photography. BSc in Photographic Science.

The Polytechnic of North London, Holloway Road, N7 (607 2789). Access: A Humanities Department offers Film Studies as part of a three year course leading to BA Humanities degree, which must comprise joint study with another subject the department offers.

The Royal College of Art, Kensington Gore, SW7, (584 5020). Department of Film and Television offers full-time post-graduate course. Two years (a 3rd year offered to exceptional students).

South Thames College, Wandsworth High Street, SW18 (870 2241). Runs DATEC courses in consultation with industry and professional organisations ie specifically vocational courses. The National Certificate Course either one year full-time and one year part-time/or one day a week for three years. Training for technicians to work in the audio visual industry. The National Diploma Course two years, full-time. Broader than the Certificate Course. Training for Audio Visual Designers and Production Assistants. The Higher National Certificate Course one day a week for two years. Experience necessary. Training for audio visual technicians seeking employment at supervisory level.

St Martins School of Art, 109 Charing Cross Road, WC2 (437 0611). Access: A. BA Fine Art degree, can choose film and video as main study option. Film and Video full-time advanced course for experienced candidates. Film and Video part-time advanced post-graduate diploma.

West Surrey College of Art and Design, Falkner Road, The Hart, Farnham, Surrey, GU9 7DS. BA Honours Degree in Art and Design specialising in one of the following: Photography; Film and Video; Animation.

Women's Groups Distributing Films and Tapes

Films can be hired for short periods (often 48 hours) to be shown at women's centres, socials, schools or by local community groups. Advice and help in using the necessary equipment is also often available from some distributors. Some will be able to send a catalogue.

Cinema of Women (COW)*, 27 Clerkenwell Close, EC1 (251 4978). Large selection of women's films covering wide range of subjects and a selection of films from other countries. Send sae for large catalogue.

Circles, 113 Roman Road, E2 (981 6828). Feminist distribution network set up by and for women to distribute women's films and videos.

Feminist Audio Books*, c/o AWP, Hungerford House, Victoria Embankment, SW1. Library of womens' books on tape for blind or partially sighted women.

Pictures of Women (POW) Productions, 245a Coldharbour Lane, SW9 (733 7207). Production group which hires out its own videos (feminist/black issues etc.). Will help with advice about their videos and how to use them, as well as selective lending of equipment. £10.00 for 48 hours (unfunded) £20.00 (funded).

Women's Education Group (WEDG)*, Women's Education Resources Centre, ILEA Drama and Tape Centre, Princeton Street, WC1 (242 6807). Access: P. A centre for teachers and youth workers. Small collection of VHS videos and slides. (A view at centre or borrow for use in schools and youth clubs. Also available as a women only space for meetings etc). Hours: Mon-Thurs 11-6, Fri 11-5. Produce three monthly subscription magazine *Gen*.

Womens' Tape Over, Box 35, 136 Kingsland High Street, E8. Feminist magazine on tape.

Women's Video Preview is a monthly event giving women working in community organisations, education and youth projects a chance to view videos that could be used in classes, groups etc. Open to all interested women. Held at: Room 908, North London Polytechnic, Ladbroke house, Highbury Grove, N5. Access: A. For details contact: Irene MacWilliam, Islington Women's Training Forum c/o IVAC, 332 Upper Street, N1 (226 4690).

Other Distributors

Other film and video organisations distribute some work by women about feminist issues. The best way of finding out what they have is to phone/write for a catalogue.

Albany Video, The Albany, Douglas Way, Deptford, SE8: Office: (692 0231 ext. 46) Distribution (692 6322). Community-based independent video workshop, distributing tapes made by its own and other community workshops. Has a number of titles dealing with specifically women's issues. Groups can preview tapes at the Albany before booking them. Some tapes come with teaching notes and Albany will give advice on ways of using or programming tapes. Have organised screenings specifically for women and for black women. All tapes VHS format. £10.00 for 48 hours.

British Film Institute (BFI), 81 Dean Street, W1 (437 4355). BFI have a viewing service. The National Film Archives produces a catalogue of films available for viewing. Offer wide selection of films send £5.00 £1.00 pp for catalogue. Also have a film/video library.

Concord Films Council, 201 Felixstowe Road, Ipswich (0473 715754). An educational charity with a large selection of broadly based 'educational films' - mainly hired by schools, colleges. Have some specifically women's films. Send £2.50 for catalogue.

Contemporary Films, 55 Greek Street, W1 (434 2623). Selection of 'alternative' films - some low-budget, some more commercial. Includes many films by women and Black people.

Inner London Education Authority (ILEA) Film and Video Library. Centre for Learning Resources, 275 Kennington Lane, SE11 (633 3892). The film and video library has a major collection of 16mm films which are available

for loan to all ILEA establishments. Videos and films available are listed in detail in the ILEA *Anti-Sexist Resource Guide* available for £3 (ILEA £2) from the Equal Opportunities (Gender) Librarian, ILEA, Centre for Learning Resources, 275 Kennington Lane, SE11 (633 5971).

London Film Makers Co-op, 42 Gloucester Avenue, NW1 (722 1728). 50% women production workshop and distribution library dealing mainly in avant garde/experimental films. Is one of the largest distributors of its kind in England and has a very wide selection of both British and foreign films for hire. (See Equipment Hire and Screening Facilities).

The Other Cinema, 79 Wardour Street, W1 (734 8508/9). Variety of films - send sae for details.

Equipment Hire and Screening Facilities

Some distributors hire their own equipment and will often advise on how to use it, as well as often operating a reasonable sliding scale price rate. Local education authorities and the ILEA are worth approaching about hiring film screening facilities, but not video. They have a good source of projectors. Commercial video hiring companies are obviously more expensive, but some reputable ones are useful as a last resort. They are efficient and will often deliver. They are listed in the Yellow Pages under Audio Visual Services and Video Services. Some have cine equipment as well as video.

Cinema Action, 27 Winchester Road, NW3 (586 7512). Have a small 60 seat cinema and post-production facilities which can be hired at a reasonable cost.

Connections, Hamersmith and Fulham Community Media Project, Project Enterprise, 16 Askew Crescent, W12 9DP (740 7271 ext. 8). Has video equipment (VHS and V-Matic for local groups).

Contemporary Films, 55 Greek Street, W1 (434 2623). Screening rooms £15.00 per hour. 16mm projectors £16.00 per day. Screen 4ft square available for hire.

Four Corners, 113 Roman Road, E2 (981 4243). Has 16mm portable projectors and 40 seat cinema for hire. Send sae for rate card; reduced rates for unfunded groups.

London Film Makers Co-op, 42 Gloucester Avenue, NW1 (722 1728). Has 16mm and Super 8 production facilities available for hire usually only to Members, but all post production facilities are available for hire. If you become a member, rates are low.

London Video Arts, 23 Frith Street, W1 (734 7410). Access: N. Non-profit-making (funded by GLC, Channel 4, GLA and BFI). Works only in video, not film. Distributors of videos with a catalogue of about 1,000 titles of art and documentary videos including many women's and overseas videos.

Lusia Films, 7-9 Earlham Street, WC2 (240 2350). Commercial company. Has wide range of equipment and facilities for hire on a sliding scale.

Newsreel, 4 Denmark Street, WC2 (240 2216). One 16mm projector, sliding scale, 9ft square screen.

Production Groups Making Film and Videos

For a completely up-to-date list of film and video companies and groups in London and nationally contact WFTVN or look in the British Film Institute's Yearbook. Many of the following groups work to produce videos and films about important issues for women to document our history and develop thought. Contact them if you want to become involved in production or have an idea for a film to be made, ie filming a women's conference or social event.

Aphra Video, 245a Coldharbour Lane, SW9 (733 7207). Women's community video group. They work with community groups, mainly women's groups, mostly producing videos with and for women on community and women's issues and sometimes produce videos covering conferences and events. They hire out some of their tapes.

Black Audio Film Collection, 89 Ridley Road, E8 (254 9527/9536). Production and welcomes ideas and participation. (See London-based Groups and Community Activities and Classes).

Broadside, c/o 74 Moss Lane, Pinner, Middlesex (866 5271). Small all-women commercial production group, mainly for television. Main aim is a commitment to non-stereotypical representation of women. Produce mainly documentaries on women's issues and some black womens issues. Are open to working with outside groups.

Cinema Action, 27 Winchester Road, NW3 (586 7512). A non-profit making production workshop. Will give advice and help to new production groups setting up as well as one-off projects.

CLIO Co-op, 91c Mildmay Road, N1 (249 2551). Produce videos concerning women's issues, specialising in older women's issues especially oral history. Non-profit making. Open to working with some outside groups.

Agender Films Ltd, 5 Gower Street, WC1 (637 7920/21). An all women production company making films with a feminist perspective.

Faction films, 7-9 Earlham Street, WC2N 9LL (379 3596). Produces progressive documentary and fiction work. Projects have included work on Ireland, Chile, Women in Technology, Black groups and so on. Organised the Irish film festival. Non commercial organisation.

Four Corners, 113 Roman Road, E2 (981 4243). Access: P. A non-profit making charity, franchised workshop very open to outside funded groups and individuals who need practical advice and help in making films - it has a large range of equipment and facilities for hire. As a production group they produce political/experimental films, many by women.

Irish Women's Film and Video Group, c/o London Women's Centre, 59 Stoke Newington Church Street, N16. Access: P.

Kuumbra Productions Ltd, 74 Newman Street, W1T 3LA (636 6696). Black production company. Encourages young Black people to enter the industry. Help with training, contacts, advice etc. There is a link up with outside workshops (eg **CEDDO**). Productions reflect a Black perspective.

Late Start, c/o Outwrite Oxford House, Derbyshire Street, E2. Black women's film video and photography group.

London Film Makers Co-op, 42 Gloucester Avenue, NW1 (722 1728). Non profit-making (funded mainly by the BFI, some help from GLC), 50% women members. Functions as a production workshop, a distribution library, and a cinema (90 seats).

London Video Arts, 23 Frith Street, W1 (734 7410). Access: N. Non-profit-making (funded by GLC, Channel 4, GLA and BFI). Works only in video, not film. Will give advice on video production.

Lusia Films, 7-9 Earlham Street, WC2 (240 2350). Commercial company. Long established commitment to independent film-making. Open to working with others groups or individuals. Has wide range of equipment and facilities for hire on a sliding scale.

Newsreel Collective, 4 Denmark Street, WC2 (240 2216). A non-profit making production workshop funded by GLC and Channel 4. Is open to doing co-production with outside groups, but cannot help unfunded groups except with advice. Hires out film editing and production equipment only (on sliding scale).

New Girls Network, c/o Carrie Bates, 27 Mount Pleasant Villas, N4 (263 5545). Very new group (GLC funded) want to produce videos concerned with women, girls and work. Only open to women already with links in broadcasting.

Penumbra Productions, 60 Farringdon Road, EC1 (251 3885). Deals with Third World issues and the Black community in Britain. There are two names under which they work. **Penumbra** deals with videos and **Azad**, the sister company, deals with mainstream TV work. Examples of work done - GLC Housing Rights. Video plus information pack to go with it. Film about domestic violence against women in the Asian Community, Pakistani settlers in Britain and what has happened to them. They are independent not commercial. There is a lot of women involvement although there is no prejudice for or against women. They do help to train women. Although the company is all Asian they are not restrictive in who works for them. Open to suggestions, ideas etc.

Pictures of Women (POW) Productions, 245a Coldharbour Lane, SW9 (733 7207). Non-profit making small womens production group working on commission basis only - therefore not really able to work with outside groups/individuals but will help women by selectively hiring out equipment. Produce films by women and Black women.

Star Productions, Basement, 61 Thistlewaite Road, E5 (986 4470). This is a film and video workshop (part of the Association of Black film and video workshops). Productions are created from an Asian point of view concentrating on Asian Life in Britain. There is positive encouragement of Asian women to become involved - they have the first Asian camera-woman! There is also a theatre project attached called the 'British Asian Theatre'. Star Productions has women-only projects running. They also intend to provide facilities for the community, including editing of equipment, a studio, etc.

Always open for ideas and suggestions.

Women in Sync*, Room 1/2, 38 Mount Pleasant, WC1 (278 2215). A women's video group whose main aim is to share skills with other women, particularly those without much experience in making tapes. They provide practical information and help to interested women.

Working Connections (formerly Co-options), 27 Clemence Street, E14 (987 3224). Contact address only. Developing own projects and interested in working with women's groups and individual women.

Complaints About Sexist Films and Programmes

TV channels are obliged to provide for, and listen to, complaints made by the public. You can phone up the duty desk of the relevant TV station at the time or after transmission of the programme.

The guidelines below were compiled by the Women's Media Action Group, a collective of women campaigning against degrading images of women in the media. The group would like to receive copies of written complaints that you make. (See Women's Media Action Group under Campaigning Groups).

TV and Radio Advertising Commercials. Write to: Independent Broadcasting Authority, Advertising Control Division, 70 Brompton Road, London SW3 - the IBA is responsible for ensuring that their Code of Advertising Standards and Practice is not contravened. They have the power to refuse to take ads or to oblige advertisers to change/withdraw them so when complaining about particular ads. use the opportunity to let them know what viewers generally find unacceptable. Send a copy to the manufacturers. Also, write to the Advertising Standards Authority, Brook House, Torrington Place, WC1, and/or ring the ASA (580 5555).

TV and Radio Programmes Telephoned Complaints: The quickest and easiest way to register a complaint about a programme is to ring up the broadcaster, either the BBC or, in the case of ITV, the IBA and the ITV company. In the case of Channel Four programmes, which are predominantly made by ITV companies or independent programme-makers, you can ring up Channel Four, the IBA and the programme-maker. See the list below:

Anglia Television (0603 615151), BBC (Television) 734 8000, BBC (Radio) 580 4468, Border Television (022 825 101), Central Television (021 643 9898), Channel Four (631 4444), Grampian Television (0224 646464), Granada (061 832 7211), HTV Cardiff (0222 21021), HTV Bristol (0272 778366), IBA (584 7011), ITN News (637 2424), NWT (261 3434), Scottish Television (041 332 9999), Television South (0703 34211), Thames Television (387 9494), TV South West (0752 663322), Tyne Tees (0632 610181), Yorkshire TV (0532 438283), S4C Wales (0222 43421)

TV and Radio - Formal Complaints

In relation to BBC television programmes, write to Programme Correspondence Section, BBC, Television Centre, Wood Lane, London W12 or preferably ring the duty officer after transmission time (743-8000). For radio programmes write to Programme Correspondence Section, Broadcasting House, Portland House, Portland Place, W1 or ring (580-4468).

● If the programme was on ITV write to the Independent Broadcasting Authority and/or the ITV company which made the programme. Write to the ITV Company's Complaints Section

● If the programme was on Channel Four, write to the Channel and/or to the programme's production company.

● Send a copy to the producer of the offending programme (the name is usually printed in the *Radio Times*);

● If you want to write a letter for other members of the public to see, write to the *Radio Times*, BBC Publications, 35

Marylebone High Street, London, W1M 4AA, or the TV Times, 247 Tottenham Court Road, W1P 0AU.

The BBC prides itself on replying to all 'serious' letters and passing an analysis of comments received to senior staff. It also has a Programme Complaints Commission which will look at your complaint if you are not satisfied with the BBC's first answer. Complaints must reach the BBC in writing within 30 days of broadcast of the offending programme. Complaints about programmes which are rung through are recorded in a log book and all the complaints are surveyed at the end of the week.

The following groups are also involved in dealing with complaints about programmes:

Campaign for Press and Broadcasting Freedom, 9 Poland Street, W1 (437 2795). Broad based organisation, made up mainly of media workers, that researches and campaigns for greater accountability, access and diversification of media and advises on redress against misrepresentation. Now establishing a 'Right to Reply Unit' and a right of reply pack - comprehensive information on how to make complaints. Has a women's group based in London. Has developed a code of conduct (provisionally accepted by NUJ and ACTT at present) - copies available from above address. Pamphlets on media sexism, racism, anti-gay/lesbian and anti-disabilities. Organise regular events and conferences and a 'free press' bulletin bi-monthly for members.

National Union of Journalists (NUJ) Head Office, Acorn House, Grays Inn Road, WC1 (278 7916). Has an Equality Council and Race Relations Working Party, which strive for rights of women and Black NUJ members within their profession which covers news and research work in television and radio, in addition to editorial work in press and publishing. There are two options for complaints, one informal - by phoning the Equality Council and they will take up your complaint for you, the other formal - by contacting NUJ Head Office for advice on the procedure to carry through a complaint. The latter can be complicated but a booklet on how to complain is available from NUJ Head Office. From March 1986 there will be an 'Ethics Council' which should make the procedure more straightforward and effective.

Music

London is exceptionally well provided for with women musicians and groups, and with many opportunities for making music.

For general information on many different types of music/musicians, see the weekly listings magazine *City Limits*. For more information on women's bands and benefits, see *Spare Rib* (monthly) magazine, and notice boards at women's bookshops (see Women's Publications) and women's centres (see **Borough Information**).

For all information on specific women's bands (all women and mixed) available for booking, workshops, publications, sound engineering, women DJs, tours, festivals etc. send sae to: Music Resource Agency, c/o 98 Hazellville Road, N19 3NA.

Young women - (see **Young Women's** section for music projects, which are often set up in youth clubs specifically for girls/young women). Women's discos - (see **Lesbian** section of this book).

Music Participation

Chat's Palace, 42-44 Brooksby's Walk, E9 (986 6714). Community Centre with a range of activities. Open Mon-Sat. Runs music workshops for girls/young women in Reggae and other types of music. Access: A.

Interchange, 15 Wilkin Street, NW5 (267 9421). Facilities for making demo tapes and learning to record (4 track) available. Women's night programmed, call for details. Access: N.

Kentish Town Women's Workshop*, 169 Malden Road, NW5 (267 0688). 10-6 pm. Mon-Fri. Space available for women's groups evenings and weekends. Wide range of workshops and classes, including voice and rhythm classes. Access: A.

Lewisham Academy of Music, 77 Watson's Street, Deptford, SE8 (691 0307). Music workshops for women - young women, mothers and unemployed women. Outreach music workshops for people with disabilities, at day centres, etc. Access: N in main building, but out-building has Access: A.

Moonshine Community Arts Workshop Ltd., 1090 Harrow Road, Kensal Green, NW10. (960 0055). Range of activities include studio recording and sounds workshops for women and girls, day and evening. Access: P.

Pink Singers: Contact Ron (881 0076) for information on this group which invites lesbians and gay men to join. Rehearsals at County Hall, SE1 weekly at 2.30 pm. (Room number at reception).

West London Women's Music Project, Metrostore, 231 The Vale, Action, W3 (740 9285). Musical instrument and voice tuition (Guitar, piano, percussion) on a one to one basis at very reasonable rates. Workshop space available for practice sessions. Access: A.

Music Resources

Music Resources Agency, 98 Hazellville Road, N19 3NA (272 2304). New centre for general music resources for women-identified projects. Information about tours, festivals, professional and educational music and sound engineering workshops, publications, contacts for bands, women sound engineers. Newsletter to be arranged.

OVA, 122 Holly Lodge Mansions, Oakeshot Avenue, N6 (341 4967). OVA currently run music workshops for women in Voice and Rhythm (percussion and drumming), and workshops in PA sound at different venues throughout London. (Phone for details). In the very near future they will be opening a women's music resource centre which will have a Sound Recording Studio for women to use and space for workshops as above. Premises for this not yet finalised. Contact address and number will not be changing.

WEFT*, Sound Recording Studio, 90 De Beauvoir Road, N1 (254 6536). 16 Track Sound Studio for recording and training for women only. Also porta studio for hire. Access: P.

Wesley House*, 70 Great Queen Street, WC2 5AX (430 1076). This is a multi-purpose Women's Resource Centre which includes music and performance facilities.

Useful Contacts

London Musician's Collective, 42A Gloucester Avenue, NW1 (722 0456). Access: N.

Musicline, 64 Palatine Road, N16 (249 5492). Service for all musicians or would-be musicians offering 'introductions to like-minded amateur music-makers of every style and standard'. Join for £6 (£3 unwaged) and get their newsletter/contact list available from above address.

Women's Revolutions per Minute (WRPM), 82 Woodstock Road, Birmingham B13 9BN (021 449 7041). Main distributors of women's music both from this country and abroad, with extensive catalogue of American women's music. All records and tapes on sale at Sisterwrite and Silver Moon Bookshops (see Women's Booksellers) or send SAE for list.

Photography

Many adult education institutes run courses on photography. Details of these are available from your local public library. The ILEA *Floodlight* guide to adult education (available at libraries and from most newsagents - June-Sept, 50p) is very thorough. (See also Film/Video section as some groups listed there also run photography courses for women).

Acton Community Arts Workshop (ACAW), Action Hill Church, 1b Gunnersbury Lane, W3 (993 3665). ACAW is a women's arts group working with women's groups on photographic and graphic exhibition work - graphic and photographic exhibitions/poster series /leaflet work - covering local, London-wide and national issues. The women's groups provide the information, and ACAW handles the technical work, with design, layout and image selection jointly discussed. Facilities - fully equipped black and white darkroom, and layout area for planning exhibitions and posters.

Albany Community Centre, Douglas Way, Deptford, SE8 (691 0231/7223 and 692 0231). Large, modern active communtiy centre with darkroom facilities. Runs classes and special projects in photography for women. Access: A.

Battersea Arts Centre, 177 Lavender Hill, SW11 (223 6557/8). Large, active community centre, with darkroom facilities. Runs photography classes

for women, and arranges special events for women, eg viewings. WEA funded photography class on Thurs has creche facilities available. Access: A.

Cambridge House Literacy Scheme, 131 Camberwell Rd, SE5 0HF (701 4221). From time to time runs photography courses for women, with creche facilities. Contact for details. Access: P.

Camerawork, 121 Roman Rd, E2 (980 6256). This is a women's only day community photographic centre. Darkroom, gallery, quarterly magazine (back issues available), and 50 touring photographic shows. Workshops include women's workshop and Black representation workshop. Courses run for beginners (women only and mixed). Outreach work with local community. Special darkroom for people with disabilities, and toilet. Access:A.

Chat's Palace, 42-44 Brooksby's Walk, E9 (986 6714). Community centre runs photography classes for women on Thurs, with creche facilities. Access: A.

Cockpit Gallery, Princeton St, WC1 (405 5334). Gallery 10 am - 6 pm Mon-Fri. Also from time to time, photography courses for women, girls only courses, and courses for women teachers of photography. Ring for details. Access: N.

The Drill Hall, 16 Chenies St, WC1 (631 5107). Runs photography courses for women and has darkrooms available for low charge. Hours: 10 am - 6 pm (some evenings available: phone for details). Access: P.

Format Photographers*, 25 Horsell Rd, N5 (609 3439). Commercial agency representing nine women photographers who produce pictures on a great range of subjects for magazines, newspapers and other media. Coverage includes women's issues, anti-sexist and anti-racist material. Office hours: 10 am - 6 pm weekdays. Access: N.

Interchange, 15 Wilkin St, NW5 (267 9421). Courses in photography available. Darkroom facilities available for hire by local women's groups. Access: N.

Island Arts Centre, Tiller Rd, Isle of Dogs, E14 (987 7925). Community arts centre with a range of facilities including photography and video and screen printing. Weekly women's group. Special courses for women. Also, open to special projects with groups from ethnic minorities. Outreach work with other community centres and groups in the community undertaken. Access: A (phone in advance). Creche: Weds.

Lee Centre, 1 Aislibie Road, SE12 (852 4700). Daytime photography courses for women, Mon-Fri, with creche facilities. Access: A.

Lenthal Road Women's Workshop, 81 Lenthal Rd, E8 (254 3082). Feminist community arts workshop offering darkrooms and other facilities. Offers skill-sharing, space and resources. Also supplies photographs for use in publications. Hours: 10 am - 6 pm weekdays. Access: P.

Monocrone, c/o Blackfriars Settlement, 44 Nelson Sq, SE1 (928 9521). Monocrone is a photography project for women presently sharing the resources of the Blackfriars Photography Project. Monocrone runs day and evening courses in photography for women, does tape/slide work, and has produced a handbook of photography. Their photographic exhibition on women and amateur photography is available for hire. Access: N.

Moonshine Community Arts Workshop Ltd, 1090 Harrow Rd, Kensal Green, NW10 (960 0055). Activities include women only classes in photography, day and evening. Access: P.

North Paddington Community Darkroom, 510 Harrow Rd, W9 (969 7437). Faciilities available for groups and campaigns both locally and throughout London. Also runs training courses. Hours: 10 am - 4 pm weekdays (phone first). Access: N.

Parkview Youth Centre, Parkview Rd, Southall, Middx, UB1 3HJ (574 7836). Women and girls' night (Fri) includes a photography class, as well as karate, table tennis and pool. Contact Jackie Clayton. Access: A.

Wesley House*, 70 Great Queen Street, WC2 5AX (430 1076). This multi-purpose Women's Resource Centre has slide/tape facilities.

West London Media Workshop, 118 Talbot Rd, W11 (221 1859). Video and photography workshop, access for local groups/womens groups. Photography classes every Monday for women - some outreach work. Access N.

Women Artists' Slide Library, share BAC premises (above). Different phone no. 228 5771. WASL publishes a newsletter.

Theatre

For general theatre listings, 'fringe', and women's theatre, see weekly listings magazines such as *City Limits*. For an up-to-date register of women's theatre groups and other performers, contact Women in Entertainment (see below).

Artsline, 5 Crowndale Rd, NW1 1TU (388 2227). Good phone-in advice service on the Arts and Entertainment in London for people with disabilities. Mon- Fri 10 am - 4 pm; Sat 10 am - 2 pm. Access: A.

Fringe Theatre Box Office, Duke of York Theatre, St Martin's lane, WC2 (379 6002). Tickets availabe for most of London's fringe theatre. Credit card bookings over the phone. Access: A.

Equity Women's Committee, 8 Harley St, WC1 (637 9311). Advice, information and women's campaigning branch of Actor's Equity, the actors' trade union.

Women in Entertainment, 7 Thorpe Close, W10 (969 2292). National pressure group of volunteers working for non-sexist work in the entertainment industry. Runs workshops, conferences and aims to act as an advice and resource centre with up-to-date register of women's theatre groups and performers.

Women's Playhouse Trust, Office: 60 York Way, NW1 9AO (833 4781), Friends' Membership Secretary, 141 Hamilton Terrace, NW8. Group formed to record and document women's experiences in theatre and currently raising funds to buy and establish a theatre building in Central London which will be a permanent and secure platform for women's plays.

The following London based companies present shows (theatre, cabaret, etc) which take up issues of interest and concern to women. They are available for hire to perform at schools, women's centres and theatres; phone them for details of current productions or details of performances close to you. Many are also able to present workshops. All are all-women companies unless otherwise stated.

Burnt Bridges Theatre Company, 4 Birdhurst Road, Colliers Wood, SW19 (540 9080). Touring company. All female based. Try to express the female experience and find a new theatrical language in which to do so.

Clean Break, Basement, 34a Stratford Villas, NW1 (485 0367). Workshops and productions written and performed by criminalised women on theme of women and the law.

Consenting Adults in Public, Thornhill Neighbourhood Centre, 199 Caledonian Rd, N1 (278 9500). Theatre workshop for all lesbians and gay men. Access: P.

Gay Sweatshop, Lesbians and gay men (625 4670).

Graeae Theatre, Diorama, Peto Place, NW1 (935 5588/8999). Actors with physical disabilities.

Hesitate and Demonstrate, St James Institute, Pollard Row, E2 6NB (729 1815). Mixed visual theatre company, rehearsal space to rent.

Labyrinth Theatre Company, Basement flat, 9A Upper Park Road, Belsize Park, NW3 (708 0147). Aims to illuminate the power of women's writing. They have contact with international women. Also organise women's workshops.

Little Women Theatre Company, 33 Osbaldeston Road, N16 7DJ (806 6565). Aims to entertain and challenge the roles tradition presents to women both on and off the stage.

Monstrous Regiment, 4 Elder Street, E1 6DT. Aims to provide exciting political theatre which places womens' experiences centre stage. (247 2398). Mixed.

ReSisters Theatre (671 0338). Women and self-defence.

The Rubber Jennies, Charlotte Ashton, c/o Cockpit Theatre, Gateforth Street, Marylebone, NW8 8EH (262 7907). Young women's theatre.

Access: A up to four wheelchairs. No toilet facilities.

Scarlet Harlots (272 4973).

Sensible Footwear Company (482 2633)

Siren Theatre Company (806 5327). London and Brighton based all women theatre collective. Content of their work relates very explicitly to the position of women in our society; how women occupy different social positions according to our class, disabilities, race, creed and sexuality.

Spare Tyre, 86 Holmleigh Road, N16 (800 9099). Present cabaret shows and humerous musical plays on women's issues particularly women's health and compulsive eating. Also help set up and run workshops for women with eating problems.

Tara Arts, 356 Garrat Lane, SW18 4EF. Access: A. Three Functions: Professional Asian touring company; Education - tour around schools performing plays; Arts Centre. Although an Asian group it is not specifically aimed at an Asian audience/market. (871 1458/9).

Women's Theatre Group, 5 Leonard St, EC2 A4AQ (251 0202). Feminist touring company. Aim to perform plays by women and for women. They explore the cultural, political and social themes from a woman's point of view.

Vukani, 86 North Hill, N6 4RL (348 0254). A multi-racial group who use theatre as a medium to expose racism. Company orientated.

Theatre of Black Women, Box 6, 136 Kingsland High St, E8 2NS (249 1660). Aims to reflect the life of Black women. Provides a view of Black women's lives based on the truth of their own experience. Challenges racist and sexist stereotypes while examining and redefining Black women's self image. Aim is to portray Black women in a positive light.

Munirah Theatre Co, 136 Allisin Road, N8 0AS (340 3190). All Black women's touring theatre company. Deals with issues affecting African people, in particular women. Have workshops.

The theatres and centres below regularly present women's companies and many also offer other facilities such as meeting rooms available for hire, run training courses, darkrooms for photographers and workrooms. Telephone for current programme of events or check the Theatre sections of the weekly *City Limits* magazine.

Africa Centre, 38 King St, WC2 (740 7271). Access: P.

The Albany Empire, Douglas Way, SE8 (691 3333). Access: A.

Arts Theatre, 6 Great Newport St, WC2 (836 2132). Good children's programmes. Access: N.

Battersea Arts Centre Theatre, Old Town Hall, Lavender Hill, SW11 (223 8413). Good children's programmes. Access: A.

The Drill Hall, 16 Chenies Street, WC1E 7ET (631 1353). Offers free childcare on Mon, Fri, Sat. Access: P.

The Factory, 1 Chippenham Mews, W9 (286 1656). Access: N.

Greenwich Theatre, Crooms Hill, SE10 (858 7755). Access: P.

Half Moon Theatre, 213 Mile End Rd, E1 (790 4000). (Also: **Half Moon Young People's Theatre Company.**)

Hoxton Hall, 130 Hoxton St, N1 (739 5431). Access: A.

Jacksons Lane Community Centre Theatre, Archway Rd, N6 (340 5226). Access: A.

Old Red Lion Theatre, St John St, EC1 (837 7816). Access: P.

Oval House, 54 Kennington Oval, SE11 (735 2786). Access: A.

Tricycle Theatre, 269 Kilburn High Rd, NW6 (328 8626). Access: possible (phone first).

Women's Theatre at Lauderdale, Lauderdale House, Waterlow Pk, Highgate Hill, N6 5HG (348 8716). Access: A. No toilet facilities.

Visual Arts

The listings below provide details of arts projects, and galleries which provide specific facilities for women. The Minority Arts Advisory Service, Women Artists Slide Library and Institute of Contemporary Arts will advise on relevant publications according to your particular interest or need.

Black Art Gallery, 225 Seven Sisters Road, N4 (263 1918). Access: A. This gallery is part of the Organisation for Black Art Advancement and Leisure Activities (OBAALA). The gallery provides a forum for Black artists who have previously had little opportunity to show and share their work. Open: Tues-Sat 11am-6pm.

Black Women's Creativity Project, Women's Education Resource Centre, ILEA Drama and Tape Centre, Princeton Street, WC1 (242 6807). The project aims to meet the needs of and be receptive to Black women's creativity. The project organises exhibitions etc. Open 10am-5.30pm.

FAN, Feminist Arts News, 195 Station Road, Kingsheath, Birmingham, 14 7TP. Feminist arts news service.

Minorities Arts Advisory Service, Beauchamp Lodge, 2 Warwick Crescent, W2 (286 4154). Advisory service on all aspects of Black and ethnic minority arts.

Pentonville Gallery, 7/9 Ferdinand Street, NW1 (482 2948). Access: A. Exhibitions cover all types of artwork ie Black, Irish, etc. Open: Wed-Sat 11am-6pm. Sun 11-3pm.

People's Gallery, 72 Prince of Wales Road, NW5 (267 0433). Access: A. No toilets. Aims to provide an outlet for those who have attained a high standard of work but have been denied access to exhibit, due to race, sex or class. Giving opportunities to disabled artists is an important part of the gallery's activities.

Round House Theatre, Chalk Farm Road, NW1 8PB (482 5245). Has an art gallery for Black Art.

Women Artists Slide Library, c/o Battersea Arts Centre, Lavender Hill, SW11 5TJ (228 5771). Access: A. The Library is a national resource, and has three sections:- historical, documentary and contemporary slides of women artists. There is a book and catalogue section and cuttings file. Projects run:- Black Women Artists Index, Irish project, history project, women and papermaking, mural project, video and performance project, current book list. All run by volunteers. Open: Tues-Wed 10am-5pm, Thurs-Fri 10-6pm. Open to all practising women artists.

Women's Eye Gallery, Lauderdale House, Waterlow Park, Highgate Hill, N6 (348 1794).

Publishing and Books
Women's Publications

This is a list of just some of the magazines and newsletters that are available. Most can be found at Silver Moon and Sisterwrite bookshops in London (see below) you can also obtain subscription details by forwarding an sae. Some are now available on tape for blind/partially sighted women. Some are women-only publications not meant for men to read; please respect this.

Many women's groups, centres, campaigns and organisations also produce regular newsletters which are a valuable source of information and contacts.

Black Feminist Newsletter, c/o AWP Hungerford House, Victoria Embankment, WC2.

FAN (Feminist Arts News), 195 Station Road, Kingsway, Birmingham, 14 7TB. Covers women's work and writings in the visual arts.

Feminist Review*, 11 Carlton Gardens, Brecknock Road, N19 5AQ (485 8420). Published three times annually. A journal aimed at developing the theory ofthe women's liberation movement.

For The Likes of Us, c/o Julia Tant, 3 Kestrel Avenue, SE24. Working class women's writing newsletter.

GEN*, c/o Women in Education, Drama and Tape Centre, Princeton Street, WC1. (01-242 6087) Anti-sexist, anti-racist education magazine with reviews, articles and contacts.

ISIS International Women's Journal, via S. Maria d'ell Anima 30, 00186 Rome, Italy. Giving indepth coverage to the issues women around the world are working on. Also, Women in Action newsletter bringing news of conferences, events, information about groups and resources.

Lysistrata, 11 Princes Street, Brighton. Jewish, Black women's magazine with emphasis on peace issues. Available on tape.

m/f, 24 Ellerdale Road, NW3. Feminist theory journal.

Mukti,* 213 Eversholt Street, NW1. Asian women's magazine published in Belgali, English, Gujerati, Hindi, Punjabi and Urdu.

Older Feminist Newsletter, c/o A Woman's Place, Hungerford house, Victoria Embankment, WC2 (836 6081). Regular newsletter for older women with discussions and details of meetings and social events.

Older Lesbian Newsletter, BM OLN, WC1N 3.

Outwrite Women's Newspaper*, Oxford House, Derbyshire Street, E2 (729 4575). Anti-racist, anti-imperialist feminist newspaper campaigning against women's oppression.

Panakaeia, 1 Ravenstone Road, N8. A journal of feminist psychics and alternative healing.

Revolutionary/Radical Feminist Newsletter, 17 Kensington Terrace, Leeds 6. Irregular feminist newsletter for women-only. Available on tape.

SEQUEL, BM Sequel, WC1N 3. National lesbian feminist magazine.

Shifra, Box No. 2, 59 Cookbridge Street, Leeds 1. Jewish feminist magazine.

Spare Rib*, 27 Clerkenwell Close, EC1R OAT (253 9792). Monthly women's liberation magazine. Available on tape.

Trouble and Strife, PO Box MT16, Leeds, LS17 5PY. A radical feminist magazine published three times annually. Available on tape.

We Are Here, c/o A Woman's Place, Hungerford House, Victoria Embankment, WC2 (836 6081). Regular newsletter for Black feminists only.

Women for Life on Earth Newsletter, 2 Branshill Gardens, NW5 1JH. Magazine of unifying network for feminists and ecology.

Women's News, c/o Box WN, 7 Winetavern Street, Belfast, BT1. Belfast women's paper.

Women's Studies International Forum, c/o The Editorial Group, Rossetti House, SW3. Regular information about improvements in women's studies debates and publications.

Women's Tape Over, c/o A Woman's Place, Hungerford House, WC2 (836 6081). Feminist magazine produced on tape for blind partially sighted women.

Women's Review, Old Loom House, Back Church Lane, London E1 ILS (265 1719). Monthly books and arts review produced by women.

Working with Girls Newsletter, Keswick House, 30 Peacock Lane, Leicester, LE1 5NY. Bi-monthly newsletter useful to youth workers and all women working with girls.

Women's Publishing Houses

There are now many women's publishing houses in Britain and Ireland which concentrate on promoting women's writings. Their books are available in London at Silver Moon, and Sisterwrite and Virago bookshops and should also be available at most other bookshops in the Greater London Area. If you have trouble getting hold of a particular title, please telephone the sales manager of the publisher concerned and they will give you details of your local stockists.

Ultra Violet Enterprises, Top Floor, 25 Horsell Road, N5 (607 4463). Women's publishing consultancy service offering advice on all aspects of publishing.

Women In Publishing, c/o Susannah Charlton, 87 Newman Street, W1 (637 0341 day). Umbrella organisation for all women involved in the book trade. Offers training courses, meetings and produces a newsletter. Also awards The Pandora Award annually for 'The Greatest Contribution to the Position of Women in Publishing'.

Attic Press, 48 Fleet Street, Dublin 2 (0001 716367). Irish feminist publishing house concentrating on books by and about Irish women. Also connected to Irish Feminist Information which runs a nine month Women and Community Publishing Course, partially funded by the European Social Fund.

Battle Axe Books, Kim Werts (603 1139) Mon, Wed, Thurs. Concentrating on humour, fiction, education, history and non-fiction.

Black Woman Talk, PO Box 222, N1 2YL. First British Black women's publishing co-operative. Committed to promoting books written by women of African and Asian descent living in Britain.

Onlywomen Women Press, 38 Mount Pleasant, WC1 (837 0596). Concentrating on radical feminist and lesbian literature.

Pandora Press, 14 Leicester Place, WC2H 7PH (437 9011). Feminist books concentrating on contemporary issues.

Sheba Feminist Publishers, 10A Bradbury Street, N16 (254 1590). Independent feminist co-operative which concentrates on producing feminist fiction by women, anti-racist, anti-sexist children's books, poetry and Black women's writing. Committed to working as racially mixed collective.

Stramullion, 43 Candlemaker Row, Edinburgh, EH1 2QB (225 2612). Women's publishing house, concentrating on books written by Scots women.

Virago Press, 41 William IV Street, WC2 (379 6977). Publishes reprints of important books written in the past as well as contemporary list.

Women's Community Press, 144 East Essex Street, Dublin 2, Eire (0001 712149). Irish Feminist Publishing Co-operative with an emphasis on community publishing.

Women's Press Ltd, 124 Shoreditch High Street, E1 6JE (729 5257). Feminist publishers of fiction and non-fiction by and for women. Also produces postcards. Runs bookclub by post-phone for details.

General publishers

Many other publishing houses are now also concentrating on women's books or have specific 'Women's Lists' including Bogle L'Ouverture, Chatto & Windus, George Allen & Unwin, Harper & Rowe, Harvester, Methuen (with a new list of women's plays), Quartet, Pluto.... and more. Many community bookshops also have active community publishing programmes - see Bookshops (below) for details.

The following have a strong commitment to a particular area of women's writings:

Arlen House, 69 Jones Road, Dublin 3, Eire (0001 786913). Irish publishing house with strong women's list.

Brilliance Books, 14 Clerkenwell Green, EC1 (01-250 0730). Lesbian and Gay men's fiction and non-fiction publsher.

Change, 29 Great James Street, WC1N 3ES (01-405 3601). Researching and publishing reports on the condition and status of women internationally for use by teachers and lecturers.

The Federation of Worker Writers and Community Publishers, 178 Whitechapel Road, E1 (01-791 1165). Active organisation focussing on local community and working class writers' groups.

Heinemann Educational Books, 22 Bedford Square, WC1 3HH (01-637 3311). Specialist range of books by writers from England, Africa and the Caribbean.

Hutchinson Educational, 17/21 Conway Street, W1P 6JD (01-387 2811). Publishes Explorations in Feminism; a specific series covering a wide range of feminist research.

Zed Books, 57 Caledonian Road, N1 9BU (01-837 4014). Major publisher of books by or about people in the third World, fiction and non-fiction, with a particularly strong Black women's list.

Women's Booksellers

London now has three bookshops which are owned exclusively by women and which have a special commitment to promote women's writings.

Silver Moon, 68 Charing Cross Road, WC2 (01-836 7906). Bookshop and women-only cafe and art gallery in the basement.
Hours: Shop; 10.30am-6.30pm Tues-Sat. Cafe; 12 noon-6pm. Closed Sun/Mon. Access: A to shop only.

Sisterwrite Bookshop, 190 Upper Street, N1 (01-226 9782). Bookshop with women-only facilities for making tea and coffee upstairs. Hours: Tues/Wed/Fri 10am-6pm; Thurs 10am-7pm; Sat 11am-6pm. Closed Sun/Mon. Access: A to shop only.

Virago Bookshop, 34 Southampton Street, WC2E 7HE (01-240 6638). Bookshop with women's Art Gallery in basement. Hours: 9am-7pm Weekdays; 10pm-6pm Sat. Closed Sun. Access: P to shop only.

Other women's bookselling organisations:

Feminist Audio Books,* 52/4 Featherstone Street, c/o A Woman's Place, Hungerford House, WC2 (no phone contact). Feminist service supplying women's books on tape for blind or partially sighted women.

Letterbox Library, 1st Floor, 5 Bradbury Street, N16 9JN (01-254 1640). Children's bookclub specialising in anti-racist, anti-sexist children's books and books for young women. Mail order service. Hours: Mon-Fri 9.30am-3.15pm (phone first). Access: N

The Women's Press Bookclub, 124 Shoreditch High Street, E1 (01-729 4751). Britain's only feminist mail order bookclub carrying books by women from more than 20 different publishers. Quarterly catalogue.

Local bookshops with good stock of women's books

Balham Food and Book Co-op, 92 Balham High Road, SW12 (01-673 0946). Book-Tokens; Bookstalls arranged; Library supplier. Hours: 9.30am-6pm Mon, Tues, Thurs, Fri. 9.30am-5.30pm Saturday. Wed/Sun closed. Access: A for bookshop, food shop only. Cafe, toilets upstairs not accessible.

Battersea Arts Centre Bookshop, Old Town Hall, Lavender Hill, SW11 (01-223 5063). Bookshop in active Community Arts Centre. Hours: 11.30am-9.30pm Wed to Sun. Access: A

Black Ink, 258 Coldharbour Lane, SW9 (733 0746). Stock includes emphasis on promotion of Black people's non-sexist writings, in particular the experiences of young Black people. Access: P

Boat's Bookshop, 2 Brook Street, Kingston-Upon-Thames, KT1 2HA (546 7592). General bookshop. Hours: 9am-5.30pm Mon to Sat. Access: A to ground floor only.

Bogle L'Ouverture, 51a Chignel Place, Ealing, W13 (579 4920). Specialising in books about Africa and the peoples of African descent. Mail order to libraries, schools and institutions. Access: A. Hours: 10am-6pm Mon-Sat. Closed Sunday. Access: A.

Bookmarks, 265 Seven Sisters Road, Finsbury Park, N4 2DE (802 6145/8773). Books on trade union studies, Labour history and international politics. Hours: 10am-6pm Mon to Sat (till 7pm Wed). Access.

Bookplace/Peckham Publishing Project, 13 Peckham High Street, SE15 (701 1757/0720). Community bookshop with publishing project and Adult Education Centre. School and Library suppliers. hours: Mon, Tues, Wed, Fri, Sat 10am-6pm. Access: A.

Booksplus, 23 Lewisham Way, SE14 (691 2833). General bookshop with good stock of feminist titles, radical books and non-sexist children's books. Hours: Mon and Fri 10am-5pm; Tues, Wed, Thurs, Sat 11am-6pm. Access: A.

Centreprise, 136 Kingsland High Street, E8 (254 9632). Multi-purpose community centre with bookshop, cafe and publishing project with a women-only writers' group. Hours: Tues, Wed, Fri, Sat 10.30am-5.30pm, Thurs 10.30am-2pm. Access P.

Compendium, 234 Camden High Street, NW1 (485 8944). General bookshop with lots of American imports. Hours: Mon-Sat 10am-6pm. Access: P.

Deptford Book Traders, 55 Deptford High Street, SE8 (692 8339). Bookshop and Literacy Centre with extensive multi-cultural children's book section. Hours: Tues-Sat 9.30am-5.30pm (1.30pm Thurs). Closed Sun/Mon. Access: A to shop only.

Gay's The Word, 66 Marchmont Street, WC1 (278 7654). New, secondhand and out-of-print lesbian and gay men's books. Hours: Mon-Sat 11am-7pm, Sun 12 noon-6pm. Access: A.

Housmans, 5 Caledonian Road, N1 (837 4473/4). Pacifist bookshop, with stock that includes feminist, anti-racist and anti-sexist titles.

Kilburn Bookshop, 8 Kilburn Bridge, Kilburn High Road, NW6 (328 7071). General bookshop with specialised sections including feminism and children's books. Hours: Mon-Sat 9.30am-6pm. Access: A.

Mew Beacon Books, 76 Shroud Green Road, N4 3EN (272 4889). Specialises in books by Afro/Caribbean writers and Black politics. Hours: Tues to Sat 10.30am-6pm. Closed Mon/Sun. Access: N.

Owl Bookshop, 211 Kentish Town Road, NW5 (485 7793). General bookshop with large children's and women's book section. Also with much academic stock as Polytechnic close by. Hours: Mon to Sat 9.30am-6pm. Access: A.

Paperback Centre, 10 Atlantic Road, SW9 (274 8342). General bookshop specialising in Afro/Caribbean books, women's politics, lesbian and gay men's books. Hours: Mon-Sat 9.30am-5.30pm (2pm Wed). Access: A.

Page One, 53 West Ham Lane, E15 (534 6539). Radical bookshop (and wholefood shop) with stock including many feminist/non-sexist and non-racist titles. Hours: Mon, Tues, Fri 9.30am to 5.30pm; Thurs 9.30am to 1pm; Sat 9.30am to 5pm. Access: A.

Reading Matters, 10 Lymington Avenue, N22 (881 3187). Community bookshop with good women's fiction and non-fiction and politics. Also small publishing group, Hours: Tues-Sat 11am-5.30pm. Access: A.

Soma Books Ltd, Commonwealth Institute, Kensington High Street, W8 6NQ (01-603 0754). Bookshop providing materials related to the commonwealth countries with emphasis on the Black commonwealth and a wide range of women's books. Hours: Mon-Sat 10am-5.30pm, Sun 2pm-5pm. Access: A.

THAP Bookshop (Tower Hamlets Arts Project), 178 Whitechapel Road, E1 (247 0216). Lively general East End bookshop linked to multi-media arts project. Hours: Tues-Fri 10am-6pm, Sat 10am-5pm. Access.

Webster's Bookshop, 1063 The Whitgift Centre, Croydon (686 7032). General bookshop. Hours: Mon to Fri 9.30am-5.30pm (6pm Sat). Access: A to part of shop only.

Book Distribution

If you can't find a particular book either telephone the Sales Manager (see Women's Publishing Houses), or contact one of the following distributors to find out where you can buy it:

Airlift Book Company, 14 Baltic Street, EC1 (257 8608). Major distributor of American women's presses throughout Britain and Europe including many lesbian books.

Third World Publications, 25 Horsell Road, N5 1XL (607 4463). Specialist distributor of books by and about the Third World; strong Black women's list.

Turnaround, 27 Horsell Road, N5 1XL (609 7836). Distributor for many English Scots and Irish publishing groups and specialise in radical publications.

Libraries

Some Public Lending Libraries now have special sections for women's/feminist books but all Libraries should order a book for you if you can't find it on the shelf. Also, many women's centres have extensive resources including books, pamphlets and leaflets (see **Borough Information**.)

Fawcett Library, At The City of London Polytechnic, Old Castle Street, London, E1 (283 1030 x570). Extensive Library of British Women's History containing many rare and interesting books and journals dating back hundreds of years. Hours: Mon-Fri 10am-5pm; (1pm-8.30pm Mon during term). Closed Fri/Sat/Sun. Access: A.

Feminist Library, 1st Floor, Hungerford House, Victoria Embankment, WC2 (930 0715). Lending Library; Women's Studies Course Lists; Index to current research being done - also expanding their journals in Arabic, Persian Asian and European languages. Hours: Closed Sun/Mon. Tues-Sat 11am-5.30pm; Thurs 11am-7.30pm. Access: Not possible; but they will service women downstairs in A Woman's Place if requested.

Lesbian Archive, BCM Box 7005, WC1N 3. Planned resource Library for the lesbian community, currently looking for suitable premises. Also produces newsletter on tape detailing activities and providing list of material already acquired.

Wiser Links*, 173 Archway Road, N6 (341 4403). International Women's Resource Centre and Library with special section focusing on Black British women and women from British ethnic groups. Hours: 2pm-7pm Mon to Fri (phone first). Access: N.

Women Artists' Slide Library, c/o Battersea Arts Centre, Old Town Hall, Lavender Hill, SW11 (228 5771).

Hours: Tues/Wed 11am-5pm; Thurs/ Fri 11am-7pm.

Women in Libraries, 8 Hill Road, NW8 (286 9088). Umbrella organisation for women working in (or interested in) libraries which aims to improve jobs and the provision of women's books available to the borrowing public. Meets regularly, produces a newsletter, holds annual conferences and keeps an up-to-date job-share register.

Older Women

Older women are a growing presence in our society. More women are living longer than ever before in our history. Over 40% of the female population in London is aged 45 and over. Yet despite their numerical strength and the valid contribution that they have made to society older women are discriminated against, given low status by society as a whole and their needs often ignored.

The main areas of concern to older women are media presentation, health, housing, transport and the treatment of elderly women by professional services. These issues have been highlighted in consultation with older women carried out by such groups as Older Feminist Network, Older Lesbian Network, Pensioners' Link and the Standing Conference of Ethnic Minority Senior Citizens.

The media presentation of old age is generally biased and incorrect and relies on caricatures; older women are either characterised as 'cosy, ineffectual grannies' or feeble-minded, incompetent and pathetic creatures incapable of making decisions about their own lives. Nothing could be farther from the truth and this was one of the main issues of concern to older women highlighted in consultation with them, by the GLC Women's Committee.

Many older women experience trivialisation of their health problems, particularly those classified as non-acute chronic conditions. The length of waiting lists for non-acute operations affecting older people such as hip replacement and cornea grafting is evidence of the fact that treatment of chronic ailments affecting old people is considered a poor investment by society.

The housing needs of older women tend to be ignored since it is assumed that they are settled, usually in a household headed by a man: yet figures show that a substantial number of elderly women live alone and head a one-person household, 38.3% of elderly women compared with 18.2% of elderly men.

Women generally are greatly dependent on the public transport system and have less access to private transport than men. Only three out of ten women hold a driving licence and this figure falls to one in ten for women aged 65+. Older and elderly women are also more concerned about security and safety on public transport which probably accounts for their reluctance to travel alone at night.

A lack of awareness amongst staff working with the elderly on the specific needs of Black and ethnic minority women deny them access to the support services necessary for a decent standard of living. A lack of understanding of the cultural, linguistic and religious background of Black and ethnic minority elderly coupled with fixed stereotypical ideas, bears little relation to reality. For example, there is a common assumption that Black and ethnic minority elderly people have extended family support networks which will take care of the elderly in the community, but evidence indicates that this is not always the case.

In accordance with the GLC's policy of promoting equal opportunities for women, a Forum for the Elderly was set up to identify the specific needs of older and elderly women and to work to ensure that all policies and initiatives it develops are designed to meet those needs. The Women's Committee had an advisory member with particular reference to Older Women and established an Equalities Team to ensure, amongst other matters, that the welfare and interests of older women were being adequately met. Work involved included consultation with older women, the support and development of projects which seek to counteract ageism and resourcing projects specifically for older women such as the Older Women's Project at Pensioners' Link, a series of locally based workshops, and the production of an *Older Women's Bulletin*.

It is the Social Services Dept in each borough that is responsible for the care of the elderly in the borough. Some boroughs produce guides/pensioners' handbooks: contact your Town Hall (see **Borough Information**).

This section describes how ageism works and provides information about groups which campaign around older women's issues as well as groups and centres which offer support, advice and social amenities. Although there are day centres for older people throughout London only a few so far have special women's groups - check with your Social Services or Age Concern / Pensioners Link. (Also, see specific sections in the Handbook such as **Health, Sport, Housing, Disability** and **Carers** for further information about provision for older women).

This section is ordered as follows: *Ageism, Campaigning Groups, Voluntary Sector Organisations, Pensioners' Trade Union Organisations and Campaigns), Organisations for Black and Ethnic Minority Older People, Educational Opportunities for Older People, Further Organisations and Support Groups, Locally Based Projects, Publications.*

Ageism

Ageism is defined as the discrimination by individual acts and institutional processes against persons and groups on account of their age. Ageism operates through social institutions to deprive older and younger women of their rights to participate in democratic decision-making processes. All too often, policies affecting older and younger women are made without reference to their specific points of view.

Despite the negative effects of ageism, older women are organising autonomously to confront the stereotypical images that society holds and to present themselves as they really are - diverse, creative and dynamic.

Campaigning Groups

Age Concern Greater London, 54 Knatchbull Road, SE5 9QY (737 3456). Large organisation with branches/centres all over London. Contact above number for your local centre. Advice on welfare rights, special (eg Christmas) activities, clubs, minibus transport, outings, practical help, visiting, help for housebound. Also aids on loan, day centres, luncheon clubs and holiday schemes. Some centres also offer bereavement counselling, chiropody, good neighbour scheme, service for hard of hearing, pop-ins, newsletters and sale of welfare foods. Many useful publications. Contact main Age Concern for provision in your area (and see **Carers**).

Help the Aged, 16/18 St. James' Walk EC1R (253 0253). Campaigning and fund-raising organisation which provides a number of services including grants for pensioners' projects and help with housing, eg for elderly people living by themselves. Produces a wide range of publications. Access: P.

National Federation of Old Age Pension Associations, Melling House, 91 Preston New Road, Blackburn, Lancs. BBN 6BD (0245 52606). National campaigning body with branches all over London and the rest of Britain. The Federation asks for higher pensions and an equal retirement age for women and men. They describe their aims as 'a better deal for pensioners'. Contact for local group or to get regular news-sheet, *Pensioner's Voice.*

Older Feminist Network, c/o 5 Fanthorpe Street, SW15 (785 9324). Meets every five weeks (Saturdays), always welcomes new women. Newsletter published. For details of meetings see *City Limits* (Action section), or newsletter. Hoping to get an older women's centre established. 'Older' is self-defined: from late 30s onwards to 80s and above. Social, political, campaigning, discussions and other activities. Meetings always fully accessible for wheelchair users.

Older Lesbian Network, BM OLN, WC1N 3XX. Formed subsequently to OFN above, and plan meetings (monthly, Saturdays) so that they don't clash with OFN as some OLN members go to both. Newsletter, details from above. Discussions, action, social events. Older: self-defined. Mainly 30s upwards. Meetings always fully accessible.

Pensioners' Link Older Women's Project,* (age 50+). Pensioners Link Central office, 17 Balfe Street N1 9EB (278 5501/4). The project is a focus to bring older women together to initiate and develop work with older women throughout London. Priority is given to making the project representative of and relevant to Black and ethnic minority women. The project seeks to give a voice for older women campaigning for recognition of their needs and abilities. A 9-panel exhibition, and a publicity pack is now available. Social meetings are organised around important issues. Women who are interested should contact: Pam Wright, above. Access: N at head office. Access: P at centres.

The Standing Conference of Ethnic Minority Senior Citizens, 5-5a Westminster Bridge Road, SE1 7XW (928 0095). Campaigning for rights and will give information on day centres, clubs and activities all over London relevant to Black and ethnic minority older people. Access: A.

West Indian Women's Association. (WIWA), c/o Marie Ologbosere, Co-ordinator, or Gerry Williams, Pensioners' Officer, 71 Pound Lane, Willesden, NW10 (451 4827). Has cultural groups in the evening - dance, arts and crafts (eg pottery and silk screening) to which older women come. Access N.

WIWA (As above), Granville Centre, Granville Road, NW6W 1WA. Run workshops on a Wednesday afternoon for older women, on arts and crafts. At the moment they are doing screen printing. There is a lunch club run by WIWA at the Granville centre, four days a week which has a high membership of older women. WIWA also give welfare rights advice. They are about to appoint a Women's Development Officer and will be looking into ways of increasing their work with older West Indian women. Access: P. The Centre is not directly accessible, but helpers are available to assist women who are disabled.

Voluntary Sector Organisations for Older People

In London, the two main organisations are Age Concern and Pensioners Link. Both advise on welfare rights and offer a range of services supplementing statutory local authority social services provision.

Age Concern Greater London, 54 Knatchbull Road, SE5 9QY (737 3456). Large organisation with branches/centres all over London: contact above number for your local centre. Advice on welfare rights, special (eg Christmas) activities, clubs, minibus transport, outings, practical help, visiting, help for housebound. Also aids on loan, day centres, luncheon clubs and holiday schemes. Some centres also offer bereavement counselling, chiropody, good neighbour scheme, service for hard of hearing, pop-ins, newsletters and sale of welfare foods. Many useful publications. Contact main Age Concern for provision in your local area (and see **Carers**).

Pensioners' Link. Large help and advisory service, working in partnership with pensioners, offering legal help, advice, support, social events and useful local contacts. For all pensioners with many centres having activities of specific interest to women. (Formerly called **Task Force**).

Pensioners' Link Central Office, 17 Balfe Street, N1 9EB (01 278 5501/4). Concerned with finance, administration and the development of work for centres everywhere. Ring with general enquiries. Access: N.

Barnet Pensioners Link, Park House, 16A High Road, N2 (01 883 1075). Particular interest in welfare rights to the housebound throughout Barnet, and health education including evaluating health courses. Access: N.

Brent Pensioners' Link, Carlton Centre, Granville Road, NW6 (01 624 3480 / 328 2688). Irish pensioners group, a women's group, a health group. Organises volunteers for people with disabilities. Involved in Campaign Against Post Office Closures.

Camden Pensioners' Link, 52 Grafton Road, NW5 (01 267 3381/1). Organises a school visiting scheme, works with pensioners' campaigning groups. Welfare Rights advice. Also co-ordinates a 'Telephone Link Up' group for people with disabilities. Access: P.

Ealing Pensioners' Link, Bedford Hall, Bedford Road, W13 (567 8017/840 1748). Welfare Rights, odd jobs school visiting scheme, arranges outings and parties. Access: N.

Greenwich Pensioners' Link, Old Town Hall, Polytechnic Street, SE18 (854 2835). Social and action groups, Black pensioners' groups, organises odd jobs, education in schools and does reminiscence work with housebound pensioners to build up factual picture of local history and produce useful educational material for schools. Access: N.

Hackney Pensioners' Link, 33 Dalston Lane, E8 (241 2224). Organises odd jobs, Pensioner's Groups, health courses and education work. Runs 24 hour emergency service for people at risk from the cold: 'Cold Line' 01-533 1218. Access: N.

Haringey Pensioners' Link, Tottenham Town Hall, Town Hall Approach, N15. (801 6522/808 1000). Campaigning groups, welfare rights advice, handicraft courses, Black pensioners' group, West Indian disabled/housebound group, Asian women's pensioners' group and keep fit classes. Access: N.

Islington Pensioners' Link, Manor Gardens Centre, 6/9 Manor Gardens, N7 6LA. (281 2700). Welfare rights advice to housebound pensioners. Runs health courses, arranges odd jobs and decorating. Projects in schools. Access: N.

Kensington Pensioners' Link, 7 Thorpe Close, W10 5EX (969 9105/6). Welfare rights, social and action groups, has peace group and arranges schools visiting pensioners at home. 9 am-1 pm week days, but can arrange to meet in local coffee shop - please phone for information. Access: N.

Lewisham Pensioners' Link, 74 Deptford High Street, SE8 (691 0938). Publishes a newspaper, has anti-racist project, offers welfare rights and odd jobs service. Action groups and women's self-defence groups. Works on reminiscence with pensioners in local area. Access: N.

Wandsworth Pensioners' Link, 170 Garratt Lane, SW18 (870 7171/7272). Outings and parties, odd jobs and visiting schemes and support for carers. Access: N.

Westminster Pensioners' Link, 1a St Mary's Terrace, W2 (723 7663). Offers practical help, Luncheon Club, newsletter for the housebound and schools visiting. Access: N.

Pensioners' Trade Union Organisations and Campaigns

The British Pensioners' and Trade Union Action Association, Fred Baker MBE, The General Secretary, 97 Kings Drive, Gravesend, Kent DA13 5BQ (0474 61802). Branches throughout Britain. Also produces a journal, *The British Pensioner*, available from Tom Mitchell, The Asst Secretary, 68 Crawley Green Road, Luton, Beds. (0582 24254).

Greater London Pensioners' and Trade Union Action Association, 28a Highgate Road, NW5 (267 6151). Campaigning organisation for all pensioners, whose demands include: higher pensions, better social services provision and adequate housing, abolition of the Standing Charge on Gas and Electricity. Has 25 locally based groups throughout London area, contact above for nearest contact or write to Peter Jones, Secretary, GLP & TUAA 194 Queensbridge Road, London E8. Affiliated to organisation below.

London Joint Council for Senior Citizens, c/o TGWU Retired Members Association, Room 703, TGWU, Transport House, Smith Square, Westminster, SW1P 3JP (828 3806). Access: N.

Organisations for Black and Ethnic Minority Older People

ASRA, 5-5a Westminster Bridge Road, SE1 7XW (928 9379). Specialised Housing Association which develops and manages sheltered housing for elderly Asians and for single Asian women aged 18 and above, with and without children. Access: A.

Standing Conference of Ethnic Minority Senior Citizens, 5-5a Westminster Bridge Road, SE1 7XW (928 0095). Information on all groups; ring for details re your area. Access: A.

North

Black Pensioners' Group, c/o Lord Morrison Community Centre, Chestnut Road, London N17. Tues 10-12 pm. Access: No information. Contact for above group: Annexe B, Tottenham Town Hall, Town Hall Approach, London N15. (801 6522). Access: N.

Cypriot Elderly and Handicapped Centre*, Cypriot Community Centre, Earlham Grove, Wood Green, Haringey N22 (881 2329). Access: A.

Heads, Community Centre, 128 Rectory Road, N16. Lunch club and meeting place for West Indian elderly, used by many older women. Access: No information.

Unity Pensioners' Group, c/o Triangle Community Centre, 93 St Ann's Road, London N15. Mon 1-3. Access: A.

West Indian Community Centre, 91 Tollington Way, N7.

West Indian Women's Association. (WIWA), c/o Marie Ologbosere, Co-ordinator, or Gerry Williams, Pensioners' Officer, 71 Pound Lane, Willesden, NW10. (451 4827). Has cultural groups in the evening - dance, arts and crafts (eg pottery and silk screening) to which older women come. Access: N.

East

Dame Colet House*, Ben Johnson Road, E1 (790 9077). Wed. 10am-12 Arts and Crafts: 2-4pm Keep Fit. Access: A.

Health Group, Chelmer Road, E9. Discussions on health issues, mainly women. Fri mornings. Would welcome new members.

South

Abeng Centre, 7 Gresham Road, SW9 (737 1628). Thurs pm. Access: N.

Asian Community Action Group, 322a Brixton Road, SW9 (733 7494) Mon-Fri 9.30am-5.00pm Access: N.

Battersea Black Elderly Group, c/o York Gardens Community Centre, Lavender Road, SW11 (223 7961). Thurs 1-4pm. Access: A.

Brixton Neighbourhood Community Association, 1 Mayall Road, SW4. Mon-Fri normal office hours.

The Calabash Day Centre, 26 George Lane, SE13 (461 3420). Day Centre and lunch-club for Afro-Caribbean pensioners offering day care, and to be used by older women. Access: A.

50 Plus Association meets at Abeng Community Centre, 7 Gresham Road, SW9 (274 7722 ext 2167); postal address is c/o CCRL, 441 Brixton Road, SW9 8HE. Caters for the needs of Afro-Caribbean elderly and pensioners. Regular discussion groups, offers welfare advice and arranges visits to other similar clubs for exchange of information. Tues 10.30am-12.30pm Weds 10am-2pm Discussion group Fri 12 noon - 4pm. Access: N.

Lambeth Age Concern. 1/5 Acre Lane, SW2 5DG, (274 7722 ext 2009). Will give information on groups in Lambeth for Black and ethnic minority older people. Access: A but no toilet facility.

Milap Day Centre, Town Hall Annexe, Southall, Middlesex (574 2311 ext 223) 10am-5.30pm Mon-Sat This centre is mainly used by Asian Groups. Access: A.

Seventh Day Adventist Church. Day Centre for the Elderly, Santley Street, SW9 (674 2592) Mon-Wed 10am-3pm. Access: A.

St. Martins Pensioners' Health Group meets at Roupall Court Elderly Peoples' Home, Roupall Road, SW2. 1.30 - 3.30pm Weds., fortnightly. Enquiries c/o 6 Bell House, Ewen Crescent, SW2.

West

Asian Pensioners' Group, The Oak Tree Community Centre, Osbourne Road, South Acton W3 (992 5566). Weds videos; Fri religious ceremony 2-5 pm Access: A.

Dutchpot (Black Pensioners' Club), 510 Harrow Road, W9 (960 8504). Access: A.

The Pepperpot Club. Westway Information and Aid Centre, 140 Ladbroke Grove, London W10 (969 2433) - ask for Pepperpot Club. Access: A.

Educational Opportunities for Older People

The Forum on the Rights of Elderly People to Education (FREE), Bernard Sunley House, 60 Pitcairn Road, Mitcham, Surrey CR4 3LL (640 5431). Brings together many organisations and individuals wishing to promote all kinds of educational opportunities for older people. Produce a quarterly information bulletin giving details of local initiatives, research and publications. Also organises occasional discussion forums. Access: P.

The University of the Third Age, c/o The Executive Secretary, 6 Parkside Gardens, SW19 5EY. Many local groups organise 'mutual aid' learning groups, some are connected to educational institutions. UTA involves older people in teaching as well as in learning, as researchers and organisers and it makes education available at home and in local communities. A manual on setting up new groups is available.

Workers' Education Association, London District Office, 32 Tavistock Square, WC1H 9EZ (387 8966). Branches all over London, with some courses particularly aimed at older people. Ring central office for details.

Open University, London Region, Parsifal College, 527 Finchley Road, NW3 7BG (794 0575). Seven per cent of all OU students are over 60, studying either for degrees or on shorter courses. There is a four part course on the pre-retirement theme. Self-help study groups are often organised for students on the same course. Access: A.

The **Pre-Retirement Association of Great Britain and Northern Ireland**, 19 Undine Street, Tooting, SW17 8PP (767 3225). Arranges courses in work places for pre-retirement workers, publishes magazine entitled *Choice, a magazine for retirement planning*. Access: N.

(For other educational opportunities see **Education and Further Education**)

Further Organisations and Support Groups

Age Exchange, 15 Camden Row, Blackheath, SE3 (postal address only). (318 9105/852 9293). Group working on touring photo exhibitions, books based on reminiscence work (ie oral history) with older people and theatre company which has produced two plays about women's issues. Office address 11A Blackheath Village, SE3. Access: N.

All Party Parliamentary Group for Pensioners, House of Commons, SW1A 0AA, (219 4082).

Centre for Policy on Ageing, Nuffield Lodge Studio, Regent's Park, NW1 4RS (586 9844). An independent policy unit promoting better services for older people. Aims to promote informed debate about issues affecting older people, to formulate and promote policies, and to encourage the spread of good practice. Several publications available.

The Computer Group, c/o Islington Pensioners Link (281 2700). Working with computers to visit day centres, sheltered blocks and individuals to check that they are receiving the correct benefits.

Cruse, Cruse House, 126 Sheen Road, Richmond TW9 1VR (940 4818/9047). National organisation for the widowed and their children. Offers bereavement counselling, social groups etc. Seven branches in London - ring for details.

The Gay Bereavement Project, c/o Dudley Cave, Unitarian Room, Hoop Lane, NW11 8DS (Phone Gay Switchboard 01 837 7324). Run by volunteers, this group offers immediate support on the death of a gay partner. Advice on funeral costs, burial ceremonies, legal problems (especially wills) relating to gays relationships and death of partner.

National Association for Widows, c/o Stafford Voluntary Services Centre, Chell Road, Stafford ST16 2QA (0785 45465)(24 hours). Benefit advice and support nationally. Access: N.

National Council for Carers and their Elderly Dependants, 29 Chilworth Mews, W2 3RG. (262 1451). Provides support and advice on benefits available, produces bi-monthly newsletter, maintains list of volunteer helpers. Mixed. Access: A.

Pensioners for Peace, 7 Sandfield, Bromsberrow Heath, Ledbury, Hereford, HR8. (0531 84185).

Reminiscence work - being carried out all over London. Includes oral history projects (some involving work with schoolchildren), video work etc. Towards valuing the experience of older people, and working against patronising attitudes about 'dwelling on the past'. Details of projects c/o Chio co-op (video group · working with older women), 91c Mildmay Road, N1 4PV (249 2551).

Locally Based Projects

Brent Women's Centre. (See **Borough Information**). Has an older womens' group.

Camden Old People's Welfare Association, c/o Mr L Rofay, 335 Grays Inn Road, WC1X 8PX. (278 1585/837 3777). This organisation co-ordinates the work of various groups and agencies in the Borough and provides direct help for elderly people in need. Access: N.

Charteris Community Sports Centre, Charteris Road, NW6 (625 6451). Wed all-women day with special classes in sports for older women. Access: A.

Hackney Forum for the Elderly, (now Age Concern Hackney), 22 Dalston Lane, E8 (254 0715). Planning, campaigning and information on services in the borough. Hairdressing service, Jewish holiday scheme, outings for housebound. Access: P.

Haringey Women's Centre* (see **Borough Information**). Has an older lesbian group.

Kentish Town Women's Workshop* (see **Borough Information**). Has an older womens' group.

Priory Centre for Community Programmes, Petersfield Road, Acton W3 8NY. Tues. 1 pm Social group, mainly older. Contact Winifred Miller, (992 5566 ext 2305) Mon, Tues, Weds. Access: A.

Southwark Pensioners' Action Group, 186 Crompton Street, Walworth SE17 (701 8955). Federation for Pensioner groups in the Borough produces quarterly newsletter free. Campaigning currently focuses around post office closure, pavement parking and Social Security Benefits. Contact above for information on local groups.

Southwark Pensioners' Forum, contact Town Hall, Peckham Road, SE5 8UB (703 6311 ext 2386). The Forum is a sub-committee of the Council's Community Affairs Committee. There are regular meetings with representatives of pensioners' groups. The Forum has a campaigning function mainly focused on social services, pensions and health care. Access: A.

The White Hart Lane Project, Devonshire Library Hall, Compton Crescent, N17 (801 2589). Women's day every Tues. with general drop-in, tea and coffee and women's drama group. Many activities for older women. 10 am-3 pm Access: P. (Side door help).

Useful Reading

Age Concern Quarterly Newsletter, concentrates on special topic each time eg health, heating. Subscription £1 a year. Age Concern (as above).

Begin Again, Margaret Torrie (founder of Cruse), £2.50 & 50p Postage and Package from Cruse (see in listings above).

Beyond Tea, Bingo and Condescension, G Buckingham, Daisy Truscott, B Dimmock. Evaluates new approaches to care for the elderly. £2.25 from 1 Thorpe Close, off Cambridge Gardens, W10 5XL.

British Pensioner, Six times yearly, published by British Pensioners and Trade Union Action Association (see above.)

The Chronicle, Ten times a year, free to members (membership £3.50) from Cruse (see in listings above).

Handbook For Widows, J Hemer and A. Strange. (Virago Press £1.50).

Help Yourself to London, guide to leisure opportunities for pensioners, 30p (includes post). Age Concern, 54 Knatchbull Road, SE5 9QY (737 3456).

Older Feminist Newsletter, See in listings under Older Feminist Network.

Older Lesbian Newsletter, See in listings under Older Lesbian Network.

On Your Own, handbook on many aspects: housing, finance, DIY etc. Jean Shapiro, (Pandora Press £6.95).

Pensioners' Voice, Published monthly by National Federation of Old Age Pension Associations (see above).

Senior Citizen, British Pensioners and Trade Union Association, 11/12 Castle Market Buildings, Exchange Street, Sheffield S2 5TS.

Your Rights, Lists benefits and wide range of rights and how to get them. Includes information for Black and ethnic minority pensioners. 85p, Age Concern (as above).

A Wealth of Experience, The Lives of Older Women, collection of writings, ed Susan Hemmings, (Pandora Press £3.95).

Peace

The women's peace camp at Greenham Common cruise missile base is just one example of a major initiative taken by women to express their views and feelings about peace issues. The camp has been supported by a significant number of women from Greater London who have visited the camp, lived for a period on the site or expressed their support in other ways by lobbying institutions of local or national government.

In making such representations, women have set peace issues in the wider context of male power and domination, on a personal level and on a national and international level. The women's peace movement has been slow to develop an understanding of the situation of Black women and the importance of listening to Black women's views on peace issues. This is now acknowledged by more women in the peace movement.

The GLC's awareness of the concerns expressed by women, especially in London, about the escalation of the arms race and the siting of Cruise missiles in this country, combined with their responsibility for civil defence functions in London, led to the Council deciding to promote peace in London by declaring 1983 a 'Peace Year'. During 1983 the Council declared Greater London to be a 'nuclear free zone', and organised a programme of activities and media promotion which led to other local authorities following suit in subsequent years.

The GLC Women's Committee has, through a consultative process with women in London, drawn up a Programme of Action which includes a section on Peace. The draft Programme received a large number of written responses from women which put forward a range of proposals.

These were the main proposals:

● That the GLC should provide information to Londoners about the arms race and the dangers of nuclear war.

● That the GLC should encourage the development of peace education in London.

● That the GLC should liaise with a wide range of peace groups in London.

● That opportunities should be created for public debate.

● That the Women's Committee should encourage the development of a common set of objectives by women in London in furthering the cause of peace.

- That the GLC should create the opportunity for greater international understanding by Londoners, including the possibility of organising or sponsoring exchanges.
- That the GLC should investigate and publicise the number of firms involved with arms production in London.
- That the Women's Committee should support the women at Greenham Common.
- That the GLC should encourage initiatives seeking conversion from arms production to socially useful products.

The GLC Women's Committee took a number of steps to respond to these proposals, including the setting up of a Peace Working Group to examine particular issues in relation to women, grant aid to women's peace groups and holding meetings open to the public on such issues as defence and disarmament.

There are many different peace groups, with varied campaigning emphases. The list below should help you to get in touch with groups if you are interested, or simply to read more about the subject.

This section is ordered as follows: ***Women's Peace Groups, Medical Campaigns, Nuclear Disarmament, Nuclear-Free Zones in London, Peace and Anti-Militarism, Publications.***

Women's Peace Groups

Greenham Women In London, 52 Featherstone Street, EC1 (608 0244). Access: A.

Greenham Common Women's Peace Camp, USAF Greenham Common, Newbury, Berks. There are currently six camps around the base described as a 'vigil'. The women are there because they are appalled at the threat of nuclear weapons, especially Cruise because it is a first-strike weapon. Each woman goes as an individual to express a personal protest, and tries to live in ways which challenge the nuclear mentality and to find better ways to live.

South East London Women Oppose the Nuclear Threat (WONT), c/o 52 Malpas Road, SE4.

South East London Greenham Women, c/o 58 Waveney Avenue, SE15.

Women's International League for Peace and Freedom (WILPF), 17 Victoria Park Square, E2 9PB (980 1030). Founded in 1915 by women active in the suffrage movement. international organisation working on issues of peace, development and human rights. Access: N.

Women's Peace Alliance, Box 240, Peace News, 8 Elm Avenue, Nottingham. An alliance of women's peace groups promoting peace in all its aspects and enabling women to support each others' initiatives for disarmament and the prevention of war. Provides information and resources. Has published a *History of the Women's Peace Movement*, (60p) and has a bi-monthly newsletter (20p). Access: N (0278 422632).

Women for World Disarmament, International Centre, North Curry, Taunton, TA3 6HL (0823 490207). Works closely with the United Nations Association (see below) to involve women worldwide in the peace movement and setting up groups internationally. Access: A.

Medical Campaigns

The Medical Association for Prevention of War, Secretary: Dr Alex Poteliakhoff, South Bank House, Black Prince Road, E1 7SJ (435 1872). Concerned with the ethical responsibility of doctors towards the question of war, studies the effects of war and the psychological mechanisms which cause acceptance of it. Opposes the use of medical science for anything but the relief of suffering and propose the reallocation of resources to the fight against disease and malnutrition. Publishes a very expensive journal. Access: A.

Medical Campaign Against Nuclear Weapons, 7 Tenison Road, Cambridge (0223 313828). Advocate nuclear disarmament and compile information. Membership open to all healthcare workers. Publish a variety of leaflets on the medical and human consequences of nuclear war. Access: N.

Nuclear Disarmament

Armament and Disarmament Information Unit, Science Policy Research Unit, Mantell Building, University of Sussex, Falmer, Brighton BN1 9RF (0273 686758). Maintains a data base on the British defence industry including information on women in the military. Publishes regular reports and fact sheets. Access: N.

Campaign for Nuclear Disarmament (CND) (and Youth CND), 22-24 Underwood Street, N1 7JQ (250 4010). Umbrella campaign for the unilateral abandonment of nuclear weapons, bases and alliances as a prerequisite for a British foreign policy of worldwide abolition of nuclear, chemical and biological weapons. Can give information on local groups. Publishes *Sanity* (monthly 65p) and *Campaign* (monthly 20p). Access: N.

European Nuclear Disarmament, South Bank House, Black Prince Road, SE1 7SJ (587 1563). Works for the creation of a European nuclear-free zone. Fosters contacts between peace activists East and West, Britain and Continent. Publishes the *END Journal* (£1) and various special reports, booklets and pamphlets. Access: A

Pensioners for Peace (London Group), Co-ordinator: Mrs Janet Pott, 56 Addison Avenue, W11 4QP (603 5301). London branch of a national organisation working with other peace and pensioners' groups to continue to work for peace and world disarmament including nuclear, biological and chemical warfare.

People to People, Secretary: Rae Street, Calder Cottage, Hare Hill Road, Little Borough, Lancs (0706 78043). Works to create links between people in Britain and Europe to work together to end the arms race. Helps local peace groups establish twinning relationships with US groups or individuals to become 'peace pen-pals'.

World Disarmament Campaign (UK), Secretary: Carla Wartenberg, 238 Camden Road, N1 9HE (485 1067). Supports People to People and seeks to promote links between peace groups. Publishes *Letter News* (quarterly 50p, free to unwaged). Access: N.

Nuclear-Free Zones in London

The GLC and many London boroughs have declared nuclear-free zones. Each borough has its own policies, but the main aim is to oppose the conscription of councils into war planning, as the public cannot be adequately protected from the effects of nuclear war, and the provision of 'civil defence' may help encourage the illusion that 'limited' nuclear wars can be fought and won. Some boroughs also have a policy banning the siting of nuclear weapons and some ban any kind of nuclear weapons and industry. The following boroughs are nuclear-free: Hounslow, Brent, Camden, Islington, Haringey, Hackney, Waltham Forest, Tower Hamlets, Newham, Greenwich, Lewisham, Southwark, Lambeth. The GLC was declared nuclear-free in 1983. No nuclear weapons are to be sited, no nuclear materials or weapons to be transported through and no power station to be sited in the GLC area (although the GLC has no powers to control the transport of nuclear materials through London on BR networks for example). The GLC is against statutory provision for nuclear civil defence and is campaigning against the implementation of new regulations concerning civil defence. The GLC also attempts to use only contractors who have no connection with the nuclear industry.

Peace and Anti-Militarism

The Bertrand Russell Peace Foundation, Bertrand Russell House, Gamble Street, Nottingham NG7 4ET (0602 784504). Works to further the cause of peace, freedom of thought and non-exploitative forms of human association. Opposes the unrestricted manufacture and stockpiling of nuclear weapons. Access: A.

Campaign Against the Arms Trade (CAAT), 5 Caledonian Road, N1 (278 1976) and 11 Goodwin Street, N4 (281 0297). Access: A. Campaigns against the manufacture and trade of arms of any kind, proposes the conversion of military industries to socially useful production, and opposes the abuse of human rights supported by the arms trade. Publishes a wide range of informative pamphlets and a regular newsletter (15p).

Concord Films, 201 Felixstowe Road, Ipswich, Suffolk IP3 9BJ (0473 715754). Has a range of films on peace available for hire. Access: A.

Labour Action for Peace, Secretary: Cynthia Roberts, 291 Clarence Lane, SW15 (878 2955), is the official Labour Party peace group working with constituency parties and trade unions to keep peace in the forefront of Labour politics. Monthly newsletter (10p).

The National Peace Council, 29 Great James Street, WC1 (242 3228). Umbrella organisation servicing the peace movement and linking groups with different priorities. Can give information and contacts. Publishes reports and pamphlets, monthly newsletter free to members.

Peace Advertising Campaign, PO Box 24, Oxford, OX1 3JZ. Founded by Quakers, encourages local peace groups to buy hoarding space for peace posters.

Peace Pledge Union, 6 Endsleigh Street, WC14 0DX (387 5501). Pacifist organisation campaigning against militarism, especially war toys and the conditioning of children into the general public acceptance of the existence of trained killers in society, and of war. Has a Peace Education Project liaising with schools and produces a range of non-sexist children's books, other publications and newsletters. Access: N.

Peace Tax Campaign, 13 Goodwin Street, N4 3HQ (263 2246). Campaigning for an extension of the law permitting conscientious objection to military service to allow individuals to refuse the use of their taxes for military purposes on conscientious grounds. Access: N.

United Nations Association, 3 Whitehall Court, SW1 (930 2931). British branch of the World Federation of United Nations Associations which supports the aims of the UN. Access: N.

War Resisters International, 55 Dawes Street, SE17 1EL (703 7189). Links, supports and serves people all over the world who are fighting non-violently against war, militarism, racism, economic exploitation and other causes of war. Sympathetic to feminist input. Published *Piecing it Together* jointly with the Feminism and Non-Violence Study Group on the links between feminism and non-violence. List of other publications available. Access: P.

Publications

Peace News, 8 Elm Avenue, Nottingham 3, (40p). Fortnightly paper 'for non-violent revolution', covering peace, third world, anti-nuclear, political and feminist issues. Mixed collective committed to feminism. Also produce a number of pamphlets including *It'll Make a Man of You* (a feminist view of the arms race) (95p).

Women for Life on Earth 2 Bramshill Gardens, NW5. Journal covering women's peace activities as well as ecology, holism and similar issues.

Keeping the Peace, ed Lynne Jones, (The Women's Press 1983, £3.75). Anthology of ideas, views, experiences, from women in many countries with practical information and resources for women's peace actions.

Over Our Dead Bodies, ed Dorothy Thompson, (Virago 1983, £3.50). Varied anthology of prose, poems, arguments by women deeply concerned by the nuclear threat.

Breaching The Peace, (Onlywomen Press 1983, £1.25). Strong arguments for and from the women's liberation movement raising reservations about the 'large' cause of the peace movement.

Black Women and the Peace Movement, Wilmette Brown, (Falling Wall Press £2.95).

'Who Feels It Knows It - Rethinking the Peace Movement' by Gail Lewis in *Outwrite* (issue 32).

'Challenging Imperial Feminism' by V. Amos and P. Parmar in *Feminist Review* (issue 17).

'The Nuclear Question - *A Third World Perspective'*, by Rada Gungaloo in *Spare Rib* 142 (special issue on peace, 70p).

Trouble and Strife, issues 1, 2, 3, many articles analysing Greenham politics.

Outwrite, Spare Rib, Feminist Review, Trouble and Strife - (see **Media and Arts**, Women's Publications). All these publications continually discuss/report on women's role in peace movements and struggles; contact them re: back issues, normally available.

'Black Women and the Peace Movement' by Claudette Williams, *European Nuclear Disarmament Journal*, May 1985. Address above.

Films/videos: many on this issue, and several on Greenham. Contact feminist film distributors - (see **Media and Arts**).

Planning

The planning and design of the built environment of London has a major impact on women's lives, but the way in which decisions are made about the use of buildings and space is a mystery to many women. It is women who bear the brunt of poorly designed houses and estates, of walking miles to the shops, of town centres which are deserted at night and therefore unsafe.

The concerns and needs of women have major implications for the way in which land is used. For example, many women need and want paid work and their income is vital to keeping large numbers of households out of poverty: So a planning policy which fosters light industry as opposed to warehousing on vacant land near their homes would be beneficial for local women.

What is planning? When the Planning legislation was first drawn up after the war the fundamental aims were to:

- Control development so the limited land available was used to facilitate economic recovery and improve the general environment.

- Give priority to community interests, especially by improving the environment for those living in bad conditions.

- Ensure that decisions about the kind of places our cities, villages and countryside become, are determined by the communities themselves through our elected local and national representatives.

Local authorities have a duty under law to control building *development* in their areas. They do this through the planning application procedures. If you want to build a new building, alter an existing building (eg adding on a new bathroom) or even just change the use of existing buildings or land, you must make a planning application. The decision on your application will be made by considering your proposed design, the effect it will have on the area (by overshadowing or overlooking the property next door or by generating traffic or rubbish) and its relation to any other planning policies of that authority regarding the use of land.

Land-use policies are usually set out in *local plans* which are periodically drawn up by the *local authority* (the boroughs, in London) which contain policies on issues like employment, housing, shopping, open space, transport and conservation. Different authorities have different policies. Local Planning Authorities have a statutory obligation to consult the public over local plans so in theory women's groups can press for things they want. The arguments, if couched in terms that fall within the planner's powers can be extremely effective. For instance, in Westminster the growing number of sex shops in Soho was challenged on the grounds of the threat to the amenity of local residents, of the viability of a small community if certain shops were lost, of housing need and of the effect on local school children.

Decisions on planning applications and on local plans are made by elected councillors at committee or council meetings on the advice of officers in the Planning Department.

Local *planning departments* may vary in the way they are organised. Some departments are split into two sections - the 'development control' section dealing with planning applications and the other dealing with policy making and local plans. Some are organised geographically into area teams which are responsible for both types of work. However the department is organised, only a very small proportion of planners are women.

In Greater London, up till the abolition of the GLC, the GLC has been responsible for drawing up a *structure plan* for the use and development of land. This served as a framework for the boroughs who draw up detailed local plans for their individual areas. The GLC through the Greater London Development Plan has attempted to guide borough councils on the strategic implications of community services and facilities, to ensure facilities such as meeting rooms for elderly people (most of whom are women) are integrated into the communities which they serve.

When the GLC goes, each individual borough will have to prepare a development plan which combines the features of a structure plan and a local plan with strategic guidance from the Secretary of State for the Environment.

What is planning for? Put it another way, how do our urban land and the buildings in our city end up the way they are? The main point we must remember is that we in Britain do not live in a 'planned society'. For instance, in the urban planning sphere, land and building are valuable and the major reason for developing a site is usually to make the maximum profit - scant attention is paid to the impact on local communities or to the needs of women.

Broadly speaking, the aim of the planning system is to control private development 'in the public interest', and to reduce the amount of chaos. Thus, planning is political in that it tries to balance conflicting interests and the planning process can be made to act as a brake on private development. For this reason the current government has taken steps to undermine the planning system. For instance, in Docklands planning decisions are no longer controlled by an elected council but by the London Docklands Development corporation. The government has also introduced measures to speed up the planning process with the result that the time allowed for public participation and consultation has been reduced.

GLC policy on planing - The GLC during this administration has developed and pursued a policy of needs-led planning and its actions in the field of planning have included:

- The revised *Greater London Development Plan* (GLDP) with new policies for equal opportunities including a chapter on women. This challenges stereotypes about gender roles and recognises the reality of women's lives as they are affected by age, disability, ethnic origin and class.

- Support for London's residential community groups which provide a local voice in planning and redevelopment matters, by providing assistance and finance for initiatives in community areas.

- Policies and funding for improvements to over 100 town centres to spread facilities more evenly across London and to help ensure that essential shopping, employment and community services are within reach of everyone, and that town centres offer a safe and convenient environment for people with disabilities or those accompanied by young children or encumbered with shopping and for ethnic groups

- Developing a London Industrial Strategy which shows how the economy can be rebuilt in the interests of the people who live and work in London.

Central to all the policies has been the concept of the absolute necessity to consult with and involve the women and men of London in planning decisions.

The Women's Committee has been instrumental in initiating or providing support for the work which has resulted in these policies. In particular, it pioneered the consultation process in the discussions it organised prior to writing the chapter on Women for the *GLDP*.

Through the *GLDP* and *Programme of Action* for Women the need for borough local plans to tackle the issues of equality has been raised and the Transport and Development Department has established a new Equality Structure to enable Equal Opportunities issues to be raised both from the point of view of the consumers and the officers working in the Planning Department.

The Women's Committee has also co-funded a survey into the shopping patterns of Londoners. Interviews were carried out with 3,000 people in three areas of London. The intention of the survey was to gather information on such factors as gender of shopper, ethnic origin, household composition and income with patterns of retail expenditure and attitudes towards different types of shopping centres. It was also designed to look at ways in which shopping centres could be improved for the benefit of all shoppers and in particular women. For example, few shopping developments at present provide creches, nappy changing facilities, comfortable and pleasant places for breast feeding, seats at check-out areas so that elderly women, pregnant women and women carrying young children can sit while waiting. Another aspect of planning and shopping is location: is there good access by public transport? Is a halal butcher situated within the main shopping centre so that ethnic minority women can combine their meat shopping with other shopping?

As has been said before, the present government does not share our commitment to positive planning for people's needs and is more and more allowing market forces to dictate planning decisions. During recent years the government has sought not to concentrate on regional and strategic planning but to tinker with minor aspects of the planning system. With the erosion of the mechanism for ensuring that the needs of society as a whole are considered for the use of land and the provision of co-ordinated services, all of us will suffer the consequences. Many of the progressive policies the GLC has initiated will be at risk and we women too could be losers.

However, from our experience of the last few years we have proved that if women want to, or discover that we have to, get involved in the planning process, there is a lot that we can achieve. For example, look at the advances in the women's Chapter of the *GLDP,* and look at the way the women of Tindlemanor through persistence, careful argument and heavy lobbying eventually obtained the planning permission they needed for their new building. We must now together ensure that our gains are not lost and that the process which has been begun continues so that women's needs and involvement becomes an integral part of planning.

This section is ordered as follows: *Borough Contacts, Community Organisations and Campaigns, Other Environmental Groups, Technical Aid Services (a)for women, b) other), Local Groups and Projects, Useful Reading.*

Borough Contacts

All Boroughs have their own planning departments. Contact yours through your local Town Hall. (see **Borough Information**).

Community Organisations and Campaigns

There are a number of campaigns and organisations concerned with planning and development, putting the needs of the community first.

Campaign for Homes in Central London, 5 Dryden Street, WC2 (240 2430). Umbrella group campaigning for an environment which meets social need and against development oriented towards offices, tourists and luxury. Emphasise need for housing, local shops, services and employment, transport and development that is well-designed and affordable. Has a good awareness of women's needs and seeks to ensure that their interests are well represented. Can given help and advice to groups and campaigns and put people in contact with groups active around these issues. Access: N.

Community Land and Workspace Services Limited, 245A Coldharbour Lane, SW9 8RR (274 7700).

Community Work Service (part of London Voluntary Service Council), 68 Chalton Street, NW1 (388 0241). Regional resource centre for community groups in London, servicing campaigns in all areas. Has produced *Community Technical Aid* (directory of technical aid centres serving community groups in London, ed Tim Young £1.50). Very useful, covering housing

services, planning advice and design services. Access: N.

Inquire, 85 Chalton Street, NW1 (388 0094). Access: A (no toilets)

The Neighbourhood Use of Buildings and Space, 15 Wilkin Street, NW5 (267 9421).

People's Plan Centre, 10 Pier Parade, North Woolwich (476 6692). Access A (no toilets)

Planning Aid for Londoners, (part of the Royal Town Planning Institute - a professional organisation), 26 Portland Place, W1 (580 7277). Gives free advice to individuals rather than groups concerning planning permission, for people unable to afford professional consultation, inspired by the legal aid scheme.

Reuse of Industrial Buildings Service (RIBS), c/o URBED, 99 Southwark Street, SE1 0JF (928 9515). Access: N.

Streetwork, c/o Nottingdale Urban Studies Centre, 189 Freston Road, W10 6TH (968 5440). National organisation promoting urban studies in school and education. Access: N (but can be organised).

Tower Hamlets Environment Trust, 192-6 Hanbury Street, E1 5HU (377 0481/2).

Town and Country Planning Association, 17 Carlton House Terrace, SW1Y 5AS (930 8903). Campaigns for better planning and environment, somewhat old-fashioned in its approach. Has a **London Planning Aid Service** giving advice to groups in London and help with planning applications, legal advice and general enquiries about planning. Also has a library and various publications available. Access: N.

Other Environmental Groups

Airfields Environment Federation Trust, 17/19 Redcross Way, SE1 1TB (378 6766).

British Trust for Conservation Volunteer, 2 Mandela (Selous) Street, NW1 (388 3946).

The Ecological Parks Trust, Gina Douglas, c/o The Linnaen Society, Burlington House, W1V 0LQ (734 5170).

London Wildlife Trust, 1 Thorpe Close, W10 (968 5369).

National Federation of City Farms, Harry Gallery, c/o Dean City Farm, Batsworth Road, Mitcham, SW19.

People Before Profit, 52 Dewhurst Road, W14 (603 6493).

Technical Aid Services

If you have a piece of land which you want to develop, or a building that you want to change, as well as advice on planning, you may need advice on the existing state of the building, what the best plans would be for what you want, what heating system to put in, help with finding a suitable builder. This technical advice is offered (for a fee) by architects and surveyors. There are now a number of groups which offer technical aid services particularly for community groups. Some of these are listed in the LPA's manual 'Planning Advice for Women's Groups' (see Useful Reading).

Women

At present in London there are 2 groups offering technical services specifically to women. These are:

Matrix,* 8 Bradbury Street, N16 8JN (249 7603). Provides architectural services primarily for women's groups including a free advice service. Are very aware of the particular needs of women with disabilities and women from ethnic minorities. Producing a

handbook on accessibility for women with disabilities and a handbook on nurseries. They also provide careers advice. Acccess: N.

Women's Design Service, 1 Ferdinand Place, NW1 8FE (485 5799). Free service providing feasibility studies for women's groups prior to purchasing premises including costs, design, planning permission, accessibility, and can put women in contact with women builders and tradespeople. Strongly emphasise the needs of women with disabilities and women from ethnic minorities. *Women and the Built Environment*, available from above address.

If you are an architect or studying architecture, or are interested in the field you may be interested in:

Feminist Architects' Network, c/o Support, 106a Shakespeare Road, SW9. Network of feminist architects meeting monthly to discuss issues related to architecture and design from a feminist perspective. Quarterly newsletter.

Other Technical Arts Centres

Community Land and Work-Space Services, 61-71 Collier Street, N1 19DF (833 2909).

Free Form Arts Trust Ltd, 38 Dalston Lane, E8 (249 3394).

Neighbourhood Use of Buildings and Space, John Knights, Inter-Clause (Trust Ltd), 15 Wilkin Street, NW5 (267 9421).

Support - Community Building Design Ltd, 106 Shakespeare Road, SE24 0QQ (735 9318).

Local Groups and Projects,

Advice Centre in the Blue, Rotherhithe Community Planning Centre, 190 Southwark Park Road, SE16 (231 2471).

Battersea Neighbourhood Aid Centre, 22 Battersea Park Road, SW17 (720 9409).

Battersea Power Station Community Group, c/o 68 Dunston Road, SW11 5YA (223 2308).

Bedford Park Society, 40 Rusthall, Bedford Park, W4 1BP.

Brixton Town Development, 31 Nursery Road, Brixton, SW9 8BS.

Bromley South Action Group, 32 Beadon Road, Bromley, Kent.

Clapham Community Project, Clapham Community Centre, St Anne's Hall, Venn Street, SW4 0BW (720 8731, 622 2042).

Covent Garden Community Association, 45 Short Gardens, WC2 (836 3355).

Covent Garden Forum, 204-205 Bedford Chambers, Covent Garden, WC2 E8HA (836 7017).

Docklands Forum, The Brady Centre, 192-196 Hanbury Street, E1 5HU (377 1822).

Federation of Heathrow Anti-Noise Groups, 23 Palace Road, East Molesey, Surrey, KT8 9DJ.

Finsbury Park Action Group (15 Finsbury Park Road), Alexandra National House, 330 Seven Sisters Road, N4 (802 2612).

Fitzrovia Neighbourhood Association, 39 Tottenham Street, W1 (580 4576).

The Greenwich Society, 6 Pond Road, SE3.

The Hackney Society, 133 Ball's Pond Road, N11.

Hackney Urban Studies Centre, 6-8 Lower Clapton Road, E5 ONS (985 5682).

Heart of Bromley Residents Association, 21 Holwood Road, Bromley, Kent (460 3163).

Joint Docklands Action Group, 2 Carole Street, E1 8JG (480 5324).

Lambeth Planning Resource Centre, 23 New Park Road, SW2 4DU (674 9188).

The Lee Valley Association, Mick Molloy, 41 Rheola

Limehouse Development Group, The Arches, 21-23 Trinidad Street, E14 (515 1480).

Newham Docklands Forum, People's Plan Centre, 10 Pier Parade, North Woolowich (476 6692).

North Southwark Community Development Group, 56 Southwark Bridge Road, SE1 (928 0711).

Paddington Federation of Tenants and Residents, 1 Crompton Street, W2 (724 4832).

Peckham Urban Studies Centre, Peckham Urban Studies Centre, Staffordshire Street, SE15 5TF.

Pimlico Neighbourhood Aid Centre, 1-3 Charlwood Street, SW1 (821 1608).

The Smithfield Trust, 14-16 Cowcross Street, EC1M 6DR.

Southwark Docklands Campaign, 190 Southwark Park Road, SE16 3RP (231 2472).

Thornhill Neighbourhood Project, Arkney House, 199 Caledonian Road, N1 (278 9500).

Tower Hamlets Environment Trust, 192-196 Hanbury Street, E1 5HU (377 0481).

Vauxhall Cross Amenity Trust, 115/116 Market Towers, 1 Nine Elms Lane, SW8 5NG (627 0686).

Vishwa Hindu Parishad (UK), 60 Richmond Road, Ilford, Essex, IG1 1JZ.

Wimbledon Town Centre Co-ordinating Group, 4 Hartfield Road, Wimbledon, SW19 3TJ (879 0446).

Useful Reading

Planning Advice for Women's Groups, TCPA LPAS Community Manual No.6 £1.50.

GLDP September 1984. Contains a chapter 'Women in London'.

Built Environment Vol.10 No.1, Women and the Environment.

Making Space: Women and the Man-Made Environment, Matrix. (Pluto £5.95).

Women and the American City, ed. Stimpson, Dixler, Nelson and Yatrakis. (Chicago Press £7.50).

Heresis Vol.3, No.3, Issue 11.

Geography and Gender, Women and Geography Study Group of the IBG.

The Grand Domestic Revolution - Dolores Hayden. £9.95.

Women and the Planned Environment - Proceedings of a conference held at Polytechnic of Central London, November 1982. (From Planning Unit, PCL, 35 Marylebone Road, NW1 £2.50.)

Community Action (from 27 Clerkenwell Close, EC1).

WEB Quarterly Newsletter of Women and the Built Environment (from 1 Ferdinand Place, NW1).

Planning for the Future of London, GLC Transportation and Development Department (SBN 7168 14013) plus Issue Papers.

Community Areas Policy - A Record of Achievement. GLC Transportation and Development Department (SNB 7168 15222).

Erosion of the Planning System. GLC (ISBN 7168 15192).

Policing

Many crimes committed against women are due to male violence and yet women feel the emphasis of policing is not responsive to women's needs and concerns. (See **Violence against Women**.)

Sir Kenneth Newman, the Metropolitan Police Commissioner, endorsed this when he categorised domestic disputes along with 'stranded people, lost property and stray animals' as not 'real crime work' (*The Times* 4.10.83).

Many women argue that the whole legal framework within which rape, domestic violence and assault of women are treated is prejudicial to women. The type of evidence sought and the woman's role in the case operate effectively to put the burden of proof on her and to put her on trial.

For these reasons many women are reluctant to report violent incidents against them to the police, and thus recorded figures at present vastly misrepresent the numbers of these attacks. Black women are often particularly reluctant to report incidents to the police because of the racism in the police force (well documented in the Policy Studies Institute Report on the Metropolitan Police), and where the attack is racial because of the inadequate response of the police in such cases. (See **Housing,** Race and housing.) Where Black men are involved, many Black women are particularly reluctant to report incidents to the police, because of their knowledge of how the information could be used to 'trawl' the Black community and also to stop and detain Black men on 'suspicion', a method often illegally used by the police at present.

Irish women too are particularly vulnerable to police surveillance and harassment, under the Prevention of Terrorism Act.

Women want a change in the style and priorities of policing rather than an overall increase in police powers. Many have added their opposition to that of the GLC and community groups in opposing the new Police and Criminal Evidence Act, the major provisions of which will be implemented by January 1986. The Act will give the police unprecedented power to stop and search, set up roadblocks, detain without charge, seize evidence of any offence when carrying out a search, search premises of people not suspected of any offence and confiscate evidence held by innocent third parties. The Act does not contain comparable safeguards to protect individuals, or to increase the accountability of the police, or to curb the abuse of existing police powers.

In conjunction with this, the new strategy for policing devised by Sir Kenneth Newman does not take into account any of the concerns voiced by women. The new strategy blurs the distinction between public order and crime, and places emphasis on public bodies and members of the public in a 'multi-agency' approach to assist the police in clearing up crime. To this end, the police have prioritised 'high crime' areas and the targeting and surveillance of individuals and locations within them. Neighbourhood Watch Schemes were set up in September 1983. It involves intelligence gathering with no safeguards that unsubstantiated information received through the scheme could be entered into the police computers and remain on record regardless of the accuracy or relevance of such information.

The goal of the new approach was spelled out by Sir Kenneth Newman: '...it would be better if we stopped talking about crime prevention and lifted the whole thing to a higher level of generality represented by the words 'social *control*' (*FT* 23.3.83).

Social control and the countering of social unease is inherently different from 'traditional crime detection', and the targeting and surveillance of designated areas and individuals could lead to an increase in tensions between the police and various community groups already most vulnerable to the police. It also raises fundamental questions about civil liberties.

There is no evidence that the proposals will lead to a reduction of crime and for many of the crimes of violence suffered by women - rape, domestic violence, racial attacks, assault - the new strategies are irrelevant.

The GLC Police Committee is setting up a 'Public Safety Unit' to promote the role of local government rather than the police in creating safer environments and to look at the safety of communities, groups and individuals prone to attack. Women are one such group. The Police Committee was set up to give information on policing practices, the organisation of the police, and to campaign for a more accountable and responsive police force. It funds various police monitoring groups and research projects in connection with policing and has a worker specifically working on women and policing issues, and has produced broadsheets on *Women and Policing in London,* and an exhibition on the same topic.

The GLC Women's Committee works closely with the Police Committee on issues of women and policing, in particular the organising of a Women and Policing Conference in November 1985. It looks at the implications for women of the Police and

Criminal Evidence Act and has jointly funded a survey into violence against women and the police response to it, in Wandsworth.

While the police continue to carry out investigations into complaints about their behaviour without recourse to an independent body, most women have little confidence that it is worth complaining. However, if you do decide to complain always get advice first from a police monitoring team (see below), or an advice centre (see **Borough Section**). Sometimes the police call without an appointment while investigating complaints. You should ask them to call again at a set time, and make sure you have taken advice meanwhile and, preferably, have a friend with you to support you. (Also see **Prison, Prostitution, Violence against Women, Housing**.)

This section is ordered as follows: *Police Monitoring Groups, Useful Reading.*

Police Monitoring Groups

(and other groups concerned with policing policies)

Barnet Police Monitoring Group, Room 321, Trafalgar House, Grenville Place, NW7 3SA (959 2972) (24 hour answer phone).

Camden Policing the Police, 213 Eversholt Street, NW1 (387 2777).

CAPA (Community Alliance for Police Accountability), Oxford House, Derbyshire Street, E2. (729 2652). Access: P

Children's Legal Centre, 20 Compton Terrace, N1 2UN (359 6251). Also two other groups in same premises - Black and In Care, National Association of Young People in Care. Access: N.

Public Order, Research Group (Cities of London and Westminster), 9 Poland Street, W1. (734 5831) Access:P.

Hackney Legal Defence, 50 Rectory Road, N16 (254 9849). Access:P.

Haringey Independent Police Committee, 5 Annexe B, Tottenham Town Hall, Town Hall Approach, N15. (801 2837). Access:N.

Hayes Police Monitoring Group, Basement Office, Westbourne House, Station Approach, Hayes (573 6582). Access:N.

Institute of Race Relations, 2-6 Leeke Street, WC1X 9HS. (837 0041).

Inquest (investigating, for instance deaths in police custody), Alexandra National House (Ground Floor), 330 Seven Sisters Road, N4 (802 7430). Access:N.

Lespop (Lesbian's and Policing Project),* 38 Mount Pleasant, WC1X 0AP (833 4996/9). Access: N.

Lewisham Action on Policing, 192 Evelyn Street, Deptford, SE8 (692 1308). Access: N.

Libertarian Research and Education Trust (Neighbourhood Watch Project), 9 Poland Street, W1 (434 4220). Access: P.

NAVSS (National Association of Victim Support Schemes), 17a Electric Lane, SW9 8LA (737 2010). Access: N.

National Council for Civil Liberties,* 21 Tabard Street, SE1 4LA. (403 3888). Access: N.

Newham Monitoring Project, 382 Katherine Road, E7. (555 8151). Access: N.

Release, c/o 347a Upper Street, N1 (485 4440).

Rights of Women,* 52-54 Featherstone Street, EC1 (251 6577).

Southall Monitoring Group, Top floor, 50-52 King Street, Southall (843 2333). Access: N.

Southwark Monitoring Project, 8 Camberwell Green, SE5 (703 1906). Access: N.

Waltham Forest Police Monitoring Group, 226 High Street, E17 (520 4333). Access: N.

Wandsworth Policing Campaign, 248-250 Lavender Hill, SW11 (223 8655). Access: N.

Useful Reading

Women, Crime and Criminology, Carol Smart, (Routledge & Kegan Paul).

Prison

The number of women in prison is on the increase - currently about 1,500 women are in prison. Prostitute women, for example, are now more, not less, likely to serve a sentence - for non-payment of the fine which was originally supposed to be an alternative to prison (see **Prostitution**).

Overcrowding, and harsher attitudes, along with the idea that women who offend are 'sick' rather than 'bad', have led to poor conditions, deprivation of rights (for instance exercise, and, in the case of young prisoners, the right to education), and misuse of tranquilising and other drugs - massively over-prescribed in women's prisons.

There are eight women's prisons in England, five of which are closed prisons and three of which are open. Holloway, a closed prison, is London's only women's prison, but is a major dispersal prison, so women from London can be sent to prisons elsewhere, which often makes it very difficult for their families to visit.

Most women are in prison for fine default and stealing. Only 7.5% of women are in prison for violent crime.

The racism of the courts coupled with the penal system ensures that a vastly disproportionate number of Black women are held in prisons, and that they receive harsher sentences (and face racist attitudes and treatment from staff and co-prisoners). A similarly high proportion of Black women are committed to mental institutions because of the powers of the police under the Mental Health Act; and the racist assumptions of white mental health workers. (See **Health**, Mental Health and **Disability**, Mental Health.) In both cases, Black women are often separated from their families with inadequate provision being made for their children, who are then taken into care. All women prisoners with children find it difficult to re-establish contact once released: this is increased for Black women, who are even more likely to be assumed to be unfit mothers once they have been kept in an institution.

Recently women, many of them ex-prisoners, have brought to light the injustices practised against women in prisons and conditions which have led, in some cases, to women seriously harming themselves. Black women have been organising around the treatment of Black women prisoners: a conference on this matter was organised jointly by the Black Female Prisoners's Scheme and the GLC Women's Committee Support Unit and held in March 1985.

Women in London have also organised to support women held in Armargh Prison, Northern Ireland, for political reasons, and have campaigned against ill-treatment and strip-searching (see **Black and Ethnic minority women,** Irish women).

The GLC Women's Committee recognised that many of the women in prison are among the most socially and economically deprived, was concerned about the treatment of women in prison and was aware of how little concrete information is available on women in prison. The Women's Committee has funded women's groups working with and for women prisoners, has highlighted with other prison groups the conditions in Holloway Prison, and has commissioned a major research project into women in prison.

This section is ordered as follows: *Women's Organising and Campaigning Groups, other Campaigning Groups and Advice Services,Useful Reading.*

Women's Organising and Campaigning Groups

Women in Prison, * Unit 3, Cockpit Yard, Northington Street, WC1 2NP (430 0767/8). Seeks to unite women of all classes, ethnic backgrounds and sexual orientation in a campaign which whilst highlighting, and attempting to redress, the injustices presently suffered by Britain's hitherto neglected women prisoners, will also contribute to the wider campaigns for democratic control of the criminal justice systems. **Women in Prison** - campaigning for women prisoners - demands:

● Improved safety conditions, particularly in Holloway Prison where women have been burned to death in their cells.

● The introduction of a range of facilities (eg more visits, including family and conjugal visits in relaxed surroundings, more association with other prisoners, fewer petty rules) aimed both at reducing tension and, subsequently, the number of drugs prescribed for behaviour and mood control rather than the benefit of prisoners.

● Improved, non-discriminatory and non-paternalistic education, job-related training, leisure and work facilities.

● Improved training and supervision of prison officers, aimed at reducing their present discriminatory practices against women from ethnic minorities, lesbians and disabled or mentally or emotionally disturbed women.

● A mandatory and non-discriminatory income entitlement to meet the basic needs of women prisoners.

● Improvement of the existing child-care facilities in prisons together with the introduction of a whole range of child-care facilities for mothers receiving a custodial sentence (eg new centres specially for mothers and children with local nurseries and parents' groups).

● Improved medical facilities in general and specialised facilities for women during pregnancy, childbirth and menstruation.

● Dismantling of the punitive disciplinary structure coupled with the development of official recognition of prisoner participation in the organisation of the prison.

- Non-discriminatory sentencing of women.
- Unrestricted access to the Boards of Visitors for representatives from women's organisations and community, ethnic minority and other minority (eg lesbian) organisations.

And for *all* prisoners:

- Suspension of Official Secrets Act restrictions on the availability of information about prisons; public accountability of the Home Office Prison Department for its administration of the prisons; public inquiries replacing Home Office internal inquiries into the deaths of prisoners, injuries and complaints in general.
- Increased funding for non-custodial alternatives to prisons together with greater use of the existing sentencing alternatives.
- Abolition of the Prison Medical Service and its replacement by normal National Health Service provision.
- Provision of a law library in prisons so that prisoners may have access to information about their legal rights in relation to DHSS entitlement, employment, housing, marriage and divorce, child-custody, court proceedings etc.

For full details of the Women in Prison campaign demands, send SAE to address above. This organisation also gives advice and support to ex-prisoners on all relevant issues. Access: A

Black Female Prisoners' Scheme,* 141 Stockwell Road, SW9 (733 5520). Aims to provide a service with a view to reintroducing women prisoners (Afro-Caribbean and Asian) into the community. This involves mediating with the families of ex-prisoners, making provision for housing, helping in the search for jobs and giving careers advice. Acts as an education and recreation unit for ex-offenders and also single parents. In the past,

great emphasis has been centred around Black men in the penal system. There has been a corresponding lack of information and concern about Black women prisoners who, although fewer in numbers suffer the same racism inside prison and on their release. Access: N.

Women Prisoners' Resource Centre, 1 Thorpe Close, Ladbroke Grove, W10 5XL (968 3121). Provides independent advice, information and support for women leaving custody and returning to the Greater London area, on welfare rights, housing, education, health, employment, training and issues such as alcoholism, drug abuse and domestic violence. Access: A.

Other Campaigning Groups and Advice Services

Apex Trust, 31-33 Clapham Road, SW9 0JE (582 3171). Runs an employment placement service from its head office in Clapham Road and operates four employment resource centres in Haringey, Hackney, Wandsworth and Hounslow offering specialist counselling and pre-employment training to all ex-offenders. Access: N.

Camden Community Relations Council, 58 Hampstead Road, NW1 2PY (387 1125). Setting up support group for Black prisoners and their families, also to act as a pressure group on local authorities and the Home Office on Black prisoners. Access: P.

Creative and Supportive Trust (CAST), Basement, 34a Stratford Villas, NW1 9SG (485 0367). Offers supportive environment in which women ex-prisoners can gain work skills and generate self employment tuition and workshop space available for weaving, pottery, painting, knitwear and silk screen printing with the aim to produce saleable items. Organises exhibitions. Also offers advice and counselling on problems related to imprisonment, courts, drugs and housing. Access: N.

Clean-Break, Basement, 34A Stratford Villas, NW1 9SG (485 0367). Touring theatre company open to all women ex-prisoners, producing original work based on central theme of women and the law. Runs two regular workshops, one of these is for women from Black and ethnic cultures. Hopes to move into more accessible premises next year. Access: N.

Howard League for Penal Reform, 322 Kennington Park Road, SE11 (735 3317). Access: N.

Inquest, Ground Floor, Alexandra National House, 330 Seven Sisters Road, N4 2PJ (802 7430). Looking into deaths in police custody and prison deaths. Access: N.

NACRO (National Association for the Care and Resettlement of Offenders), 169 Clapham Road, SW9 0PU (582 6500). The principal non-statutory organisation concerned with community provision for offenders, alternatives to prison and the prevention of crime. Contact above for general inquiries about provision in your area. NACRO manages projects which help offenders and others to resettle in the community. The projects are in the fields of housing, youth training, adult employment, education, day centres, safe neighbourhoods, and leisure activities

for youth. There are more than 170 projects. NACRO staff are organised in specialist teams, each of which provides a range of services. For details, ring main office above. Access: N.

Prisoners Advice and Information Network, BM PAIN, WC1N 3XX (542 3744). Collective of PROP, RAP, WIP, BFPS and Inquest giving information and advice to ex-prisoners, prisoners and prisoners' families, with a back-up legal and medical service.

Prisoners' Wives and Families Society, 254 Caledonian Road, N1 (278 3981). Aims to help in any way possible the families (wives, husbands, parents, dependants) and friends of prisoners by giving advice and moral support and overnight accommodation for those travelling long distances to visit their husbands in London prisons, or short-term stay for homeless wives and children. Advice on welfare rights. Access: P.

Prisoners' Wives Service, 51 Borough High Street, SE1 1NB (403 4091). Provides volunteer visitors to families of prisoners in their own homes in the Inner London area, to offer friendship and support during the man's imprisonment. Also gives advice and information by telephone or letter to families of prisoners anywhere in Britain. Access: N.

Prison Reform Trust, Nuffield Lodge, Regents Park, NW1 4RS (722 8871/ 586 4978). Charity aiming to provide public debate about prison conditions by encouraging community interest in penal establishments and by advocating reforms of prison rules and penal policy generally. Access: P

PROP (National Prisoners' Movement) BM PROP, WC1N 3XX (542 3744). Ex-prisoners group concerned with welfare and support of prisoners inside prison.

RAP (Radical Alternatives to Prison), BCM Box 4842, WC1. Publish quarterly journal The Abolitionist.

Useful Reading

The Abolitionist - from RAP, as above.

Criminal Women, autobiographical accounts by Pat Carlen, Diana Christina, Jenny Hicks, Josie O'Dwyer, Chris Tchaikovsky (Polity Press £4.95).

NAPO Probation Directory (lists all local probation and after-care services). Available from NAPO (National Association of Prison Officers) 3-4 Chivalry Road, SW11 (223 4887/223 7393)

Women on Trial, Susan Edwards. A study of the female suspect, defendant and offender in the criminal law and criminal justice system (Manchester University Press £14.50)

Women's Imprisonment, Pat Carlen. A study in social control (Routledge £5.95).

Prostitution

Prostitution continues to be an issue on which society is divided, and men's double standards are most obvious. Said to be the 'oldest profession' in the world, prostitution has been used to divide women into 'good' and 'bad'. Laws have been harsh and illogical towards women who work as prostitutes. Prostitution has been, and continues to be, one way in which women have been able to earn money. Women working as prostitutes have said repeatedly that the reasons for their work are economic.

Many women, from economically depressed areas in the North of England travel to London to find jobs. With so many areas of employment closed to women, and those that remain concentrated in low paid work, it is not surprising that prostitution remains a positive option to many women, nor that prostitution is concentrated around areas like Kings Cross, near to the terminus of trains from the North of England.

Feminist debates on prostitution have attempted to expose the hypocrisy of judges, police, lawyers and legislators - who are predominantly male — in criminalising and prosecuting prostitutes. What has been clear amongst all feminists concerned about the issue is that it is a matter of social, not moral concern.

The recent Sexual Offences Act makes kerb-crawling illegal, and men engaged in the practice liable to arrest. The supporters of this Act claim to be seeking to alleviate the harassment that all women experience from the unwelcome attention of men in cars stopping women on the street. However, many women working as prostitutes pointed out that the Act would make the job harder, by forcing them to lose their independence and reinforce the power of pimps. Black organisations also objected to the increased possibility of Black men being singled out by the police on the pretext of kerb-crawling.

The Act, supposedly aimed at protecting 'decent' society, does nothing to deal with the forces that make prostitution an economic reality for over one million women in Britain today. All organisations representing women working as prostitutes have demanded that prostitution be decriminalised. Whilst agreeing with decriminalisation, they oppose prostitution as an institution and would not wish to support state run or state endorsed prostitution. Many of the debates are concerned with the difficulties of supporting individual women engaged in the prostitution industry, whilst at the same time objecting to the existence and nature of prostitution.

The two areas of public policy in which prostitution particularly features are planning (the local effects of prostitution in an area) and the legal system. In both instances the impact of the public involvement is to 'penalise' prostitutes rather than to secure any improvement or solutions to the overall issue.

Some local authorities, including the GLC, have begun to take a more rounded view of the complex issue of prostitution, looking at the problems and solutions from the point of view of residents generally, prostitute women, non-prostitute women, safety, traffic, the impact of racism on how measures to tackle prostitution affect Black men and women, and so on.

As far as the law is concerned it is an outdated hotch-potch of measures which weigh heavily against prostitute women themselves. There are offences relating to loitering and soliciting (prostitution itself is not an offence), brothel keeping, advertising services, living off immoral earnings (men) and controlling a prostitute (women). Fines are the common penalty (reinforcing women's need to engage in prostitution) and many women are imprisoned for non-payment of fines for example. The punitive and judgemental basis to the laws means many women are reinforced in resorting to prostitution. Once a woman has a conviction, police are more likely to pick her up for loitering while waiting on the street for friends, at bus stops etc.

This section is ordered as follows: **Campaigning and Advice Groups**

Campaigning and Advice Groups

English Collective of Prostitutes, Kings Cross Women's Centre, 71 Tonbridge St, WC1. Campaigning for the abolition of all laws against prostitute women.

Legal Action for Women, address as above. Specialising in Legal advice for prostitutes, social security, immigration, rape and divorce.

Rights of Women (ROW)*, 52-54 Featherstone St, EC1 (251 6577), has compiled information on the policing of prostitution all over London. Runs telephone legal advice service, Tues and Thurs, 7-9 pm and campaigns on the law.

(See also **Police, Prison** and **Borough Information** for legal advice agencies. See **Housing** for advice on homelessness, hostels etc. **Young Women** for young people's advice centres and **Planning** for the local effects of prostitution in an area).

Sport

Over the past thirty years there has been an unprecedented growth in sports as a commercial activity. Although still very much a male dominated activity the number of women and girls participating has also risen. Wide media coverage has helped to stimulate and deepen interest in sports activities generally. However, this is neither neutral nor value free. Coverage of women's sports activities often stress sexuality and other superfluous information, such as clothes and hair designs. This trivialises women's contribution to the sports world and perpetuates the prevalent sexist images such as masculinity equals strength, competitiveness and determination.

In general, sports provision for women and girls in London revolves around the more 'sedate' or 'safe' sports such as tennis, badminton, netball, swimming and keep-fit. There are few opportunities for women and girls to gain entry to traditionally male sports, particularly those which require strength and physical contact.

In 1983 the first London-wide Women's Day of Sport was organised by the GLC Women's Committee. It was designed to heighten awareness of women's needs in sport and recreation at a local level. It was highly successful both in numbers of women participating on the day and in the reaction and subsequent action by sports providers, particularly local authorities.

A questionnaire was circulated to participants on the day and further analysis revealed a number of common barriers to participation.

- Women felt they were not asked what types of classes they preferred or the best times for scheduling such activities.

- Marketing of courses and classes generally was criticised for not reaching areas accessible to women. Women reliant on public transport were extremely wary of travelling to certain centres at night or within 'high risk' areas.

- Black and ethnic minority women often felt alienated from the sports and recreation pursuits on offer. What may be acceptable and suitable for some women may be frowned upon and rejected within certain cultures. Many centres stress a mode of dress which excludes participation for cultural or religious reasons.

- In an increasingly violent society all women feared attack. Black women were also faced with the possibility of racial attack and racist attitudes among sport providers.

- The cost of sports and recreation pursuits is generally prohibitive to the lower paid. In the present economic climate many women, some of whom are single parents, find themselves living on a limited budget barely able to meet minimal needs. As a result recreation activities are seen as 'luxuries' or treats.

- There is a tendency within wider society to view people with disabilities as neuter, consequently the needs of disabled women are usually confined to problems of accessibility. Many disabled women wish to be involved in planning for disabled sports provision at centres.

This section deals largely with sports courses and classes currently available and is aimed primarily at the non-professional sportswoman. These programmes are subject to alteration and it is worth contacting the local centre or leisure services department for an updated list of activities. If the required activity is not available it is usually worthwhile lodging a request as it may be borne in mind at a later date.

The Young Women's Christian Association (YWCA) organises special sports classes and events. You could also try contacting your local Women's Centre (see **Borough Information**) or Community Centre for individual contacts in your area. Many local Girls' Projects organise activities for girls such as football, self-defence (see **Young Women**).

It is also worth checking with Further Education Institutes and the Youth Service programmes for sports programmes and facilities.

This section is ordered as follows: *General Section, Sporting Organisations specifically for people with disabilities, Specific Sports, Sports facilities catering specifically to women, and Sports and Leisure Centres.*

General

Sportsline, a telephone information service can give details of all local sports/leisure centres throughout Greater London as well as information on neighbourhood sports projects and groups. Sportsline will know about special sessions for women, and also have details of concessionary rates for unemployed, pensioners, etc in sports centres. Telephone 222 8000 weekdays.

Floodlight. To find a local group for a specific sport either phone Sportsline or look in *Floodlight*, which is the guide to part time and evening Adult Education classes and includes many sports activities, particularly for beginners. It's available from most newsagents in July/September or from ILEA, Room 80, County Hall, SE1 7PB - 50p.

The City Limits Guide to Sporting London, published by Wildwood House, for comprehensive details of sports for specific groups, eg older people, unwaged, and details of the governing bodies of a wide range of sports. *The City Limits Guide* has an A-Z of Sports in London that covers sports centres in every borough and council district officers to contact for details of sports and recreation in your area. Available at most newsagents and your local library should have a reference copy, (if not ask them to order one). See also *City Limits* magazine sports section or details of participation events, and *Time Out, What's On* and *Where to Go*, as well as local newspapers, libraries and sports centres. See also The Sports Council magazine *Sport and Leisure*, (available from 16 Upper Woburn Place, WC1, (778 7060).

The Sports Council, 16 Upper Woburn Place, WC1 (778 7060). Grants and loan schemes to improve sports facilities. Sometimes runs leadership courses aimed primarily at women. Regional structure - see GL & SE Region below. See their magazine *Sport and Leisure.*

Sports Council Greater London and South East Region, PO Box 480, Crystal Palace National Sports Centre, Ledrington Rd, SE19 2BQ (778 8600). Contact for details of governing bodies of the various sports. A regional handbook is being prepared which will give full details of these.

Foundation for Afro-Asians in Sport, 5 Westminster Bridge Rd, SE1 (928 7858). Educational and pressure group aimed at increasing the participation of Black people in sport. Organises courses and events, some for Black women in particular.

Sports and Disability

The British Sports Association for the Disabled (London Region), The Cottage, Tottenham Sports Centre, 703 High Rd, N17 (801 3136). Large organisation working throughout the Greater London area to encourage disabled people to take part in physical recreation and sport for pleasure, for physical, emotional and social benefit and as an aid to rehabilitation. Have six branches throughout London (phone 801 3136 for local contacts) and also aims to further opportunities, through sport, for integration with the able bodied community.

British Amputees' Sports Association, c/o 110 Speed House, Barbican, EC2Y 8AU.

Cerebral Palsy International Sport and Recreational Association, c/o Mr Howard Bailey, Spastics Society, 16 Fitzroy Sq, W1 (387 9571).

British Deaf Sports Council, Mr R Haythorntwaite, 38 Victoria Place, Carlisle, CA1 1HU (0228 48844).

UK Sports Association for People with Mental Handicap, Mr Roger Biggs, 62c Grand Parade, Haringey, N4 (885 2315).

British Paraplegics' Sports Society, Ludwig Guttmann Sports Centre, Barnard Crescent, Aylesbury, Bucks HP21 8PP (0296 84848).

Les Autres, c/o Bob Churchill, 5 Marne Avenue, Welling, Kent. A sports association for people with a range of disabilities other than those listed above.

British Association for Sporting and Recreational Activities of the Blind, 51 Westfields, Railwayside, Barnes, SW13 0PJ (221 0721) or (878 7788).

Specific Sports

Falcon Ladies' Basketball Club Islington Green School, Prebend St, N1 (609 4878). New members welcome. Contact the Secretary or just go along to the practice sessions at Islington Green School, Tues from 7.15 to 9 pm and Sat from 2 to 4.30 pm.

London Ladies' Basketball Association, c/o 74 Murillo Rd, Lewisham.

Women's Amateur Athletics Association, Francis House, Francis St, SW1 (828 4731).

English Ladies' Golf Association, c/o Mrs Coombe, Greensleeves, Bitchet Green, Sevenoaks, Kent (0732 61838).

All England Women's Hockey Association, c/o Mrs T Morris, Argyll House, 29-31 Euston Rd, NW1 (278 6340).

Women's Cricket Association, c/o Mrs Daley, 16 Upper Woburn Place, WC1 (387 3423).

All Women's Lacrosse Association, c/o Mrs Cantell, 16 Upper Woburn Place, WC1 (387 4430).

The Women's Football Association Limited, c/o Linda Whitehead 11 Portsea Mews, Marble Arch, W2 (402 9388). Has information on girls' and women's football teams and leagues. Also publishes WFA News.

The Women's Squash Rackets Association, 345 Upper Richmond Rd West, East Sheen, SW14.

London Gay Tennis Club, 5 Caledonian Rd, N1.

England Women's Softball Team, c/o 16 Packholme Rd, E8.

Women's Facilities

National Federation of Women's Institutes, 39 Eccleston St, SW1W 9NT (730 7212). National organisation which arranges sports activities for women, particularly older women. Recently appointed a special sports officer to further these activities. Contact above for your local group.

The Women's Sports Foundation, c/o GES, Sheffield City Polytechnic, 51 Broomgrove Rd, Sheffield S10. Aims to promote the interests of all women in and through sport, to increase sporting opportunities for women, to campaign against discrimination and to encourage women's confidence in starting new sporting activities. Information exchange. Write for details of local contacts.

Outdoor Woman, c/o A Woman's Place, Hungerford House, Victoria Embankment, WC2. Women's group meet regularly to make outdoor pursuits accessible to all women and girls and to share organising, equipment and resources. Good contact point for meeting other women interested in particular sports. Write for details of meetings.

Camden Sports Development Officer (John Mann), Camden Town Hall, Euston Rd, NW1 2RU (278 4444 ext 2134). Contact for details of women's sport sessions and activities throughout the borough. A 10-week pilot scheme which took place at the University of London Union (ULU) offered aerobics, weight training, snooker, squash, swimming, badminton and much more to women on Sunday afternoons, with creche facilities provided, was a great success. Camden hope to carry on this type of women only session, but the venue may change, so contact for information. Also, Mornington Sports Centre has weight training and self-defence for women. Details of these and much more from the Sports Development Officer. Sports workers cover different areas of the borough. For details of women's football in Swiss Cottage, contact the Winchester Project (586 8731).

Hackney Action Sport, 380 Old St, Shoreditch, EC1 9BT (729 0218). Contact for details of a wide range of classes for women - self-defence, yoga, aerobics, badminton, swimming, dance and more - based in local community centres and day nurseries as well as sports/leisure centres. A yoga class for Asian women takes place in Stoke Newington Day Nursery. Any group of eight women or more, interested in taking up a particular activity, can get in touch with Hackney Action Sport for help in finding a suitable location and qualified instructors.

Haringey Women's Sports Group, The Cottage, Tottenham Sports Centre, 703 High Rd, N17 (801 8233). Has details of all women's sports activities in Haringey. Also produces *Ready Steady, Go*, the Haringey Women's Sports Magazine. Contact for details of special events for women, eg Women's Days of Sport.

Hounslow Youth and Community Education Department, Thornbury Rd, Isleworth, Middx (586 3697). Contact Paul Levy or Paul Coxon at the above for details of the range of sports available at sports centres and Adult Education Centres throughout the borough. Another source of information for what is happening is the Arts and Recreation Department, Civic Centre, Lampton Rd, Hounslow (570 7728).

Islington: North Islington Women's Sports Clubs, 115 Manor Rd, N16 (contact address) (800 0471). Informal club where women can meet and play their favourite sport or learn a new activity. Main base at the George Orwell School Annexe. Access: N, with badminton, table tennis, self-defence, football. Also, weight training at Hornsey Rd Baths and T'ai Chi at Crouch Hill Recreation Centre. Also, massage classes. (Ring 800 0471 for details of all these).

North Kensington Action Sport, c/o North Kensington Amenities Trust, 1 Thorpe Close, W10 (969 0992). Contact for details of the following activities for women and girls which take place at the Westway Outdoor Sports Centre, 10 Crowthorne Rd, W10, or at local venues in the community - keep fit and aerobics, racket ball and squash, weight training and multigym. There are facilities for women's football, and also netball coaching and playing for women and girls. A women's sports night is planned for the near future.

Southwark Action Sport, c/o Elsie Sharples, 22 Colombo St, SE1 (261 0115). Contact for details of women's cricket, also, football for women (training and playing) self-defence for women and other sports activities for women and girls. The following are available at present, but it is safer to check: weight training, keep fit, indoor tennis and badminton for women on Fri mornings 10 am - 12 noon, (cheap sessional rates and creche facilities), at the Colombo St Community Centre. Multisports for women Fri 3 - 5 pm at the Elephant and Castle Leisure Centre (free). Netball, volleyball and rounders for women at Geraldine Mary Handsworth Park, SE1 (928 8501 for details). Netball for women Mon 7.30 - 9 pm at Camberwell Sports Hall, Church St, SE5 (free).

Tower Hamlets Recreation Department, 227-233 Commercial Rd, E1 2BU (790 1818 ext 269). Check for up-to-date activities for women and girls in Tower Hamlets. Here is a sample of what's on offer: Wapping Sports Centre, Tench St, E1 (488 9421) has a women's morning every Tues with creche 10.30 am - 12 noon. Also, girls (under 16) gym club on Wed 6.00 - 8 pm. George Green Sports Centre, Manchester Rd, E14 (515 5154) has two women's mornings, Tues and Wed 10 - 12 noon, both providing creches. Also, jazz dance on Tues 10 - 12 noon has a creche. There is also a sports club for people with disabilities on alternate Saturdays from 1 - 5 pm. Langdon Park Community Centre, Byron St, E14 (987 3575), has women's keep fit to music on Wed 10.30 - 11.30 am and aerobics for women of all ages Thurs 7.30 - 8.30 pm. Spitalfields (Brady) Centre, 192 Hanbury St, E1 (247 0346) have keep fit for women on Wed 8 - 10 pm, also, aerobics for women on Tues 7 - 9 pm. Tower Hamlets Action Sports, based at the Spitalfields (Brady) Centre on 247 1286, have details of activities for the over 50s in local community venues in Poplar, Bethnal Green and Bow as well as the Brady Centre. Also, activi-

ties for the unemployed including multisports and canoeing (Shadwell Basin).

Waltham Forest Recreation Services, Sales Office, 112a High St, E17 7JY (521 7111). Open for information on all aspects of leisure in Waltham Forest (sports, entertainment, hall hire, catering, bars, and allotments) - from 10 am - 6 pm Mon, Tues and Wed, 10 am - 8 pm Thurs, 10 am - 4.00 pm Sat. (Ansaphone outside these hours). Also see *Let's Go*, recreation page, in the *Waltham Forest Guardian* on the last Fri of every month.

Wesley House*, 70 Great Queen Street, WC2 5AX (430 1076). This is a multi-purpose women's resource centre which includes a multi-gym, saunas, hydro massage pool and showers.

Sports/Leisure Centres

Brixton Recreation Centre, Brixton Station Rd, Brixton, SW9 (274 7774). Multi-purpose sport and leisure centre with women-only sessions. Access: A.

Charteris Community Sports Centre, Charteris Rd, NW6 (625 6451). Wed all-women day. Extensive activities for all women ranging from special classes for pregnant women, older women, disabled women in a variety of sporting activities. Self-defence for women. Access: A.

Jubilee Hall Recreation Centre, Central Market Sq, Covent Garden, WC2 (836 2799/4835). Access: N (Being redeveloped in 1986 with full access then).

Michael Sobell Sports Centre, Hornsey Rd, Islington, N7 7NY (607 1632). Women's recreation sessions - keep fit, badminton, squash and sauna. Free for unemployed women. Access: A.

Westcroft Leisure Centre, Westcroft Rd, Carshalton, Surrey (669 7026). Access: A.

Crystal Palace National Sports Centre, Norwood, SE19 (778 0131).

Queen Elizabeth Centre, Meadway, EN5 5JX (441 2933). Mon nights - swimming for women. Aerobics class is mostly women. Access: A.

Ashmole Sports Centre, Burleigh Gardens, Southgate, N14 (368 4984). Aerobics and keep fit for women. Has outdoor swimming pool. Access: P.

Kingfisher Leisure Pool, Fairfield Rd, Kingston-upon-Thames, Surrey (546 1042). Women's learn to swim sessions. Body conditioning sessions for women. Mothers and babies splash sessions. Access: A.

Redbridge Sports Centre, Forest Rd, Barkingside, Essex (501 0019). Women only sessions Mon and Fri 9 am - 12 noon, also, Wed 1 - 3 pm. Activities available are racket sports (tennis, table tennis, badminton and squash), keep fit, netball and volleyball. Coaching is available in all sports activities. The Redbridge Sports Centre also runs ante natal and post natal exercise classes. (Ring for details). Access: N.

Wanstead Sports Centre, Redbridge Lane West, Wanstead, E11 (989 1172. Netball for women only, every Mon 6.30 - 9.30 pm. The 'Wanstead Work Out' session on Mon eves are mainly women. Access: P.

Last Chance Centre, 87 Masbro Rd, W14 (603 7118). Women only evening on Mon 6 - 9 pm (50p), has netball, football, multigym and circuit training. Access: A.

Wood Lane Sports Centre, Dagenham, Essex (592 7706). Women only sessions for weight training, pop mobility, aerobics, keep fit, body conditioning, dance, netball and basketball. Also, women only days for using the sauna and solarium. Contact for details. Also, details of football pitch at Parsloes Park for booking from B&D Town Hall. Access: P.

Dormer Wells Lane Sports Centre, Dormers Wells Lane, Southall (574 2311). Special women only sessions in weight training, slim and trim, netball and hockey. Contact for times.

Vale Farm Sports Centre, Watford Rd, Sudbury, Middx. (Nr East Lane) (908 2528). Women's recreation sessions on Thurs 10 am - 12 noon offer squash, table tennis and badminton, with creche provision. Also, keep fit for women on Mon at 7.30 pm and Wed and Thurs at 8 pm. Mother and baby swimming sessions every Thurs at 2 pm, and every Fri at 10 am. Access A.

Lee Valley Leisure Park, PO Box 88, Enfield, Middx. (Lee Valley 71771, 971 7711 from London, and 24-hour information service on 976 1333/Lee Valley 761333). A leisure kit is available from the above address (free) which gives details of a huge range of recreational activities in and around the Greater London area.

Picketts Lock Centre, Picketts Lock Lane, Edmonton, N9 (803 4756). Open Mon-Fri 10 am - 10.30 pm. Sat 9 am - 11 pm. Sun 9 am - 10 pm. Golf, bowls, squash, swimming, roller skating and much more. All activities mixed except for women's sauna and solarium sessions. The bonus is that a purpose built creche, with qualified supervision is available weekdays, bookable on the hour or half hour up to a maximum of three hours. Access: A.

Lea Bridge Riding Centre, Lea Bridge Rd, Leyton, E10 (556 2629). Open Tues-Fri 9 am - 8.30 pm. Sat-Sun 9 am - 5.30 pm. Can cater for people with disabilities. Access: A.

Eastway Sports Centre, Quarter Mile Lane, Leyton, E10 (519 0017: phone for opening times for different activities). Women only sessions in weight training and keep fit, martial arts, pop mobility and basketball. Access: A.

Eastway Cycle Circuit, Temple Mills Lane, Stratford, E15 (534 6085). Open 8 am - 8 pm daily. Pedal cycling activities, walking and running on road circuit. Access: A.

Lee Valley Ice Centre, Lea Bridge Rd, Leyton, E10 (533 3151). Access: A. The Lee Valley Leisure Park has a lot more to offer in the way of countryside activities - caravan parks, lidos, narrowboats on the Lee river, chalets, farms to visit.

Banbury Sailing Centre, Greaves Pumping Station, North Circular Rd, E4 (531 1129). Access: P.

King George Sailing Club, Lea Valley Rd, Chingford, E4. Access: P. Apart from sauna and solarium women only sessions the Lea Valley Leisure Park centres have as yet no other specific activities for women only. However, they are keen to develop more women only activities. (971 7711 for details).

Kelmscott Leisure Centre, Mark House Rd, E17 8RN (520 7464/5). Morning recreation sessions for women on Tues and Fri 10.30 am - 12.30 pm: keep fit, badminton and trampolining. Playgroup for under fives. Also evening sessions for women in weight training, aerobics and keep fit. Phone for times. Access: A.

Leytonstone Recreation Centre, Cathall Rd, E11 (539 8343/4). Sauna/solarium with women only sessions (contact centre direct for times). Special swimming sessions for mothers and babies. Also a swimming club for people with disabilities, aerobics and keep fit for women. Contact Recreation Services Sales Office (521 7111) for

details of swimming and keep fit sessions. Access: A.

Waltham Forest, has three swimming pools, one outdoor. All have mother and toddler sessions. Contact Recreation Services Sales Office for details on (521 7111). Waltham Forest has special concessions for single parent families and unemployed for renting allotments.

The Walnut Grove Sports Centre, Orpington Kent (667 0533). This centre has a Ladies and Housewives Recreation Club every weekday (phone for times) offering squash, badminton, table tennis, football, netball and volleyball. Creche facilities available. Also yoga and keep fit for women, and a ladies' self defence club take place at this centre. Access: A.

Plumstead Sports Centre, Plumstead High St (854 9217). A Mums' Club at this centre offers a variety of sports and activities including keep fit and netball, with a creche facility available. (Ring for times). The centre also has women's leagues in netball and hockey. Access: P.

Lachmere Leisure Centre, (871 7470). Keep fit for women. Also, mothers' and toddlers' swimming sessions. A new leisure centre which may develop more sports and leisure activities for women if there is a demand from women in the borough. Access: A (ring first).

Romford YMCA, Rush Green Rd, Romford (706 6211). Sessions for women with creche available in the following - table tennis, aerobics, badminton, basketball and basketball for disabled people. Access: A.

Harrow Leisure Centre, Christchurch Avenue, Harrow (863 5611). Ladies' recreation sessions offer badminton, squash and keep fit. Also slim and trim sessions and women only sessions in the fitness studio. The centre's swimming pool has mother and toddler sessions (phone for times). Creches sometimes arranged. The centre will provide creches so contact them in advance if you need one. Access: A.

Crook Lodge Sports Centre, Brampton Rd, Bexley Heath (304 5386). Women only sessions in keep fit, archery, basketball and weight training. Creche facility available. Contact the centre for details of creche and times of sessions. Sessions on Sundays for people with disabilities in all activities. Access: A.

Tolworth Recreation Centre, Fullers Way North, Surbiton, Surrey (391 1882). Women only sessions in keep fit, aerobics, basketball, self-defence. Body conditioning and weight training days for women. Women only training sessions in squash. An hour every day with an instructor for women's fitness and weight training. Contact for times of all these sessions. Access: A.

Britannia Leisure Centre, 40 Hyde Road, Shoreditch, N1 5JU (729 4485). Women only sessions Mon 10-12, Fri 11-12 with creche provided. Various evening sessions in keep-fit, aerobics, pop mobility, sauna. Access: A.

Cranford Sports Hall, (897 6609). This community school/sports centre has women only sessions in keep fit, weight training, dance, self-defence and indoor hockey. Access: P.

Heathland School Sports Centre, Wellington Rd, South Hounslow (572 6775). Games (netball, hockey or whatever is demanded and possible), exercise and pop mobility sessions for women only. Also volleyball for women and shape-up-to-music. Access: P

Hounslow Manor Sports Centre, Cecil Rd, Hounslow (572 7582). Women only sessions in netball and oxygen dance (pop mobility and aerobics combined). Access: P.

Ealing Northern Sports Centre, Greenford Rd (422 4428). Recreation sessions for women offering badminton, squash, table tennis and trampolining. Also, keep fit for women, weight training sessions for women in the body conditioning room, and women only days in the sauna. Access: P.

Waltham Forest YMCA, Forest Rd, Walthamstow, E17 (520 4019). Women only sessions in weight training and aerobastics (a form of aerobics). The 'Y' has facilities for a wide range of sports - worth contacting to start women only sessions in any of these. Access: P.

Wimbledon YMCA Sports Centre, 200 The Broadway, SW19 1RY (540 7255). Every morning Tues-Fri 10 am - 12 noon. Women only sessions in keep fit, yoga and body conditioning. Creche for morning activities. Ring to book a place. Mon evening - keep fit for women 2 classes, 8 - 9 pm and 9 - 10 pm. Fitness studio - Ladies' Night Wednesday. Other mixed activities table tennis, badminton, volleyball, basketball, circuit training, drama, chess, bridge.

Training

Training, particularly training linked to other positive action initiatives, has a crucial role to play in breaking down job segregation and improving women's employment opportunities. For many women in London, training (or retraining) is the only route out of low paid, low graded women's work. For increasing numbers of women, it has become the only way of getting into work of any kind. Training for women has never been taken as seriously as training for men, because of all sorts of notions like ' a woman's place is in the home', 'women only work for pin money', 'they're always leaving to have children' or 'women can't do men's work'. While some improvements have been made, women still find it a constant struggle to gain access to training opportunities, especially in areas that are still regarded as men's. Although there seem to be a large number of bodies providing training, both public (eg colleges), and private (eg organisations like 'Sight and Sound'), there is no real training strategy which is aimed at women. Men still get much more than their fair share of opportunities, and women still in the main receive training which reinforces rather than changes the traditional sexual division of labour.

Despite the Sex Discrimination Act, the education that boys receive in school is still geared more towards scientific and technical jobs than girls' education. Careers advice in some schools is still very poor, with careers teachers having very traditional ideas about the sort of work women should do. As a result, the majority of craft apprenticeships go to boys.

Once at work, young women are much less likely than young men to receive training, even in predominantly female industries. A recent study sponsored by the EOC shows that in 1981 women made up only 18% of all young people between 16 and 18 released by their employers for day-release study.

Adult women receive even less training than young women. Training in industry is still largely confined to young people, which makes it difficult for older women to overcome the effects of past discrimination. Many women are in unskilled or semi-skilled jobs or areas of work which are considered to be 'dead-end' and where little or no formal training is given. In many organisations training for women is confined to 'induction' on entry or to 'sitting by Nellie' for a few weeks after joining. Women are also less likely to be given training which will enable them to move into higher graded or paid jobs. Without systematic appraisal systems and career development schemes, women tend not to be put forward for training and many women lack the confidence to put themselves forward.

New areas of work, like micro-electronics, have not given women access to new and higher valued jobs. Women's involvement in micro-technology has been mostly at the word-processing end, with all the health hazards and isolation that come with it. Some firms and local authorities now have 'positive action' policies, where they encourage women to take training in areas which up to now have not been open to them. But these employers are very few and far between and trade unions are constantly trying to get them to put into action their equal opportunities policies.

Childcare facilities or even allowances are still not available in most education and training establishments - and many courses in traditionally male areas are full-time. The Manpower Services Commission (MSC), the body responsible for implementing government training policy, does not provide childcare facilities or allowances on its schemes.

Many women have been out of work for several years after bringing up a family and are now desperate to return. This can be a daunting experience for women who feel they do not have the right qualifications or confidence to go for a training course or apply for jobs. Many colleges and institutes are now offering courses, often with names like Fresh Horizons, Second Chance or Wider Opportunities for Women, that are designed to give women the confidence to re-enter the job market. (See **Education and Further Education** for full details). Some of these schemes are funded by the government and, like all other areas of government spending, are likely to be cut.

Black and ethnic minority women encounter additional barriers. The process which pushes Black women to the bottom of the labour market starts at school with an unsuitable and often discriminatory education system and inadequate and often racist careers advice. Training to achieve promotion and greater opportunities within large organisations is also comparatively rare and Black women are frequently excluded because of racist and sexist practices, despite stated equal opportunities policies. Little attention has been paid to the specific training needs and demands of Black and ethnic minority women.

Women with disabilities face particular problems. Even where they do not encounter negative attitudes they find few training projects and courses which are equipped and accessible (in the widest sense) to people with disabilities.

Women already in employment need positive training opportunities to enable them to break out of dead-end 'women's work'. Positive training initiatives are also needed to overcome the effects of past discrimination. This is particularly important for older women who in the past did not have the same opportunities as men to obtain skills or other qualifications. Women also need opportunities to enable them to move out of jobs and industries which are particularly vulnerable because of technical change or the effects of restructuring. For example, women are over-represented in certain parts of the engineering industry, in banking and insurance and in low paid production work and office work, all of which are threatened by changes in technology and in industries like clothing which are declining. For women not in employment, either because of domestic responsibilities or because they are unemployed, training or re-training is needed mainly to get back into work of any kind, and certainly into better paid, lasting areas of work. In addition, women often need special preliminary or refresher training to give them the confidence, support and basic skills they need to be able to either enter more traditional male areas of training or to undertake training for higher levels of work in general.

The GLC has taken initiatives on women's training opportunities in two major areas: as an employer and through the activities of the Greater London Training Board (GLTB). The Council developed 'access' schemes to allow women and ethnic minority employees to reach the standards needed for entry to apprenticeships or clerical and administrative training schemes and provided additional courses or sponsorships for women and ethnic minority employees over 19. It also provided basic skills courses for women cleaners; adult traineeships in painting and decorating, particularly aimed at women over 19; and 'second chance' schemes which enabled people without the necessary qualifications or work experience to work and study for up to a year on a full-time salary.

The GLTB created new opportunities for women by investing in women's training in London. All GLTB projects aimed to recruit women teachers and trainees and to provide childcare and flexible hours. The Training Board has deliberately tried to meet the needs of older women who have been denied opportunities in the past. It has funded centres run by and for women to increase training opportunities especially in non-traditional areas. With the abolition of the GLC, those projects currently funded by the Training Board have no guarantee of being funded by any other source. This, together with cuts in government training schemes, has very serious implications for the advancement of women in London.

This section will look at courses and schemes that are open to women in London. Priority will be given to courses that require no or very few qualifications and to courses which are either very cheap to do or have some kind of allowance attached to them. The emphasis is on giving information about non-traditional areas - such as engineering, craft skills, etc - as this is often difficult to come by through the usual channels, but training in 'traditional' areas like secretarial skills is considered and addresses given.

The listings are by no means comprehensive. However, a list of useful general agencies and training directories is also included at the end of the section. (Also see **Education and Further Education, Employment and Unemployment.**)

This section is ordered as follows: *Discrimination, Women-only Training Centres/Facilities, Centres Offering Women-only Courses, Manpower Services Commission (MSC), TOPS Courses, Skillcentres, Wider Opportunities for Women (WOW), Project Full-Employ, Youth Training Scheme (YTS), Apprenticeships, Local Authority Provision, Training Opportunities in Nationalised Industries, Opportunities in Private Industry, Further Education Colleges Offering Vocational Training, Educational Advice and Counselling Services for Adults, Useful Sources of Information.*

Discrimination

The Race Relations Act and the Sex Discrimination Act make it illegal for training bodies to discriminate on the grounds of either race or sex when affording access to vocational training facilities to any person who wishes to undergo this training in order to increase their chances of employment. These training bodies include: Industrial Training Boards, the MSC, the Employment Service Agency, the Training Services Agency and Employers' training associations. However, Sections 47 and 48 of the Sex Discrimination Act allow training bodies and employers to discriminate positively in favour of one sex for training for particular areas of work where no-one or very few people of that sex have been doing that work

during the last 12 months.

If you think that you are being turned down for training either because you are Black, or a woman (or both), get advice from:

Commission for Racial Equality, Elliott House, 10-12 Allington Street, SW1 (828 7022)

National Council for Civil Liberties,* 21 Tabard Street, SE1 (403 3888: ask for the Women's Officer)

The Equal Opportunities Commission, Overseas House, Quay Street, Manchester M3 3HN (061 833 9244: ask for the Legal Officer)

Rights of Women,* 52-54 Featherstone Street, EC1 (251 6577)

Women-only Training Centres/Facilities

These centres have been created in response to a demand from women for training in what were once traditionally 'men only' skills. Training generally is provided by women tutors in workshops which recognise the need for developing women's confidence, and provide support and childcare, either in the form of creche facilities or by payment of the childminding costs of the women trainees. All of them are open to adult women and priority is given in most groups to the doubly discriminated against, such as Black women, working class women, single parents and disabled women. Some provide part-time courses; many offer 'taster' schemes which allow women to try out new areas of work before opting for a full course.

Haringey Women's Training and Education Centre. This training centre offers full and part-time courses for women, with priority to Haringey residents. Courses are aimed at working class women over 25, with priority to Black women, women from other ethnic minority groups, single parents, and lesbians. Places are reserved for disabled women. No formal entry requirements. Help is given with literacy and numeracy. Training advice is provided.

Courses: Computing, electronics, both one year full-time, training up to City and Guilds level; taster courses (run twice yearly); carpentry, electrics and plumbing, all 12 weeks part-time and could lead to TOPS courses. Science and technician skills - 12 weeks part-time. (Part-time day and evening adult education classes are also run). Course fees: None; training allowances paid for full-time trainees, expenses paid for part-time trainees, travel and child-minding allowances paid; on-site creche, for women attending AEI courses or using the Centre's drop-in facilities. Access: A. Contact: HWT EC, Former Somerset Lower School, Lordship Lane, N17 (801 6233).

Lambeth Women's Workshop. This centre is open to all women living in the Greater London area. The course is aimed at women over 25 years, with priority to Black and white working class women, single parents, women who have applied for TOPS courses and want to learn basic skills before starting. No formal qualifications required. A high standard of achievement by the end of the course. Could lead to City and Guilds and TOPS courses or adult apprenticeships.

Course: Carpentry and joinery - 16 weeks, part-time; training and child-minding allowances paid; travel costs might be met; hours flexible to suit women with school age children. Access: P - lift and wide doors but no toilet facilities. Contact: Lambeth Women's Workshop, Unit C22, Park Hall Trading Estate, Martell Road, West Norwood, SE21 8EA (670 0339).

Lewisham Women's Training Centre. This is a new training centre for Lewisham residents only. It is aimed at women over 25. No formal qualifications are required, and priority will be given to women with no further education, single parents and Black women. Training will be up to City and Guilds level. Protective clothing will be provided.

Courses: Basic electrical installation and Basic plumbing, both one year full-time. Course fees: None; training and childminding allowances paid; fares may also be paid; on-site nursery. Access: A (planned). Contact: Pat Quirke, Lewisham Women's Training Centre, 78A Blackheath Hill, SE10 (691 3550).

Newham Women's Employment Project. This project provides taster courses for unemployed women living in Newham. The training is aimed at women over 25 with no further education, ethnic minority groups and single parents. There are no formal entry requirements; courses are run three times per year, three days per week. 19 places on each course.

Courses: Taster courses in manual trades and in computing. Course fees: None, no training allowance but travel cards provided for the trainees; on-site nursery; courses held between 10.00 am and 3.00 pm and co-ordinated with school terms. Access: N (at present - hope to develop). Contact: Heather or Janis, Newham Women's Employment Project, 339 Barking Road, E13 (474 7189).

Southwark Women's Training Workshop. Run by Southwark Council, and is open only to Southwark residents. Training is aimed at women over 25. No formal qualifications necessary, although some previous woodworking experience an advantage. Help is given with literacy and numeracy. Course aims to provide training up to first year City and Guilds level, and trainees are encouraged to go on to further training.

Course: Carpentry and joinery for the construction industry - six months full-time; one day each week is spent on site. Course fees: None; training allowance; childminding allowances given. Access: P - hope to provide full access soon. Instruction for the deaf. Contact Southwark Women's Training Workshop, 164 Union Street (2nd Floor), SE1 0LH (261 0575/6).

South West London Women's Electrics and Electronics Workshop. This new training centre is open to women resident in Wandsworth and Lambeth. It is aimed at women aged 19-25 (50% of intake) and women aged 25 and over (50% of intake). No formal qualifications required. Women will be trained up to City and Guilds level. The Centre runs initial taster courses so that women can decide which skill they wish to take up. Priority will be given to women who have had least access to education. Protective clothing, tools and all other equipment will be supplied.

Courses: Digital electronics - one year part-time; electrical installation - one year full-time. Course fees: None; training and childminding allowances; travel expenses may be met; on-site nursery and after school and holiday childminding allowances for school-age children; full disabled access is planned. Contact: Sian or Barbara, South West London Women's Electric and Electronics Workshop, 460 Wandsworth Road, SW8 (622 9208).

Wesley House,* 70 Great Queen Street, WC2 5AX (430 1076). This is a multi-purpose women's resource centre, continually running workshops and classes on a wide variety of subjects. Access: A.

Women's Education in Building. The Centre is open to all women living in the Greater London area and provides training in various aspects of the building industry. Protective clothing and tools are provided. Courses start in September and March, and all are aimed at women aged 25 and over. No formal qualifications required. The trainees are encouraged to take the relevant City and Guilds courses, and to apply for TOPS courses, apprenticeships and improverships. Priority is given to women who have not previously had educational opportunities, single parents, Black and ethnic minority women, lesbians and disabled women.

Courses: Bricklaying - six months part-time. Provides a basic knowledge of the trade by the end of the course; carpentry and joinery - one year part-time, trainees should have basic knowledge and experience of the trade, trainees should attain a fairly high degree of competence by the end of the course; electrics - one year part-time, trainees will have gained a basic knowledge of domestic installations by the end of the course; plastering - one year part-time, aims to give trainees a basic knowledge of the trade by the end of the course; plumbing - six months full-time, trainees should have a basic grasp of the trade by the end of the course.

Course fees: None; Training and childminding allowances and travel expenses are paid; on-site nursery. Access: P. Contact: Women's Education in Building, 12 Malton Road, W10 (968 9139).

Women's Motor Mechanics Project. Open to all women living in the Greater London area. The Project is aimed at women over 18, with priority given to ex-prisoners, single parents, Black women, working class women. No formal qualifications necessary. Course leads to a recognised qualification at the end.

Course: Basic motor mechanics course - six months part-time. Course fee: None, training allowance paid, which includes travel, tools and protective clothing; childminding allowance given. Access: P (ramps). Contact: Cindy Smart, Jane Freeston, Women's Motor Mechanics Project, Bay 4R, 1-3 Brixton Road, SW9 6DE (582 2574).

ICOM Women's Link Up. The Centre works with London boroughs participating in the Link-Up scheme to set up short training courses (100 hours each) within these boroughs. Courses are on three levels, for women who are thinking either of re-entering the job market or of starting a co-op. Priority is given to Black and ethnic minority women. Access: P.

Module A Course: Helps women gain confidence to seek work, explore further education and training opportunities, or to think about starting a co-op.

Module B Course: Helps women identify ideas and assess the feasibility of starting up their own co-ops.

Module C Course: Provides further training and support for women, once the co-op has started up, or who are still investigating starting up.

For more information, contact: ICOM Women's Link-Up, 393-395 City Road, EC1 (837 7020).

Centres Offering Women-only Courses

Camden Training Centre. This centre offers some women-only courses as well as mixed training courses. Preference is given to Camden residents, and the courses are aimed at people aged over 19 years, who are unemployed. The Centre aims to have intakes of 50% men and women and 40% ethnic minorities. No formal qualifications required. All courses are at a basic level, but are geared to fit into further training courses, for example at further education colleges. Some courses are to City and Guilds Stage I.

Women-only Courses: Co-op Training - ten weeks part-time; introduction to business skills - 10-12 weeks part-time; Return to Work - six weeks, four days per week; setting up a business - ten weeks full-time. Contact: Elizabeth Dobbie - Women's Worker, Camden Training Centre, 57 Pratt Street, NW1 (482 2103).

Mixed Courses: Building maintenance - 22 weeks full-time; carpentry and joinery - 30 weeks full-time, trainees expected to have relevant experience; catering - full-time, two courses are run - one of 26 weeks, one of nine weeks; micro-electronics - 14 weeks full-time, trainees have to undergo an aptitude test; Printing - 24 weeks full-time, trainees expected to be fit and healthy. Course fees: None; TOPS allowance for full-time trainees;

on-site nursery. Access A (though not ideal). Contact: Local Job Centre or Camden Training Centre, 57 Pratt Street, NW1 (482 2103).

Charlton Training Centre. This independent training centre is open to all living in the Greater London area and offers mixed training courses, as well as women-only courses. The Women's Unit has various courses aimed at women over 16 with priority to ethnic minority groups and people with disabilities. No formal qualifications necessary. Help and advice will be given on employment and apprenticeship prospects. Literacy, numeracy and ESL classes are also provided.

Women-only Courses: Domestic House Maintenance; Taster Course - 13 weeks, where women try out such skills as carpentry and joinery, co-operative and business development and plumbing. Course fees: None; training allowance may be paid; creche facilities and childminding allowances. Access: A. Contact: Marcia, Charlton Training Centre Women's Unit, Westminster Industrial Estate, Ferranti Close, Off Westfield Street, SE18 (317 9636).

Mixed Courses: Most are full-time (6-9 months) and will lead to a qualification. They are aimed at people over 16 with priority to ethnic minority groups, women, people with disabilities, and those with no formal qualifications. Literacy, numeracy and ESL classes also provided; catering; co-operative/business development; industrial electronics; office skills - using high technology; record press/entertainment services; sheet metal working; vehicle body repair and spray; vehicle repair and maintenance. Course fees: none; travel and childminding allowances, creche facilities. Access: A. Contact: Isha, Sue, Jayesh, Charlton Training Centre, Westminster Industrial Estate, Ferranti Close, Off Westfield Street, SE18 (317 9636).

Deptford Skillcentre - Women's Unit. This skillcentre offers a full-time women-only ten week taster course aimed at women aged 19 years and over. No formal entry qualifications are required. Women can try at least four of the skills offered. Some trainees go on to TOPS courses (see TOPS later in this section). 97% of women taking the course complete it successfully.

Course: Introduction to manual skills: includes bricklaying, carpentry, electrics, electronics, engineering, motor vehicle repair, painting and decorating, plumbing, welding. Course fees: None; training allowance and lunch allowance paid; On-site nursery and childminding allowances paid to women from Lewisham, Greenwich and Southwark; no disabled access. Contact: Local Job Centre or Annie Green, Deptford Skillcentre - Women's Unit, 2 Deptford Church Street, SE8 (691 5012).

London New Technology Network. This is a mixed training centre, which offers a women-only course in microcomputer technology. This course is six months full-time and is aimed at women over 25 living in Greater London. Applicants must have a background in electronics, as the course will be up to City and Guilds Stages 2 and 3.

Course: Micro-computer technology - City and Guilds 756, Parts 2 and 3. Course fees: None; either a training allowance or expenses will be paid; creche on site. Access: P. Contact: Women's Project Worker, London New Technology Network, 86-100 St Pancras Way, NW1 9ES (482 3816).

Tower Hamlets Advanced Technology. This centre offers a mixed training course in computing and microelectronics, aimed at people over 25 who are unemployed and live in Tower Hamlets. Women, people from ethnic minority communities and disabled people are encouraged to apply. No formal entry requirements. Training is up to RSA level and a certificate of completion is given at the end of the course. Courses start in September.

Course: Introduction to New Technology. Course fees: None; training and childminding allowances and travel expenses paid; creche on site. Access: A, (not ideal at present but will be improved). Contact: Co-ordinator, Charlie Buxton, Tower Hamlets Advanced Technology, Unit 3.2, Whitechapel Technology Centre, 75 Whitechapel Road, E1 (247 4682).

Manpower Services Commission

Increasingly, training provision in Britain is provided by the Manpower Services Commission (MSC). The MSC provides the bulk of its training opportunities for adults through its Training Opportunities Scheme (TOPS) and for young people through the Youth Training Scheme (YTS). The proportion of women on these courses is much higher than in the early 70s but their training still tends to be for traditional female areas of work. The MSC has, however, set up a small programme of positive action to meet the special training needs of women and girls. The wider opportunities for women courses (WOW, higher WOW for women returning to supervisory and managerial work and WOW for women wanting to work in fields related to new technology) provide training specifically for women returning to work after a period of domestic responsibility. The MSC is also carrying out experimental management and introductory Skillcentre courses for women only.

While all these schemes are to be welcomed, they affect overall only a very small number of women. Most of the MSC training women receive reinforces rather than alters the traditional division of labour. For example, most women on TOPS courses are taking clerical, secretarial or commercial courses. Furthermore, training opportunities in these traditional female areas are being cut while training in non-traditional areas is not being increased. Women are less likely than men to obtain integrated work and training experience under YTS. Under Mode A of YTS employers recruit their own trainees which has meant that a lower proportion of women, particularly ethnic minority women, have been taken on to these courses.

The MSC's policy on adult training is largely aimed at those in employment or about to start a new job. This suggests that the MSC is unlikely to initiate further positive adult training measures on any significant scale either for unemployed women, women returning to work or women trapped in lower-graded jobs.

The MSC does not provide childcare allowances or facilities, even for courses such as WOW which are aimed at women with domestic responsibilities. This lack of provision means that those women who might particularly benefit from such schemes may not be able to attend. Also, courses such as WOW and most other MSC courses are not offered on a part-time basis.

While the MSC has a stated commitment to equal training opportunities for women, it has not so far taken positive and practical steps to ensure that women are aware of and encouraged to go on to courses in non-traditional areas and that more women are taken on to employer-based schemes such as Mode A of YTS. More positive outreach programmes are needed as well as systematic and regular monitoring of schemes to ensure women receive equal treatment.

Examples of schemes are given below but further information can be obtained from these addresses and from Job Centres (listed under Manpower Services Commission in the phone book):-

MSC Regional Information Section: Selkirk House, 166 High Holborn, WC1V 6PF (278 6363).

North London: 6th Floor, 19-29 Woburn Place, WC1 0LU (837 1288).

North East London: 3rd Floor, Cityside House, 40 Adler Street, E1 1EW (377 1866).

South East London: Skyline House, 200 Union Street, SE1 0LX (928 0800).

South and West London: Lyric House, 149 Hammersmith Road, W14 (602 7227).

Office Training Centre: 17 Lansdowne Road, Croydon CR9 2DA (680 1411)

TOPS Courses

These are different types of vocational training offered at SkillCentres, business schools and colleges of further education. They are open to people over 19 years who are unemployed and have been out of full-time education for at least two years, and who have not done a TOPS course in the last three years.

The courses are full-time and can last up to one year. A weekly training allowance is paid, with possible additions for travel and meals. In general, no childcare facilities are offered. Although you are not required to have 'O' or 'A' levels, there is a maths and English test to be taken before you can start a course. The mark required to get on certain courses, eg secretarial, is very high, and the tests are not easy. For certain courses you are asked to take an extra test, eg in maths for those who wish to do accounting courses. If you find the test too difficult, it may be possible to go on to a Pre-TOPS course, but again cuts in MSC spending means that these are gradually disappearing.

The majority of courses are run along traditional lines, ie some courses are seen as 'suitable' for women (typing, shorthand, catering, general clerical) and others for men (carpentry, plumbing, plastering). If a woman wishes to be trained in a traditionally male skill, she will need to be persistent and convince the Job Centre that she is serious in her intention, otherwise she could be fobbed off with a traditional women's skill. As courses often change, and new courses set up, women should contact the MSC Regional Information Section (address above) for the most up to date information.

To apply for a TOPS course, go to your Job Centre or Unemployment Office (see phone book under Employment, Department of) but be prepared. Cuts in spending mean that you will probably be interviewed by an untrained person who has only ten minutes to spare - not really enough to help you decide on your future. If you would like to talk to someone in more detail, it may be better to go first to one of the advice centres for adults (see listing) or one of the groups listed under Useful Information. In particular, if you would like to train for a traditionally male area of work, contact Women and Manual Trades (see Useful Information below) for advice on how to go about it.

Skillcentres.

These centres generally offer TOPS courses in manual skills, such as carpentry, bricklaying, plumbing, etc. and so tend to be male dominated. As well as having to convince the Job Centre staff that you are serious about wanting to learn a manual skill, you will also have to be prepared to deal with the isolation you might experience in male dominated workshops and any prejudice from male trainees or staff. Also, in general, most courses start early in the morning, which proves a barrier for a woman with school age children, and there are no childcare facilities at the workshops for children under five. At present, only three out of 100 trainees are women.

The Women's Assessment Unit at Deptford Skillcentre (see above) is attempting to meet the needs of women by offering women-only taster courses in manual skills and childcare facilities. However, women must be prepared to wait as the unit is open to women from all over London, and there is a long waiting list. Camden Training Centre also has an on-site nursery. To apply for a Skillcentre course, apply to your local Job Centre or Unemployment Office.

Some Skillcentres are considering

introducing access courses and new technology courses which would particularly benefit women. Be sure to ask about these.

Skillcentres have regular 'Open Days'. Anyone interested in a course can go along, have a look around and talk to the instructors. Contact local Skillcentres to find out the date of the open day.

Barking: 25 Thames Road, Barking IG11 0HR (591 2662).

Deptford: 2 Deptford Church Street, SE8 4SJ (691 5721).

Enfield: Bilton Way, Enfield, Middlesex EN3 7NZ (805 1365).

Lambeth: Units 13-14, 11 Lyham Road, SW2 (274 4106).

Perivale: Walmgate Road, Perivale, Greenford, Middlesex UB6 7NE (998 1451).

Twickenham: Industrial Estate, Rugby Road, Twickenham TW1 1DT (892 6285).

Annexe: Avondale Gardens, Hounslow TW4 5HX (572 2256).

The MSC is planning to close some of its Skillcentres, thus further restricting training opportunities for women and men. The Women into Skillcentres campaign c/o Women and Manual Trades (see Useful Sources of Information) and trade unions are campaigning to prevent these closures.

Wider Opportunities for Women (WOW)

These courses are aimed at women who are planning to return to work after being out of the workforce. They are available for women over 19 who have never worked, or who have been out of work for at least 2 years because of domestic responsibilities and who are not sure what kind of work they would like to do. The courses are six weeks full-time, with a TOPS allowance payable, and give women the opportunity to try out various skills to see which ones they have an aptitude for. The women also get practice in applying for jobs and help with litera-

cy and numeracy and confidence building.

These courses are generally available at further education colleges, but there have been cuts in this area. For more information, contact either your local Job Centre or MSC Area Office (above).

Project Fullemploy

This is an MSC mixed scheme aimed primarily at the Black and ethnic minority communities, women and single parents. The training is generally in office skills, and is for people aged 19 and over. Most courses include training in social skills. No formal qualifications are required. No childcare facilities or allowances are available. Only Greenwich and Clerkenwell have disabled access. There are various locally based training centres.

For Greenwich residents: TOPS course in office skills - Trainees will get work experience with various firms. Priority given to Black and ethnic minority. Course fees: None; TOPS allowance paid if the course full-time. Access: P, but no toilet facilities. Contact: Local Job Centre or Joyce Shepherd, Project Fullemploy Greenwich, 5th Floor, Riverside House, Woolwich High Street, Woolwich, SE18 6EN (855 7969).

For residents of Hackney and adjacent boroughs: Electronics office course - 20 weeks full-time, including four weeks work experience. Trainees get a certificate of completion at the end of the course. Course fees: None; training allowance, travel expenses may be met. Access: P. Contact: Local Job Centre or Louise Hunger, Project Manager, Project Fullemploy Hackney, 47 Great Eastern Street, EC2 (729 5255).

Project Fullemploy Hackney also offers a full-time Business Studies BVA Course for people aged 19 and over with no formal qualifications. For further details, contact Project Fullemploy Hackney.

For residents of Islington and adjacent boroughs: Tops Clerical Course - 20 weeks full-time with three weeks work experience, trainees get a certificate of completion at the end of the course, and can also take Pitmans typing exams. Priority to Black and ethnic minority women. Course fees: None; TOPS allowance; travel expenses may be paid. Access: N. Contact: Local Job Centre or Project Fullemploy Islington, 7-15 Rosebery Avenue, EC1 (833-1501).

For residents of Kensington and adjacent boroughs: Combined Clerical and Retail Course - 18 weeks full-time. Course fees: None; training allowance; travel expenses may be met. Access: N. Contact: Project Fullemploy Kensington, 383 Ladbroke Grove, W10 5AA (960-8484).

For Lambeth residents: Office Skills Course - 21 weeks full-time, including three weeks work experience, help is also given with literacy and numeracy, trainees get a certificate of completion at the end of the course. They can also take the RSA Stage I typing certificate. A three-day GPO telephonist course is also offered, with a certificate of completion. Priority given to Black and ethnic minorities. Course fees: None;

training allowance, travel expenses may be met; Contact: Local Job Centre or, Carlene or Steve, Project Fullemploy, 444 Brixton Road, SW9 8EJ (733 3338).

For Lewisham residents: TOPS clerical course - Help is given with literacy and numeracy, 20 weeks full-time, including six weeks work experience, trainees get a certificate of completion, and are encouraged to take exams in Pitmans Typing - Stages I, II, and III, and Pitmans English for Office Use. Access: N. Course fees: None; training allowance, travel costs may be paid; Contact: Local Job Centre or, Project Manager, Project Fullemploy Lewisham, 23 Mercia Grove, SE13 (852-3423).

For Clerkenwell residents: Self-employment Project - This is a course for people aged 18 and over who wish to become self-employed. Training is offered in sales, marketing, finance, the law and book-keeping, three months full-time. Course fees: None; training allowance, travel costs may be paid. Access: A. Contact: Local Job Centre or Jane Straw, Project Fullemploy Clerkenwell, Unit 120 Clerkenwell Workshops, 31 Clerkenwell Close, EC1 (251-4083 / 6037).

Project Fullemploy - Adult Advisory Unit: This adult advisory scheme in Kensington offers a short confidence and direction course to help those people who are unemployed, working part-time or wishing to change their job. Employment and training advice is exactingly given. Contact: Derek Brown (969-1397).

Youth Training Scheme (YTS)

The MSC provides school leavers with one year full-time training, with 13 weeks spent at college and rest of the year on work experience or training. A weekly allowance is paid. A two-year scheme is to be introduced in April 1986.

YTS can either be based with employers in private industry or the public sector (eg local authorities), in further education colleges or in training workshops. Although training in general is still based on traditional divisions, a few schemes offering training in non-traditional skills positively encourage applications from young women. The standards of schemes vary so young women wishing further advice or information should either contact the London Women in Youth Training Research and Support Project or Women and Manual Trades (see below). Because of the variety of schemes being offered, it is impossible to provide comprehensive information here, but a few examples of what is on offer are given. Local Careers Offices and Job Centres will have information on YTS.

YTS Schemes aimed at Black and Ethnic Minority Communities

Aimed at Greenwich residents. Combined retail and office training - six months work experience, includes computing, word processing, English, Maths, life and social skills, young people should be able to apply for employment as either junior office workers or sales assistants at the end of the course. Access: P, no toilet facilities Contact: Project Fullemploy Greenwich, 5th Floor, Riverside House, Beresford Street, SE18 (855 7969)

Aimed primarily at Hackney residents. Silk screen printing, photography and graphic design - four weeks work experience, includes English, Maths. Young people get a certificate of completion at the end of their training. Contact: Project Fullemploy Hackney, 47 Great Eastern Street, EC2 (729 5255).

Example of College Based YTS

London College of Furniture. Course: Furniture Crafts - Practical work in the use of materials relating to various processes in furniture production, leading to City and Guilds Part I during the years training. Musical Instrument Technology - Course designed to provide a firm foundation in

the trade. Trainees can either do a general course in Musical Instruments or a course in stringed Keyboard Instruments which can lead to City and Guilds Part 1. Upholstery and soft furnishings - practical work in the use of materials relating to various processes in upholstery and furnishing production. Trainees can take a City and Guilds basic skills certificate during the years training. The College is seeking young women for this course in NW1, Archway and Islington areas. Sponsor companies will be available. Contact: YTS, c/o Senior Administration Officer, London College of Furniture, 41 Commercial Road, E1 1LA (247 1953).

Nottingdale Information Technology Centre, 191 Freston Road, W10. (969 7527). Course: Electronics and Computing - includes office skills, building equipment and practical skills, fault-finding, programming. More young women are needed on the course. Further information on ITECs available from the MSC and Job Centres.

Examples of YTS Training Workshops

Course: Cabinet making, carpentry, carpentry and joinery, mechanics - three days are spent in the workshops and two days on education. Training is up to City and Guilds level. The workshops would be happy to have more young women apply for training. Contact: North London Training Workshop, 96a Bartholomew Road, NW5 (485 5170).

Courses: Carpentry, office skills, painting and decorating, textile design - work experience placements in community settings. The workshop is keen to have young women on the manual skills, and 50% of the places on the scheme are kept open for them. Contact: Springboard Islington, 338 Upper Street, N1 (226 0508).

Information Technology Centres. Information Technology Centres (ITECs) have been set up to provide training in micro-electronics, computer skills and office-type business skills. Examples include:

Central London Youth Project, 99-103 Long Acre, WC2E 9NR (240 8377). This project provides a broader skills programme than most ITECs. It includes electronics as well as operation and provides links to employers and services community groups. Some women tutors and women positively encouraged to apply.

Haringey Information Technology Centre, Course: Electronics, Computing and Business Administration - trainees can go on to further education or training at the end of the course Contact: Braemar Road, N15 (800 5689).

Lewisham Information Technology Centre, Course: Micro-computer Applications - includes word processing, typing, computing, basic electronics, some maintenance and training. Young women are positively encouraged to apply. Contact: Drake House, 18 Creekside, Deptford, SE8 3DZ (692 7141).

Apprenticeships

Apprenticeships have always been the route into skilled and better paid jobs - but usually only for young, white males. Less than one in twenty of London's apprentices are girls, and most of these are in hairdressing. Many local authorities and nationalised industries offer apprenticeships or schemes of their own. Some companies have an equal opportunities policy - for example, some of the Industrial Training Boards eg The Engineering Industry Training Board, have schemes to encourage girls to apply - but it is still a struggle for girls who want to take an apprenticeship in a traditionally male job.

Thames TV's 'Help' Programme have published a booklet of useful information on apprenticeships for young women. Woman and Manual Trades should also be able to provide more comprehensive information for any woman interested in appren-

ticeship schemes. See Useful Information below for publications.

Local Authority Provision

London's local authorities are major employers of women. Though they employ large numbers of women and some of them are equal opportunities employers, women are still mainly concentrated in the lowest paid jobs, and in a narrow range of jobs where their skills are undervalued and poorly paid.

Most local authorities provide training and educational programmes for their staff, but there are considerable differences in provision between authorities. Overall, those who benefit most are mainly white men.

Here is a brief outline of the range of training opportunities offered, and some examples of innovative schemes which have been introduced in recent years. These illustrate the types of schemes and facilities which women throughout London should be pressing for in their workplaces.

Most authorities provide a variety of short training courses for employers. These include induction and short courses on specific areas like health and safety, first aid, interviewing techniques, and report writing, and service related courses, for example, short courses related to housing, social services, childcare or clerical work.

If women want to take up the opportunities available, it is important that they find out for themselves what is available and apply for it, as the training needs of women are not seen as an important priority by many employers. Contact your training officer for information and advice.

Some local authorities have begun to recognise the extent to which women have missed out on educational and training opportunities, both at school and in employment. They are attempting to redress these imbalances by setting up special short courses for women. Authorities such as Camden, Greenwich, Hackney, Hammersmith and Fulham, Islington,

Lambeth, Lewisham and Southwark provide courses for women like assertion training, women's development courses (to encourage women to plan their lives and careers) and stress management (usually for women in management positions). These courses are usually open to all women employees in the authority organising the course; they are usually advertised widely and a positive attempt is made to encourage Black women and women from lower grades to attend. They are held in work time and do not cost anything. Some local authorities have women's units and/or women's training officers. They should know if your authority provides this type of course. Where there is no women's unit or women's training officer, it is best to approach the training officer.

Most local authorities provide qualification related training which covers a wide spectrum of courses and exam levels, ranging from 'O' and 'A' level, BEC, general, City and Guilds Crafts to post-degree professional qualifications. It is usually provided outside of the authorities' internal training programme through a combination of day and block release and full-time secondment courses.

There is not a consistent selection pattern throughout London although similar practices do operate. Most authorities require the training to be relevant to the job (opportunities are rarely provided to enable someone to move from one job type to another) and approved by the employee's head of the section as contributing towards providing a better service.

As compared with most short courses, time off is given for attendance at the courses, exam fees are paid and some authorities make a contribution towards travel, meals and books. Technically, post-entry training is open to all employees, provided they meet the above conditions, but in practice men benefit most. They tend to attend the higher level and technical courses while women mainly do lower level and the cheaper courses. Cam-den Council has attempted to break this tradition by setting up Affirmative Action Schemes which aim to improve the employment position of disadvantages workers. One of these schemes is within the Social Services Department. Six new posts were created for mature people interested in entering social work. The people recruited are taken for four years; after a range of practical experience and college-based courses during their first two years with the authority, they are seconded to a relevant social work course to complete their professional qualification. People are recruited from both existing staff and through the usual recruitment procedures. The course is specifically orientated to Black people.

Craft Apprenticeships and Adult Traineeships

Most apprenticeships in all area of work usually go to young white heterosexual males. Some local authorities now take positive steps to counter this discrimination. (See **Borough Information** for councils with equal opportunities policies).

Craft apprenticeships are one of the few examples of council-sponsored training and go to people not already working for the council. People are taken on to train for three-four years according to the skill which they are learning and are given training both on and off the job. Day or block release to do the relevant City and Guilds exams at colleges is provided. While training, young people are paid between £60-90 according to the skill they are learning. College fees are also paid.

Some Councils now specifically encourage young women to apply for apprenticeships. Some also offer traineeships to enable adults to train for the same craft skills as apprentices.

Below are examples of boroughs which are attempting to recruit women into training for traditionally male skilled areas of work.

Camden Council. Camden offers apprenticeships in the building trade in carpentry, plumbing, painting and decorating, glazing, and electrics. In the Parks Department they offer gardening. Until this year apprenticeships were only open to school leavers under 18, but this policy is currently under review. No educational qualifications are required, but young people are expected to pass a test. Young women and Black people are positively encouraged to apply. The council run a creche which is available for use by staff. Recruitment takes place from February for courses to start the following September. To find out more information, contact: Camden Careers Office or, Apprentice Training Section, Camden Town Hall (278 4444).

Greenwich Council. Greenwich offers apprenticeships in painting and decorating, electrical, plumbing, carpentry, bricklaying and gardening. Open to young people between 16-17. Good CSEs and an interest or experience in the trade they are applying for required. They have to pass an aptitude test. Recruitment takes place around Easter, advertisements are put in the local paper and information sent to the local Careers Office. There is positive policy of encouraging young women to apply; a special booklet directed at young women has been produced. From January 1986 an adult training scheme will be offered giving preference to women. For more information, contact: Mrs Irene Morley, Personnel Section, Peggy Middleton House, 50 Woolwich New Road, Woolwich SE18 (845 8888).

Hackney Council. Training is offered in the following crafts: electrical, heating and ventilating, motor vehicle fitting, painting and decorating, bricklaying, carpentry and plumbing.

Open to school leavers. No formal qualifications are required, but young people are expected to pass an aptitude test. Preference is given to Hackney residents, but people from outside Hackney are not excluded. A positive effort is made to recruit young women. Priority for Black and ethnic minorities on some courses. Informa-

tion is available through the Careers Services and the advertisements are placed in the local papers. Hackney Council hopes to recruit a woman officer with responsibility for supporting and encouraging young women apprentices. Access: P disabled. For further information contact Mr Norton, Netil House, 1-7 West Gate Street, E8 3RW (986 3123).

Hackney recognises the need to provide training in the craft trades for adults as well as for young people and provides roughly ten adult improvership places per year. This scheme is for people with some previous training like TOPS or some other recognised training. Open to Hackney and non-Hackney residents. Women are positively encouraged to apply. The scheme is seen as being of particular relevance to women and advertisements are sent to relevant women's groups in the area. The council has offered a nursery for children of the staff. People are taken on as improvers for 18 months during which time they are given access to day release courses. At the end they are recognised as fully qualified craftspeople. Recruitment takes place in the summer, and the scheme starts in November 1985. Access: A. For further information contact: Personnel, in the Building Division, (986 3210). Netil House, 1-7 West Gate Street, E8 3RW.

Islington Council. Training is provided in the building trades, carpentry, painting and decorating, plumbing and in engineering skills.

This year, for the first time, apprenticeships will be open to all age groups. No educational qualifications are required, but applicants are expected to have an interest in the trade and to pass an aptitude test. Preference is given to people from Islington, but outsiders are also taken on. Young women are positively encouraged to apply through publicity campaigns in the schools. For further information contact: Careers Service, or write to: Staffing Office, Building Works Department, Orleston Road, N7.

Lambeth Council. Training offered in: carpentry, glazing, wood-machining, welding, roofing, bricklaying, plastering, electrics, plumbing. For school leavers. No educational requirements, but applicants are expected to pass a test and write an essay. It is not restricted to Lambeth residents. Girls are positively encouraged to apply, visits are made to schools and exhibitions mounted, etc. Access: P. For further inforamtion contact: Local Careers Office or Apprentice Training Officer, 87 South Lambeth Road, Vauxhall, SW9 (274 7722).

Lambeth also offers training for adults for three-four years depending on the skill. About 25 places per year are provided in the above trades. No age barrier and no previous academic experience is required, but applicants are given the same tests as the apprentices. Knowledge of and experience of the trade are an advantage. Women are positively encouraged to apply, in fact the scheme already has a high number of women trainees. In line with the borough's equal opportunities policy, they also encourage Black people and disabled people to apply. Applications should be submitted by the end of the year, for training which starts in the following September. For further information contact: Apprentice Supervisor (274 7722).

Lewisham Council. Lewisham Employment and Training Divison offers an Apprentice Support Scheme.

It gives grants to companies who are willing to take on apprentices for three years. Currently there are 30 places in building, electronics, catering and hairdressing firms. Apprentices are paid by the firm, given access to day release in return for grant aid from the council. Open to school leavers and adults, though it is mainly for young people. It is for Lewisham residents only. A positive effort is made to recruit young women and Black people. For further information contact: Lewisham Employment and Training Division (690 4343).

Southwark Council. Apprenticeships are offered in the following trades: painting and decorating, carpentry, plumbing, heating and ventilating, electronics, motor vehicle maintenance, mastic asphalting, bricklaying and plastering. No previous educational standards are required. Applicants are expected to pass a maths test. Preference is given to Southwark residents, though people from outside the borough are also taken on. For school leavers. Young women are positively encouraged to apply through publicity directed to them. For further information contact: Local Careers Service or Craft Apprentice Trainer. (703 0977).

The borough also currently offers seven adult training places, in carpentry. Recruitment is mainly from existing council staff and from Southwark Women's Training Centre. The person is required to have worked in the trades as an unskilled person for two years, or attended a recognised training course. Applicants are not expected to have had any previous educational experience, but are given a similar test as the apprentices. Training is provided for two-three years depending on previous experience. Day release is also provided.

Women are positively encouraged to apply - six out of the current seven adult trainees are women. For further information contact: Craft Apprentice Trainer. (703 0977).

Some local authorities are attempting to implement equal opportunities policies to ensure more equal access to training and jobs, to counter the discrimination previously faced by Black people and women. But many still do not see the need. Their belief is that all jobs are equally accessible to everyone, though the evidence suggests that there are no or few women doing those jobs which have always been done by men. There is still a lack of action amongst local authorities about meeting the training needs of disabled people. Overall, very little has been done to date.

Training Opportunities in Nationalised Industries

Most nationalised industries have apprenticeships and training schemes for young people, which are open to both women and men. The training is generally between two-four years, combining practical training/experience with study at a further education college, and will lead to a qualification in City and Guilds, ONC, HNC or TEC levels. Below are examples from two industries.

British Rail. BR offers a variety of training schemes for school leavers, which are open to young women and young men alike. Examples are given, but note that these are only a fraction of the training schemes available. For more information, contact: The nearest British Rail regional or area office.

Course: Craft Apprenticeship Scheme For 16-18 year olds. No formal entry requirements, but a background in Maths and Science is useful, and applicants must show an aptitude for practical engineering. Contact: Area Personnel Manager, British Rail, London (West Coast), Willesden Junciton, NW10 4UY (387 9400) ext 6203.

Course: Civil Engineering Technician Training Scheme for school leavers under 19. Four GCE 'O' levels or four CSE Grade 1 are required - must include English, Maths and Science; Railway Engineering Technician Scheme: For 16-18 year olds. GLC 'O' levels or equivalents are required. Must include Maths, English, and Physics (or combined Science with Physics). Contact: Regional Civil Engineer, British Rail, Stephenson House, 67-87 Hampstead Road, NW1 2PP (387 9400 ext 2957).

London Electricity Board. LEB offers a variety of training schemes which are open to both women and men alike. Examples of training schemes for young people are given, but further information on other schemes can be obtained from the address given below. Most training courses start in September. Training Schemes: Craft Careers in Electrical Fitting, metering (repair, service and conditioning) and electrician. No formal entry requirements but CSEs in Maths, English, Metal or Woodwork would be an advantage. Drawing Office Careers for 16-18 year olds. No formal entry requirements, but CSEs in Maths and English and Technical Drawing would be an advantage. There is also a selection test. Electrical Engineering Careers for people aged 18 and over. Maths and Science 'A' levels are required. Selection is by interview. Contact: The Education and Training Manager, London Electricity Board, 64 Pratt Street, NW1 OEJ.

Opportunities in Private Industry

Employers in the private sector also provide apprenticeships, day release and other forms of training. With the abolition of Industrial Training Boards (ITBs) in many industries, and the recession, employers are providing fewer training opportunities for all their employees. Few organisations in any case provide positive training initiatives for women.

There have been attempts by some ITBs to introduce positive measures to improve women's training opportunities although these too have largely been confined to young women workers. The Engineering Industry Training Board, for example, has sponsored several schemes in conjunction with the EOC which seems to have had some (very limited) success in increasing the numbers of women in craft, technical and managerial jobs in engineering. The EITB has provided scholarships for girls to undertake technician education and training, undergraduate bursaries for young women studying to become professional engineers and a residential scheme called 'Insight' which allows girls to learn more about professional engineering. However many of these Training Board initiatives have now ceased or are in danger because of the transfer of funding for Training Boards from central government to industry itself and thus it seems likely that there will be even fewer such schemes in future.

Positive training measures are usually an integral part of positive action programmes. Companies such as Thames Television have, for example, run an evening course on the basics of making a television programme which has led to some secretaries moving into techical jobs. (See Resources for Women Workers in **Employment and Unemployment** for details of women's networks and groups in various industries and occupations who are working to improve employment and training opportunities within their workplaces). Also contact the Training Officer in your firm for information about training opportunities available where you work.

Further Education Colleges offering Vocational Training

(For more detailed information see **Education and Further Education**). The courses mentioned here are examples of colleges offering vocational training either for women only, or which could be of interest to women (because they are non-traditional skills). Many further education colleges now offer various courses, including TOPS courses, so contact your local further education college for more information.

Haringey College, Park Road, N11 (888 7123) **Course**: Fresh Start in Science and Technology - a course with Women in Mind: one year, 20 hours pw. Aimed at women over 19. Includes Introduction to Science, Craft Skills, Information Technology, Numeracy, Communications and Life Skills. Students are encouraged to do further courses. No formal qualifications required. Course starts in September. Course fees: contact college; Grant: None; Childcare facilities: No creche facilities at present. Timet-

able allows women with school age children to take them to and from school. Access: A, but college at present restricted to eight wheelchair bound students. Access to be improved from September 1986; Contact: Eileen Loucaides, Course Tutor.

South East London College. Course: Switch on to Science: one year part-time, starts in September. Designed primarily for women over 19. No formal qualifications required. Course will bring students to TEC level or 'O' level course in Science, Maths and English; Course fees: £1 for people on supplementary benefit. Other applicants should check fee payable with college; Grant: None; Childcare facilities: creche facilities might be available. Check with college. Access: A. Contact: Paul Rispoli, South East London College, Goudhurst Road, Downham, Kent (698 5000/1720 ext 28).

Vauxhall College. This college offers two courses for women only, open to women living in Greater London area.

Course: Construction and Land Use Foundation Course: 15 places, one year full-time. Aimed at women over 25. Course can lead on to further training; Course fees: None; Grant: Paid to women over 25. £41.55 pw. Travel expenses might also be paid; Childcare facilities: College has a creche for children of students and staff, but places are limited. Access: N. Contact: Sue Sandle, Vauxhall College, Belmore Street, Wandsworth Road, SW8 (928 4611).

Course: Women's Painting and Decorating Course - 14 places, 36 weeks, 20 hours pw. Aimed at women aged 16 and over, Can lead on to City and Guilds; Course fees: check with college; Grant: None; Childcare facilities: As above: Disabled access: None; Contact: Mr Smith, Department of Building Crafts, Vauxhall College, Belmore Street, Wandsworth Road, SW8 (928 4611).

Westminster College. Course: Vocational Preparation for a Future in Fashion - 18 places, one year full-time.

Course mainly for young people aged 16 and over. The year is spent exploring various areas of the fashion industry, including design construction, marketing and theatre wardrobe. Three CSE Grade 3 required. Applicants also have to complete a small project before attending for interview; Course fees: Contact college; Grant: ILEA grant might be available; Childcare facilities: None; Access: N; Contact: Mrs Tregiddon, Course Tutor, Westminster College, Battersea Park Road, SW1 (720 2121).

Sir John Cass. The Department of Silversmithing, Jewellery and Allied Crafts runs mainly full-time art and design courses and some day release and evening classes. One course which might be of interest to young people is:

Course: Pre-Apprenticeship Course one year full-time. For students between 16 and 17. Course aims to provide a high level of design and practical education. Students select one main area of study from silversmithing, jewllery and engraving and gain a working knowledge of the other two subjects. Study is towards City and Guilds levels; Course fees: Contact department; Grant: Grant might be available. Students should contact their LEAs; Childcare facilities: creche available for use by students. Access: P - contact Course Organiser; Contact: Head of Department of Silversmithing and Jewellery, Sir John Cass - Department of Silversmithing, Jewellery and Allied Crafts, (Part of City of London Polytechnic), Central House, Whitechapel High Street, E1 (283 1030).

The Cordwainers Technical College. Course: Pre-entry course in Footwear and Leathergoods Manufacture: one year full-time. For 16-17 year olds. No formal entry requirements, but applicants must satisfy the Principal and Head of Department that they have an aptitude for and will benefit from the course. Includes, pattern cutting, introduction to design, leather and art craft, handbag making. Course up to City and Guilds Stage 1; Course fees: contact college; Grant: grant might be payable; Contact: Senior Administrative Officer, The Cordwainers Technical College, Mare Street, E8 3RE (985 0273/4).

Course: Craft Course in Leathergoods Manufacture (sponsored by the MSC): six months full-time. Applicants must be aged 19 or over and have previous industrial experience. Includes handbag making, pattern production, leather art and craft, introduction to hand tool equipment and sewing machines; Course fees: contact college; Grant: Students can apply for an MSC award. Access: N. Contact: Senior Administration Officer, The Cordwainers Technical College, Mare Street, E8 3RE (985 0273/4).

Polytechnic of the South Bank. Course: HNC in Electronics for Women Only: Starts in September 1985. One year full-time. Includes electronics, computer planning, maths, computer engineering, industrial law and administration. During the year students can either go on an industrial placement for eight weeks or take an Engineering Applications course at the Poly. Applicants must have four 'O' levels and one 'A' level - including Maths and Physics; Course fees: check with college; Grant: full grant guaranteed for students under 25; Childcare facilities; creche is available for students and staff, but places are limited. Access: A. Contact: Department of Electrical and Electronic Engineering, Polytechnic of the South Bank, Borough Road, SE1 0AA (928 8989 ext 2261).

Work Base - Trade Union Education and Skills Projects - Southwark. This project, which is linked to the South East Regional Trade Union Congress Basic Education Committee, seeks to offer educational opportunities to manual workers on a paid release basis. Courses in basic education are held in the student's own workplaces for groups of up to eight employees. The aim of the project is to widen the opportunities of manual workers, through using the combined support of trade unionists, employers and educationalists. Advice is given to manual workers on how to get paid educational leave. For more information: Contact: Work Base, Southwark Institute, Tabard Branch, Hunter Close, Weston Street, SE1 (403 1866).

Lambeth Employment Training Scheme. Lambeth Council runs 20 week full-time courses. They are aimed at unemployed people aged 19 and over living in Lambeth, and train them in a variety of semi-skilled areas of work. No formal entry qualifications. Areas include: general clerical, garage operative, typewriter operative, catering, soldering and assembly, domestic appliance servicing; Course fees: None; Training allowance: MSC allowance, fares might also be paid; Contact: Carol Williams, Directorate of Town Planning and Economic Development, London Borough of Lambeth, Courtenay House, 9-15 New Park Road, SW2 4DU (674 9844) x 313).

New Directions. A one year training course in youth and community work aimed at the Black community, aged 24-40. Training leads on to further professional qualifications. A training allowance might be paid. Contact: New Directions, 1 Larch House, Clyde Street, Deptford SE8 (692 2608).

Turning Point Apprenticeship Training in Community Work: a two year full time course. Ten places per intake, equal numbers of Black and white people. Trainees spend three days in practice, two days in study. Aimed at people aged 23-50. No formal entry requirements, but applicants must show a sustained commitment to community work. Certificate in Community Work from Goldsmith College awarded at the end of the course; Course fees: None; Grant: LA grant might be available; Childcare facilities: None; Contact: Rooney Martin, Turning Point, 23 Albany Street, Deptford, SE8 3PT (691 3204).

Educational Advice and Counselling Services for Adults

London has a network of training and education advice centre as below. Most have drop-in and appointment facilities - phone for details. (Further listings are provided in **Education and Further Education**).

Camden: Camden Adult Learning Advice (CALA), 58 Phoenix Road, NW1 (388 4666).

Greenwich: Greenwich Education and Training Advice (GRETA), 12-14 Wellington Street, SE18 (854 2993)

Hackney: Hackney Education Advice Service (HEAS), 263 Mare Street, E8 (986 8446).

Hammersmith & Fulham: Education and Training Advice for Adults, 241 Kings Street SW6. (741 8441)

Islington: Education Advice Service for Islington Adults (EASIA), c/o ILEA Learning Materials Service, Highbury Station Road, N1 (226 9143).

Kensington & Chelsea: Kensington and Chelsea, Learning Advice for Adults, Wornington Road, W10.

Lambeth: Lambeth Educational Opportunities (LEO), Strand Centre, Elm Park, SW2 (671 2961).

Southwark: Education and Training Shop (INSET), 175 Rye Lane SE15 (635 9111).

Tower Hamlets: Tower Hamlets Education Advice (THEA), The Education Shop, 75 Roman Road, E2 (981 3164).

Wandsworth: Wandsworth Education Shop, 248 Lavender Hill, SW11 (350 1790).

Useful Sources of Information

Apprenticeships for Girls: Issued by Thames TV's 'Help' programme (388 5199).

INSET Education and Training Shop, 175 Rye Lane, SE15 (635 9111).

The London Women in Youth Training Research and Support Project This project provides advice, support and inforamtion on the location and availability of training resources available for young women. It also aims to provide/organise training sessions relevant to women's needs (eg racism and sexism) and to explore how far the structure of YTS reflects young women's needs and the problems they face on the schemes. For more information contact: Nadia Edmond and Yvonne Bentley, London Women in Youth Training, Room 125, South Bank House, Black Prince Road, SE1 7SJ (582 9761).

Opportunities for Adults: Basic Education, Access and Training in North East London; contact: North Islington Neighbourhood Education Project, 43 Henley Road, N4 or Newham Parents Centre, 147 Barking Road, Dagenham, Essex RM9 5QA.

South East London Women's Training Directory The director provides information on education and training courses available to women over 19 in the London boroughs of Lewisham, Greenwich and Southwark. It is aimed at women who have had little or no access to educational or training opportunities. It attempts to put together in a more comprehensive way that information which is already available, though not often easily accessible. It consists of eight booklets, the first one an introductory pamphlet, covering areas like childcare, money, how to get on courses, access and basic education courses. The remaining seven cover the following: Arts, Craft and Media; Women and Technology; Cookery; Working with People; Starting your own Business; Business and Office Skills; Manual Trades. It is available from women's organisations and educational institutions in the three boroughs. Copies can also be obtained from: Lewisham Women's Employment Project, 179 Deptford High Street, SE8 (691 3550).

Training Opportunities for Women in Lambeth: Published by Lambeth Women and Work Group, c/o 460 Wandsworth Road, SW8 3LX. (662 9208).

Women and Manual Trades (WAMT) is a group of women working in non-traditional manual jobs, who provide support, information and advice for other women who either work in manual trades or who are trying to get into these trades. The information they provide is practical, comprehensive and useful. WAMT publishes a *Yellow Pages of Training*. Women can either phone, write or visit the project. For more inforation Contact: WAMT, 52-54 Featherstone Street, EC1 (251 9192).

(See **Employment and Unemployment** for detailed information on Resources for Women Workers in different industries and localities. See also **Education and Further Education** for other sources of information).

Transport

Getting around in London - on foot, by bus, by tube, by bike, by car - plays a vital part in women's lives. Travelling gives us the opportunity to get to a job, to the hospital, to the shops, to visit friends or relatives. But the transport system is designed with the male journey to work very much in mind. Little thought is given to women's needs. Yet, as the *Women & Transport Survey* carried out by the GLC Women's Committee has shown, these needs are very real.

Looking around the streets of London it's obvious that many people use a car to get from A to B. Much public spending goes on providing roads and parking for cars. But most of the drivers are men. Twice as many men as women hold a full driving licence. Even where a car is available it is usually the man in the household who uses it.

Women are far more likely to walk than drive. The GLC Women and Transport Survey showed that 55% of women walk all the way to their destination on at least five days a week. But walking along noisy and polluted roads, through dark subways, across busy traffic, is not pleasant. Women often have to accompany dependants on journeys because they are unsafe. There is little thought or finance given to the needs of pedestrians: kerbs are rarely dropped for people in wheelchairs and pushing pushchairs, street furniture (signposts, lamp-posts, benches etc) clutters routes for those with sight problems, pavements are obstructed by parked vehicles and insufficient action is taken to discourage pavement parking, pedestrian routes are rarely direct and well lit.

Buses are also an important means of getting around for women, who are the majority of bus users in London. But services do not always meet our needs. Why are the steps onto a bus so high and why isn't it possible to get on a bus in a wheelchair, to keep a child sitting in her buggy on the bus, to have space for shopping trolleys? Many women prefer having a conductor on the bus yet one-person-operation is increasing, threatening our jobs, our safety and our mobility. Short hop journeys which many women make are more expensive than longer journeys. Services are less frequent when women need to use them in the off peak period, and often services to areas where many Black and working class women live are poor, restricting their access to jobs and other services.

A high proportion of women from all areas of London are reluctant to travel at all because of the threat of violence or harassment. Women feel unsafe waiting at unlit bus stops, on lonely underground stations or travelling in trains at night. For Black and ethnic minority women there is the additional fear of racist attack or harassment. Given the will, there is much that transport operators and designers could do to improve safety on public transport: improved staffing levels, supervision of waiting areas, adequate alarm systems, improved lighting would all help.

As the transport services are geared up to male journeys so the transport industry is geared to male jobs: drivers, engineers, planners, mechanics, managers. The mechanical and technical skills associated with such jobs are often difficult for women to obtain. In London Regional Transport (LRT) only 10% of the staff are women. The majority of these are in lower paid and undervalued jobs - catering, cleaning, conducting, ticket collecting - where job conditions are poor. Such jobs are threatened by LRT's policies on one-person-operation and on privatisation. These losses will be severe for the many Black women employed in these areas.

Transport unions too are male dominated as are the majority of organisations making decisions about transport policy. The transport politicians and planners at the GLC were no exception but with the existence of a Women's Committee thinking changed.

The GLC, as the London-wide transport authority, put emphasis on providing an integrated transport network which prioritised public transport; managed the road network to benefit buses, pedestrians and cyclists; restrained the use of the private car and recognised the varied needs of different groups of the public including women, people with disabilities and Black and ethnic minority groups. As existing public transport does not provide a safe door-to-door service and women can be at danger from racist and sexist harassment or attack, the GLC Women's Committee and Borough Women's Committees have also funded a number of women's groups to buy their own minibus or to set up women's taxi services.

In June 1984 the GLC lost control of London Transport to LRT and since this date the policies pursued by LRT have led to a considerable deterioration in services which hit hardest at women. With abolition of the GLC other transport responsibilities will also fall to central government. London will lack a democratically elected transport authority where women's needs can most effectively be voiced and addressed.

It is important that women challenge the existing transport policies and campaign for a transport system that meets our needs. This section lists groups which campaign around a broad range of transport issues. More specific campaigns are listed under relevant headings eg Disability. There is one group set up by women to campaign specifically for women's transport needs, Women for Improved Transport (WIT, see below). Some mixed groups working on such issues as improved public transport, reduction of traffic, better facilities for pedestrians or cyclists, have also begun to address women's needs. Other broader campaigns also focus on transport issues. Many of these groups can put you in touch with local campaigns in your area.

This section is ordered as follows: *Campaigns, Community Transport, Cycling, Dial-A-Ride, Disability, Employment, Motorcycling, Motor Mechanics, Pedestrians, Pollution, Public Transport, Roads, Women's Taxi Services, Publications.*

Campaigns

Campaign to Improve London's Transport, (CILT) Tress House, 3 Stamford Street, SE1 9NT (928 9179). A campaign uniting workers and passengers committed to fighting for improved and democratically controlled public transport. Very active on women's issues. Will advise on how to mount a local campaign and how to channel complaints. Access: N.

Capital (Campaign to Protect and Improve London's Transport), 308 Grays Inn Road, WC1 (833 4022/3719). Set up with similar aims to CILT and also very active on women's issues. Produces a free monthly bulletin. Working on a Women's Information Pack to be available free during 1986. Also advises on how to mount a local campaign and how to channel complaints. Access: A.

Friends of the Earth (FOE), 377 City Road, EC1V 1NA (837 0731). Access: N.

London Amenity and Transport Association (LATA), 3/7 Stamford Street, SE1 (928 1440). Access: N.

London Centre for Transport Planning (address as LATA). Research, education and advice.

Socialist Environment and Resources Association (SERA), 9 Poland Street, W1V 3DG (439 3749).

Traffic, 377 City Road, EC1 (837 0731). Access: N. Concerned with women's issues.

Transport 2000, 358 Pentonville Road, N1 9JY (388 8386). Access: N. Concerned with women's issues.

Women for Improved Transport (WIT), c/o 12 Bartholomew Villas, NW5.

(See also **Planning**)

Community Transport

CT organisations hire out mini-buses and vans, usually to community groups. They are voluntary organisations usually funded partly by local authorities. Some are also prepared to administer vehicles owned by other community groups or to allow such groups to administer and control vehicles owned by the CT group. Most have at least one vehicle fitted with a tail-lift for full access and some have a vehicle fitted out specifically for children. Some CT schemes are run by Black and ethnic minority groups.

National Advisory Unit for Community Transport, Tavistock House North, Tavistock Square, WC1H 9HX (388 6542). Access: A. Will advise and provide research for groups wishing to set up new schemes.

London Community Transport Association, London Production Centre, Broomhill Road, SW18 (871 5052). Can provide you with a list of local community transport schemes.

Cycling

More women are now using bikes to travel in London and - despite fumes, dangerous roads and sexual harassment - find it an enjoyable and cheap way to travel. There are no specific women's campaigns but mixed groups seem keen to recruit women cyclists.

Friends of the Earth (See Campaigns above).

London Cycling Campaign, Tress House, 3 Stamford Street, SE1 9NT (928 7220). Access: N. Lobbies the bodies concerned for better conditions for cyclists. Stress that they are anti-sexist and have a woman lawyer who can give advice on accidents, consumer complaints and harassment. Also gives general advice on cycling. Publish a bi-monthly bulletin the *Daily Cyclist* (40p) and a booklet *On Your Bike* (90p) in conjunction with FOE (above), covering all aspects of cycling. 1 year membership costs £3.

Dial-A-Ride

Dial-a-ride schemes have been set up to help provide for the transport needs of the elderly, people with disabilities or people otherwise unable or unwilling to use public transport. Women are the major users of these schemes. The GLC funded schemes with the aim of providing a London-wide network. The Federation can put you in touch with your nearest scheme.

Federation of London Dial-A-Ride (FOLDAR), 25 Leighton Road, NW5 2QD (482 2325).

Transport and Disability

Transport is of vital importance to women with all types of disability - physical, visual, aural, mental - yet much of our public transport system is inaccessible and unsafe for all but the able-bodied.

Transport in London Group, Liberation Network of People with Disabilities, c/o Houseman's, 5 Caledonian Road, N1.

(See also **Disability**)

Employment

Although male dominated some of the transport unions have equal opportunities officers and have women active within them. LRT (see Public Transport below) also has an equal opportunities officer.

Transport and General Workers Union (TGWU), Transport House, Smith Square, SW1P 3JB (828 7788).

National Union of Railwaymen (NUR), Unity House, 200 Euston Road, NW1 2BL (387 4771).

Transport Salaried Staffs Association (TSSA), Walkden House, 10 Melton Street, NW1 2EJ (387 2101).

South East Regional TUC (SERTUC), Caxton House, 13-16 Borough Road, SE1 0AL (636 4030 x214). Active Transport Working Party, contact Julie Hayes.

Associated Society of Locomotive Engineers and Firemen (ASLEF), 9 Arkwright Road, NW3 6AB (435 6300). **LT Equal Opportunities Pressure Group**. An unofficial group outside the union structure, addressing race issues. Convener: W.M. Tucker, SCI, GP Planning, Albany House, 55 Broadway, SW1.

(See also **Employment and Unemployment**)

Motorcycling

National Motorcycle Training Scheme Federation, 2309 Coventry Road, Sheldon, Birmingham. London Booking Agent: Mary Grant (764 7022). Provides mixed training courses for motorcycle riders, ring for details of your nearest scheme.

South London Women's Centre,* 55 Acre Lane, SW2 (274 7215). Holds women-only motorcycle maintenance workshops on Sunday afternoon (held in basement). Access: N.

Motor Mechanics

There are a number of women-only car mechanics courses available in London. The Women's section of *Floodlight* (available in public libraries or from ILEA Education Information Service, County Hall, SE1 7PB) lists women-only courses in Inner London. For outer boroughs contact your Local Education Authority.

Bigends Garage, Arch 199, Prebend Gardens, W6 (994 1165). Garage run by women for women doing repairs and maintenance. Access: A.

Women in Manual Trades, 52-54 Featherstone Street, EC1 (251 9292). A campaign group supporting women in manual trades and can advise or put women in contact with courses and workshops. Access: P.

Women's Motor Mechanics Project, Bay 4R, 1-3 Brixton Road, SW9 (582 2574). Set up by women for women to provide free training in motor mechanics, oriented towards employment. Access: A.

Young Lewisham Workshop, 346 Lewisham High Street, SE13 (690 4957). Runs free women-only car maintenance courses, Thurs morning for girls aged 16 up, Wed evening for married women. Hoping to set up motorcycle mechanic courses. Access: A.

(See also **Training**)

Pedestrians

Pedestrians Association, 1 Wandsworth Road, SW8 2IJ (582 6878).

Pollution and Noise

Campaign Against Lead in Petrol (CALIP), 171 Barnet Wood Lane, Ashtead, Surrey (03722 75977). Campaign for legislation for lead-free petrol. Children are especially at risk, diet can minimise effects, CALIP has a diet-sheet for children available, also fact-sheets and leaflets. Briony Jones (603 5778) can put you in touch with a London group and has information on environmental issues.

Campaign for Lead Free Air (CLEAR), 2 Northdown Street, N1 9BG (278 9686). Access: N. Campaigning for lead-free petrol and reduction of lead levels in paints. Can give information and book lists. Publish a booklet *Lead-Free Air - A Legacy for our Children* (£1.50) and a free newsletter.

National Society for Clean Air, 136 North Street, Brighton, BN1 1RG (0273 26313). Access: N. Old, established campaign concerned with air pollution, especially acid rain, lead, traffic and industrial pollution, noise etc. Gives advice and information.

(See also **Planning**)

Public Transport

London Regional Transport (LRT) have overall control of the buses and tubes in London. They are accountable only to the Secretary of State for Transport. The buses and tubes are now run by two subsidiary companies of LRT: London Buses Ltd and London Underground Ltd. Trains in London are run by British Rail. There is an official body representing passengers (London Regional Passengers' Committee see below) which is generally sympathetic to women's concerns and a number of mixed campaigns which are also active on women's issues (see Campaigns above.) If you want to complain about the service you are getting (or not getting), complain first of all in writing to the operator (LRT or BR) at their head office and the local district office or garage. You should also register your complaint with the London Regional Passengers Committee. Campaigns such as WIT and CILT listed above will advise you on how to channel your complaints and how to mount a campaign.

London Regional Passengers' Committee, Golden Cross House, Duncannon Street, WC2 (839 1898).

London Regional Transport (LRT), 55 Broadway, SW1H 0BD.

London Buses Ltd, at above address.

London Underground Ltd, at above address.

LRT Unit for Disabled Passengers Tony Shaw/John Wagstaff, above address (227 3176).

British Rail, Euston Square, PO Box 100, NW1 2DZ

Roads

With the abolition of the GLC responsibility for roads in London will be split between the Secretary of State for Transport and the boroughs. Restraints on major road building will disappear as the Department of Transport has earmarked £15,000 million for spending on London's roads. Major road building can have disastrous effects on local communities and there are a number of local groups active in their opposition to road proposals (see Campaigns above).

Secretary of State for Transport, Marsham Street, SW1.

Women's Taxi Services

These schemes have been set up by women for women to provide a safe means for women to get home late at night. Some have been funded by the GLC so fares are low, but others are self-financing.

Safe Women's Transport,* The Albany, Douglas Way, SE8 (692 6009). Operates Mon-Fri, 6.30pm-12pm, 50p one journey, 25p OAP and children under 14. Recommend booking one day in advance. Are adapting a minibus for full access. Access: A.

Stockwell Women's Lift Service,* (274 4641). Operates Fri and Sat from 11pm-1am in and around the Lambeth area. No fares but donations welcome. Access: A.

Ladycabs, 57 Stoke Newington Church Street, N16 (254 3501/3314). All-woman taxi company charging standard fares (except no surcharge after midnight). Operates all over London but mileage due from Stoke Newington. Access: A.

Publications

There is little material available that deals specifically with women's transport issues in a non-technical way but the following may be useful:

Women on the Move - GLC Women's Committee series of publications of the results of their Women and Public Transport Survey. Free. 1. Initial Research Preliminary to Survey: Women's Group Discussions. 2. Survey Results: The Overall Findings

Future booklets will include:- Survey Results: Safety, Harassment and Violence, Survey Results: Different needs of different women, Survey Results: Black women, The Survey Methodology, Ideas for Action.

GLC Women's Committee Bulletin, Issue 25 Aug/Sept 1985. Special issue on transport. Free.

Getting Around: Transport Today and Tomorrow, Gavin Smith, (Pluto 1984 £2.95).

52% Getting Women's Power into Politics, Barbara Rogers (The Women's Press £4.50) has a chapter on transport.

Violence against Women

The extent of violence towards women by men is under-reported and not sufficiently recognised or legislated against.

Statistically, women are more likely to be attacked violently by a close family member (husband, lover, relative) in their own homes, than attacked by a stranger in the street. Twenty-five percent of reported violent crime is 'wife' assault. The Rape Crisis Centre estimates that 54% of rapes are committed by someone the woman knows well and the Child Sexual Abuse Preventative Education Project estimates that one in five women are survivors of child sexual abuse.

Violence in these contexts can be physical, psychological, sexual and economic or all of these reinforcing one another. Many women are unable to speak about their experiences until a long time afterwards. The effects of violence on women - physical pain, illness, depression, living in constant fear, loss of self-esteem and lack of confidence - can have a long-term effect on women's mental health. Particularly where the attack has been by a stranger, outside the house, the woman may modify her behaviour, so as never to go out alone, or after dark, thus severely restricting her freedom and mobility.

Lesbians are often the victims of male violence as a result of their sexuality and also face discrimination and harassment on this account. Some women in violent relationships with men are lesbian and this may inflame the man's violence. It is likely also to make the choice to leave particularly difficult if there are children involved, because of the woman's justifiable fear that she may lose custody of her children on account of her sexuality.

In addition to all the above, Black women experience racist attacks, which often take the form of sexual violence. In areas where racist attacks are a frequent occurrence, in the streets and on people's houses, usually on housing estates, Black women are often vulnerable to attack.

The police response to racist attacks has been widely criticised and a Home Office report on racial attacks made it clear that detection and prevention of racial harassment had not so far been seen as policing priority. Often the failure of the police to respond quickly to incidents and their reluctance to prosecute means that the police response is often totally ineffective. (See **Housing**, Race and housing).

Black and ethnic minority women are often reluctant to report cases of violence to the police. Because of the level of personal and institutional racism within the police force, as recently highlighted in the Policy Studies Institute's report on the Metropolitan Police, Black women are often taken less seriously when reporting attacks, or themselves become targets for racist abuse from the police. (See **Policing**).

The Police have also been widely criticised for their response to women who are the victims of domestic violence, rape or sexual attack. Unenlightened attitudes in society often reinforce the view that domestic violence is less serious than other forms of violence, that the man is merely exercising his 'rightful control' or that it is an individual problem in a private domain. Unfortunately, this view is compounded by the response of the Courts and police, who often fail to apply the legal remedies available as deterrents to the violent man and do not respond as promptly and sympathetically as they might.

Where a woman reports a rape or sexual attack she undergoes an immediate interview at the time which involves long hours spent at a police station and adds to her distress. This and the often gruelling questioning she will face in Court often discourage many women from reporting violent crimes.

Even when victims do feel confident enough to report a violent attack, the police often do not record it as a crime because they do not believe that they have sufficient evidence to bring a successful prosecution. The Metropolitan Police have now announced that they intend to record attacks which might previously not have been recorded thus figures should rise to reflect more accurately the incidence of rape.

The Metropolitan Police have also opened special 'victim examination suites' at nine centres, where the emphasis will be placed on the victim's welfare rather than seeking to identify the culprit immediately.

For a long time many women have, however, been resisting and effectively challenging men's violence and have set up support groups, refuges, advice centres and self-defence training. By giving support, information and shelter to women who are the victims of violence, women no longer 'have to put up with it' but are able to make more informed and realistic choices about their future and to take shelter in safety.

The GLC Police and Women's Committees have recognised violence against women to be a crucial issue, with a wide-reaching effect on women's lives. The Police Committee produced special supplements on women and policing (which have highlighted police response to violence against women), and have undertaken a number of initiatives in this area (see **Policing**). The Women's Committee has highlighted that environmental factors like inadequate street lighting can increase women's feeling of vulnerability and has set out recommendations in relation to environmental improvements, improved security on housing estates and safe public transport (underground stations and bus stops). It has also funded a number of women's groups specifically working round the issues of violence towards women, and in conjunction with the GLC Housing Committee funded the majority of Women's Aid groups in London.

This section describes the various forms of violence which women and children may experience and lists the groups which offer support and advice.

This section is ordered as follows: *Domestic Violence, Women's Aid Refuges, Rape, Indecent Assault, Indecent Exposure, Violence Against Lesbians, Sexual Abuse of Children, Incest, Sexual Harassment - strategies for dealing with it: Assertiveness Training, Confrontation, Self-defence, Racism and Sexual Harassment, Sexual Harassment in Schools/Colleges, Sexual Harassment at Work, Sexual Harassment on Public Transport, Groups around London offering Support and Advice, Useful Reading.*

Domestic Violence

Legal Points

If you are living with a man or were living with him until he assaulted you, and he is physically violent towards you or your children, you can apply to a County Court for an injunction. If you are married, you can apply instead to the Magistrates' Court for an order which has the same effect as an injunction. Generally, though, the powers of the County Court judge are more flexible and the atmosphere in the County Court is usually less intimidating, and the procedure less distressing.

If you are married, you do not have to decide, before getting an injunction, whether or not you want a divorce or separation.

Solicitors: you need to consult one if

you want to get an injunction. You may be eligible for emergency Legal Aid. If you don't know of a solicitor who is likely to be sympathetic, ask your local Citizens Advice Bureau or Law Centre (see **Borough Information**), or Women's Aid Federation (see below) or Rights of Women (see below).

The point of an injunction is to order a person to stop doing something. In the case of domestic violence the following orders are often included: not to assault or interfere with you; not to assault your children; to leave your home by a certain date and not return; to keep a certain distance from your home; to let you back into your home. It is not easy to get an injunction ordering the man to leave the home ('ouster order'), but you should tell your solicitor all about his violence and behaviour which makes it impossible for you and your children to live with him. A full report from your doctor to your solicitor may be helpful. Note: if you are not yet at the injunction stage in your mind, but are sustaining strain, stress, and/or injuries, visit your doctor and ensure s/he makes a note of it, as you may need this later.

However, an injunction ordering the man not to assault you can, with your solicitor's help, be obtained fairly quickly (about two days); meanwhile you can discuss with your solicitor whether/how to apply for an 'ouster order'.

Power of arrest can be attached to an injunction - meaning that the man could be taken by the police and held if he breaks the orders: this type of injunction therefore gives you better protection. Normally it can only last for three months unless renewed.

Whether or not you apply for an injunction, you should get advice on your housing rights (see **Housing**). Violence and threats from a person you are living with are recognised in law as causing 'homelessness' and give you the right to be rehoused away from the fear of it if you are in 'priority need' - have children or are 'vulnerable' in some other way. The council should not insist on you getting an injunction, although they may require some independent evidence in support of your rehousing application (doctor, solicitor, social worker). Get advice from a solicitor, Law Centre or Women's Aid before approaching your council's Emergency Homelessness Section. (see **Housing**, Registration/Homelessness).

Rights of Women,* (Legal advice by and for women), 52-54 Featherstone Street, EC1 (251 6577). Telephone advice sessions Tues-Thurs 7-9pm. Access: A.

Women's Aid Refuges

These hostels, all over London (and nationally), provide refuge and accommodation for women and children who have been physically, mentally or sexually abused by a man. This can provide a temporary breathing space while a woman decides her future, or, if she has decided that the crunch has come and she needs to live apart from him, they can provide help with getting the legal side sorted out, with social security matters, and with getting rehoused. The locations of refuges are kept secret so that the violent husband/man will not know where you are. We therefore list below the addresses and phone numbers of the Women's Aid Federations, and they will put you in touch with the most appropriate refuge.

London Women's Aid, 52-54 Featherstone Street, EC1 (251 6537/251 6538). Ring at any time. At weekends or in the evening their ansaphone will give you the emergency number. Access: P

Women's Aid Federation England (WAFE), 52-54 Featherstone Stree, EC1 (831 8581).

Black Women's Aid Group, c/o Women's Aid Federation, as above. (Information on refuges for women of many nationalities.)

Lambeth Asian Women's Resource Centre (ASHA), 27 Santley Street, SW4 (274 8854). Refuge, young women's hostel.

Southwark Asian Women's Resource Centre (ASHA), PO Box 484, SE5 OHS.

Information on refuges in Eire, Northern Ireland, Scotland, Wales and all areas of England: contact WAFE, as above.

Rape

The Law: Rape involves sexual intercourse - the penis must penetrate the vagina. Assault with any other weapon, even if it penetrates, is considered 'indecent assault' and carries a much lighter sentence (see Sexual Abuse of Children below). For a man to be guilty of rape, it must also be unlawful: this means that rape in marriage is not recognised by the law. Women have been campaigning for changes in the law over all these matters since the last century.

Consent: A man commits rape if at the time he knows the woman does not consent to it or is reckless of whether she consents to it.

Sentences vary alarmingly. Rape carries a maximum of life imprisonment - and no minimum sentence. The maximum penalty now for attempted rape is also life imprisonment. In 1983 a man served three weeks for raping a six year-old girl.

The racial dimension of rape also contributes to the variance in sentences. A significant case in May 1985 involved a black woman, Jackie Berkeley, who had alleged she had been raped by police officials in a Manchester police station the year previously, and was sentenced at the end of the trial to three months imprisonment, suspended for a year, for wasting police time. The Jackie Berkeley Defence Committee organised support expressing Black people's concern at their experience of policing and the courts.

Indecent assault: This is any assault on a woman or girl which does not include penetration of the vagina by the penis (see Rape above). It is defined as any act which will cause a person to fear an assault in circumstances of indecency (except buggery , which is a separate crime and illegal act, even with a consenting woman). The offence covers even the most serious sexual assaults short of actual intercourse. Consent is not a defence if the woman is under 16, but in practice prosecutions are rarely brought against 'boyfriends'. The Sexual Offences Act which came into force on 16 September 1985 increased the maximum penalty for indecent assault to 10 years in all cases.

Indecent exposure: There are two types - in common law it is an offence to commit an act which outrages public decency or corrupts public morals in a place when two or more people could see it. This need not be a public place. The offence can be committed by a woman. Secondly, under the Vagrancy Act (1824), it is a crime for a man to expose his penis with intent to insult a woman.

Rape Crisis Centre, PO Box 69, WC1 (278 3956/837 1600 - 24 hours). Advice, counselling, practical help including medical and legal.

Women Against Rape, c/o Kings Cross Women's Centre, 71 Tonbridge Street, WC1 (837 7509) or PO Box 287, NW6 5QU.

Women's Anti-Violence Organisation,* 73-75 Stockwell Rd, SW9 (326 1228).

Women Against Violence Against Women (WAVAW), general feminist campaign. Since 1981 WAVAW have been campaigning against male violence in all its forms, and groups form according to need. Women interested in starting up or being in a WAVAW group can contact A Woman's Place (836 6081) for up-to-date information, or their local women's centre (see **Borough Information**).

(See **Childcare and Children** for advice centres for children. They will help you, whether you are young yourself, or contacting them on behalf of a young person.)

Violence Against Lesbians

Lesbians on their own or with other lesbians face the threat of sexual and racial harassment and physical violence, ranging from muttered abuse, shoving, stoning, spitting, attack on their homes through to assault and murder.

Men are often the recipients of sympathy and reduced sentencing if the woman they attack or murder was in a relationship with another woman. The media often single out Black lesbian projects as being laughable examples of 'wasted ratepayers' money' exacerbating Black lesbians' vulnerability to homophobia. Like other women, lesbians receive little or no assistance if they report attacks to the police.

(See **Lesbians** for information on all lesbian groups and see Self-Defence under Sexual Harassment later in this section. Also see **Policing** for possible increased police harassment of lesbians.)

Lesbian Police Monitoring Unit, LESPOP,* (833 4996), is monitoring experiences lesbians have with the police, and offers support and advice to lesbians in this matter. Inquiries from lesbians welcome (lesbian workers in this project).

Lesbian Line, * (251 6911). Help, advice, support (Tues-Thurs 7-10pm; Mon and Fri 2-10pm).

Lesbians Against Male Violence, c/o LAMV, A Woman's Place, Hungerford House, Victoria Embankment, WC2 (please enclose SAE). Meet and campaign.

Gay Legal Advice, BM Glad, WC1N 3XX (821 7672), 7-10pm nightly.

Black Lesbian Support Network, c/o Black Women's Centre, 41a Stockwell Green, SW9.

Sexual Abuse of Children

A recent Mori Poll conducted for Channel 4 TV found that 1 in 10 of all children had experienced sexual abuse. This is a far more common experience for girls than for boys and in most cases the abuser is a close relative. Sexual abuse of children covers a whole range of offences. It may involve exhibitionism (displaying the genitals), touching or manipulating the child's genitals, oral sex, oral rape and vaginal rape. It may occur once or be repeated over a number of months or years.

Incest: The law: incest is separated from other forms of sexual assault on girls or women and means a man having sexual intercourse with a woman he knows to be his granddaughter, daughter, sister or mother. It does not include assault by step fathers, adopted fathers, uncles or other relatives. Many women, however, define incest to include all sexual abuse of children by any adult in a position of trust and many define it as rape.

Incest Survivors Group, c/o A Woman's Place, Hungerford House, Victoria Embankment, WC2 (please enclose SAE). ISG provides a campaigning and support group for women and mothers of children who have been sexually abused. They have drop in centres at:

South London Women's Centre, * 55 Acre Lane, SW4. Tues 10.30am-12.30pm each week.

Waltham Forest Women's Centre, * 109 Hoe Street, Walthamstow, E17. Access: A

These centres offer support, advice, including legal advice, in confidence and in an informal non-professional situation. They have set up a self-help network, and Black women and disabled women survivors can get support in exclusive groups. Creches are available. In Hackney there is a refuge for girl survivors and a drop-in service. (Contact ISG as above.)

Child Sexual Abuse Preventative Project. This group is open to all women. Its aim is educational and is aimed at reaching girls in schools, and professionals working with young women. They can be reached through the same contacts as ISG above.

Sexual Harassment - Strategies for dealing with it

Sexual harassment continues to be a serious and widespread problem faced by women in the home, community and at work. It includes many forms of unwanted 'attentions' from men, from embarrassing comments, 'jokes', pin-ups, advertisements, touching, rape, and actions which intimidate, undermine and threaten women.

There are various ways to deal with it: you will want to take into account where it happens, who is around at the time to support you, and whether there is any formal procedure through which you can complain and get redress.

Assertiveness training: Confidence-building women-only courses, available at low cost (concessions for unemployed) all over inner London. Lists in *Floodlight*, Inner London Education Authority's guide to part-time day and evening courses, published annually (early autumn, before term starts), 50p from bookshops and newsagents. Or in public libraries. Or try your local women's centre (see **Borough Information**). For teachers see below under Self-Defence.

Workers' Education Association, 32 Tavistock Square, WC1 (387 8966), also runs courses in many parts of London, including outer boroughs.

Confrontation: A method used more in North America but sometimes here too. It is relevant where harassment has taken place when the man is known. The woman who has been harassed confides in a group of about six friends. They go together and confront the harasser, telling him precisely what it is about his behaviour which is causing offence and that he must stop it. It is the woman centrally concerned who says how he has upset her, the others provide support. It is crucial to practise first in role play, anticipating his responses. With six women the man is not likely to become violent; there is less chance, also, that things will get out of control than if a large group of women go. Forms of confrontation can be useful in sexual harassment settings where there is no formal complaints procedure.

Further forms of response related to confrontation, tried out successfully in North America, are: encouraging women to discuss ways of watching out for each other on the streets or estates; organising at work to deal with harassment; encouraging women to respond to cries for help; printing and distributing details of harassers' descriptions, names etc, in the areas they are known to operate, both as a form of embarrassing the harassers, and warning other women.

All these strategies developed in the context of strong work on anti-racism which is crucial because of racism and racist myths surrounding violence against women. Women participating in these methods should thoroughly discuss and resolve any racist implications of confrontation before taking action.

Self-defence: Special classes for women are run all over London - not counting the many courses in karate, aikido and other self-defence sports/skills which are also plentiful (and sometimes women-only). Courses listed in *Floodlight* (see above under Assertiveness) and from WEA (as above); also contact your local woman's centre (see **Borough Information**), and your local sports' centre (see **Sport**).

List of women self-defence teachers available (sae) from ILEA, Room 77, County Hall, SE1 7PB; (633 1066). Will also sometimes advise woman assertiveness trainers.

Martial Arts Commission, First Floor, Broadway House, 15-16 Deptford Broadway, SE8 (691 3433). Information on all martial arts except judo.

A Woman's Place,* Hungerford House, Victoria Embankment, WC2 (836 6081) will also advise on self-defence and assertiveness trainers. Send sae if writing.

Racism and Sexual Harassment

Black women have set up Black women's refuges, support networks and women's groups for Black women who are the victims of domestic violence, rape, incest and racial and sexual harassment. There are also a number of mixed Black groups which have set up to monitor and give advice on racist attacks (see **Housing**, Race and housing and **Policing**, Racial Harassment).

Asian Women's Resource Centre,* 134 Minet Avenue, NW10 (961 6549)

Black Incest Survivors' Group, Brixton Black Women's Centre, 41 Stockwell Green, SW9 (274 9220/7696).

Sexual Harassment in Schools and Colleges

Girls and young women, and their women teachers and tutors, are growing more openly concerned and angry about sexual harassment from boys, male students, male teachers and tutors. (For details of anti-sexist work in schools, see **Education** and **Young Women**).

In many colleges there are women's groups which are supportive in helping you to deal with sexual harassment. This has often proved the most effective way of curbing sexual harassment from fellow students and getting sexist events cancelled and sexist 'jokes' and material removed from student publications (or college prospectuses). If you do not have a women's group, these may be good issues to start one about. Take it from there to the students' union.

If you need to confront male tutors: go in a supportive group (see Confrontation above) either to see the man concerned or his superior; be well prepared in advance. Sympathetic women tutors exist in most colleges. Organise a joint meeting between women tutors and students on the issue, and discuss strategies to raise the issue more widely in the college. Or approach one tutor individually in confidence.

National Union of Students Women's Unit, 461 Holloway Road, N7 (272 8900 ext 280 - Women's Officer), is currently (1985) carrying out a large survey on sexual harassment in colleges, polys and universities, and are campaigning around the issue. They also can advise you on women's groups in colleges to whom they send regular bulletins. Also, if you are having trouble getting support in cases of harassment, ring them for advice. Access: P

Sexual Harassment at Work

Though the battle is still by no means won, some unions, and the Trades Union Congress (TUC), are now taking seriously the issue of sexual harassment at work. The TUC pamphlet, *Sexual Harassment at Work* (1983), defines it as including repeated and unwanted verbal or sexual advances, sexually explicit derogatory statements or sexually discriminating remarks made by someone in the workplace which are offensive to the worker involved, which cause the worker to feel threatened, humiliated, patronised or harassed, or which interfere with the worker's job performance, undermine job security or create a threatening or intimidating work environment. It includes the following examples: leering, ridicule, embarrassing remarks or jokes, unwelcome comments about dress or appearance, deliberate abuse, the offensive use of pin-ups, pornographic pictures, repeated and/or unwanted physical contact, demands for sexual favours, physical assault.

The law: Sexual harassment is not specifically recognised in the Sex Discrimination At, but certain conduct fitting this description could amount to discrimination, since you are treated less favourably than a man would be, or subjected to a detriment that a man would not be. Also, under this Act employers must not allow an offensive working environment to continue.

If you resign following sexual harassment you could claim 'constructive dismissal' and therefore take your case up with an Industrial Tribunal, claiming compensation. Get advice from your local law centre (see **Borough Information**).

If you are a member of a union, and suffering sexual harassment (or supporting a woman who is), find out through your representative or regional office what procedures, if any, are laid down to make your complaint. Some employers are 'equal opportunities' employers: they will have, or will be developing, procedures for complaints in sexual harassment cases; your manager should have the necessary information.

Many women workers (about one third) do not belong to a union. Even women who are members may well want to avoid formal channels of complaint, especially as these are not always easy or pleasant to negotiate. Or women may want to try informal steps as the first stage. As the NUJ Equality Council suggest in their pamphlet *Sexual Harassment*: 'Don't try to tackle it on your own. Talk to sympathetic colleagues first. You may find others who have had similar experiences, and in any case their support may help you decide how best to deal with the offender. Once you have this support, try telling the offender to stop the behaviour you find unwelcome. Once the offender understands clearly that you and others disapprove, this may be enough to put an end to it.'

Whether or not you are unionised, organising with other women is a helpful strategy in dealing with sexual harassment. Assertiveness, self-defence and confrontation techniques (see above) are all relevant - two or more of you could go on a course together. Whatever course of action you decide to take, on your behalf or for other women, always remember to keep a clear record of what the harasser does, where and when. This evidence is essential for both formal and informal remedies. For further information contact:

Equal Opportunities Commission (EOC), Overseas House, Quay Street, Manchester 3 (061 833 9244).

Unions with policies condemning sexual harassment at work:

London Print Campaign Against Sexual Harassment (for those in unions to do with print/publishing): c/o Equality council, NUJ, Acorn House, 314 Grays Inn Road, WC1.

National Union of Public Employees (NUPE).

National Association of Teachers in Further and Higher Education (NATFE).

Electrical, Electronic, Telecommunications and Plumbing Union (EETPU).

Banking, Insurance and Finance Union (BIFU).

Civil and Public Service Union (CPSU).

National Union of Journalists (NUJ).

National Association of Local Government Officers (NALGO).

National Graphical Association (NGA).

Society of Graphical And Allied Trades 82 (SOGAT).

Sexual Harassment on Public Transport

Sexual harassment and violence is often experienced by women on public transport, or while waiting. Women do not experience safety in taxis, unless driven by other women. (See

Transport for details of women's transport campaigns and safe women's transport projects).

See earlier under Sexual Harassment for possible forms of defence and action against harassment and violence on transport and elsewhere.

Groups around London offering support and advice

Aico House, Alexander Road, Hounslow, Middlesex. Hindi, Urdu, Gujarati speaker available.

Asian Women's Resource Centre,* 134 Minet Avenue, NW 10 (961 6549). Hindi, Urdu, Gujarati, and Punjabi available. Access: P

Black Incest Survivors Group, Brixton Black Women's Centre, 41 Stockwell Green, SW9 (274 9220/7696).

Islington Girls Project,* 8 Manor Gardens, N7 (263 6276). Urdu, Punjabi speaker available. Access: P

Plumstead Community Law Centre, 105 Plumstead High Street, Plumstead SE18 (855 9817). Hindi available. Access: A

South London Women's Centre,* Drop in Centre, 50 Acre Lane, Brixton SW2. Tues 10.30am-12.30pm.

Waltham Forest Women's Centre,* 109 Hoe Street, Walthamstow, E17. Access: A

Womens Anti-Violence Organisation,* 73-75 Stockwell Road, SW9 (326 1228). Access: N

London Women's Aid, 52-54 Featherstone Street, EC1 (251 6537/6538). Access: P

Sexual Violence - the Reality for women (Women's Press £3.50).

Stand Your Ground, K. Quinn, (Orbis £3.99).

Well Founded Fear, Nanner and Saunders (Hutchinson £3.50).

Useful Reading

Father Daughter Rape, Elizabeth Ward (Women's Press £4.95).

Incest - Facts and Myths, S. Nelson (Stramullion £3.50).

Leaving Violent Men, Val Binney and others (Women's Aid Federation)

Preventing Child Sexual Assault, Michelle Elliot - offers a practical guide for parents.

Young Women

Young women in London today who are under 21 have benefited from the revolution in the education system made possible by the 1944 Education Act and comprehensive education. 'Equality of Opportunity' has been their birthright yet still young women face discrimination. They are subjected to the discrimination of sex role stereotyping, so that the pattern of their education and achievements is still quite different from that of boys. Early socialisation within the family, at school, by the media and in society generally often limit the lifestyles and choices available to young women. Society's expectations of what young women can and should do has a serious debilitating effect upon their life chances. These attitudes, reinforced by 'ageism' (see **Older Women**), mean that many see no choices or opportunities open to them at the end of their schooling, with qualifications which offer no way out of low paid work or unemployment.

Unemployment amongst young people has reached catastrophic proportions and for young women, particularly Black and ethnic minority young women, the situation is particularly bad. Alternatives to unemployment, such as Youth Training Schemes (YTS), often reinforce traditional divisions of labour, and restrictions in social security benefits to young people leave many young women without access to income or housing, even if they are single parents.

Despite the reality of young women as parents, having family and work responsibilities, and being sexually active, society's expectations are very different. This attitude is typified by the legal action taken by Mrs Victoria Gillick in 1984 who tried to stop prescription and advice on contraception to under 16s without parental consent. The emphasis of this action was on the unacceptability of girls (no mention of boys) having anything to do with sex. Young women aged under 16 were to be denied the right to seek confidential advice and guidance on sexuality from caring professionals when this advice and guidance was not forthcoming from their own families.

The taboo on young women being sexually active also means that discussing their sexuality openly within the family is also difficult for most young lesbians. In a recent research survey conducted by the London Gay Teenage Group, 60% of young lesbians chose to discuss their sexuality first with a friend as opposed to 7% with their mothers.

Little attention is given to young women by any statutory or non-statutory bodies, though the Youth Service has traditionally been seen as the service which aims to enable young people to fulfil their potential. Although over 50% of those aged 5-21 are female, the participation by young women in youth service provision both statutory and voluntary, does not match their numerical strength. Youth clubs and centres are dominated by boys who have exclusive use of the facilities, equipment and youth workers' attention. The growth of 'girls work' in London is testimony to the fact that more needs to be done within the youth service to meet their specific needs. Work with Asian and Afro-Caribbean young women has been a notable part of this growth in 'girls' work'. It is girls, young women and women youth workers who are taking the initiative, organising autonomously and making demands to counter discrimination.

For its part in International Youth Year 1985, the GLC and Inner London Education Authority jointly funded the London Youth Festival to organise a programme of major events to take place across London throughout 1985 and also to assist projects organised by and for 15 to 25 year olds which contributed towards the themes of International Youth Year - Participation, Peace and Development.

The listings in this section are arranged mainly on a borough by borough basis to enable you to find your nearest girls' or young women's project. They also include counselling agencies for young people, unemployment projects, young mothers' projects and some young lesbian projects (also see **Lesbians**). You do not necessarily have to live locally to go to one of these - ring to check first if you are unsure.

For additional sources of legal and welfare rights, see agencies specialising in children's rights in **Childcare and Children** (eg school matters, adoption, in care, 'at risk' etc) or contact one of the legal centres listed in **Borough Information**. For anti-sexist, anti-racist policies at school, see **Education**; for advice on incest, sexual abuse, sexual harassment, see **Violence Against Women**. For accommodation and hostels which take young women, see **Housing**. For signing-on, see **Employment and Unemployment**, and for apprenticeships and courses, see **Training and Further Education**.

This section is ordered as follows: **Contacts for General Enquiries, Girl's and Young Women's Projects etc (by borough), Family Planning Clinics, Useful Reading**

Contacts for General Enquiries

Girls' Work Unit, National Association of Youth Clubs (NAYC), 30 Peacock Lane, Leicester (0533 29514). Provides information, resources including video library, training and support for youth workers developing their youth work practice with girls/young women. Newsletter *Working with Girls*, 6 issues £5.50 individuals, £12.00 institutions. NAYC have also published *Coming in from the Margins*, a book about girls' work by V Carpenter and K Yeung.

London Union Of Youth Clubs (LUYC), Girls Work Unit, 64 Camberwell Road, SE5 OEN (701 6366). For youth workers in London, offering support, resources, information, advice and training.

National Youth Bureau (NYB), Albion Street, Leicester LE1 6GD (0533 554775). Has extensive library of youth work publications and a number for sale, eg *Beyond Street Level; detached work with young women.*

Association of Jewish Youth, 50 Lindley Street, El (790 6407).

Association of Muslim Youth, 41 Gwendolen Road, Leicester (0533 730058).

Borough Addresses
Barking
Important: in the following borough listings, the *first* address in each borough will be able to give up-to-date information about local groups/activities.

Youth and Community Office (North Area), Japan Road Club, Japan Rd, Chadwell Heath, Romford (590 4966). For Chadwell Heath and Marks Gate Estate area.

Youth and Community Office (East Area), The Longhouse Centre, Charlecote Rd, Dagenham, Essex (592 1803). For areas west of Rivers Rom and Beam.

Youth and Community Office (West Area), The New Cambell Club, Arden Crescent, Dagenham, Essex (592 7793). For Thames View, Gascoigne and Eastbury Estates area.

Carousel Twirlers, Thomas Arnold (Junior School) Rundowns Rd, Dagenham. Majorette Training age range 11 years +.

Dagenham Girls' Pipers, Dagenham Priory School, Vicarage Rd, Dagenham. Marching, Piping, Drumming and Highland/Scottish Dancing. Mon, Tues and Wed - 7.30-9.30, age range 11 years +.

Vineries Young Adult Centre, 321-329 Heathway, Dagenham, Essex (593 3931). A confidential information and counselling service available to young adults, Mon to thurs-afternoons and evenings, Fri afternoons only, age range 16-25 years.

Barnet
For up-to-date information about new groups, activities and events (such as the Girls' Gynastics Championships or Girls' Five a Side Football) contact:
Youth and Community Service, Town Hall, Friern Barnet, N11 3DL (368 1255).

Off the Record, 5 Woodhouse Rd, Tally Ho Corner, Finchley N12 9EN (445 0888). Confidential counselling for young people. Mon-Fri, 10am-4.30pm by appointment.

Rendezvous Youth and Community Centre, Coppetts Rd, N10 1JS (444 7839). Girls' night one evening a week.

Sangam: Association of Asian Women, 235-237 West Hendon Broadway, NW9 7DH (202 4629). Women's meetings once a month and regular sewing and music classes plus advice and information.

Bexley

The Youth and Community Office, Education Department, Town Hall, Crayford, Kent DA1 4EN (303 7777). 9am-5pm.

Danson Youth Centre, Brampton Rd, Bexleyheath, Kent DA7 4EZ, (303 6052). Contact: Ruth Flavin. Run activity groups (such as gymnastics) for girls and young women only.

Welling Youth Centre, Lovel Avenue, Welling, Kent DA16 3JQ (854 1639). Danson Youth Centre (see above). Girls' night every Thurs 7-9.45pm, age range 11-20yrs.

Brent

Youth and community services are divided into 6 areas in Brent. To find out where your nearest youth club or centre is, and for up-to-date information about new groups or activities contact the Neighbourhood Development Worker in your area:

Neighbourhood 1 (Chalk Hill, Kenton, Kingsbury, Neasden), 369 Greenings Walk, Chalk Hill Estate, Wembley, Middx, (908 2979/904 5811).

Kingsbury Youth and Community Centre, Roegreen, (at the rear of the swimming pool), Kingsbury High Rd, NW9 (206 1672). Girls' Night Thurs, 7-9pm, age range 14-19yrs.

Nutshell, 105 Gold Beaters Walk, Chalk Hill Est, Wembley, Middx, (908 0404). Black young womens' group, meets weekday afternoons to evenings, age range 14-25yrs.

Neighbourhood 2 - Wembley, Wembley Youth and Community Centre, London Rd, Wembley, Middx, (903 6948).

Tokyngton Youth Club, St Michaels Church Hall, St Michaels Ave, Wembley, Middx, (903 0799). Separate activities and a girls only area in the youth club, age range 14-16yrs.

United Indian Youth Centre, Kingsbury High School, Sports Hall, Prices Ave, NW9. Girls' Night for asian girls and young women, Weds 7-10pm, age range 4-11yrs and 14yrs +.

Neighbourhood 3 (Gladstone Park, Neasden, Church End Green + Cricklewood, 59-60 Yuletide Close, Churchend St, Churchend Estate, NW1 (451 5120).

Asian Girls Group, c/o Asian Women's Resource Centre, 134 Minet Avenue, NW10, (961 5701).

Brent Young Peoples' Law Centre, 272 High Rd, NW10 (451 2428). Legal advice and represetation of young people aged up to 21, who live or work in Brent.

Neighbourhood 4 (Stonebridge and Harlesden), the Hilltop Club, 17 Stonebridge Shopping Centre, Hillside, NW10 (961 1562).

Brent Black Women's Group, Youth Aid Centre, 38 Craven Park Rd, NW10 (961 4600). Organise groups and activities for Black women of all ages. Phone for details.

The Crescent Club, Sladebrooke School, Brentfield Rd, NW10. (at

Neighbourhood Office) Girls' night Wed 4-7pm.

Brent Youth Advice Centre, 38 Craven Park Rd, Harlesden NW10 (961 4100/1/2/3). Advice and information mainly for ethnic minority young people.

Neighbourhood 5 (South Kilburn), (625 5880).

Granville Afro-Caribbean Centre, 80 Granville Rd, NW6 (328 4454). Young womens' netball team Tues and Thur age range 14yrs. Also other activities. Phone for details.

Oxford and Kilburn Club, Denmark Rd, NW6 (624 6292). Girls only group, Thurs 3.30-5pm, age range 7-11yrs.

Neighbourhood 6 (Kensal Rise, Kensal Green, Harrow Rd, 71a Pound Lane, NW10 (451 4758).

Moonshine Community Arts Workshop, 1090 Harrow Rd, NW10 (corner of Victor Rd and Harrow Rd), (960 0055 office; 969 7959). Many groups for girls and young women only such as: Afro-Caribbean women and their daughters, photography, print, reggae, sands, recording studios, super 8 animation, video. Access A. Phone for details.

Roundwood Community Association, Roundwood Estate, NW10. Girls' night Mon 7-10pm. Age range 10-20yrs, keep fit Tues from 7pm.

Titherton Youth and Community Centre, Wrentham Ave, NW10 (969 4454). Netball and dressmaking Mon 7-10pm; keep fit Tues 7-10pm.

Bromley

The Youth Service, Town Hall, Wodmore Rd, Bromley, Kent BR1 1SB, (464 333 ext 4574).

Bromley 'Y' Project, 17 Ethelbert Rd, Bromley, BR1 1JA, (464 9033). Advice and counselling for young people, age range 15 to 25 years.

Bromley and Downham Boys Club, 41 Valeswood Road, Downham, Bromley (698-4333). Runs separate activities for girls and young women - football, netabll, unihock, trips out

and much more. Mon, Wed, Fri, age range: juniors 8-11 years, seniors 11-19 years. Access P.

Spitfire Youth Centre, Church Rd, Biggin Hill, Westerham TN16 3LB, (0959 74835). (night is run by women workers). Girls' night every Thurs - starting soon - 7.30-10pm, age range 14-21yrs. Access P.

Camden

Camden Girls Centre Project, 4 Caversham Rd, NW5 (267 2898). (Mon 11am-4pm). Runs the following groups - ring for more details:

> **Young Lesbian Group** Mon 7.30-10-30, 16-21yrs (263 5932 during group time for more information on the Project)

> **Young Mothers Group**, Tues 12.00-6.00pm, 16-19yrs. Transport and creche provided. Meets at 71b Agar Grove, NW1. Sportsnight Alternate Tues eves, 8yrs-21yrs. Meets at Maitland Park Gym

> **Afro-Caribbean Young Women's Group**, Tues 2.00pm-5.00pm, 16-20yrs olds

> **Young Women's Music Workshop**, Thurs 8.00-11.00pm, 14-21yrs. Meets at 8 Manor Gdns, N7.

> **Bengali Girls' Group**, Thurs 2.00-5.30pm, 14-21yrs. Meets at Surma Community Centre.

> **Asian Girls' Group-Boundary Road**, Sat 10.00am-1.00pm, 14-21yrs.

Bedford House Girls Project, 35 Emerald Street, WC1 (405 2379). Girls and young women's programme Mon-Fri. Phone for details.

Camden Youth Unemployment Project, 2-6 Camden High St, NW1 (388 4343). Offer advice and information to young people plus activities and groups, some for young women only.

Fleet Community Education Centre, Agincourt Rd, NW3 (485 9988). Many groups plus classes for young people plus Bengali girls' group Mon 4.00pm - 6.00pm; Women's self defence and women's carpentry.

Kings Corner Project, 90 Central St, EC1 (253 6754). Football for young women, Wed 7.30-8.30pm (held at Finsbury Leisure Centre, Central St, EC1) 16 years +.

Kingsgate Community Centre, 107 Kingsgate Rd, NW6 (328 9480, 624 8661). Girls' group, Tues 6.30-9.30pm, age range 15-17yrs.

Resources and Information for Girls, 25 Bayham St, NW1 (387 7450). Run 5 young womens activity groups - some at Bayham St and some at community centres. Two groups are for Black young women, one of these is a photo visual group. Also Black young lesbians group on Tuesdays, phone for details, age range 16-21yrs. Other groups are for Black and white young women. Age ranges vary 11-21yrs Phone for details. Access P at Bayham St, A at Community Centres.

Thomas Coram Foundation Project, 71b Agar Grove, NW1 (267 6944). Runs young mothers' with Camden Girls' Centre Project and runs unemployed young womens' group with Camden Youth Unemployment Project.

The Winchester Project, Old Winchester Arms, 21 Winchester Rd, NW3 3NT, (586 3731). Wednesday 2pm-4pm Creche provided and transport available.

Croydon

The Youth Office, Taberner House, Park Lane, Croydon, CR9 1TP (686 4433).

Croydon (Arnhem) Ladies' Football Club, meets at Ashburton Park Sun 2-5pm; Monks Hill Sports Centre 8-9pm; Sylvan Sports centre 6-7pm. (777 0805).

Croydon Modern Rhythmic Gymnastic Club, John Newnham High School, Selsdon Park Rd, South Croydon. (657 3267). Meets Mon-Wed 6-10pm.

Drop In (Youth Counselling Service), 132 Church St, Croydon, Surrey, (680 0404). Counselling, support and information for young people, age range 14-25yrs. Women counsellors are available.

Phillip Game Youth Centre, 38 Morland Ave, Addiscombe, Croydon, (654 6260), (night is run by women workers). Girls' night every Thurs 7-9pm. Age range 11-18yrs. Transport available to take young women home. Access: P.

Ealing

For up-to-date information about activities, events and groups for girls and young women only contact: The Education Office, 79-81 Uxbridge Road, W5 5SU (579 2424 ext. 2584). Contact: Mrs Joy Thomas.

Acorn Youth Information and Advice Centre, 55 High Street, Acton W3 (992 5566 ext. 2253). General information, advice and counselling for young people aged 12-25 years. Mon to Thurs 10.00-5.30pm. Fri 10.00-4.30pm. Legal advice on Fridays. Asian languages available on Fridays. French and Spanish available all week.

Featherstone High School, Montague Way, Southall. Self defence group for young women. Thurs 4.00-5.00pm.

Golflinks Estate, Brindley Pavilion, Brindley Way, Southall (574 3537). Girls' Club - keep fit, netball, table tennis.

Havelock Centre, Havelock Road, Southall (571 2241). Contact: Jackie Clayton.Various groups and activities for girls and young women only, such as: aerobics, self defence, Indian dancing, Indian music, Asian Arts groups.

Parkview Youth Club, Parkview Road, Southall (574 7836). Girls' group (including photography project), Fri 6.00-9.30pm. Self defence.

Southall Evangelical Church Hall, Norwood Road, Southall (574 1991). Girls' club, Fri 4.30-6.30pm.

Unified Community Action, Southall Library, Ostley Road, Southall (574 2466). Aims to encourage women's groups and has a lot of information about new groups for up-to-date information.

Villiers High School, Boyd Avenue, Southall. Self defence/karate Mon

6.00-8.00pm.

Youth Advice Centre, Southall Library, Osterley Park Road, Southall. Drop-in for advice and information for young people Wed 3.00-5.00pm, Thurs and Fri 3.30-6.30pm.

Greenwich

Greenwich Girls' Project, c/o Greenwich Youth Office, 20 Passey Place, SE9 (859 4236).

Avery Hill Youth Club, Anstridge Road, SE9 (850 8577). Girls' night every Tues 7-9pm.

Blackheath Bluecoat Youth Centre, Old Dover Road, SE3 (853 3224).

Enysham Youth Club, 2 Penmon Road, SE2 (310 6114). Girls' night every Wed 7-10pm.

Ferrier Youth Club, Kidbrooke Park Road, SE3 (856 6739). Young Women's session every tues 12-3pm.

Greenwich Youth Unemployment Project, c/o YMCA, Woolwich Dockyard, Woolwich SE18 (317 7594). Occasionally organises groups and activities for unemployed young women. Contact: the Project for details.

Hawksmoor Youth Club, Bentham Rd, SE28, (310 9754). Girls' night every Thurs 7.30-10pm. Age range 11 years upwards. Access: A.

Kings Park Youth Centre, 131 Eltham Palace Rd, SE9 (850 1599). Girls' night every Mon 7-9pm.

Rathmore Youth Centre, Rathmore Rd, London SE7 (853 4192). Run some groups and activities for girls and young women only 14-21yrs. Access: A.

St Thomas's Youth Club, Woodland Terrace, SE7 (316 0619). Girls' night every Thurs 7-9pm.

Simba Project, Artillery Place, Woolwich, SE18 (317 0451). Offer a range of activities and services to the Afro-Caribbean community. Some women only groups day and evenings. Phone for details.

Thomas Tallis Youth Centre, Kidbrooke Park Rd, SE3 (856 2703). Provides safe transport to and from the centre for girls and young women.

Every Mon and Fri evening. Age range 11 years upwards.

Trinty Youth Centre, Burrage Rd, SE18 (317 7940). Young women's session every Friday, 12-3pm.

Waterfield Youth Centre, Bentham Rd, SE28 (310 8562). Girls and young womens' activity groups (computing, games + disco dance). every Saturday. 10am-2pm age range 11yrs upwards. Access (P).

Hammersmith and Fulham

Fulham Girls' Project, 683 Fulham Rd, SW6 (736 7696).

Clem Attlee Youth Club, Community Hall, Clem Attlee Estate, Lillie Rd, SW6 (385 8524). Girls night every Thurs, 7.15-8.15pm, age range 12yrs plus.

Fatima Youth Club, Fatima Community Centre, Commonwealth Ave, W12 (740 0477). Black young womens group afternoons starting soon.

Fulham Cross Youth Club, Bayonne Rd, W6 (385 7339). Club is run by a committee of girls and has lots of groups and activites for girls and young women only. Age range 14yrs plus. Access: A.

Fulham Girls' Project, 683 Fulham Rd, SW6 (736 7696). Young Mothers' Group Mons and Thurs 1.30-4.30pm, age range 16yrs + Girls' group Fri 6.30-9pm, age range 11-13yrs.

Hammersmith Teenage Project Youth Club, Bulwer Street, W12 (749 1847). Girls' Group Wednesday afternoons.

Lancaster Court Youth Club, Lancaster Court Community hall, Lancaster Court, Fulham Rd, SW6. Girls' night every 4th Monday 6-10pm age range 11 yrs +. Access: P.

St Mathews Hall, Margarvine Rd, W6. Young women's music group, Mons 7-9pm, age range 16-22 yrs.

Project Upfront, St Pauls Youth Club, Gliddon Rd, W14 (741 1119). Young Mother's group, Weds 10-3pm, age range 16-22 yrs, creche provided. Access: A.

Sands End Detached Project, 59-61 Broughton Rd, SW6 (736 0827). Girls' groups Weds and Thurs.

Townmead Youth Club, St Michaels Centre, Townmead Rd, SW6 (736 8776). Girls' night Mon evenings 5-7pm, age range 12 years plus. **The Upstairs Project**, 182 Hammersmith Rd, W6 (741 3335). Counselling, advice and information for young people, age range 16-25yrs.

West Kensington Estate Youth Club, Tenants Hall, Thaxton Rd, W14. Girls' night Weds 6.30-9.30pm, age range 11 years +.

W14 Youth House, 73 Talgarth Rd, W14 (602 1972). Full time youth project for girls and young women. Groups run during day and evenings. Transport available to take young women home.

White City Detached Project, White City Community Centre, India Way, W12 (740 5857). Arrange activities and outings for girls and young women. Can put young women in contact with interest groups such as drama, football, music, skating, swimming. Also trips out, summer holidays plus advice and information.

The following adventure playgrounds have girls' nights, or girls only activities and organise girls only holidays. Age range is 6-17yrs. For further details contact the playgrounds:

Bishops Park Adventure Playground, Bishops Park, Fulham Palace Rd, SW6 (731 5441).

Coningham Adventure Playspace, Coningham Rd, W12 (743 2957).

Distillery Adventure Playground, Distillery Rd, W6 (748 9224).

Thaxton Adventure Playground, Thaxton Rd, (385 5132).

Hackney

Hackney Girls' Project, South Hackney School Building, Cassland Road, E9. (985 5463). Phone for details.

Chats Palace Youth Club, 42-44 Brooksbys Walk, E9 (986 6714). Girls' night every Monday, 6-8pm.

Dalston Community Centre, 62A Montague Rd, E8 (241 2675). Girls' night every Wednesday, 7-10pm.

Frampton Park Youth Club, Frampton Park Estate, Wells St, E9 (533 0210). Girls' night every Friday, 6.30-9.30pm.

Hackney Downs Youth Centre, Hackney Downs School, Downs Park Rd, E5 (985 5920). Girls' night Tues and Wed, 6.30-9.30pm, age range 11 yrs +.

Hackney Youth Unemployment Project, Daniel House, Clissold Road, Stoke Newington, N16 (249 7266). Young Mothers' Group, every Weds 12.30-5pm. Creche provided. Young women's music group, every Thurs 3.30-6.30pm, age range 16-25 yrs. Access: P.

HEADS, 128 Rectory Rd, N16. Offer separate activities for girls and young women Mon evenings.

Homerton Detached Project, 109 Homerton High St, E9 (533 1011). Girls' night every Tues 7.30-10pm.

Hoxton Hall, 130 Hoxton St, N1 6SH (738 5431/739 6593). Girls night every Weds 6.30-8pm.

Huddleston Centre, 30 Powell Rd, E5 (985 9089). Centre for young people with disabilities and provides transport to and from all groups. Provisions for girls and young women Mon 6.30-9.30pm; Tues 6.30-8.30pm; Thurs 6.30-8.30pm.

Off Centre, 25 Hackney Grove, E8 (985 8566/986 4016/7). Counselling and advice service for young people aged 13yrs-25yrs. Mon 10am-6pm; Weds 10am-6pm; Thurs 10am-8pm; Fri 10am-6pm.

Pedro Youth Club, 175 Rushmore Rd, E3 (985 2801). Girls' night every Thurs 6-9pm.

Stamford Hill Youth Club, 124 Stamford Hill, N16 (802 8414). Separate activities for girls every Thurs 6.30-10pm.

Troubridge Youth Club, Gainsborough School Site, Berkshire Rd, London E9. Girls' night every Thurs 6.30-9.30pm.

Wenlock Provost Youth Club, 41 Provost St, N1 (251 6588). Separate activities for girls Mon and Wed evenings.

Wrens Park Youth Club, Warwick Grove, Upper Clapton, E5 (806 1344). Girls' night every Mon 6.30-9pm.

Haringey

Youth and Community Office, 48-62 Station Road, Wood Green, N22 4TY (881 3000 Ext. 3112).

Gladesmore Community Association, Gladesmore Road, Tottenham, N15 (802 7624)

Muswell Hill Youth Centre, Hillfield Park, Muswell Hill, N.10 (883 9508).

Open door; Hornsey Young People's Consultation Service, 12 Middle Lane, Crouch End, N8 8PL (348 5947/348 6235). General advice, information and counselling young people aged 13-25 years.

Walk-In-Centre, 42 Turnpike Lane, N8 0PS (888 3138). General advice, information counselling and support for young peopled aged 16-25 years.

Harrow

Youth and Community Service, Education Department, Civic Centre, PO Box 22, Harrow Middx, (863 5611).

Pinner Centre, Chapel Lane Car Park, Pinner Middx, (868 8865). Contact: Dorothy Weir.

Havering

Albemarle Youth and Community House, Gooshays Drive, Harold Hill, Romford RM3 9FU, (0423 401610).

Hallmead Youth Office, Marborough Gardens, Cranham, Upminster, (Upminster 27985).

Hillingdon

Youth and Community Services, Civic Centre, Uxbridge, Middlesex UB8 1UW, (Uxbridge 50111 ext 3622).

Grange Centre, Pine Place, Hayes, UB4 8RA, (573 2961). Has a girls' only group one evening a week, age range 11-15yrs.

Links: Youth Consultation and Advisory Service, Crossways, Whitehall Rd, Uxbridge, Middlesex, UB8 2DF, (Uxbridge 38884). Advice on housing and rights, confidential counselling for young people, age range: 14-25yrs.

Rendezvous, Unit Two, West Drayton Centre, Harmondsworth Rd, West Drayton, WB7 9JS, (West Drayton 421230). Girls' night one evening a week, age range 14-18yrs.

Hounslow

Youth and Community Office, Spring Grove Centre, Thornbury Rd, Isleworth, (568 3967).

Asian Women's Community Centre, moving to new premises, phone for new address, (572 2484). Shama - Asian girls' group every Thurs 4-6pm; every Mon self-defence 6-7pm.

Hanworth Youth Centre, Hounslow Road, Hanworth, (898 0892). Girls' group Thurs 8-10pm, age range 14-21yrs.

Islington

Islington Girl's Project, * 8 Manor Gardens, N7 (263 6270). Young Lesbian Group, Mon 7.30-10.30pm, Tues 4-6 pm.

Battlebridge Youth Centre, Copenhagen School, Treaty Street, N1 (837 2627). Activities include judo, climbing, canoeing, modern dance, rock music, football, self-defence for Asian girls and computer. Age range 11yrs+.

Caxton House, 129 St John's Way, N19 (263 3151). Girls' night every Mon 7-9.30pm.

Factory Basement, 107 Mattias Road, N16 (249 8909). Contact Claudette. Girls' night every Wed 6.30-9 pm.

Hanley Crouch, The Laundry, Sparsholt Road, N19 (263 1067). Girls' night every Mon 7-9 pm.

Highbury Grove Youth Centre, Highbury New Park, N5 (226 7993). Girls' night Fri 7-9.30pm. Swimming, judo, basketball and other activities. Contact Centre for details.

Highbury Roundhouse, 71A Ronalds Road, N7 (354 2418). Girls' night Tues 7-9 pm. Young mothers' group Wed 2-5pm.

Highview Youth Group, c/o Crouch Hill Recreation Centre, Hillside Road, N19 (272 4243). Contact group for details.

Holloway Neighbourhood Project, 8a Annette Road, N7 (607 9794). Girls' night Mon 7.30-9pm. Also trips arranged specifically for girls like holiday trips and residential weekends.

Islington Boat Club, City Basin, 16-34 Graham Street, N1 (253 0778). Sailing and canoeing Wed 4.30-7.30pm. During summer more outdoor activities boating and swimming. Term time activities are flexible to the needs of the girls. During holiday there is a girls whole day in summer. Winter activities - go-carting, ice skating, indoor games, arts and crafts. Future activities - dark room for photography. Trips out for members.

Islington Bus Company, Palmer Place, N7 (609 0226). Music sessions Thurs eves, Sat 10am-1pm, once a month Woman's Tapeover for partially sighted women.

Islington Girls' Project*, 8 Manor Gardens, N7 (263 6270). Young Lesbian Group Mon 7.30-10.30pm. Asian Girls' Group Tues 4-6 pm. Young mothers' Group Thurs 2-5pm. Music group Mon 6-9pm. Other groups and activities run for short periods of time (eg self defence, depression). Contact the Project for details.

Islington Green Youth Centre, Prebend St, N1 (226 4919). Football and trampolining Wed and Fri 6.30-9.30pm. Gymnastics Thurs 6.30-9.30pm. Clothes making Tues and Thurs. Photography Thurs, Dance Mon.

Kings Corner Project, 92 Central Street, EC1 (253 6776). Mixed football (held at Finsbury Leisure Centre) 7.30-8.30pm.

Magnus Wookshop, Penton Rise, WC1 (833 0613). Girls' night Tues 6-8pm. Women's night Monday 7.30-9.30pm.

New Grapevine, 416 St Johns St, EC1 (278 9147). Counselling, advice and information on sexuality, personal relationships, contraception and pregnancy etc. Tues 2.30-6.30pm. Wed 2.30-8.30pm. Thurs 2.30-6.30pm. Age range under 25 years. Also run post abortion support groups for young women. Sex education sessions for young people, also.

Peel Youth Club, 33 Lloyd Baker St, WC1X 9AB (837 6082). Girls night Wed 7-10pm for 10yrs+. Weekends away for girls.

Pluto Project, North London college, 444 Camden Road, N7 (607 0947). Welfare rights information and advice for unemployed young people, and housing and prospectuses for FE Courses.

St Josephs Youth Club, Highgate Hill, N19 (272 1434). Girls football 10am-1pm. Girls' group Mon 7.30-9.30pm.

St Mary's Neighbourhood Centre, Upper St, N1 (354 1387). Girls only room, dance, football, every Mon 7-9pm, rollerskating every Tues 8.30pm. Badminton Thurs 6.30-7.30 Juniors, 7.30-9pm Seniors.

Shelburne Youth Centre, Hornsey Road, N7 (609 0487). Girls' football. Mon and Thurs 7-9pm. Age range 11yrs+.

Tollington Park Youth Centre, Trule Road, N4 (272 4000). Netball Fri 7.30-9.30pm. Music Mon 7-9pm. Age range 11yrs+.

Thomas Coram Foundation, 29 Newington Green, N16 (267 9693). Young mothers' group Wed afternoons, creche provided. Thurs and Fri 10-4pm for unemployed young women, courses run for 6 weeks, programme available.

Whittington Youth Club, Rupert Rd, N19 (263 1443). Girls eve every Tues. Other activities (netball, electronics, craft, hair fashion also available. Contact the club for details.

White Lion Youth Centre, White Lion St, N1 (278 5223). Girls' afternoon, every Sun 2-4pm. Other activities during the week for young women only, such as weight training, judo, drama, self defence, dance. Contact the centre for details. Age range 12-21 yrs.

York Way Club, Delhi St, N1 (837 4694). Girls activities in a mixed club.

YPCA, 62 Eden Grove, Holloway, N7 (607 5176). Girls' night and hairdressing, dance, drama, cooking, photography, arts and outings holidays at times. Thurs eve from 6.30 pm. Age range 11 yrs +. Also run groups (eg health) from time to time. Contact YPCA for details.

Kensington and Chelsea

Kensington and Chelsea Youth Office, 11 Westbourne Grove, W2 4UQ (727 1552).

Bangladesh Centre, 24 Pembridge Gdns, London W2, (229 9404). Girls' and young women's group, weekends mostly. Phone for details.

Chelsea Youth Centre, Hortensia Rd, SW10 (352 2905). Activities for girls and young women (eg, body popping, marquetry and Keep fit). Every Mon, Wed, and Fri evening. Age range 11yrs+.

Kensal Community Centre, 1 Bosworth Rd, W10 (960 0896). Girls' night every Tues, age range 10yrs-21yrs.

Ladbroke Youth Centre, Lancaster Rd, W11 (727 3105). Moroccan girls' sewing group Mon and Wed 4.30-6.30pm age range school age. **Lancaster West Play Centre,** (727 8390). Girls' night every Wed.

Lancaster Youth Club, 128A Lancaster Rd, W11 1QS (727 1800). Women's night every Wed, creche provided.

Lancaster West Youth Club, (727 4512). Young lesbian group, phone for details.

Quest Girls' Club, Community Hall, Willsham St, W11. Girls' club Wed 6-9pm age range 5-16yrs.

Portobello Project, 49-51 Porchester Rd, W2, (221 4413). Information, advice and counselling for young people, age range 14-25yrs.

Rugby Club, 223 Walmer Rd, W11 (229 7097). Run various groups for young women. Contact the club for further information. Daytime.

St Clement's Youth Club, Sirdar Rd, W11 (229 9259). Girls' night every Fri.

Tabernacle Community Association, Powis Square, Wll (221 5172).

Third Feathers Club, 17 Bramham Gardens, SW5 OJJ (373 2681). Young women's evening, every other Sun 7pm-11pm, age range 17yrs-25yrs.

Venture Club, Wornington Rd, W11 (969 6516). Girls night every Wed.

Lambeth

Lambeth Girls' Project, Vauxhall Primary School, Vauxhall St, SW11 (735 8803/4).

Abeng Youth and Community Centre, 7 Gresham Rd, SW9 (274 5261/737 1628). Young women's group Tues 3.30-9pm.

Alford House, Aveline St, SE11 (735 1519). Young women's group Wed 7-10pm.

Beaufoy Youth Centre, Beaufoy School, Lollard St, SE11 (735 9461). Young women's group Mon 6-8.30pm.

Chesnut Lodge, 48 Palace Rd, SW2 (671 8342). Young women's group, Thurs 11am-4pm, creche provided.

Clapham Community Project, Venn St, SW4 (720 8731). Young women's group, Thurs 7-10pm.

Clapham Youth Centre, Lyham Rd, SW2 (274 3011). Young women's group Tues 8-9pm.

Dorset Road Club, 1 Sherbourne Hse, Bolney Rd, SW8 (582 1032). Young women's group Mon 7-10pm.

Gypsies Youth Club, Clive Rd, SE21 (670 1901). Young women's group Tues 7-9pm.

Heath Brook Play Centre, Rhule St, SW8 (720 4353). Young women's group Wed 7-9pm.

Immanuel Youth Centre, Buckleigh Rd, SW16 (764 5944). Young women's group, Tues 7.30-9.30pm.

Kendoa Youth Club, 20 Kendoa Rd, SW4 (720 1410). Young women's group Thurs 5-7pm.

Lambeth Girls' Project, Vauxhall Primary School, Vauxhall St, SE11 (735 8803/4). Contact the Project for details of current groups.

Lambeth Youth Aid, 16 Thornton St, SW9 (274 6760). Young women's group Fri 6-8pm.

Lansdowne Youth Club, 278-280 South Lambeth Rd, SW8 (622 8223). Young women's group Tues 7.30-10pm.

Lillian Baylis School, (Milton room), Lollard St, SE11 (735 2884). Young womens group Fri 9am-1pm.

Marcus Lipton Youth Centre, Minet Rd, SW9 (737 2837). Young womens' group Wed 7-10pm.

Mostyn Road Nursery, Mostyn Rd, SW9 (274 6760). Young women's group, Thurs 1-4pm, creche provided.

Patmore Youth Club, Thessaly Road, SW8 (622 6005). Young women's group Mon 1-4pm (creche provided); Tues 7-10pm.

Rathbone Centre, 8 Chatsworth Way, SE27 (670 7842). Young women's group Tues 9am-3pm.

Vassall Neighbourhood Centre, 145 Brixton Rd, SW9 (735 1378). Young women's group Wed 7-9pm.

Woodvale Girls' Group, Woodvale Tenants Hall, Woodvale Estate, Norwood High St, SE27 (761 3923) (old library). Young women's group Wed 7-9pm.

Lewisham

Young Women's Resource Project, c/o St Mary's Centre, Ladywell Road, SE13 (690 0613).

Athelney Youth Centre, Athelney School, Athelney Street, SE6 (698 5834). Separate activities for girls and young women.

Catford and Bellingham Boys' Club, Randlesdown Road, SE6 (698 4126). Volleyball for girls only, Thurs 7-9pm 12-19 years.

Crofton Youth Centre, Manwood Road, SE4 (690 7213). Young women's group Wed 7-9pm, 16 years plus. Also jewellery classes on Tues and netball on Thurs.

Deptford Green Youth Centre, Deptford Green School, Amersham Vale, (off Edward Street), Deptford, SE14 (692 9383). Girls' group Tues 7-9pm 11-21 years. Netball on Weds and typing on Thurs. Access: P.

Forest Hill Youth Centre, Forest Hill Boys' School, Dacres Road, SE23 (699 9343). A girls-only room with pool and snooker. Girls only groups: Mon - typing and cookery; Tues - haircare, dance, drama, dressmaking and design; Thurs - dance and Unihock. 11-18 years. Access: P.

Grove Centre, 2 Jews Walk, Sydenham, SE26 6PL (659 9363). Girls' night Wed 7.30pm, 14yrs+.

Hearsay Centre, 17 Brownhill Road, Catford, SE6 (697 2152/697 7435).

Advice and information for young people.

Honor Oak Youth Club, 50A Turnham Road, Brockley, SE4 2JD (732 4978). Girls' night Wed 7.00-10.00pm 11yrs+.

Lewisham Way Centre, 138 Lewisham Way, SE14 (692 1190). Black young women's evening every Mon 7-10pm, 16 years plus. Starting soon on Mons. workshop on sexuality and reproduction.

Moonshot Youth Club, Fordham Park, Pagnall Street, New Cross, SE14 (691 8935). Women youth workers available in evenings. Girls only activities: basketball Thurs; netball Mons and Weds; needlecraft Mons and Weds; all at 6-9pm. Trampolining every afternoon 1-4pm. Seven years upwards. Young mothers' club starting soon.

Platform One, Station Approach, 2-4 Devonshire Road, SE23 (291 2428). Young women's group (drama and video), Mon 4-6pm, 15-16 years upwards. Young mothers' group (c/o Joy Robinson), Tues from 1pm (meets in a near-by hall).

Riverside Youth Club, Corner of Oxtails Road, and Grove Street, Deptford, SE8 (692 4611). Girls' night Tues 6.30-8.30pm 13-21 years.

Rockbourne Youth Club, 41A Rockbourne Road, SE23 (699 0163). Black young women's group Mon, Weds, and Fri 11am-3pm, 16 years plus. Creche.

St Andrews Youth Group, St Andrews Centre, Brockley, SE4 (692 5041). Girls' night Fri 8-10pm 14-25 years.

St Mary's Youth Club, Ladywell Road, SE13 (690 2501). Girls only netball Thurs 8pm onwards, 16-18 years.

Schoolhouse, 10 St Johns Vale, SE8 (691 7102). Girls' group Mon 6-9pm, 12-14 years.

South London Gay Youth Group, (697 7435). Mixed gay youth group Mon 7-10pm; young lesbian group Tues 7-10pm. 16 years upwards.

Young Lewisham, 31 Manor Park, Lee, Se13 (318 4509). Unemployed young women's group Wed 12-3pm, 16 years plus. Girls' group at St Swithins Church, 6.30-9.30pm, 16-13 years; other groups from time to time, plus advice and information.

Young Lewisham Motor Vehicle Workshop, 31 Manor Park, Lee, SE13 (690 4957). Run regular courses in car maintenance for girls and women. Young women's morning course in mechanics Thurs 10am-1pm for unemployed young women.

Young Mothers' Project, moving to a new address, contact Young Lewisham (above). Runs groups and activities for young women with children.

Youth Aid, 17 Brownhill Road, Catford, SE6 (697 2152). Catford Young Women's Group Fri 11am-3pm, under 25 years. Includes social events in the evenings and holiday trips. Creche provided. Access: P.

Kingston Upon Thames

Youth and Community Service, Guildhall, Kingston upon Thames, Surrey KT1 1EU, (546 2121 Ext 2710).

Barnfield Youth Club, Parkfields Rd, Park Rd, Kingston upon Thames, (546 6982). Girls night every Thurs 7-10pm, age range 12-21yrs.

Merton

Youth and Community Office, Town Hall, Wimbledon, SW19 7NR (946 8070 ext 24).

Newham

Community Links, 81 High Street South, E6 (472 6652). Girls' group Tues 5.30-7.30pm, 10-13 years. Advice and information session for women (including pregnancy testing) Thurs 6.30-7.30pm. Young mothers' group Fri 10.30am-12.30pm Up to 24 years. Also girls-only summer and Easter holiday projects for 6 to 20 year olds. Mon to Fri 10.00am-4.00pm. Access (A).

East London Black Women's Organisation, 745 Barking Road, Plaistow, E13 9ER (552 1169). A new organisation, interested in developing a young women's section. Phone for more information.

Hartley Centre, Barking Road, E6 (472 1021). Girls' group Thurs 6-8pm, 13 years plus.

Mayflower Centre, Vincent Street, E16 (474 3798). Girls' night Mon from 7pm.

Mayflower Club, Hammersley Avenue, Canning Town, E16 (474 3798). Sports for young women only (hockey, netball, volleyball, etc) Tues 10.30am-12.30pm, 16-25 years.

Out of Work Centre, 66B Sebert Road, Forest Gate, E7 (534 8592). 16-25 years. Presently running groups for black, unemployed women - activities include: learning electrics and computing; mothers and toddlers; swimming; relaxation; and help with numeracy and literacy.

Shipman Youth Centre, Fernhill Street, E16 (474 1189). Girls' night Thurs 7-9.30pm.

Stardust Youth Centre, meets at: Labour Party Rooms, 241E High Street North, E12 (534 6428). Asian Girls' Group Tues from 4.30pm.

Trinity Community Centre, East Avenue, E12 (472 8947). Girls group Tues 4.30-6.30pm, 11 years +.

Upton Centre, Resource Centre for the Unemployed, Plachet Road, E13 (472 1056). Wed is a women only day for 16-25 year olds. Keep fit. Creche available.

Vicarage Youth Centre, Vicarage Junior School, Room 1, Vicarage Lane, E6 (472 3258). Girls' only activities (sports, self defence, drama etc) Tues 7.30-9.45pm. Girls' football team ('Vicarage Wanders') Thurs from 6.30pm.

Westham Youth Centre, Deanery Lane, E15 (534 1771). Girls' night Thurs 6.45-9.45pm.

Redbridge

Education Department, 255-59 High Rd, Ilford, Essex 1G1 1NN, (478 3020). (Principal Youth Officer).

Loxford Youth Centre, Loxford High School, Loxford Lane, Ilford, Essex, (478 4306). Run activity groups (such as dance and self defence) for girls and young women. Groups change all the time so contact the centre for up to date information.

Richmond Upon Thames

The Youth and Community Officer, Town Hall, Regal House, (891 1433).

Townmead Youth Club, Mortlake Rd, Kew, (878 1731). Girls' night every other Sun 6.30-9.30pm, age range 13yrs+.

Southwark

Southwark Girls' Project, New Images, 68b Old kent Rd, SE1.

Blackfriars Settlement Youth Project, 44 Nelson Sq, SE1 (928 9521/633 0383). Young mothers' group Wed 2-4pm; creche provided. Other groups from time to time phone for details.

Charterhouse, The Ark/Rainbow, Crosby Row, SE1 (407 5666). Regular girls groups Mon. Age range 12-14; 14-16; 14-18.

Crossed Swords Youth Club, Lorrimore Sq, SE17 (735 6882). Youth club is open for girls only. Phone for details.

Manor and Ninth Feathers Club, Roseberry St, SE16 3PB (237 6170). Girls' night Thurs 7-9.30pm, age range 13+.

Rockingham Detached Youth Project, 1A Banks House, Rockingham Estate, SE1 (407 3949/403 6168). Runs a girls' project, phone for details.

Southwark Unemployed Youth Project, 58 Comber Grove, SE5 OLD (701 0952). Run groups for young women with children on North Peckham and Brandon estates. Also other groups, information and advice. Age range 16yrs +.

St Giles Youth Centre, Benhill Rd, SE5 (703 5989). Girls' night, one evening a week.

Squires Youth Club, Harper Rd, SE1 (407 3949). Girls' night Tues 7-10pm.

Teenage Information Network, 102 Harper Rd, SE1 (403 2444). Advice, information and counselling for young people. Also run groups (literacy arts and crafts). Phone for details, age range 13-25yrs.

Sutton

Youth and Community Office, Westcroft, Westcroft Rd, Carshalton, Surrey, SM5 2TG (661 5783/661 5784).

Tweedale Activity and Adventure Centre, 66 Tweedale Rd, Carshalton, Surrey SM5 1SQ, (641 2467). Girls' night every Thurs 7-10pm, age range 14-21yrs.

Open Door, 31 West Street, Sutton, SM1 1SJ, (643 3277 day; 643 2440 evening). Confidential counselling service for young people.

Tower Hamlets

Tower Hamlets Girls' Project, The Basement, Old Ford Methodist Church Hall, 522 Old Ford Road, E3 (981 7218).

Asian Girls Project, East End Mission, 583 Commercial Road, E1 (790 3366).

Avenues Unlimited, 162A Brick lane, E1 (247 0933). Have a girls-only room at the Project and also other activites.

Row Baths Community Centre, Sutherland Rd, E3 (981 0666). Girls night Tues 7-10pm. Other girls and young women's activities during day and evenings.

Bow North Young Women's Group, 161-7 Parnell Rd, E3 (980 0438).

Burdett Matchbox Girls' Club, Burdett Matchbox Centre, Burdett Estate, E14 (987 6297).

FBY Montefiore Centre, Deal St and Hanbury St, E1 (247 8818/9). Girls' and women's groups starting soon. Phone for details.

Greenlight Youth Club, c/o THCRE, Montefiore Schoolkeeper's House, Hanbury St, E1 (274 9472). Groups for Afro-Caribbean young women.

Kingsley Hall Community Centre, Powis Rd, E3 (981 5017). Girls' night one evening a week.

Montifiore Community Education Centre, Deal St, Hanbury St, E1 (247 5028). Various girls' and young women's groups, including Bengali girls' and young women's groups. Day and evenings.

Ranwell Girls' Group, (981 3202). Girls' and young women's group, 7-10pm.

Saxon Youth Club, Saxon Rd, E3 (980 0054). Girls' night one evening a week.

'Shejuti', Mulberry School for Girls, Richard St, Commercial St, E1 (790 3366). Girls' group for asian girls, Mon 6-9pm. Badminton Thurs 11-23yrs.

Tower Hamlets Youth Unemployment Project, 212 Whitechapel Rd, E1 (247 4948). Contact: Barbara Sansome. Groups for unemployed young women. Advice and information.

Wessex Community Centre, Wessex St, E2, (980 2588). Groups for girls and young women.

Waltham Forest

Youth and Community Service, Town Hall, Forest Rd, E17 (527 5544 Ext 5157).

Asian Centre, Oxford Rd, E17, (520 4511). The Centre's social and recreational facilities are available to girls and young women only every Wed, 6-10pm. Access: P.

Daytime Provision Unit, Pastures Youth Centre, Davies Lane, E11 (556 2326). Young mother's groups every Thurs, 12.30-4pm. 16-25yrs; creche provided. Access: A.

Leyton Youth Centre, Crawley Rd, E10 (539 1924). Young mother's group every Tues and Fri, 1.30-4.30pm. 16-25yrs; creche provided.

Pastures Youth Centre, Davies Lane, E11 (539 5469). Girls' night every Thurs 7-10pm. 13 years upwards. A creche can be provided. Access: A.

Under Twenty-One, Chesnuts house, 398 Hoe St, E17 (558 0811/558 3163). Information, advice counselling and pregnancy testing for young people, Mon to Fri 10am-7pm.

Waltham Forest Girls' Project,* 397 High St, Leyton, E10 (556 5849). Educational and social activities for girls and young women; age range 14yrs upwards.

Walthamstow Youth Centre, Markhouse Rd, E17 8BD (520 5761). The centre has a girls only unit which may be used when the centre is open. On Tues there is a youthworker just for girls. Starting soon will be girls only groups at the two local girls schools.

Warwick Youth Centre, Barrett Rd, E17 (520 2434). Young mother's group every Thurs afternoon, 16-25yrs.

Wandsworth

Youth Office, 92 St John's Hall, SW11 (228 6693).

Alton Youth Club, Dilton Gardens, SW15 (788 1830). Girls night Tues 7pm-10pm, 13yrs-21yrs.

Ashburton Youth Club, Westleigh Ave, Putney, SW15 (788 5151). Girls night Weds 7-10pm.

Balham Youth Centre, Hydeburn School, Chestnut Grove, SW12 (673 2635). Young Women's Group (basketry, sewing, keep fit, netball and trompoline). Fri - 6-8pm, 15 years upwards - creche available.

Balham Youth Project, 91 Bedford Hill, SW12 (673 8313). Girls' night Wed 6.30-9.30pm, 12-18 years.

Battersea Project, Old Chesterton School, 100-116 Battersea Pk Rd, SW11 4LY, (622 9231). Unemployed young women and young mothers group. Fridays 10.30am-4pm. Creche provided (held at Shillington Adult Education Institute, Est Rd, SW11). Asian young womens group Fri 1-4pm, 20-25yrs.

Battersea Youth Advice Centre, 22 Battersea Pk Rd, SW11 4HY (720 9409). Advice and information (including legal advice) for young people.

Brocklebank Youth Club, Anchor Mission, Garratt Lane, SW18. Girls only activities Tues 7-10pm.

Central Wandsworth Project, 92 St Johns Hill, SW11 (228 6693). Activities for girls + young women.

Central Wandsworth Youth Advisory Service, 97 East Hill, SW18 2QD (870 5818). Advice, information and confidential counselling for young people, 15yrs-21yrs.

Devas Youth Club, 2A Stormont Rd, SW11 5EN (223 0297). Girls night Activities for girls only. 11yrs-14yrs.

Fitzhugh Youth Centre, Fitzhugh Estate, Trinity Rd, SW18 (874 6253). Girls' group Mon evenings, 12yrs plus.

Garfield Youth Group, Garfield Community Centre, 64 Garfield Rd, SW11, (223 8220). Girls' night Mon 7-10pm, 11yrs-16yrs.

Katherine Low Settlement, 108 Battersea High St, SW11 (223 2845). Girls' group Fri 6-8pm.

Lara Youth Club, 92c St Johns Hill, SW11 (223 1828/2422). Girls' night Weds evenings.

The Rock Youth Club, Magdalen Rd, SW18 (947 5109). Girls night Wed 7.30-10pm, 14yrs-22yrs.

Roehampton Boys Club, Holybourne Ave, Roehampton, SW15 (788 9255). Football, five-a-side, netball and dancing for girls only. Mon and Thurs, 7-10pm, age range 9yrs-21yrs.

Shaftesbury Christian Centre, 3 Austin Rd, SW11 (622 4360). Girls group Tues 7-9.30pm.

St Boniface Youth Club, St Boniface Church, 185 Mitcham Rd, SW17 9PG (672 2345). Girls' night Mon 7-10pm.

Tooting Youth Project, St Peters Church Hall, Beechcroft Rd, SW17 (672 9562). Activities for Afro-Carribbean young women.

Westhill Project, Ackroyden Estate, Windlesham grove, SW19 (874 4730). Activities for girls and young women.

Westside Club, Windlesham Grove, SW19 (788 1338). Girls' night Thurs 7-10pm, 14yrs-20yrs.

Wilditch Youth Clubm, Windlesham Grove, SW19 (223 9990). Girls night Thurs, 7-10pm, 14-20yrs.

Wandsworth Unemployed Youth Project, 92 St Johns Hill, SW11 (228 7136). Groups and activities for girls + young women only (including a womens sounds group). 16yrs +.

York Gardens Community Centre, Lavender Rd, SW11 2UQ (223 7961). Girls night Wed 7-9pm, 12yrs +.

Westminster

Westminster Girls' Project*, 48 Great Peter Street, SW1 (222 6327).

Avenues Project, 3-7 Third Avenue, W10 (969 9552). Girls night one evening a week.

The Base, Bravington Rd, (Off Harrow Rd), (960 5029). Rastafarian women's cultural group, every Wed, daytime.

The Base, Maryfields Study Centre, Bravington Rd, W9 (960 5029). Girls' night one evening a week.

The Centre at St Martin, 12 Adelaide St, WC1 (930 2561). Young women's groups, 16-24yrs.

Cockpit Theatre, Gateforth St, NW8 (262 6935). Girls' night, music and drama groups, one evening a week.

Cosway Street Detached Project, Marylebone/Paddington AE1, 29 Cosway St, NW1 (723 6564). Girls' night one evening a week.

Ebury Bridge Youth Club, 1 Ebury Bridge Rd, SW1 (730 0571). Girls' night one evening a week.

Elimu Project, 470 Harrow Rd, W9 (289 7320). Girls' night for Black young girls.

Fourth Feathers Youth Club, 12 Rossmore Rd, NW1 6NU (723 8308). Girls' night one evening a week.

Lillington Gardens Youth Club, Community Cente, (Under Morgan house), Lillington gardens, SW1 (834 0777). Girls' night one evening a week.

Moberly Youth Centre, Kilburn Lane, W10 (969 4083). Drama work with young women. Contact Liz York.

The Mozart Project, 62 Third Ave, W10. Unemployed young women's group meets during the day.

North Paddington Boys Club, 235 Lanark Road, W9 (624 4089). Girls' work one evening a week. Contact Mavis Phipps.

Oneness group, 27-37 Broadley Terrace, NW8. Single parent's group, daytime meetings.

Quintin Kynaston School, Youth and Community Centre, Marlborough Hill, NW8 (722 8141). Girls' night one evening a week.

Sarah Siddons Youth Centre, North Wharf Rd, W2 (723 2522). Girls' night one evening a week. Asian young women's group starting.

Westminster Girls Project, 48 Great peter Street, SW1 (222 6327). Unemployed young women's group and many other evening events for young women.

Westminster Youth Advisory Service, 22 Mozart St, W10 (969 3825). General information and counselling for young people, 14-22yrs, Mon-Fri 2-5pm.

Family Planning Clinics for Young People

Times given are for young people's sessions.

Barnet

Vale Drive Clinic, Vale Drive, Barnet (441 0745). Thurs 6.30-8.30pm.

Brent

Pound Lane Clinic, Pound Lane, NW10 (459 5116). Tues 5.30pm. Appointments as necessary.

Chalk Hill Health Centre, Chalk Hill Estate, Wembley Park, Middlesex (908 0404). Wed walk-in clinic 5.30-7pm.

Bromley

Bromley Youth Advisory Service, Beckenham Hospital, Croydon Road, Beckenham, Kent (650 0125). Tues 7-9pm.

Camden

Brook Advisory Centre, 233 Tottenham Court Road, WC1 (267 4792). Appointment only, daily 10am-5pm.

Croydon

The Annexe, Lodge Road Clinic, Croydon, Surrey (684 9123). Tues 5-7pm, appointments unnecessary.

Parkway Health Centre, Parkway, New Addington, Surrey (664 2117). Wed 3.30-5.30pm.

Purley Hospital, Brighton Road, Purley, Surrey (660 0177). Mon 7-9pm.

Dulwich

Youth Advisory Clinic, Dulwich Hospital, East Dulwich Grove, SE22 (274 6222 Ext 2662). Wed 5pm.

Ealing

Youth Advisory Session, 13 Mattock Lane, Ealing, W5 (567 2006). Wed 5.30pm.

Enfield

Silver Street Clinic, Silver Street, Edmonton, N18 (807 8321). Tues 6.30-8.30pm.

Greenwich

Blackheath Family Planning Clinic, Welfare Centre, Langton Way, SE3 (858 8898). Mon 7pm.

Hackney

Richmond Road Centre, 136 Richmond Road, E8 (254 6374). 1st Tues in month 5.30-7.00pm, Thurs 5.30-7pm.

Hammersmith

The Family Planning Association, 160 Shepherd's Bush Road, W6 (602 2723). Wed 9.30am-3.30pm 6pm. Sat 9.30am.

Haringey

Fortis Green Clinic, 150 Fortis Green Road, N10 (444 9754). Thurs 6.30pm.

Harrow

Caryl Thomas Clinic, Headstone Drive, Wealdstone, Middlesex (863 7004). Mon 4.45pm.

Cecil Park Clinic, Cecil Park, Pinner, Middlesex (863 7004). Tues 4.45pm.

Islington

Finsbury Health Centre, Pine Street, EC1 (837 6363/4) Mon 5.30pm.

Brook Advisory Clinic, Manor Gardens Centre, 6-9 Manor Gardens, N7 (580 2991). Tues 1.30-4pm, Thurs 4.30-7pm.

Lambeth

Brockwell Clinic, 47 Tulse Hill, SW2 (674 3502). Tues 4.30pm.

Brook Advisory Centre, Moffat Centre, 65 Sancroft Road, SE11 (703 7880). Wed 4.30pm.

Lewisham

Central Lewisham Hospital, 410 Lewisham High Street, SE13 (703 9660/7880). Wed 4.30pm.

Merton

Patrick Doody Clinic, Pelham Crescent, Wimbledon, SW19 (543 4777). Tues 4pm.

Richmond

Kings Road Clinic, Kings Road, Richmond, Surrey (948 0251). Tues 6.30pm.

Romford

Eastern Road Clinic, 49 Eastern Road, Romford, Essex (704 4702). Thurs 5.45pm. Appointments only.

Southwark

Brook Advisory Clinic, 153A East Street, SE17 (703 7880). Daily 9.30am-7.30pm, Sat 9.30am.

Kings College Hospital, Denmark Hill, SE5 (274 6222 Ext 2662). Wed 5.30pm.

Sutton

St Helier Hospital, Wrythe Lane, Carshalton, Surrey (644 4343). Mon 6.30pm.

Tower Hamlets

Gill Street Health Centre, Gill Street, E14 (987 4433). Thurs 4.30pm.

Waltham Forest

Leyton Green Clinic, Leyton Green Road, E10 (539 8646). Tues 6.30pm.

Wandsworth

Brook Advisory Clinic, St Christopher's Health Centre, Wheeler Court, Plough Road, SW11 2AY (703 9660 and 223 7222 (session times only). Tues 4.30-8pm, Fri 4.30-8pm.

Westminster

Youth Advisory Clinic, 21 Portnall Road, W9 (969 3825). Wed 5.30pm.

There are also **Brook Advisory Clinics** (specialising in advice to young people) in: Newham, Brixton, Stockwell, and Lewisham. Ring Brook Advisory Centre (580 2991) for details.

Useful Reading

Changing Bodies, Changing Lives, Ruth Bell. Published by Random House. An American book covering the physical and emotional aspects of adolescence and sexuality. £4.80.

Girls are Powerful, edited by Susan Hemmings. Sheba. A collection of writings by young women first published in *Shocking Pink* and *Spare Rib* magazine.

Growing Up, published by Guide Books. A health book for young people of Afro-Caribbean descent, published in Jamaica. £2.90.

Have you started yet?, Ruth Thomson. Piccolo (a book about periods). £1.25.

Make it Happy, Jane Cousins. Penguin. A book for young people about sex and sexuality. £1.50.

Young Gay and Proud, Sasha Alyson. Alyson Publications. A book about gay and lesbian young people. £1.95.

Notes

Notes

Notes

Notes

Borough Information

This section gives details about what is available in the individual boroughs. The information in this section is listed in alphabetical order of the 32 London Boroughs plus the City of London. Within each borough the following information is listed:

MPs

Who the borough's MPs are and what political party they represent. All MPs can be written to c/o Member's Lobby, House of Commons, SW1 AA.

GLC Councillors Note that on abolition of the GLC there are no longer GLC councillors.

Borough Councils

This entry begins with details of where to address general enquiries to at the council. Some Councils have a good information service and can tell you about a wide range of things to do with the area of London. Others see their role as limited to information about the Council services.

Several London boroughs now have a Women's Committee with a Support Unit, a Women's Sub-Committee or Women's Policy Advisor of some kind. Depending on their resources and policies they work to change the role of women, as employees, within the council itself and to improve women's participation in decision-making at local government level; to improve the overall services of the council for women; and to provide information and to promote the welfare and interests of all women in their local communities. A Women's Committee will often involve the active participation of 'co-opted members' from the local community to keep them informed of local opinion and advise on specific issues: eg employment, housing, and on the needs of specific groups: eg women with children, Black women and women from other ethnic groups, lesbians, women with disabilities, older and younger women. Make direct contact if you have an enquiry, or a complaint, or if you would like to receive their publications or be informed of any local advisory meetings. It is sometimes possible to obtain childcare/dependency allowances so that you can attend these meetings. Ring them for details.

Also listed are the contact details for a council's Ethnic Minorities Committee, Race Relations Advisor or equivalent and details of any lesbian and gay working party's that exist. For enquiries and issues concerning people with disabilities most councils refer to the

Social Services Department. Finally, where a council has an equal opportunities policy we have listed that council's equal opportunities 'statement' as it appears in job advertisements. Sometimes, despite considerable effort, it was not possible to get information from a council about equal opportunity matters - hence 'no information' appears in that section.

Women's Centres

Women's Centres are valuable places for local women to meet and talk. A variety of services can be provided including pregnancy testing, social security advice, self-defence classes, skill-sharing and many other activities. Some run a creche on the premises. They are women-only spaces and have notice boards announcing socials and services offered. Most can give details and contacts for women's groups that meet regularly in your local area. As they are often staffed by only one worker it's best to telephone first before visiting. If there isn't a centre in your borough phone A Woman's Place (see **Women's Resources and Campaigning**) for a local contact, advertise in *Spare Rib* magazine Classifieds Section (see **Media and Arts**, Women's Publications) or contact the nearest women's centre in a neighbouring borough.

Advice Centres

These are listed in the following order: Community Relations Councils, Advice and Law Centres, Citizen's Advice Bureaux and then a selection of agencies that either specialise in a particular area, run women's advice sessions or provide the service in translation as indicated.

Barking and Dagenham

MPs

Barking Jo Richardson (Lab), Dagenham B Gould (Lab).

Borough Council

General enquiries to Press and Public Relations Office, Civic Centre, Dagenham, Essex, RM10 7BN (592 4500). Access: P. Equal Opportunities: 'no information'.

Advice Centres

Barking and Dagenham Councils for Racial Equality, First Floor Office, Methodist Church Building, London Road, Barking, Essex, IG11 8AL (594 2773). Access: N (but will visit by appointment).

Barking Citizens Advice Bureau, Methodist Church, London Road, Barking, Essex (594 6715). Mon 10-12, Wed 6-8, Thurs 10-12, Fri 10-12. Access: A. Also session at Centre for the Unemployed, Abbey Hall, Axe Road, Barking Mon and Fri 1.30-3.30.

Dagenham Citizens Advice Bureau, 383 Heathway, Dagenham, RM9 5AG (592 1084). Mon, Tues, Wed, Fri 10-1, Thurs 2-3.30., 6-7 Access: A.

Barnet

MPs

Chipping Barnet Sydney Chapman (Con), Finchley Margaret Thatcher (Con), Hendon North John Gorst (Con), Hendon South Peter Thomas (Con).

Borough Council

General enquiries to Information Office, The Burroughs, Hendon, NW4 4BE (202 8282). Access: A. Enquiries regarding people with disabilities to the Social Services Committee, Services for Physically Handicapped, Fiboard House, Oakleigh Gardens, N20 (446 4354). Equal Opportunities: Barnet Council is taking positive action to ensure that in all aspects of its role as an employer it is totally non-discriminatory, giving equal opportunity to all.

Women's Centres

Women in Barnet Action Group*, 3rd Floor, 375a Regent's Park Road, Finchley Central, N3 1DE (346 8858) 10-4 (phone first). Access: N (although they organised courses for women at separate premises with disabled access.)

Barnet Mobile Centre, c/o 375a Regent's Park Road, N3 (801-345 8858). Converted ambulance with lift for wheelchairs, which travels the local Borough working as resource centre, creche and meeting place for women. Has library, with non-sexist children's books and is available for use by other groups in Barnet, especially women's groups.

Advice Centres

Barnet Community Relations Council, 1 Friern Park, North Finchley, N12 9DE (445 6051). Access: N.

Barnard House, 158 Burnt Oak Broadway, Burnt Oak, Edgware, Middlesex. Legal advice on housing, employment, immigration, welfare benefits, children and family law, personal injury, crime, consumer advice (LB of Barnet only). Tues 6.30-8 Correspondence: 64 Sunny Gardens, Hendon, NW4 (203 1338).

East Barnet Citizens Advice Bureau, Town Hall, Station Road, New Barnet, Herts (449 9181 ext.24; 441 2384). Advice and information Mon-Wed, Fri 10-4, Thurs 10-1. Legal advice Tues 6-7 (by appointment).

East Finchley Neighbourhood Centre, 42 Church Lane, N2 (444 6265). General advice Mon-Fri 10-12, Mon-Wed 2-4.

Edgware and District Citizens Advice Bureau, Watling Community Centre, 145 Orange Hill Road, Burnt Oak, Edgware, HA8 0TR (959 0915). Advice and information Mon, Thurs 10-1, Tues 1-5, Sat 10-12.30.

Finchley Citizens Advice Bureau, Hertford Lodge Annexe, East End Road, N3 (349 0954). Advice and information Mon-Fri 9.30-12.30, Thurs 6.30-8.30.

Friern Barnet Citizens Advice Bureau, Priory Hall, Friern Barnet Lane, N11 3LU (361 0727). Advice and information Mon, Tues, Thurs 10-3; Fri 10-1.

Grahame Park Citizens Advice Bureau, The Concourse, Grahame Park, Hendon, NW9 5XA (205 4141). Advice and information Mon 10-1, 3-7; Tues-Fri 10-5.

Hendon (Bell Lane) Citizens Advice Bureau, 25 Bell Lane, Hendon, NW4 2BP (203 5801). Advice and information Mon-Fri 10-5. Legal advice alternate Weds 6.30-8 (by appointment). Financial advice Wed 6.30-8 (by appointment).

Hendon West Citizens Advice Bureau, 133 West Hendon Broadway, NW9 7DX (202 5177). Advice and information Mon 10-1, 4.30-7.30, Tues-Fri 10-5. Legal advice alternate Mons 6-7 (by appointment).

Sangam Association of Asian Women, 235-237 West Hendon Broadway, NW9 7DH (202 4629). Consultation and advice on social welfare, health, housing, employment, legal and immigration issues, family and marital problems Mon-Tues 10-6.30, Thurs 10-5.30, Fri 11-7, Saturday 10-2. Group discussions held at 154 Station Road, NW4.

Bexley

MPs

Bexley Heath Cyril Townsend (Con), Erith Crayford D. A. Evennett (Con), Old Bexley Sidcup Edward Heath (Con)

Borough Council

General enquiries can be made to the Civic Offices, Broadway, Bexleyheath, DA6 7LB (303 777). Access: A. Enquiries regarding people with disabilities to the Social Services Sub-Committee, c/o Housing and Personal Services Secretary at address above. On Equal Opportunities the Council's policy is not to discriminate either for or against any person on the grounds of colour, race, creed, nationality, ethnic or national origin, sex or marital status.

Advice Centres

Bexley Council for Racial Equality, Riverside Baths, 3 Walnut Tree Road, Erith, Kent, DA8 1RA (0322 340316). Access: N.

Bexleyheath Citizens Advice Bureau, Graham Road, Bexleyheath, Kent, DA6 7EG (304 5619). Advice and information Mon-Fri 10-1, Mon, Thurs 1-4. Legal advice alternate Weds evenings. Access: A.

Erith Citizens Advice Bureau, 1 Walnut Tree Road, Erith, Kent (Erith 40481). Advice and information Mon-Tues 10-4, Wed, Fri 10-1.

Sidcup Citizens Advice Bureau, 7 Hadlow Road, Sidcup, Kent, DA14 4AA (300 7804). Advice and information Mon, Tues, Fri 10-4, Wed-Thurs 10-1. Financial advice alternate Tues 7.30-9. Legal advice Tues, Wed 2-4.

Thamesmead Citizens Advice Bureau, 97 Binsey Walk, SE2 9TX (310 0108). Advice and information Mon-Fri 10-1, Mon 1-4. (Chinese/Vietnamese interpreters available Tues, Thurs mornings.) Access: A.

Welling Citizens Advice Bureau, Springfield Road Car Park, Welling, Kent (303 5100). Advice and information Mon, Thurs 10-4, Tues, Wed, Fri 10-1. Correspondence c/o The Pop In Parlour, Rear of 99 High Street, Welling, Kent, DA16 1TY. Access: A.

Brent

MPs

Brent East Reginald Freeson (Lab), Brent North Dr Rhodes Boyson (Con), Brent South Laurie Pavitt (Lab)

Borough Council

General enquiries to Chief Public Relations Officer, Brent Town Hall, Forty Lane, Wembly, HA9 9HX (903 1400 ext.8206). Access: A.

The Council has a Women's Sub-Committee with a liaison Chair only. Ellen Reynolds, the Women's Information and Resource Worker can be contacted at the Town Hall (903 1400 ext.8257).

Hazel Taylor is the Equal Opportunities Adviser in the Education Department, Chesterfield House, Wembley, Middlesex (903 1400 ext.8577).

There is a Race Relations Sub-Committee. Russell Profitt is the Principal Race Relations Adviser. There are five workers in the central unit Room 78 at Town Hall (903 1400 ext.8357) and five workers in other departments.

On Equal Opportunities the Council's Draft Code of Practice lists no discrimination on the grounds of 'race, colour, nationality, or ethnic or national origins, age, marital status, sex, sexual orientation, disability or is disadvantaged by conditions or requirements which cannot be seen to be justified'.

Women's Centres

Brent Women's Centre*, 232 Willesden High Road, NW10 (459 7660). Hours 10.30-5.30 Weds/Thurs/Fris. Creche on Mon/Tues/Wed/ Thurs. Access: A.

Asian Women's Resource Centre (Brent)*, 134 Minet Avenue, NW10 (961 5701). Hours 10-6 Tues/Thurs/Fri. Access: A to ground floor only (no toilet).

St Raphael Women's Workshop, 46 Henderson Close, NW10 (459 2501). Hours 9-5 weekdays/Creche 8.30-4 weekdays. Access: A.

Advice Centres

Brent Community Relations Council, 194 High Road, Willesden, NW10 (451 4499 and 4490). Access: A.

Brent Law Centre, 190 High Road, Willesden, NW10 (451 1122 - answering machine outside working hours).

Brent Young Person's Law Centre (for people up to the age of 21), 272 Willesden High Road, NW10 (451 2428) Mon-Fri 9.30-6.

Brent Mobile Citizens Advice Bureau, various sites around the Borough. Advice and information taken to areas and client groups (e.g., disabled or elderly people) who find it difficult to get to advice services. Correspondence to 154 Manor Park Road, NW10 4JR (965 5821).

Cricklewood Citizens Advice Bureau, 87 Cricklewood Broadway, NW2 (450 2407). Advice and information Mon-Fri 10-3; Tues 6.30-7.30. Legal and financial advice Tues 6.30-7.30 (by appointment).

Harlesden Citizens Advice Bureau, 156 Manor Park Road, NW10 (965 5821). Advice and information by appointment. Open Mon, Tues, Fri 10-12.15, Wed 2-4 for making appointments or for advice on urgent problems.

Wembley Citizens Advice Bureau, 501 High Road, Wembley, Middlesex, HAO 2DH (902 5177). Advice and information Mon, Tues, Thurs, Fri 10-4, Mon 7-8.30. Legal advice Mon 6-7, two weeks out of three (by appointment). Financial advice Mon 6-7, one week out of three (by appointment).

Willesden Citizens Advice Bureau, 270-272 High Road, Willesden, NW10 (451 4355). Advice and information Mon-Wed, Fri 10-12, 2-3, Thurs 10-12. Legal advice Tues 6.30-8 (by appointment).

Asian Rehabilitation Community Projects, 25 Dagmar Avenue, Wembley, Middlesex (903 7579, 24-hour service). General and legal advice, and Tribunal representation Mon-Fri 9.30-5.30. (Preferably by appointment.)

Brent Community Law Centre, 190 High Road, Willesden, NW10 (451 1122 during office hours. Answering machine outside working hours.) Advice and assistance on legal and administrative matters, for people who live or work in the LB of Brent only, by appointment only. Office hours Mon, Tues, Thurs, Fri 9.30-1, 2-5.30, Wed 2-5.30.

Brent Irish Advisory Service, Information Centre, 76 Salusbury Road, Kilburn, NW6 6NY (624 9991). Information, advice and welfare support, for Irish people Wed 3-7. Other times, by appointment Mon-Fri 9.30-1, 2-5.30.

Harlesden Advice Centre, 25 High Street, NW10 (965 2590 or 7305). Advice and information on housing, welfare, employment, immigration and nationality rights, fuel debts Mon, Wed 10.30-12.30, Tues, Thurs 2-4, other times by appointment.

London Borough of Brent Youth Advice Centre, 38 Craven Park Road, Harlesden, NW10 4AB (961 4100/4101/4102/4103). Advice and information, mainly for ethnic minority young people Mon-Wed, Fri 10-6, Thurs 10-1.

Ten Twenty Project, 1020 Harrow Road, NW10 5NS (960 3043 or 969 7474). Advice and information Mon-Thurs 10-1, 2-5, Fri by appointment. Estate Officer last Tues of month, 2pm. Councillor third Thurs of month, 6pm. Career Officer fortnightly. (Spanish, Hindi, Gujerati, West Indian languages spoken.)

Bromley

MPs

Beckenham Sir Philip Goodhard (Con), Chislehurst Roger Sims (Con), Orpington Ivor Stanbrook (Con), Ravensbourne: John Hunt (Con)

Borough Council

General enquiries to Bromley Civic Centre, Rochester Avenue, Bromley, BR1 3UH (464 333). Access: A. There is also an enquiry point in the Education Department at the Town Hall, Widmore Road, Bromley, BR1 1SB. For people with disabilities contact Director of Social Services, Mike Carpenter at the Town Hall.

Advice Centres

Beckenham Citizens Advice Bureau, The Old Town Hall, Church Avenue, Beckenham, Kent (650 1617). Advice and information Mon. Tues, Fri 10-4, Wed 10-1. Access: A (ring).

Bromley and Chislehurst Citizens Advice Bureau, 83 Tweedy Road, Bromley, Kent (464 6023 or 460 8161). Advice and information Mon-Fri 9.30-5, Sat 10-12. Solicitor, Accountant and Surveyors Aid Scheme Wed evening (by appointment). Access: A.

Orpington Citizens Advice Bureau, Wallis House, 1 Church Hall, Orpington, Kent (Orpington 27732). Advice and information Mon-Fri 10-4. Legal advice Wed 6-7. Access: P (not wheelchairs).

Penge and Anerley Citizens Advice Bureau, St John's Church Annexe, High Street, Penge, SE20 (778 0921). Advice and information (Penge and Anerley) General public Mon, Fri 10-4, Tues, Thurs 10-2. Legal advice Mon evenings (by appointment). Access: A.

Camden

MPs

Hampstead Highgate G Finsberg (Con), Holborn St Pancras Frank Dobson (Lab)

Borough Council

General enquiries to Public Relations Officer, Camden Town Hall, Euston Road, NW1 2RU (278 4444). Access: A.

The Council's Women's Committee is chaired by Anna Bowman and serviced by a Women's Unit. Contact Judy Watson, Room 710E at the Town Hall (278 4444 ext 2738).

The Race and Community Relations Community is chaired by Hugh Bailey and serviced by a Race Relations Unit headed by Rashid Mofti.

For the Disabled Person's Liaison Group (Social Services) contact Social Services. For the Mental Health Liaison Group (Social Services) contact Caroline Gladstone in the Communications Unit on 837 3363.

For the Disabled Persons Sub-Committee (Staff and MS) contact Dave McDonnell. Lesbian issues are dealt with by the Women's Unit (see above). Lesbians and gay men (employees only) contact Sue Olley in the Equal Opportunities Unit at the Town Hall.

Camden's Equal Opportunities Policy states, 'Applicants are considered on the basis of their suitability for the post. Applications are invited from women, ethnic minorities, lesbians and gay men, and people with disabilities and regardless of marital status, age, creed/religion and unrelated criminal conviction. All posts are open for job-sharing.'

Women's Centres

Camden Women's Mobile Bus Advice and Information Centre*, c/o 213 Eversholt Street, NW1 (380 0304). Mobile Women's Centre working as information and advice centre in Camden area and active in local campaigns. Feeds ideas into the Council's Women's Committee.

Camden Lesbian Centre, c/o 2 Malden Road, NW5. Currently looking for new premises but hopes to open soon. Telephone 267 1402 for details.

Cromer Street (Kings Cross), 90 Cromer Street, WC1 (278 0120). Hours 10-5 Mon/Tues/Fri, 10-1 Wed. Access: A.

Kentish Town Women's Workshop*, 169 Malden Road, NW5 (267 0688). Hours 10-6 weekdays. Access: A.

Tonbridge Street (Kings Cross) Women's Centre, 71 Tonbridge Street, WC1 (837 7509). Hours 11-5 weekdays. Access: P.

West Hampstead Women's Information and Employment Advisory Centre, 55 Hemstell Road, NW6 (328 7389). Hours 11-5 weekdays (phone first as they are often working outside). Access: A.

Advice Centres

Camden Committee for Community Relations, 58 Hampstead Road, NW1 2PY (387 1125). Access: P.

Camden Community Law Centre, 146 Kentish Town Road, NW1 (485 6672 Mon, Tues, Wed, Fri 10-6, Thurs 2-6, and 24 hour emergency service). Legal advice on housing, employment, race and immigration, mental health, education and other general advice, for people who live or work in Camden, north of Euston Road and east of Finchley Road, Mon, Wed 10-5, Fri 10-4 (languages include Bengali, Hindi and Punjabi). Access: P.

Central London Community Law Centre, Fitzrovia Neighbourhood Association, 39 Tottenham Street, W1. Legal advice on housing, employment, immigration, planning, social security, for people who live in Fitzrovia, Wed 5.30-7. Correspondence 13 Ingestre Place, W1 (437 5764 Mon-Fri 10-5.30). Access: N.

West Hampstead Community Law Centre, 59 Kingsgate Road, NW6 (328 4501 or 328 4523 Mon-Fri 10-6, 485 6672 in emergency, 24 hours). Legal advice and representation on employment, housing, juvenile crime, immigration/nationality, race, women's rights, social welfare, for people who live or work in West Hampstead only, and local community groups Mon, Tues, Fri 11-2, Wed, Thurs 4-7. Other times, Mon-Fri 10-6, by appointment. Access: A.

Hampstead Citizens Advice Bureau, Oriel Hall, Oriel Place, NW3 1QN (435 4200 or 435 0048). Advice and information Mon-Wed, Fri 10-4, Thurs 10-1. General advice Mon evening (by appointment). Legal advice Mon 6-8 (by appointment). Access: N.

Highgate New Town Citizens Advice Bureau, 60 Chester Road, N19 5BZ (272 5519). Advice and information Mon-Wed, Fri 10-1, 2-5, Thurs 10-1, 5-7.30. Legal advice Thursday 5-7.30 (by appointment). Local MP and local Councillor third Thurs each month. Access: N.

Kentish Town Advice Bureau, 242 Kentish Town Road, NW5 2AB (485 7034 or 267 1150). Advice and information, with specialist consumer unit Mon-Wed, Fri 10-3, Thurs, Sat 10-1. Legal advice Sat 10-1 (by appointment). Session for Vietnamese Thurs 10-1. Access: P (no WC).

Kings Cross Citizens Advice Bureau, 74 Marchmont Street, WC1 (837 9341). Advice and information Mon-Wed, Fri 10-4, Thurs 10-1, 6-8. Legal advice Thurs 6-8. Financial advice Thurs 6.30-7.30 every two weeks (by appointment). Access: P (no WC).

Swiss Cottage Citizens Advice Bureau, 94 Avenue Road, NW3 3EX (722 3228 or 586 3882). Advice and information Mon-Wed, Fri 10-4, Thurs 10-1, 6.15-8. Legal or financial advice Thurs 6.15-8 (by appointment). Access: A.

West Hampstead Citizens Advice Bureau, 200 Kilburn High Road, NW6 (624 5906 or 624 2007). Advice and information, with specialist advice in consumer and Small Claims Court matters Mon, Wed 10-5, Tues, Fri 10-3, Thurs 10-1. Legal advice Mon 6.30-8 (by appointment).

Camden Girls Centre Project, 4 Caversham Road, NW5 (267 2898). Advice and information on family and personal matters, social security benefits, health, housing and leisure, for young women, aged 16-21, Mon 11-4. Groups for young women, young mothers, Afro-Caribbean, Asian/Bengali, etc. meet at various times (enquiries initially to the Project).

Chinese Information and Advice Centre*, 152-156 Shaftesbury Avenue, WC2 (836 8291 or 379 5098). General advice, and specialist advice on housing, employment, welfare and family rights, racial or sexual discrimination, immigration and nationality, student problems Sun 11-4, Mon-Wed, Fri 11-5. Staff meetings and training Thurs 11-1, 2-6, but clients seen if they turn up at the Centre. (Mainly serves the needs of the Chinese Community in Greater London.)

Kings Cross Women's Centre, 71 Tonbridge Street, WC1 (837 7509). Information, advice and referral services for women, including support for problems of racial and sexual assault or harassment, rape, prostitution, immigration, social security, child benefit, custody, health, and housing Mon-Fri 11-5. Legal Action for Women Thurs 6-8 (Legal advice from women lawyers). Correspondence PO Box 287, NW6 5QU (837 7509).

Mary Ward Financial Advice Centre, 42 Queen Square, WC1N 3AJ (831 7079). Advice on tax, debt-handling, bankruptcy, redundancy pay, social security and welfare benefits for people who cannot afford the services of an accountant Mon, Wed 6.30-8.30. Home visits to house-bound clients in the Camden area (by appointment).

Mary Ward Legal Centre, 42 Queen Square, WC1N 3AJ (831 7000). Legal advice to clients and other agencies Mon-Wed, Fri 9.30-5.30, Thurs 9.30-7. Home visits to disabled people in the Camden area (by appointment).

Network for the Handicapped Ltd, 16 Princeton Street, WC1R 4BB (831 8031 or 831 7740). Legal advice, assistance and information, for disabled and handicapped people and their families Mon-Fri during office hours (by appointment only). House-bound clients are visited in their homes.

Network for the Handicapped Ltd, Bedford House, 35 Emerald Street, WC1N 3QL (405 2370 or 405 2379 Thurs evenings only). Legal advice, assistance and information, for disabled and handicapped people and their families Thurs from 7.30 (by appointment only). Correspondence: 16 Princeton Street, WC1R 4BB (831 8031 or 831 7740).

Croydon

MPs
Croydon Central John Moore (Con), Croydon NE Bernard Weatherill (Con), Croydon NW H J Malins (Con), Croydon South Sir William Clark (Con)

Borough Council
General enquiries to the Town Clerk, Croydon Town Hall, Taberner House, Park Lane, Croydon, CR9 3JS (686 4433). Access: A. No information given on Equal Opportunities.

Women's Centres
Croydon Women's Centre*, 13 Woodside Green, South Norwood, SE25 (656 2369). Hours 9.30-4.30 weekdays. Access: P.

Advice Centres
Croydon Council for Community Relations, 70 Park Lane, Croydon, CR0 1JE. Access: A.

Addington Citizens Advice Bureau, 1a Overbury Crescent, New Addington, Croydon, CR0 0LR (Lodge Hill 46890). Advice and information Mon-Wed, Fri 10-3.30, Thurs 10-12, 6-7.30. Legal and financial advice Thurs 6-8 (by appointment).

Coulsdon and Purley Citizens Advice Bureau, 105 Brighton Road, Purley, Surrey, CR2 4HD (660 6800). Advice and information Mon, Tues, Thurs, Fri 10-3.30, Wed 10-12, 2.30-7.30 (by appointment). Legal and financial advice Wed 6-7.30.

Croydon Citizens Advice Bureau, Eldon House, 78 Thornton Road, Thornton Heath, Surrey, CR4 6BA (684 9661). Advice and information Mon, Tues 10-12.30, 2-4, Wed 2-4, 6-7.40, Thurs 10-3.30, Fri 10-12.30, 2-3.30. Legal and financial advice Wed 6-7.30 (by appointment).

South Croydon Extension Citizens Advice Bureau, United Church Hall, Aberdeen Road, South Croydon, Surrey, CR0 1EQ (681 3728). Advice and information Mon, Tues, Thurs 11-3. Correspondence Coulsdon and Purley

Citizens Advice Bureau, 105 Brighton Road, Purley, Surrey, CR2 4HD (660 6800).

Upper Norwood Extension Citizens Advice Bureau, United Reformed Church, St Aubyn's Road, off Church Road, Upper Norwood, SW19. Advice and information Tues, Thurs 10-2. Correspondence Croydon Citizens Advice Bureau, Eldon House, 78 Thornton Road, Thornton Heath, Surrey, CR4 6BA (684 9661).

Legal Advice Centre (Croydon Council for Community Relations), 45 Wellesley Road, Croydon, CRO 2AJ (686 8014 or 686 8524). Advice and information Wed 6.30-8.

Ealing

MPs

Ealing Acton Sir George Young (Con), Ealing North Harry Greenway (Con), Ealing Southall Sydney Bidwell (Lab)

Borough Council

General enquiries to Public Relations Officer, Ealing Town Hall, New Broadway, W5 2BY (579 2424). Access: N (main building - but Annexe accessible). Equal Opportunities 'No information'.

Women's Centres

Milap Ladies' Centre (for elderly women), Milap Day Centre, Town Hall Annexe, Southall, Middlesex (574 2311 ext 223). Hours 10-5.30 Mon to Sat. Access: A.

Southall Black Women's Centre* (for Asian and Afro-Caribbean Women), 86 Northcote Avenue, Southall, Middlesex (843 0578). Resource centre and base office for Southall Black Sisters organisation. Hours 9-6 weekdays. Access: A.

West London Women's Centre*, Metrostore, 231 The Vale, Acton, W3 (743 0326). May be moving; phone for details. Hours Wed 10-7. Access: P.

Advice Centres

Ealing Community Relations Council, 2 The Green, High Street, Ealing, W5 5DA (579 3861). Access: A.

Ealing Community Law Centre, Action Green Methodist Church, Steele Road, W4 (995 5127). Opening Hours Mon-Fri 9.30-5.30, Tues 9.30-1, Thurs 2-5.30. Additional sessions at The Viking Centre, Northolt Village Community Centre, Wed 2-5 and 10-1.

Southall Community Law Centre, 14 Featherstone Road, Southall, Middlesex, UB2 5AA (574 2434). Legal advice and representation Mon-Fri 10-6 by appointment. Legal advice for women Thurs morning at the Hindi Temple, King Street and Thurs afternoons at the Hardrick Centre, Hardrick Street (languages: Punjabi and Hindi).

Hanwell Citizens Advice Bureau, Hanwell Community Centre, Westcott Crescent, W7 1PD (578 0171). Advice and information Mon 10-1, 7.30-9, Tues 1.30-3.30, Thurs, Fri 10-1.

Northolt Extension Citizens Advice Bureau, St Richards Church Hall, Sussex Crescent, Northolt, Middlesex (422 9653). Advice and information: Mon, Thurs 10-1. Correspondence Hanwell Citizens Advice Bureau, Hanwell Community Centre, Westcott Crescent, W7 1PD (578 0171).

Acorn Youth Information and Advice Centre, 55 High Street, Acton, W3 (992 5566 ext 2253). General information, advice and counselling for young people aged 12-25 Mon-Thurs 10-5.30, Fri 10-4.30. Counselling preferably by appointment. Legal advice preferably on Fridays. Asian languages on Fridays. French/Spanish available all week.

Acton Rights Legal Advice Panel, Action Hill Church Centre, Woodlands Avenue, Acton, W3 (933 3331). Legal advice and information Mon-Thurs 6.30-8.

Ealing Community Relations Council (Acton office), Acton Hill Church Centre, Woodlands Avenue, W3 (922 8479 or 933 3331). Advice on housing, consumer protection, DHSS benefits, matrimonial problems, immigration and nationality, employment Mon-Thurs

10-6.30. Legal advice Mon-Thurs 6.30.8.30.

Ealing Community Relations Council (Legal advice), 2 The Green, High Street, Ealing, W5 5DA (579 3861 or 579 3862). Legal advice and information Mon-Fri 9.30-5.30. Legal advice, from qualified lawyers Fri 6.30-8.

Southall Black Women's Centre, 86 Northcote Avenue, Southall, Middlesex (843 0578). Resources centre, for Asian and Afro-Caribbean women. Legal advice Mon 2-7. Health advice Thurs 2-6.

Southall Rights, 54 High Street, Southall, Middlesex (571 4920). General advice Mon-Sat 10-9. (Session for women only Tues 6-9). Legal advice Mon-Fri 6-9, Sat 10-1. (Punjabi, Hindi, Urdu, Gujerati, spoken.)

Enfield

MPs

Edmonton I D Twinn (Con), Enfield North Tim Eggar Con, Enfield Southgate C M Portillio (Con)

Borough Council

General enquiries to PO Box 50, Civic Centre, Silver Street, Enfield, Middlesex, EN1 3XA (366 6565 ext 2147). Access: A.

Disabilities are the responsibility of the Social Services Committee. Contact Director of Social Services, PO Box 59 at the Civic Centre.

The Council has an equal opportunities policy 'directed against unlawful discrimination on grounds of race, sex or marital status, rather than towards the protection of any particular group. The sole exception is the disabled, towards whom preferential treatment is allowed under the statutory quota system and this is referred to in the policy'.

Advice Centres

London Borough of Enfield Community Relations Council, Enfield Highway Library, 258 Hertford Road, Enfield, EN3 5BN (805 6121). Access: N (phone for visit).

Citizens Advice Bureau, Edmonton County Court, 59 Fore Street, Edmonton, N18. Landlord and tenant problems, on possession order days only. (Serves the area covered by the Court: Epping, Waltham Cross, Cheshunt, Broxbourne, Waltham Forest, Haringey, Enfield.) Correspondence Southgate Citizens Advice Bureau, Town Hall, Palmers Green, N13 (882 5940).

Citizens Advice Bureau, Public Library, Ordnance Road/Hertford Road, Enfield. Advice and information Tues 10.30-4. Correspondence Enfield Citizens Advice Bureau, 10 Little Park Gardens, Enfield (363 0928).

Edmonton Citizens Advice Bureau, Methodist Church, Lower Fore Street, N9 (807 4253). Advice and information Mon-Fri 10.30-12.30, Mon, Thurs 1.30-4, Wed 7-8.30. Legal advice Wed evening. Access: P.

Enfield Citizens Advice Bureau, 10 Little Park Gardens, Enfield, EN2 6PQ (363 0928). Advice and information Mon-Fri 10.30-4. Access: N.

Southgate Citizens Advice Bureau, Town Hall, Palmers Green, N13 (882 5940). Advice and information Mon-Thurs 10-4, Fri 10-12. Legal advice alternate Tues 2.30-4 (by appointment). Access: A.

Network Community Advice Centre, All Saints Church Hall, Church Street, Edmonton, N9. Advice on legal, financial and welfare rights problems Mon 7.30-9.30. Correspondence Network Community Services, Millfield House, Silver Street, Edmonton, N18.

Greenwich

MPs

Greenwich Guy Barnet (Lab), Eltham Peter Bottomley (Con), Woolwich John Cartwright (SDP)

Borough Council

Greenwich Town Hall, Wellington Street, Woolwich, SE18. Access: A. Council's Information and Advice Centre is at 41/43 Wellington Street, SE18. Access: P.

Women's Sub-Committee c/o Community Affairs Committee) is serviced by a Women's Unit. Contact Kathryn Riley, Women's Unit, Riverside House, Beresford Street, SE18 (854 888 ext 2080).

The Race Relations Committee is serviced by a race unit. Contact Ms L. Coleman and/or Mr M Luthra at Riverside House, Beresford Street, SE18.

The main contact for people with disability is the Employment Officer for the Disabled (Tony Davis), Social Services Department, Peggy Middleton House, Woolwich New Road, SE18.

The Council has an Equal Opportunities Policy and 'positively welcomes applications from women, ethnic minorities and disabled people'.

Women's Centres

Greenwich Women's Centre, 14 Ebden Way, Ferrier Estate, Kidbroke, SE3 (856 3808). Hours 10-5 weekdays but telephone first as also have mobile women's centre (bus) and may be out of the office. Access: N.

Greenwich Women's Bus, c/o, 14 Ebden Way, Ferrier Estate, Kidbroke, SE3 (856 3808). Travels the Borough of Greenwich with information for women on welfare benefits, housing, childcare, training opportunities and local activities and campaigns. Often invite women with expertise in specialist areas to travel with them and answer enquiries. Also visits local schools.

Greenwich Asian Women's Centre, 307 Plumstead High Street, SW18 (no phone yet). Hours 9-5 weekdays. Access: A.

Greenwich Lesbian and Gay Rights Centre. Currently looking for new premises but hopes to open soon. Phone 854 8888 Ext 2048 for details.

Advice Centres

Greenwich Council for Racial Equality, 115-123 Powis Street (2nd Floor), Woolwich, SE18 (855 7191-4). Access: N.

Greenwich Law Centre, East Greenwich Community Centre, Christchurch Way, Greenwich, SE10 9AL (853 5212 pm only).

Plumstead Community Law Centre, 105 Plumstead High Street, SE18 1SB (855 9817). Legal advice on housing, employment, family, welfare, race and immigration, for people who live or work in LB of Greenwich Mon, Wed 6.30-8, Fri 10-12. (Cases limited to SE7 and SE18.) Access: A.

Abbey Wood Extension Citizens Advice Bureau, William Temple Church, Eynsham Drive, SE2 9PT (310 0957). Advice and information Wed 1.30-8.30. Legal advice Wed evening (by appointment). Correspondence Woolwich Citizens Advice Bureau, 41 Wellington Street, Woolwich, SE18 (854 9607 or 854 9608).

Eltham Citizens Advice Bureau, Eltham Library, High Street, SE9 1TS (850 6044). Advice and information Mon, Tues, Thurs, Fri 9.30-4. Legal advice, advice on taxation and Surveyors Aid Scheme - by appointment.

Ferrier Extension Citizens Advice Bureau, 1 Ebdon Way, SE3 9PE (319 2715). Advice and information Tues 9.30-12.30, 4.30-7.30. Correspondence: Eltham Citizens Advice Bureau, Eltham Library, High Street, SE9 1TS (850 6044).

Woolwich Citizens Advice Bureau, 41 Wellington Street, Woolwich, SE18 (854 9607 or 854 9608). Advice and information, and debt counselling Mon 10-1, Tues 1-4, Thurs 10-1 and 5.30-7.30, Fri 10-1. Wed by appointment only.

Woolwich Simba Project (Advice Unit), 48-50 Artillery Place, Woolwich, SE18 4AB (317 0451). Advice and information for ethnic minorities, particularly Afro-Caribbean Mon, Wed-Fri 10-5, Thurs 2-5.

Hackney

MPs

Hackney North, Stoke Newington E Roberts (Lab), Hackney Shoreditch B Sedgemore (Lab)

Borough Councils

General enquiries to Public Relations Officer, Hackney Town Hall, Mare Street, E8 1EA (986 3123). Access: A.

Women's Rights Sub-Committee (sub-group of Policy and Resources Committee) serviced by Women's Support Unit, Room 112, Hackney Town Hall (533 1459).

Race Relations Committee (sub-group of Policy and Resources Committee) serviced by Race Relations Unit, Town Hall (986 3123).

Disability Officer, Karen Buck, Hackney Town Hall (986 2123).

Equal Opportunities 'no information'.

Women's Centres

Claudia Jones Organisation Black Women's Centre*, 47 Barrett's Grove N16 (241 1646) moving to 103 Stoke Newington Road, N16.

Hackney Women's Centre*, 20 Dalston Lane, E9 (986 0840). Hours 9.30-5 weekdays. Access: A.

Lenthal Road Women's Workshop, 81 Lenthal Road, E8 (254 3082). Women's 'services' centre offering darkroom, screen printing and other facilities. Aims to offer skill-sharing with local women. Hours 10-6 weekdays. Access: P.

Mameisia (for African women), 135 Clarence Road, Lower Clapton, E5 (985 0147). Hours 10-5 weekdays. Access: N.

Advice Centres

Hackney Council for Racial Equality, 1 Crossway, N16 8LA (241 0097). Access: N.

Hackney Advice Bureau and Law Centre, 236-238 Mare Street, E8 1HE (986 8446 Mon-Fri 10-5). Advice and information, including consumer advice Mon, Wed, Thurs 10-1, Tues

5-7. Legal advice by appointment.

Dalston Citizens Advice Bureau, 491-493 Kingsland Road, E8 (249 8616). Advice and information Mon-Wed, Fri 11-2.30, Mon 6-7. Legal advice Mon 6-7.

Cypriot Centre, 5 Balls Pond Road, N1 (254 8605). Advice and assistance on welfare rights, housing, immigration, matrimonial problems, education, consumer rights, etc, for Cypriot men and women Mon-Tues 10-2, Wed 10-1, Thurs 3-6.

Hackney African Organisation, Hackney African Centre, 4 Dalston Lane, E8 (241 2720 or 241 2740). Counselling, advice and information, for ethnic minority groups, particularly Africans Mon-Fri 10-6, Sat 10-2. Legal advice usually Mon-Fri 6-9.

Hackney Citizens Rights Group, Centerprise, 136-138 Kingsland High Street, E8 (254 9632). Advice on housing, welfare rights, debt management, immigration and nationality, employment etc, and tribunal representation, for people who live or work in Hackney Tues 11-1. Legal advice Thurs 6.30-7.30.

Hoxton Centre, Hoxton Hall, 130 Hoxton Street, N1 6SH (739 5431 or 739 6593). Legal advice Wed 7-8.

Stoke Newington Advice Group Service, Manor Road United Reformed Church, 102 Manor Road, N16 5NU (809 0641, during office hours 802 7949, during sessions only). Advice and information employment, social security, immigration, housing, consumer affairs etc, Mon, Wed 7-8.

Hammersmith and Fulham

MPs

Hammersmith Clive Soley (Lab), Fulham Martin Stevens (Con)

Borough Council

General enquiries to Information Centre, Town Hall, King Street, W6 9JU (748 3020). Access: phone to arrange visit. Equal Opportunities 'no information'.

Advice Centres

Hammersmith and Fulham Council for Racial Equality, Palingswick House, 241 King Street, Hammersmith, W6 (741 5715). Access: A.

Hammersmith and Fulham Community Law Centre Ltd, 106-108 King Street, W6 0PQ (741 4021 Mon-Fri 10-5.30, 741 8228 emergency service outside office hours). Legal advice for people who live or work in LB of Hammersmith and Fulham. (Cases limited to homelessness, possession, illegal eviction, health and safety, equal pay, immigration and nationality, racial and sexual discrimination, juvenile crime, mental health, care proceedings), Mon-Fri 10-5.30 (by appointment only). Advice for women Wed 10.30-1.30. Advice on immigration and nationality Tues 5.50-7.30.

Fulham Citizens Advice Bureau, 50 Greyhound Road, W6 (385 1322). Advice and information, negotiation and representation Mon, Wed-Fri 11-2, Tues 3-7. Legal and employment advice Tues 7-8 (by appointment only).

Asia Community Centre, 239 Uxbridge Road, W12 (740 6940). Advice on housing and social services for Asians Mon-Fri 10-4.30, Sat 10-2. (Interpretation in Hindi and Urdu languages.)

Fulham Legal Advice Centre, 510 Fulham Road, SW6 (731 2401). Legal advice Mon-Fri 9.30-4.30. Advice from solicitor Mon, Tues, Thurs 6.30-8 only.

Notting Dale Community Law Centre, 2 Bramley Road, W10 6TF (229 3544). Legal advice Mon-Fri 10-5.

Shepherd's Bush Advice Centre, 338 Uxbridge Road, Shepherd's Bush, W12 7LL (743 6953 Mon-Fri during office hours). Advice and information Mon 9.30-12, 6-8, Tues 2-4, Wed 6-8, Thurs, Fri 9.30-12, Sat 9.30-12 (alternate weeks). Legal advice Mon, Wed 6-8 by appointment. Financial advice by appointment.

Haringey

MPs

Tottenham Norman Atkinson (Lab), Hornsey Wood Green Sir Hugh Rossi (Con)

Borough Council

General enquiries to the Public Relations Officer, Civic Centre, High Road, Wood Green, N22 4LE (881 3000). Access: P (no toilet).

Women's Committee is contacted at the Civic Centre and is serviced by a Women's Unit, Education Building, 48/62 Station Road, Wood Green, N22 (881 3000 ext.3879). Contact: Sheila Fletcher. Access: A.

There is an Ethnic Minorities Joint Consultative Committee, contact the Committee Secretary at the Civic Centre, and a Race Relations and Ethnic Adviser post and departmental ethnic minority liaison officers.

No special committee for the disabled, but four co-opted members to the full Social Services committee represent the disabled c/o Civic Centre. The Council are currently discussing establishing a gay and lesbian working party.

Haringey is an Equal Opportunities employer and welcome applications 'which will be considered on merit, irrespective of race, marital status, sex or any disability'

Women's Centres

Haringey Women's Centre*, 40 Turnpike Lane, N8 (889 3912). Hours: 10-6 weekdays. Closed Sat/Sun. Access: N.

Advice Centres

Haringey Community Relations Council, 14 Turnpike Lane, N8 0PT (889 6871/4). Access: A.

Tottenham Law Centre, 15 West Green Road, N15 (802 0911).

Haringey Women's Centre*, 40 Turnpike Lane, N8 (889 3912). Advice, information and support on health, relationships, housing, children, unemployment, legal matters, for women Mon-Thurs 12.30-4.30, Sat 1-4.

Pregnancy testing Tues 6-8, Sat 10-12. Legal advice Mon 7-9, by appointment. Advice for women in violent relationships Wed 1.30-3.30.

Hornsey Advice Bureau, Hornsey Town Hall, The Broadway, N8 9JJ (340 3626). Advice and information, mediation and advocacy, for people who live or work in LB of Haringey: Mon-Wed, Fri 9.30-1, Thurs 1-7.30. Legal advice, by appointment Wed from 10, Thurs from 6. Financial advice, by appointment Thurs from 6.30.

Iranian Community Centre*, 465a Green Lanes, N4 1HE (341 5005). Advice on welfare, immigration and education for Iranians in London Mon-Sat 10-1, 2-6.

Tottenham Community Project, 628 High Road, N17 9TP (808 4754). Unemployed workers' centre Mon-Fri 9.30-5. Legal advice Mon 7-9. (Provision for under-fives.)

Tottenham Neighbourhood Law Centre, 15 West Green Road, N15 5BX (802 0911, emergency number: 802 9497). Legal advice and representation juvenile crime, housing, employment, welfare rights. General advice service Mon 10-6, Tues 10-2, 7-8, Wed 4-7, Fri 10-2. Legal advice Tues 7-8. Access: P.

Turnpike Lane Advice Bureau, 16 Turnpike Lane, N8 0PT (888 4233 Mon-Fri 9.30-5). General advice for people who live or work in LB of Haringey, and Greek and Turkish Cypriots: Mon 1-7.30, Tues-Fri 9.30-1. Legal advice, by appointment Mon 6-7.30, Tues 10-12. (Advice in English, Greek and Turkish.)

Wood Green Advice Bureau, Civic Centre, Room 41, 2nd floor, High Road, Wood Green, N22 (888 0152). Advice and information, mediation and advocacy for people who live and work in LB of Haringey Mon, Wed-Fri 9.30-1, Tues 1-7.30. Legal advice, by appointment Tues 6-7.30, Thurs 11-1.

Harrow

MPs
Harrow East Hugh Dykes (Con), Harrow West A J Page (Con)

Borough Council
General enquiries to Public Relations Officer, PO Box 2, Civic Centre, Harrow, HA1 2UH (863 5611). Access: A. Equal Opportunities 'no information'.

Advice Centres
Harrow Community Relations Council, 64 Pinner Road, Harrow, HA1 4HZ (427 6504). Access: A.

Harrow Free Law Centre, Holy Trinity Church, Wealdstone, Harrow, Middlesex (no telephone). Legal advice Tues 7-8.15. Access: A.

Harrow Free Law Centre, The Welldon Community Centre, Welldon Crescent, Harrow, Middlesex (861 0762). Legal advice Thurs 7-8.15. Correspondence Holy Trinity Church, Wealdstone, Harrow, Middlesex.

Harrow Citizens Advice Bureau, adjacent Civic Centre, Station Road, Harrow, HA1 2XH (427 9443). Advice and information Mon, Tues, Thurs 10-4, Wed, Fri, Sat 10-12. Legal and financial advice alternate Tues evenings (by appointment). Access: A.

Harrow South Extension Citizens Advice Bureau, Baptist Church Hall, 270 Northolt Road, South Harrow, Middlesex. Advice and information Tues, Thurs 10-12. Correspondence Harrow Citizens Advice Bureau, adjacent Civic Centre, Station Road, Harrow, HA1 2XH (427 9443).

Havering

MPs
Hornchurch Robin Squire (Con), Romford Michael Neubert (Con), Upminster Sir Nicholas Bonsor (Con)

Borough Council
General enquiries to Public Relations and Information Department, Romford Town Hall, Romford, RM1 3BD (70 46040). Access: A.

The Public Relations and Information Department organise a women's 'conference' four times a year for local women's clubs and organisations, but this is more social/visits than policy formulating.

People with disabilities contact Mr F Dickinson, Head of Social Services Department, Mercury House, Mercury Gardens, Romford, Essex (Romford 66999).

The Council does not have a formal equal opportunities policy but has an employment policy to recruit the most suitable candidate regardless of race or sex within the terms of the anti-discrimination laws.

Advice Centres

Havering Community Relations Council, 21 Sims Close, Romford, Essex, RM1 3QT

Hornchurch Citizens Advice Bureau, 73 North Street, Hornchurch, Essex, RM11 1ST (Hornchurch 45893). Advice and information Mon-Fri 10-4, Thurs 6-8. Legal advice Thurs 6-8.

Rainham Extension Citizens Advice Bureau, Family Centre, 21 Broadway, Rainham, Essex (Rainham 20350). Advice and information Mon, Wed, Thurs 10-12.30. Correspondence Hornchurch Citizens Advice Bureau, 73 North Street, Hornchurch, Essex (Hornchurch 45983).

Romford Citizens Advice Bureau, 221 South Street, Romford, Essex (Romford 63414). Advice and information Mon-Wed, Fri 10-4, Thurs 10-1.

Hillingdon

MPs

Hayes Harlington Terry Dicks (Con), Ruislip Northwood J. Wilkinson (Con), Uxbridge Michael Sheresby (Con)

Borough Council

General enquiries to the Information Centre, 22 High Street, Uxbridge, UB8 1JN (0895 50600). The Civic Centre is in the High Street, Uxbridge, UB8 1UW (0895 50111). Access: A.

The Social Services Department has responsibility for people with disabilities. Contact the Director of Social Services at the Civic Centre.

Hillingdon are an Equal Opportunities employer (no wording) and are currently considering creating a post with responsibility for equal opportunities.

Women's Centres

Hillingdon Women's Centre* - not yet established in premises. Contact Vivien Woodcock (Development Worker) on Ruislip 37248 for further information.

Advice Centres

Hillingdon Community Relations Council, 65 High Street, Uxbridge, Middlesex, UB8 1JP (0895 56536). Access: N.

Hillingdon Legal Resource Centre, 12 Harold Avenue, Hayes, Middlesex (561 9400 during sessions). Legal advice, for people who live or work in LB of Hillingdon Mon-Fri 10-1, 2-6 (by appointment only, except in emergency). Mon, Fri 6-8 (no appointments). Access: A.

Hayes and Harlington Citizens Advice Bureau, 16 Botwell Lane, Hayes, Middlesex (561 0261 or 573 4507). Advice and information Mon, Tues, Thurs, Fri 9.30-12.30, 2-4, Tues 5-7. (Asian languages spoken.) Access: A.

Hillingdon Citizens Advice Bureau Legal Service, Darren House, 65 High Street, Uxbridge, Middlesex, UB8 1JP (Uxbridge 33302 or Uxbridge 34028). Legal advice by appointment only. Access: N.

North wood Citizens Advice Bureau, Oaklands Gate, Northwood, Middlesex, HA6 3AA (Northwood 22506). Advice and information Mon 10-4, Thurs 1-4. Correspondence Ruislip Citizens Advice Bureau, The Manor Farm, Ruislip, Middlesex, HA4 5SY.

Ruislip Citizens Advice Bureau, The Manor Farm, Ruislip, Middlesex, HA4 5SY (Ruislip 35212 or Ruislip 74928). Advice and information Mon, Tues, Thurs, Fri 10-4.

Uxbridge Citizens Advice Bureau, 65 High Street, Uxbridge, Middlesex (Uxbridge 56511). Advice and information Mon-Fri 10-4.

Yiewsley and West Drayton Citizens Advice Bureau, 106 High Street, Yiewsley, West Drayton, Middlesex (West Drayton 442007). Advice and information Mon, Wed, Fri 10-1, Tues, Thurs 10-4. Access: A

Hounslow

MPs
Brentford/Isleworth B Hayhoe (Con), Feltham and Heston R P Ground (Con)

Borough Council
General enquiries to Senior Information Officer, Civic Centre, Lampton Road, Hounslow, TW3 4DN (570 7728). Access: A.

Strategy Group on Women contact Dr P Whelan in Committee Administration at the Civic Centre.

Under the Ethnic Minorities Strategy Group the Chief Executive has an overall co-ordinating responsibility for race relations matters.

Ethnic Minorities Liaison Sub-Committee contact Mr J Tatum, Personal Assistant to Chief Executive. There are also officers in a number of council departments with ethnic minority responsibilities. (Hounslow's Community Relations Council has a race relations officer/unit and runs an information interpreting and translation service in 34 languages. A mobile information unit tours the borough. Contact Mr I Uppal, Senior CRO, 51 Grove Road, Hounslow, TW3 3PR, 570 1168.)

Hounslow is currently formulating an equal opportunities policy. Contact Civic Centre for details.

Advice Centres
Hounslow Community Relations Council, 51 Grove Road, Hounslow, Middlesex, TW3 3PR (570 1168). Access: A.

Hounslow Law Centre, 51 Lampton Road, Hounslow, Middlesex (570 9505). Legal advice and representation employment, immigration problems, care, welfare rights, housing, women's rights, mental health, for people who live or work in LB of Hounslow Mon, Tues, Thurs, Fri 10-6, Wed 2-6. Access: A.

Brentford and Chiswick Citizens Advice Bureau, Town Hall, Heathfield Terrace, Chiswick, W4 (994 4846). Advice and information Mon-Fri 10-3, Tues 8-9. Legal and financial advice by appointment. Access: A.

Feltham Citizens Advice Bureau, 77 Bedfont Lane, Feltham, Middlesex (890 2213). Advice and information Mon-Tues, Thurs 9.30-3.30, Fri 9.30-2.45. Legal advice Tues 5.30-7 (by appointment). Access: P.

Hounslow Citizens Advice Bureau, 1 Treaty Road, Hounslow, Middlesex (570 2983). Advice and information Mon, Tues 10-3, Wed 1-4, Thurs, Fri 10-4. Legal advice Tues 6-8 (by appointment). Access: N

Islington

MPs
Islington North J Corbyn (Lab), Islington South/Finsbury. C Smith (Lab)

Borough Council
General enquiries to Information Officer, Islington Town Hall, Upper Street, N1 2UD (226 1234). Access: A.

There is a full Women's Committee serviced by a Women's Support Unit at the Town Hall (226 1234 ext.3133).

Race Relations Committee with a Race Relations Unit at the Town Hall, contact Chief Officer Richard Crowson.

For people with disabilities there is the specialist service group five - Physically Handicapped. Contact Colin Groves, Assistant Director of Social Services, 4 Highbury Crescent, N5 (226 1234).

The Council has a gay and lesbian (policy) Sub-Committee. No specific officer contact. Write to Town Hall.

The Equal Opportunities Policy states that 'applications are welcome from candidates regardless of race, sex and sexuality and we have a positive attitude towards the employment of disabled people'. The Equal Opportunities Unit is in the Personnel Department, Northway House, 257/258 Upper Street, N1 1RW (226 1234).

Advice Centres

Islington Race Relations Officer, London Borough of Islington Town Hall, Upper Street, N1 (226 1234 ext.3150). Access: A.

North Islington Law Centre, 161 Hornsey Road, N7 (607 2461). Legal advice (and representation in certain circumstances) for people in LB of Islington, north of the North London railway line Mon 10.30-3.30, Tues 7-9, Wed 10.30-3.30, Thurs 1.30-5.30, 7-9, Fri 9.30-1.30.

South Islington Law Centre, 131-132 Upper Street, N1 1QP (354 0133 Mon-Fri 9.30-5.30). Legal advice employment, housing, immigration and nationality, sexual and racial discrimination, racial harassment and violence, care proceedings and wardship, for people in LB of Islington, south of the North London railway line, by appointment.

Finsbury Citizens Advice Bureau, 106 Old Street, EC1. Advice and information Mon 1.30-4, Tues 3-6, Wed 1.30-4.30, Thurs 12-2, Fri 10-12.30. Legal advice Tues evening, Wed 1.30-4.30 at Social Services, 121 Rosebery Avenue, EC1. Access: P (no toilet).

Highbury Corner Citizens Advice Bureau, 326-328 St Paul's Road, N1 (359 0619). Advice and information Mon 3-6, Tues, Thurs, Fri 10-1, Wed 1-4. Other times by appointment. Financial advice by appointment. Vietnamese advice session 2.30-4.30, one day each week.

Holloway Citizens Advice Bureau, Caxton House, 129 St John's Way, N19 3RU (272 5577). Advice and information Mon-Wed, Fri 10-1, Thurs 3-6. Tax advice by appointment.

Advice Rights Centre for the Handicapped, 133 St John's Way, N19 (263 8622). Advice, information, counselling and advocacy, for people with disabilities Mon-Fri 10-3.

Advisory Service for Squatters, 2 St Paul's Road, N1 2QN (359 8814). Legal and practical advice, for squatters and homeless people Mon-Fri 2-6.

Islington Cypriot Centre, 15 Hercules Street, N7 (272 4143). General advice Mon-Fri 12-5, Housing advice Thurs 2-5.

Islington Legal Advice Centre, The Vestry, St Mary's Church, Upper Street, N1. Legal advice on housing and planning, immigration, employment, family and personal consumer and business affairs Tues 7-8, Wed 10.30-1, 2-4, Thurs 7-8.

Islington People's Rights, 2 St Paul's Road, N1 2QN (359 2010). Advice on welfare rights, social security, housing benefit, simple taxation Mon, Tues, Thurs 10-1, 2-5. (Local resource for local authority workers and voluntary agencies.) Access: A.

Islington Women's Advice Group, legal advice for women Fri 1-3. Moving soon - for new address ring North Islington Law Centre (607 2461).

New Grapevine, 416 St John Street, EC1V 4NJ (278 9147). Counselling, advice and information on sexuality, personal relationships, contraception, pregnancy, etc., for young people aged under 25 Tues, Thurs 2.30-6.30, Wed 2.30-8.30. Sessions held in youth clubs and schools, by arrangement.

North London Bangladeshi Welfare Association, 251 Pentonville Road, N1 (278 0877). Advice and information for the Bengali community Mon-Fri 10-5.

Union of Turkish Women*, 129 Newington Green Road, N1 (226 7544). Advice on legal, sexual and racial problems, for Turkish-speaking women Sun 10.30-7.30, Mon-Fri 9.30-7.30, Sat 10.30-9. Group work Thurs 7.30-9.

Union of Turkish Workers, 129 Newington Green Road, N1 (226 7544). General advice, and advice on immigration, welfare, housing, for the Turkish-speaking community Sun 12-8, Mon 9.30-9, Tues 9.30-8, Wed 9.30-9, Thurs, Fri 9.30-9, Sat 12-9.

Kensington and Chelsea

MPs

Chelsea Nicholas Scott (Con), Kensington Sir Brandon R Williams (Con)

Borough Council

General enquiries contact Chief Information Officer, Town Hall, Kensington, W8 7NX (937 5464). Equal Opportunities 'no information'.

Advice Centres

Kensington and Chelsea Community Relations Advisers, Westway Information and Aid Centre, 140 Ladbroke Grove, W10 5ND (969 2433). Access: A.

North Kensington Law Centre, 74 Golborne Road, W10 (969 7473). Legal advice, information about legal rights, and representation for juvenile crime, care, landlord and tenant, employment, complaints against the police, for people who live or work in North Kensington Mon-Fri 10-6 (24 hour emergency service).

Chelsea Citizens Advice Bureau, Chelsea Old Town Hall, Kings Road, SW3 5EE (351 2114). Advice and information Mon 10-1, Tues 3-7, Wed 10-1, Thurs, Fri 10-1. Legal and financial advice Tues 7-9 (by appointment).

Citizens Advice Bureau, Westway Information and Aid Centre, 140 Ladbroke Grove, W10 (960 3322). Advice and information Mon, Wed, Fri 10-12, Tues 2-4. At other times Mon-Fri 9-5 (by appointment). (Moroccan, Arabic, Spanish, Portuguese spoken).

Black People's Information Centre, 303 Portobello Road, W10 (969 9825). General advice Mon-Fri 10-6, Sat 11-4. (Lawyer available for legal advice at all times).

North Kensington Unemployed Centre, Venture Community Centre, Wornington Road, W10 (969 6516). Advice and information on welfare benefits, education and training, for unemployed or semi-employed people Tues, Wed 11-5 (Wed: Women only).

Nucleus - Earls Court Community Action Ltd, 298 Old Brompton Road, SW5 9JE (373 4005). Advice, particularly on housing, social security, employment and immigration law Mon, Tues 12-6, Wed 2-6.30, Thurs 12-6, Fri 12-5. Legal advice Wed 7-9 (by appointment).

Kingston upon Thames

MPs

Kingston Norman Lamont (Con), Surbiton R Tracey (Con)

Borough Council

General enquiries to Information Services, Guildhall, Kingston-Upon-Thames, Surrey, KT1 1EU (546 2121). Access: A. Equal Opportunities 'no information'.

Women's Centres

Kingston-Upon-Thames Women's Centre*, 66 London Road, Kingston-Upon-Thames (541 1964). Hours: 9-4.30. Note: temporary office/moving into new centre in 1985. Access: Currently N/ new centre A.

Advice Centres

Kingston Group for Racial Understanding, c/o KCVS, 29 St James's Road, Kingston-Upon-Thames, Surrey.

Chessington and Hook Citizens Advice Bureau, Hook Community Centre, Hook Road, Chessington, Surrey, KT9 1EJ (397 6187). Advice and information Mon, Tues 10.15-3.30, Wed 10.15-2, 6-8, Thurs, Fri 10.15-2. Legal advice alternate Wed 6-7.

Kingston Citizens Advice Bureau, 31 St James's Road, Kingston, Surrey (549 0818). Advice and information Mon-Fri 10-4. By appointment Wed from 6.15.

Malden and Coombe Citizens Advice Bureau, 41 Blagdon Road, New Malden, Surrey (949 4179). Advice and information Mon, Tues, Thurs, Fri 10.30-3.30, Wed 10.30-12.30, Sat 10.30-12. Legal advice monthly Tue 6.30-7.30, Thu 2.30-3.30 and tax advice by appointment.

Surbiton Citizens Advice Bureau, Library Extension, Ewell Road, Surbiton, Surrey, DT6 6AF (399 2360 or 399 7873). Advice and information Mon-Fri 10-4, Wed 6-8. Legal advice Wed 6-8 (by appointment only).

Lambeth

MPs

Streatham W J M Shelton (Con), Norwood John Fraser (Lab), Vauxhall Stuart Holland (Lab)

Borough Council

General enquiries from the Information Desk, Lambeth Town Hall, Brixton Hill, SW2 1RW (274 7722). Access: A. Lambeth Women's Committee is chaired by Helen Crossfield and has a Support Unit - contact Juliet Coke at the Town Hall. The Community Affairs Committee has responsibility for race relations and is chaired by Vincent Lean. Phil Sealey is the Principal Race Relations Adviser. Contact both at the Town Hall.

The Social Services Department has responsibility for people with disabilities. Contact the Director of Social Services at the Town Hall.

The Lesbian and Gay Working Party Contact through Committee Clerk (274 7722.

Lambeth's Equal Opportunities Policy states 'Applications are welcome from people regardless of race, creed, nationality, disability, age, sex, sexual orientation or responsibility for children or dependents.' Further enquiries c/o Management Services, 18 Brixton Hill, SW2 (274 7722).

Women's Centres

Asha, 27 Santly Street SW4 7QF (274 8854) Primarily a resource and advice centre, also has refuge for Asian women on separate premises. Hours Drop-in session sessions Wed 9.30-5.30, other weekdays phone first between 9.30-5.30. Access: N.

Brixton Black Women's Centre, 41a Stockwell Green, SW9 (274 9220/7696) has details of all black women's group throughout London. Hours 10-6 weekdays (except 10.00a.m.-10.00p.m. Thursdays). Also publishes black women's newsletter, 'Speakout'. Access: N.

Lambeth Women and Children's Health Bus* c/o South Western Hospital, Landor Road, SW4 (769 3042). Travelling women's health and resource centre with creche on board for tenants groups, housing estate advice and information centre for women in Lambeth.

South London Women's Centre*, 55 Acre Lane, SW2 (274 7215), 10-6 weekdays. Access: A

Advice Centres

Council for Community Relations in Lambeth, 441 Brixton Road, SW8 8HE (274 7722 ext. 2388). Access:A.

Brixton Community Law Centre, 506-508 Brixton Road, SW9 8EN (733 4245). Legal advice for people who live or work in Brixton Mon, Tue, Fri 10-12.30 Wed 6-8.

North Lambeth Law Centre, 381 Kennington Lane, SE11 (582 4373 or 582 4425 emergency 24-hour service). Legal advice on housing, immigration, employment, planning, welfare rights, for tenants, employees, claimants etc. Mon-Fri 10-6 (by appointment only).

Stockwell and Clapham Law Centre, 337 Wandsworth Road, SW8 2JQ (720 6231, 24 hour emergency service). Legal advice and representation on education, employment, low pay, social security, housing, immigration and nationality. Employment, low pay and social security advice Tue 6-7.30 General legal advice Wed 6-7.30 Education advice Thurs 4.30-7. Other times, by appointment.

Citizens Advice Bureau Community Action Team, advice sessions on housing estates and in hospitals, day centres, Homeless Families Units, etc mostly for people who do not normally have access to advice. (Times of sessions vary according to location.) Correspondence 323 Kennington Road, SE11 (582 8420).

Clapham Citizens Advice Bureau, 361 Clapham Road, SW9 (733 1946). Advice and information Mon 1-4, Tue 4-7, Thurs 1-4. Vietnamese session Fri 1.30-3.30 (with Cantonese and Vietnamese interpreter).

North Lambeth Citizens Advice Bureau, 323 Kennington Road, SE11 (735 9551). Advice and information Mon. 10-12 Wed 4-7 Fri 10-12. Legal advice Wed 4-7.

Norwood Extension Citizens Advice Bureau, Old Congregational Church, Chapel Road, SE27 0UR (761 0515). Advice and information Tue, Thu 10-3. Correspondence Streatham Citizens Advice Bureau, 93 Streatham Hill, SW2 4UD (674 8993).

Brixton Neighbourhood Community Association, 1 Mayall Road, SE24 0PW (737 3505). General and legal advice, and advice from local MP Mon-Fri 10-1, 2-6, Mon 6-8, Fri 6-6.30, Sat 11-1.

Centre 70 Community Association, 138 Christchurch Road, Tulse Hill, SW2 3DQ (674 6671). Advice, information and assistance Mon 10-1, 7-8.30, Tue 1-4, Thurs 10-1, Fri 1-4. Legal advice Mon 7-8.30.

Centre 70 Community Association, 22 Norwood High Street, SE27 (761 1528). Legal advice Thu 7-8.30. Correspondence 138 Christchurch Road, Tulse Hill, SW2 3DQ.

Clapham Town Advice Centre, Clapham Community Project, St Anne's Hall, Venn Street, SW4 (720 8731). Housing and fuel advice, legal advice, and youth advice (by arrangements with youth worker) Mon, Wed. Fri. 12-4. Legal advice Tue, Thu 7-8.

Family Support Service, 36 Stockwell Green, SW9 (737 4775 or 737 2830). Advice and counselling, support and activities for one-parent families Mon-Thu 9.30-1, 2-6, Fri 9.30-1, 2-5 (Thu 6-7 by appointment).

Latin American Community Project, 14 Brixton Road SW9 6DU (737 3617). Advice and assistance social security, immigration, health, education, housing and other problems, for individuals and Latin American community groups Mon-Fri 10-1, 2-6.30, Wed 6.30-8 for people unable to come at other times.

Myatts Field Centre, 40 Bramah Green, SW9 (582 6885). Advice on social security, housing and legal problems Mon, Thu 1-4, Tue, Wed 2-4.

One Parent Families: South London Advice Centre, 20 Clapham Common South Side, SW4 (720 9191). Advice (mainly by telephone) for one-parent families and other agencies Mon-Fri 9.15-1, 2-5.15.

Stockwell and Vauxhall Neighbourhood Centre, 157 South Lambeth Road, SW8 (735 5051). Advice and information on immigration, education, family and personal matters, social security, health and housing Tue, Thu 10-1, Sat 11-1. Legal advice Tue 6.30-7.30.

Waterloo Action Centre, 14 Baylis Road, SE1 7AA (261 1404). Advice on welfare rights, housing, health problems etc for people who live or work in the Waterloo area Mon-Fri 10.2. Legal advice on employment, housing, accidents, insurance and compensation, matrimonial and consumer affairs Thu 6.30-8.

Lewisham

MPs

Lewisham Deptford John Silkin (Lab), Lewisham East C B Moynihan (Con), Lewisham West J C Maples (Con)

Borough Council

Lewisham Town Hall, Catford, SE6 4RU, Tel. 690 4343. Access: A. General enquiries to: Borough Information Centre, Borough Mall, Lewisham Centre, SE13 7EP, Tel 318 5421 (entrance via Renell St). Access: P (toilet nearby). Also: Information Point, Town Hall Chambers, Rushey Green, SE6 4RY, Tel 690 4343 ext 529. Access: A.

Women's Committee chaired by Margaret Sandra. Contact Women's Policy Adviser, Irene Payne, 27 Rushey Green, SE6, Tel. 698 6121, line 1.

Race Relations Committee chaired by Russell Profitt. Contact Principal Race Relations Adviser, Neville Adams, 27 Rushey Green, SE6, Tel. 698 6121, line 4.

For people with disabilities: Social Services Committee chaired by Paulette Goudge. Contact Director of social Services, Grank Hatton, Eros House, Brownshill Road, SE6 2EG, Tel. 698 6121.

The Council has an Equal Opportunities Policy which states 'jobs are open equally to all races and both sexes'. The Equal Opportunities Unit is at Riverside Offices, 68 Molesworth Street, SE13, Tel. 852 9121.

Women's Centres

Lewisham and Deptford Women's Centre, 74 Deptford High Street, SE8 (692 1851). Hours 10.00 am-4.00 pm weekdays. Closed Sat/Sun. Access: N.

Advice Centres

Lewisham Council for Community Relations, 48 Lewisham High Street, SE13 5JH (852 9808). Access: N.

North Lewisham Law Centre, 28 Deptford High Street, SE8 3NU (692 5355 Mon-Fri 10-5.30). Legal and representation Tue 2-7, Fri 10-1, Sat 10-12.

Catford Citizens Advice Bureau, 120 Rushey Green, SE6 4HQ (690 8455). Advice and information Mon-Fri 10-3, Mon 5-7. Financial advice Thurs 6.45-8.15. Access: A.

Lewisham Citizens Advice Bureau Community Service, 8-12 Eltham Road, SE12. Advice and information Wed 10-12.30. Correspondence 120 Rushey Green, SE6 4HQ (690 4343 ext 264).

Lewisham Citizens Advice Bureau Community Service, Wesley Halls Community Centre, Shroffold Road, Downham, Kent. Advice and information Fri 10-4. Correspondence 120 Rushey Green, SE6 4HQ (690 4343 ext 264).

New Cross Citizens Advice Bureau, 2 Lewisham Way, SE14 (692 6654). Advice and information Mon, Thurs, Fri 10-2, Tue 4-6. Legal advice Wed 6.30-7.30 (by appointment).

Bellingham Legal Advice Centre, Community Flat, 99 Lushington Road, Bellingham, SE6. Legal advice, information and advocacy Mon 7-8.30. Correspondence Lewisham Citizens Advice Bureau Legal Service, 120 Rushey Green, SE6 (690 5360).

Downham Legal Advice Centre, Wesley Hall, Shroffold Road, Downham, Bromley, Kent. Legal advice, information and advocacy Tue 7-8.30. Correspondence Lewisham Citizens Advice Bureau Legal Service, 120 Rushey Green, SE6 4HQ (690 5360).

Sydenham Citizens Advice Bureau, 299 Kirkdale, SE26 4QD (659 1764). Advice and information Mon, Tue, Thurs, Fri, 10-1, Weds 2-7, Phone answering service Mon, Tue, Fri. Legal advice Weds, Fri, (by appointment).

Hither Green Legal Advice Centre, The Crypt, St Swithun's Church, St Swithun's Road, Hither Green Lane, SE13. Legal advice Thurs 7.30-8.30. Correspondence 191 Hither Green Lane, SE13.

Honor Oak Legal Advice Centre, Forman House, Frendsbury Road, SE4 (693 9103 during sessions). Legal advice and counselling Wed 6.30-8, Thurs 6-8.

New Cross Legal Advice Centre, 170 New Cross Road, SE14 (732 9716). Legal advice Thurs 6.30-8.

Telegraph Hill Neighbourhood Council, 170 New Cross Road, New Cross SE14 (732 9716 or 732 9717). Welfare rights and general advice Mon-Fri

9.30-12.30, 1.30-4. Legal advice Thurs 6.30-8.

Welfare Rights Unit, The Albany, Douglas Way, SE8 (692 0231). Benefit advice and appeal tribunal representation Mon-Wed, Fri 10-1.

Women's Advice and Counselling Service, The Albany, Douglas Way, Deptford, SE8 (692 6268). Counselling, legal, welfare rights and sexual advice, for women Mon 7-10.

Merton

MPs

Mitchan and Morden Angela Rumbold (Con), Wimbledon Sir Michael Havers (Con)

Borough Council

General enquiries to Information Centre, Merton Council, Crown House, London Road, Morden SM4 5DX (543 2222). Access: N at present, to be provided.

Joint Consultative Committee on Ethnic Minorities. Equal opportunities 'no information'.

Advice Centres

Merton Community Relations Council, 36 High Street, Colliers Wood, SW19 2AB (540 7386). Access: A (1 step).

Colliers Wood Extension Citizens Advice Bureau, Colliers Wood Community Centre, High Street, Colliers Wood, SW19. Advice and information Tue, Fri 10.30-12.30. Correspondence Wimbledon Citizens Advice Bureau, 30 Worple Road, Wimbledon, SW19 4EF (947 4946 or 947 4947). Access: A.

Merton and Morden Citizens Advice Bureau, 80 Kingston Road, SW19 1LA (542 9061). Advice and information: Mon, Tue, 10-3, Wed 2-7, Thurs 10-3, Fri 10-1. Legal advice Wed 6-7 (by appointment). Access A.

Mitcham Citizens Advice Bureau, 326 London Road, Mitcham, Surrey (648 1910 or 648 4000). Advice and information Mon, Wed-Fri 10-4, Tue 10-1, 4-7. Legal and financial advice by appointment. Access A.

Pollards Hill Extension Citizens Advice Bureau, Pollards Hill Day Centre, (679 0305). Advice and information Tue, Thurs 10.30-12.30. Correspondence Mitcham Citizens Advice Bureau, 326 London Road, Mitcham, Surrey (648 1910 or 648 4000).

Wimbledon Citizens Advice Bureau, 30 Worple Road, Wimbledon, SW19 4EF (947 4946 or 947 4947). Advice and information Mon, Tue 10-4, Wed 10-12.30, Thurs, Fri 10-4, Sat 10.30-12.30. Access: A.

Merton Community Bus Welfare Rights Campaign, 226 London Road, Mitcham, Surrey CR4 3HD (648 5588). Advice on welfare rights, housing rights, and rights at work Mon-Fri 10-1, 2-4.30.

Merton Resource Centre, 240 Merton Road, South Wimbledon, SW19 1EQ (542 6223). Legal advice Tue 7-8.30. Correspondence 30 Branksome Road, SW19 3AW (540 6454 evenings).

Newham

MPs

Newham NE Ronald Leighton (Lab), Newham NW Tony Banks (Lab), Newham South Nigel Spearing (Lab)

Borough Council

General enquiries to Information Centre, Newham Town Hall, East Ham, E6 2RP, Tel 472 1430. Access: P.

Women's Committee Support Unit, address as above (472 1430 ext 3465/3466).

Race Relations Unit, address as above (472 1430 ext 3472).

The Council has just adopted a new Equal Opportunities Policy which aims 'to ensure that no job applicant or employee will receive less favourable treatment on the grounds of race, colour, nationality, or ethnic or national origins, age, marital status, sex, sexual orientation, disability ...'.

Advice Centres

Newham Race Relations Association, 175 Upton Lane, E7 (471 4621), Access: N.

Newham Rights Centre, 285 Romford Road, Forest Gate, E7 9HJ (555 3331). Advice and information on employment, crime, welfare rights, housing, immigration and nationality Mon, Wed, Fri 9.30-11.30, 2.30 -4.30, Tue 6.30-7.30.

Newham Rights Centre, Ambedkar International Mission, 84 Dacre Road, Plaistow, E13. Legal advice Thurs 6.30-7.30. Correspondence 285 Romford Road, Forest Gate, E7 9HJ (555 3331).

Newham Rights Centre, Canning Town Information Centre, 57 Barking Road, E16. Legal advice Mon 6.30-7.30. Correspondence 285 Romford Road, Forest Gate, E7 9HJ (555 3331).

Newham Rights Centre, Congregational/Methodist Church, Wakefield Street, East Ham, E6. Legal advice Thurs 6.30-7.30. Correspondence: 285 Romford Road, Forest Gate, E7 9HJ (555 3331).

Newham Rights Centre, Newham Immigration and Social Advice Service, Barnardo's Hall, Upton Lane, E7. Legal advice Wed 7-8. Correspondence 285 Romford Road, Forest Gate, E7 9HJ (555 3331).

Beckton Mobile Citizens Advice Bureau, (474 8467). Advice and information, in various localities Mon 4-6 Custom House Library, Prince Regent Lane, E16, Tue 1-012 at St John's Centre, Albert Road, North Woolwich, E16, Tue 12.30-2.30 at Newlands Street, Silvertown, E16, Tue 3.30-5.30 at Strait Road, East Beckton, (Cyprus), E6, Thurs 9.30-11.30 at Custom House Library, Prince Regent Lane, E16, Thurs 12.30-2.30 at Hanameel Street, West Silvertown, E16 (near Barnwood Court and Jubilee PH), Thurs 3.30-5.30 at Woodman Street, North Woolwich, E16. Correspondence 3 Pier Parade, Pier road, North Woolwich, E16.

Plaistow Citizens Advice Bureau, 661 Barking Road, E13 (471 5223). Advice and information Mon, Fri 10.30-12.30, Wed 5-7, (Tue, Thurs by appointment). Legal advice Tue 6-7.30 (by appointment). Financial advice first Thurs in month, 3-5 (by appointment).

Canning Town Information Centre, 57 Barking Road, E16 4HB, (474 0931). General advice service Mon 6.30-7.30, Tue 10-1, 2-5, Wed 10-1, Thurs 10-1, 2-5. Other times, by appointment.

Community Links, 81 High Street South, East Ham, E6 4EJ (472 6652). Advice and information Mon-Fri 9.30-12, 2-4.30, Thurs 6.30-7.30. Advice for women Thurs 6.30-7.30, Fri 9.30-12.30. Advice for young people Tue 4-6. Advice for handicapped people, by appointment.

Redbridge

MPs
Ilford North Vivian Bendall (Con), Ilford South Neil Thorne (Con), Wanstead/Woodford Patrick Jenkin (Con)

Borough Council
General enquiries to Information Centre, Redbridge Town Hall, High Road, Ilford, Essex, IG1 1DD, Tel 478 3020. Access: N (plans to alter). Responsibility for people with disabilities comes under the Social Services Department. Contact: Social Services Enquiries Office, Social Services Department, 17/23 Clements Road, Ilford, Tel 478 3020.

'Redbridge welcomes applications from all sections of the community.' At the moment an Equal Opportunities Policy is under discussion with the trade unions. For further information contact Michael Bailey, Asst Director of Administration and Legal Services (Personnel) at the Town Hall.

Advice Centres
Redbridge Community Relations Council, Methodist Church Hall, Ilford Lane, Ilford, Essex IG1 2JZ, (514 0688). Access: N.

Hainault Extension Citizens Advice Bureau, Community Centre, Manford Way, Chigwell, Essex (500-3281). Advice and information Mon, Wed 10-4, Fri 2-4. Correspondence Ilford Citizens Advice Bureau, Fellowship

House, Green Lane, Ilford, Essex (514 1314).

Ilford Citizens Advice Bureau, Fellowship House, Green Lane, Ilford, Essex (514 1314). Advice and information Mon-Fri 10-4. Legal advice Thurs 6-7.30 (by appointment).

Woodford Extension Citizens Advice Bureau, 112 High Road, South Woodford, E18 (505-3965). Advice and information Mon 10-12, Tue Wed 2-4. Correspondence Ilford Citizens Advice Bureau, Fellowship House, Green Lane, Ilford, Essex (514 1314).

Crossroads Centre, 48 Ilford Hill, Ilford, Essex, IG1 2AS (478 1572). Employment advice Mon-Fri 9.30-1, 2-5.30. Money advice Tue, Thurs, Fri 10-12, 2-4 (but available at other times, telephone 514 5107).

Ilford and District Jobless Centre, 203 Ilford Lane, Ilford, Essex (514 5116). Welfare benefits advice for unemployed people Mon, Wed, Fri 9-5, Tue, Thurs 9-1. Sessions for women only Tue morning. Claimants Union Wed 2.

Richmond

MPs
Richmond and Barnes J Hanley (Con), Twickenham Toby Jessel (Con)

Borough Council
General enquiries to Press and Public Relations Department, York House Municipal Offices, Twickenham TW1 3AA (891 1411). Access: N.

Responsibility for people with disabilities is under the Social Services Department, Head Office, 42 York Street, Twickenham, TW1 3LZ (891 1422).

'Richmond is an equal opportunities employer'. The Equal Opportunities Officer is Christine Kerr, Personnel Department, York House (see above).

Advice Centres
Barnes Citizens Advice Bureau, Sheen Lane Centre, Sheen Lane, SW14 8LP (876 1513). Advice and information Mon-Fri 10-4, Sat 10-12.

Legal and financial advice by appointment.

Ham Extension Citizens Advice Bureau, The Health Clinic, Ashburnham Road, Ham, Surrey (940 1200). Advice and information Mon, Fri 10-12.30, Correspondence Richmond Citizens Advice Bureau, The Vestry House, 21 Paradise Road, Richmond, Surrey (940 2501 or 948 5091).

Richmond Citizens Advice Bureau, The Vestry House, 21 Paradise Road, Richmond, Surrey (940 2501 or 948 5091). Advice and information Mon-Fri 10-4, Sat 10-12. Legal advice Tue (by appointment) Financial advice first Wed in month (by appointment). Surveyor's advice by appointment.

Twickenham Citizens Advice Bureau, 25 London Road, Twickenham, Middlesex TW1 3SX (892 5917). Advice and information Mon-Fri 10-4, Wed 7.30-8.30, Sat 10-12. Legal advice Wed 7.30-9 (by appointment).

Southwark

MPs
Southwark/Bermondsey Simon Hughes (Lib), Dulwich G F Bowden (Con), Peckham Harriet Harman (Lab)

Borough Council
General enquiries to Southwark Town Hall, Peckham Road, SE5 8UB, (703 6311). Access: A.

Council Women's Unit in Room 411 at the Town Hall (703 6311 ext 2174).

Race Equality Unit at the Town Hall, (703 6311 ext 2384).

The Council has an Equal Opportunities Policy that protects 'women, ethnic minorities and registered disabled persons'.

Women's Centres
Peckham Black Women's Centre*, St Giles Parish Hall, Benhill Road, SE5 (701 2651). Hours 10-5 Monday to Friday. Access: P.

Southwark Women's Centre, 6 Peckham High Street, SE15 (701 2564). Hours 10-6 weekdays, 11-3 Saturdays, closed Sundays. Access: A. Also has mobile bus (women's centre) for use for meetings, giving out information etc (bus adapted for disabled access).

Advice Centres

Southwark Council for Community Relations, 352/354 Camberwell New Road, SE5 (274 8793). Access: N.

Southwark Law Centre Project, Information and Advice Centre, 29-35 Lordship Lane, SE22 (299 1024). Legal advice and representation for people with low incomes, ethnic minorities, tenants etc Tue 4.30-6.30, Fri 10.30-12.30. Access: A.

Southwark Law Project, Bermondsey Health Centre, 108 Grange Road, SE16. Access: P. Legal advice and representation for people with low incomes, ethnic minorities, tenants etc. Thurs 5-7. Correspondence, Information and Advice Centre, 29-35 Lordship Lane, SE22 (299 1024).

Peckham Citizens Advice Bureau, 97 Peckham High Street, SE15 5RS (639 4471 or 639 4472). Advice and information Mon, Tue, Thurs, Fri 1-3, Wed 5-7. Legal and financial advice alternate Wed 5-7 (by appointment). Welfare rights advice alternative Thu 1-3 (by appointment).

Southwark Citizens Advice Bureau, York Mansions, 199 Walworth Road, SE17 1LP (703 4198). Advice and information Mon, Tue, Fri 9.30-12, Thu 5-7.30 (Wed, Thurs 2-4 by appointment). Vietnamese session Thurs 2-4. Bengali session Thurs 1-3. Legal advice (employment and personal injury) Thurs 6-8 (by appointment). Access: A.

The Advice Centre in the Blue, 190 Southwark Park Road, SE16 3RP (231 2471). Advice and information, representation and advocacy Mon, Wed, Fri 10.30-12, 2-3.30, Thurs 6.30-8. Other times by appointment. Access: P (not WC).

Afro-Asian Advisory Service, Cambridge House, 137 Camberwell Road, SE5 0HB (701 0141). Advice on immigration and nationality, and welfare rights, including representation at appeals Mon-Thurs 9-1, 2-7, Fri 9-1, 2-6.30.

Age Concern - Southwark, 33 Peckham Road, SE5 8UH (703 6105). General advice for elderly people Mon, Wed, Fri 10-4, Tue, Thurs 10-1.

Bellenden Neighbourhood Advice Centre, Copleston Centre, Copleston Road, SE15 4AN (639 8447 Mon-Fri 9-1). General and legal advice, and advice on nationality and immigration Mon 6.30-8.30, Tue 10-12, Wed 6.30-8.30, Sat 11-1. Other times by appointment.

Cambridge House Legal Centre, 137 Camberwell Road, SE5 0HF (703 3051 or 701 9499 Mon-Fri 9.30-1, 2-4.45). Legal advice, assistance and representation Mon-Wed, Fri 10.30-12.30, 2.14-4.30, Tue, Thurs 7-8.30. Access: N.

Southwark Disablement Association, Room 48, Aylesbury Day Centre, Boyson Road, SE17 (701 1391). Advice and information for disabled people and other agencies Mon 1.30-3.30, Wed 10-12, 6.30-8.30, Fri 1.30-3.30.

Southwark Disablement Association, Peckham Citizens Advice Bureau, 97 Peckham High Street, SE15 5RS (639 4471). Advice and information for disabled people Thu 1-3. Correspondence Room 48, Aylesbury Day Centre, Boyson Road, SE17 (701 1391).

Walworth Advice and Community Work Project, 186a Crampton Street, SE17 (701 1038). General advice Mon, Tue, Thu 9.30-12.30, Tue 6.30-8.30. Legal advice, by appointment Wed 10-12. Access: A.

Sutton

MPs

Sutton and Cheam Neil MacFarlane (Con), Carshalton/Wallington Nigel Forman (Con)

Borough Council

General enquiries to Public Relations Officer, Sutton Civic Offices, St Nicholas Way, Sutton, Surrey, SM1 1EA (661

5000). Access: A. Enquiries regarding people with disabilities contact the Occupational Therapy Unit, (661 5559). Equal Opportunities 'no information'.

Women's Centres
Sutton Women's Centre, 3 Palmeston Road, Sutton (661 1991). Hours 9.30-7 weekdays. Access: P.

Advice Centres
Sutton Community Relations Council, 46 Tudor Avenue, Sutton, Surrey.

Beddington and Wallington Citizens Advice Bureau, 16 Stanley Park Road, Wallington, Surrey, SM6 0EU (669 3435 or 661 5509). Advice and information Mon-Fri 10-4. Legal advice Tue 5-7 (by appointment). Access: A.

Housing Aid Centre, St Nicholas' Way, Sutton, Surrey (661 5049). Housing advice Mon-Sat 10-4. (Other times, by appointment).

North Cheam Citizens Advice Bureau, Priory Crescent, North Cheam, Sutton, Surrey, SM3 8LR (641 0889 or 661 5468). Advice and information Mon-Fri 10-4. (Mon-Fri evenings, by appointment).

St Helier Citizens Advice Bureau, Hill House, Bishopsford Road, Morden, Surrey, SM4 6BL (648 1209 or 640 4170). Advice and information Mon-Fri 10-4. Access: A.

Sutton Citizens Advice Bureau, Central Library, St Nicholas Way, Sutton, Surrey, SM1 1EA (643 5291 or 643 5292). Advice and information Mon-Fri 10-4. (Mon-Fri evenings, by appointment).

Worcester Park Extension Citizens Advice Bureau, Worcester Park Library, Windsor Road, Worcester Park, Sutton, Surrey, KT4 8ES (337 1609). Advice and information Mon, Thu 1-4. Correspondence North Cheam Citizens Advice Bureau, Priory Crescent, North Cheam, Sutton, Surrey, SM3 8LR (641 0889 or 661 5468).

Tower Hamlets

MPs
Bethnal Green/Stepney Peter Shore (Lab), Bow and Poplar Ian Mikardo (Lab)

Borough Council
For general enquiries contact the Public Relations Officer, Town Hall, Patriot Square, E2 9LN (980 4831). Access: P (no WC).

The Ethnic Minorities Committee is chaired by A Downes. The Principal Race Relations Adviser in the Chief Executives Office is Mr Kimpton Ndlovu at the Town Hall.

Responsibility for people with disabilities is under the Social Services Committee chaired by B Holmes. enquiries to the Director of Social Services, Head Office, Southern Grove Centre, Southern Grove, E3 (980 7111). The Equal Opportunities Policy states 'applicants are considered on the basis of their suitability for the post regardless of sex, racial origin, marital status, disablement or age'. Further enquiries to the Head of Personnel and Management Services at the Town Hall.

Advice Centres
Tower Hamlets Association for Racial Equality, Oxford House, Derbyshire Street, E2 6HG (729 1946). Access: A (phone first).

Tower Hamlets Law Centre, 341 Commercial Road, E1 2PS (791 0741). Legal advice for people who live or work in the London Borough of Tower Hamlets Mon-Fri by appointment or in emergency. Access: A.

Tower Hamlets Law Centre, The Berner Club, Ponler Street, E1. Legal advice on immigration and nationality only Tue 6.30-8. Correspondence 341 Commercial Road, E1 2PS (791 0741).

Tower Hamlets Law Centre, Poplar Legal Advice Session, Langdon Park Community Centre, Byron Street, E14. Legal advice Wed 7-8.30. Correspondence 341 Commercial Road, E1 2PS (791 0741).

Tower Hamlets Law Centre, Stepney Green Legal Advice Session, Dame Colet House, Ben Jonson Road, E1 (790 9077). Legal advice Tue 7-8.30 (by appointment only). Correspondence 341 Commercial Road, E1 2PS (791 0741).

Tower Hamlets Law Centre, West Stepney Legal Advice Session, 414 Cable Street, E1. Legal advice Mon 7-8.30. Correspondence 341 Commercial Road, E1 2PS (791 0741).

Tower Hamlets Law Centre, Bethnal Green Legal Advice Session, Bethnal Green Rights Shop, 296 Bethnal Green Road, E2. Legal advice Wed 7-8.30. Correspondence 341 Commercial Road, E1 2PS (791 0741).

Bethnal Green Citizens Advice Bureau, St Margaret's House, 21 Old Ford Road, E2 9PL (980 2390). Advice and information Mon, Tue 10-3, Wed 10-12.30, 4.30-6.30, Thurs 10-12.30, Fri 10-3. Debt counselling Thurs 1-3 (by appointment). Access: N.

Bow Citizens Advice Bureau, 86 Bow Road, E3 4DL (980 3728). Advice and information Mon-Wed, Fri 10-12.30, 2-4, Thurs 10-1. Legal advice by appointment. Access: N (5 steps).

Poplar South Citizens Advice Bureau, Old Council Offices, Woodstock Terrace, E14 (987 6040). Advice and information Mon, Tue, Thurs, Fri 10-1, Mon 3.30-6. Legal advice Mon 6-7 (by appointment)

Stepney Green Citizens Advice Bureau, Dame Colet House, Ben Jonson Road, E1 (790 9077). Advice and information Mon-Fri 10-1. Access: A.

Toynbee Hall Citizens Advice Bureau, Toynbee Hall, 28 Commercial Street, E1 6LS (247 4172). Advice and information Mon-Fri 10-3, Mon 5-7. Financial advice alternative Mon 5-6.30 (by appointment).

Asian Outreach Unemployment Project, Montefiore Education and Community Centre, Hanbury Street, E1 (377 8456 or 247 2399). Advice on welfare rights, employment, low pay, education Mon-Fri 10-1, 2-5.

Bethnal Green Rights Shop, 296 Bethnal Green Road, E2 (739 4173). General advice on welfare rights, health, housing and legal problems Mon 9.30-1, Thurs 9.30-1, Fri 9.30-4.30. Housing rights group Mon 2-4. Unemployed rights Tue 10-1. Bethnal Green Claimants Union Tue 2-5. Women's Drop-in Group Wed 1.30-3.30. Legal advice Wed 7-8. Women's Health Group Thurs 1.30-3.

East London Claimants Union, Dame Colet House, Ben Jonson Road, E1 (790 9070). Self-help group for claimants, providing assistance with claiming DHSS or local benefits and representation at DHSS Appeals Tribunals, etc Wed from 7. Access: A.

Spitalfields Housing and Planning Rights Service, 192 Hanbury Street, E1. Housing and planning advice, including legal advice and representation Mon, Wed-Fri 1-2, Tue 6-8. (Other times by appointment). Access: N.

Toynbee Hall Legal Advice Centre, Toynbee Hall, 28 Commercial Street, E1 6LS (247 4172 messages only). Legal advice Wed 6.30-8.

Waltham Forest

MPs
Chingford Norman Tebbit (Con), Leyton H Cohen (Lab), Walthamstow Eric Deakins (Lab)

Borough Council
General enquiries to the Information Office, Town Hall, Forest Road, Walthamstow, E17 4JF (527 5544). Access: A.

The Council has a Race Relations Adviser as part of a Policy Analysis Team c/o Town Hall.

The Council has an equal opportunities policy that states 'All applicants are considered for their suitability for the post regardless of disability, race, sex, and marital status.' Further enquiries to Mr Kama, Equal Opportunities Officer, Personnel Department at the Town Hall.

Women's Centres

Waltham Forest Women's Centre*, 5 Pretoria Avenue, E17 (520 5318). Moving in the Spring, new address 109 Hoe Street, E17. Phone for hours. Access: A.

Advice Centres

Waltham Forest Community Relations Council, 25 Church Hill, Walthamstow, E17 3AB (521 8851/2/3). Access: N.

Waltham Forest Citizens Advice Bureau, 167 Hoe Street, Walthamstow, E17 (520 0939). Advice and information Mon, Wed, Fri 10-1, Tue 2-5, Thurs 4-7. Advice at other times by appointment. Legal advice Thurs 5.30-7 (by appointment only). Financial advice alternate Tue 6.30-7.15 (by appointment only).

The Aid Centre, 807 High Road, Leyton, E10 7AA (558 0033). Advice and information on housing, rent and rates, employment law, welfare rights, council services, landlord and tenant and consumer law Mon-Fri 10-6, Sat 9-1.

Disablement Information and Advice Line, Old School Building, 1a Warner Road, Walthamstow, E17 (520 4111). Advice on all aspects of disability, for disabled people, doctors, social workers etc Mon-Fri 10-4.

Legal and Welfare Rights Advice Service, Marlowe Road, Walthamstow, E17 (520 8141). Legal advice, and social work advice (by Waltham Forest Social Services Department) Thurs 6-7.30. Correspondence 20 Church Hill, Walthamstow, E17 (521 6766).

Wandsworth

MPs

Battersea Alfred Dubs (Lab), Putney David Mellor (Con), Tooting: Thomas Cox (Lab)

Borough Council

General enquiries to the Information Office, Wandsworth Town Hall, Wandsworth, SW18 2PU (871 6000). Access: A.

An officer with responsibility for race relations is in every relevant Council department. Contact above for details.

The Director of Social Services at the Town Hall is responsible for services affecting people with disabilities.

Wandsworth is an Equal Opportunities employer. 'All applicants are considered on the basis of their suitability for the job irrespective of disablement, race, sex or marital status'. Contact Denis Candy, Equal Opportunities Officer, Central Personnel Department at the Town Hall for more details.

Advice Centres

Wandsworth Council for Community Relations, 57 Trinity Road, SW17 (767 3631). Access: A.

Springfield Legal Advice Project (Law Centre), Springfield Hospital, Glenburnie Road, SW17 (767 6884).

Tooting and Balham Law Centre, 107 Trinity Road, SW17 7 SQ (672 8749).

Wandsworth Legal Resource Project (Law Centre), 248 Lavender Hill, SW11 (228 2566 or 228 9462, 24 hour emergency service). Legal advice Mon-Fri 10-6, Tue 7.30-9.

Wandsworth Legal Resource Project, Balham Family Centre, 91 Bedford Hill, SW12. Legal advice Thurs 7-8.30. Correspondence 248 Lavender Hill, SW11 (228 9462).

Wandsworth Legal Resource Project, 347 Garratt Lane, Earlsfield, SW18. Legal advice Tue 7-8.30. Correspondence 248 Lavender Hill, SW11 (228 9462).

Wandsworth Legal Resource Project, The Open Door Community Centre, Beaumont Road, Southfields, SW19. Legal advice Wed 7-8.30. Correspondence 248 Lavender Hill, SW11 (228 9462).

Wandsworth Legal Resource Project, Roehampton Family Centre, 1 Portswood Place, Danebury Avenue, SW15. Legal advice Mon 7-8.30. Correspondence 248 Lavender Hill, SW11 (228 9462).

Wandsworth Legal Resource Project, 92c St Johns Hill, Battersea, SW11. Legal advice Thurs 7-8.30. Correspondence 248 Lavender Hill, SW11 (228 9462).

Wandsworth Legal Resource Project, Threshold Centre, 101a Tooting High Street, SW17. Legal advice Thu 7-8.30. Correspondence 248 Lavender Hill, SW11 (228 9462).

Wandsworth Legal Resource Project, York Library, Wye Street, Battersea, SW11. Legal advice Mon 7-8.30. Correspondence 248 Lavender Hill, SW11 (228 9462).

Battersea Citizens Advice Bureau, 177 Battersea High Street, SW11 3JS (228 0272 or 228 9391). Advice and information Mon-Fri 10-12.15, Mon 5-6.30. Legal 7 (by appointment only).

Roehampton Citizens Advice Bureau, 1 Portswood Place, Danebury Avenue, SW15 4ED (876 6909). Advice and information Mon-Fri 10-1.

Tooting Bec Hospital Citizens Advice Bureau, Tooting Bec Hospital, Tooting Bec Road, SW17 8BL (767 7537). Advice and information for patients, relatives and staff of Tooting Bec Hospital Tue, Thurs 2-4. (Other times by appointment.) Visits arranged to patients unable to leave their wards.

Wandsworth Citizens Advice Bureau, 609-613 York Road, SW18 2PU (870 6552 Mon-Fri 10-12.30). Advice and information Mon-Fri 10-12.30, (Other times by appointment). Legal advice Mon 6-9 (by appointment only).

Advice and Legal Representation Project, Springfield hospital, Glenburnie Road, SW17 (767 6884). Legal advice and representation, for patients in Springfield Hospital Mon-Fri 10-6.

Battersea Neighbourhood Aid Centre, 22 Battersea Park Road, SW11 4HY (720 9409). Advice and information Mon-Fri 10.30-12.30, Tue 2-4. Legal advice Thurs 7-8.30.

Battersea Youth Advice Centre, 22 Battersea Park Road, SW11 4HY (720 9409). Advice and information for young people Tue-Thu 2-5.30. Legal advice Thu 7-8.30.

City of Westminster

MPs
Westminster North John Wheeler (Con)

Borough Council
General public enquiries to Westminster City Hall, Victoria Street, SW1 (828 8070). Access: P (not public WC's).

'The policy of the Council is to appoint the best candidate for any appointment irrespective of race, colour, creed, marital status or sex except where membership of a particular sex or race is a genuine occupational qualification.'

Women's Centres
North Paddington Women's Centre*, 119 Portnall Road, W9 (969 8897 or 7937). Hours Mon-Fri 10-5. Access: P. Black Women's Group Mon-Fri 10-6.

Advice Centres
Westminster Community Relations Council, 472 Harrow Road, W9 3RU (289 2277-8). Access: A (no toilet).

Central London Community Law Centre, 13 Ingestre Place, W1 (437 5764 Mon-Fri 10-5.30). Legal advice relating to housing, employment, immigration and social security, for people who live or work in Central London Wed 12-2, 5-7. Employment advice Tue 3-5. Other times by appointment. Access: N.

Paddington Advice and Law Centre, 441 Harrow Road, W10 (960 4481). Advice and legal representation on immigration, supplementary benefit, housing, employment, domestic violence, care proceedings, juvenile crime, for people in W2, W9 and the parts of W10 in Westminster who cannot afford to pay for legal representation Tue 10-12, Wed 5-7, Thu 1-3, Fri 11-1. Immigration and nationality Thu 1-3. Session for women only Wed 10-12 (at North Paddington Women's Centre, 115 Portnall Road, London W9). Access: A.

Charing Cross Citizens Advice Bureau, 33 Charing Cross Road, WC2H 0AH (839 2825). Advice and information Tue, Wed and Fri 11-3, Thu 3.30-6 (Thu 2-3.30 by appointment).

Pimlico Citizens Advice Bureau, 99 Tachbrook Street, SW1 (834 5727). Advice and information Tue-Fri 10-4, Wed 5.30-7. Legal advice Wed 6-7 (by appointment). Access: A.

Royal Courts of Justice Citizens Advice Bureau, Royal Courts of Justice, Strand, WC2 (405 2225 or 405 7641 ext 3880). Advice, information and practical help for people involved in High Court litigation Mon-Fri 10-12.30, 1.30-4.30. Access: N.

St Marylebone Citizens Advice Bureau, Westminster Council House, Marylebone Road, NW1 (486 6425 or 828 8070 ext 4157). Advice and information Tue, Wed 10-2, Thu 3-7, Fri 10-1. Legal and financial advice by appointment. Access: N (porter can help with advance notice).

Chinese Community Centre, 2nd floor, 44 Gerrard Street, W1V 7LL (439 3822). General advice (in Chinese) with interpretation and translation service for the Chinese community: Sun, Mon 11-5, Tue-Fri 2-5.

Chinese Community Centre, Community House Information Centre, Derry House, Penfold Street, NW8. Advice (in Chinese) for the Chinese community Tue 10-12. Correspondence 2nd floor, 44 Gerrard Street, W1V 7LL (439 3822).

Community House Information Centre, Derry House, Penfold Street, NW8 (402 6750). Advice and information including legal advice, taxation, welfare rights, housing, education, immigration, nationality and citizenship for people who live or work in the Lisson Green, Church Street, St Johns Wood, Maida Vale, Edgware Road, Paddington Green area Tue-Fri 10-4. Legal advice Wed 6-8.

Gay Legal Advice, Pimlico Neighbourhood Aid Centre, 1-3 Charlwood Street, SW1 (821 7672). Legal advice for gay men and lesbians, by telephone only daily 7-10 p.m.

Paddington Migrants and Immigrants Employment Rights Unit, 439 Harrow Road, W10 (960 5746). Information and advice to Migrants (Spanish, Portuguese, Moroccans, Latin Americans, Filipinos, Bengali, Chinese) Mon-Fri 10-6.

Pimlico Neighbourhood Aid Centre, 1-3 Charlwood Street, SW1 (821 1608). Housing and legal advice for people who live or work in South Westminster. Housing advice Mon, Thu 12.30-3.30. Legal advice Tue 7.30-9. Visits to people at home, by appointment. Also disabled self-help group. Access: A.

CITY OF LONDON

MPs

City and Westminster S Peter Brooke (Con)

Corporation of London: General enquiries to the Public Relations Officer, P O Box 270, Guildhall, EC2P 2EJ (606 3030 ext2455). Access: A. Equal Opportunities 'no information'.

Notes

Notes

Women's Resources and Campaigning

Where To Go And How To Get Involved

This section pulls together a listing of central and all-London women's groups, organisations and campaigns for easy reference. All of them appear elsewhere in the Handbook either in the topic sections at the front or in **Borough Information.**

First, though, is some information on joining community or women's groups and projects, raising issues you are concerned about with local councillors or MPs, getting more involved and taking action in other ways.

The Handbook lists hundreds of organisations which offer advice, information and, often, useful services. Most of them also welcome anyone who wants to join them and take part in planning and carrying out their work. Some groups are mainly campaigning groups, concerned about an issue such as discrimination against women in the social security system or racism in the provision of health care. They might meet together, discuss the issues in detail drawing on everyone's experience and information. They might produce leaflets or newsletters to let a wider group of people know about the issues, go to speak to other groups, contact the press, media, councillors or MPs, and organise protests or other activities to highlight the issues. They may have a set of proposals for changes needed which may be based around a particular local incident or case, for example, the proposed deportation of a local Black woman or the closure of a children's ward in a hospital.

Many such groups also run facilities themselves which help and support women affected by the problems the group is concerned with - an advice service or a playgroup or a training course. You could be involved in this type of activity too if you're interested. Even where groups have funding or paid workers there are often tasks that depend on members of the group doing them. Most groups also have a management committee, steering group or collective which takes responsibility for premises, the group's finances, organising events, developing the group's work and so on. If you are interested in playing this sort of role the group could let you know when and how you could stand for election.

In some areas there are few existing women's organisations and so you may have to start by finding other women locally who share your concerns or ideas. Asking around and talking to neighbours, other parents, women at a local healthcentre or community organisation like a youth club, Community Health Council or lunch club should mean you find some interest. Advertising for other interested women to contact you and have a meeting is a good first step too. You can always go and talk to groups in other areas about how they got started.

Part of any group's activities will usually be trying to win recognition, financial support and action for change from local councillors, MPs, political parties. Advice on how to do this most effectively is useful - many existing local groups have a lot of experience and there are long-established national or issue-based campaigns which can also give advice. The National Council of Voluntary Organisations (NCVO) or London Voluntary Service Council (LVSC) (see **Funding**) can also advise you.

If you are an existing group it is well worth your while spending time, energy (and money if you have any) on producing good quality and attractive printed material about your group and the issues it is dealing with and spending time distributing it widely. There are groups that will help with design, advice on the technicalities of printing and how to get your message across. Some of them are based in community centres and others are women's projects. (See **Borough Information** and **Funding**.)

Contacting other groups can provide you with other useful things - women's groups can share and co-operate on things like transport, photocopying, skills, childcare equipment and creche sessions. Use the Handbook to make more contacts and strengthen your group.

Women's Centres and Advice Agencies London-wide (see Borough Information for local centres).

A Woman's Place*, Hungerford House, Victoria Embankment, WC2 (836 6081). Main central London women's liberation meeting place with bookshop and meeting rooms. Supplies details of women's groups meeting throughout Greater London area and is the mailing address for many women's groups and campaigns. 12 noon-7pm weekdays; 12 noon-6pm Saturdays. Closed on Sun except for meetings. Access: A.

Brixton Black Women's Centre*, 41a Stockwell Green, SW9 (274 9220/7696). Details of all Black women's groups in London. Advice and support sessions. 10-6 weekdays (10-10 Thurs). Access: N.

Irish Women's Centre*, Cabin Y, 25 Horsell Road, N5 (609 8916) but moving to 59 Stoke Newington Church Street, N16. Has details of all Irish women's groups throughout London. 10am-5pm weekdays. Access: P.

London Lesbian and Gay Centre, 67-69 Cowcross Street, EC1 (608 1471). A multi-purpose centre for lesbians and gay men, with separate facilities for women. Creche. Details available upon request. Women's facilities include meeting rooms, workshop spaces, large, comfortable lounge. Hours: Open Tues-Sun, with late nights Fri and Sat. Access: A.

London Women's Aid Federation. The Women's Aid Federation exists to give women advice, information and shelter. Any woman needing to leave a man for any reason can contact LWAF for advice, support and refuge. In the London region there are over 25 refuges. The London office at 52-54 Featherstone Street, EC1 is open from 10am-5pm Mon to Fri and can put you in contact with your local or another refuge. Telephone the 24 hour emergency service line on 251 6537.

Rights of Women (ROW)*, 52-54 Featherstone Street, EC1 (251 6577). Legal advice for women, by letter, or by telephone Tues, Thurs 7-9 only.

Wesley House*, 70 Great Queen Street, WC2 5AY (430 1076). The GLC's Women's Committee has undertaken the renovation and restoration of a large building in central London which will serve as a multi-purpose women's resource centre. It will house much office accommodation for a wide variety of women's organisations and will have childcare facilities on the premises for both visitors and employees. There will be three floors of public space available for arts and recreational facilities including: a gig/performance space with a full PA and lights (capacity 200 seated); conference hall (capacity 80 seated); U matic video camera and editing suite; small sound proofed rehearsal room; tape/slide, film projection and overhead projection equipment.

The building will also house a cafe and bar and a Sports Centre for women which will include a fully equipped gymnasium and saunas. The centre is aimed at a diverse range of interests to attract all women living in the Greater London area and will have full wheelchair access for the disabled and other suitable facilities. Due to open early in 1986.

INDEX

Notes

Notes

Notes

Notes